The
SCHOOLS FOR
SPECIAL NEEDS
GUIDE

The SCHOOLS FOR SPECIAL NEEDS

GUIDE

7TH EDITION

A COMPLETE GUIDE

GABBITAS
Educational Consultants

KOGAN
PAGE

Publisher's note
The information supplied in this Guide has been published in good faith on the basis of information submitted by the schools listed. The views expressed by the authors of this Guide are not necessarily those of the publishers. Neither Kogan Page nor Gabbitas Educational Consultants can guarantee the accuracy of the information in this guide and accept no responsibility for any error or misrepresentation. All liability for loss, disappointment, negligence or other damage caused by the reliance on the information contained in this Guide, or in the event of bankruptcy or liquidation or cessation of trade of any company, individual or firm mentioned, is hereby excluded.

Photographs on front cover supplied with kind permission of (left to right) St Vincent's School for Blind and Partially Sighted Children, Liverpool; Headlands School, Penarth, South Glamorgan; and Exhall Grange School, Coventry.

First published in 1995
This edition published in 2001

Kogan Page Ltd
120 Pentonville Road
London N1 9JN

E-mail: kpinfo@kogan-page.co.uk

© Gabbitas and Kogan Page 2001

British Library Cataloguing in Publication Data
A CIP record for this book is available from the British Library
ISBN 0 7494 3597 6

Typeset by Bibliocraft Ltd, Dundee
Printed and bound in Great Britain by Bell & Bain Ltd, Glasgow

Contents

PART ONE:
SPECIAL NEEDS – GUIDANCE FOR PARENTS

PART TWO:
DIRECTORY OF SPECIAL SCHOOLS AND COLLEGES

PART THREE:
PROFILES OF SPECIAL SCHOOLS AND COLLEGES

PART FOUR:
INDEPENDENT MAINSTREAM SCHOOLS
WITH SPECIALIST PROVISION

PART FIVE:
REFERENCE SECTION

Tomorrow's Achievers...

...or society's misfits?

Today's gifted children should be among the outstanding entrepreneurs, business leaders, scientists and artistic performers of the 21st century.

Sadly, many are at risk of falling by the wayside or, through lack of fulfilling outlet, turning their talents to crime. Gifted children often go unrecognised at school, where they may become bored, isolated and disruptive. Some are dyslexic; others are loners and may be bullied or ostracised by classmates. Others deliberately underachieve so as not to be different. Many suffer the added disadvantage of living in socially depressed areas, where they are even less likely to be recognised.

Tomorrow's Achievers is a new initiative to ensure that gifted children receive the extra stimulation and support they need. Through a nationwide programme of proven specialist masterclasses, to be developed over the next five years, we shall be able to give 15,000 gifted children the chance to make the most of their abilities.

"NAGC gives Gabbitas its wholehearted support in this vitally needed initiative." Peter Carey, Director, National Association for Gifted Children.

By investing in today's gifted children, you can make a vital contribution by giving them the tools to become tomorrow's success stories.

PART ONE: SPECIAL NEEDS – GUIDANCE FOR PARENTS

1.1

Introduction

Gabbitas Educational Consultants

Special educational needs remain the focus of much debate. Developments in recent years reflect the increasing attention now paid to the important tasks of assessing and defining the educational needs of each child and ensuring that suitable provision is made.

Parents, however, often face difficulties and frustrations during the complex and sometimes lengthy process of assessment, agreement on the nature of provision required, and identification of a suitable school.

Schools for Special Needs – A Complete Guide is designed specifically for parents, offering a step-by-step guide to all aspects of finding the right school for a child with special educational needs, including essential information on parents' rights and the duties of the Local Education Authority. We are delighted that it has met with so much interest and appreciation from parents and professionals alike.

This seventh edition has been fully revised and updated in line with the latest developments. Following requests from readers, this edition also introduces a number of new features, including:

- A guide to assessment methods used to identify a child's individual needs (see Part 1)
- Information on the system of special needs provision in Scotland (see Part 1)
- More detailed information on the nature and extent of provision offered by independent mainstream schools (see Part 4)

The bibliography in Part Five offers suggestions for further reading and has been compiled with the kind assistance of our editorial contributors.

Part One

Part One of the guide provides parents with extensive guidance written by experts on the many aspects of assessment, statementing and provision as well as on choice of schools, special arrangements for examinations, education planning at 16+, social security benefits for children and carers and advice for parents overseas.

Part Two

Information about individual special schools is given in Part Two, which contains a comprehensive directory of independent and non-maintained special schools, plus details of colleges and other establishments providing training and support services for students aged 16+. Each entry includes the name, address and telephone number of the school or college; the name of the Head or Director; the sex, number and age range of pupils or students; whether residential accommodation is available; and details of all the types of special needs for which the school or college provides. There is a separate section for state schools, which includes details of those that responded to our request for information. For ease of reference, the primary or principal need catered for is shown in bold (wherever this information was made available). Entries also indicate which schools offer 52-week care.

Part Three

The listings in Part Three are contributed by schools and offer more detailed information about individual special needs establishments.

Part Four

Part Four contains a directory, profiles and indexes of independent mainstream schools. The vast majority of these schools do not take children with statements, but offer provisions for a limited range of special needs. The most frequently available provision is for specific learning difficulties or dyslexia, although some can also offer help in other areas (see Part 4.1). For this new edition, each school listed has been asked to classify the level of provision offered for individual special needs in order to help parents identify appropriate options.

Part Five

In Part Five parents will find a quick reference guide to independent and non-maintained special schools and colleges catering for specific types of need, together with suggestions for further reading, an extensive list of useful addresses and associations and details of schools registered under CReSTeD (Council for the Registration of Schools Teaching Dyslexic Pupils).

We are indebted to all those who have helped us in the preparation of this guide, as advisors and authors, and to the Heads and Principals who contributed so much information about their schools, colleges and support services, without which publication would not have been possible.

We should particularly like to acknowledge with thanks the support given to us by the following:

Rosemary Ayles, BA (Psychol), AFBPsS, CPsychol, FRSA
Consultant Educational Psychologist; Honorary Fellow, University of Reading

Tony Britton, Publicity Manager
Association for Spina Bifida and Hydrocephalus (ASBAH)

British Epilepsy Association

Dr Steve Chinn
Principal, Mark College, Somerset

Dr Deborah Christie, C.Clin.Psychologist AFBPsS
Consultant Clinical Psychologist, Department of Child and Adolescent Psychological
Services, Middlesex Hospital

CReSTeD (Council for the Registration of Schools Teaching Dyslexic Pupils)

Cystic Fibrosis Trust

Down's Syndrome Association

Ken Dutton, Principal Educational Psychologist, Scottish Borders Council

The Dyslexia Institute

The Dyspraxia Foundation

Jonathan Fogell, Chartered Educational Psychologist

John Friel, Barrister-at-law, Gray's Inn
Member of the Governing Council of Dyslexia Institute
Council Member and former Chair of the Advisory Centre for Education
Chair of the Special Needs Group of the Educational Law Association.

Lyn Fry, MA, DipEdPsych, AFBPsS, CPsychol, Chartered Educational Psychologist

Nick Goss, Education Officer
Royal Association for Disability and Rehabilitation (RADAR)

Alban Hawksworth
Disability Alliance

Joint Council for General Qualifications

Dr Richard Lansdown, Chartered Psychologist

Muscular Dystrophy Group

Mrs Carol M Orton
The British Dyslexia Association

Matt Parsonage, Information Officer
Royal National Institute for the Blind (RNIB)

David Potter
The National Autistic Society

Arno Rabinowitz, BA, AFBPsS, CPsychol
Chartered Educational Psychologist
Specialist Psychological Services

Jonathan Roberts, Assistant Information Services Manager
AFASIC – unlocking speech and language

SCOPE (formerly The Spastics Society)

Paul Simpson, Education Adviser
National Deaf Children's Society

SKILL (National Bureau for Students with Disabilities)

Jennifer Steeples, Special Needs Co-ordinator
Founder, Special Needs Support Group for the Diplomatic Service Families Association, now the London Dyslexia Association Resource Centre

Gabbitas Educational Consultants

Having celebrated its 125th year in 1998, Gabbitas is uniquely placed to offer parents a wealth of professional expertise, an understanding of their concerns and a personal knowledge of independent schools throughout the UK. Each year Gabbitas helps thousands of parents and students in the UK and abroad who seek guidance at all stages of education:

- choice of independent preparatory and senior boarding and day schools;
- choice of independent sixth form or further education colleges;
- educational assessment services;
- sixth form options – A and AS Levels, the International Baccalaureate, vocational courses;
- university and degree choices and UCAS applications;
- careers assessment and guidance.

Familiar with the requirements of students from overseas, Gabbitas also advises on specialist areas such as transferring into the British education system, guardianship for children from overseas attending boarding schools in the UK and testing for overseas students in English, Maths and Science.

In this guide we aim to provide a comprehensive and practical source of advice based on our knowledge and experience – a unique reference source to help you through all stages of your search for the right school for your child.

Gabbitas Educational Consultants

May 2001

1.2
Sources of Help: A Guide for Parents

Arno Rabinowitz, Chartered Educational Psychologist,
Specialist Psychological Services

There are many sources of help for parents who are worried about any aspect of their child's development. The range can often seem bewildering. With so many professions that exist to help children it is important for parents to know what each does and how to access this help if they are to gain access to the right support for their children and themselves. The list that follows is not exhaustive but includes the main groups with whom parents might come into contact during the course of an assessment of their child's needs.

Educational psychologists

Educational psychologists (EPs) are trained to understand how young children learn, think and behave. All EPs are trained teachers who have taught for a minimum of two years and, in many cases, very much more. Their training begins with an Honours degree in Psychology and then, after teaching experience, further postgraduate training lasting a year.

Most EPs work for Local Education Authorities, but some – an increasingly large number – work privately. They use a variety of tests and techniques to find out the general level of a child's ability to learn, and whether the child has any areas of specific learning difficulty. Referral to sources of help, including Child and Family Consultation Services, can be arranged through EPs and some are actually based at these centres. EPs have special knowledge of schools and similar provision and play a key part in the formulation of psychological advice that contributes to a Statement of Special Educational Needs. EPs who work for Local Education Authorities cannot normally help children who attend non-maintained schools. In such cases an independent EP will have to be approached. Independent EPs can also help in presenting cases to, and supporting parents at, Special Educational Needs Tribunals.

Clinical psychologists

Clinical psychologists work more from the perspective of health and community care. They are not trained teachers but their training, like that of EPs, is long and rigorous. Clinical psychologists usually work in the health service, in health centres, GP surgeries, hospitals and outpatient clinics.

Both clinical and educational psychologists are members of a profession, which is strictly regulated and chartered. Only people recognised by the British Psychological Society can call themselves chartered psychologists – a legally recognised title authorised by the Privy Council. They have agreed to follow a strict code of conduct and are answerable to a disciplinary system in which non-psychologists are in the majority when complaints are considered.

Child psychotherapists

Child psychotherapists work in Child and Family Consultation Centres (or Child Guidance Centres as they were more generally called) and also in health centres, hospital wards and centres for adolescents. Their work is mainly with children, teenagers and their parents, and their training gives them a particular understanding of the inner worlds of children and of how early childhood experience influences everyday life. Most child psychotherapists work with children individually, though some may work with groups of children and families. A number of child psychotherapists work independently but the majority are employed within the health service.

Child and Family Consultation Services

Child and Family Consultation Services (CFCS) are centres where parents can discuss worries about their children and where a range of professional workers can co-operate to help the child and family resolve problems. In most CFCS you will find an EP or clinical psychologist, a psychotherapist, a child psychiatrist, a specially trained social worker, a community psychiatric nurse and other specialised therapists. They work as a team to address problems but usually only one worker will work with a child or his or her family. CFCS are free and open to all. The service is confidential except where a child is at risk. Referral can be arranged through a GP, social worker, EP or teacher and many CFCS accept self-referral from families.

Child psychiatrists

Child psychiatrists are doctors who are specially trained to work with children who show signs of emotional distress or difficulty. They work within teams in clinics and hospital departments and will usually offer treatment or therapy in clinical settings or schools. Working with them may be a similarly trained range of specialised medical personnel: nurses, social workers and sometimes occupational and speech and language therapists.

Occupational therapists

Occupational therapists are trained in understanding how the body functions and how it works as a system. They can assess the way a child interacts with the physical world around him and can arrange therapy where this is needed. Usually they work within health centre or hospital settings but an increasing number work independently.

Speech and language therapists

As their name implies, speech and language therapists are concerned not only with articulation but also with the development and extension of language abilities and skills. They are, as are all the workers mentioned here, members of a carefully regulated profession with high professional standards of conduct. They work on programmes for individual children that can be implemented in school, as well as provide individual therapy in appropriate cases.

All the workers mentioned above are there to help and support parents. Sometimes, though, the most valuable help comes through contact with parents and others who have had similar experiences. Finding these groups is not always easy. Each Local Authority, at your town, county or shire hall, has a list of voluntary groups. As well as the groups and organisations listed at the end of this book, there are many umbrella groups which exist to inform parents about help available.

Contact-a-Family (020 7608 8700) has links with about 9000 independent self-help and mutual support groups and contacts throughout the country. Young Minds (020 7336 8445) and the Advisory Centre for Education (020 7354 8321) can help parents find similar groups in the field of mental health and education. For help with children in any form of education in London, Parents in Partnership (020 7735 7735) has many contacts and there are many similar organisations that offer support for parents of children with special needs. Network 81 (01279 647415) is a national network of support groups of parents of children with special educational needs while In Touch (0161 905 2440) offers information and contact for children who have rare handicapping conditions. Specialist Psychological Services (020 8874 1569) can help in finding the most appropriate professional for your child. The most important thing for parents is to find information and, for once, the truism is accurate: if you seek, you will find!

1.3
A Guide to the Classification
of Special Needs

Attention Deficit/Hyperactivity Disorder
(Lyn Fry, MA, DipEdPsych, AFBPsS, C.Psychol)

Do you recognise this child?

- Jo can't dress himself in the morning because he gets distracted by anything that is around him.
- Alex can't stay at a meal table without constantly getting up.
- Sarah has always had teachers writing in her reports that she must learn to concentrate.
- David's teachers complain because he daydreams.
- Homework is a nightmare with Sam. He can't settle to it and then he keeps popping up unless supervised by an adult.
- Jacob is just like his Dad. Both of them talk constantly and are always on the go.
- Victoria drives other kids mad because she is always touching their things.
- Other children don't like Ben because he spoils their games. He does silly things and forgets about rules.

From time to time all children have difficulty in sitting still, listening to what the teacher says, or being distracted by their friends. For those children with Attention Deficit Disorder (ADD), the difficulties are more pervasive. Because of this, they have considerable difficulty in keeping their behaviour under control. ADD is not easy to diagnose and can often be confused with other conditions. Children whose behaviour is not well managed, those with a language disorder, or those who are deaf, for example, often have difficulty in staying focused in class.

The American Psychiatric Association has a Diagnostic and Statistic Manual (DSM-IV) that attempts to break all conditions down into their key requirements, in order to differentiate them from other conditions. For attention-deficit/hyperactivity disorder they divide it into two parts: 'Inattention' and 'Hyperactivity-Impulsivity'. For Inattention, they require that 'at least six of the following symptoms of inattention have persisted for at least 6 months to a degree that is maladaptive and inconsistent with developmental level:

a) often fails to give close attention to details or makes careless mistakes in schoolwork, homework, or other activities;
b) often has difficulty sustaining attention in tasks of play activities;
c) often does not seem to listen to what is being said to him/her;
d) often does not follow through on instructions and fails to finish schoolwork, chores, or duties in the workplace (not due to oppositional behaviour or failure to understand instructions);
e) often has difficulties in organising tasks and activities;
f) often avoids or strongly dislikes tasks (such as schoolwork or homework) that require sustained mental effort;
g) often loses things necessary for tasks or activities (eg school assignments, pencils, books, tools or toys);
h) is often easily distracted by extraneous stimuli;
i) is often forgetful in daily activities.

For Hyperactivity-Impulsivity they require that 'at least four of the following symptoms of hyperactivity-impulsivity have persisted for at least 6 months to a degree that is maladaptive and inconsistent with developmental level:

a) often fidgets with hands or feet or squirms in seat;
b) leaves seat in classroom or in other situations in which remaining seated is expected;
c) often runs about or climbs excessively in situations where it is inappropriate (in adolescents or adults, may be limited to subjective feelings of restlessness;
d) often has difficulty playing or engaging in leisure activities quietly.

Impulsivity:

e) often blurts out answers to questions before the questions have been completed;
f) often has difficulty waiting in lines or awaiting turn in games or group situations.

In addition, symptoms should have been present before the child turns 7 and must be present in two or more situations. The latter is particularly important, since children frequently show their symptoms in one situation (such as home) but not in another (such as school). DSM-IV goes on to stress that the disturbance must cause 'clinically significant distress or impairment in social, academic or occupational functioning'.

It is important for parents to appreciate that children with ADD are not always hyperactive. In fact, some children cause considerable concern to their teachers by daydreaming or showing poor concentration in class without ever being overactive or impulsive. In addition, children do tend to become less hyperactive as they get older (usually after about 7 or 8 years of age) although difficulties with concentration will remain into adulthood.

The troublesome thing about ADD is that it does not occur all the time. Many children have no difficulties watching television or videos or playing computer games. These are highly visually stimulating with images changing many times every minute.

Causes

The cause for this condition is not fully understood. It clearly has a neuro-biological basis. Research has also shown that there is a genetic link. Thus, many children with ADD also have parents who have similar difficulties.

Making The Diagnosis

A number of steps need to be taken before a firm diagnosis can be made. Parents should start with a medical opinion about the child's physical health, in order to exclude any obvious causes like vision, hearing or thyroid dysfunction. Other medical conditions should also be considered.

There are a variety of ways of going about assessing for ADD. These include:

- In-depth interview with the parents, looking at the child's development, education and behavioural history.
- Evidence from the child's school or social groups.
- Use of a checklist such as the Conners' Checklist. The Conners' Checklist is a set of questions that differentiates between diagnoses of ADD (distinguishing between with hyperactivity and with distractibility/impulsivity) and other conditions such as oppositional defiant disorder, cognitive and learning problems, social difficulties.
- Observation in a clinical setting, together with testing that looks at a child's hyperactivity, distractibility and impulsivity in a standardised way.

Assessment of pre-schoolers is particularly difficult, since most of them are very active at one time or another. They also develop at different rates, so that while they may be very immature at one point they will then go through a developmental spurt and calm down. Nevertheless, there are some pre-schoolers who are very much more active, unable to entertain themselves, demanding and more easily bored than others.

In about 30 per cent of cases ADD exists alongside another problem, such as a specific learning difficulty or dyslexia.

Treatment For Attention Deficit Disorder

It is very important that the appropriate steps are taken in finding suitable help for a child, since inappropriate treatment and continuation of the disorder can lead to poor self-esteem, academic under-achievement and social isolation.

There has been considerable research interest in ADD since it was first identified a hundred years ago. Some approaches have been scientifically proven to be effective while others have been shown to have little or no effect. Those that are effective include:

- Parent training in behaviour management techniques
- Appropriate measures taken in the classroom
- Counselling and therapy for the individual or the family
- Medication if necessary. Between 70 to 80 per cent of children with ADD do respond well to medication.

All other treatments have either been shown to have little impact or have been researched inadequately.

Factors that have been shown to have an occasional or small impact, such as the levels of sugar, food additives and colouring in the diet, are being studied.

What can be done at school?

It is important that the teacher sees this as a situation that needs to be attended to, and not something that is simply going to improve by telling the child to concentrate.

Through the Educational Research and Improvement Clearing House, the US Department of Education has summarised the research and has come up with a variety of recommendations for teachers. They suggest that:

1. *The 'proper learning environment' must be established.* This means that children with ADD should be seated away from distractions in the classroom. They should be near the teacher's desk but as much apart from the class as possible. They should be surrounded by good role models. They have difficulty in handling change well, so need to be carefully supervised at transition times in class and in the less structured lessons.

2. *Instructions must be given carefully* to children with ADD. The teacher should be making eye contact with the child, keeping directions clear and concise and repeating the instructions if necessary. Sometimes it is important to get feedback from the child, to ensure that they have heard the whole instruction. A daily assignment notebook may help. The teacher should check that homework is written down correctly. This notebook may also be used for communication with parents.

3. *Giving assignments.* Only one task at a time should be given. The teacher should be monitoring frustration, since this may lead to a breakdown in good behaviour patterns. The child may need extra time for some tasks. Many children cope better if the assignment is broken down into manageable parts, often called 'chunks'. For example, a teacher wants a class to do 20 sums. For the ADD child, however, she might ask them to do 5 and then show them to her. This sets a reasonable target and gives the child an acceptable way to have a short break.

4. *Modifying behaviour and enhancing esteem.* The teacher needs to remain calm and have pre-established consequences for behaviour. It is important for the teacher to remember that this is not the child's fault and if things are not going well then other behavioural strategies will need to be considered. It is often best for a teacher to reward outcomes (such as completion of a task) rather than on task behaviour, since praise at this point may serve to distract the child. ADD children often respond better when inattention is drawn to their notice. Response/cost programmes will often work well. Children do need to be rewarded more frequently than they are punished. The child needs to be encouraged frequently and aspects of success need to be drawn to the attention of the whole class. It is also important for a teacher to be wary of using the child's name too often as a means of helping them to refocus. Constantly hearing one child's name can make the rest of the class increasingly aware of his unacceptable behaviour. Children with ADD need frequent feedback about when they are on task.

5. It is important to have an *individual education plan* with a specific plan for modifying unacceptable behaviour. This should be reviewed at approximately two-weekly intervals so that changes can be made if necessary. It is also important to keep trying for this period of time before judging a programme to be a failure.

Some children respond to social skills training. This will often help them to be less impulsive and socially inappropriate in a group.

Children with ADD do not cope well with team sports such as football, since they have difficulty in sustaining concentration for that length of time. They often do better at individual sports, such as tennis, gymnastics, skiing, swimming, karate.

Parenting The Child With Attention Deficit Disorder

Children with ADD present a special challenge for parents. Reasoning and explaining are poor techniques, since these children have difficulty in listening carefully.

Above all, these children respond well to clear rules and routines. They do not cope well with sudden changes of plan. Using charts and other reward systems will work well, as long as the parents start by tackling small targets. It is also important that parents should start with the most important issues first, such as temper tantrums or rudeness. These two issues will undermine any behaviour management systems. Thomas Phelan devised a system called "1,2,3, Magic!" for use with ADD children with behaviour management difficulties, which has been shown to be very successful over the years.

Homework is often a problem. This needs to be done in a distraction free environment. It should always be done with the television off (as should most other activities for ADD children). There should be a set time during which absolutely nothing else happens. Parents also need to look after each other. It is a stressful business having a child who is hyperactive, distractible and impulsive.

Where Can I Get More Information?

One of the best places for parents to find extra help is through the Internet. They should start with the C.H.A.D.D. Website, which can be found on www.chadd.org. This has a variety of fact sheets, research bulletins and information, including contacts for parents.

- "Is your Child Hyperactive, Inattentive, Impulsive, Distractible: Helping the ADD/Hyperactive Child" by Stephen Garber, Marianne Garber and Robyn Spizman, 1990, Villard Books, Random House.
- "Power Parenting for Children with ADD" by Grad L Flick, Prentice Hall International, 1996
- "1,2,3, Magic" by Thomas Phelan, Child Management Incorporated, 1996.
- "Understanding A.D.H.D." Christopher Green, Kit Chee, Roger Roberts, Random House, 1998.

References

American Psychiatric Association (1994). *Diagnostic and Statistical Manual of Mental Disorders*. Fourth Edition. Washington, DC: American Psychiatric Association.

Autism
(Information supplied by the National Autistic Society)

Autism is a complex developmental disability which affects social and communication skills. People with autism can often have accompanying learning disabilities but everyone with the condition shares a difficulty in making sense of the world. In most children with autism, some types of skills will be better than others so that their development will not only be slower than usual but will also be uneven and different from that of other children with learning disabilities.

An autistic spectrum disorder is a life-long disability and is not, at present, curable, but there are ways of helping, especially if a child is diagnosed and receives appropriate intervention early in life. Specialised education and structured support can really make a difference to a child's life, helping to maximise skills and achieve full potential in adulthood.

Autism affects the way a child communicates and relates to people around him or her. Although it describes a condition with wide ranging degrees of severity (hence the description, 'autistic spectrum disorder'), all those affected have a triad of impairments. These affect

- social interaction (difficulty with social relationships, eg appearing aloof and indifferent to other people or making odd, one-sided, naïve social approaches);
- social communication (difficulty with verbal and non-verbal communication, eg not really understanding the meaning of gestures, facial expressions or tone of voice);
- imagination (difficulty in the development of play and imagination, eg having a limited range of imaginative activities, possibly copied and pursued rigidly and repetitively).

In addition to this triad, repetitive behaviour patterns and a resistance to change in routine are notable features.

Particular points are worth noting. Firstly, the severity of impairment differs from person to person, and different aspects of the behaviour pattern are more obvious at some ages than at others. In addition, three-quarters of children with autism also have mild or severe learning disabilities. A child's personality, education and social environment can also markedly affect their behaviour. Finally, children with autism may also have other associated disabilities including epilepsy, cerebral palsy and sensory impairments.

Autism also includes the condition known as Asperger Syndrome. This term is used to describe people at the higher functioning end of the autistic spectrum. Most are of average or above average intelligence and generally have fewer problems with language, often speaking fluently, though their words can sometimes sound formal or stilted. Unfortunately, because their disability is often less obvious, a person with Asperger Syndrome may be more vulnerable. They can, sadly, be an easy target for teasing or bullying at school. The exact cause of autism has not yet been fully established. It is, however, evident from research that autism can be caused by a variety of conditions which affect brain development and which occur before, during or after birth. They include, for example, maternal rubella, tuberous sclerosis, lack of oxygen at birth and complications of childhood illness such as whooping cough and measles. In many instances, genetic traits appear to be important, though the sites of the relevant genes have yet to be identified.

As yet there is no cure for autism, but specialised education and structured support can help maximise a child's skills and minimise any behaviour problems. The right kind of education and care programmes are essential. They make a real difference to the child's life enabling each individual, whatever their level of disability, to achieve as great a degree of independence as possible.

It is crucial that autism is recognised early in a child's life to enable effective intervention and management of the condition. Early diagnosis and intervention are also essential to ensure that families and carers have access to appropriate services and professional support.

Certainly the signs are there to be recognised. In most cases, the triad of impairments emerges in the first two to three years of life. Indeed, there are often indications of developmental problems within the first year. However, because autism is a complex condition it is easy to miss important clues.

Autism is a pattern of abnormal development which unfolds over time, so diagnosis depends upon obtaining a detailed history of the child's development and a careful assessment of skills and abilities.

In infancy one of the most important indications that autism could be present is the absence, or very delayed development, of drawing the attention of parents and others to objects or events. In normal childhood development, by 12–18 months, children are usually pointing at things and trying to engage the interest of the person they are with to invite them to look too. They can also gain attention by bringing toys and making eye contact when doing so. If this behaviour does not occur or begins very late and is limited to the child's own interests, an autistic disorder should be suspected.

If you suspect that autism is present it is essential that you refer the child for a specialist diagnosis and assessment as early as possible – either to your local GP, the Child Development Centre or Child and Family Guidance Centre, or, if you are a teacher, to your Local Education Authority's educational psychologist.

The National Autistic Society runs 21 education and adult centres for people with autism, supports local authorities in the development of specialist services, provides publications, conferences and training programmes, offers specialist diagnosis and assessment services and supports local groups and families around the country. For more information, please contact the National Autistic Society, 393 City Road, London EC1V 1NG, tel: 020 7833 2299, fax: 020 7833 9666,
Website: www.oneworld.org/autism_uk Email: nas@nas.org.uk

Cerebral Palsy
(Information supplied by SCOPE, formerly The Spastics Society)

Cerebral palsy is not a disease or an illness. It is the description of a physical impairment that affects movement. The movement problems vary from barely noticeable to extremely severe. No two people with cerebral palsy are the same – it is as individual as people themselves.

Cerebral palsy is most commonly the result of failure of the part of the brain to develop, either before birth or in early childhood. This is sometimes because of bleeding or blocked blood vessels, complications in labour, or extreme prematurity. Infections during pregnancy, eg rubella, or infancy and early childhood, eg meningitis or encephalitis, can also lead to cerebral palsy. Occasionally it is due to an inherited disorder. In such cases genetic counselling may be helpful. It is sometimes possible to identify the cause of cerebral palsy, but not always.

The main effect of cerebral palsy is difficulty in movement. Many people with cerebral palsy are hardly affected, others have problems walking, feeding, talking or using their hands. Some people, for example, are unable to sit up without support and need constant enabling.

Sometimes other parts of the brain are also affected, resulting in sight, hearing perception and learning difficulties, and some people are also affected by epilepsy.

People with cerebral palsy often have difficulty controlling their movement and facial expressions. This does not necessarily mean that their mental abilities are in any way impaired. Some are of higher than average intelligence, other people with cerebral palsy have moderate or severe learning difficulties, although most people with cerebral palsy are of average intelligence.

Cerebral palsy includes a variety of conditions. The three main types correspond to injuries on different parts of the brain and many people will have a mixture of the following types and effects:

- People with spastic cerebral palsy find that some of the muscles become very stiff and weak, especially under effort. This can affect their control of movement.
- People with athetoid cerebral palsy have some loss of control of their posture, and tend to make unwanted movements.
- People with ataxic cerebral palsy usually have problems with balance. They may also have shaky hand movements and irregular speech.

The needs of children with cerebral palsy are very wide and often very complex. Some are able to integrate into mainstream schools with minimal support whilst others require the help of a welfare assistant, special furniture and adaptations to the environment. The mainstream experience can vary greatly according to the individual challenges faced by each child, the available expertise, resources and environment and the commitment of all involved. However, the needs of some children cannot easily be met with integrated mainstream provision.

In many cases, it is the complexity of needs as a result of cerebral palsy, for example communication, visuo-motor and visual perceptual problems, physical ability and medical conditions such as epilepsy and dietary needs that lead parents to seek out specialist education.

It is now widely agreed that early intervention is very important. The early diagnosis of a disability, coupled with appropriate specialist intervention, can do much to lessen its effects upon the development of children, and thus reduce the potential of the disability to result in functional handicap. This is no less true in the case of cerebral palsy than of any other disability.

The effectiveness of such a strategy in the early years is enhanced greatly by the active participation of the parents and family of a disabled child. Their involvement is central to the success of such programmes. During recent years, there has been a recognition of the role of parents as the prime educators of young children with whom other professional groups must work in genuine partnership.

Access to the National Curriculum is enhanced when children with cerebral palsy have opportunities to develop stable sitting, head control, hand/eye co-ordination, gross/fine motor skills, effective communication, independence in standing, walking and self-help skills.

Many children need additional time to achieve writing and manipulation activities and, in order to keep pace with their peers, require up to date micro technology and/or communication aids to support their learning.

Methods of teaching vary and professionals from many disciplines can be involved, eg teachers, occupational therapists, physiotherapists, conductors, nursery nurses, speech and language therapists, psychologists, as well as a variety of medical professionals. There are traditional educational methods within mainstream and special schools. Some mainstream schools have special units attached. Multi-disciplinary teams of staff are involved in teaching and providing for the needs of individual children. Children attending a mainstream school will usually require time out to attend therapy sessions. This may be within the school or can involve attendance at a child development centre.

Children attending a special school will usually receive their therapy support in the school. Some therapists see the children in their classroom as well for individual sessions. Another option is Conductive Education, developed by Professor Andra Peto in Hungary. Conductive Education is a holistic learning system which incorporates teaching and learning, and may help some children with cerebral palsy to become as independent as possible, encompassing all their learning needs.

For further information on cerebral palsy and SCOPE, contact the Cerebral Palsy Helpline, SCOPE, PO Box 833, Milton Keynes, MK12 5NY. Telephone 0808 800 3333 (freephone).

Cystic Fibrosis
(Information supplied by the Cystic Fibrosis Trust)

Cystic Fibrosis (CF) is the UK's most common inherited, life-threatening disease, affecting about 1 in 2,500 children. CF affects the glands which secrete body fluids, causing damage to major organs including the lungs, pancreas and liver and the digestive and reproductive systems. Before the discovery of antibiotics children with CF did not live very long. However, modern treatment means that today most live into adulthood with the condition kept under control. CF affects children in different ways and can vary in severity from one month to the next, so it is important to examine the special needs of each child on an individual basis.

One person in 25 is a carrier of the faulty gene which can cause CF in their children. Carriers are, however, completely healthy because they also have a normal gene which overrides the defective gene. If both parents are carriers of CF, any child they have has a 25 per cent chance of having CF (by inheriting faulty genes from both parents), a 50 per cent chance of being completely healthy but being a carrier (by inheriting a faulty gene from one parent and a healthy gene from the other) and a 25 per cent chance of being completely unaffected (by inheriting normal genes from both parents). Screening is now possible to enable prospective parents to find out if either is a carrier.

Medical complications

Children born with CF produce an abnormally thick mucus in the lungs which can block smaller airways and cause infections, leading to long-term damage. The most noticeable effect is a persistent cough which is non-infectious but may cause distress in front of classmates, particularly if severe, which may lead to coughing up mucus. Digestive problems, in widely varying degrees, may be caused as a result of damage to the pancreas, which produces insulin to regulate sugar levels in the blood and enzymes which aid digestion.

Other less common health problems associated with CF include sinusitis, hayfever, arthritis, diabetes, heart strain and cirrhosis of the liver. Sexual maturity may be delayed and boys with CF may become sterile.

Treatment for cystic fibrosis

Treatment for CF aims to keep the lungs functioning as normally as possible. Physiotherapy and breathing exercises to clear the lungs of any harmful mucus are a vital part of each child's daily routine. Many will require it two or three times a day, from 15 minutes to an hour at a time, depending on the child's needs. Parents are taught to do physiotherapy as soon as CF is diagnosed, but older children can do part of the treatment themselves and often become completely independent.

Physiotherapy may be combined with nebuliser treatment, in which liquid medication is converted to a fine mist which is inhaled and works directly in the lungs. Antibiotics are also taken regularly to prevent or treat infections. Digestive problems can be alleviated by replacing missing enzymes with a substance called pancreatin, taken with meals to aid good absorption of food.

Special Educational Needs

A child with CF may have special educational needs if the condition prevents or hinders him or her from making use of educational facilities of a kind provided for children of the same age in schools covered by the Local Education Authority (see Part 1.5 on The Code of Practice on the Identification and Assessment of Special Educational Needs). Most children with CF can be provided for within a mainstream school without the need for a statement. Schools should, of course, involve parents and seek their views at all stages.

All schools have the service of a Medical Officer or equivalent, but not always on site. Teachers, therefore, must be willing to allow parents or other helpers to come into school when a child requires treatment. The school's medical room or another suitable room will need to be made available.

Teachers may also need to arrange supervision at mealtimes to ensure that children eat well and take any necessary medication and food supplement capsules.

CF does not affect a child's intellectual or academic abilities but may mean long periods away from school because of chest infections or hospital stays. However, schools may be able to set work to be done at home or in the hospital if the child is well enough. Physical exercise is usually very good for children with CF because it helps to loosen mucus in the lungs, but teachers should be aware that children may feel unusually tired after a cold or chest infection. Teachers should remember that children with CF may need to use the toilet urgently and more frequently than other pupils. Therefore, consideration should be made for them to leave the classroom for privacy to cough and visit the toilet.

Children with CF may be teased at school because of their persistent cough and the fact that they may be small for their age. Some may find it embarrassing to take medication in front of their classmates. Friends must be supportive and encouraged to understand the importance of physiotherapy sessions which may sometimes interfere with the social timetable. The adolescent years can be particularly traumatic. Some teenagers may display rebellious behaviour by neglecting physiotherapy and diet and refusing to recognise the potential seriousness of the condition. Sympathetic counselling can be valuable to help teenagers cope with the stresses associated with delayed sexual maturity, to advise girls of the risks associated with pregnancy and offer support to boys who face possible sterility.

The pressures of coping with CF place great strain on family life and relationships. Brothers and sisters may feel resentment at the attention given to their sibling with CF and may feel guilty as a result. This can give rise to bad behaviour, withdrawal or other problems at school. All members of the family will be affected by the psychological pressures arising from the severe nature of CF, uncertainty about the future, genetic aspects and tiring routines. Families may also have to face the prospect of death. Medical advice, support and bereavement counselling are available to help families to cope with these pressures.

Teachers can help by meeting parents before a child comes into class and by understanding the problems which may arise within the family. They may be able to offer practical help by administering medication or supervising children taking it. There are no national guidelines for teachers on giving medication to children at school and teachers are not obliged to do so. If parents consent, however, there is no reason why teachers should not help in this way, provided they are insured by their employer. Teachers can also explain to classmates the reasons for coughing, physiotherapy and so on and encourage a positive attitude.

Special arrangements can be made for candidates with CF taking GCSE examinations. Additional time and supervised breaks may be allowed, or permission given for candidates to take examinations in hospital or at home (see section on GCSE & GCE examinations – Special Arrangements for Candidates with Special Assessment Needs).

For further information parents should contact the Cystic Fibrosis Trust, 11 London Road, Bromley, Kent BR1 1BY, tel: 020 8464 7211, fax: 020 8313 0472, E-mail: enquiries@cftrust.org.uk Website: www.cftrust.org.uk

Down's Syndrome
(Information provided by the Down's Syndrome Association)

Down's syndrome is the most common form of learning disability (previously known as mental handicap). It is caused by an accident before or around the time of conception, which gives rise to an extra number 21 chromosome in each of the person's cells. Instead of the usual 46 chromosomes, a person with Down's Syndrome has 47 chromosomes. This results in a disruption of the growth of the developing embryo, and a degree of developmental delay in the child.

The presence of the extra chromosome also gives rise to a number of physical characteristics, which are often shared by people who have the condition. These include:

- short stature;
- eyes that slant upward and outward – the eyelids often have an extra fold of skin (epicanthic fold) which appears to exaggerate the slant. (This does not mean there is anything wrong with the eyes – they just look different.);
- small ears;
- short fingers;
- poor general muscle tone, although this tends to improve as the child grows.

The presence or absence of these characteristics bears no relation to the child's intellectual ability. It cannot be stressed enough that each child will have his or her own personality and traits of character, just like any other child.

Certain medical problems are more common among people with Down's Syndrome than in the rest of the population. These include:

Hearing loss

Children with Down's Syndrome are particularly prone to colds and often find them more difficult to 'shake off'. The Eustachian tubes which connect the ear to the nose can be particularly narrow in children with Down's Syndrome and become easily blocked with mucus. This, in turn, can lead to middle ear infections (otitis media) and cause temporary deafness. Usually, when the cold gets better, the Eustachian tube clears and the mucus which caused the infection drains away.

Sometimes, however, a single infection, or repeated upper respiratory infections such as colds, or infected or enlarged adenoids, can cause more long-term obstruction of the middle ear space which never drains away. The fluid in the ear gradually changes from a watery substance to become more like jelly (or glue) and hearing is affected, a condition known as 'glue ear'. This can happen in all children, but is more frequent in children with Down's Syndrome.

Vision Problems

Many children wear glasses, but a small proportion of children with Down's Syndrome also have a degree of visual impairment. However, this is far less common than hearing problems. As with other pupils who wear glasses, teachers must make sure that the child actually does wear them when necessary. Visually-impaired children have a partial or total lack of vision in both eyes. Most LEAs employ advisory teachers for visually-impaired students, and these specialists will be able to give guidance to teachers in mainstream schools. It is estimated that 75–80 per cent of classroom activities are based on vision, so a child who is visually disadvantaged will need considerable support.

Lack of muscle tone

Many babies with Down's Syndrome have poor muscle tone and tend to be 'floppy' (hypotonic). In most cases, this characteristic reduced muscle tone improves as the child grows. However, in some children, it can contribute to a delay in acquiring fine and/or gross motor skills. This means that skills such as running, skipping, throwing and catching may cause a child with Down's Syndrome more difficulty than the other children in the class, but there is nothing to prevent that child from acquiring these skills eventually. As with all children, the opportunity to practise these skills is necessary and it is important not to restrict such opportunities because the child is perceived to have certain limitations.

Poor muscle tone can also affect fine motor skills such as writing. Again, most children will eventually be able to write quite well, but may take longer to acquire such skills.

Heart defects

It is estimated that about 40 per cent of children born with Down's Syndrome also have a heart defect. Such defects can range from relatively minor problems to severe malformations of the heart, which can require surgery and/or medication. Most children of school age who have an operable defect should already have undergone surgery. Successful treatment will allow the child to lead as active a life as he/she wants.

Speech and language problems

Nearly all children with Down's Syndrome have significant delay in language acquisition and understanding. This is caused by a combination of factors, some of which are purely physical and some due to the overall developmental delay that usually accompanies the condition.

The main physical obstacle is the ratio between the size of the tongue to the size of the mouth. Many children with Down's Syndrome have a small mouth cavity which means that their tongues seem too big for their mouths. This, along with poor muscle tone in the tongue and mouth, can cause children varying degrees of difficulty in actually producing the sounds required for talking clearly.

Other speech and language problems of children with Down's Syndrome stem from delayed understanding of language or difficulty in processing words. It is common for children with Down's Syndrome to have problems with auditory short-term memory, which has limited capacity for storing and processing information they hear. This difficulty can sometimes make the child seem disobedient or stubborn when, in fact, he or she has been given too much information at once and is unable to process it. This can be helped in a number of ways, principally by breaking down information into smaller units which the child can deal with more easily, giving him/her time to process the information and respond. Speech and language therapists will be able to suggest strategies for improving any language problems.

Since the 1981 Education Act, the trend has been towards the integration of children with Down's Syndrome into ordinary schools rather than special schools. However, a significant number of children with Down's Syndrome are successfully placed in special schools and some will spend time in both.

The variance in the abilities of children with Down's Syndrome means that they are as individual as members of the general population and should be assessed as such when a choice of school is made.

Dyscalculia
(Information supplied by Dr Steve Chinn, Mark College, Somerset)

Dyscalculia is a specific learning difficulty which hinders the learning of mathematics. It may occur as a single learning difficulty for a child or it may co-occur with other specific learning difficulties, the most likely of which is dyslexia.

Research on dyscalculia is minimal and research papers on mathematics difficulties in general are far less prevalent than papers on reading difficulties. Yet the occurrence of general maths difficulties is said to be over 6 per cent of children and the occurrence of dyscalculia as a single problem, that is not alongside say, reading problems, is probably around 2 per cent. These percentages represent a large number of children.

There has been some recent research which suggests that maths difficulties may have a genetic factor. However, it is difficult to separate the inherent problems of a child from the influences of his or her environment and experiences, which include home and school. Maths is a subject where anxiety and attitude are significant factors and both of these have a huge effect on the child's future learning of maths. These combinations create a wide range of levels of difficulty and a wide range of response to remediation.

To illustrate some of the difficulties of maths, imagine a pupil with dyscalculic problems attempting a long multiplication problem such as 387×362. Some children will look at the question and not make any attempt to start. They will be overwhelmed. Assuming the pupil starts, he or she has to have enough spatial skills to present the work on paper correctly. He has to be able to write the numbers legibly and in the correct sequence. He will probably know the two times table facts well enough to start, but will not know the six times table facts for the next step. As he tries to work out the three times facts, slowly and probably inaccurately, his short term memory will be failing to cope with the number of steps in the process.

The key difficulties for children with dyscalculia or with maths difficulties occurring alongside dyslexia are memory and spatial skills. For example, a good short term memory is essential for mental arithmetic and may also affect written maths. Long term memory deficits, especially failure to remember and retrieve from memory the basic facts, can be damaging.

While most people can compensate for poor recall of addition and subtraction facts by finger counting, few can create compensatory strategies for times table facts. Being unable to learn the times tables is one of the key characteristics of dyscalculia. It can be circumvented and is not a feature unique to dyscalculics.

One of the (inexplicable to me) demands of maths is speed of working. A child with difficulties tends to work more slowly. Sympathetic teachers might like to consider weeding out unnecessary examples.

Sometimes a pupil can start maths quite successfully and then, inexplicably, fail. For example, a child might be happy when little written work is required and then fail when he has to document procedures. Alternatively, a child may be surviving early demands for learning facts but not be able to appreciate or absorb the patterns and generalisations which can be used to organise information in more manageable and memorable forms as demands increase. Maths is a very developmental subject and any area of failure or insecure knowledge can have severe implications for future progress.

Another of the frequent and important influences on progress is anxiety. Children are usually aware of their difficulties, especially if those difficulties are confined to one subject and that subject is as important as maths. Anxiety has a negative effect on learning and can be serious enough to block children from attempting to learn maths.

Pupils who are failing in maths will first of all need an understanding of their individual problems. They will need encouragement and the experience of success. Clear explanation of fundamental ideas, using structured, multisensory methods, will be essential. There are many suggestions on how to provide this in *Mathematics for Dyslexics: A Teaching Handbook* (Chinn and Ashcroft, published by Whurr).

Dyslexia
(Information supplied by the Dyslexia Institute)

Dyslexia is a specific learning difficulty which hinders the learning of literacy skills at any level of intellectual ability. The problem is neurologically based and tends to run in families. Other symbolic systems, such as mathematics and musical notation, can also be affected.

About one child in every 25 is affected to some degree and will need specialist tuition at some point in their school career. About three times as many boys as girls present for assessment and specialist tuition. It is also evident that individuals with a dyslexic relative are eight times more likely to have dyslexia.

It has been established that there is a genetic disposition to dyslexia involving at least two genes. Genes are not the full answer, however. Environment, both before and after birth, also plays a part. Most importantly, it is known that environmental enrichment, including focused teaching, can bring about change in an individual's ability to learn and succeed.

It is the tiny neurological anomalies present in the brains of dyslexic people which create difficulties with processing information. Research has established that there are anomalies in lower levels where sensory information is coming into the brain and in higher levels where languages and codes are being organised, sequenced and retrieved.

A pre-school dyslexic child will often have difficulties with spoken language. He may be late in learning to talk and in learning common sequences, and may confuse sounds beyond the age of four.

Typically, at five years the child will have difficulty with letter knowledge, in linking sounds with symbols and in blending letters. He is also likely to have difficulty in learning by heart such things as the months of the year, or songs and rhymes, and is frequently disorganised in much of what he does.

Difficulties in reading, writing, spelling and learning to do sequential activities like learning tables arise as a result. In addition he may become increasingly reluctant to go to school during his first few years, or may develop emotional or behavioural problems.

Unidentified early problems persist and become more complex as they undermine the learning process. Children with dyslexia are puzzling to their parents and to their teachers. Often they appear (because they are) much more able than their work suggests. Occasionally it is only the complex writing and comprehension tasks required at secondary school which expose the problems.

Dyslexia affects some people more severely than others. This depends on the amount of neurological disruption and whether the environment has been able to provide the support needed. The greater the disruption, the greater the support needed. The later the condition is identified, the greater the impact. Success breeds success; conversely, failure breeds failure. Degrees of difficulty should be identified as early as possible so that effective remediation can be put in place.

The effects of dyslexia can be alleviated by skilled specialist teaching and committed learning. All children benefit from well structured phonically based early learning at school; all benefit from practice to make the learning permanent. Dyslexic children must have this type of teaching and, because of their difficulties, a multi-sensory approach which integrates seeing, hearing and doing is also critical to them.

If by six and a half a child is failing to gain early reading, writing and spelling skills (or earlier if dyslexia exists in the family), a psychologist's assessment should be considered. A good quality teacher assessment can also be very valuable in the early years. The aim is to identify strengths and weaknesses and make recommendations for action.

The majority of dyslexic children can, and should, be educated in ordinary schools alongside their peers, They will need some specialist teaching to enable them to reach their full potential. Only a tiny minority with severe and complex problems, which are frequently exacerbated by other conditions such as attention deficit or dyspraxia, need to be educated in specialist schools.

The key is the quality of teaching – in the normal classroom and by the specialist teacher. The specialist support in an ordinary classroom might range from one and a half to three hours per week over two to three years in primary school. Further targeted help is likely to be needed in the secondary years.

In conclusion, dyslexic children need to be taught in structured classrooms and must be identified and given focused specialist teaching as early as possible. Wherever possible they should be placed in schools which can nurture their latent talents – they frequently have creative and lateral thinking abilities. If their education is well-managed and they are prepared to work hard, dyslexic children can, and do, succeed in a wide range of careers.

Dyspraxia
(Information supplied by the Dyspraxia Foundation)

The Dyspraxia Foundation defines dyspraxia as 'an impairment or immaturity of the organisation of movement and, in many individuals, there may be associated problems with language, perception and thought'.

The term normally used is Developmental Dyspraxia or Developmental Co-ordination Disorder.

The condition is thought to affect up to 10 per cent of the population in varying degrees. It is probable that there is at least one dyspraxic child in every classroom requiring access to a specific treatment programmes.

Symptoms are evident from an early age. Youngsters are generally irritable from birth and many exhibit significant feeding problems. They are slow to achieve expected developmental milestones, often not sitting independently by the age of 8 months. Many fail to go through the crawling stage as babies, preferring to 'bottom shuffle' and then walk. Children with dyspraxia usually avoid tasks which require good manual dexterity and depend upon well developed perceptual skills. Inset puzzles, Lego and jigsaws are difficult.

Between the ages of 3 and 5, children with dyspraxia may demonstrate the following types of behaviour:

- Very high levels of motor activity, including feet swinging and tapping when seated, hand clapping or twisting and an inability to stay in one place for more than 5 minutes.
- High levels of excitability, with a loud/shrill voice. Children may be easily distressed and prone to temper tantrums.
- Awkward movement. Children may constantly bump into objects and fall over. Associated mirror movements, hands flap when running.
- Difficulty pedalling a tricycle or similar toy.
- Poor figure and ground awareness. Children may lack any sense of danger, illustrated, for example, by jumping from an inappropriate height.
- Continued messy eating. Children may spill liquid from drinking cups and prefer to eat with their fingers.
- Avoidance of constructional toys, such as jigsaws or building blocks.
- Poor fine motor skills, demonstrated by difficulty in holding a pencil or using scissors. Drawings may appear immature.
- Lack of imaginative play. Children may show little interest in 'dressing up' or playing appropriately in a home or Wendy House.
- Limited creative play.
- Isolation within the peer group. Rejected by peers, children may prefer adult company.
- Laterality still not established. Problems crossing the mid-line.
- Persistent language difficulties. Children are often referred to a speech therapist.
- Sensitivity to sensory stimulation, including high levels of noise, being touched or wearing new clothes.
- Limited response to verbal instruction. Children may exhibit a slower response time and problems with comprehension.
- Limited concentration. Tasks are often left unfinished.

If the condition is not identified, problems can persist throughout school life causing increasing frustration and a lowering of self-esteem.

Between the ages of 5 and 7, behaviour may include the following traits:

- Problems adapting to a more structured school routine
- Difficulties with PE (Physical Education)
- Slow at dressing and inability to tie shoe laces
- Barely legible handwriting
- Immature drawing and copying skills
- Limited concentration and poor listening skills
- Literal use of language
- Inability to remember more than 2–3 instructions
- Slow completion of class work
- Continued high levels of motor activity
- Motor stereotypes – hand flapping or clapping when excited
- Tendency to become easily distressed and emotional
- Problems co-ordinating a knife and fork
- Inability to form relationships with other youngsters, isolation in class
- Sleeping difficulties, including wakefulness at night and nightmares
- Reporting of physical symptoms, such as migraine, headaches or feeling sick

Poor handwriting is one of the most common symptoms of dyspraxia and, as the child progresses through the education system, requirement for written work increases. By the age of about 8 or 9 the children may have become disaffected and poor school attendance is much in evidence in secondary education.

With access to appropriate treatment, the majority of dyspraxic youngsters could have their needs accommodated within the mainstream setting.

Parents concerned about their children should refer to their GP or health visitor if the child is aged under five or the special needs co-ordinator if in full-time schooling. A referral may then be made to an outside professional, for example, a paediatrician, educational psychologist, physiotherapist, occupational therapist or speech therapist for assessment.

When an appointment has been made, write down all your concerns. In an unfamiliar setting your child may not behave in the expected manner or give sufficient attention to the tasks set. Assessment usually involves giving a detailed account of your child's developmental history, examination of gross and fine motor skills and a test of intellectual ability.

Treatment is available from specialists in health and education when the condition has been identified. Movement programmes may be offered by therapists and additional support can be made available in school.

If you require further information about dyspraxia or how to help your child, contact the Dyspraxia Foundation, 8 West Alley, Hitchin, Herts, SG5 1EG, tel: 01462 454 986.

Epilepsy
(Information supplied by the British Epilepsy Association)

Epilepsy is a tendency for the brain to experience recurrent seizures in which total or partial consciousness may be lost. The brain is a complex sensitive organ carefully protected inside the bony skull. It regulates and controls everything we do. To accomplish its many functions the brain's nerve cells (neurones) must work in smooth harmony. An epileptic seizure is caused by a brief disruption of brain function involving abnormal electrical activity in the nerve cells.

Epilepsy can begin at any age, but the incidence is high in childhood. Some children have epilepsy as a result of damage to the brain through, for example, injury, birth trauma or stroke (symptomatic epilepsy). Others have no known or identifiable cause but have epilepsy as a result of being born with a low epileptic seizure threshold (idiopathic epilepsy). Everyone has a seizure threshold; having a low seizure threshold means that a person has a lower resistance to seizures than people in general.

Children who have 'uncomplicated epilepsy', that is those without any additional physical disability or mental handicap, have exactly the same range of intelligence and abilities as unaffected children. For this reason the majority of children with epilepsy are educated in mainstream schools, usually without any extra educational provision. A number of children with epilepsy do experience behavioural problems and/or learning difficulties. However, the possible causes for this vary. The following factors may have a bearing:

- The severity of the epilepsy. If seizures occur frequently, a child's everyday life may well be affected.
- As epilepsy is a symptom rather than a condition in itself, it may well be that any damage to the brain may cause learning difficulties as well as epilepsy.
- The type of seizure. For example, when someone is experiencing a complex partial seizure they may appear to others as if their behaviour is strange or abnormal.
- Subclinical seizure activity, that is ongoing epileptic activity which is taking place in the brain without any obvious outward signs. This may also affect a child's learning or behaviour.
- The duration of seizures. Prolonged seizure activity (non-convulsive status epilepticus) may be accompanied by confusion, inappropriate behaviour, etc.
- Anti-epileptic medication. This may also be a possible cause for behaviour problems/learning difficulties and therefore needs careful monitoring by the child's specialist.
- Psychological and social factors, such as family and peer attitudes as well as self-image.

There is also some evidence to suggest that some children with uncomplicated epilepsy do experience specific learning problems with particular subjects, often reading or arithmetic. For all these children, it is important that individual educational assessments are made, together with advice from the relevant education professionals to ensure that all children achieve their full potential.

Finally, there are some children with epilepsy who will need to attend schools particularly for children with this condition. There are very few schools in this category, but the following are specialist centres for children with epilepsy and associated problems: St Piers Lingfield, St Piers Lane, Lingfield, Surrey RH7 6PW tel: 01342 832243; St Elizabeth's School, South End, Much Hadham, Herts SG10 6EW tel: 01279 844270;

and the David Lewis School, Mill Lane, Warford, Nr Alderley Edge, Cheshire SK9 7UD tel: 01565 872613.

Further information about epilepsy and education can be obtained from the British Epilepsy Association Helpline (0808) 800 5050. The Helpline has a 24-hour answering machine, on which a message can be left to obtain the information you require. Alternatively, you can speak directly to an Advice and Information Officer. This service is available from 9.00am to 4.30pm Monday to Thursday and 9.00am to 4.00pm on Friday.

Gifted children
(Arno Rabinowitz, Chartered Educational Psychologist, Specialist Psychological Services)

In every group of children there are some who show more creativity, have more interest in learning and who are quicker to learn. Researchers estimate that these children make up about 2 per cent of the school population and these are the ones that are often called gifted. The word gifted, though, is not so often used now: schools prefer to use more accurate terms like able and talented or exceptionally able. Whatever term is used, the education of these children poses many special problems. The first problem is identifying the child with unusual or special abilities. From the very beginning the child will have been specially responsive to new ideas and insatiably curious, often severely testing the limits of parents' patience. A powerful sense of observation, an early ability to use logic and to read, an easy growth of lateral thinking and usually a good ability to express ideas and feelings are other early indictors of exceptional ability. Sometimes too, allied with these, is early development of good co-ordination, ingenuity in managing mechanical problems and a degree of determination and persistence that can be exhausting for the adults involved. If you link this with a special interest and ability ahead of usual developmental levels in activities such as music, you have a good profile of an average child with special abilities. The main thing to remember, though, is that there is no average specially able child. Each one is very different and has very different needs.

Once the child gets to school he or she may be quite quickly recognised as specially able by alert teachers. They will notice that the child is good at reasoning and dealing with abstract ideas and can do both of these remarkably quickly The child's vocabulary and ability to use it will be better than most. Reading will have usually developed easily and quickly, but this does not always happen. There are many dyslexic gifted children. For most, though, problem-solving appears to be a pleasure, as is the ability to put solutions into effect. Linked with this is often a very low boredom threshold and consequent displacement behaviour. The more able are not always the best behaved in class.

As a result, problems do sometimes arise. Teachers, particularly those who lack appropriate resources and training, may misinterpret signs of exceptional ability if a child is naughty or disruptive or has learning difficulties such as dyslexia or dyspraxia or conditions such as Asperger Syndrome (see p15) which gives rise to additional frustrations for the child. If parents believe that their child's exceptional abilities have not been recognised at school, tact, diplomacy and persistence will be required in tackling this issue.

Tests by educational psychologists, arranged through the school or through one of the relevant organisations, can give a very good idea of the child's academic potential. They can show, too, if a child is underachieving. However, a combination of the observations of parents and teachers, together with formal tests, is usually the best way of achieving a clear idea of a child's ability. What is particularly important in all testing is that any results are related to the National Curriculum and the levels to be expected. If this does not happen then it is very difficult for schools to make proper use of any estimations of potential ability.

Identification is the first problem. The second is understanding the need for these special children to have as normal a childhood as possible. Without this it is difficult for the child, as an adult, to make complete use of his or her special abilities.

Although more able children learn more quickly, their rate of emotional development is not always equally swift. For intellectual activities the child may need to be in a group doing higher level work but will still require the friendship, companionship and stimulation of a group of people of the same age and social interests.

People often think that the best way to help more able children is to accelerate them through classes so that they spend time learning with older and higher-achieving children. This is not always the right course. An enhanced curriculum, for which the National Curriculum makes good provision, is usually better for the child's development. The more able also need more opportunities for activities and the development of interests so as to prevent the onset of boredom. The most helpful way to provide this is often through evening and weekend clubs at school and activities organised by the major voluntary societies.

When the child reaches secondary school the extension of the curriculum is easier to organise. This can be arranged through the provision of differentiated work in conjunction with a school extension programme for the most able. Some schools allow the student to work with more advanced groups while retaining a link with their class or tutor group. Some can arrange for students to work at a local college for part of the curriculum. What is needed is a degree of imagination and resourcefulness in curriculum design while at the same time remembering the important principle that the normal process of personal and emotional development needs to be given as much care as does the narrowly academic process.

Sometimes difficulties arise when more able children show behaviour problems or appear to be unrecognised or underachieving. If this should happen, the first approach for parents should be to the child's tutor or to the school's special educational needs co-ordinator. Discussion should result in some agreement about the child's ability and needs. If not, parents should ask the school to bring in an educational psychologist (EP) to observe or test the child . It is sensible to ask for a copy of the school or LEA policy as soon as possible. Sometimes, if there is no agreement or if the school has no access to a psychologist, parents arrange for an independent assessment. This can be organised through the National Association for Gifted Children (01908 673677). The British Psychological Society (0116 254 9568) publishes a list of chartered psychologists and this is usually available in public libraries.

It is important that able children are helped to achieve everything they can. It is equally important that, in doing this, they do not become isolated from their friends and from groups in school; otherwise they will lose as much as they may have gained from early achievement. Balance, as in all things, is very important. Finding out your child's capabilities, working with the school to ensure that the child is stretched but not isolated, and allowing the child as much of a normal childhood as possible is the ideal prescription, the one to be aimed at. Intelligence and wisdom are two very different qualities. Finding the right prescription for a child will mean that these qualities both grow together and result in happiness and appropriate achievement.

[The Gabbitas, Truman and Thring Educational Trust manages a programme of masterclasses and residential courses for exceptionally able children. For details of 'Tomorrow's Achievers' and a list of courses contact Patricia Morse (see p.viii)]

Deafness/Hearing impairment
(Information provided by the National Deaf Children's Society)

About deafness

There are three types of deafness:

1) *Conductive.* In these cases sound may not pass into the middle ear or to the nerve of hearing. This is caused by blockages in the ear canal or fluid in the middle ear. If untreated, this can sometimes lead to the second type.
2) *Sensori-neural* (nerve deafness). This is where the nerve of hearing does not process sound effectively.
3) *Mixed Deafness.* This describes instances where both conductive and sensori-neural deafness are present.

Few deaf children are totally deaf. Most have some hearing, on some frequencies at certain volumes.

A central principle of recent reforms has been the need for a 'continuum of provision' to match 'a continuum of needs'. This principle for deaf children, if not for children with other learning difficulties, appears increasingly at risk. Past closures of schools for deaf children (independent and maintained) due to falling rolls attest to this and are mainly a result of pressure on LEA budgets to keep children within county or borough schools. This is not to say that all LEAs are recommending placements they think they can afford rather than in line with the child's individual needs; but the NDCS has evidence from its advocacy service and SEN tribunal experience that some children are being required to attend or remain in unsuitable local provision where the exact terms of the statement cannot be met. Deaf children learn better in small groups and many parents are turning, especially at secondary level, to independent or non-maintained schools for deaf children for more favourable teacher-pupil ratios. In some cases parents would prefer a local placement but a suitable school within reasonable travelling distance might not always be available. However, it is hoped that forthcoming SEN legislation with emphasis expected on regional planning for children with low incidence disabilities may open up more options for parents with deaf children.

What do deaf children need?

Choices

NDCS sees the extension of choice as the main challenge for the education of deaf children and has launched a Charter (which closely follows the good practice recommended in the Code of Practice introduced with the 1996 Education Act) to encourage LEAs to promote choice. Parents need:

- good quality, unbiased information on maintained and independent schools within and outside the LEA area (a legal requirement of the Education Act 1996);
- face to face support from teachers of the deaf, educational psychologists, school staff or health and social services professionals to enable them to reach the best decision on the communication method and school.

Information must be delivered at the right time, not just after diagnosis, and with sensitivity (taking into account the culture of deaf parents whose first language is British Sign Language and parents from ethnic communities). Parents value jargon-free, easy to follow information about their rights and responsibilities, especially with reference to the complex statutory assessment and statementing process. NDCS has recently produced 'Quality Standards in the Education of Children' which offers service providers valuable benchmarks.

Sufficient and well co-ordinated support services

The development of market forces in education and with it the current requirement for LEAs to delegate no less than 95 per cent of the potential school budget to schools may restrict LEAs' ability to hold vital support services centrally. The creation of new unitary authorities raises doubts about the capacity of these smaller LEAs to take advantage of economies of scale and many parents worry about loss of expertise if cities are set adrift from the old shire counties or metropolitan boroughs. It is hoped that the unitary authorities will share expertise and resources with hearing-impaired services within the counties or boroughs in the new scenario. Indeed, it is hoped that new law will discourage LEAs from 'going it alone' and facilitate greater sharing of resources, facilities and expertise.

Teachers of the deaf

Teachers of the deaf fulfil many vital functions which include:

- home visits to newly diagnosed and pre-school children to help parents develop involvement in their child's early education and social development;
- the development of language, whether signed or spoken or both (as in Total Communication Approaches);
- checking of audiological equipment (although parents, support staff and deaf young people could be taught to check hearing and radio aids);
- advising and helping to train school staff to meet legal requirements, identifying and acting upon the needs of deaf children, with or without a statement of special educational needs. This might also mean advising staff on appropriate

testing and assessment tools and teaching methods (eg Derbyshire Language Programme).

In the latter part of the last decade there was great concern about a future shortage of teachers of the deaf. NDCS research found that the majority of qualified specialist teachers were aged 40+ and that there were insufficient numbers of young people to replace them once they retire. It remains to be seen whether LEAs will be able to fund existing teachers to complete the additional mandatory teacher of the deaf qualification, thus ensuring a more healthy supply.

Speech therapy

Speech and language therapists have a wealth of knowledge about speech and language development (which goes beyond teaching the child to articulate sound) and may work with oral or signing children to develop competence in lip-reading or British Sign Language (BSL). Some may use Signed Supported English (where a sign is used to follow the significant words in an English sentence). Unlike BSL, SSE is not a language but is used to develop English vocabulary.

Despite a favourable high court ruling and the Code of Practice's granting of 'ultimate responsibility' for speech therapy to LEAs, the provision of speech therapy continues to be an on-going problem. However, the government will be looking at the problems again in the foreseeable future.

Audiological equipment

Many deaf children, especially those in schools which emphasise the development of spoken language, are now exposed to a range of highly sophisticated aids to hearing to help them make use of any residual hearing which may exist at certain sound frequencies. It should be emphasised that whilst spectacles can correct long or short sight, no aid will restore hearing. Cochlear implants (high-powered hearing aids which are surgically attached to the skull) will open up to about 40 or more frequencies to deaf people. Although this can make a significant difference to a child's ability to access sounds, it should be remembered that hearing people are able to access thousands of frequencies. Most commonly used in schools, especially in whole class teaching, are radio aids. A sound receiver is body-worn by the pupil and is linked to a transmitter worn by the teacher. The advantage over a traditional behind the ear or in the ear aid is that it creates a direct link between teacher and pupil, eliminating unhelpful extraneous sounds within the class-room.

Acoustic environment

Statements or Individual Education Plans for some deaf children may feature 'an acoustically treated environment' or at least 'quiet space or room within the school/classroom'. Carpets, curtains and blinds help to muffle background noise. However, whilst many units attached to mainstream schools are acoustically treated, the rest of the building may not be so, and recent government initiatives, such as the Schools Access Initiative, will need to be more generous. The Disability Discrimination Act does not currently apply to schools.

Whilst recent developments covering maintained schools are to be welcomed, it is not surprising that some parents of deaf children seek an education for their child in deaf schools in the independent or non-maintained sector. These are generally well-placed to offer small classes, good access to teachers of the deaf, speech therapists and deaf-friendly school staff, a sizeable and appropriate deaf peer group, access to audiological aids and a good acoustic environment. NDCS acknowledges the improvements and good work in the state sector but believes that with the right allocation of resources and approach on the part of LEAs, maintained mainstream schools could be made to work more effectively for the 93 per cent deaf children being educated alongside their hearing peers.

For further information, please contact Anne-Marie Hall, Education Adviser, NDCS, 15 Dufferin Street, London EC1Y 8PD. Tel: 020 7250 0123. Fax: 020 7251 5020. Parents' freephone 2–5pm weekdays 0800 252380.

Leukaemia
(Dr Deborah Christie, C. Clin. Psychologist AFBPsS, Consultant Clinical Psychologist, Middlesex Hospital Adolescent Unit)

Leukaemia is a cancer of the blood where the white blood cells stop working properly. The malfunctioning (malignant) cells can also invade internal organs and can get into the central nervous system. Early symptoms include anaemia, problems with infection and abnormal bruising. Current treatment for leukaemia has resulted in up to 80 per cent of children achieving cure. The treatment involves intensive chemotherapy, which will last up to two years. The child may also undergo radiotherapy. The small number of children who relapse will undergo additional chemotherapy and/or radiotherapy. They may also be given a bone marrow transplant.

Associated learning difficulties

Associated learning difficulties on treatment may include tiredness, nausea, poor appetite and hair loss, which are the most common acute side effects of the drugs. Some children can lose a lot of weight. Steroids may cause dramatic weight increases and irritable behaviour. Regular hospital appointments in addition to these side effects can make getting back to school difficult for the recently diagnosed child. Children on treatment must also be careful to avoid direct contact with certain viral illnesses, a factor which will also disrupt regular school attendance.

Children can have different emotional reactions to their diagnosis. Some children become angry, argumentative and demanding. Other children become withdrawn, anxious and depressed. Both reactions are quite normal and usually lessen as time goes on. All these problems can make it hard to concentrate, learn and participate in 'normal' school life.

Accurate and honest information about the disease is important for everyone in the school. While the child is in hospital, the school might send a tape, video or newsletter about what is happening. The school can also help by sending class work to the child at home. Liaison with the hospital school can reassure children that they will not fall behind in topic work during admissions or time at home. A school assembly about cancer can help classmates (and parents) understand what is happening to their friend and answer some fantasies and worries they may have (for example, classmates may be worried about catching the cancer). Advance warning about the possible changes may help them to be less frightened by changes in appearance. This can also reduce the incidence of teasing or bullying. Working closely with parents can also help reassure teachers about how much to expect of the child.

Research has shown that the combination of chemotherapy and radiotherapy caused learning difficulties in up to 40 per cent of children treated for leukaemia. For children who receive a second course of treatment the chance of developing learning difficulties is much higher. Many children experience a similar pattern of difficulties.

The most common problem is a drop in overall intellectual ability (IQ). The two most important factors in predicting long term effects of treatment are (a) age at treatment and (b) gender. Children treated at a younger age are more likely to develop problems than older children. In particular they may have difficulty with abstract verbal reasoning. Girls show greater vulnerability to treatment effects than boys, whatever their age at treatment. They develop impairments in a wider range of intellectual functions, with a selective reduction in verbal skills compared with non verbal abilities.

For those children who appear to maintain their overall IQ levels, short term memory, attention and concentration can often be selectively impaired. Many children have problems remembering several instructions or have difficulty processing and remembering visual information. This may make it difficult for them to copy quickly and accurately from the blackboard. Children with attention or concentration problems may be unable to concentrate for more than a few minutes or have problems completing or finishing tasks. This will make it difficult for them to keep up with lessons or complete assignments. Their behaviour can be seen as deliberately naughty or disruptive which results in them being constantly criticised. This can cause them to be unhappy and demotivated.

Curriculum

In many children the consequence of this pattern of cognitive impairment occurs in tandem with levels of reading, spelling and maths that are well below that which might be expected given their IQ. Some children will have problems in all areas of the curriculum while others will have specific problems with reading and spelling, making them appear to be like children who are dyslexic.

Many children find it difficult to learn how letters and sounds go together while other children with a poor visual memory struggle to remember how a word 'looks'. Maths may cause particular problems as short term memory and poor sequencing can contribute to difficulties with written maths and automatic memory-based number skills like learning tables. Older children may struggle to copy information from the blackboard quickly and accurately. Understanding and remembering class work or homework may also be difficult. Although, as mentioned above, having leukaemia may mean missing quite a lot of school, this is not the major contribution to these problems. The children who show the greatest difficulties in school have usually been diagnosed and treated before they began attending school.

The best way to address these problems is to try and determine levels of ability at time of diagnosis. Regular monitoring of progress is required and at the first signs of difficulty the school should set up additional support. A detailed neuropsychological assessment can help identify patterns of strengths and weaknesses that may be related to treatment (Christie et al, 1995).

Emotional concerns

Emotional concerns should also be taken into account. As children get older and the illness becomes ever more part of the past they may still have worries about how it has affected them. They may also worry about the cancer coming back. If their friends do not know about the cancer children may worry about them finding out. Being worried or anxious can make it difficult to concentrate in class. Some children may appear to have a 'short fuse' and lose their temper more easily than other children. For all children, being unable to 'keep up' feeds into a vicious cycle of failure and poor self esteem. This can produce emotional adjustment difficulties that make the learning difficulties more entrenched and severe.

The majority of children can remain in mainstream schooling with varying degrees of support. Some children however may develop moderate to severe learning difficulties that make it harder for them to function in a mainstream school without intensive teaching support and will require a special needs environment. It is possible to identify and assess those children who are at greatest risk for developing problems as they progress through the education system. Appropriate long term remedial support can help children readjust their learning strategies and develop compensatory strategies to help them deal with difficulties that are the consequence of treatment.

References

Christie, D, Leiper, AD, Chessells, J M and Vargha-Khadem, F. 'Intellectual Performance after presymptomatic treatment for lymphoblastic leukaemia: effects of age, time since treatment and sex'. *Archives of Disease in Childhood* 1995 (73) 136–140.

Loss of, or damage to, limbs
(Information supplied by the Royal Association for Disability and Rehabilitation)

Children may be born without a limb or part of one (limb deficiency), or they may lose all or part of a limb as a result of an accident, or through medical necessity (amputation).

Artificial limbs (prostheses) are usually provided for young children, both to encourage development of strength in the muscles and patterns of movement and, perhaps most importantly, to encourage independence. Learning to use artificial limbs is self-evidently not a natural process and takes time and practice, according to the motivation and skills of each child. Some may need encouragement, whilst others may need help to prevent them being too ambitious. For children born with digits missing or who have a partial hand, prostheses are not available or appropriate.

Staff will need to be aware of a child's needs before they start school. Parents will be able to advise on the medical aspects of the limb loss and in most instances a child will be able to explain their own needs, eg how he or she operates the arm, what he or she can and cannot do and how much help might be needed. It is important for a pupil to be given the opportunity to say when he or she prefers to wear or remove the artificial limb, for example for PE, or during hot weather when the residual limb may become uncomfortably hot in the prosthesis.

A child who is fitted with a prosthesis will be in regular contact with a prosthesist, who will be able to advise on any problems in using the prosthesis, or in new tasks to be learned. As children grow, prostheses need to be replaced regularly. If the child has had an amputation, they may need surgery from time to time to check the growth of the residual limb.

There are no learning difficulties specifically associated with limb deficiency or amputation. However, teachers may have to seek extra time for students sitting examinations if it is considered that the student's writing speed is affected by the limb loss. Written forms of language can be produced on typewriters, personal computers or a voice-activated computer system, and access to word-processing can be tailored to the requirements of the pupil. Other solutions include accessing the word processor via single or multiple switches, which may be in the form of rollerballs or joysticks.

The artificial arms usually supplied to children are made of metal or plastic and have a grasp mechanism. They are normally covered in foam and toning plastic to improve the appearance. With practice pupils develop the skills needed to use the arm and grasp mechanism. Most children do not learn to write with their artificial arm. Some prefer to use their own ways of managing instead of, or as well as, using an artificial arm. A pupil's preference is important but it is also advisable to check with the parents, prosthesist and/or occupational therapist to ensure a consistent approach.

Children with no upper limbs who do not use artificial arms have to learn methods of managing their own personal needs. Initially they may require assistance, but with time many of them develop the skills needed to be fully independent. Children who have lost one or both legs, above or below the knee, will be able to use artificial limbs, but are still likely to have some mobility difficulties. Some may use sticks or crutches and some may use a wheelchair. Mobility needs should be taken into account when considering emergency procedures.

Children who have limb deficiency should be encouraged to take part in PE as far as possible. Physical fitness is as important for these pupils as for all others. Children will often develop strategies for participating within their limits but may need encouragement. If advice is needed a physiotherapist will be able to help. If the child chooses to participate without the artificial limb, it is important it is stored safely and securely. If the limb is hidden as a prank this can be very distressing for the child.

Children who lose a limb following an accident or through medical necessity often find it difficult to adjust to their impairment and changed body image. They, their parents and possible siblings may need counselling to help them work through the emotional stress of the loss of a limb. Emotional stress is an almost universal experience amongst amputees, their families and carers.

Any child who is physically 'different' is at risk of being teased. It may be helpful to ensure that the child concerned has a simple explanation and is ready to satisfy the curiosity of their peers. A matter-of-fact attitude on the part of the adults will help to reduce any embarrassment felt by a pupil and their peer group.

Good communication between parents, professionals and the pupil must be encouraged to ensure proper resources are in place. The expertise of parents and pupil should be utilised, and inter-agency collaboration will help smooth the way for the pupil's academic and social development. The transition from school to adult life can often be a stressful time and the process of transitional planning is therefore essential.

Further information is available from:

The National Co-ordinator
REACH – Association for Children with Hand or Arm Deficiency
12 Wilson Way
Earls Barton
Northamptonshire
NN6 0NZ
Tel: 01604 811041

Limbless Association
Roehampton Rehabilitation Centre
Roehampton Lane
London
SW15 5PR
Tel: 020 8788 1777

Muscular dystrophy
(Information supplied by the Muscular Dystrophy Campaign)

Muscular dystrophy (MD) is a name given to many different conditions which have in common the breakdown of muscle fibres leading to weak and wasted muscles. More than 20,000 children and adults in the UK have MD or a related neuromuscular condition.

Each of these neuro muscular conditions has a different cause; they are mostly genetic, but some are autoimmune (where a person's immune system attacks healthy cells within the body itself). Symptoms of some disorders show very early on, even at birth, but in others symptoms may only start to show later in childhood or adulthood. Severity is variable: several conditions are very disabling or life-threatening; the rest can cause moderate or mild disability. Most of the conditions cause progressive weakening of the muscles but some remain stable. Different conditions affect different muscles and various other body systems. The inheritance risks vary. There can also be a wide variation in the degree of severity not only between one type of dystrophy and another but also between individuals with the same type.

In some conditions, particularly Duchenne muscular dystrophy (DMD) and myotonic dystrophy, some individuals may have a degree of intellectual impairment. This may be reflected particularly in poor reading ability, word comprehension and memory skills.

This intellectual impairment is not directly related to muscle weakness, however, and is not progressive.

Children's educational needs depend, of course, on the individual concerned and the nature of their condition and disability. Some children may need to attend special schools but many will be able to continue with mainstream schooling right through to college or university. Help needed within school will also vary widely depending on the physical limitations of the individual. Many children with a significant disability will need a great deal of support.

Some conditions also have other complications which need to be carefully monitored, such as heart and breathing problems and allergy to anaesthesia. Muscle weakness can also cause additional mobility problems such as contractures (tightening of joints) and scoliosis (curvature of the spine).

Anyone can be affected by these conditions. They are usually inherited from the parent(s) but can appear out of the blue, in a family with no history of the condition. Males and/or females can be affected depending on the genetic cause of the condition. For example, DMD is usually inherited from the mother by the son. Apart from very rare exceptions females are the only carriers of DMD and are not affected themselves. In myotonic dystrophy either the mother or the father is affected and can pass the gene on. In spinal muscular atrophy neither parent is affected but both must carry the faulty gene for it to be passed on to their children. The conditions are not infectious.

It is not possible to 'catch' muscular dystrophy or any of the related conditions. However, if someone is found to be affected, their relatives might also have the condition because the disrupted gene may run in the family.

Although there are as yet no treatments or cures available for the majority, physiotherapy is helpful and symptoms can be alleviated through careful management. However, it is possible to treat the symptoms of myotonia congenita effectively. Immunological treatment is possible for polymyositis, dermatomyositis, myasthenia gravis and other immunological neuromuscular conditions. These treatments may involve the use of immunosuppressive drugs such as steroids, plasma exchange and intravenous immunoglobin.

Researchers are trying to find treatments and cures for the rest. Where the cause is genetic, identification of the genetic fault is the first vital step towards understanding the condition and then finding a treatment. Muscular Dystrophy Campaign researchers are at the forefront of international research; they already know the genetic faults responsible for several conditions and are investigating several possible treatments.

A fact sheet entitled 'Children with muscular dystrophy in mainstream schools' is available from the Muscular Dystrophy Campaign, 7–11 Prescott Place, London, SW4 6BS Tel: 020 7720 8055.

Speech and language difficulties
(Information supplied by Afasic)

The ability to use language and communicate effectively is the basis of all learning and social interaction. Without these skills, education will not achieve its goals. It follows that the development of language and communication skills is central to all education.

The vast majority of children with special educational needs have one or other kind of communication difficulty. There is also a group of children who do not develop language skills normally, irrespective of any obvious intellectual or physical disability. These children are often said to have a specific or primary speech or language impairment, which may be in isolation or alongside another disability.

It is estimated that 1 in 500 school-age children will have severe long-term impairments, while at least 6 per cent will experience some degree of difficulty at some time which could interfere with his or her educational progress.

Characteristics

Some children are unable to understand or express themselves clearly, while others have near normal understanding but experience difficulty in speaking intelligibly. Some may not be able to form words and sentences correctly, have limited vocabulary, may produce strings of unintelligible sounds or repeat spoken language correctly without knowing the meaning of what they say. Some will have difficulty with the beginnings and endings of words. Others may display 'autistic tendencies'.

Identification of difficulties

Any of the following can be an indication of a language impairment:

- late onset of speech;
- a discrepancy between verbal and non-verbal skills or between receptive and expressive language;
- lack of concentration;
- history of 'glue-ear';
- difficulty with fine and/or gross motor skills;
- short-term memory;
- word-finding difficulties;
- poor interaction with peers.

As language skills develop very rapidly in the early years, much is gained if difficulties are identified as early as possible. 2–3 years of age is not too early. Where help is provided at this age, a child is often able to join a mainstream school at 5 years of age. If the difficulties are not tackled in the early years, and the child struggles through primary schooling, difficulties can be seriously compounded by the time secondary age is reached. In a mainstream school the child is unlikely to be able to master the necessary conceptual understanding and complex social interactions expected in such a setting and may well become confused, disorientated, suffer emotional stress and succumb to bullying. Special schooling is then likely to be the only way to begin to provide effective help.

Assessment of difficulties

If there is cause for concern and a speech and language therapist has not already been seen, referral should be arranged following discussion with parent(s). It is obviously important to identify a child's particular strengths and weaknesses at the first possible opportunity. Speech and language therapists have the skills to undertake such an assessment and to advise how any weakness may be overcome. Where a child's difficulties are particularly severe it is likely that a full assessment has taken place, or is underway, and that a statement has been drawn up.

Ways to help

Those with severe difficulties are best helped in a special school or language unit or class, with teachers and speech and language therapists working very closely in partnership. In the latter, intensive language work can take place with integration into the host school as and when appropriate. There are about 400 such units throughout the country, but few, as yet, are available for secondary-aged pupils.

Even where difficulties are not said to be severe, input from a speech and language therapist is recommended, as different approaches and programmes can be discussed, the most appropriate selected and queries clarified. Advice from an occupational and/or physiotherapist should be sought for those with co-ordination difficulties.

Because these children do not acquire language spontaneously as others do, they need to be taught appropriate skills in a structured setting.

- A planned approach should be used to teach speaking and listening skills and reading and writing for all pupils.
- Activities should encourage the development of turn-taking, rhythms and rhyme and the building up of self-esteem and confidence.
- Where a child has difficulty in learning the order of a task, it helps to structure the sequence of skills and to simplify each step.
- The use of computers and a combination of sight, sound, touch or movement can be valuable.
- Small group work (4–8 pupils) is essential to achieve national curriculum targets successfully.
- Social skills and the use of social or functional language must be developed.

It can be especially helpful to relate work to a child's own interests or family.

For further information please send a stamped, addressed envelope to Afasic, 69–85 Old Street, London EC1V 9HX.

Spina Bifida and/or Hydrocephalus

(Information supplied by the Association for Spina Bifida and Hydrocephalus)

What is Spina Bifida?

Spina bifida is a congenital disability that affects babies very early in pregnancy. It is a fault in the development of the spine, when one or more vertebrae fail to close properly. Spina bifida usually affects the lower limbs, where there will be a lack of sensation of pain and temperature and perhaps problems with circulation. Many people with spina bifida will have continence problems, which need to be managed effectively if self-image is not to be damaged.

What is Hydrocephalus?

Hydrocephalus happens when the fluid in the brain cannot drain away into the blood-stream because the normal pathways are blocked. The excess pressure must be relieved quickly to minimise brain damage.

New drainage pathways are opened, either by inserting a fine tube (called a shunt) inside a space in the brain or by making a small hole in the floor of one of these spaces, this operation is called a ventriculostomy.

Many people with spina bifida also have hydrocephalus, but it can occur by itself, especially after meningitis, a head injury, stroke, or in babies born prematurely.

Hydrocephalus may affect motor skills, vision, speech and language, and behaviour.

Neither spina bifida nor hydrocephalus is associated with any particular level of general intelligence.

Educational issues for children with spina bifida and/or hydrocephalus

Time off in hospital
Children with spina bifida and/or hydrocephalus may require repeated admission to hospital or hospital visits as out-patients. During prolonged stays in hospital, arrange-ments will probably need to be made for formal education to be continued.

Physical access
Consideration may need to be given to access issues, especially wheelchair access, or access to the cirriculum through specialist equipment or classroom assistance before a child starts at a particular school.

Learning
Hydrocephalus, whether it has or has not been shunted, may affect (1) a child's co-ordination and visual-spatial perception, (2) short-term memory and ability to solve problems, and concept of time and (3) social and emotional development.

(1) Co-ordination and perception
Some children appear to be clumsy and have balance problems. Many tire very easily. Hand-eye co-ordination may be poor, and there is often a weak handgrip.

Visuo-spatial perception may be affected, resulting in a distorted view of the world. There may, for instance, be difficulty in distinguishing between a step and a line drawn on the ground. Many children have squints, some may have tunnel vision, or nystagmus. Work in mathematics and geography may be affected.

For some children, some abilities can improve through time, although appropriate experiences should be provided at an early age. However, careful observation is needed to identify ways in which residual visual problems (squints, tunnel vision) may be affecting a child's performance, eg in copying from the blackboard and organising their belongings.

Help and understanding may be needed in the following situations:

- walking long distances and walking down stairs
- colouring-in and hand-writing; using scissors and other tools; fastening buttons; tying laces
- moving in crowded spaces without bumping into furniture or other people
- 'finding' objects that are mixed up with other objects, interpreting diagrams and maps
- noticing things on their desk and table, which are immediately in front, or to one side
- 'tuning in' to one voice, against a background of chatter and hypersensitivity to noises like clapping, laughter or lawn mowers.

(2) Memory, problem-solving and concept of time

Long-term memory for details of events is usually very good. However, many children have short-term memory problems, especially in retaining spoken words long enough to understand what they mean. The 'verbal' ability of many children can lead others to presume that they understand the instructions and conversations when this may not be so. Most children will have short concentration spans. Many will have problems in self-correcting, expressing observations and giving explanations, and these children will find it difficult to 'make connections' between different items of information. Most children will need extra time and help to learn new ideas, and to develop the thinking strategies they need to deal with unfamiliar information.

Again for some children, some abilities can improve if appropriate experiences are provided. However, unless they are also helped to recognise their own competencies and what is expected of them, many still experience a great deal of anxiety in relatively unfamiliar situations, which may include formal tests.

Help and understanding may be needed in the following situations:

- concentrating on tasks, and self-monitoring
- switching from one activity to another
- finding their way in an unfamiliar environment
- understanding and remembering verbal instructions
- giving clear accounts – there can be a tendency to focus on isolated, unconnected details
- self-organisation – where to start, what to do next
- problem-solving – reluctance to engage in 'difficult' work without help
- thinking ahead – tendency to act or speak before they think.

(3) Social and Emotional Behaviour

Hydrocephalus is sometimes linked with developmental delay in physical development in infancy and also in language development.

Although children with hydrocephalus are very 'sociable' some may have problems in adjusting their own behaviour to different social contexts. Some can tend to treat everyone as a 'friend'. Some may be very shy, or overly domineering with their peers. Lack of self-esteem is common and some people become withdrawn and depressed, while others show challenging behaviours.

Children with hydrocephalus can be helped to learn social skills and have more confidence in themselves, and the chances of this teaching being effective are greater if begun before the beginning of Key Stage 2.

Help may be needed to develop skills in the following areas:

- self-inhibition, eg learning to wait their turn to speak
- addressing different people in appropriate ways
- peer relationships
- anticipating unfamiliar situations
- participating in family and classroom chores

Support in mainstream

Behavioural problems may be evident in school but not at home, and vice versa. It is important not to attribute blame in either context. Open and trusting relationships between parents and teachers are essential, as is a problem-solving approach to any perceived difficulties.

Good school-home partnerships will ensure that information relating to possible medical problems and physical difficulties is shared and understood, and that the 'strategies' to be used to solve behavioural problems are consistent. No strategy will succeed unless the child is also involved.

If learning support assistant time is available in class, target it on developing the skills the children will need to work and socialise independently. This may be a matter of gradual withdrawal of support, eg as children develop the ability to listen to whole-class instructions and carry them, the assistant may begin to use prompts instead of repeating the whole instructions on a one-to-one basis.

Making a point of observing and noting the outcomes of the approaches that are used, and to modify them as necessary after discussions. If the children can begin to think positively about the skills and knowledge they are developing, this will provide the confidence for more difficult tasks.

ASBAH produces a pack of ten topic sheets, a book titled Hydrocephalus and You. These are available from: Information, ASBAH National Centre, 42 Park Road, Peterborough, PE1 2UQ, Tel: 01733 555988, Email: gillw@asbah.org

Gilles de la Tourette Syndrome
(Dr Deborah Christie, C. Clin. Psychologist, AFBPsS, Consultant Clinical Psychologist, Middlesex Hospital Adolescent Unit)

Gilles de la Tourette Syndrome (TS) was first identified over 100 years ago. It is an inherited condition. There are often other members of the family who will have either TS themselves or some of the symptoms. It is associated with dysfunction in areas of the brain responsible for movement and the control of inhibition and impulsivity. These difficulties are thought to be connected with an excess of a brain chemical (neurotransmitter) called Dopamine. Medication which alters the amount of Dopamine in the brain can often help reduce many of the symptoms.

TS is found in three times as many boys as girls. Peak onset is around seven years of age and for many children a period of inattentiveness and impulsiveness precedes the onset of the tics. This may often be diagnosed as attention deficit disorder (ADD) – with or without hyperactivity, although over time it becomes clear that the attentional problems are not the primary difficulty. Very often the medication prescribed for ADD can exacerbate or initiate the onset of tics.

Tics

The main symptom in TS is the involuntary movements (motor) or noises (vocal) known as tics. These can be simple (eye blinks, head nod, sniffs, grunts) or complex (twirling, jumping, shouting or repeating things). One feature of the tics is their tendency to change over time. They may become more or less frequent or intense or may alter completely.

Attentional problems

Children with Tourette's syndrome can have problems with attention or concentration. It is estimated that 50 per cent of children with TS may be inattentive, impulsive and overactive, which are the core manifestations of AD/HD (see p.10). This does not necessarily mean the child has AD/HD. He or she may be unable to concentrate for more than a few minutes or have problems finishing tasks. This will make it difficult for the child to keep up with lessons or complete assignments. Teachers may see behaviour as deliberately naughty or disruptive, which may result in the child being constantly criticised.

Obsessive Compulsive Behaviour

Beside the tics, 50–70 per cent of children with TS suffer from obsessive compulsive behaviour. An obsession is an overwhelming thought or image that produces significant distress and anxiety. To reduce this anxiety the individual feels a compulsion to complete a stereotyped behaviour or action. Children with TS may be unable to stop themselves touching something (or someone). They may need to do things in a particular way. These could be short routines, like flicking light switches, counting up to a certain number all the time or turning taps on and off. They may need to get dressed in a certain way. If anyone interrupts the routine, they may have to start all over again. Teachers may see this as stubborn or awkward behaviour. It can also cause conflicts with classmates.

Making friends

Many children with TS have problems making and keeping friends. They may not know how to 'stick to the rules', how to start a conversation, take turns or listen. Children with TS may have a 'short fuse' and lose their temper more easily than other children of the same age. Sometimes other children make fun of the habits and behaviours. Whatever the reason, having TS can make it hard to make friends.

Emotional problems

Although the motor and vocal tics (or habits) may not cause specific learning difficulties, they may result in emotional problems. The psychological sequelae of TS include aggressive behaviour, social difficulties, poor peer relationships, low self esteem, anxiety and depression. These can be both a part of the disorder and a response to how adults and other children respond to it. Teasing and bullying before or after being diagnosed can make the child feel bad about themselves. They may be withdrawn and unhappy at school or at home. Some children become defensive and angry in response to comments about habits or behaviour over which they have no control.

Intelligence

Although most children with TS are of normal intelligence, there is a tendency for verbal skills to be better developed than non verbal ones. They may also have specific problems with organising work, memory and copying. This means they may have difficulty copying information quickly and accurately from the blackboard. Maths may cause particular problems. There may also be difficulty in understanding and remembering class work or homework. A clinical or educational psychologist can complete a comprehensive assessment to see if your child has some of the difficulties that are often described in children with TS.

Living with tics

Although the tics described are involuntary, many children are also able to suppress them. The effect of this, however, is rather like putting a cork into the mouth of a kettle. There is a gradual increase in pressure (usually paralleling a wearing off of medication) and for many children there is an explosion of symptoms when they get home. The physical and psychological effort of suppressing the tics during the school day can cause children to be totally exhausted when they get home. They may also get a release of high levels of aggressive thoughts/behaviours that they have also been holding on to during the day. This can make it very difficult for homework to be completed efficiently or easily.

The relationship between stress, anxiety and the symptoms can be used to help children. Relaxation sessions in drama can help reduce tension (and stress). An accepting environment which acknowledges and responds sympathetically to the symptoms can initially produce an increase in tics as the child feels less need to suppress the movements/behaviours. Ultimately, however, the child becomes so comfortable that the frequency of the tics does reduce without the accompanying build-up of pressure. Another way of helping is building energy breaks into the day to help the child expel some of the built-up anxiety.

Parents may find it helpful to contact the Tourette Syndrome (UK) Association, PO Box 26149, Dunfermline KY12 9WT. Email: enquiries@tsa.org.uk

Visual impairment
(Information supplied by the Royal National Institute for the Blind)

There are more than 24,000 blind and partially sighted children and young people under the age of 16 in the UK today.

While visual impairment is a 'low incidence' disability with only about two children in every thousand being blind or partially sighted, these children have very individual and important information and support needs.

Although a few children have no sight at all, most have some vision. For example, some can tell the difference between light and dark, some have central vision and can only see things in front of them, while others can see out of the sides of their eye but not the middle.

Some people see everything as a vague blur, others as a patchwork of blanks and defined areas. Some see better in bright light, some when it is darker, and others find it impossible to adjust between light and dark.

Children with a sight impairment but no other significant additional needs

It is increasingly common for blind as well as partially sighted children to be included in mainstream schools. For some children, inclusion will be appropriate throughout their education. Others may need special schooling for part or all of their school lives. Some children move in and out of mainstream education as their needs change.

Many children do need some level of special school education. Depending on the individual, this may be in a school for blind and partially sighted pupils or in another type of special school.

Each child should be assessed as soon as possible so that the level of educational support needed can be planned in conjunction with the local education authority (LEA) visual impairment specialist. The RNIB can provide names of local LEA visual impairment specialists and also offers a wide variety of assessment services.

Whether the child is in a mainstream or special school, he or she will need some specialised materials, equipment, or adaptations to the standard of work of sighted children in order to follow the National Curriculum fully.

Children with some residual vision may be able to use enlarged materials, whether enlarged on a photocopier or specially printed in a larger print size. Some examination boards provide pre-enlarged exam papers, and all Key Stage examination papers are available in both enlarged and modified enlarged formats.

If visual impairment prevents a child from reading enlarged print, he or she may learn to read and write braille and may also make extensive use of audio tapes. There are organisations, including the RNIB, which can supply text books to blind and partially sighted children spanning a wide range of subjects at all levels.

Computers and other technology are also valuable supplements to a child with impaired vision. There are many different ways for blind and partially sighted children to use technology. Examples include:

- a closed-circuit television (CCTV). This enables a student to place a regular piece of print underneath a small moving camera, while the CCTV shows the enlarged print on a monitor. The students can then move the camera across a page and read a whole page of standard print.
- computer packages which can convert words on a computer screen into synthesised speech, and read computer files back to a blind or partially sighted student.
- devices which can be attached to a computer and allow the user to have a braille display of what is on the computer screen.
- packages which can convert computer text into a braille print-out. One device allows a child to braille onto a Perkins brailler, then produce a print copy for a sighted teacher.
- portable braille note-takers, which allow individuals to braille information into a small machine and retrieve it later by hooking it to a computer.

The RNIB offers advice to LEA staff, in-service training, and help in setting up new inclusion schemes. For individual schools and pupils, the RNIB has facilities for trying out special equipment and can help with particular aspects of the curriculum.

Blind and partially sighted children with additional needs

More than one child in every three with a visual impairment also has additional disabilities. Due to the range of causes of visual impairment, a child may also have a hearing impairment, learning difficulty, physical difficulty or a combination of impairments.

A full multi-disciplinary assessment of all of the child's educational needs will determine whether a special or mainstream school is most appropriate. There is a small number of specialist schools for blind and partially sighted children with additional needs, including four RNIB schools which cover the 3–9 age range. The RNIB also offers assessment services for children who have a complex range of impairments.

Technology is also used extensively with multiply-disabled children, particularly in the form of multi-sensory rooms using lights and sounds to stimulate the sensory-impaired child or touch screens and switch technology to help develop communication skills and provide access to the National Curriculum.

A large number of books and factsheets have been published by the RNIB and others about the education of blind and partially sighted children, many of which are available from the RNIB. For details of any aspect of the education of a blind or partially sighted child, including the services mentioned above, please contact the RNIB Helpline Tel: 0845 766 9999.

1.4

'Just like any other child only more so': Some Reflections on the Continuing Debate over Emotional & Behavioural Difficulties (EBD)

Jonathan A Fogell*
Chartered Educational Psychologist

Recent years have seen a deluge of government initiatives designed to redefine education. These have included the introduction and subsequent pruning of the National Curriculum, SATs, the rise and fall of Grant Maintained schools, league tables, OFSTED inspections (a flurry of naming and shaming), and many more. Most pupils meantime have continued their education with its array of minor triumphs and traumas, with relatively few complications despite the debate surrounding these innovations. For some there has even been evidence of improved educational performance.

Schools have continued their core business of developing well-adjusted young people fit to take their place in the world, equipping pupils with indelible memories and values, most of which are not unpleasant.

For those children at the margins, however, school life can be fraught with complications. Sometimes the child's unusual response to his or her environment is the source of difficulties. There has in recent years been greater understanding of the impact of a number of neurological syndromes/conditions which may affect the ability of a child to manage their behaviour:

- autistic spectrum disorder including Asperger Syndrome;
- Tourette's Syndrome;
- attention deficit (hyperactive) disorder;
- dyspraxia;
- specific learning difficulties;
- anxiety and panic disorder.

Most often for children with emotional and behavioural difficulties they have experienced or are enduring life circumstances that no one should be expected to tolerate. For this small but significant group there has been continuing evidence of growing dissatisfaction

---

* Jonathan Fogell is a Senior Educational Psychologist for West Sussex County Council. He is writing here in a personal capacity.

and disillusionment with schooling. The increasing rate of exclusion and truancy from our schools provides evidence of this.

The number of pupils excluded from schools remains small overall but it has risen sharply and then levelled in recent years:

Year	Number of permanent exclusions primary, secondary *and special schools*
1991/2	4,000
1996/7	13,500+ (Godfrey & Parsons, 1998)
1997/8	12,300 (DfEE, 1999)

In addition, there were some 135,000 temporary exclusions in 1996/7 (Smith, 1998).

Godfrey & Parsons (1998) and the Cabinet Office *Social Exclusion Unit Report* (1998) suggest the following reasons for the increase in exclusions:

- high levels of family stress;
- poor acquisition of basic skills, particularly literacy;
- limited aspirations and opportunities;
- poverty;
- poor relationships between pupils and parents or teachers.

Peter Smith (1998) summarised the evidence in relation to pupils temporarily excluded. He concluded that they faced considerable risks, they . . . 'are relegated to the margins of society while teachers find it difficult to cope, and the public picks up the cost for children who drift onto the streets without qualifications and skills where they can easily gravitate towards crime and prison'.

It has been argued, notably by some teachers' professional organisations, that if certain pupils are not excluded other children can be at a considerable disadvantage. Such arguments emphasise the teacher's right to teach and the pupils' right to learn. After all, the behaviours cited for exclusion are not pleasant reading:

- bullying;
- fighting and assaults on peers;
- disruption, misconduct and unacceptable behaviour;
- verbal abuse to peers;
- verbal abuse to staff;
- theft;
- defiance and disobedience;
- drugs (smoking, alcohol, cannabis);
- vandalism and arson;
- physical abuse and assaults on staff.

The list suggests that head teachers administer the majority of exclusions in a bid to protect the wider student community and therefore presents difficulties in formulating strategies to reduce exclusions because of the need to continue to protect pupils. Any head teacher introducing a policy of reducing exclusions might incur opposition from parents who want to see school tackling poor behaviour.

The argument at its simplest would be as follows: schools should make behavioural boundaries explicit, especially the conditions that will result in a pupil being excluded. They should then rigorously implement their policies. Local Education Authorities (LEAs) should in turn make adequate provision, in the form of special schools or units, for those excluded. Teachers could then get on with the task of teaching children who want to learn. So what's wrong with that?

The central problem with exclusions as a sanction is the apparent arbitrary nature of its usage. A number of groups are disproportionately likely to be excluded:

- children with statements of special educational needs, especially EBD;
- African-Caribbean children;
- looked-after children;
- boys (84 per cent of excluded pupils in 1997/8 were boys);
- pupils at Key Stage 4 (67 per cent aged 13–15).

While the exclusion rates vary greatly from school to school, they tend to be higher in areas of social deprivation. In addition, it is clear from current evidence that pupils with statements of special educational needs for EBD are amongst the groups most vulnerable to exclusion.

Moreover, one outcome of exclusion is to place further pressure on vulnerable families, potentially hastening the need for Social Services Department or other Agency involvement. Thus the problem is not so much solved as shifted elsewhere.

Hayden (1996) identified the risk factors determining likelihood or otherwise of a child being excluded from school. She described a complex interplay between pupil factors, family/environmental factors and school factors. A similar interplay exists in relation to emotional and behavioural difficulties. However, not all children excluded from school can be described as having special educational needs arising from emotional and behavioural difficulties. A label of EBD will only be appropriate if the problem behaviour presented by the child includes the following features:

- seriousness;
- frequency;
- persistence;
- irrationality;
- resistance to change;
- absence of alternative explanations for the behaviour.

The rise in emotional and behavioural difficulties is inextricably linked to the position of children in society. There is compelling evidence that our society is becoming more complex for children. Burghes (1994) observed that 'marked differences and poorer average outcomes are found for children from families disrupted by separation and divorce compared with those intact families'. Cockett and Tripp (1994) report that children whose families undergo a series of disruptions and changes are more likely to experience social, educational and health problems than those whose families remain intact. The message from these and many other reports appears to be that children can achieve stability and sound emotional growth within a wide range of family structures but the risk of emotional damage increases when the following factors, or a combination of them, exist:

- domestic conflict;
- poverty;
- inconsistent parenting;
- violence;
- abuse;
- poor housing;
- recent traumatic incident;
- time spent in care of Social Services Departments.

Concern about the cyclical effects of these difficulties is reflected by the decision of The Cabinet Office, Social Exclusion Unit, to focus on truancy and exclusions from school as one of the first areas for investigation. Their report refers to the need for 'joined-up thinking' in tackling deeply rooted complex problems. Solutions to problems are more likely to emerge from the variety of perspectives of the individual affected and the agencies working with them. The end result should be more creative solutions using the resources of a number of different agencies. The National Health Service (NHS) thematic review (1995) 'Child & Adolescent Mental Health Services: Together we stand', promotes a similarly inclusive approach. It concludes that mental health in young people is indicated by the following capacities:

- a capacity to enter into and sustain mutually satisfying personal relationships;
- continuing progression of psychological development;
- an ability to play and learn so that attainments are appropriate for age and intellectual level;
- a developing moral sense of right and wrong;
- the degree of psychological distress and maladaptive behaviour being within the normal limits for the child's age and context.

The National Children's Bureau (1997) advocates a future for supporting vulnerable children and young people that draws together Health, Education, Social Services Department and Voluntary Agencies. It acknowledges a helpful start in the Children Act (1989) requirement for local authorities to produce joint Children's Services Plans to map out local services from a range of different departments. Further attempts at co-ordinating services to support vulnerable pupils can be seen in the government circulars 10/99 and 11/99. Circular 10/99 explains the law and good practice on:

- pupil discipline and behaviour;
- reducing the risk of disaffection;
- school attendance and registration; detention
- proper use of exclusion; and
- reintegration of excluded pupils.

For those pupils who do not respond to action to combat disaffection (or more likely continue to present unacceptable standards of behaviour), this circular describes the use of Pastoral Support Programmes. This process does not replace the use of Statutory Assessment, and for pupils with statements of special educational needs, pastoral support programmes can be set up through their individual education plans. The main principles of a Pastoral Support Programme are described as follows:

- it is a school-based intervention;
- it should identify precise and realistic behavoural outcomes for the child to work towards;
- it should be overseen by a nominated member of staff;
- administration should be kept to a minimum;
- it should be automatically set up for a pupil who has had several fixed term exclusions.

Circular 11/89 explains the administrative and legal responsibilities of LEAs for:

- managing attendance, including legal action for enforcing attendance;
- providing education outside school;
- pupils at risk of exclusion;
- education and reintegrating excluded pupils; and
- pupil referral units.

The Government's green paper, 'Excellence for All Children: Meeting Special Educational Needs', of November 1997 and its subsequent action plan, Meeting Special Educational Needs: A Programme of Action, of October 1998 both acknowledge the complexities of work with children who present emotional and behavioural difficulties. The Government set the following agenda in this area:

- the need for a national programme to help primary schools tackle emotional and behavioural difficulties at a very early stage;
- enhancing opportunities for all staff to improve their skills in teaching children with emotional and behavioural difficulties;
- supporting schools that cater for pupils with emotional and behavioural difficulties when they are experiencing problems;
- supporting young people with EBD at Key Stage 4.

Inevitably much of the focus has been on those pupils who present conduct-disordered behaviour. This statistically small group of pupils often dominates the concerns of teachers because of the threat they pose to other pupils, the social control of the school community, the psychological well being of the class teacher, and of course to themselves. Those pupils who experience emotional difficulties often demand less attention from teachers and administrators. Yet these children may be showing the antecedents of many of the greater problems later on.

This is recognised in the DfEE Circular 1/98: 'The legal requirement to produce behaviour support plans focuses on pupils with behavioural difficulties. However, behavioural difficulties can frequently stem from emotional difficulties and so pupils with emotional difficulties are identified as one of the vulnerable groups. Some services which provide for pupils with behavioural difficulties – in mainstream schools or other settings – would be likely to include pupils who have so far only experienced emotional difficulties, as well as pupils who have experienced behavioural difficulties or a combination of the two.'

Whilst recognising the needs of these two groups under the umbrella term Emotional and Behavioural Difficulties (EBD) it is important to match carefully the style of support given to pupils displaying different patterns of behaviour. The growing awareness in recent years of the impact of various conditions or syndromes referred to earlier, has produced evidence of strategies more likely to work well with specific behaviour patterns. There are clearly dangers in labelling associated with locating the difficulty within the child. This can have the effect of obscuring other possible explanations for the child's difficulties, ie concerning family systems or school organisation. Conversely, the lack of reference to categories with emotional and behavioural difficulties has led to the 'unfortunate delusion that all children classified as having EBD have similar problems and therefore require similar treatment' (Cooper, 1996).

Increased understanding of the impact and effects of specific disorders, as well as of trauma and abuse, on behaviour, can help in designing appropriate behaviour programmes. Establishing the best type of strategy to help a child overcome his or her problem behaviour increases the likelihood of a successful outcome

Fogell and Long (1996) group a range of strategies under five different broad groupings. For those presenting disordered conduct or 'acting out' behaviour, they divide strategies into those appropriate for:

1) Children who can't behave appropriately (learning difficulties or communication disorders) and
2) Children who won't behave appropriately (children with average or above ability who present disturbed, angry or aggressive behaviour).

For those children presenting emotional or 'acting in', they identify three separate groups:

3) Unhappy
4) Anxious
5) Depressed.

Sometimes teachers need to look beyond their personal resources for ideas to help children with complex problems. They may also seek confirmation that they are following an appropriate strategy. There are boundless sources of advice on how to meet the needs of children with Emotional and Behavioural Difficulties. It is important therefore, that careful observation and monitoring of the child is undertaken when devising behaviour programmes.

DfEE circular 9/94 suggests behaviour programmes should include Formulation, Implementation, Monitoring and Evaluation. I would contend that there should be one further stage in the cycle, namely consideration of when the child has made sufficient progress to have the behaviour programme stopped. The following process forms the basis of an action learning cycle that can provide support but also informs the teachers and parents about the nature and complexity of the child's difficulties.

Formulation

1) Identify the behaviours which are of concern.
2) Explore the behaviour from the pupil's perspective:

- What are the triggers which set off the behaviour?
- What does the pupil gain from the behaviour?
- What does the pupil lose by the behaviour?
- When does this behaviour not occur?

3) Explore the process from the teacher's perspective:

- When was this behaviour at its worst?
- On a scale of 1–10, where 1 is the point at which you were most concerned and 10 is a point at which there are no concerns, where would you rate your level of concern now?
- What would be a reasonable point to aim for on that scale as a first step to tackling the behaviour?
- What would tell you that this point had been reached?

4) Actively involve the pupil's parents.
5) Identify indicators of success for the behavioural programme.
6) List the changes to be made in order to construct the behavioural programme.
7) What support will teachers need from colleagues?
8) How will the pupil be encouraged to continue to make improvement?
9) How long will the behaviour programme last?

Implementation

1) Agree a date/time to start the behavioural programme.
2) Ensure, wherever possible, that the pupil understands the desired outcome.
3) Where the pupil does not understand the intentions of the teacher, make sure that the desired behaviour is rewarded and undesired behaviour is not.
4) Agree contingency plans in case the pupil or staff experience difficulties.

Monitor

1) Keep record sheets as simple as possible. This means that they are more likely to be filled in.
2) Record small steps towards the ultimate goal.
3) Be consistent across all the pupil's school experiences in recording success.
4) Involve the child in the monitoring process.

Evaluate

1) Agree a time to evaluate the programme.
2) Seek feedback from all of the participants in the programme to ensure that evaluation is as comprehensive as possible.
3) Be tough on the issues but understanding of constraints on people.

For pupils at the extreme end of the EBD spectrum, ie those who present challenging behaviour, the above process still pertains. Indeed, the detail in the joint planning is one of the keys to success in addressing challenging behaviours. This term is usually applied to children with severe learning and/or communication difficulties. With children presenting such extremes of dangerous, distressing or self harming behaviour there will be a need for senior management teams and LEA support staff to help teachers and classroom support assistants to deal with the strong feelings such behaviour can develop in them. In such complex work there is a need constantly to question even basic assumptions.

When I once asked a teacher of children with autism, 'How do you respond to challenging behaviour?', she responded: 'The first thing I ask is, what is this child trying to say to me?'

Harris (1995) surveyed professionals working with children presenting challenging behaviour. Strategies identified as being most likely to be effective included the following:

- Forming a positive relationship with one particular adult;
- Examining and amending the system of rewards and sanctions;
- Matching learning task to known strengths and weaknesses of the pupil;
- Focusing on teaching language and communication;
- Working on language and communication necessary for meeting individual needs in everyday settings;
- Helping the child to anticipate sequences of events in activities;
- Allowing the child to opt out of specific activities;
- Conveying adult expectations clearly and providing constant feedback;
- Ensuring all staff are aware of new working methods or behaviour plans;
- Providing a written protocol to all staff describing how to respond to each challenging behaviour.

I find it reassuring that the above list consists of examples of good practice planned and delivered more systematically.

The future agenda for Emotional and Behavioural Difficulties will remain complex. The report by Chris Woodhead during his time as HM Chief Inspector of Schools recognised a number of outstanding concerns in relation to progress in special schools for pupils with EBD. It also identified progress in a number of areas, highlighting in particular a marked improvement in schools for pupils with emotional and behavioural difficulties and noting the most commonly identified components of good teaching as:

- High quality of teachers' planning;
- Teachers' subject knowledge (especially at Key Stage 4);
- An accurate match of lesson plans to the needs of all pupils in the teaching group.

This serves to emphasise that the key to successful teaching of pupils with emotional and behavioural difficulties is the same good practice as for all pupils but with adequate back-up and resources to cope with the behavioural demands presented by pupils. Good teachers of pupils with emotional and behavioural difficulties are just like any other teacher, only more so.

The future agenda for EBD will need to be wide ranging. There is still much to do in implementing the recommendations of the Elton Report, let alone all the complications that have developed since its publication in 1989. The following 'shopping list' is not exhaustive but does identify some of the issues which must be addressed in order to develop a range of coherent services for pupils with EBD:

- Greater clarity is needed in the use of terms to describe groups of pupils. 'Disaffected', 'disruptive', 'delinquent', 'challenging' and 'EBD' are not necessarily interchangeable.
- Efforts must continue to be focused as much on emotional as on behavioural difficulties. Early recognition of emotional difficulties can avoid the development of conduct disordered behaviour.
- The over-representation of boys, various ethnic minorities, and age groups within the EBD spectrum needs further investigation.
- The role of EBD special schools must be re-examined if they are not to continue being over-represented in the failing schools group.
- There must be a continued emphasis on the development of high quality learning and teaching for pupils with EBD.
- Teachers require better training and support in preventing and, where necessary, responding assertively to difficult behaviour in the classroom.
- Schools should be supported to develop and implement positive policies that change attitudes and develop behavioural management skills.
- The DfEE must go beyond the Circulars on Social Inclusion to examine the relationship between school systems and the incidence of EBD to ensure that systems do not exacerbate behaviour difficulties.
- SEN co-ordinators and learning support assistants will also require appropriate training in EBD.
- Early identification and intervention is essential. Poor language development and communication skills can act as indicators of potential problems.
- As in all areas of SEN, a multi-agency approach is required for effective provision.

Schools can be joyful places providing the best experiences and memories for all children and young people. Teachers and allied professionals working in partnership with parents rightly take pride in the care and support they give to their children. For some children they must work harder to achieve their goals and that can be very difficult in the face of challenging behaviour. Emotional and behavioural difficulties present many more dilemmas than other special educational needs. The fundamental question posed is, how can we create a safe environment for all our pupils? Achieving success in the face of adversity can, however, be extremely rewarding. For a teacher, the knowledge that he or she has made a difference for the better in the life of a vulnerable child can give a sense of job satisfaction that is matched in few other professions.

References

Burghes L (1994) *Lone Parenthood and family disruption: the outcomes for children, Occasional Paper 18*, Family Policy Studies Centre

Cabinet Office (1998) *Social Exclusion Unit Report, Truancy and School Exclusions*, The Stationery Office

Cockett M and Tripp J (1994) *Children Living in Re-ordered Families*, Joseph Rowntree Foundation

Cooper P (1996) Giving it a Name: The value of descriptive categories in educational approaches to emotional and behavioural difficulties. In *Support for Learning V11N4*, NASEN

DfEE (1994) Circular number 9/94 *The Education of Children with Emotional and Behavioural Difficulties*, DfEE

DfEE (1997) *Excellence for All Children: Meeting Special Educational Needs*, The Stationery Office

DfEE (1998) Circular number 1/98 *Behaviour Support Plans*, DfEE

DfEE (1998) *Meeting Special Educational Needs: A Programme of Action*, The Stationery Office

DfEE (1999) Statistical Press Notice: Permanent Exclusions from Schools in England 1997/98 and Exclusion Appeals Lodged by Parents in England 1997/98

DfEE (1999) Circular number 10/99 *Social Inclusion: Pupil Support*, DfEE

DfEE (1999) Circular number 11/99 *Social Inclusion: Pupil Support*, DfEE

Elton, Lord (1989) *Discipline in Schools. A Report of the Committee of Enquiry*, HMSO

Fogell J and Long R (1996) *Spotlight on Special Educational Needs: Emotional & Behavioural Difficulties*, NASEN

Godfrey R & Parsons C (1998) *Report on Follow-up Survey of Permanent Exclusions from Schools in England – 1996/9*, ATL

Hayden C (1996) *Children Excluded from School: Policies & Practices in England & Wales*, ERSC

Harris J (1995) Responding to pupils with severe learning disabilities, who present challenging behaviour. *British Journal of Special Education V.22 N.3*, NASEN

National Children's Bureau (1997) *Childfacts 6 Nurturing Healthy Minds: Prevention and early intervention in child adolescent mental health*, NCB

NHS Health Advisory Service (1995) *Child & Adolescent Mental Health Services – Together We Stand*, HMSO

Smith R (1998) *No Lessons Learnt: A Survey of School Exclusions*, The Children's Society

Woodhead C (1999) *Ofsted Annual Report 1997/98*, Ofsted

1.5

The Code of Practice on the Identification and Assessment of Special Educational Needs*

John Friel, Barrister-at-law, Gray's Inn

The parents of a child who believe that there is a problem will not normally wonder whether their child has a special educational need (SEN). It is obvious to the parents, possibly to the child, and often the teacher that something is wrong.

The intention of the Education Act 1996 and the Code of Practice is that children with special educational needs are provided, if possible, with adequate help by their ordinary school. If such help, or enough help, is not available, or if the child needs extra specialist help or a specialist environment, then that provision should be made. At the time of writing, a new Code of Practice with important revisions is expected to be published towards the end of 2001 or early 2002. The present Code of Practice, which is now of limited duration, is explained below. Details of the substantial changes are discussed at the end of the article.

The Code of Practice

The Code is designed to ensure that children with special educational needs receive adequate help in school or, if not available, in a specialist environment.

In light of this, the following questions become central to the identification and assessment of special educational needs:

1) Is this a case where the child clearly needs extra provision, a statement, very specialised provision, or a specialist school?
2) What evidence is there that immediate intervention by way of an assessment is required?
3) Given the extent of the problems, is this the sort of difficulty for which we would expect an ordinary school to have provision readily available? Would one normally expect LEA intervention? (Examples of this are children in an ordinary school who require speech and language therapy; for example, where the difficulty is dyspraxia or hearing impairment.)
4) If there is a difference of viewpoint between the parents and the school, is there clear professional evidence, the results of psychometric testing which establishes at

---

* This article was originally compiled from *Children with Special Needs* by John Friel, published by Jessica Kingsley Publishers (1995) and is revised annually.

least in the balance of probabilities that the child is not slow to learn, or suffering from stress due to some family problem, but has a learning difficulty, which requires special educational provision?

5) Is there evidence of emotional problems, stress or illness interrelated with stress exhibiting itself, which shows that the child needs immediate assessment, and more help?

6) Every report must contain a list of the child's needs and the provisions to meet those needs.

Everybody working in this field must have a copy of the Code of Practice: a very long document, which will not be described in detail here. However, its fundamental principles are that:

- the needs of all pupils who have special educational needs either throughout, or at any time, during their school careers must be addressed; the Code recognises that there is a continuum of needs and a continuum of provision, which may be made in a wide variety of different forms;
- children with special educational needs require the greatest possible access to a broad and balanced education, including the National Curriculum;
- the needs of most pupils will be met in the mainstream, and without statutory assessment or statement of special educational needs. Children with special educational needs, including children with statements of special educational needs, should, where appropriate and taking into account the wishes of the parents, be educated alongside their peers in mainstream schools;
- even before he or she reaches compulsory school age, a child may have special educational needs requiring the intervention of the LEA as well as the health services;
- the knowledge, views and experience of parents are vital. Effective assessment and provision will be secured where there is the greatest possible degree of partnership between parents and their children and schools, LEA and other agencies.

The practices and procedures essential in pursuit of these principles are that:

- all children with special educational needs should be identified and assessed as early as possible and as quickly as is consistent with thoroughness;
- provision for all children with special educational needs should be made by the most appropriate agency. In most cases, this will be the child's mainstream school, working in partnership with the child's parents: no statutory assessment will be necessary;
- where needed, LEAs must make assessments and statements in accordance with the prescribed time limits; must write clear and thorough statements, setting out the child's educational and non-educational needs, the objectives to be secured, the provision to be made and the arrangements for monitoring and review; and ensure the annual review of the special educational provision arranged for the child and the updating and monitoring of educational targets;
- special educational provision will be most effective when those responsible take into account the ascertainable wishes of the child concerned, considered in light of his or her age and understanding;

- there must be close co-operation between all agencies concerned and a multi-disciplinary approach to the resolution of issues.

The guidance in the Code is drafted subject to the matters set out above and must be borne clearly in mind.

The essential feature of the Code is that it is a three-stage school-based procedure of assessment and provision, which, as necessary, calls upon the help of external specialists. At Stages 4 and 5 (basically the assessment stages) the LEAs are expected by the Code to share the responsibility with schools.

The Special Educational Needs Tribunal (see Part 1.7) will have regard to any provision of the Code, which appears to the Tribunal to be relevant to any question arising on appeal. The principles of the code are designed to be actioned in partnership with parents to secure appropriate provision for children with special needs and to minimise disputes, thereby avoiding appeals. The overriding interest of the Code and all concerned is to make sure that provision is made for the child with special educational needs.

In relation to the criteria for making an assessment, detailed guidance is given by the Code, and it is likely that the Tribunal will order an assessment in the following circumstances:

1) Where the disability is obviously a disability that needs extra help and resources, which are not normally available in an ordinary school;
2) If parents can show that the school has not adequately coped and/or does not adequately understand the child's needs and problems, so that intervention is necessary even if the school is of the view it can cope;
3) Where there is an obvious need for immediate action, such as emotional problems developing into a severe difficulty, development of medical problems or psychiatric problems, where the child refuses to attend school (school phobic), or where the needs are misunderstood or undetected and the child is far behind.

These illustrations are not, of course, exhaustive. An important consideration will obviously be where, on the facts, in light of the child's special educational needs and requirements for provision, it is obvious that the school itself does not have available adequate provision.

It is important for parents to remember that if they are contemplating bypassing the early assessment procedures in the Code, they will have to justify their case clearly. Equally, there will be cases where it is obvious that the child's learning difficulties are sufficiently severe to justify moving forward more quickly to the statement process.

School-based stages of assessment and provision

It is probable from statistics available for some counties, and local authorities, that the actual number of children who should be statemented has always been greater than 2 per cent. Whether that be so or not, the Code makes it clear that this is a broad national estimate, and the proportion of children with special needs will vary significantly from area to area.

Duties of the School Governing Body

The Code is drafted on the basis of the respective responsibilities of the school governing body (section 317), and the local education authority. In particular, the governing body must carry out the following tasks:

- do their best to secure that the necessary provision is made for any pupil who has special educational needs;
- secure that, where the 'responsible person' – the head teacher or the appropriate governor – has been informed by the LEA that a pupil has special educational needs, those needs are made known to all who are likely to teach him or her;
- secure that teachers in the school are aware of the importance of identifying, and providing for, those pupils who have special educational needs;
- consult the LEA; as appropriate, the Funding Authority and the governing bodies of other schools, when it seems to them necessary or desirable in the interests of co-ordinated special educational provision in the area as a whole;
- report annually to parents on the school's policy for pupils with special educational needs;
- ensure that the pupil joins in the activities of the school together with the pupils who do not have special educational needs, so far as that is reasonably practical and compatible with the pupil receiving the necessary special educational provision, the efficient education of other children in the school, and the efficient use of resources;

(section 317)

- have regard to this Code of Practice when carrying out their duties toward all pupils with special educational needs.

(section 313)

It is the responsibility of the governing body to decide how best to provide for children with special educational needs. The Code of Practice recommends that the governing body delegate their responsibility to an individual member of the body, the head teacher or the co-ordinator of the special educational needs (SEN) team. The Code expects, however, that arrangements are made for the governing body to monitor closely the work of the school on behalf of pupils with special educational needs. The Act reinforces the duty on the governing body by requiring by regulation prescribed issues to be addressed in the school's policies, which include:

1. Basic information about the school's special educational provision:
- the objectives of the school's SEN policy;
- the name of the school's SEN co-ordinator or teacher responsible for the day-to-day operation of the SEN policy;
- the arrangements for co-ordinating educational provision for pupils with SEN;
- admission arrangements;
- any SEN specialism and any special units;
- any special facilities which increase or assist access to the school by pupils with SEN.

2. Information about the school's policies for identification, assessment and provision for all pupils with SEN:
- the allocation of resources to and amongst pupils with SEN;
- identification and assessment arrangements, and review procedures;
- arrangements for providing access for pupils with SEN to a balanced and broadly based curriculum, including the National Curriculum;
- how children with special educational needs are integrated within the school as a whole;
- criteria for evaluating the success of the school's SEN policy;
- arrangements for considering complaints about special educational provision within the school.

3. Information about the school's staffing policies and partnership with bodies beyond the schools:
- the school's arrangements for SEN in-service training;
- use made of teachers and facilities from outside the school, including support services;
- arrangements for partnership with parents;
- links with other mainstream schools and special schools, including arrangements when pupils change schools or leave school;
- links with health and social services, educational welfare services and any voluntary organisations.

> Educational (Special Educational Needs) (Information)
> Regulations, Regulation 2 and Schedule 1

The Code expects there to be an SEN co-ordinator responsible for the day-to-day operation of the school's SEN policy, advising class and subject teachers, taking the lead in managing provision for pupils, particularly at stages 2 and 3, updating and allowing for the keeping of records of all pupils with special educational needs, working with the parents of the children, and liaising with external agencies. It is doubtful, in fact, whether before the 1993 Act, these tasks were adequately addressed nationally in some schools. The Code certainly requires a substantial change in practice in many areas by schools.

Chapter 2, paragraph 2.16 of the Code, emphasises the importance of early identification assessment and provision for any child who may have special educational needs. The earlier the action is taken, the more responsive the child is likely to be, and the more likely it is that the child will be successfully helped without undue intervention. Equally, the Code fully appreciates that if there is an early start, it is more likely that intervention will be successful within the ordinary school.

Chapter 2 of the Code also emphasises the importance of record keeping during school-based assessment stages, and of using the expertise of the health services and the local authority social services, and particularly the importance of partnership with parents. The Code accepts that the relationship between parents and the school has a crucial bearing on the child's educational progress and on the effectiveness of any school-based intervention. The Code expects the attitude of the school to be a working partnership with parents which is a practical and effective scheme. The school's arrangements for parents of children with special needs, (Chapter 2.33 onwards of the Code of Practice), should include the following:

1. *Information on:*
- the school's SEN policy;
- the support available for children with special educational needs within the school and LEA;
- parents' involvement in assessment and decision-making, emphasising the importance of their contribution;
- services such as those provided by the local authority for children 'in need' (eg, under the Children Act 1989);
- local and national voluntary organisations which might provide information, advice or counselling.

2. *Partnership arrangements, including:*
- arrangements for recording and acting upon parental concerns;
- procedures for involving parents when a concern is first expressed within the school;
- arrangements for incorporating parents' views in assessment and subsequent reviews.

3. *Information regarding access for parents, including:*
- information in a range of community languages;
- information on tape for parents who may have literacy or communication difficulties;
- a parents' room or other arrangements in the school to help parents feel confident and comfortable.

The involvement of the child

The Code equally recognises that the effectiveness of any assessment and intervention will be influenced mainly by the involvement and interests of the child and young persons concerned. Equally the Code accepts (Chapter 2, paragraph 2.3436) that the child or young person has important and relevant information, and further, that children have a right to be heard and should be encouraged to participate in the decision making about provision to meet their needs. The school should make every effort to identify the assessable views and wishes of the child and young person about his or her current education. The Code invites all to consider how they:

- involve pupils in the decision making processes;
- determine the child's level of participation, bearing in mind the age, ability and past experience of the child;
- record the pupil's views in identifying their difficulties, setting goals, agreeing a development strategy and monitoring and reviewing progress;
- involve pupils and implement individual educational plans.

Maintenance of appropriate medical records

In appropriate instances, where the difficulties seen at school exhibit medical conditions (whether related to educational needs or whether the disability itself involves a medical condition or one has developed), the child health services must be involved. In particular, where the case gives cause for concern to the general practitioner, health visitor, school health service, or the community paediatrician – whichever is the appropriate expert – the relevant advisory teacher should be consulted. If parents express anxiety about an aspect of development, they should be involved and the relevant professionals consulted. Where such advice is necessary, useful and relevant, the SEN co-ordinator should ensure its confidentiality and maintain effective systems in school for:

- keeping medical records of children with SEN;
- drawing together information available from the general practitioners, school health service, health visitor, community paediatrician, child and adolescent mental health service, or hospital children's department;
- the transfer of relevant medical information between phases for ensuring thorough co-operation with the relevant professionals, and the elimination of medical causes as a possible explanation for observable learning and behavioural difficulties;
- identifying early signs of depression and abnormal eating behaviour and substance misuse.

Social services and education welfare service

Schools should be aware of the range of social services provided by the education welfare service and the Social Services Department to support children regarded as being in need. They should also be aware of the Social Services Department duty under section 17 of the Children Act 1989:

(1) It shall be the general duty of every local authority (in addition to the other duties imposed on them by this Part)

    (a) to safeguard and promote the welfare of children within their area who are in need; and

    (b) so far as is consistent with that duty, to promote the upbringing of such children by their families, by providing a range and level of services appropriate to those children's needs.

(2) For the purpose principally of facilitating the discharge of their general duty under this section, every local authority shall have the specific duties and powers set out in Part 1 of Schedule 2.

(3) Any service provided by an authority in the exercise of functions conferred on them by this section may be provided for the family of a particular child in need or for any other member of his family, if it is provided with a view to safeguarding or promoting the child's welfare.

(4) The Secretary of State may by order amend any provision of Part 1 of Schedule 2 or add any further duty or power to those for the time being mentioned there.

(5)   Every local authority:
    (a)   shall facilitate the provision by others (including in particular, voluntary organisations) of services which the authority have power to provide by virtue of this section, or section 18, 20, 23 or 24; and
    (b)   may make such arrangements as they see fit for any person to act on their behalf in the provision of any such service.

(6)   The services provided by a local authority in the exercise of functions conferred on them by this section may include giving assistance in kind or, in exceptional circumstances, in cash.

(7)   Assistance may be unconditional or subject to conditions as to the repayment of the assistance or of its value (in whole or in part).

(8)   Before giving any assistance or imposing any conditions, a local authority shall have regard to the means of the child concerned and of each of his parents.

(9)   No person shall be liable to make any repayment of assistance or of its value at any time when he is in receipt of income support or family credit under the Social Security Act 1986.

(10) For the purposes of this Part a child shall be taken to be in need if:
    (a)   he is unlikely to achieve or maintain, or to have the opportunity of achieving or maintaining, a reasonable standard of health or development without the provision for him of services by a local authority under this Part;
    (b)   his health or development is likely to be significantly impaired, or further impaired, without the provision for him of such services; or
    (c)   he is disabled,
    and 'family', in relation to such a child, includes any person who has parental responsibility for the child and any other person with whom he has been living.

(11) For the purposes of this Part, a child is disabled if he is blind, deaf or dumb or handicapped by illness, injury or congenital deformity of such other disability as may be prescribed; and in this Part
    'development' means physical, intellectual, emotional, social or behavioural development; and
    'health' means physical or mental health.

The Code asks the school to provide an integrated approach to education, health and welfare needs of children with special educational needs. It also requires schools to co-operate with the social services department where it is considered that the child is at risk of abuse or neglect.

A social services department should designate an officer or officers, who are responsible for working with schools (Chapter 2, paragraph 2.54). This officer should be available so that schools and the LEA can refer cases for advice. Schools are required to have suitable arrangements for:

- liaising with social services;
- registering concern about a child's welfare;
- putting into practice any local procedures relating to child protection issues;

- liaising with the local authority when a child is accommodated by that authority;
- obtaining information on services provided by the local authority for children in need.

The 1981 Act was under-used for children with learning difficulties, when the Children Act assessment processes were used. Equally, the Children Act assessment processes apply to children with learning difficulties, even if they come from a supporting parental background. The powers under section 17, section 43 and Schedule 2 of the Children Act were often ignored, and where a child had a multiplicity of problems and needs, but supportive parents, the Children Act was not used. The Code of Practice directs attention to the necessity of looking at a child in light of these statutory duties.

Summary of school-based stages of assessment

The school-based stages should be seen as a continuous and systematic cycle of planning and intervention. There should be the necessary reviews within the school to check progress. It is intended to enable the child with special educational needs to learn and make progress.

Stage 1

This envisages class or subject teachers consulting the SEN co-ordinator and identifying the child's special educational needs, assembling information and putting into place any special arrangements to meet those needs and informing the head teacher.

Stage 2

The SEN co-ordinator now takes the lead responsibility for managing the child's special educational provision, working with the child's teachers to devise a more comprehensive set of strategies, and informing the head teacher.

Stage 3

The SEN co-ordinator continues to lead and should always consult and inform the head teacher. Specialist staff from outside the school, such as the educational psychologist, and advisory teachers with special qualifications, are brought in to help the school support a child with more complex needs. Should the child still not progress satisfactorily, a specialist will help the school consider whether the child is likely to meet the criteria for statutory assessment.

At the end of each stage, the Code indicates that the progress of the child should be reviewed, following each stage of planned intervention. The class teacher and the SEN co-ordinator will decide whether they are applying each stage to:

- continue the child's current educational arrangements;
- seek further advice; or

- draw up a plan using the expertise within the school, initially, and at the end of each stage;
- review the progress made by each child;
- the effectiveness of the education plan;
- the updated information and advice available in light of the child's progress or lack of progress; and
- decide on future action.

At each stage it will be decided either that no further help is needed, or that the child remains at the same stage, or that the child should move forward into the next stage.

Each stage requires an education plan for the child, as well as a review of any decision making process. Stage 2, the more sophisticated stage, involves consideration of non-curriculum issues such as the pastoral care arrangements, medical requirements and the like.

Stages 3, 4 and 5

Obviously stage 3 is the stage which can be regarded in normal cases as the threshold to a statement. If intervention is effective, then it is a success. If stage 2 does not work, one would certainly expect an assessment, and very possibly a statement. However, stage 3 is not simply a stage that should be used following stages 1 and 2.

The Code makes it clear that in some cases children will need early intensive intervention, but not necessarily an assessment or statement. In the cases of such children the SEN co-ordinator, teachers and parents should discuss the issues, and the SEN co-ordinator, having consulted the head teacher, can put into place early intensive intervention and bring in external support where it is immediately necessary.

Such support will come from teachers in learning or behaviour support services, peripatetic teachers, educational psychologists, child health or mental health services, social services and advisers or teachers with knowledge or information of technology. Equally, where help is available from special publications, or from organisations that deal with particular problems of the disabled, such as the National Council for Educational Technology, this should be sought. The SEN co-ordinator is expected by the Code to be familiar with the relevant information and local practices.

Stage 3 is therefore also, on a less sophisticated basis, an alternative form of assessment to the assessment procedures envisaged by statute and regulation. The SEN co-ordinator will review the position, assuming the child has gone through stages 1 and 2. This will include information gathered at that point and the report compiled at the end of review stage 2.

Equally, stage 3 should lead to consideration as to whether an assessment is necessary at this stage and the decision made should include consideration of whether further advice is necessary, the drawing up of a new education plan, including the involvement of the support services. The Code at this stage requires a much more detailed individual education plan, which is reproduced below:

Stage 3 – Individual Education Plan

- nature of the child's learning difficulty;
- action – the special education provision;
- school staff involved, including frequency and timing of support;
- external specialists involved, including frequency and timing;
- specific programmes/activities/materials/equipment;
- help from parents at home;
- targets to be achieved in a given time;
- any pastoral care or medical requirements;
- monitoring and assessment arrangements;
- review arrangements and date.

It is important that a review date be set, which may be within half a term but should always be within a term. The SEN co-ordinator should agree with the pupil's teachers and the external specialists who are involved in arrangements about the means of monitoring the child's progress against the objectives that are established in the plan. The SEN co-ordinator should convene a review meeting at the end of the review period and it should focus on:

- progress made by the child;
- effectiveness of the education plan;
- whether a child is likely in the future to be referred for statutory assessment, an important part of the decision-making process;
- updated information and advice;
- future action.

Obviously, the outcome of the review can be a continuation at stage 3 if progress is satisfactory or non-proven, a reversion to stage 2 if progress is at least satisfactory, or a referral by the head teacher to the LEA for a statutory assessment if progress is not satisfactory. The Code expects the head teacher to work together with the SEN co-ordinator on this issue.

The Code expects the following to be available should there be a reference for a statutory assessment:

- the recorded views of parents and, where appropriate, children on the earlier stage of assessment and any action and support to date;
- evidence of health checks, for example relevant information on medical advice to the school;
- when appropriate, evidence relating to social services involvement;
- written individual education plans at stages 2 and 3 indicating the approaches adopted, the monitoring arrangements followed and the educational outcomes;
- reviews on each individual education plan indicating decisions made as a result;
- evidence of the involvement and views of professionals with relevant specialist knowledge and expertise outside the normal competence of the school.

If the school does not keep the required documentation some LEA officers believe this is a reason to refuse an assessment. Equally, the school may not strictly apply the Code.

However, if a parent appeals, the real issue will be the child, and his or her education, not whether the school has applied the Code.

Stages 4 and 5 are the statutory assessment and the decision to make a statement. These stages, and the Special Educational Needs Tribunal, are considered in Parts 1.6 and 1.7.

A revised Code of Practice

Proposals for significant changes in the Code and the law currently include the Special Educational Needs and Disability Bill, which would extend parental rights and rights of children with special educational needs. Associated with the proposals is a move by the Government to substantially revise the SEN Code of Practice. Recent statements indicate that a new Code is likely for September or October, but it could be later.

Between July and October 2000, a consultation took place in regards to a new Code. Over 2000 responses were received from a wide range of people and organisations. There was also consultation about the assessment regulations that provides for the assessment of children with special educational needs, who may or may not require a Statement. The consultation on the revised Code of Practice drew a considerable number of positive responses, often from parents, parental organisations, national SEN organisations and others. It also gave rise to considerable criticism. The positive responses were that the draft Code highlighted the following:

- The earliest possible identification of a child with special educational needs;
- Effective school based provision to help children with SEN to progress;
- The need to work with parents as partners in their children's education;
- The need to take account of the views of children with SEN;
- The need to reduce unnecessary paper work without damaging the quality of help for pupils.

However, substantial criticisms were also identified as follows:

- Firstly, the absence of an adequate description of the strategic responsibilities of LEAs and schools themselves for pupils with SEN was noted. Currently there is no method of checking whether a school actually spends, on a pupil, the money attached to his or her Statement of Special Educational Needs.
- It was felt that a system of accountability was needed to check on the funding delegated to schools for children with Statements for special educational needs.
- Creating links and revising the proposed Disability Rights Code which has arisen as a result of the Special Educational Needs and Disability Bill.
- Currently the law requires that Statements of SEN must be specific in describing the provision to be made for the child's needs. There was criticism that the revised Code attempted to water down this requirement, as did the revised regulations. The criticism was accepted.
- It was felt that a system of accountability was needed to check on the funding delegated to schools for children with statements of SEN.

- It was also suggested that the Code should relate to other proposed guidance for children with special educational needs issued by the Department for Education and Employment (DfEE). This would clearly be beneficial.

The revised code is intended to cover these deficiencies. Additionally the Code, in its revised form, gives guidance on parent partnerships and support for the SEN co-ordinator so that Heads and Governors recognise that the SENCO will need time and support in order to be able to co-ordinate the school's SEN activity.

In addition, the Special Educational Needs and Disability Bill provides for a Disability Rights Commission which will prepare a Code of Practice to explain and illustrate the legislation on disability to education providers, disabled people and others.

In light of the criticisms made about the proposed revisions to the Code, it has not yet been issued. However, the current Code is now of limited duration and is likely to be changed substantially by the new Code coming into force either later in 2001 or early in 2002. Parents should therefore check current developments and obtain a copy of the relevant Code from the Department for Education and Employment (see page 538).

1.6

Children with Special Needs:
The Legal Implications*

John Friel, Barrister-at-law, Gray's Inn

As noted in the previous chapter, the Special Educational Needs and Disability Bill is intended to change substantially rights in this field. This represents a significant step forward in helping schools and Local Educational Authorities to improve educational opportunities for children with special educational needs and in securing rights for disabled people. Parents should not underestimate the existence of new rights.

Part I of the Bill makes changes to existing law in the Education Act 1996 for children with special educational needs to:

1. Strengthen the right of children with special educational needs to be educated in mainstream schools. Section 1 amends Section 316 of the 1996 Act to provide a duty to educate children with special educational needs in mainstream schools. In fact, the change is not as substantial as it seems. The 1981 Act contained a similar provision, which was watered down in the 1996 Act. It should be appreciated that in relation to the assessment provisions for children with special educational needs and the provisions relating to Statements of SEN, the new Act will make a change in the law in that it will improve the rights of those parents who seek to integrate their children into mainstream schools. As it stands local authorities are able to defeat those rights and the change to the Act will help eliminate this.

2. Allow LEAs to arrange for parents of children with special educational needs to be provided with advice and information on SEN issues.

3. Enable a means of resolving disputes between schools or LEAs and parents of children with special educational needs (by adding Section 322B to the Education Act 1996). If there was some form of dispute resolution procedure available, many disputes would not need to go to Appeal to the SEN Tribunal or to the Courts.

4. Require schools to tell parents if the school is making special educational provision for their child. Again this matches the provision in the Code of Practice to make schools and LEAs become accountable for expenditure of SEN budgets on children with special educational needs, which is not currently being addressed.

---

* This article was originally compiled from *Children with Special Needs – Assessment, Law and Practice: Caught in the Acts*, published by Jessica Kingsley Publishers (1995).

5. Allow schools to request a statutory assessment of a pupil with special educational needs. There are many cases at present where schools would like such an assessment but are prevented from requesting one, the implementation of this would be welcome.

Part II of the Bill addresses disability discrimination in education. It places new duties on LEAs and schools. In summary those duties are:

1. Not to treat disabled pupils less favourably, without justification, than non-disabled pupils.
2. To make reasonable adjustments so that disabled pupils are not disadvantaged when compared with pupils who are not disabled.
3. To plan strategically and progress in increasing physical accessibility to school premises and the curriculum.

In addition, Part II places new duties on further education institutions, higher education institutions and LEAs in respect of education and Education Youth Services. These duties are:

a) Not to treat disabled students less favourably, without justification, than non-disabled students.
b) To make reasonable adjustments to ensure that people who are disabled are not substantially disadvantaged compared with people who are not disabled in accessing further and higher secured LEA Education.

The Act extends the jurisdiction of the Special Educational Needs and Disability Tribunal so that the Tribunal has powers under the new proposed Act. It also alters the 1995 Disability Discrimination Act in relation to admissions to school under the School Standards and Framework Act 1998 and exclusions, either where discrimination against a child with special educational needs is alleged to the New Tribunal or where there has been a fixed term exclusion. In cases concerning discrimination, the Tribunal has power to award compensation in all aspects of discrimination which includes admissions and exclusion. This is a substantial advancement in the law.

The Bill also requires the Disability Rights Commission to provide a new Code of Practice to explain and illustrate the legislation.

The following is a summary of the current legal process required to achieve a Statement for a child with special educational needs. For parents requiring more information, the book – *Children with Special Educational Needs – Assessment, Law and Practice: Caught in the Acts* (Jessica Kingsley Publishers) currently outlines the law. This publication will be revised once the new Codes of Practice, the new Act and the new Regulations are fully known.

Is there a problem?

Before a parent or an education authority can know whether or not there is a legal obligation to make provision under the Education Act 1996 for a child's needs, a child must first be assessed.

Identification of children with special needs

The local education authority (LEA) is required to exercise its powers with a view to securing or identifying those children who have special educational needs and for whom it is necessary for the authority to determine the special educational provision. Where the authority forms the opinion that a child has special educational needs, and it is necessary for the authority to determine the special educational provision which any learning difficulty calls for, the authority must serve a notice on the child's parents that it proposes to make an assessment. For those who are not subject to assessment or who have been assessed but who are not statemented, the duty to provide help lies with the school.

Preparing a request for an assessment

If possible, a parent who can afford independent advice should consider such advice essential. This is so, even if the school wishes to have the child assessed and supports the idea of an assessment or statement. An independent expert report is very useful, and certainly, if the school is not recommending an assessment, or agreeing that there is a problem, it is an essential aid to the parent.

Obviously, many children with special needs have conditions that require medical treatment or the oversight of doctors. In all such cases medical reports should be obtained. Where there is a need for reports on particular forms of therapy, particularly speech therapy, physiotherapy and occupational therapy, it is clearly essential that an independent report be obtained, wherever possible.

The last important requirement of an expert report is that it considers the provisions of the Code of Practice. In conclusion, the report by any adviser whether a psychologist, doctor or therapist employed by the parents, or indeed the LEA, should finish with a clear conclusion, if possible summarising the issues with details of the recommended provision. If an assessment or statement is needed, the report should say so. Unfortunately experience has proven that without such evidence LEAs do not make expensive specialist help available.

Decisions of the Courts have strengthened parents' rights in this field. A Statement must be a diagnosis of and a prescription for a child's special educational needs (see R -v- The Secretary of State for Education ex parte E1992 FLR page 377). Further Statements must be specific so that the provision in a Statement is ascertainable, identifiable and quantified (L -v- Clarke and Somerset 1998 Education Law Reports page 128, confirmed in the Court of Appeal SENT -v- Bromley 1999 Education Law Reports page 260). Experts must prepare their reports with these principles in mind. Expert reports should address specifically what provision is required. If they fail to do so they cannot be relied upon either to support a request for assessment or at a later stage if an Appeal to the Tribunal takes place. It should also be remembered that the Local Education Authority can not be expected to understand the parent's case if the expert report does not make clear what is needed.

The intention of the 1996 Act and the Code of Practice

The intention of the Act and the Code of Practice is that children with special educational needs are provided with adequate help, if possible, by their ordinary school. If such help, or enough help, is not available, or if the child needs extra specialist help or a specialist environment, then that provision should be made.

Assessment procedure

Where the parent sends a written request for an assessment under Section 323 of the Act, the authority is under a mandatory statutory duty if it considers that it is necessary to conduct such an assessment. If the authority does not consider it necessary, the parent has the right of appeal under the provisions of Section 32 to the SEN Tribunal. As aforementioned, unless parents lay the groundwork for the request in advance, it is likely that an appeal will be necessary. If, however, the parent prepares the case properly and obtains adequate reports to justify the request, then a LEA will normally assess under Section 323. In making such a request it is important that parents clearly illustrate the issues, the cause for concern, and whether the child's needs have been adequately met at present, and if not, why this has occurred. The request should also be accompanied, if possible, by expert reports. I would suggest it is reasonable to summarise the conclusions of those reports in support of the parental request for a statutory assessment.

The LEA has a month to make a decision, and must inform the child's head teacher of the request, and ask the school for written evidence about the child, in particular the school's assessment of the child's learning difficulty and the school's account of the provisions which have been made. The Code of Practice requires that the psychology service and other bodies, such as the designated medical officer or social services, should be informed.

Provision: practical issues

The Education Act 1944 imposed a duty on the local education authority to assist children who required special educational treatment. The Education Act 1981, which came into force in 1983, replaced the concept of special educational treatment with that of 'special educational needs'. The 1996 Act provides greater power to assist children with special educational needs.

Provision made by the 1996 Act must be *special educational provision*, not special provision or merely educational provision. This is an important distinction, because the child may need provision to be educated. For example, a child with a speech difficulty may need speech therapy, which may be either educational or medical; in most cases, it is in fact both. If it is essential to the child's education, it will be a special educational need.

A social or religious factor arising out of a child's family background or community could also be a special educational need that requires special educational provision. For example, a child from a strictly religious background with a disability, such as Down's Syndrome, may not be able to cope in a secular school. Factors such as diet, religious observance, moral habits and teaching may be significantly different. This will affect the child's ability to learn if he or she is puzzled, stressed or unhappy in such circumstances. The local education authority has power not only to arrange provision, which is educational but also non-educational and medical matters.

However, a social services requirement is not special educational provision. For example, unless a residential educational provision is educational, not social, it is not regarded as an LEA duty, but a social services matter. Social services are very reluctant to provide help away from home on solely educational grounds.

In fact, the boundary between educational and social services provision, particularly where children are more disabled or who have conditions which affect their functions during the waking day, is much less distinctive. The Courts have recently had cause to consider such cases, and in Bromley -v- The SENT 2000 Education Law Reports page 260 the Court of Appeal made it clear that Parliament did not contend there to be a clear boundary between educational and non-educational provision. In some cases non-educational provision will be obvious, ie a wheelchair; in other cases where residential provision is required, it is possible to describe the child's requirements for provision as being partly social and partly medical. So long as it falls overall within the definition of educational, it is appropriate to consider such provision as educational. This decision has been extremely helpful to parents.

Age

Section 312 defines a child as any person who has not attained the age of 19 years and is a registered pupil at the school. This responsibility is therefore being adopted by an LEA for a child by way of a statement. The jurisdiction of the Act continues until the age of 19 years or until the child leaves school, whichever is the earlier.

The involvement of the child and the role of social services and the education welfare service

As discussed in Part 1.5, the Code also emphasises the importance of involving the child and his or her views and of the need for an integrated approach by the school to take account of the education, health and welfare needs of the child.

School-based stages of assessment

The school-based stages of assessment (stages 13) are summarised in Part 1.5.

Stage 3 is the stage that can be regarded, in normal cases, as the threshold to a statement. If intervention is effective, then it is a success. If stage 3 does not work, one would certainly expect an assessment, and very possibly a statement. Stages 4 and 5 are the statutory assessment and the decision to make a statement.

Stages 4 and 5: statutory assessment and the decision to make a statement

What is a statement?

The 1981 Education Act introduced the new concept of a statement of a child's special educational needs. In so doing, Parliament adopted the recommendation of the Warnock Report CMND7212, the report of the Committee of Enquiry into the Education of Handicapped Children and Young People. The Warnock Committee recommended that it be agreed that special help and protection were necessary for children with the more severe or complex special educational needs. For that purpose a statement of special educational needs was the recommended method of assisting the child.

Obviously a child with a problem which is less severe will soon become a child with a severe problem if no help is given or if inadequate help is given.

A statement of special educational needs requires an assessment of the child's needs under section 323. In section 323 the test is whether the local authority is of the opinion that the child for whom they are responsible falls, or probably falls, within the section.

An assessment must be made in statutory form. The process of assessment gives careful consideration to all aspects of the child's needs. It requires the authority to obtain professional advice from a number of sources.

The Courts have considered the contents and nature of a Statement on frequent occasions because of the legislation. In R -v- Secretary of State ex parte E 1992 Family Law Reports page 377 the Court of Appeal made it clear that a Statement was in part II a diagnosis of the child's special educational needs and in Part III a prescription. The High Court and Court of Appeal, in considering how a Statement was constructed, decided that the Statute and Regulations require Statements normally to be specific, so that provision in Part III not only matches Part II but is specific, ascertainable and quantifiable (see L -v- Clarke and Somerset 1998 Education Law Reports page 128 confirmed by the Court of Appeal in Bromley -v- SENT 2000 Education Law Report pge 260). Thus a Statement must define in Part II a child's needs, provide for the needs in Part III and be specific as to what is to be done in Part III.

The process of assessment

The first step is to inform the parents. This applies, however, once the assessment is commenced. Having given notice to the parents, the LEA must send copies of the relevant notice to:

(a) the social services authority;
(b) the district health authority; and
(c) if the child is registered at school, the head teacher of the school.

The notice served must describe to the recipient what help the authority is likely to request.

Service of documents in an assessment

Documents and notices required to be served under the Act or Regulations may be served or sent, or a notice may be given by properly addressing, pre-paying and posting a letter containing any such document or notice.

Regulation 4(2) defines the proper address of a person as:

(a) in the case of a child's parents, his last known address;
(b) in the case of the head teacher and other members of staff at the school, the school's address;
(c) in the case of any other person, the last known address of the place where he carried on business, his profession or other employment.

Where first class post is used, the document or notice is treated as served, sent or given on the second working day after the date of the posting, unless the contrary is shown. If, therefore, it is contended that service has not been effected, there is a presumption that it was effected two days after it was served, sent or given.

Advice to be sought

The authority is required to seek the following advice:

(a) from the child's parent;
(b) educational advice;
(c) medical advice from a district health authority;
(d) psychological advice;
(e) advice from social services;
(f) any other advice that the authority considers appropriate for the purpose of arriving at a satisfactory assessment.

The requirement is that the advice shall be written advice relating to the educational, medical, psychological or other features of the case (according to the nature of the advice sought) which appear to be relevant to the child's educational needs (including his likely future needs); how those features could affect the child's educational needs and the provision which is appropriate for the child.

Consultation

The expert from whom the advice is sought has a discretion, if it appears to him expedient, to consult some other person. The local education authority has power to specify that a consultation should take place.

Reassessment

If there is a reassessment within a short period of time, the only obligation on the authority is to seek parental advice. However, the authority could, under this regulation, be required to obtain some but not all of the earlier advice.

The timetable for the process

The first task for the LEA, having notified the parents that the statutory assessment might be necessary or having received a request from the parents or a grant maintained school, is to decide whether a statutory assessment must be made. The timetable in each case is as follows:

1. Either the LEA concludes that it may be necessary to make a statement and serves the statutory notice giving 29 days to make representations. Six weeks after issuing a notice the LEA must tell parents whether they will or will not make a statutory assessment. Alternatively parents request a statutory assessment. The LEA must decide within six weeks of receiving the request whether they will or will not make a statutory assessment and inform the parents.
2. Making the assessment: the period from the LEA's decision to make the statutory assessment and the LEA's decision whether or not to make a statement must normally be no more than ten weeks.
3. Drafting the proposed statement or a note in lieu of a statement: the period from the LEA's decision whether to make a statement to the issue of a proposed statement or a notice of the LEA's decision not to make a statement must be within two weeks.
4. Finalising the statement: the period from the issue of the proposed statement and the final copy of the statement must normally be no more than eight weeks. Total 26 weeks, although there are some exceptions.

In practice, delays are likely to occur where the parents want to submit their own evidence in relation to assessing the child's needs by an independent expert, if they have not obtained expert advice in advance of the decision to assess, or where they wish to make representations in relation to the draft statement. A draft statement must be served prior to a final statement.

Draft statement and the right to make representations

Having obtained all the advice, if the LEA decides it is necessary to determine the special educational provision and any learning difficulties the child may have calls for, the authority makes the statement of his special educational needs. Having served a draft statement, the next step is for the parents either to accept it or to make representations.

Prior to the making of the statement in final form, the education authority is obliged to serve on the parent of the child concerned:

(a) a copy of the proposed statement; and
(b) notice explaining the arrangements and the right to appeal.

The final statement

The statement contains the assessment of a child's special educational needs. It contains:

(a)   any representations made by the child's parents;

(b)   any evidence submitted by or at the request of the child's parents;

(c)   the advice obtained by the LEA under Regulation 6;

(d)   the type of school or other institution which the local authority considers would be appropriate for the child;

(e)   the provision for the child.

1.7
Statements of Special Educational Needs and the Special Educational Needs Tribunal

John Friel, Barrister-at-law, Gray's Inn

It is important to make clear at the outset that statements for children with special needs are reserved for those children with the greatest difficulties, normally referred to as severe or complex.

Many parents reading this book will be seeking a school for children who have considerable difficulties. A significant number of schools in this book deal with children who are the subject of statements of special educational needs. Not every school is suitable for children with statements. It is only those registered by statute under the Education Act 1996 by the DfEE for the express purpose of taking children with statements or those approved on a case by case basis that are suitable. The DfEE will not approve every school that makes a provision. The cost of placement at (a specialist) school is such that in many cases it is only a Local Education Authority (LEA) or those with substantial means, (which includes parents from abroad), who can afford the fees. Specialist schools dealing with dyslexic children are the exception: although the schools listed take statemented children, there are a substantial number of fee-paying parents at these schools. Indeed, in most such schools, fee-paying parents will be the majority.

The 1981 Education Act set up after the Warnock Report provided for a new system for the assessment of children with special educational needs and the making of a statement for those who had more severe and complex needs. This system gave rights to parents who disagreed with LEAs. There were considerable defects with the new system and it was improved by the 1993 Education Act, which created the Special Educational Needs Tribunal. The 1993 Act also introduced the concept of a National Code of Practice in order to increase standards of practice and awareness in ordinary schools (see Parts 1.5 and 1.6).

Generally, the duty to provide for children with special needs in an ordinary school is imposed by section 321 of the Education Act 1996. This Act has now replaced the 1993 Education Act.

The 1981 Education Act and its successors, which now include the 1996 Act, have created two categories of pupils with special educational needs. The first category is those children who can be educated in an ordinary school. For those who have more severe and complex needs, the Acts have created the concept of a statement of special educational needs. A statement amounts to a diagnosis of the child's needs and a prescription to meet the needs of that child. These must be set out in a statement. The Court of Appeal approved this concept of a statement in the well-known case of R v Secretary of State for Education and Science, ex parte E (1992) FLR 377, in the leading judgement of Lord Justice Balcombe. It is where there is a statement that local authorities will pay for the schools in this book.

Parents who are interested in obtaining a statement have to apply for a statutory assessment. The LEA is bound only to assess or make a statement if it is necessary for the LEA to determine the special educational provision required by any child with a learning difficulty (section 323 of the Act). The Code of Practice defines a three-stage process of assessment which, if it is successful, means that a statement is not required. However, the Code is only guidance. Cases will occur which do not fit into the Code. If, however, a child goes beyond stage 3 of the Code, a statutory assessment is necessary and eventually, unless the assessment produces the answer to the child's problems, a statement is made.

Where a statement is made, the LEA must arrange the special educational provision required by the child and also arrange an appropriate school. Under the statutes, parents have a right to request a statutory assessment and are given specific appeal rights. The rights of appeal mean that parents can appeal to an independent Tribunal, established under the 1993 Act, with a legally qualified Chairman and two lay experts. The Chairman of the Tribunal, together with the President of the Tribunal, is appointed by the Lord Chancellor. The lay members are a panel of persons who may serve as lay members and are appointed by the Department for Education and Employment.

Rights of appeal

The rights of appeal as created by the statutes are as follows:

1. Against the LEA's refusal to make an assessment following a request from the parents to assess a child's special educational needs under section 323 of the 1996 Act.
2. Against the refusal of the LEA to re-assess a child who has a statement under section 329.
3. Against the LEA's refusal to make a statement for a child under section 325 of the Act.
4. Against the LEA's assessment of a child's special educational needs, the provision specified in the statement of special educational needs, or, if no school is named in the Statement, against that under section 326. This appeal includes appeals against decisions to amend statements. This appeal, in all its aspects, will include a request to have a particular school named in the statement.
5. Against the LEA's decision not to change the name of a school specified in a statement; this is only applicable to a state-maintained or grant-maintained school and is not applicable to independent schools.
6. Against the decision of the LEA to cease to maintain a statement under paragraph 2 of Schedule 27 of the Act.

As a result of these statutory powers, the Tribunal can order an assessment of a child's special educational needs, if necessary; order a statement, or change a statement, which includes consideration of the correct school. Where the LEA ceases to maintain a statement, the Tribunal can reverse their decision, thus ordering the LEA to continue to pay for a school.

Issues not for the Tribunal

The Tribunal clearly has power over the wording of the statement, which includes the name of the school. However, the Tribunal has no power to compel a local education authority actually to obey the statement and enforce the contents of the statement or the Tribunal's Order. If an LEA does not obey its statutory duty, that is a matter for the High Court and not for the Tribunal. Equally, the Tribunal does not have power over social services functions. A large number of specialist schools, which are residential – particularly those dealing with children with a more unusual or severe problem – have children who have been placed there by joint funding paid by social services and the education department.

Where issues go outside the Tribunal's jurisdiction, these are matters for the High Court on judicial review, the system which enables parents to challenge a decision made by a public body – in this instance, the LEA. It is relevant to note that where the case is within the High Court jurisdiction, the child is entitled to Legal Aid in the child's own right and the parent means are irrelevant. Regrettably, this is not the case in relation to the Tribunal where no Legal Aid is available.

On appeal from the Tribunal, Legal Aid is available for proceedings in the High Court, but to the parent and not the child. On appeal to the High Court from the Tribunal parental means are irrelevant when determining whether Legal Aid will be granted. However, there are legal insurances available to parents in these circumstances. There is unfortunately an unfairness in the law, which has been commented on in Parliament and elsewhere: parents of children with special educational needs are not eligible for Legal Aid and are discriminated against, whereas parents of children who do not have such problems can simply obtain Legal Aid in their children's own right if issues arise.

The appeal to the Tribunal

In some cases, no appeal is needed as the LEA will agree a child needs a specialist school. However, about 900 cases a year go to the Tribunal. The working of the Tribunal is considered by Professor N Harris in his book, *Special Educational Needs and Access to Justice* (Jordans, 1997).

The Tribunal's timescales

The rules of procedure in the Tribunal provide for an appeal to be lodged within two months of the final statement, and if a parent does not lodge within time, it is highly unlikely that the appeal will be preserved. The Statutory Instrument 1995/3113 sets rigid time limits, which the Tribunal normally enforces in an extremely strict manner.

Preparation of a case

There are few books dealing with preparation of cases to the SEN Tribunal. A good, simple guide is published by the Advisory Centre for Education (ACE). However, for parents, I regret to say that my own book, *Children with Special Educational Needs – Assessment, Law and Practice: Caught in the Acts* (Jessica Kingsley Publishers) remains the only alternative specifically designed for parents. There are two further books which are more technical by nature: Austin & Oliver, *Special Educational Needs and the Law* and Friel & Hay, *Special Educational Needs and the Law* (Sweet and Maxwell Publishers). Both of these are really lawyers' guides, rather than parental guides, to the Tribunal and the system. The Code of Practice, which is free, is an extremely useful document. It is available from the Department for Education and Employment (see Part 5.4, Bibliography).

Parents would be strongly advised, if they are going into the statementing process and seeking a specialist school – whether it is a maintained or grant-maintained specialist school, or an independent school – to use independent experts to advise them. An experienced independent educational psychologist is obviously essential. Where children have medical difficulties, reports from clinical psychologists, paediatricians and consultants in the field of expertise governing the child's specific medical disability, are clearly essential. Bearing in mind the timescales used by the Tribunal, these reports must not be late: they should be obtained at about the time of the appeal, or if possible before the appeal, in order to persuade the authority of the parents' case.

In cases that involve speech therapy, a report of an independent speech therapist is normally essential. The local authority normally obtains reports from the Health Service, which do not sufficiently specify the required level of speech therapy. This is often important, as the Health Service is under no obligation to provide to the Education Authority the speech therapy required by the children under its care.

Health Authority reports often deal only with the help a Health Authority will offer. As a matter of law, the local education authority must provide the special educational provision necessary, which means that, if necessary, it must pay itself for speech therapy and provide it (R v Harrow London Borough Council, ex parte M, *The Times*, 15 October 1996). Equally, in cases where occupational therapy and physiotherapy is important, specialist reports should be obtained.

Legal Aid and legal representation

As outlined previously, Legal Aid is not available for the Tribunal. It is available for appeals to the High Court, subject to means, from the Tribunal to the High Court. For parents who are outside the Legal Aid limits, legal representation – particularly if parents are seeking a school that is listed in this book – is in my view essential, if at all possible. Such cases are often extremely complex. The cost of a placement at LEA special schools is expensive, and very expensive indeed at the more specialised schools, whether LEA or independent.

The cost of a placement at a specialist speech and language school for five years can be £125,000–£150,000. For children with autism, severe learning difficulties or emotional and behavioural problems, costs may be higher still and a placement can cost in excess of £40,000 a year. Nobody would seek to recover sums of this nature in the High Court or in the County Court without proper legal representation. For this reason alone, legal representation in this field is worthwhile.

For those who are on Income Support, Legal Aid can be obtained simply to give advice for Tribunal cases. This can be extended to cover an expert report in some cases. The Legal Aid situation is considered in *Special Educational Needs and the Law*, as mentioned above. Despite changes in the Legal Aid system, Legal Aid for education cases will remain much the same so far as can be presently predicted.

The Tribunal, in its publicity documents, maintains that parents can conduct cases without representation. There is considerable disagreement on this issue between practitioners and advisers in this field and the Tribunal. Some charities, in my view, quite wrongly take the view that legal representation is not necessary or is actually wrong. While inexperienced lawyers may offer no help to a case, the use of an experienced lawyer makes a large difference. Clearly, too formal an approach is unhelpful. Representation by some charities is excellent, but the quality varies greatly, even within the same charity from area to area. The Tribunal itself takes the clear line that representation is not necessary. Although this is obviously desirable so that parents do not incur costs, in practice, legal representation may well assist in obtaining the desired outcome in favour of parents.

Obviously not all legally-represented appeals will be successful, but I regularly have to look at cases where the wrong result has been obtained and where the parent was not represented or was represented by a charity with insufficient experience. Professor Harris in his work, *Special Educational Needs and Access to Justice* (Jordans, 1997) did not look at the quality of legal representation directly. He recorded the reservations of various bodies, which I have mentioned above. He did find that most legal representation was good and cases well prepared. He came to no conclusion as his research did not deal with the issue. His work, however, indicates that legal representation is effective. In practice, it proves effective in my view.

The Tribunal does a very good job and does try to conduct its business in order to assist parents with problems who are unrepresented. Nonetheless, mistakes are made. A good example of this is the case of a dyslexic child – Burbridge v Birmingham City Council (Unreported) Court of Appeal, Transcript: Friday 6 September 1996 – where the Court of Appeal decided that the Tribunal had applied completely the wrong test and looked at the wrong issues. The local authority maintained that no statement was necessary, nor a statutory assessment, although it had been helping the child for about four years, during which time he had actually worsened rather than improved. At the time of the case before the Tribunal, he was virtually four years behind in literacy and four years behind in numeracy. The Tribunal refused the appeal. The parents were not represented. Had they been represented, they should have succeeded.

This area of law should be dealt with by experienced solicitors or lawyers. Lawyers operating in this field should be members of the Education Law Association which can be contacted through its Secretary, Jowan Hazelden, Education Law Association, 370 Grimston Avenue, Folkestone, Kent CT20 2QD, Tel: 01303 211570. The Association keeps a list of lawyers who practise in this field.

Recommendations represent only a personal point of view, of course, but I would recommend to parents, solicitors who normally act on a set fee basis. This means that parents know the extent of expenditure on a case.

Voluntary organisations

A number of voluntary organisations provide representation in this field. I have long-standing personal experience of the British Dyslexia Association, which operates a befrienders scheme through the local associations. The Head Office is at 98 London Road, Reading Berkshire RG1 5AU, tel: 0118 966 8271. In London, the Law Centre, Disability Law Service, Ground Floor, 39–45 Cavell Street, London E1 2BP, tel: 020 7791 9800 provides an excellent service, but is limited to the London area in normal circumstances. Where parents are simply seeking advice, the Advisory Centre for Education, Unit 1C, Aberdeen Studios, 22–24 Highbury Grove, London N5 2DQ, tel: 020 7354 8321, is a good resource. The charity IPSEA (Independent Panel for Special Education Advice), 4 Ancient House Mews, Woodbridge, Suffolk IP12 1DH provides advice and, in many cases where requested, will assist with representation.

Conclusion

The author's view is that if parents can afford it, they would be wise to obtain representation and advice prior to any appeal rising. If the case is properly prepared, they may not even need to go to appeal. It is worth consulting expert lawyers who can assist parents by recommending expert educational psychologists, speech therapists, doctors etc, prior to an appeal arising and not after it.

1.8
Enforcing Your Rights: What Can You Achieve?

John Friel, Barrister-at-law, Grays Inn

The Special Educational Needs Tribunal (discussed in Part 1.7) is intended to resolve disputes, but parents may often feel that they would benefit from a wider awareness of their rights, whether or not they have legal representation. This article offers additional guidance to parents on their entitlement to Legal Aid and other options.

The Special Educational Needs and Disability Bill will extend the jurisdiction of the Tribunal to issues under that Act, which will include the admission and exclusion of children with special educational needs. Although these are welcome developments, this book is really about obtaining specialist education for those children who have exceptional problems and who cannot for whatever reason, be given the provision required in a mainstream school. However, the new Bill also introduces procedures for the resolution of disputes between LEAs concerning children in their area. These arrangements are not intended to affect the entitlement of a parent to appeal to the Tribunal (see Clause 6 of Section 3 of the new Bill). There is provision for the resolution of disagreements between authorities and parents, and between the parents of the child and the proprietor of the school about special educational provision made for that child. Parents should bear in mind these possible changes for the future, but at present, the law has not changed. In setting up such a procedure LEAs will have to have regard the guidance given by the Secretary of State in England or the National Assembly of Wales in Wales. The procedure is designed to be independent and may well be an important means of resolving disputes without going to the Tribunal. Obviously, the system will have to be considered once it is in place, and once it is known what advice is given. Under the 1981 Act parents were able to negotiate frequently without going to the Tribunal, sometimes with expert help when attending meetings with LEAs. This practice appears to have been abandoned with the introduction of the Tribunal with many Local Authorities.

This article is not intended to be anything other than assessment based on experience. However, the information used is gathered from many sources. Overall, the system has become much fairer and more usable by parents since the 1981 Education Act. The reforms introduced by the 1993 Education Act have meant that the Special Educational Needs Tribunal does provide a useful and effective means of resolving disputes between parents and local education authorities (LEAs), albeit only for children with, or entitled to, Statements of Special Educational Needs.

As mentioned in the previous section, a Tribunal can only deal with certain limited issues, it cannot enforce its own orders. Secondly, the Tribunal is based on the idea that parents will represent their own case, however complex a child's difficulties actually are, and however difficult the presentation. It should be remembered that, unless the child is reaching the end of his or her school years, such decisions are not necessarily final if things change or if new evidence or new approaches come to light. The Tribunal is certainly willing to look again at cases, particularly where intervention argued for and promoted by local education authorities has not worked, or has not worked effectively.

However, the Tribunal is attempting to do a cheap, effective job in very complex cases. In any ordinary court, disputes of this nature would take days to resolve, while within the Tribunal a case that takes two days is wholly exceptional. A court would resolve such disputes at a very much greater cost and certainly much greater length. Many parents who present their own cases find, despite the efforts of the Tribunal to create a friendly and informal atmosphere, that for them it is far from friendly and informal. Experience also shows that while the Tribunal may resolve a number of disputes adequately, to the satisfaction of all concerned, in cases where the parents are dissatisfied, there appears to be substantial evidence to support parental complaints.

A lawyer like myself will only analyse cases that have been argued by parents who go to appeal to the High Court. However, in a large number of cases, parents achieve a satisfactory settlement before the hearing in the High Court or the parents succeed following argument in the High Court. It should be remembered that cases argued before the High Court exclude a proportion of the stronger cases (ie, from the parents' perspective). Those cases will have been settled to the parents' satisfaction before the hearing. However, where appeals have a realistic chance (some are argued that do not have a realistic chance), a high proportion of such appeals succeed when compared with other jurisdictions.

Overall, therefore, the Special Educational Needs Tribunal represents a realistic and effective means of resolving disputes. Experience, however, shows that parents presenting the cases, even sometimes with charitable support, feel overtaken or overwhelmed by the way in which the Tribunal conducts its procedure. In such cases, when looked at either by the High Court, or by outside lawyers, there appears to be substantial grounds for the parental complaint. Most people would not conduct such cases without legal advice and representation if they were involved in a serious road accident. I believe that a number of these problem cases would be more effectively resolved had parents used professional advisers, normally lawyers, educational psychologists and appropriate experts in dealing with a child's case. A substantial proportion of these problems could be solved if those who could afford to pay for appropriate support did so. This factor is counterbalanced by the Tribunal's stance that cases do not need such support and that the Tribunal will take care of everything. Overall, however, the latest Legal Aid reforms indicate that Parliament and our society is expecting people to pay for such professional services as and when necessary. It is regrettable that in this field the idea is, to some extent, actively discouraged.

For those without income the Legal Aid Green Form is available. This entitles parents who qualify for the scheme to a consultation with a lawyer for a low, fixed sum. There are very many parents with children with special educational needs, including those with the severest disabilities, who can afford little or nothing. The Legal Aid scheme still gives these parents access to advice and enables them to obtain professional reports. It can also be used to obtain representation at a court hearing. The same applies to advice and assistance available through some charities and/or Law Centres. Again, in my view, this method to support parents with no or low income is underused.

However, the Tribunal cannot enforce its own orders, and there are all too many cases where the Tribunal's orders are not ultimately implemented by local education authorities. In such cases, as this is a breach of statutory duty, the correct remedy in my view is judicial review (a system which enables the parents to challenge a decision made by the LEA). As the statutory duty is owed to the child, the child is eligible for Legal Aid and parental means are irrelevant. It is therefore ironic, and in my view unfair, that the Legal Aid system will be supporting children to a greater extent than it supports parents. The child often needs the parent to appeal or take action, which is vital for the support of the child. Judicial review will ensure that the Tribunal's order is enforced.

Judicial review also provides an important remedy in cases where children are excluded from school. Exclusion happens in a large number of cases, but it also includes children with Statements of Special Educational Needs, or children who are on the verge of obtaining a statement. There is a duty upon the LEA to provide either temporary out of school education and/or home tuition imposed by section 19 of the 1996 Act, which is often ignored. The second feature of section 19 is that it imposes a duty to provide temporary out of school education, which may involve considerable expertise to deal with special educational needs for those who are ill or who cannot attend school for other reasons. Overall, as a remedy, judicial review is extremely effective, but underused. Few cases actually go to a final hearing because either the service of proceedings or an initial hearing results in appropriate action being taken.

Overall, Section 19 has become much more important due to the fact that many children with special educational needs have unfortunately been excluded from mainstream school, or have become unable to attend due to illness, often arising from stress and depression. In these circumstances it is unfortunate that the authorities do not frequently deliver a home tuition or unit-based provision. Parents therefore have to resort to Judicial Review much more regularly. However, it is not generally known that Circular 11/99 gives guidance on the provision for children who are out of school. Chapter 5 of the circular provides for what is in fact a very detailed provision for children out of school whether they are excluded from school or unable to attend school due to illness or for some other condition (Section 19 (1). Therefore, LEAs must regard the advice given by the Secretary of State. The existence of this circular, and particularly Chapter 5, is extremely important. Parents are increasingly resorting to Judicial Review to obtain a reasonable education for children who are out of school. Unfortunately, more and more children are unable to attend school due to recognised problems with stress and depression and this right has become an important means of at least covering this situation on a temporary basis.

Additionally, parents have the right to complain to the Secretary of State (which derives from ss. 497 of the Education Act 1996). Despite the wide-ranging powers that the law apparently gives to the Secretary of State to intervene when LEAs and governing bodies act illegally or unreasonably, few of these cases attract attention. Overall, the complaint power of the Secretary of State is a less effective remedy than judicial review. Firstly, unless parents can afford it, legal representation is not available. The drafting of such complaints, however, normally requires some technical knowledge, even in the simplest of cases. Secondly, the procedure appears to be slow, erratic and not necessarily comprehensive.

The last remedy to be considered is a complaint to the Local Government Ombudsman/Commissioner. Such a complaint must be made within a year of the decision or action subject to complaint. Where litigation has taken place, the Local Government Commissioner would not normally intervene, but he retains discretion. This remedy is useful for failures in the past and the Local Government Commissioner can recommend compensation, but it is ineffective when dealing with present situations.

Leaving aside the complaint to the Secretary of State, which is rarely used, it is clear from experience in the courts with judicial review certainly from reported cases, as well as the reported decisions of the Local Government Commissioner that parents can achieve a great deal. It is, however, often a matter for expert consideration as to which remedy is appropriate, and how and when to make the complaint.

This article would not be complete without mentioning the duties under the Children Act to assess children in need. The definition of children in need includes all children who are disabled and the definition of disability is extremely wide (see section 17 of the Act). The 1989 Act provides for a social services assessment of needs, and the Secretary of State has issued guidelines. These guidelines require a social services' assessment of needs to be placed into a care plan, which has some similarities with a statement. In cases where residential provision is sought, serious consideration to social services' assessment should be given.

Although children are known to social services and the local education authority, it is surprising that in most cases there is no care plan and very often no assessment, yet there is a dire need for services, home help or respite care, for example. If no provision is made and there is no care plan, the correct remedy is normally judicial review for breach of statutory duty.

Disputes as regards care plans can, in rare cases, be subject to judicial review, but will more often be subject to the internal complaints procedure. Nonetheless, a knowledge of this area of law is most useful in cases where children have more unusual and severe problems or are more clearly and obviously disabled. Again, experience has shown that parents who exert legal pressure where there is a breach of duty with Legal Aid have achieved considerable success.

Overall, therefore, my conclusion is that parents in many cases need great determination and recourse to expert advice, which if possible should include legal advice, and may well need to attack on more than one front. Nonetheless, despite the complexity of this area and the expertise required, parents can achieve a great deal.

1.9

Special Educational Needs in Scotland

Ken Dutton, Principal Educational Psychologist – Scottish Borders Council*

The legislative system

The special needs system in Scotland broadly follows similar principles and processes to the parallel requirements in England. However, this is defined by separate laws in Scotland (the Educational (Scotland) Act 1980, as amended by the 1981 Act) and the detail of the process is different in many significant ways. In general, the processes tend to be less bureaucratic than their English law Counterparts.

The Education Committee of the Scottish Parliament is presently undertaking a comprehensive review of provision for special needs in Scottish schools. Significant changes are possible, particularly in the way needs are identified, assessed and then provided for, and significant changes in legislation are being mooted. The review is also expected to underline the 'social inclusion' political agenda which is now modus operandum of most councils and Educational Departments. The committee is expected to report during 2001; the description, which follows below, describes present arrangements for children with educational needs.

Assessing and documenting special educational needs

The principle vehicle currently for the definition of needs in Scotland is the Record of Needs Process which is the equivalent of the Statementing practice south of the border. Most authorities in Scotland have a staged system for supporting all pupils, similar to the 'Code of Practice (COP) in England and Wales. There are recommended stages listed in the equivalent Scottish 'Manual of Good Practice', but this is guidance for authorities rather than the legally enforced prescriptive practice laid out in the Code of Practice.

Most school-age children with learning difficulties requiring the protection of a Record of Need would be identified in schools via the staged systems of identification, assessment and support. The local authority must open a Record of Need for any child who has severe, specific or complex needs which are required to be kept under review by the local authority.

* Ken Dutton is Principal Psychologist at Scottish Borders Council; the article above, however, is written in a private capacity and the views expressed are not necessarily those of the Council or Education Department.

Educational Departments are required to identify and record children with severe complex needs from the age of two. Such children, not yet within the formal school system, are usually brought to the attention of the authorities by multi-agency links with paediatric services, GPs & health visitors, visiting paediatric therapists and, often parents themselves.

Any parent can request a multi-disciplinary assessment to see if a Record of Need is required for their child. An authority must carry out such an assessment unless it feels it is an unreasonable request, and clearly must have evidence to support such a decision. If a parent does not accept an authority's decision either to carry out, or to not carry out, an assessment, they may appeal to the Scottish Executive Education Department (S.E.E.D) to have that decision scrutinised.

If the assessment is carried forward then an authority must obtain reports from the school, the school's educational psychologist and clinical medical officer/ paediatrician. The local authority also must seek the parent's view as to what is considered best for the child. Since the enactment of the Children (Scotland) Act 1995, the child's own views must also be obtained, directly if they are over 12 years of age and able to express their views, or via their parents if younger or not considered able to express their own views.

When all the reports have been obtained, the authority collates them, and makes a decision whether or not to open a Record. If it decides to proceed, a draft version of the Record of Need is then sent (or, in some authorities, taken by the educational psychologist) to the parents for their approval. If approved this is then issued as a final version Record of Need. If there are aspects that require edit or alteration, this is negotiated between parents and authority.

The final Record of Need is copied to parents, school and local authority; copy information can be provided to medical officers on request (normally a standardised system for such requests exists). Further copies to other personnel can be provided only with parental permission or after a parent request.

Appeals system

Parents retain rights of appeal about the various sections of the final Record of Need, if complete agreement proves difficult. The local authority appeals committee, sheriff, or Scottish Executive Education Department (depending on the specific area of disagreement) can variously hear these appeals. There is, at present, no equivalent to the tribunal system as in England and Wales though the notion of such a body has been debated as part of the (Scottish) parliamentary review of the special systems. An independent body 'Enquire', part of the Children in Scotland organisation, has been commissioned by the Scottish Executive, meantime, to act in conciliation role in the case of major disputes (which are rare, relative to the activity of the English tribunal system).

Reviewing needs

It is considered good practice to review a child's Records of Need regularly and this is usually done via the child or young person's school, annually. Parents or other professionals involved can request a review at any time, but an authority does not have to carry out a review unless it has been at least 12 months since the previous review.

Education authorities will formally review a child's Record of Needs, as a minimum, at key transition points eg transfer between nursery and primary stages, midway through the primary stages at the primary/secondary transfer point.

The authority must, by law, carry out a Future Needs Review as a child approaches school leaving age (in the year prior to their 16th birthday, the point at which a child becomes legally referred to as a 'young person'). This meeting would typically involve teachers, educational psychologists, careers officer, medical officer and social worker (if they are likely to have a statutory responsibility to provide services for the young person as he/she moves into the adult world). Any other professional who may have been providing services for the young person can also attend. The aim of the Future Needs Review is to offer the young person (and their parents) advice on what is available for them in the period beyond school, as they move into adulthood, and to plan that transition to ensure it is both smooth and effective for the young person.

As the young person leaves formal education the Record of Need is discontinued, but kept in file archives for up to five years. This is so that the young person, further education establishment or other statutory bodies may obtain required information or later references from this (but only with the young person's knowledge and permission).

Supporting individual needs

Provision of support for children with special needs varies, both in terms of the child's needs and the different local authorities' responses to education provision. Different authorities' responses are varied as a result of geography/demography as well as historical, political and philosophical standpoints.

Sparsely populated areas, such as the highlands and the border areas (Scottish Borders and Dumfries and Galloway Councils), typically tend to make provision in locally based schools and specialist provision attached to mainstream schools. Dedicated specialist centres are often non-viable both in terms of pupil numbers and the cost of establishing and running them. Some densely populated inner-city areas, such as Glasgow City, have large dedicated specialist schools as well as a spectrum of locally based and individual support arrangements.

A number of Specialist independent centres exist throughout Scotland providing very specialist (frequently residential) support for children with complex, severe low-incidence needs, occasionally involving the care and welfare as well as educational decisions. Some of the schools are listed in this elsewhere in this guide, but would include the Royal Blind School, Donaldsons School for the Deaf, Craighalbert Centre (offering Peto-type provision for children with motor impairment), etc.

Future developments

Legislation reflecting the move to inclusive policies in authorities, shortly to go before the Scottish Parliament, is likely to enact a requirement for 'presumption of mainstream' schooling as the starting point for meeting a child's needs. Only in exceptional or complex cases, or following parents' requests, would children be considered for specialist schools or resourced provision placements (which may or may not be provided locally by an education authority).

A further current trend within Scotland is a pressure for a move towards an entitlement to more extensive support resourcing for a wider range of children with learning difficulties, in all schools, not just the minority for whom Records of Needs are in place. Whilst the need to protect vulnerable young people and children is self-evident, the skewing of limited and pressurised resources/budgets to a small minority of pupils (less than 2 per cent) is increasingly seen as unfair and discriminatory to other pupils in need.

The current consultation around the proposed 'Special Educational Needs Disability Rights in Education' legislation has also underlined the need for authorities to anticipate barriers to learning for a range of children with complex needs. Education Departments will be required to audit and plan to make schools disability-friendly and the curriculum accessible, rather than the historic reactive ways of working. The changes will encompass teacher development training, school policy-making as well as physical alterations to ensure accessibility to school buildings. This change in thinking will perhaps mark one of the most fundamental changes in philosophy and practice in recent decades.

1.10
How Parents Can Help

Carol M Orton, The British Dyslexia Association

Carol Orton is experienced in helping parents through the complex and often frustrating legal and administrative processes of special education. Here she offers some practical advice to parents seeking suitable education provision for their child and emphasises the importance of an organised and positive approach.

Many parents will be reading this book because they feel, for whatever reason, that their child's difficulties are not being dealt with properly and that they want him or her to go to a school that caters specifically for them.

Once other ways of raising funds have been discarded as impractical – buying lots of lottery tickets, remortgaging the house or taking on three jobs to pay for it, they recognise the only way of paying for specialist provision is by asking their Local Education Authority (LEA) to do so.

Everyone will be at a different stage in the process so this article starts at the very beginning. Further information about the Code of Practice for the Identification and Assessment of SEN, the 1996 Education Act and other useful reading may be found in other sections of this Guide. It helps to find out as much as possible about the Law, the Code, the procedure involved and your child's learning difficulties and/or disabilities.

You know your child best. You cannot solve all their problems on your own but you can do your best to make sure that all those difficulties are fully understood and that he or she receives the right sort of help.

Before the statement

When you first begin to suspect that your child is having problems at school you will usually ask his class teacher for advice. Even at this early stage it is important to be as clear as possible just what difficulties you think he or she has and why you are worried. You have a right to express your concern and your views should be heard. The school should provide special help within the normal curriculum framework and monitor and review his/her progress. Parents should contribute to the information gathered.

If you have an independent report, for example from an educational psychologist or speech and language therapist, saying your child has severe SEN, it should be taken seriously by the school. If not, you should write to the school asking why they disagree with professional advice about both your child's difficulties and the help he or she needs. Insist on a reply in writing.

It is usually, but not always, easier to find agreement on a child's difficulties than the sort of help he or she should have. School governors have a statutory duty to 'use their best endeavours to secure that if any registered pupil has special educational needs the special educational provision which his learning difficulty calls for is made' (Section 317, 1996 Education Act). (See Part 1.5 for a summary of the governing body's responsibilities.)

The statutory assessment
The LEA only has to comply with your request to start a statutory assessment 'if it is necessary'. Your view of what is necessary and theirs may well be some distance apart. It is not enough to write a polite letter asking for an assessment. You must gather evidence and demonstrate that it is really needed, that everything else has been tried and that your child needs help that his school cannot provide.

Your child's school may support your opinion, but even so it is best if you, as the parent, request the assessment. You have a right to appeal to the Special Educational Needs Tribunal if the LEA refuses your request (see Part 1.7). Regulations state that the LEA have to make their decision within six weeks of your letter and there are no such time limits following a school's request.

It is important to describe in detail all the difficulties you know your child experiences. Describe your child's reading, for example, very precisely. What happens when he can't read a word? Does he guess wildly? Does he attempt to work it out? How successfully? In continuous reading, does he make errors, eg miss words or syllables (beginning, middle, end)? Can he read for information? A bus timetable? A computer game manual? The *TV Times*? Does he seem to be concentrating so hard on decoding, or reading so slowly, that he can't remember what he has read? Can he remember/understand a sentence/page/chapter? What strategies does he use to avoid reading? What help does he need? If certain activities at home are helpful, say so, eg 'If I read the textbook to him he can to the homework'. Examples of a child's work are useful evidence.

You may find it helpful to use headings to describe each of his difficulties. An example of possible headings is given below in the section about analysing a statement. Don't rely on your independent evidence to speak for you. Use it instead to back up what you say. Think carefully about the help he needs and say why. Say also why his local school cannot provide it. Remember that you are describing a 'difficulty in learning' or a disability that 'prevents or hinders' your child from making use of educational facilities, not simply his scores on certain tests (Section 312, 1996 Education Act).

Once the LEA has agreed to start the assessment it will seek more advice from parents, educational advice from the child's school, medical advice and psychological advice. The LEA psychologist must consult with other psychologists involved with the child, including your independent psychologist.

The quality of advice varies enormously, but the regulations, printed at the back of the Code of Practice, are quite specific:

The regulations say that advice, including parents' advice, shall relate to:

a) the educational, medical, psychological or other features of the case (according to the nature of the advice sought) which appear to be relevant to the child's educational needs (including his future needs).

b) how these features could affect the child's educational needs and
c) the provision which is appropriate for the child in the light of those features of the child's case.

When you receive all the different sets of advice you should check that they have properly detailed what your child's difficulties are and that they specify the help he needs.

If, after making the assessment, the LEA decides that an ordinary school can meet your child's needs it may decide not to make a statement. In this case they will issue a 'note in lieu' saying what his needs are and the help he requires. If you do not accept that this amount of help is adequate you have a right to appeal to the SEN Tribunal (see Part 1.7 for further information).

Analysing the statement

Once the LEA has decided 'it is necessary' for it to make a statement it will first send you a proposed statement, with all the advice gathered during the assessment. You have a right to make representations and to have a meeting to discuss the statement (Schedule 27, 1996 Education Act).

A judge has described Part 2 of the statement, which covers the special educational needs or difficulties, as a 'diagnosis', and Part 3, which specifies provision, as a 'prescription'. Part 2 must therefore describe 'all the child's needs' and Part 3 must make provision 'for each and every one' of the needs described in Part 2. A good statement is one that enables anyone reading it, even a supply teacher who does not know your child, to understand his special educational needs, and that makes it quite clear what sort of help he will receive. There should be no doubt about what is going to happen.

It is essential to analyse the proposed statement carefully. The following straightforward method may help in doing so. There should be no doubt about what is going to happen.

First make a copy of the statement and all reports. You need one clean copy and one on which you can make notes. Then take three different coloured highlighter pens! Go through all the reports, including the one you wrote yourself and your independent evidence. With one colour highlight any descriptions of your child's experiences. With another highlight any proposed provision. With the third, colour anything with which you disagree.

Use a separate sheet of paper for each of your child's special educational needs and give each a heading. For example, for a dyslexic or dyspraxic child they may be: Reading, Writing, Spelling, Maths, Memory, Organisation, Motor Skills, Language Skills, Social Skills, Self-esteem, Confidence, Behaviour and Abilities. Other learning difficulties or disabilities will have similar characteristics which your child may or may not share.

Fold the paper in half, so that you have one half for descriptions of difficulties (SEN) and one half for the suggested provision for that particular difficulty or aspect of his disability.

Go through all the reports again. Copy each highlighted phrase of a description of difficulty on to the relevant page and similarly any advice about provision. You may wish to note who said what.

You now have a list of what everyone says about each of your child's educational needs and the help they say he or she requires. Check this list against the statement. This preparation will be invaluable when the meeting is held. You can also, using the vocabulary from the reports, draft a proposed statement of your own to be used as the basis of discussion.

You will be asked to state a preference for a maintained school. You have the right to make representations for an independent school. The LEA, in that case, only has to support your request if it cannot meet your child's needs in a maintained school.

The LEA has eight weeks in which to finalise the statement, which allows for one meeting. If, after trying to negotiate, you find you still disagree with the statement you have a right to appeal to the SEN Tribunal (see Part 1.7) about the description of needs and/or provision and the name of the school.

Reviews

A statement has to be reviewed at least annually. The Code of Practice describes what should happen at the review. Most of this is endorsed by regulations, printed at the back of the Code. You will be asked to give your views. If you do not feel that the statement is adequate or wish to move to an independent school you will need to think about your report in much the same way as described for the statutory assessment. The review report, written after the meeting, should recommend amendments to the statement but the LEA does not have to follow this advice.

If the statement is amended, but you are still not satisfied, you have a right to appeal to the SEN Tribunal about the contents of the statement, including the name of the school (see Part 1.7 for further information).

General points

Keep a ring binder file with all reports and correspondence, in date order. Don't be tempted to stuff it all in a drawer! Try and keep notes of all telephone calls. Send letters to confirm in writing what has been said at meetings and on the phone and keep copies.

Maintain a diary about day to day happenings at school and at home which illustrate the difficulties your child is having. Make notes of the things your child says about his or her problems.

Prepare for meetings using the ideas in this article. The focus of the meeting should be your child. It is very easy to get distracted into a discussion about who said what and when or delays in procedure, and find that you have not said anything that really worries you about your child's difficulties.

It is a good idea to send a letter beforehand saying what you would like to discuss at the meeting. Give the school copies of any evidence in advance. If at all possible take someone with you to make sure the meeting sticks to the point and take notes. At times you may feel angry or upset if there are disagreements, but try to stay calm. Send a letter afterwards noting what was said.

And finally! Keep encouraging your child and show him or her plenty of love. Home is where your child should be safe and happy, however hard things may be at school. Try and keep any frustrations or anxieties to yourself and allow yourself to escape from the pressure sometimes. Join a support group!

More detailed information about the legal processes of assessment and statementing may be found in Parts 1.5–1.7 of this Guide. Readers should note that changes are anticipated with reference to the existing SEN framework and Code of Practice.

1.11

An introduction to assessment

Dr Richard Lansdown MA, PGCE, DipPsych, PhD, FBPsS
Chartered Educational and Clinical (Child) Psychologist

The psychological assessment of a child thought to have special educational needs is an exercise in problem solving.
First one has to pose a 'why' question, examples of which are:

Why is s/he not reading as well as we expect?
Why is s/he unable to get on well with other children?
Why is s/he having such difficulty with written work?

The problem then is to answer these questions in a way that will give indications for the child's educational future.

The first step

The very first step is to gather some general information, which involves taking a brief medical, social and educational history. Information on milestones like walking and talking, hearing and vision, serious illnesses or accidents is essential. Whether there is a history of learning difficulties of any kind in the family may be relevant and details on how many schools have been attended are also sought.

Next comes current information: what do the present teachers say about the child's attainment and behaviour? Is there any specific concern, e.g. maths or reading, or is the worry more general? What are the child's interests? What is the child's behaviour like at home? Are there any problems with sleeping or eating or with making and keeping friends?

The first hypothesis

Once this information has been gathered, a preliminary hypothesis can be made, for example, consider these four nine year olds:

Peter Doe was born after a difficult delivery and he has always been slow in his milestones. His hearing and vision are normal but he has not been able to keep up with his peers in school work and has been kept down a year in primary school. He prefers to play with younger children. He used to sleep well but now says that it is hard to get to sleep, especially in term time.

Mary Doe was a normal toddler, very bubbly and outgoing as a young child, who has always had a wide circle of friends. She was a little late in talking but is very agile and swims like a fish. She has recently been reluctant to go to school, complaining of head-aches or tummy aches and her reports have been encouraging but consistent in pointing to a difficulty with reading and spelling.

Jenny Doe has severe cerebral palsy and has no speech. She can swipe at an object with a closed fist but cannot hold or manipulate a pencil. Her parents report that she seems able to understand a great deal but they admit that they may be biased.

John Doe is described as having been a good baby, but not at all cuddly, with normal motor milestones, no illnesses but some language delay. He is solitary at school and has only one friend in the neighbourhood who shares his interest in trains. By choice, he reads nothing but train books, including out of date timetables, and will spend hours at a station. He hates change of any kind.

Each of these yields a different hypothesis. The next step is to test them, using tests and/or observations.

Testing the hypotheses

An intelligence test is the usual starting point for children with learning difficulties of any kind. Two are commonly used in the UK: the Wechsler Scales and the British Ability Scales. Both follow the same pattern of asking that children undertake a range of tasks which include verbal and non-verbal reasoning, memory, general knowledge, vocabulary and so on. The results are then aggregated to yield an IQ, with 100 as an average score. About 80 per cent of children score between 80 and 120. As a very rough rule of thumb, a score below 70 is an indication of learning difficulties, but it is of the utmost importance to note that this is only an indication, not a ticket to a special school.

Much can be learned from the scores on such a test, but also from the way the child approaches the task. Does he rush at everything, showing no sense of planning or reflection on what he is doing? Does she persist, even when the tasks are getting hard? How does he react to failure?

But an IQ is only a beginning. One needs next to look at other relevant areas, depending on the question asked.

Peter: global or specific problems?

Peter's history suggests global difficulties, but to check on this one would supplement the intelligence test with others which look at reading and maths, writing and drawing. If they all point in the same direction, one begins to firm up on a diagnosis of the learning difficulty, but it may be helpful also to consider his behaviour. Here there are two approaches. One is to rely on observations from the teachers, the parents and the psycho-logist carrying out the assessment. The other is to use a standardised rating scale which usually consists of a series of statements about children, with boxes to tick if they are appropriate for that child. This allows one to compare the child in question with others on whom the test was standardised, giving some indication of how serious any behaviour problems may be. Apart from anything else, it is useful to have data on behaviour when considering which school will be appropriate.

Mary: dyslexia?

Mary is reported to have problems with reading and spelling, so one must test those skills. Here we run into the difficulty of defining what we mean by reading. Some tests simply look at the child's ability to read single words out of context; this is useful as a screen but if there are difficulties it should be supplemented with a test of reading comprehension: how well does the child understand what is read? How much can he/she use context to guess at difficult words or phrases? Spelling mistakes can also give a clue to the next area of investigation: a child who writes 'mite' for might and 'dun' for done may have a weakness in visual memory.

If Mary's reading and/or spelling are poor when compared with her IQ, and if there are no reasons in her educational, medical or social history to explain the discrepancy, then the hypothesis of specific reading difficulty or dyslexia is likely to be upheld. It is common at this stage to assess the child's phonological awareness, which means in essence finding out how well she copes with language related sounds. There are batteries of tests to examine this, most of which include asking the child to detect words which rhyme, picking out words according to their ending sound or saying as many words as possible that begin with a certain letter in a short time. The rationale is that children diagnosed as dyslexic have often been found to have a weakness in such skills.

If it is thought that she has a memory weakness, then there are tests which examine children's memory, differentiating between visual and auditory channels.

A rating of Mary's behaviour may also be helpful, but equally important may be to look at how she sees herself. Here one uses a self concept scale, which gives some idea of whether she perceives herself as socially or academically a success, or possibly whether she feels supported at home.

A note on dyscalculia. Much is made of dyslexia, less of the maths equivalent which is known as dyscalculia. Relatively little work has been done in this area, there is some suggestion that it is related to spatial skills. The approach is similar to that used for dyslexia, with more detailed assessments of mathematical knowledge being carried out.

Jenny: a test for the tester

Jenny is quite a different matter. There are no tests standardised on children with cerebral palsy and so one normally uses instruments devised for the able bodied and interprets them in the light of the child's disability. At first it may seem impossible even to begin testing a child with no language and no hand control but much can be learned if the child can point, and swiping with a fist is often enough. For example, the British Picture Vocabulary Test consists of a series of pages with four pictures on each. The tester says a word and the child has to indicate the appropriate picture on that page. In this way one can assess vocabulary even in a child who has no speech at all. There are similar tests for spatial skills, and even one new scale which claims to assess general intelligence.

The interpretation of such tests is very much a matter of experience, for one has to take into account the fact that children with physical disabilities have not necessarily had the same breadth of life experiences that their able-bodied peers have had and may therefore not have a comparable range of vocabulary.

John: autism?

From his history, John is possibly autistic. Here one starts, not with any formal testing, but with a careful and detailed consideration of what he has done in the past and what he does now. Observations from teachers and parents are all important. One approach is to take the criteria for autism given in one of the classification[1] systems, and to look to see to what extent the child's behaviour matches them.

Once it has been established that a child can be classified, tests can be useful, and indeed are essential, to allow recommendations for the type of school that will be the best. Standard intelligence and attainment tests can often be used, although it may be necessary to rely on non-verbal scales for some children.

Behaviour ratings are also helpful, especially those which focus on activity levels, for autistic children are often overactive.

These four examples have been chosen to show that not only are different tests used according to the question put, different weights are assigned to tests or assessment approaches as well. The art of assessment is not simply in coming up with answers. It lies crucially in asking the right questions.

Questions and answers

1. A note on the IQ (intelligence quotient) and a reading age.

Psychologists usually report the results of intelligence tests using an IQ or standard score. This computation allows an age correction to be applied to children's responses: a six year old answering 20 out of 30 items correctly is clearly brighter than a nine year old who has the same raw score. Reading test results are sometimes expressed as standard scores as well (and the purists say they should be) but they are often given as a reading age which indicates the level reached by an average child of those years.

2. What effect is there when a child feels unwell, or if he or she does not like the psychologist?

It is unwise to test a child who is unwell, and most unwise to rely on scores on one who is emotionally upset. The personality of the psychologist can make a difference but if he or she has been properly trained this should be relatively small.

3. Are scores stable over time?

The older the child, the more stable the IQ will be. But a test is a snapshot, taken at one time, giving a picture of a child on that occasion and although large changes are relatively unusual in older children, they can occur and a retest after two years is advisable.

NB There can also be a practice effect on tests, that is if a child is given the same test within a few weeks the scores on the second occasion tend to be higher by up to 8 points on the full scale IQ.

4. Is IQ that important in explaining school success or failure?

Yes and no. There is no doubt that in general children with high IQs do better in school than those at the lower end, hardly surprising. But factors within children such as

---

1   There are two classification systems in use in the UK. DSM IV is American, ICD X is European. They both give detailed lists of criteria for the whole range of psychiatric disorders.

motivation, organisation and persistence play a major part, as do good teaching and support from home.

5. Do all intelligence tests give similar IQ scores?

Again, yes and no. They are likely to give more or less similar scores but the variation can be considerable. The IQ is basically a figure derived from a comparison of the child being tested with the sample on whom the test was standardised. So test A, standardised on group A, will not necessarily give the same results as test B, standardised on group B.

Of relevance here is the fact that tests get out of date and should be restandardised every twenty years or so.

6. What does an IQ of 100 really mean?

For the WISC-III^{UK} it indicates that a child has scored in the average when compared with a sample of children chosen in 1991 to be representative of the whole of the UK, geographically, ethnically and socially.

7. Why are IQ scores generally preferred to mental ages?

Mental ages are sometimes helpful but they can be misleading. Say three children have a mental age of a nine year old. There is all the difference in the world between a four year old, a nine year old and a fifteen year old with that mental age.

8. Does IQ predict success in areas other than the academic?

Not really; many other factors come into play, like the ability to get on with other people and creative ability.

9. Should we, then, talk of many different types of intelligence?

Some authorities say we should: we should distinguish, for example, between practical and academic abilities: one person may be outstanding at running a greengrocery business, always giving the right change and managing to balance the books, but may have been hopeless at the more sophisticated maths at school.

Musical or artistic skills also seem frequently to be distinct, ie a child can be very talented in either of these areas but not necessarily do well in mainstream school subjects.

1.12
Choosing a School

Mrs Rosemary Ayles
Consultant Educational Psychologist; Honorary Fellow,
University of Reading

'Children with special educational needs require the greatest possible access to a broad and balanced education, including the National Curriculum'.

The Implementation of the Code of Practice for Pupils with Special Educational Needs (OFSTED 1996).

Types of school

Most children with special educational needs will go to an ordinary state (LEA) or independent school. They will be educated with children of the same age with some supplementary help from the class teacher or a support teacher, but with no statutory assessment beyond stage 2 nor a statement of needs.

For the minority who require more specialised education, there is a range of alternative provision in special units and schools.

Special units in an LEA primary or comprehensive school

Special units attached to LEA maintained schools are provided in some areas for pupils with a range of special needs, eg partially hearing; speech and language difficulties; specific literacy difficulties; and emotional and behavioural difficulties. Pupils may share varying proportions of their time between the unit and the main school according to individual need.

LEA special school

An LEA special school will normally provide for pupils with a particular type of special need, whose degree of disability requires a more comprehensive specialist approach than can be provided in a mainstream school, eg more severe forms of visual impairment, physical disability, moderate or severe learning difficulty, speech and language difficulty (including autism and aphasia), emotional and behavioural difficulty (including ADHD). The majority are day schools but some are residential. Pupils normally attend full-time, but many schools have links with local primary and secondary schools in which pupils may spend some time each week. This is sometimes part of a longer term strategy to enable those pupils likely to benefit from a return to full-time mainstream education to do so.

Grant-maintained special school

These are schools which have opted out of LEA control and are now responsible directly to the DfEE.

In terms of the education provided, they offer the same range of facilities found in LEA schools and are subject to the same inspection procedures by OFSTED.

Independent special schools

Independent schools which have been approved by the Secretary of State for Education, as well as LEA schools, usually provide for a particular aspect of special need. They are inspected by OFSTED inspectors, but are not maintained by LEAs. Some have charitable status and are non-profit making. Fees are charged and in cases where the LEA has agreed that a pupil should attend a particular school, these are normally paid by the LEA. Occasionally the residential fee component may be paid by Social Services and medical fees (eg speech therapy, physiotherapy) may be paid by Health Services. Occasionally fees are paid by parents.

Some independent schools are not approved. They may have had approval refused or may not have requested it. LEAs are not empowered to place pupils in a school that is not approved to meet the needs outlined in a pupil's statement, without gaining prior individual agreement from the Secretary of State. This course of action is unusual.

Non-maintained special schools

These are schools approved by the Secretary of State but not maintained by an LEA or the DfEE. They are often run by major charities (eg National Children's Home, Barnardos) or by charitable trusts.

Other forms of educational provision

Children whose needs cannot be met within a school or unit are entitled to tuition either at home or in hospital. This is subject to LEA approval and inspection and is normally regarded as a short-term arrangement pending appropriate school placement.

Choosing a school

It is important to gather as much information as you can about your child's individual learning needs and aptitudes. The latter are as important as difficulties which your child may experience, since it is vital that any school you choose should provide opportunity for children to develop their strengths as well as support for their weaknesses. This information will be available from the assessments leading up to the statement, from those professionals involved in the assessments and from your own observations. Have a clear picture of what your child needs before visiting any school or unit.

The next stage, unless you are prepared to pay the fees privately, is to discuss with the key contact named in the statement the alternatives that may be available to you. In many cases there is only one appropriate school or unit available, in which case your visit will be to ensure that what is offered meets the educational needs of your child as you perceive them.

Before arranging a visit you may wish to ask for the school prospectus, the most recent annual governors' report, the special needs policy, and, if an OFSTED inspection has taken place, a summary of the OFSTED report. These should provide information on staff qualifications and areas of expertise, staffing levels, facilities (including specialist facilities and equipment), class size, extent of access to the National Curriculum, the number and range of other professionals contributing to the work of the school (eg Educational Psychologist, physiotherapist, speech therapist, occupational therapist), links with other special and mainstream schools and links with parents. Read the information carefully and prepare a list of matters on which you require further information or reassurance in relation to meeting the needs of your child.

When visiting, first impressions are important. Look for an attractive, well cared-for environment, a happy working atmosphere and genuine interest in you and your child.

There should be mutual respect between children and staff and an openness to your interest and questions. You may find it helpful to include in your list questions concerning:

- gaps in subjects offered (especially in relation to your child's area of strength and interest);
- the number of pupils in your child's class;
- how teaching is organised (eg balance of whole class teaching and specialist help);
- how pupils' work is assessed for progress (ask to see some work; is it marked and are the teacher's comments positive?);
- whether pupils take public examinations if appropriate. What is the success rate?
- whether attendance figures are high;
- the nature of transport arrangements;
- the rate of staff turnover;
- the role of visiting professionals, parents and others in the day to day work of the school;
- the procedures for establishing and maintaining close home–school links;
- the name of your key point of contact in the school;
- You should also check that you are satisfied with the provision for any physical or medical needs your child may have.

It is always helpful to take another person when visiting a school so that impressions may be discussed afterwards. After the visit the final and overriding question is 'Will my child be as happy and appropriately educated in this school as in any available alternative?' If the answer is in the affirmative you have probably made a good choice.

Making an application

If the LEA is meeting the cost in either a state or independent school it is the named person on the statement who makes application for places, although you can also let your wishes be known to the school.

If you are paying privately and in full for an independent school place you should make a personal application to the school.

1.13
Social Security Benefits

Alban Hawksworth, Disability Alliance

Many families with a child with special needs are not aware of how the social security system could help them. This article is a brief introduction to the benefits that you may be able to claim if your child has a physical disability, a learning disability, developmental delays or behavioural problems.

Getting advice

The benefits system need not be daunting or confusing. You can get information and advice from a number of sources. In the first instance you can contact your local Benefits Agency office, or call the Benefit Enquiry Line on 0800 882200. This is a national telephone helpline about benefits for people with disabilities.

You can get independent advice from a Citizens' Advice Bureau or local advice centre. There is also a number of books that give information or advice about benefits. The Disability Alliance provides information and advice about the social security benefits that disabled people can claim and publishes the *Disability Rights Handbook* and a range of other publications every year as well as providing a free telephone helpline (see useful addresses at the end of this book).

The information in this chapter uses the benefit rates current from April 2001. In addition, several of the rules affecting disability benefits for children and young people changed in April 2001. This is a short summary of those changes.

- Since 6 April 2001, young people under 20 have been able to receive Incapacity Benefits (IB) rather than Severe Disablement Allowance (SDA), which is no longer available.
- A young person who was under 20 on 6 April 2001 and already receiving SDA will transfer to Incapacity Benefit on 6 April 2002.
- Since April 2001, children of three and four years have been able to claim the higher rate of disability living allowance mobility component. The DSS estimates that around 4000 children will benefit. The lower rate mobility is still only available to children over 5 years old.

Benefits for your child

Child Benefit

You are entitled to receive child benefit for your dependent children, regardless of your other income or savings. You do not have to be the child's parent, but you do have to be responsible for him or her. You can receive child benefit for a child aged under 16, or aged under 19 and who is studying for more than 12 hours per week. You may not be entitled to child benefit if your child is in local authority care for more than 8 weeks, or if you receive a fostering allowance for that child.

Amounts
Only or eldest child	£15.50
Lone parent rate	£17.55 (*only paid to claimants who were already receiving the higher rate in April 1998*)
Each other child	£10.35

To claim child benefit, ask for a claim pack from your local office.

Children's tax credit

Since April 2001 a new children's tax credit has been introduced. You can claim if you pay tax and you have at least one dependent child under 16 living with you.

The credit is available to married or unmarried couples and single parents, and it is worth up to £520 off the tax you have to pay. If the person who receives the credit does not pay enough tax to use all the credit, they will be able to transfer the unused credit to their partner after the end of the tax year. If you or your partner pay higher tax rate, the partner with the larger income must claim the credit. When the person claiming the tax is a higher tax rate payer (on an individual income of around £32,785) the amount of the credit will be reduced. The credit of £520 is reduced at the rate of £1 for every £15 of income taxed at the higher rate. This means that you are unlikely to receive any credit if your income is around £41,000.

To claim the children's tax credit you will need to fill in a claim form available from your tax office.

Disability Living Allowance

The most important benefit for those looking after a child with disabilities is Disability Living Allowance. It is assessed purely on your child's needs – your financial circumstances are irrelevant. The benefit is assessed and paid in two parts. The care component helps with the extra costs of providing personal care, and the mobility component helps with the extra costs of going out.

The care component can be paid if your child needs supervision or extra attention in connection with their bodily functions during the day or night. It can be claimed at any age, but your child must have needed extra care for three months before any benefit is paid. All children obviously need different amounts of care at different stages in their development, and it can be difficult to explain to the Benefits Agency the amount of care that your child needs. You have to show that your child needs care or attention *substantially in excess* of that needed by other children of the same age and sex. The care component is paid at three different rates, depending on the amount of extra care needed.

The mobility component is paid at two different rates and is designed to help with the costs of going out and getting around. The higher rate can be paid from the age of three and is for children who have physical problems walking. The lower rate can only be claimed from the age of five, and is for those children who may be physically able to walk, but need extra guidance or supervision out of doors (again substantially in excess of what other children need). If you get the higher rate of mobility component you will also be entitled to exemption from road tax for one car, and you may be able to hire or buy a car under the motability scheme. You can also apply to your local authority for a blue badge for concessionary parking. Even if you don't get the higher rate mobility component you may be able to get a blue badge if your child has very substantial difficulty walking or is registered blind.

Amounts

Care Component		Mobility Component	
Higher	£55.30	Higher	£38.65
Middle	£37.00	Lower	£14.65
Lowest	£14.65		

The Benefits Agency will normally award Disability Living Allowance to your child for fixed periods. You will need to re-apply when the award expires. It is common for benefit to be renewed at *milestone* ages – five, eleven and sixteen.

Whether you are working or unemployed you should be aware of Disability Living Allowance. It is not means-tested or taxable, and it is paid on top of any other benefits you may receive. In fact your other benefits may actually be increased when you receive Disability Living Allowance.

If you think your child may be entitled, you should lodge a claim. Phone the Disability Living Allowance Unit on 08457 123456 and ask them to send you the claim forms. If you are awarded benefit it can be paid from the date of this phone call. The claim forms can seem quite complicated, so seek advice if you are not sure how to fill them in.

Benefits your child can claim at age 16

On reaching age 16 a disabled child can claim benefit in his or her own right. If s/he receives benefit s/he will cease to be your dependent and you can no longer claim Child Benefit for him or her. The benefit will be paid in his or her name, but if the young person is unable to handle his or her own claim you may apply to be their appointee and act for them.

If your child is coming up to 16 there is a very useful booklet, written by the Family Fund, entitled 'What Next'. It is full of practical advice on education and training opportunities as well as information on benefits and services. The booklet is available free to young disabled people and their carers from The Family Fund, PO Box 50, York YO1 2ZX.

Incapacity Benefit
A disabled young person can claim incapacity benefit under a special route for people who become incapable of work before the age of 20. It is very important to claim before his or

her 20th birthday, because after that age s/he will only be able to receive incapacity benefit if s/he has been employed and paid a sufficient number of national insurance contributions. There is some protection for young people in education to allow them to make a claim under these rules up to the age of 25, as long as their course of education or training began at least three months before their 20th birthday, and they claim incapacity benefit within two years of the course ending.

A young person will only be entitled to incapacity benefit after s/he has been incapable of work for 28 weeks. It is possible for these weeks to be before the young person's 16th birthday, so s/he can claim as soon as the age of 16 is reached. S/he will need a medical certificate from the doctor, and if incapacity benefit is to start straight away, the certificate will need to be backdated for at least 28 weeks. It is also possible for a new claim for incapacity benefit to be backdated for up to three months, as long as the claimant would have qualified for it at that time.

Incapacity benefit is paid at three different rates depending how long your child has been claiming it. For the first 28 weeks of a claim the short-term lower rate is paid, from 29 weeks up to the 51st week of the claim the short-term higher rate is paid, and once your child has been on incapacity benefit for one year, the long-term rate is paid. A person receiving the higher rate care component of disability allowance will receive the long term of incapacity benefit after 28 weeks. An age addition is also payable with the long term rate.

Amount – Incapacity benefit
Short term lower rate   £52.60
Short-term higher rate   £62.20
Long-term rate   £84.40
(£69.75 + £14.65 age addition if under 35)

Full time education

Incapacity benefit and severe disablement allowance cannot be paid to a student under 19 who is at school or college and is attending classes for more than 21 hours every week. When calculating the 21 hours you should ignore any time spent in study that would not be suitable for a person of the same age and sex who does not suffer from a physical or mental disability. So, if a disabled young person receives a lot of support to follow a course, or if the course is taught in such a way that would make it unsuitable for a non-disabled person, then he/she may still be able to get benefit in spite of the 21 hour rule.

Income support

A disabled young person over the age of 16 may also be able to claim Income Support. With Income Support, it doesn't matter if s/he is attending school or a training centre. If your child is still at school, s/he will have to show that s/he would be unlikely to get a job in the next year. If s/he has left school, s/he will need to be accepted by the Benefits Agency as incapable of work. In both cases, the young person should give in a medical certificate from his or her GP.

Income Support includes a personal allowance and extra amounts called premiums. A young person will be entitled to a disability premium if s/he has been incapable of work for 52 weeks, is registered blind, or gets a severe disablement allowance or any rate of disability living allowance. The enhanced disability premium is payable to a person receiving the highest rate care component of disability living allowance. Income Support cannot be paid to a young person who has more than £8000 savings. Any saving between £3000 and £7999 will reduce the amount of benefit paid.

Amounts

Income Support personal allowance (under 25)	£42.00
Disability premium	£22.60
Sub-total (if not entitled to enhanced disability premium)	£64.60
Enhanced disability premium	£11.05
Total (if enhanced disability premium payable)	£75.65

If a disabled young person receives Income Support, s/he will also be able to apply for help from the Social Fund for certain one-off expenses.

Benefits for carers

Invalid Care Allowance
You can claim this if your child receives Disability Living Allowance care component at the middle or higher rate. You must be looking after him or her for at least 35 hours every week. You can claim even if your partner is in full-time work.

You cannot receive Invalid Care Allowance if you are in full time education (21 hours of study per week) or earning above £72 net per week. It does not matter for how many hours you work, as long as you are still caring for at least 35 hours per week. To calculate your net earnings deduct tax, national insurance contributions and half of your contributions towards an occupational or personal pension. You are also allowed to deduct care costs up to a maximum of half your net earnings. This includes care for the disabled person for whom you claim ICA, or for any child under 16 for whom you claim Child Benefit, as long as the care is not provided by a close relative of yours or of the person cared for.

Invalid Care Allowance is paid at £41.75 per week, and while you are receiving the allowance your National Insurance Contribution record will be protected. Your Invalid Care Allowance will be taken into account if you or your spouse or partner are also claiming Income Support or Job Seeker's Allowance, but your overall benefit will include a carer's premium worth £24.40 per week.

To claim, get a claim form from your local office or from the Invalid Care Allowance unit on 0235 856123.

Other benefits

National Insurance contributory benefits
If you are incapable of work, unemployed, widowed or retired, you may be entitled to some benefits because of the National Insurance you have paid.

Incapacity Benefit, contribution-based Job Seeker's Allowance, Bereavement Benefit (for widows and widowers), Maternity Allowance and Retirement Pension can be paid if you have paid enough National Insurance contributions (in the case of Bereavement Benefit your husband or wife's contributions are relevant).

If you qualify for them these benefits are paid to you as an individual (although you can in some circumstances claim increases for dependents). It does not matter if you have savings or a spouse who is in full time work.

However, if these benefits are your family's only or main source of income you will usually need to claim a top-up from a means-tested benefit as well.

Income Support and income-based Job Seeker's Allowance

Income Support and income-based Job Seeker's Allowance are the benefits for people who do not have enough money to live on and who are not in full time work. You will not be entitled to these benefits if you have capital above £8,000 (£12,000 if aged over 60), and if you have savings of more than £3,000 (£6,000 if over 60) your benefit will be reduced.

You claim benefit for yourself and your family. If you have a partner you will have to claim as a couple. In most cases it will not matter which of you makes the claim, but if one of you receives Invalid Care Allowance or is incapable of work because of illness, it is usually better if that person is the claimant. This is because they may be entitled to extra amounts and may not be required to register as available for work.

Income Support can be paid to lone parents, carers, people who are incapable of work, or people over 60. Some people from abroad, who are entitled to no other benefits, may be entitled to a reduced rate of Income Support. If you do not fit in to any of the categories listed above you cannot claim Income Support and you will have to claim income-based Job Seeker's Allowance instead.

Income-based Job Seeker's Allowance is paid to people under pension age who are required to be available for and actively seeking work. You can be sanctioned, and have your benefit reduced or taken away altogether, if you refuse the offer of a job or leave a job without *just cause*.

If you own your home, Income Support and income-based Job Seeker's Allowance are particularly important as they are the only benefits which provide any help with your mortgage costs.

If you receive Income Support or income-based Job Seeker's Allowance you will be entitled to free school meals, milk tokens for children under 5, free prescriptions, NHS dental treatment and vouchers for glasses, wigs and fabric supports. You can also claim a refund of your fares to hospital. You can also apply for grants and loans from the social fund for one-off expenses.

Benefits in Work

If you or your partner are working for 16 hours or more per week, you are considered to be working full-time and you cannot claim Income Support or Job Seeker's Allowance. Depending on your family's circumstances you may be able to claim an in-work benefit, to top up your earnings.

You can claim Working Families Tax Credit if you are working for over 16 hours a week and you have at least one dependent child. The amount that you receive depends on your family circumstances and the level of your earnings. It is awarded at a fixed rate for a period of 26 weeks, and the amount will not be increased or reduced if your circumstances change. Benefit can end before 26 weeks in some circumstances – for example, if your only child leaves school.

If you or your partner have a disability you may be better off claiming Disabled Person's Tax Credit instead, which is assessed in a similar way.

You can claim either tax credit from an Employment Service JobCentre, Benefits Agency office or Inland Revenue Enquiry Centre. There is also a Tax Credit helpline on 0845 605 5858, which can advise you on how much you may be entitled to.

If you are thinking about coming off benefit and claiming a Tax Credit instead, you can ask the Benefits Agency or a local advice centre to do a 'better off' calculation, comparing your current rate of benefit with what you could be entitled to once you start work. You will need to know roughly how much you will be earning, and how much your weekly rent and council tax bills are.

When you make your decision remember to take into account your extra expenses and costs of going out to work, as well as other factors such as the loss of free school meals and milk tokens, and the loss of access to grants and loans from the Social Fund. If you own your own home remember that Income Support and income-based Job Seeker's Allowance are the only benefits that provide any help with mortgage interest.

Housing Benefit and Council Tax Benefit

These benefits are administered by your local council. You can claim them whether you are working or on benefits. Housing Benefit helps with your rent if you are a tenant. Council Tax Benefit helps with your Council Tax bill. It does not matter whether you are an owner-occupier or a tenant.

If you are on Income Support or income-based Job Seeker's Allowance you will be entitled to the maximum allowable Housing and Council Tax Benefit. Otherwise the amount of help you get will depend on the level of your family's income. The amount you get will be reduced if you have any non-dependent adults living with you.

Contact your local authority for their claim forms.

Health Benefits

- If you receive Income Support or income-based Job Seeker's Allowance you will automatically qualify for help with prescription charges, hospital travel costs, dental treatment and glasses.
- If you receive Working Families Tax Credit or Disability Person's Tax Credit you may be able to get free NHS prescriptions and optical and dental treatment, but it is not an automatic entitlement. The decision whether you will be exempt from NHS charges or not is based on how your tax credit has been worked out – your tax credit award letter should tell you whether you are exempt or not.
- If you are not on these benefits you can still claim this help on low income grounds. Claim on form HC1.

Getting further advice

This article can only give a very brief introduction to the benefits which you may be entitled to. If you want to find out more speak to a local advice centre or Citizens' Advice Bureau.

If you believe that the Benefits Agency has made a mistake about your benefit you should contact them and tell them why you think their decision is wrong. You may be able to appeal to an independent tribunal but there are very strict limits – get independent advice.

1.14

GCE (General Certificate of Education), VCE (Vocational Certificate of Education) GCSE (General Certificate of Secondary Education) and GNVQ (General National Vocational Qualification) assessment: special arrangements for candidates with particular requirements

(Information supplied by the Joint Council for General Qualifications)

Awarding bodies for GCE, VCE, GCSE and GNVQ recognise that there are some candidates who have coped with the learning demands of a course but for whom the standard arrangements for the assessment of their attainment may present a barrier. This applies both in the case of candidates with known and long-standing learning problems and candidates who are affected at or near the time of assessment. This section offers a summary of the special arrangements procedures operated in common by the awarding bodies. It is based on the Joint Council for General Qualifications (JCGQ) booklet *GCE, VCE, GCSE and GNVQ: Regulations and Guidance relating to Candidates with Particular requirements – 1 September 2000 to August 2001*. Copies of this are available direct from any of the awarding bodies, or can be downloaded from their websites. Contact details are available at the end of this section. An updated edition is issued at the start of each academic year.

Awarding body principles relating to special arrangements

In providing special arrangements for assessment, awarding bodies seek to:

- give special consideration to the performance in assessment where specific circumstances have arisen at or near to the time of assessment that were not provided for by prior special arrangements;
- ensure that neither a special arrangement nor special consideration gives an unfair advantage over other candidates;
- ensure that special arrangements do not reduce the validity or reliability of the examination or assessment;
- ensure that the provision for special arrangements and special consideration does not mislead the users of the qualification about the candidate's attainment;

- ensure that the provision for special arrangements and special consideration does not compromise the integrity or credibility of the qualification;
- determine special arrangements and special consideration in relation to the defined needs of individual candidates;
- consider the candidate's usual methods of learning and producing work when making decisions on special arrangements.

Principles for centres relating to special arrangements

The centre should:

- choose the qualification – or the option(s) within a qualification – which is most appropriate for the candidate with a known long-term or permanent disability or learning difficulty;
- diagnose the requirements of each candidate individually, making use of specialist advice from external sources as appropriate;
- ensure that all applications for special arrangements and special consideration are supported by the Head of the centre;
- ensure that the arrangements requested will assist the candidate to demonstrate his/her attainment without affecting or circumventing assessment requirements;
- consider the candidate's normal way of learning and producing work as a basis for special arrangements provided that this would not give the candidate an unfair advantage or compromise the integrity of the examination or assessment;
- ensure that the candidate has experience of and practice in the use of the arrangements requested;
- consult the relevant awarding body at the earliest opportunity if there is any doubt surrounding the acceptability of proposed arrangements for a particular candidate.

Centres should note that a candidate with a Statement of Special Educational Needs does not qualify automatically for special arrangements.

Types of special arrangements

These are summarised below. However, it should be noted that the kinds of special arrangements which are appropriate for one subject, may not be appropriate for other subjects. Separate arrangements exist for examinations in GCSE English and English Literature and awarding bodies will be able to supply details. The JCGQ *Regulations and Guidance* booklet has more detailed information on how these arrangements might apply to particular needs.

Time allowance

Additional time may be allowed in timed components in most subjects, including English, Irish and Welsh. Additional time will not normally be permitted in an examination component where performance of a task in a limited time is an assessment objective, or where a candidate's ability to demonstrate attainment in a subject is not affected by his or her special assessment need.

The amount of additional time granted must reflect the extent to which the completion of the examination is affected by the candidate's condition. For example, a candidate with a learning difficulty requiring additional time for writing should not be given additional time for examinations of a predominantly practical nature.

An additional allowance of up to 25 per cent of the total examination time should meet most needs. An allowance of more than 25 per cent may be permitted in exceptional cases with the prior approval of the awarding body.

Means of access to questions

Modification to the way the examination questions are presented may be required to enable them to be understood by candidates with particular requirements.

Modifications to the visual presentation of papers can be arranged for visually impaired candidates whose impairment is not corrected by spectacles or other forms of vision aid. Four types of modification are available:

- enlarged or large print papers
- modified print (simplification of eg layout or items of visual complexity)
- Braille version of papers
- tactile enhancement

Low vision aids and other technological devices, such as closed circuit television, OCR (Optical Character Recognition) scanners may also be permitted.

Modifications to the language used in papers may be required by severely hearing-impaired candidates who are pre-lingually deaf or hearing impaired from such an early age that vocabulary and understanding syntax are limited. Some material cannot be modified in this way, however:

- technical terms in any subject
- text and stimulus material in English and Welsh examinations
- text in the foreign language in modern foreign language papers
- literary extracts
- source material where understanding of the original material is specifically being assessed.

Reading of questions may be permitted if access to the paper is not possible through other means, except where understanding of the written word is an assessment objective.

In exceptional circumstances, the signing of questions or the oral presentation of questions using the oral/aural approach may be permitted if either approach is the usual method of communication in the classroom and access to the examination cannot be achieved by other means.

When hearing impaired candidates are taking aural tests, special amplification or reading the tests to enable lip reading is allowed.

In mental arithmetic tests, the use of flashcards or other visual presentation is allowed for hearing-impaired candidates.

Some visual difficulties are normally corrected by the use of tinted spectacles or coloured overlays and permission for the use of these aids does not have to be sought from the awarding body.

Candidates whose first language is not English, Irish or Welsh may be permitted to use bilingual translation dictionaries (ie without explanation of terms) in examinations other than in English, Irish or Welsh and in examinations in the candidate's first language. Under exceptional circumstances use of a prompter is permitted.

Means of presenting responses

The general principle applied to the presentation of responses is that candidates should use the method of answering which is quickest and most fluent for them.

For visually impaired candidates, responses may be given in Braille, although the centre must provide a transcript.

Candidates who are unable to write may use a typewriter or word processor, although they may not normally have access to any spell check, grammar check, thesaurus or other such facilities. If responses cannot be communicated through such means either, then an amanuensis may be used. Dictation of responses onto tape is not generally considered to be in the best interests of the candidate and would therefore be permitted only in the most exceptional of circumstances. In the case of a candidate's handwriting being difficult to read, the school or college may provide a transcript of the paper along with the candidate's original work.

In oral examinations, candidates who have difficulties with speech may be permitted to use augmentative speech equipment. However, it is possible that by doing so they may not be able to meet all the relevant assessment criteria.

In practical examinations or tests, use of a practical assistant or helper is allowed to ensure the candidate's safety and to support the candidate by assisting with those elements of the tasks which are not the focus of the assessment. The practical assistant must not perform tasks for which the candidate is given credit.

Alternative accommodation arrangements

It may be possible for candidates to take examinations outside the normal centre, for example at home or in hospital, provided that the relevant security and supervision requirements can be met.

Coursework

The relevant awarding body should be consulted as soon as possible if a candidate is unlikely to be able to fulfil all coursework requirements. An extension may be granted to the permitted time for completion of the coursework, but this must be formally agreed with the awarding body in advance.

Exemption

Candidates unable to fulfil a particular assessment objective may be given a special award to compensate for the missing element. However, an appropriate indication of the exemption will be recorded on the certificate.

Spelling, punctuation and grammar in GCSE

In examinations where spelling , punctuation and grammar form part of the assessment, all candidates will be assessed under the same nationally agreed criteria.

It is not considered to be in the interests of candidates to be exempted from this assessment, but if a candidate is eligible for exemption, and compensation is given in the form of an adjustment to marks, there will be an indication on the certificate that the candidate was exempt from fulfilling one of the assessment criteria in the subject.

If, in exceptional circumstances (for example, for a child with a severe physical disability or a candidate with a broken arm) permission is given for the use of an amanuensis, the candidate will not be normally be expected to dictate spelling and punctuation. If reliable alternative evidence is available, such as examples of the candidate's written work under controlled conditions, special consideration procedures will be applied to enable an assessment to be made.

Quality of language in GCE

Where this forms part of the assessment, all candidates are assessed under the same nationally agreed criteria, and no exemptions allowed.

Applying for special arrangements

Permission to allow some special arrangements is delegated to centres; in other instances form JCGQ/SA/01 must be submitted to the relevant awarding body. A copy of the form is provided in the Regulations and Guidance booklet, along with full details of evidence requirements and deadlines for applications.

Special Consideration

Special consideration is given following an examination or assessment to ensure that a candidate who has a temporary illness, injury or indisposition at the time it is conducted is given some compensation for those difficulties and the circumstances.

Further information

For more detailed guidance on special arrangements and special consideration, please contact the school or college in the first instance, since all applications must come from there.

Awarding body contact details:

Edexcel
Stewart House
32 Russell Square
London
WC1B 5DN

Tel. 0870 240 9800
Website: www.edexcel.org.uk

**Northern Ireland Council for the
Curriculum Examinations and
Assessment**
29 Clarendon Road
Belfast
BT1 3BG
Tel. 01232 261 200
Website: www.cea.org.uk

OCR
Syndicate Buildings
1 Hills Road
Cambridge
CB1 2EU

Tel. 01223 553998
Website: www.ocr.org.uk

**The Assessment and Qualifications
Alliance**
(NEAB)
Devas Street
Manchester
M15 6EX

Tel. 0161 953 1180
Website: www.aqa.org.uk

**The Assessment and Qualifications
Alliance**
(AEB/SEG)
Stag Hill House
Guildford
Surrey
GU2 5XJ

Tel. 01483 506506
Website: www.aqa.org.uk

Welsh Joint Education Committee
245 Western Avenue
Cardiff
CF5 2YX

Tel. 02920 265000 (main switchboard)
or
Tel. 02920 265150 -155 (GCSE administration)
Website: www.wjec.co.uk

1.15
Children with Special Educational Needs: Guidance for Families Overseas*

Leaving the UK

Parents leaving the UK, for example on a temporary posting, face key decisions about their children's education, including whether or not their child should accompany them or, alternatively, remain at a boarding school in the UK. In cases where a child has special educational needs, wider issues must also be considered. If you expect to live overseas for a period, the following points may be helpful in planning your child's education.

Whether your child will accompany you or remain in the UK for his or her education depends on many factors, including:

- your individual circumstances;
- expected length of stay outside the UK;
- continuity – are you likely to move again before returning to the UK?
- your child's age;
- the nature and severity of your child's special needs;
- availability and accessibility of suitable education provision and, where appropriate, medical provision and therapy in the UK and in the host country;
- your child's ability to cope with change.

It is also wise to ensure that you have a thorough understanding of the culture and attitudes towards special needs or disabilities in the country in which you will be living. You may also wish to check the general levels of physical access available to people with mobility difficulties; some travel guides provide good information on this point.

If your child has a Statement of Special Educational Needs, check with your local authority the position with reference to the maintenance of that Statement. This may vary from one local authority to another and according to your/your child's individual circumstances. If your child has been attending a day school, for example, will the LEA maintain a residential place for him or her while you are away from the UK? What happens upon your return? Depending upon circumstances, funding may be shared between education, health and welfare departments, and arrangements may be complex.

If you plan to take your child with you, life in your host country may offer a number of pros and cons. The benefits might include, for example:

---

* This article has been compiled with the kind assistance of Jennifer Steeples, Founder of the Special Needs support group at the Diplomatic Service Families Association, now of the London Dyslexia Association Resource Centre.

- better salary and employment conditions;
- better climate;
- availability of domestic help;
- good provision for your child's particular needs;
- local tax concessions;
- higher welfare benefits;
- better housing;
- travel opportunities that will broaden your child's horizons and experiences.
- better medical provision

Against this, however, there may be drawbacks, including:

- isolation;
- absence of support groups;
- lack of family support;
- language barriers;
- loss of welfare benefits;
- limited special needs provision;
- lack of facilities for the disabled;
- climate;
- housing (perhaps in a flat with no garden);
- setbacks in development;
- lack of networking opportunities to share help and ideas.
- poorer medical provision

Above all, avoid making hasty decisions. Give yourself time to make an informed choice and to consider the pros and cons for the whole family.

Points to remember

1) It may prove very helpful for your child to have a full educational and medical assessment in the UK and to have an Individual Education Plan (IEP) drawn up before you leave the UK. The IEP can then be adjusted at any new school in whichever country you settle.

2) Find out as much as you can with reference to the country in which you expect to live, for example:

- What provision is available in the host country for your child's needs?
- Is there an appropriate centre/support group where you can obtain information and advice?
- Is you child/are you entitled to any state benefits or tax concessions?

Some countries may offer highly advanced provision, others almost none. Your support group in the UK, if one exists, may be able to advise you or put you in touch with 'sister groups' in the host country or with other members of the association who have lived abroad. If experienced in working in the host country, your employer/your partner's employer may be able to guide you. It may also be worth consulting international organisations such as the

European Dyslexia Association or the British Embassy or British Council office in your host city/country, as well as the internet, for any other useful information.

3) If you know the area in which you will be living, try to make contact with sources of help, such as:

- a local doctor or hospital;
- local town hall/authority or equivalent;
- any English-speaking organisation, for example an expatriates' or women's club;
- any organisation for the disabled even if it does not focus specifically on your child's particular needs it may still be able to offer support and direct you to other appropriate organisations.

4) You may wish to consider educating your child at home. If so, make sure you have all the support you need before committing yourself. The internet is a good source of help, but check whether you will have access to it in your new destination. At the time of writing there are several useful website addresses with details of the National Curriculum and support groups. For general information try the websites for the Department for Education and Employment at www.dfee.gov.uk or for the Qualifications and Curriculum Authority at www.qca.org.uk.

5) Even if your child has little speech, talk over the move and possible changes in routine. Take care also to talk to siblings about their concerns.

6) Keep a clear diary of the help you seek, names and contact numbers.

7) Try to obtain some basic training in the treatment of the type of special needs presented by your child and research why your child has the condition or learning difficulty.

8) Keep your employer and/or your partner's employer fully briefed about your child's special needs. Most companies now have a Family Friendly Policy. Might either employer offer any help to meet additional costs associated with your child's education?

9) Take with you any reference books about the condition or learning difficulty that affects your child.

10) Join any organisation in your home country that can keep you up to date with developments and improvements in provision for the special needs your child has.

11) State clearly what you want and need for your child. Do not assume that friends and colleagues understand the kind of help and support you and your child require. Remember too that you will not be alone: at least 20 per cent of children will at some time in their lives present special needs in some form.

12) Finally, be realistic about the level of involvement you have had with your child's needs and the extent of support given by the school and other sources. How will your child cope under different circumstances?

Returning to the UK

If you are returning to the UK after being resident abroad, it is wise to contact in advance the local education authority (LEA) for the area in which you intend to live and ask for an assessment of your child's needs. At the same time, contact your support group in the UK to ensure that you are fully up to date with Department for Education and Employment (DfEE) regulations on special needs provision.

Educating your child in the UK

If you live overseas, either as a British expatriate or as a citizen of another country, but wish to have your child educated in the UK, there are a number of points to consider.

The UK offers a variety of boarding education options. The independent (fee-paying) sector offers a wide choice of boarding education with varying levels of provision for special needs. Few mainstream independent schools accept children with Statements of Special Educational Needs. Many, however, will accept children with mild or moderate specific learning difficulties provided that applicants can fulfil the normal academic entry criteria for the school. The level of provision and the number of pupils with learning difficulties admitted varies widely from school to school, and parents should take care to establish the nature and extent of special tuition available. Some schools have dedicated units to cater for children requiring special tuition and usually operate on a withdrawal basis, which means that children are withdrawn from certain lessons during the school day to have special tuition for their particular needs. Other schools offer more limited assistance, for example through extra lessons from a visiting teacher. Annual fees at independent boarding schools in 2000–2001 generally range from £7,000–£12,000 at preparatory level and from £12,000–£15,000 at senior level.

Where a child's needs are more complex or severe, and where a child has a Statement of Special Educational Needs, a special school may be more appropriate. Residential special schools usually provide for a particular type of special need. Because of the highly specialist teaching and facilities offered by independent special schools, fees are often substantial. Where the local education authority agrees that a child should attend a particular school, it will normally pay the fees (sometimes in conjunction with social services or health services), provided that the school is one that has been approved by the Secretary of State for Education and Employment. In some cases, the fees are paid by parents. Parents with no right of abode in the UK should expect to meet the full cost of fees.

State-maintained boarding schools are few in number and are open only to UK and EU nationals and others with a right of residence in the UK. Fees are charged only for the cost of boarding at these schools, while tuition is free. Annual fees are therefore generally no more than £6,000 and in some cases considerably less. As indicated above, parents should take care to find out exactly how much help will be offered to a child with special needs.

In most cases, parents based overseas should expect to meet the cost of the fees for a boarding place. A boarding allowance is made for British parents employed by the Foreign & Commonwealth Office or by HM Forces. British parents living overseas *may* be eligible for local authority support for a child being educated in the UK, but are strongly advised to take independent advice in accordance with their individual circumstances.

Non-British children of statutory school age, who are nationals of a member state of the European Union (EU) and who are being educated in the UK (whether accompanied by their parents or not), have the same rights to education in the UK as British citizens. Under reciprocal arrangements within the EU, those who hold the equivalent of a Statement of Special Educational Needs made in another EU country may be eligible for support from the local education authority covering the area of the UK in which they will be living, and parents should seek advice according to their particular circumstances. In practice, children who come to the UK unaccompanied may be more likely to attend a boarding school in the independent sector, for which parents will normally be required to meet the fees.

Unaccompanied children of statutory school age who do not have a right of abode in the UK are not normally allowed entry to take up a place at a state-maintained school. Entry to the UK for purposes of receiving an education is only permitted if the student can demonstrate that he or she has been accepted for a course of study at an independent educational institution.

It may be helpful to obtain a clear assessment of a child's needs in the home country for use in finding suitable UK schools. Some schools will reassess the child before offering a place.

Points to remember about boarding education in the UK for parents resident overseas

The choice of a suitable boarding school requires careful research. As well as providing suitable provision for your child's special needs, the school must meet your child's wider needs and offer an environment in which he or she will feel happy and at home. Find out as much as possible about schools in which you are interested and visit them before making a choice. Consider in particular:

- **Your child's academic background**
  If your child has been educated in the British system, it should not be difficult to join a school in the UK. Entry from a different national system is possible but may be less straightforward.
- **Your child's level of English**
  Is additional support required?
- **Length of stay**
  If the stay in the UK is expected to be relatively short, an international school may be more appropriate.
- **Location**
  You may prefer a location that enables your child to be near friends or relatives, but most parts of the UK are well served by air, road and rail links, so it is not necessary to limit your search to schools close to major airports.

Further advice on the choice of a suitable mainstream school is given in Part 4.1.

Also bear in mind the following points:

- If your child is attending a boarding school in the UK while you are overseas, he or she must have a guardian in the UK, preferably living near the school, who will take responsibility for your child at weekends and other times when your child is out of school. While some residential special schools offer 52-week placements, most schools have three school holidays plus half term holidays and exeats (weekends out of school). You may have friends or relatives in the UK able to care for your child during these periods, but this arrangement is not always suitable and may limit your choice of schools. If you have no contacts in the UK, talk to a reputable guardianship service provider who can find a family able to offer your child a safe and welcoming home-from-home and may also take care of other travel and administrative arrangements.

- Your child may require an escort during travel, which will incur additional costs. Some airlines issue a card to travellers who require special care and will provide the facilities requested free of charge each time a booking is made. Children with parents in the Forces may be entitled to have escorts provided by the British Red Cross or the Soldier, Sailor and Airforce Families Association (SSAFA).
- While you should receive regular progress reports from your child's school and guardian, communication with your child on a day-to-day basis may be difficult if his or her special needs give him or her limited or no speech.

Children accompanying their parents to the UK

Children accompanying parents who have the right of abode in, or leave to enter, the UK will normally be treated as dependants. Upon taking up residence in the UK, overseas parents living in the UK have the same right as anyone else with a right of abode in the UK to apply for a place at a maintained school. They also, therefore, have the same entitlement to have their child's educational needs met by their local education authority.

Whatever your requirements, you are strongly advised to seek specialist guidance in accordance with your own individual circumstances and the specific needs of your child. Further information may be available from your child's school, from any parents' support group to which you currently belong or from one of the associations listed at the back of this book.

1.16
Education and Training for Young People with Disabilities or Learning Difficulties After Age 16

SKILL (National Bureau for Students with Disabilities)

If you are nearly 16 years old, you will probably be thinking about education and training options ahead. You will need to consider what you are best at and what you would most like to do. You may also need to consider any extra support that you may need because of your disability or learning difficulty. This article explains the options available to you and the support you should expect because of your disability or learning difficulty.

What choices are available at 16?

School

You may be able to stay at the same school if it accepts students beyond age 16. You could take an academic course such as A levels, or you might wish to take a work-based course (General National Vocational Qualifications or GNVQs). You might want to consider changing to a different sixth form for a better course or better support. Your school should be able to advise you about what is best. If you are leaving school, your local careers service can help you to find a new place to learn or train (see below).

Link courses

Many schools offer what are called 'link courses'. These courses are based at school, but students attend a local further education college for part of their studies.

Further education colleges

You may find that your local further education college offers a wider range of courses than is available at your school. These might include:

- academic courses (GCSEs, A and AS levels)
- work-based courses (National Vocational Qualifications or NVQs, including RSA, Edexcel or City and Guilds Institute qualifications)

- general courses to prepare you for adult life. These courses may not always lead to a qualification.

It is important to find a course that appeals to you and to ensure that the college can offer you any extra support required because of your disability or learning difficulty.

Specialist colleges

You may find that your support needs cannot be met in a local school or college. If so, there are specialist colleges which have extensive experience of teaching students with one type of disability or a range of different disabilities. As these colleges only teach select students, they draw students from a wider area and you may have to travel to get there. Such colleges are often residential. A specialist college can help you to learn to live away from home. You may also have access to helpful equipment or support teaching that you cannot access in a local college. Some colleges offer a range of education options, including those listed above under Further education colleges.

Information on specialist residential colleges is given in the COPE Directory (Compendium of post-16 education and training in residential establishments for young people with special needs). Your local Careers Service should have a copy and they should be able to help you find the best option. You can also contact the Association of National Specialist Colleges (NATSPEC) for details of their colleges.

Higher education

If you decide to do A levels or GNVQs, you may want to go on to higher education to study for a degree or a Higher National Diploma (HND). To find out more about how to apply for higher education, seek advice from your school or college. You may also find it helpful to consult the article which begins on p138.

Work-based training opportunities

All young people are able to take up work-based training courses at 16 or 17 years. Since April 2001, training has been organised through the new Learning and Skills Council.

If you are unemployed and aged between 16 and 17, you are guaranteed a training place if you would like one. If you need to continue at school or college because of your disability or learning difficulty, you may be able to take up Youth Training at a later age.

- Work-based training for adults may also be available.
- Modern Apprenticeships give training to school leavers at a higher level within an industry; there are two levels, Foundation, which provides training up to NVQ level 2 and Advanced, which provides training to at least NVQ level 3.
- The New Deal is open to you after you reach age 18 and if you are receiving Job Seeker's Allowance. There are schemes within the New Deal to help people with disabilities to find work.

Paid time off for study or training

If you are 16 or 17 and working but do not have many qualifications you will be able to get reasonable paid time off from work to study. The types of qualification you could study for include GCSEs, NVQs, intermediate NVQs and BTECs. The study or training could be done at a local college, by distance learning or in the workplace. Contact your local Careers Service for further information.

Will all these opportunities be open to me?

Unfortunately, your choice may be limited by factors such as:

- the level and type of support you require;
- availability of a suitable specialist college nearby;
- whether or not you are prepared to travel.

There are relatively few residential colleges around the country, so it may be necessary for you to look further away from home if this type of college is right for you. Local training opportunities also differ, depending upon the number and type of local training organisations available.

How do I find out what's available?
Can anyone help me?

Careers education at school

Once you reach Year 9 at school, you should be given help to prepare for your future. There may be a teacher who is responsible for careers education. The school should give you access to careers information, such as books and leaflets about further education, training and careers. You should be able to get information in the same format as your other school work. For example, if you read Braille, you should be given access to this information in Braille.

Careers Service

When you are in Year 9 and Year 11 of school, you should speak to a member of the local Careers Service. They will be able to advise you about different jobs and the type of training courses required for the job of your choice. They should be able to tell you about local courses in schools and colleges. Careers Services can also let you know where to find your local careers library. You should be given the opportunity to write a Career Action Plan, which includes your goals in education and employment and the steps you should take to get there. You will have to register with the Careers Service, if you wish to claim:

- Jobseeker's Allowance;
- Training for Young People Bridging Allowance;
- Extended Child Benefit.

Transition plan

If you have a statement of special education needs, it should be reviewed every year. When you are 14, you should be involved in writing a transition plan. This should help you to think about what to do when you reach 16. It is important that a careers adviser helps you go through the options. You can telephone in advance to say that you would like help from a careers adviser, who then has a duty to attend. He or she should help you to find another school, college, or training course if you are unable to stay at your school after 16. If you have a disability or learning difficulty, you are also entitled to additional advice and an assessment of your needs. Your Careers Service can help if you are having problems obtaining what you need from your school or LEA. Parents or guardians should also be involved in ensuring that there is a good transition plan. In Scotland a Future Needs Assessment should be done. The Department for Education and Employment in England produces a booklet entitled *Special Educational Needs: a guide for parents*. In Scotland, a useful publication is *Your Future Needs Assessment*, published by the Children in Scotland Special Needs Forum.

Remember that the Careers Service must 'be impartial, avoid stereotyping and promote equality of opportunity for all'. If you feel that you have been judged as unable to do a job without being asked about how your disability affects you, you can ask to be seen by a different adviser.

How do I contact my local careers service?

You can contact the Careers Service directly if you have not already seen someone from the service. It should be listed in the telephone directory. The Service may have a different name, such as 'Lifetime Careers', but check under 'careers services' first. Your school or college will know which careers officer is responsible for young people in the area. You should also speak to your year tutor, who should be able to arrange for you to see a careers officer. Each area must have a specialist careers adviser who has experience of advising people with disabilities. You can request an interview with the specialist adviser if you have questions about how your disability will affect your career choices.

Social worker

Local services or social work departments are required to provide certain services to young people and adults with disabilities. If you have a statement of special educational needs, your LEA must liaise with the local social services department about your needs. This should happen when you have your transition plan written and again when you are due to leave school. This will enable them to decide whether or not you need any help from the social services or the social work department. You, or your parent or guardian, may make direct contact with the social services or the social work department if you are worried that the department is not getting involved.

Health authority

If you need medical help, you may have to seek assistance from the local health authority and social services as well as funding from your LEA or the Further Education Funding

Council (FEFC). Funding for education, personal care and medical care comes from different sources, which means that arrangements can be complicated. It is very important that the Careers Service helps you; they can speak to the different agencies involved and ensure that everything is paid for before you begin your course.

How do I find out about courses?

National Database of Vocational Qualifications

This is a detailed database of vocational qualifications. You should be able to use this database at your local careers service.

UK Course Provider

This is a CD-ROM database with information of full time courses in universities and colleges in the United Kingdom. It also gives information about access and extra support for students with disabilities in colleges and universities. You should be able to use UK Course Provider at your local careers services and there may be a copy in your school or college.

Learndirect freephone (0800 100 900)

This is a free telephone helpline set up by the Government. The helpline can give general advice about courses anywhere in the United Kingdom. It is a useful means of finding out about courses available locally, but will not provide detailed advice on disability-related support.

Will I be able to get the support or help I need because of my disability or learning difficulty?

What happens to my statement when I reach age 16?

If you have a statement of special educational needs, this will set out the types of educational support you need at school. The school has a legal duty to provide the support specified in your statement. When you reach 16, the statement will only continue to be a legal document if you stay on in a school. If you go to college, you are still entitled to disability support, but your statement will cease to give you a legal right to this support.

School

If you stay on in the same school or move to a different school, the support you have had up until now should still be available to you. As long as you remain at a school, your awarding authority (LEA, education department or education and library board) must ensure that you receive the support you need.

Local further education colleges

Many colleges offer learning support classes. You may be able to get support for personal assistance needs. Colleges can obtain extra funding to provide the support you need, for example, for a teacher for deaf students who can help with language work or for care assistants who work in the college. However, if you require significant, expensive support, it may be better to study elsewhere in a college where the support you need is already available.

Local colleges may offer study programmes specifically for people with disabilities or learning difficulties which include specialist help. These usually aim to develop literacy, numeracy and other essential skills through practical work in different departments of the college. This may be a good option if you want to increase your confidence and experience.

Specialist further education colleges

Specialist further education colleges offer types of courses different from mainstream colleges, including some which are not taught elsewhere, and provide courses and support for people with particular disabilities or needs.

If you are unable to take your chosen course at your local school or college, you can obtain funding to attend a specialist college. You will only be given money for fees at a specialist college if no local school or college can provide the support that you need.

Is further education right for me?

Schools and colleges are funded by different organisations and have separate support structures for students with disabilities. Once you have decided to move into further education, your statement will no longer be a legal record of the support that you need. Further education colleges should have a learning support co-ordinator or disability co-ordinator to help and advise students with disabilities and learning difficulties. When you are choosing a college, the college staff should consider what you would need to take part in the course. In some cases you may need to have an assessment to establish the support you require. A college which does not believe that it can cater for your support needs should not accept you.

Training

If you opt for work-based training, you should be given enough support to enable you to take part in and complete successfully the training outlined in your individual Training Plan. The Employment Service has stated that extra support should be given to allow people with disabilities to take part in mainstream training. Where this is not possible, there should be residential training available with disability-related support. You may also be able to claim back any extra money you have to spend on travelling to your placement. For further information, contact your local TEC or LEC or the Disability Employment Adviser at your local Employment Service.

How is education and training after the age of 16 paid for?

Education up to 19

Sources of funding for education up to the age of 19 vary according to the type of education chosen.

School

If you stay at a school until you are 19, the local awarding authority (LEA, education department or education and library board) pays for your education. Any statement or record of special educational needs will still legally apply. Everyone is entitled to full-time education up to the age of 18.

Local further education colleges

In England and Wales local further education colleges are normally funded by the Further Education Funding Council (FEFC). In Scotland local further education colleges are generally funded by the Scottish Further Education Funding Council.

If you are studying full time in a further education college and are aged 16–19 years in England and Wales or between 16–18 years in Scotland, you will not have to pay any tuition fees. As indicated above, a college should not accept you unless it can offer the support that you need because of your disability or learning difficulty and must provide any equipment or extra support services you need. An assessment may be needed to find out exactly what is required.

Education over 19

Funding for education should not stop when you reach 18 or 19. If you start a full-time course before you are 19, you should be funded until the end of your course. If you start a course once you are over 19, you may be exempt from paying tuition fees. Some colleges can waive fees to people who are in receipt of certain benefits. Colleges have their own policies on offering fee exemption. You should ask for a copy of the policy. If you continue at college after you are 19, the college should continue to provide the support you need. Colleges have a legal duty to produce disability statements which explain access for students with disabilities within the college. This policy may help you if you feel you are not getting the support you need. There should also be a learning support co-ordinator or disability co-ordinator to whom you can talk about any problems.

Independent specialist colleges

The Further Education Funding Councils in England and Wales can provide funding for people with disabilities or learning difficulties aged between 16 and 25 years in independent specialist colleges, which are often residential. This is only available where your needs cannot be met in local further education colleges. If you need to attend an independent specialist college for social as well as educational reasons, the local social services department should pay in part or in total for the costs of the placement. For information, contact your local Careers Service, who can write to the Further Education Funding Council on your behalf. In Scotland you may be able to obtain funding for a placement in an independent college through a bursary from the education department of your local council.

Transport help and costs

Local education authorities in England and Wales fund help for travel to and from college and school until students reach the age of 19. Funding for students with disabilities who are over 19 is problematic. Local education authorities should not have policies about not providing money for transport to students over 19. They should consider the individual situation of anyone who applies for help. Your local social services department may also help to fund transport for people over 19. It is important to get your careers adviser involved to help you negotiate this funding. All colleges also have Access Funds for students who face financial hardship. If your transport costs are very high, you can apply to the Access Fund for extra money. In Scotland local education departments may be able to help with travel bursaries.

Benefits

When you are 16, you may be able to claim certain benefits in your own right, even if you are still studying. These include

- Severe Disablement Allowance
- Income Support
- Disabled Living Allowance

If you are confused by the calculations or what you can claim, you should contact a local welfare rights unit or a Citizens' Advice Bureau for independent help with claiming benefits. You may also find it helpful to consult the article which begins on p109.

Education Maintenance Allowances (EMAs)

EMAs are currently being piloted in 12 areas around the country. EMAs are available to 16–19 year olds who stay on at school or college in the pilot areas. The allowance is paid weekly and the amount you receive depends on your household income. In order to qualify for an EMA, you and a parent or guardian must sign a Learning Agreement with the school or college and stick to the steps it sets out.

The local education authorities running pilots are Bolton, City of Nottingham, Cornwall, Doncaster, Gateshead, Leeds, Middlesbrough, Oldham, Southampton, Stoke-on-Trent, and Walsall; the four London boroughs of Lambeth, Lewisham, Southwark and Greenwich are running a single pilot. If you live in these areas, you can contact your local education authority to see if you are eligible for an Education Maintenance Allowance.

Useful publications

For a list of useful publications see the Bibliography in Part 5.

If you have any questions regarding the choices available for disabled people in post-16 education, training and employment, contact Skill's Information Service on 0800 328 5050 (voice) or 0800 068 2422 (text) (open Monday to Friday 1.30–4.30pm) or write to:

Skill
Chapter House
18–20 Crucifix Lane
London SE1 3JW

Alternatively, visit Skill's website at www.skill.org.uk, or email info@skill.org.uk

1.17
Applying to Higher Education: Guidance for Disabled People

SKILL (National Bureau for Students with Disabilities)

For many people the prospect of going to university is becoming more and more attractive but every student seeking entry to higher education should ask questions about courses and facilities in colleges. Disabled students should ask the same questions, but will probably have other concerns too. These might include, for example, provision of learning materials in Braille, wheelchair access to lecture halls or the extent to which an institution will understand the difficulties encountered by a dyslexic student. These concerns are very important, but the usual concerns of all students are just as important to disabled students as they are to non-disabled students. These include what to study and where.

What is higher education?

Higher education is any course which leads to a certain level of qualification. It includes the following:

Undergraduate studies leading to:

- a first degree (BSc, BA, BEd, LLB, BEng, BMus);
- a diploma of higher education (DipSW, DipHE);
- a Higher National Diploma (HND).

Postgraduate studies leading to:

- a master's degree (MA, MSc, MEd, MPhil);
- a doctorate (PhD)
- a Postgraduate Certificate of Education (PGCE)
- other postgraduate diplomas.

These courses are offered in universities and colleges around the country. Some further education colleges also offer higher education courses.

Higher education – is it for me?

You could go into higher education for a number of reasons. This might be in preparation for a chosen career, for the experience or as a way of empowering yourself as a disabled person. Higher education can give you the chance to learn new subjects and obtain qualifications. It can also offer opportunities to take up other activities, develop new skills, gain new experiences and meet new people.

Will I get the funding I need?

Money is a big issue for all students. If you have specific needs because of your disability you will also need to consider sources of funding for these. Universities and colleges do not always provide or pay for all the support or equipment you may need. You should check whether or not you can claim disabled student's allowances to help pay for support needs.

How do I choose the right course?

You should start your search for a university or college like any other student – by choosing a course of study. There are several questions to consider, including:

- Is the course essential for your proposed work or career plans? Would it be helpful?
- Could you still pursue your ambitions with a degree or HND in any subject?
- Which subject interests you? Is the content of a course you have in mind appropriate for this interest?
- Would you prefer to study full-time or part-time?
- Which teaching methods are used?
- Which assessment methods are used?
- What level of course do you require?
- Can you fulfil the entry requirements? Is there a related course with different requirements?
- Are you seeking a course which includes work experience or study abroad?

Where should I study?

You may be tempted to apply only to institutions which have good provision for disabled students. But take care – choosing the right institution and course for you as an individual is very important. A good way to start is to prepare a list of places which offer the courses which interest you. Then think through the following issues:

Academic considerations:	Facilities and reputation of the college? Academic support, eg personal tutor? Library facilities?
Location:	Should the institution be near your home, or not? Campus or city site?
Student community:	How many students are there? What age?

Recreation and leisure:	Town facilities, sports, hobbies, student union?
Access:	To lecture theatres and teaching rooms? To a parking space? To the bar and canteen? To sports facilities? In other ways, eg induction loops, good signage.
Experience:	Other disabled students? Staff attitude to you as a disabled person?
Accommodation:	Is it accessible? Will you be integrated with other students? Can equipment be installed or adaptations made? Will a room be provided for your personal assistant?
Support facilities:	Talk to the disabled student's adviser about the support available. Is there a suitable centre available locally for medical treatment? Any particular facilities for disabled students? eg Braille embosser, dyslexia support tutor, sign language interpreter unit, campus minibus, note-takers. If these are not available, can they be arranged in time for the start of your course?

How do I find out more about a college or university?

The prospectus

All prospectuses provide information about the general facilities in colleges or universities as well as course details. Most also give some details of facilities for disabled students. They may also give a contact name for the disability officer/adviser.

Disability statements

By law, publicly funded higher education providers in England, Wales, Scotland and Northern Ireland (and also further education providers in England, Wales and Northern Ireland) have to produce a statement of their facilities for disabled students. This should include specific support services as well as general accessibility of college premises. When requesting a prospectus, ask for a copy of the statement, plus any other information produced by the college about its services for disabled students.

Student union or association

The student union or association may produce its own information about the college or university and may have its own disability support structures and policy.

Making contact

If your questions are not answered by the prospectus or other written information, telephone or write to the institution. For information on disability related provision contact the Disability Co-ordinator or Learning Support Co-ordinator, who is responsible for services for disabled students. The internet is another useful source. Most universities have websites that contain general information and details of courses and facilities.

Making a visit

The best way to find out what a university or college is like is to visit. Many places welcome early informal 'information visits'. Try to visit during term time or semester, when you are more likely to meet other students with disabilities and will be able to form a more accurate picture.

How do I apply?

The application form

Applications for most full-time courses are made through the Universities and Colleges Admissions Service clearing house (UCAS). Application forms are available from careers services or directly from UCAS.

Your disability or impairment

Most application forms ask for details of any disability and associated individual needs. Many people worry that disclosing a disability or impairment at this stage may leave them vulnerable to discrimination. However, the following points should be kept in mind:

- Being fair to yourself: you do not want to spend the first week of term setting up support while everyone else is going to parties and making new friends;
- Being fair to the college: changes may need to be made or staff may need training before you arrive;
- Explaining something: you may need to mention your disability or impairment in order to explain something. For example, your disability may have affected your school career or you may have done exams later than most other people;
- Providing the information yourself: headteachers or tutors writing your confidential reference may mention your disability if they think it is significant;
- Discrimination: although this does still exist, more and more colleges realise that disability and inability are not the same thing. As a failsafe, UCAS and other clearing houses allow you an extra choice of college if you receive a rejection because of your disability. New legislation will also help to prevent discrimination in education. Institutions will be expected to make reasonable adjustments for disabled people and not to treat disabled students any less favourably for reasons related to their disability.

The decision about what to write is yours and you must feel comfortable with it. Beware of using terms which admissions tutors may not understand. The institution is interested in two things: how your disability or impairment may affect your studies and what they need to know to give you the right support.

If you cannot fill in the form yourself, ask someone to type or write your answers for you. Your referee can explain in his or her confidential report the method used and the reasons for it.

Selection interviews

If you are invited to attend an interview, let the institution know if you need any particular arrangements. You may be asked about your disability, for example about adapting course material to suit your needs. Be prepared to speak clearly and confidently about potential problems and solutions. It is best if these points have already been discussed during your information visit.

Offers

Admissions tutors decide whether to offer you a place and the offer will usually be a conditional offer. This means that your exam results must meet the grade requirements of the course.

Rejections

Institutions rarely give reasons for a rejection. If you think you have been rejected because of your disability, contact the institution to find out. If they confirm that they have rejected you because they do not have the facilities for your needs, UCAS will give you another choice.

What support is available?

Do not be afraid to use support. It does not make you different from other students; it is intended to help you study at the same level. You can always change your support arrangements, eg if your needs change or if the support turns out to be the wrong type.

How do I find out more?

There are many directories of higher education courses. A list of suggested titles is given in the Bibliography in Part 5. These can be found in careers, and local, libraries.

For further information about higher education for disabled people, contact Skill's information service on 0800 328 5050 (voice) or 0800 068 2422 (text); or write to Skill at:

Skill
Chapter House
19–20 Crucifix Lane
London SE1 3JW

Alternatively, visit their website at www.skill.org.uk or email: info@skill.org.uk

Expert, personal guidance on issues of interest to any student planning to enter higher education, including choice of courses and universities, gap year options, UCAS applications and interview techniques, is also available from:

Gabbitas Educational Consultants
Carrington House
126–130 Regent Street
London W1B 5EE
Tel: 020 7734 0161 Fax: 020 7437 1764
Email: admin@gabbitas.co.uk Website: www.gabbitas.co.uk

PART TWO: DIRECTORY OF SPECIAL SCHOOLS AND COLLEGES

A note on the directories and key to abbreviations

Part Two of *Schools for Special Needs – A Complete Guide* contains three directories covering establishments in England, Scotland, Northern Ireland and Wales.

1. Independent and non-maintained special schools

2. Colleges and other provision at 16+

Every attempt has been made to compile a comprehensive list of independent and non-maintained schools, and support services for students aged 16+. Each entry includes, where known, the name, address and telephone number of the school, the name of the Head, Principal or Director, the age range of students and the numbers accepted, with the number of boys and girls (B/G) or male and female students (M/F) given where available. Where applicable the number of boarding pupils or residential students is also given. Within the schools directory these are sometimes divided into full boarders (F) and weekly boarders (W).

The types of need for which the school or college makes provision are shown in abbreviated form. A key to the abbreviations is given below. The principal types of special needs catered for, where known, are shown in bold.

Schools may be Independent, DfEE Approved Independent or Non-maintained or, in Scotland, Voluntary or Grant-aided. The status of each school is given where known. Entries also indicate whether a school offers 52-week care.

3. State Maintained Schools by Education Authority

Maintained schools are listed by Local Education Authority. An index of Local Education Authorities and their corresponding page numbers appears on p200. This is not a comprehensive list, but includes information on all schools that replied to requests from Gabbitas for information.

Each school's entry includes, where known, the name, address and telephone number of the school, the name of the Head, Principal or Director, the age range and number of students accepted. Where applicable the number of residential students is also given. The number of pupils is given for both boys and girls (B/G), where known.

The types of need for which the school or college makes provision are shown in abbreviated form. A key to the abbreviations is given below. The principal types of special needs catered for, where known, are shown in bold.

Key to abbreviations used in the directories

ADD	Attention Deficit Disorder	HI	Hearing Impairment
ADHD	Attention Deficit/Hyperactivity Disorder	MLD	Moderate Learning Difficulties
		PH	Physical Impairment
ASP	Asperger Syndrome	PMLD	Profound and Multiple Learning
AUT	Autism		Difficulties
CP	Cerebal Palsy	SLD	Severe Learning Difficulities
DEL	Delicate	SP&LD	Speech & Language Difficulties
DOW	Down's Syndrome	SPLD	Specific Learning Difficulties
DYC	Dyscalculia	TOU	Tourette's Syndrome
DYP	Dyspraxia	VIS	Visual Impairment
DYS	Dyslexia	W	Wheelchair access
EBD	Emotional/Behavioural Difficulties	+	Registered with CReSTeD (see Part 5.2)
EPI	Epilepsy	*	School Profile in Part Three

2.1
Directory of Independent and Non-maintained Special Schools

ENGLAND

BERKSHIRE

ANNIE LAWSON SCHOOL*
Nine Mile Ride, Crowthorne,
Berkshire RG45 6BQ
Tel: (01344) 755508
Head: Mrs L Young
Type: Co-educational Boarding and
Day 11–19
No of pupils: 23 *No of Boarders:* F20
Special Needs: PMLD SLD W
Approved Independent
52-week care

**HIGH CLOSE SCHOOL
(BARNARDO'S)***
Wiltshire Road, Wokingham,
Berkshire RG40 1TT
Tel: (0118) 978 5767
Head: Mrs R Mahony
Type: Co-educational Boarding and
Day 6–16
No of pupils: 64 *No of Boarders:* W44
Special Needs: EBD MLD W
Non-Maintained

**THE MARY HARE GRAMMAR
SCHOOL FOR THE DEAF**
Arlington Manor, Newbury,
Berkshire RG14 9BQ
Tel: (01635) 244200
Head: Dr I G Tucker
Type: Co-educational Boarding and
Day 11–19
No of pupils: 210 *No of Boarders:* F208
Special Needs: HI
Non-Maintained

PRIORS COURT SCHOOL*
Chieveley, Newbury, Berkshire
RG18 9NU
Tel: (01635) 248209
Head: Mr R G Hubbard
Type: Co-educational Boarding and
Day 3–19
No of pupils: 100 *No of Boarders:* W13
Special Needs: ASP AUT
Independent

BRISTOL

BELGRAVE SCHOOL
10 Upper Belgrave Road, Clifton,
Bristol BS8 2XH
Tel: (0117) 973 9405
Type: Co-educational Day 7–12
No of pupils: B16 G8
Special Needs: ADD DYC DYP DYS
MLD SPLD
Independent

**ST CHRISTOPHER'S
SCHOOL***
Carisbrooke Lodge, Westbury Park,
Bristol BS6 7JE
Tel: (0117) 973 3301
Head: Ms O Matz
Type: Co-educational Boarding 6–19
No of pupils: B27 G22
No of Boarders: F48
Special Needs: AUT CP EPI PMLD
SLD SP&LD W
Independent
52-week care

THE SHEILING SCHOOL*
Thornbury Park, Park Road,
Thornbury, Bristol BS35 1HP
Tel: (01454) 412194
Type: Co-educational Boarding and
Day 6–19
No of pupils: B23 G12
No of Boarders: F28 W7
Special Needs: AUT DOW EBD EPI
MLD PMLD SLD SP&LD
Independent

BUCKINGHAMSHIRE

**THE CHARMANDEAN
DYSLEXIA CENTRE***
Tile House Mansion, Lillingstone
Dayrell, Buckingham,
Buckinghamshire MK18 5AN
Tel: (01280) 860182
Head: Mr W H Wilcox
Type: Co-educational Day 8–16
No of pupils: B40 G8
Special Needs: DYP **DYS**
Independent

**MACINTYRE SCHOOL
WINGRAVE***
The Old Manor House, Wingrave,
Aylesbury, Buckinghamshire
HP22 4PD
Tel: (01296) 681274
Head: Mrs H Willdridge
Type: Co-educational Boarding 10–19
No of pupils: 34 *No of Boarders:* F34
Special Needs: AUT EPI PMLD **SLD**
SP&LD SPLD
Approved Independent
52-week care

CAMBRIDGESHIRE

**CHARTWELL HOUSE
SCHOOL**
Goodens Lane, Newton, Wisbech,
Cambridgeshire PE13 5HQ
Tel: (01945) 870793
Head: Mr C E Wright
Type: Boys Boarding 10–16
No of pupils: 7 *No of Boarders:* F7
Special Needs: ADD DYS **EBD**
Independent
52-week care

CHESHIRE

CHAIGELEY SCHOOL
Lymm Road, Thelwall, Warrington,
Cheshire WA4 2TE
Tel: (01925) 752357
Head: Mr D Crawshaw
Type: Boys Boarding and Day 8–16
No of pupils: 72 *No of Boarders:* W24
Special Needs: ADD ADHD **EBD**
Non-Maintained

THE DAVID LEWIS SCHOOL
Mill Lane, Warford, Cheshire
SK9 7UD
Tel: (01565) 640066
Head: Mr C D Dean
Type: Co-educational Boarding and
Day 5–19
No of pupils: B48 G24
No of Boarders: F53
Special Needs: **EPI** MLD PH SLD
SP&LD W
Non-Maintained

DELAMERE FOREST SCHOOL
Blakemere Lane, Norley, Frodsham,
Warrington, Cheshire WA6 6NP
Tel: (01928) 788263
Head: Mr H Burman
Type: Co-educational Boarding and
Day 6–17 (Jewish boarders only)
No of pupils: B35 G25
No of Boarders: W44
Special Needs: ADD ADHD ASP DEL
DOW DYP DYS EBD SPI MLD
SP&LD SPLD TOU
Non-Maintained
52-week care

LAMBS HOUSE SCHOOL
Buxton Road, Buglawton,
Congleton, Cheshire CW12 2DT
Tel: (01260) 272089
Head: Mrs M S Lee
Type: Co-educational Boarding and
Day 5–16
No of pupils: 39 *No of Boarders:* F12
W8
Special Needs: **AUT**
Independent

ROYAL SCHOOL FOR THE DEAF (MANCHESTER)*
Stanley Road, Cheadle Hulme, Cheadle, Cheshire SK8 6RQ
Tel: (0161) 610 0100
Head: Mr L Reed
Type: Co-educational Boarding and Day 5–20
No of pupils: B44 G29
No of Boarders: F8 W32
Special Needs: **AUT CP HI** MLD **PH PMLD SLD** SPLD VIS W
Non-Maintained
52-week care

THE ST JOHN VIANNEY SCHOOL
(Lower School), Didsbury Road, Heaton Mersey, Stockport, Cheshire SK4 2AA
Tel: (0161) 432 0510
Head: Mr M M O'Donoghue
Type: Co-educational Day 5–11
No of pupils: 69
Special Needs: **ADD ADHD ASP AUT CP DOW DYP** MLD **SP&LD** W
Non-Maintained

TAXAL EDGE SCHOOL
Macclesfield Road, Whaley Bridge, Stockport, Cheshire SK12 7DR
Tel: (01663) 732122
Head: Ms S Wells
Type: Co-educational Day 5–16
No of pupils: 30
Special Needs: **EBD**
Independent

CUMBRIA

EDEN GROVE SCHOOL*
Bolton, Appleby, Cumbria CA16 6AJ
Tel: (01768) 361346
Head: Mr I McCready
Type: Boys Boarding and Day 8–19
No of pupils: 96 *No of Boarders:* F65
Special Needs: **ADD** ADHD ASP DYS **EBD** MLD **SP&LD TOU** W
Approved Independent

LOWGATE HOUSE SCHOOL
Levens, Kendal, Cumbria LA8 8NJ
Tel: (01539) 560124
Head: Mr G Brady
Type: Boys Boarding and Day 7–12
No of pupils: 24 *No of Boarders:* F20
Special Needs: ADD ADHD EBD SPLD
Approved Independent
52-week care

RIVERSIDE SCHOOL
Whassett, Milnthorpe, Cumbria LA7 7DN
Tel: (01539) 562006
Head: Mr G Waterhouse
Type: Co-educational Boarding and Day 10–16
No of pupils: B36 G36
Special Needs: ADD ADHD EBD MLD
Independent

WITHERSLACK HALL
Grange-over-Sands, Witherslack, Cumbria LA11 6SD
Tel: 01539 552397
Head: Mr M A Barrow
Type: Boys Boarding and Day 11–16
No of pupils: 70 *No of Boarders:* F70
Special Needs: ADD ADHD EBD SPLD
Approved Independent

DERBYSHIRE

ALDERWASLEY HALL SCHOOL*
Alderwasley, Belper, Derbyshire DE56 2SR
Tel: (01629) 822586
Head: Mr K P Hingorani
Type: Co-educational Boarding and Day 5–19
No of pupils: 176 *No of Boarders:* F146
Special Needs: **ASP** DYP DYS SP&LD
Approved Independent

EASTWOOD GRANGE SCHOOL
Milken Lane, Ashover, Chesterfield, Derbyshire S45 0BA
Tel: (01246) 590255
Head: Mr P J Brandt
Type: Boys Boarding
No of pupils: 36 *No of Boarders:* F36
Special Needs: ADD **EBD** MLD SP&LD
Independent
52-week care

PEGASUS SCHOOL*
Main Street, Caldwell, Swadlincore, Derbyshire DE12 6RS
Tel: (01283) 761352
Type: Co-educational Boarding and Day 5–19
Special Needs: **EBD**
Independent
52-week care

ROYAL SCHOOL FOR THE DEAF, DERBY*

Ashbourne Road, Derby, Derbyshire
DE22 3BH
Tel: (01332) 362512
Head: Mr T Silvester
Type: Co-educational Boarding and
Day 3–16
No of pupils: B50 G49
No of Boarders: W53
Special Needs: **HI**
Non-Maintained
52-week care

DEVON

BROOMHAYES SCHOOL

Kingsley House, Alverdiscott Road,
Bideford, Devon EX39 4PL
Tel: (01237) 473830
Head: Mrs B Dewar
Type: Boarding
No of pupils: 32 *No of Boarders:* F31
Special Needs: **AUT MLD PMLD SLD**
SP&LD SPLD
Approved Independent
52-week care

CHELFHAM MILL SCHOOL

Chelfham, Barnstaple, Devon
EX32 7LA
Tel: (01271) 850448
Head: Mrs K Roberts
Type: Boys Boarding and Day 7–13
No of pupils: 58 *No of Boarders:* F48
Special Needs: **ADD ADHD ASP EBD**
EPI MLD TOU
Approved Independent
52-week care

CHELFHAM SENIOR SCHOOL

Bere Alston, Yelverton, Devon
PL20 7EX
Tel: (01822) 840379
Head: Mrs J Marks
Type: Boys Boarding 11–19
No of pupils: 63 *No of Boarders:* F63
Special Needs: **ASP EBD MLD TOU**
Approved Independent
52-week care

DAME HANNAH ROGERS SCHOOL*

Woodland Road, Ivybridge, Devon
PL21 9HQ
Tel: (01752) 892461
Head: Mr W R Evans
Type: Co-educational Boarding and
Day 8–19
No of pupils: B34 G21
No of Boarders: F30 W20
Special Needs: **CP DEL EPI MLD PH**
PMLD SLD SP&LD W
Non-Maintained

ROYAL WEST OF ENGLAND SCHOOL FOR THE DEAF

50 Topsham Road, Exeter, Devon
EX2 4NF
Tel: (01392) 272692
Head: Mr J F Shaw
Type: Co-educational Boarding and
Day 3–19
No of pupils: 143
Special Needs: **HI**
Non-Maintained

TRENGWEATH SCHOOL*

Hartley Road, Plymouth, Devon
PL3 5LW
Tel: (01752) 771975
Head: Mrs G Pratchett
Type: Co-educational Boarding and
Day 2–19
No of pupils: B8 G12
No of Boarders: F3 W3
Special Needs: **CP DEL EPI PH PMLD**
SP&LD VIS W
Approved Independent
52-week care

VRANCH HOUSE SCHOOL

Pinhoe Road, Exeter, Devon
EX4 8AD
Tel: (01392) 468333
Head: Miss M R Boon
Type: Co-educational Day 2–12
No of pupils: 20
Special Needs: **CP** MLD **PH** PMLD
SP&LD W
Approved Independent

THE WEST OF ENGLAND SCHOOL AND COLLEGE FOR PUPILS WITH LITTLE OR NO SIGHT

Countess Wear, Exeter, Devon
EX2 6HA
Tel: (01392) 454200
Head: Mr P Holland
Type: Co-educational Boarding and
Day 2–16
No of pupils: B140 G40
No of Boarders: F40 W79
Special Needs: **PH VIS W**
Non-Maintained

WHITSTONE HEAD SCHOOL

Whitstone, Holsworthy, Devon
EX22 6TJ
Tel: (01288) 341251
Head: Mr D R McLean-Thorne
Type: Co-educational Boarding and
Day 11–16
No of pupils: B20 G3
No of Boarders: F23
Special Needs: **ADD ADHD ASP DYP**
DYS EBD MLD **SPLD TOU**
Approved Independent

**WYCHBURY HOUSE
RESIDENTIAL SCHOOL**
22 Cleveland Road, Torquay, Devon
TQ2 5BE
Tel: (01803) 293460
Head: Mr D Simpson
Type: Boys Boarding 9–16
No of pupils: 11 *No of Boarders:* F11
Special Needs: DYS EBD MLD SPLD
Independent

DORSET

THE FORUM SCHOOL
Shillingstone, Dorset DT11 0QS
Tel: (01258) 860295
Head: Mrs G Waters
Type: Co-educational Boarding 7–14
No of pupils: B34 G4
No of Boarders: F36
Special Needs: AUT
Approved Independent

LANGSIDE SCHOOL
Langside Avenue, Parkstone, Poole,
Dorset BH12 5BN
Tel: (01202) 518635
Head: Mr J Ashby
Type: Co-educational Day 2–18
No of pupils: B28 G14
Special Needs: CP DEL EPI HI PH
PMLD SLD VIS W
Approved Independent

**PHILIP GREEN MEMORIAL
SCHOOL***
Boveridge House, Cranborne,
Wimborne, Dorset BH21 5RU
Tel: (01725) 517218
Head: Mrs L Walter
Type: Co-educational Boarding and
Day 11–19
No of pupils: B13 G11
No of Boarders: F19 W3
Special Needs: ADD **ASP** DEL DOW
DYP MLD SLD SP&LD
Independent

PURBECK VIEW SCHOOL
Northbrook Road, Swanage, Dorset
BH19 1PR
Tel: (01929) 422760
Head: Mrs S Goulding
Type: Co-educational Boarding 11–19
No of pupils: B40 G4
No of Boarders: F44
Special Needs: AUT
Independent

**THE WESSEX AUTISTIC
SOCIETY, PORTFIELD
SCHOOL**
4 Magdalen Lane, Christchurch,
Dorset BH23 1PH
Tel: (01202) 486626
Head: Mr P Gabony
Type: Co-educational Boarding and
Day 2–19
No of pupils: 42 *No of Boarders:* W16
Special Needs: AUT
Independent

ESSEX

DOUCECROFT SCHOOL
163 High Street, Kelvedon,
Colchester, Essex CO5 9JA
Tel: (01376) 570060
Head: Mr K Cranmer
Type: Co-educational Boarding and
Day 2–19
No of pupils: B22 G4
Special Needs: ASP AUT
Approved Independent

ST JOHN'S RC SCHOOL
Turpins Lane, Woodford Green,
Essex IG8 8AX
Tel: (020) 8504 1818
Head: Sister M Galvin
Type: Co-educational Day 5–19
Special Needs: MLD SLD SP&LD
Non-Maintained

WOODCROFT SCHOOL*
Whitakers Way, Loughton, Essex
IG10 1SQ
Tel: (020) 8508 1369
Head: Ms F Khan
Type: Co-educational Day 2–11
No of pupils: B20 G4
Special Needs: ADD ADHD ASP AUT
CP DOW DYP DYS **EBD** EPI HI MLD
PH PMLD **SLD** SPLD SP&LD VIS W
Approved Independent

GLOUCESTERSHIRE

COTSWOLD CHINE SCHOOL*
Box, Stroud, Gloucestershire
GL6 9AG
Tel: (01453) 837550
Head: Ms S Rieser
Type: Co-educational Boarding 10–16
No of pupils: 42 *No of Boarders:* F40 W2
Special Needs: ADD ADHD ASP AUT EBD EPI MLD SLD SP&LD SPLD TOU W
Approved Independent
52-week care

ST ROSE'S SCHOOL*
Stratford Lawn, Stroud,
Gloucestershire GL5 4AP
Tel: (01453) 763793
Head: Sister M Quentin
Type: Co-educational Boarding and Day 2–18
No of pupils: B37 G31
No of Boarders: F17 W16
Special Needs: ASP CP DEL DYP EPI MLD PH SLD SP&LD SPLD VIS W
Non-Maintained

HAMPSHIRE

COXLEASE SCHOOL
High Coxlease House, Clay Hill,
Lyndhurst, Hampshire SO43 7DE
Tel: (023) 8028 3633
Type: Boys Boarding 9–17
No of pupils: 45 *No of Boarders:* F45
Special Needs: ADHD EBD MLD
Approved Independent
52-week care

GRATELEY HOUSE SCHOOL
Grateley, Andover, Hampshire
SP11 8JR
Tel: (01264) 889751
Head: Mr A Sumner
Type: Co-educational Boarding 11–16
No of pupils: B25 G8
No of Boarders: F33
Special Needs: ADD ADHD ASP DYP TOU
Approved Independent

HILL HOUSE SCHOOL
Rope Hill, Boldre, Lymington,
Hampshire SO41 8NE
Tel: (01590) 672147
Head: Ms J Wright
Type: Co-educational Boarding 11–19
No of pupils: B17 G5
No of Boarders: F22
Special Needs: AUT SLD
Approved Independent
52-week care

HOPE LODGE SCHOOL
22 Midanbury Lane, Bitterne Park,
Southampton, Hampshire SO18 4HP
Tel: (023) 8063 4346
Head: Mrs M Filley
Type: Co-educational Boarding and Day 4–19
No of pupils: 46 *No of Boarders:* W27
Special Needs: ASP AUT SLD SP&LD
Approved Independent

LODDON SCHOOL
Wildmoor, Sherfield-on-Loddon,
Hook, Hampshire RG27 0JD
Tel: (01256) 882394
Head: Ms M Cornick
Type: Co-educational Boarding 8–18
No of pupils: 27 *No of Boarders:* F27
Special Needs: ADD ADHD AUT EPI SLD SP&LD
Approved Independent
52-week care

MORDAUNT SCHOOL
Rose Road, Southampton,
Hampshire SO14 6TE
Tel: (023) 8022 9017
Head: Ms C M Spiller
Type: Co-educational Day 2–19
No of pupils: B15 G12
Special Needs: AUT CP EPI PH PMLD SP&LD SPLD VIS W
Approved Independent

ST EDWARD'S SCHOOL*
Melchet Court, Sherfield English,
Romsey, Hampshire SO51 6ZR
Tel: (01794) 884271
Head: Mr L P Bartel
Type: Boys Boarding 10–17
No of pupils: 68 *No of Boarders:* F68
Special Needs: ADD DYS EBD MLD
Approved Independent

THE SHEILING CURATIVE SCHOOLS*
Ashley, Ringwood, Hampshire
BH24 2EB
Tel: (01425) 477488
Type: Co-educational Boarding and Day 6–19
No of pupils: B31 G20
No of Boarders: F49 W1
Special Needs: AUT CP DOW EBD EPI MLD PMLD SLD SP&LD
Independent

SOUTHLANDS SCHOOL
Vicar's Hill, Boldre, Lymington,
Hampshire SO41 8QB
Tel: (01590) 675350
Head: Ms S Gething
Type: Boys Boarding 8–19
No of pupils: 61 *No of Boarders:* F61
Special Needs: ASP AUT
Approved Independent

TRELOAR SCHOOL*
Upper Froyle, Alton, Hampshire
GU34 4LA
Tel: (01420) 526400
Head: Mr N Clark
Type: Co-educational Boarding and
Day 5–16
No of pupils: B88 G52
No of Boarders: F108
Special Needs: CP DEL DYC DYP HI
MLD **PH SP&LD** SPLD VIS W
Non-Maintained

HEREFORDSHIRE

**HILLCREST PENTWYN
SCHOOL**
Clyro, Hereford, Herefordshire
HR3 5SE
Tel: (01497) 821420
Head: Mrs E Hudson
Type: Boys Boarding 11–17
No of pupils: 12 *No of Boarders:* F12
Special Needs: ADD ADHD DYP DYS
EBD MLD SPLD
Independent

ROWDEN HOUSE SCHOOL*
Winslow, Bromyard, Herefordshire
HR7 4LS
Tel: (01885) 488096
Head: Mrs H Hardy
Type: Co-educational Boarding 11–19
No of pupils: B22 G6
No of Boarders: F28
Special Needs: AUT DOW EPI PMLD
SLD TOU W
Approved Independent
52-week care

HERTFORDSHIRE

**MELDRETH MANOR
SCHOOL***
Fenny Lane, Meldreth, Royston,
Hertfordshire SG8 6LG
Tel: (01763) 260771
Head: Mr E Nash
Type: Co-educational Boarding and
Day 5–19
No of pupils: 77 *No of Boarders:* F74
Special Needs: AUT CP EPI HI **PH
PMLD SLD SP&LD** VIS W
Approved Independent

**RADLETT LODGE SCHOOL
FOR AUTISTIC CHILDREN**
Harper Lane, Radlett, Hertfordshire
WD7 9HW
Tel: (01923) 854922
Head: Mrs L Tucker
Type: Co-educational Day and
Boarding 3–11
No of pupils: 49 *No of Boarders:* W18
Special Needs: **AUT**
Approved Independent

ST ELIZABETH'S SCHOOL*
South End, Much Hadham,
Hertfordshire SG10 6EW
Tel: (01279) 844270
Head: Mrs C A Walker
Type: Co-educational Boarding and
Day 5–19
No of Boarders: 53
Special Needs: AUT DOW DYP DYS
EPI MLD PH SLD SP&LD TOU VIS W
Non-Maintained

ISLE OF WIGHT

ST CATHERINE'S SCHOOL*
Grove Road, Ventnor, Isle of Wight
PO38 1TT
Tel: (01983) 852722
Head: Mr G E Shipley
Type: Co-educational Boarding and
Day 7–18
No of pupils: B55 G12
No of Boarders: F56 W5
Special Needs: **SP&LD**
Non-Maintained

KENT

**BREWOOD EDUCATION
CENTRE***
86 London Road, Deal, Kent
CT14 9TR
Tel: (01304) 363000
Head: Miss C Simcox
Type: Co-educational Boarding and
Day 7–14
No of pupils: B8 G2
Special Needs: ADD ADHD ASP DYC
DYP DYS EBD HI MLD SP&LD TOU
VIS
Independent

CALDECOTT COMMUNITY
Ashford, Kent TN25 5NH
Tel: (01233) 503954
Head: Mr D Marshall
Type: Co-educational Boarding 5–16
No of pupils: B34 G34
No of Boarders: F68
Special Needs: DYS **EBD**
Non-Maintained
52-week care

CONEY HILL SCHOOL
Croydon Road, Hayes, Bromley, Kent
BR2 7AG
Tel: (020) 8462 2017
Head: Ms S Harris
Type: Co-educational Boarding and
Day 5–16
No of pupils: B15 G7 *No of Boarders:* F3
W8
Special Needs: CP EPI PH PMLD
VIS W
Non-Maintained

**DON BUSS LEARNING
OPPORTUNITIES**
The Old School, Ringwould Road,
Ringwould, Deal, Kent DT14 8DW
Tel: (01304) 381906
Head: Mr M Tipping
Type: Co-educational Boarding and
Day 11–16
No of pupils: B20 G1
Special Needs: ADD ADHD ASP EBD
Approved Independent

**DON BUSS LEARNING
CENTRE PRIMARY**
The School, The Street,
Womenswold, Canterbury, Kent
CT4 6HE
Tel: (01227) 831236
Head: Miss L O'Keefe
Type: Boys Boarding and Day 7–12
No of pupils: 9
Special Needs: ADD ADHD ASP EBD
Approved Independent

EAST COURT SCHOOL
Victoria Parade, Ramsgate, Kent
CT11 8ED
Tel: (01843) 592077
Head: Dr M E Thomson and E J
Watkins
Type: Co-educational Boarding and
Day 8–13
No of pupils: B58 G11
No of Boarders: F15 W38
Special Needs: DYC DYP DYS SPLD
Independent

HELEN ALLISON SCHOOL
Longfield Road, Meopham, Kent
DA13 0EW
Tel: (01474) 814878
Head: Mrs J Ashton-Smith
Type: Co-educational Boarding and
Day 5–19
No of pupils: 66 *No of Boarders:* W27
Special Needs: ASP AUT
Approved Independent

**MEADOWS SCHOOL
(BARNARDO'S)***
London Road, Tunbridge Wells, Kent
TN4 0RN
Tel: (01892) 529144
Head: Mrs S Paterson
Type: Co-educational Boarding and
Day 11–16
No of pupils: B36 G10
No of Boarders: W26
Special Needs: EBD MLD W
Non-Maintained

RIPPLEVALE SCHOOL
Ripple, Deal, Kent CT14 8JG
Tel: (01304) 373866
Head: Mrs R Howells
Type: Boys Boarding and Day 10–16
No of pupils: 45 *No of Boarders:* F24
Special Needs: **EBD**
Approved Independent

ROYAL LONDON SOCIETY FOR THE BLIND
Dorton House, Seal, Sevenoaks, Kent
TN15 OED
Tel: (01732) 592650
Head: Mr B Cooney
Type: Co-educational Boarding and
Day 3–16
No of pupils: B56 G38
No of Boarders: W52
Special Needs: VIS
Non-Maintained

THE ROYAL SCHOOL FOR DEAF CHILDREN MARGATE AND WESTGATE COLLEGE FOR DEAF PEOPLE
Victoria Road, Margate, Kent
CT9 1NB
Tel: (01843) 227561
Head: Mr D E Bond
Type: Co-educational Boarding and
Day 4–25
No of pupils: B122 G53
No of Boarders: F10 W145
Special Needs: HI
Non-Maintained
52-week care

WESTWOOD SCHOOL*
479 Margate Road, Broadstairs, Kent
CT10 2QA
Tel: (01843) 600820
Head: Mr C L Walter
Type: Co-educational Day 11–16
No of pupils: B18 G3
Special Needs: ADHD EBD MLD
Independent

LANCASHIRE

BEECH TREE SCHOOL
Meadow Lane, Bamber Bridge,
Preston, Lancashire PR5 8LN
Tel: (01772) 323131
Head: Ms L Bayliss
Type: Co-educational Boarding 7–16
No of pupils: B14 G1
No of Boarders: F15
Special Needs: AUT EBD EPI HI PH
PMLD SLD SP&LD VIS W
Approved Independent
52-week care

BIRTENSHAW HALL SCHOOL*
Darwen Road, Bromley Cross,
Bolton, Lancashire BL7 9AB
Tel: (01204) 304230
Head: Mr C D Jamieson
Type: Co-educational Boarding and
Day 3–19
No of pupils: 30 *No of Boarders:* F22
Special Needs: CP DEL EPI MLD PH
PMLD SLD W
Non-Maintained

CEDAR HOUSE SCHOOL
Kirkby Lonsdale, Via Carnforth,
Lancashire LA6 2HW
Tel: (01524) 271181
Head: Mr A W Cousins
Type: Co-educational Boarding and
Day 9–16
No of pupils: 70 *No of Boarders:* F56
Special Needs: ADD ADHD EBD SPLD
Approved Independent

CROOKHEY HALL SCHOOL
Garstang Road, Cockerham,
Lancaster, Lancashire LA2 0HA
Tel: (01524) 792618
Head: Mr J Rider
Type: Boys Day 11–16
No of pupils: 64
Special Needs: EBD SPLD
Approved Independent

CROWTHORN SCHOOL (NCH ACTION FOR CHILDREN)*
Broadhead Road, Edgworth, Bolton,
Lancashire BL7 0JS
Tel: (01204) 852143
Head: Mr S Forster
Type: Co-educational Boarding and
Day 8–16
No of pupils: 56 *No of Boarders:* F50
Special Needs: EBD MLD
Non-Maintained

NUGENT HOUSE SCHOOL*
Car Mill Road, Billinge, Wigan,
Lancashire WN5 7TT
Tel: (01744) 892551
Head: Mrs J L G Bienias
Type: Boys Boarding and Day 7–19
No of pupils: 92 *No of Boarders:* F62
Special Needs: ADD ADHD ASP AUT
DYS EBD SPLD TOU
Approved Independent
52-week care

PONTVILLE SCHOOL*
Black Moss Lane, Ormskirk,
Lancashire L39 4TW
Tel: (01695) 578734
Head: Mr R Farbon
Type: Co-educational Boarding and
Day 9–19
No of pupils: B39 G12
No of Boarders: F21
Special Needs: ADD ASP EBD MLD
TOU
Non-Maintained

ROSSENDALE SPECIAL SCHOOL
Moorside Farm, Bamford Road,
Ramsbottom, Lancashire BL0 0RT
Tel: (01706) 822779
Head: Mr D G Duncan
Type: Co-educational Boarding and
Day
No of pupils: B50 G10
No of Boarders: W15
Special Needs: ADHD ASP DYP EBD
TOU
Approved Independent

ROYAL CROSS PRIMARY SCHOOL
Elswick Road, Ashton-on-Ribble,
Preston, Lancashire PR2 1NT
Tel: (01772) 729705
Head: Mrs R Nottingham
Type: Co-educational Day 4–11
No of pupils: 48
Special Needs: HI SPLD W
Non-Maintained

UNDERLEY GARDEN SCHOOL*
Kirkby Lonsdale, Carnforth,
Lancashire LA6 2DZ
Tel: (01524) 271569
Head: Mrs P Redican
Type: Co-educational Boarding 9–16
No of pupils: B21 G28
No of Boarders: F49
Special Needs: ADD ADHD ASP EBD
MLD SPLD
Approved Independent
52-week care

UNDERLEY HALL SCHOOL*
Kirkby Lonsdale, Carnforth,
Lancashire LA6 2HE
Tel: (01524) 271206
Head: Ms L Rosehr
Type: Boys Boarding 9–16
No of pupils: 70 *No of Boarders:* F70
Special Needs: ADD ADHD EBD MLD
SPLD
Approved Independent
52-week care

LINCOLNSHIRE

KISIMUL SCHOOL*
The Old Vicarage, Swinderby,
Lincoln, Lincolnshire LN6 9LU
Tel: (01522) 868279
Head: Mrs S Shaw
Type: Co-educational Boarding and
Day 10–19
No of pupils: 28 *No of Boarders:* F26
Special Needs: AUT DOW EPI SLD
SP&LD SPLD
Approved Independent

LONDON

BLOSSOM HOUSE SCHOOL*
8 The Drive, Wimbledon, London
SW20 8TG
Tel: (020) 8946 7348
Head: Mrs J Burgess
Type: Co-educational Day 3–12
No of pupils: 90
Special Needs: DYP EBD SP&LD
SPLD
Independent

CENTRE ACADEMY*
92 St John's Hill, Battersea, London
SW11 1SH
Tel: (020) 7738 2344
Head: Mr F J O Regan
Type: Co-educational Day 8–18
No of pupils: B40 G15
Special Needs: ADD ADHD DYC DYS
SP&LD SPLD
Independent

FAIRLEY HOUSE SCHOOL*†
30 Causton Street, London
SW1P 4AU
Tel: (020) 7976 5456
Head: Mrs J Ferman
Type: Co-educational Day 6–12
No of pupils: B69 G27
Special Needs: ADD ADHD DYP DYS
SPLD
Independent

**HOME SCHOOL OF STOKE
NEWINGTON**
46 Alkham Road, London N16 7AA
Tel: (020) 8806 6965
Head: Mrs C Allen
Type: Co-educational Day 11–16
No of pupils: B11 G2
Special Needs: ASP DYC DYP DYS
SPLD
Independent

**HORNSEY CONDUCTIVE
EDUCATION CENTRE**
54 Muswell Hill, London N10 3ST
Tel: (020) 8444 7242
Head: Miss C Hewitt
Type: Co-educational Day 0–7
No of pupils: B15 G10
Special Needs: CP PH
Approved Independent

KISHARON DAY SCHOOL
1011 Finchley Road, London
NW11 7HB
Tel: (020) 8455 7483
Head: Mrs Lehman
Type: Co-educational Day 3–16
(Jewish pupils only)
No of pupils: B14 G13
Special Needs: ADHD ASP AUT CP
DOW EBD MLD SP&LD
Approved Independent

THE MOAT SCHOOL
Bishop's Avenue, Fulham, London
SW6 6ED
Tel: (020) 7610 9018
Head: Mr R M Carlysle
Type: Co-educational Day 11–16
No of pupils: B27 G5
Special Needs: ADD DYC DYP DYS
SPLD
Independent

**THE NEW LEARNING
CENTRE**
211 Sumatra Road, London
NW6 1PF
Tel: (020) 7794 0321
Head: Ms N Janis-Norton
Type: Co-educational Day 6–14
No of pupils: 15
Special Needs: **ADD ADHD** ASP DYC
DYP DYS EBD MLD SPLD
Independent

PARAYHOUSE SCHOOL*
Old Ellerslie Site, South Africa Road,
Shepherds Bush, London W12 7BP
Tel: (020) 8740 6333
Head: Mrs S L Jackson
Type: Co-educational Day 8–16
No of pupils: B27 G3
Special Needs: ADD ADHD ASP CP
DEL DOW DYP EPI HI **MLD**
SP&LD
Independent

**THE SPEECH, LANGUAGE &
HEARING CENTRE**
Christopher Place, Chalton Street,
London NW1 1JF
Tel: (020) 7383 3834
Head: Ms A Harding
Type: Co-educational Day 0–5
No of pupils: 60
Special Needs: DYP HI SP&LD W
Independent

**WILLOUGHBY HALL
DYSLEXIA CENTRE***
1 Willoughby Road, London
NW3 1RP
Tel: (020) 7794 3538
Head: Mr W H Wilcox
Type: Co-educational Day 6–12
No of pupils: B26 G7
Special Needs: **DYS** DYP
Independent

GREATER MANCHESTER

DIDSBURY SCHOOL
611 Wilmslow Road, Didsbury,
Manchester, M20 6AD
Tel: (0161) 448 7022
Head: Mr H Millerman
Type: Co-educational Boarding and
Day
No of pupils: B13 G4
Special Needs: **EBD**
Independent

**THE ST JOHN VIANNEY
SCHOOL (UPPER SCHOOL)**
Rye Bank Road, Firswood, Stretford,
Greater Manchester M16 0EX
Tel: (0161) 881 7843
Head: Mr J Cusick
Type: Co-educational Day 11–16
No of pupils: 96
Special Needs: **MLD**
Non-Maintained

MERSEYSIDE

**BIRKDALE SCHOOL FOR
HEARING IMPAIRED
CHILDREN***
40 Lancaster Road, Birkdale,
Southport, Merseyside PR8 2JY
Tel: (01704) 567220
Head: Mrs A Wood
Type: Co-educational Boarding and
Day 5–19
No of pupils: B21 G23
No of Boarders: F4 W18
Special Needs: ASP DYP DYS **HI** MLD
SP&LD
Non-Maintained

CLARENCE HOUSE SCHOOL
West Lane, Freshfield, Formby,
Merseyside L37 7AZ
Tel: (01704) 872151
Head: Ms M A Bird
Type: Co-educational Boarding and
Day 9–16
No of pupils: B58 G13
No of Boarders: F25
Special Needs: **EBD**
Approved Independent
52-week care

**PETERHOUSE SCHOOL FOR
PUPILS WITH AUTISM**
Preston New Road, Southport,
Merseyside PR9 8PA
Tel: (01704) 506682
Head: Ms B Matthews
Type: Co-educational Boarding and
Day 5–19
No of pupils: B38 G10
No of Boarders: F3 W14
Special Needs: ASP **AUT** W
Approved Independent
52-week care (3 places only)

RNIB SUNSHINE HOUSE SCHOOL
2 Oxford Road, Birkdale, Southport, Merseyside PR8 2JT
Tel: (01704) 567174
Head: Mrs J Bell
Type: Co-educational Boarding and Day 2–11
No of pupils: 18 *No of Boarders:* W8
Special Needs: CP EPI PH PMLD SLD VIS W
Non-Maintained

ROYAL SCHOOL FOR THE BLIND
Church Road North, Wavertree, Liverpool, Merseyside L15 6TQ
Tel: (0151) 733 1012
Head: Mr J P Byrne
Type: Co-educational Boarding and Day 2–19
No of pupils: B39 G17
No of Boarders: W17
Special Needs: EBD HI MLD PH PMLD SLD VIS W
Non-Maintained

ST VINCENT'S SCHOOL*
Yew Tree Lane, West Derby, Liverpool, Merseyside L12 9HN
Tel: (0151) 228 9968
Head: Mr A MacQuarrie
Type: Co-educational Boarding and Day 4–17
No of pupils: B44 G49
Special Needs: ASP CP DEL EPI HI MLD PH SP&LD SPLD VIS W
Non-Maintained

WARGRAVE HOUSE SCHOOL
449 Wargrave Road, Newton-le-Willows, Merseyside WA12 8RS
Tel: (01925) 224899
Head: Mrs P M Maddock
Type: Co-educational Boarding and Day 4–19
No of pupils: 62 *No of Boarders:* W20
Special Needs: ASP AUT
Approved Independent

WEST KIRBY RESIDENTIAL SCHOOL
Meols Drive, West Kirby, Wirral, Merseyside L48 5DH
Tel: (0151) 632 3201
Head: Mr G W Williams
Type: Co-educational Boarding and Day 6–16
No of pupils: B55 G40
No of Boarders: W35
Special Needs: ADD ASP EBD MLD SP&LD TOU
Non-Maintained

MIDDLESEX

PIELD HEATH SCHOOL
Pield Heath Road, Uxbridge, Middlesex UB8 3NW
Tel: (01895) 258507
Head: Sister J Rose
Type: Co-educational Boarding and Day 7–19
No of pupils: B50 G50
No of Boarders: W30
Special Needs: ADD ASP AUT CP DEL DOW DYP EPI MLD PMLD SLD SP&LD SPLD VIS
Non-Maintained

RNIB SUNSHINE HOUSE SCHOOL
33 Dene Road, Northwood, Middlesex HA6 2DD
Tel: (01923) 822538
Acting Head: Mrs L Stewart
Type: Co-educational Boarding and Day 2–11
No of pupils: 50 *No of Boarders:* W12
Special Needs: CP EPI MLD PH PMLD SLD SP&LD TOU VIS W
Non-Maintained

THE SYBIL ELGAR SCHOOL
Havelock Court, Havelock Road, Southall, Middlesex UB2 4NZ
Tel: (020) 8813 9168
Head: Ms C Phillips
Type: Co-educational Boarding and Day 11–19
No of pupils: B76 G10
No of Boarders: W24
Special Needs: AUT SP&LD
Approved Independent

NORFOLK

BANHAM MARSHALLS COLLEGE
Mill Road, Banham, Norwich, Norfolk NR16 2HU
Tel: (01953) 888656
Head: Mr R Wilson
Type: Co-educational Boarding and Day 6–16
No of pupils: B80 G40
No of Boarders: F50 W40
Special Needs: ASP EBD SP&LD SPLD W
Approved Independent

CHURCH HILL SCHOOL
Banham, Norwich, Norfolk NR16 2HN
Tel: (01953) 887815
Head: Mrs H Wilson
Type: Co-educational Boarding 8–16
No of pupils: B7 G1 *No of Boarders:* F8
Special Needs: ASP AUT
Independent

ST ANDREW'S SCHOOL
Lower Common, East Runton, Norfolk NR27 9PG
Tel: (01263) 511727
Head: Ms G Baker
Type: Co-educational Day 6–12
No of pupils: B6 G1
Special Needs: ASP DYP DYS MLD SPLD
Independent

**SHERIDAN HOUSE CHILD &
FAMILY THERAPY UNIT**
Sheridan House, Southburgh,
Thetford, Norfolk IP25 7TJ
Tel: (01953) 850494
Head: Mrs S Sayer
Type: Boys Boarding and Day 10–16
No of pupils: 12 *No of Boarders:* F12
Special Needs: EBD
Approved Independent
52-week care

NORTHAMPTONSHIRE

**POTTERSPURY LODGE
SCHOOL**
Towcester, Northamptonshire
NN12 7LL
Tel: (01908) 542912
Head: Miss G Lietz
Type: Boys Boarding and Day 8–16
No of pupils: 49 *No of Boarders:* F15
W17
Special Needs: ADHD **ASP** DYP **EBD**
TOU
Approved Independent

**RNIB RUSHTON HALL*
SCHOOL**
Rushton, Kettering,
Northamptonshire NN14 1RR
Tel: (01536) 710506
Head: Mrs R Kirkwood
Type: Co-educational Boarding and
Day 4–19
No of pupils: 45 *No of Boarders:* F35
Special Needs: CP EPI MLD PH PMLD
SLD **SP&LD VIS** W
Non-Maintained

THORNBY HALL SCHOOL
Naseby Road, Thornby,
Northamptonshire NN6 8SW
Tel: (01604) 740001
Head: Mrs R Jelly
Type: Co-educational Boarding 13–18
No of pupils: 17 *No of Boarders:* F17
Special Needs: DYS EBD EPI MLD
Independent

NORTHUMBERLAND

**NUNNYKIRK CENTRE FOR
DYSLEXIA†**
Netherwitton, Morpeth,
Northumberland NE61 4PB
Tel: (01670) 772685
Head: Mr S Dalby-Ball
Type: Co-educational Boarding and
Day 7–16
No of pupils: B38 G5
No of Boarders: W20
Special Needs: DYS SPLD
Non-Maintained

NOTTINGHAMSHIRE

I CAN'S DAWN HOUSE SCHOOL*
Helmsley Road, Rainworth,
Mansfield, Nottinghamshire
NG21 0DQ
Tel: (01623) 795361
Head: Mrs M Uden
Type: Co-educational Boarding and
Day 5–16
No of pupils: B59 G18
No of Boarders: W47
Special Needs: **SP&LD** W
Non-Maintained

RUTLAND HOUSE SCHOOL*
1 Elm Bank, Mapperley Road,
Nottingham, Nottinghamshire
NG5 3AJ
Tel: (0115) 962 1315
Head: Mrs C A Oviatt-Ham
Type: Co-educational Boarding and
Day 5–19
No of pupils: B17 G13
No of Boarders: F18 W6
Special Needs: CP EPI HI PH PMLD
SP&LD VIS W
Approved Independent

SUTHERLAND HOUSE SCHOOL (PRIMARY DEPARTMENT)
Sutherland Road, Nottingham,
Nottinghamshire NG3 7AP
Tel: (0115) 987 3375
Head: Mrs M Allen
Type: Co-educational Day 7–11
No of pupils: B25 G5
Special Needs: AUT
Approved Independent

SUTHERLAND HOUSE SCHOOL (SECONDARY DEPARTMENT)
'Westward', 68 Cyprus Road,
Mapperley Park, Nottinghamshire
NG3 5ED
Tel: (0115) 969 1823
Head: Mrs C Byles
Type: Co-educational Day 11–16
No of pupils: 14
Special Needs: AUT
Approved Independent

OXFORDSHIRE

BESSELS LEIGH SCHOOL*
Bessels Leigh, Abingdon,
Oxfordshire OX13 5QB
Tel: (01865) 390436
Head: Mr J Boulton
Type: Boys Boarding 11–16
No of pupils: 38 *No of Boarders:* F38
Special Needs: ADHD DYS EBD SPLD
Non-Maintained
52-week care

BRUERN ABBEY SCHOOL*
Chesterton Manor, Bicester,
Oxfordshire OX26 1UY
Tel: (01869) 242448
Head: Mr S S Stover
Type: Boys Boarding and Day 8–13
No of pupils: 34 *No of Boarders:* F30
Special Needs: DYP **DYS** SP&LD
SPLD
Independent

MULBERRY BUSH SCHOOL*
Abingdon Road, Standlake, Witney,
Oxfordshire OX29 7RW
Tel: (01865) 300202
Head: Mr R R Rollinson
Type: Co-educational Boarding 5–12
No of pupils: B22 G14
No of Boarders: W36
Special Needs: **EBD**
Non-Maintained

PENHURST SCHOOL*
New Street, Chipping Norton,
Oxfordshire OX7 5LN
Tel: (01608) 647020
Head: Mr R Aird
Type: Co-educational Boarding 5–19
No of pupils: 24 *No of Boarders:* F21
Special Needs: CP EPI HI PH PMLD
SP&LD VIS W
Non-Maintained

SWALCLIFFE PARK SCHOOL*
Swalcliffe, Banbury, Oxfordshire
OX15 5EP
Tel: (01295) 780302
Head: Mr R Hooper
Type: Boys Boarding and Day 11–19
No of pupils: 62 *No of Boarders:* F57
Special Needs: ADD ADHD ASP EBD
MLD
Non-Maintained

UNICORN SCHOOL*†
Stroud Court, Oxford Road,
Eynsham, Oxfordshire OX8 1BY
Tel: (01865) 881820
Head: Mrs E Christie
Type: Co-educational Day 6–12
No of pupils: B30 G2
Special Needs: ADD ADHD DYC DYP
DYS SPLD W
Independent

RUTLAND

**THE GRANGE THERAPEUTIC
SCHOOL**
Knossington, Oakham, Rutland
LE15 8LY
Tel: (01664) 454264
Head: Mr D R Lee
Type: Boys Boarding 8–16
No of pupils: 60 *No of Boarders:* F60
Special Needs: **EBD**
Approved Independent

SHROPSHIRE

COTSBROOK COMMUNITY
Higford, Shifnal, Shropshire
TF11 9ET
Tel: (01952) 750 237
Head: Mr J Airth
Type: Co-educational Boarding 11–16
No of pupils: B13 G5
No of Boarders: F18
Special Needs: **EBD**
Approved Independent

CRUCKTON HALL
Cruckton, Shrewsbury, Shropshire
SY5 8PR
Tel: (01743) 860206
Head: Mr P D Mayhew
Type: Boys Boarding 8–19
No of pupils: 68 *No of Boarders:* F68
Special Needs: ADHD ASP AUT DYC
DYP DYS EBD EPI MLD SPLD
Approved Independent
52-week care

ORCHARD SCHOOL
Near Middleton, Shropshire
SY21 8EW
Tel: (01743) 884145
Head: Mr J W Kwaterski
Type: Co-educational Boarding 11–19
No of pupils: B6 G2 *No of Boarders:* F8
Special Needs: AUT DOW EBD EPI
PH SLD W
Independent
52-week care

OVERLEY HALL SCHOOL
Wellington, Telford, Shropshire
TF6 5HE
Tel: (01952) 740262
Head: Mr S West
Type: Co-educational Boarding 9–19
No of pupils: B14 G4
Special Needs: ADD ADHD ASP **AUT**
DOW DYC DYP DYS EBD **EPI** MLD
SLD SP&LD TOU
Independent

**RNIB CONDOVER HALL
SCHOOL***
Condover, nr Shrewsbury,
Shropshire SY5 7AH
Tel: (01743) 872320
Head: Dr A Best
Type: Co-educational Boarding and
Day 5–19
No of pupils: 60
Special Needs: MLD PMLD SLD
VIS W
Non-Maintained

SOMERSET

EDINGTON AND SHAPWICK SCHOOL†
Shapwick Manor, Shapwick,
Bridgwater, Somerset TA9 9NJ
Tel: (01278) 722012
Head: Mr D C Walker and J P
Whittock
Type: Co-educational Boarding and
Day 8–18
No of pupils: B132 G39
No of Boarders: F115 W15
Special Needs: DYC DYP **DYS** SPLD
Approved Independent

THE MARCHANT-HOLLIDAY SCHOOL*
North Cheriton, Templecombe,
Somerset BA8 0AH
Tel: (01963) 33234
Head: Mr J M Robertson
Type: Boys Boarding and Day 7–12
No of pupils: 38 *No of Boarders:* F33
Special Needs: ADD ADHD ASP DYS
EBD SPLD
Approved Independent

MARK COLLEGE*†
Blackford Road, Mark, Highbridge,
Somerset TA9 4NP
Tel: (01278) 641632
Head: Dr S J Chinn
Type: Boys Boarding and Day 10–16
No of pupils: 80 *No of Boarders:* F60
Special Needs: DYC DYP **DYS**
Approved Independent

NORTH EAST SOMERSET

FARLEIGH COLLEGE
Newbury Manor, Farleigh
Hungerford, Bath, North East
Somerset BA2 7RW
Tel: (01373) 814980
Head: Mr S W Bradshaw
Type: Co-educational Boarding and
Day 11–18
No of pupils: B56 G10
Special Needs: **ASP**
Independent

STAFFORDSHIRE

BLADON HOUSE SCHOOL*
Newton Solney, Burton upon Trent,
Staffordshire DE15 0TA
Tel: (01283) 563787
Head: Mrs B Murfin
Type: Co-educational Boarding and
Day 5–19
No of pupils: B80 G34
Special Needs: MLD SLD SP&LD
Approved Independent
52-week care

LONGDON HALL*
Longdon Green, Rugeley,
Staffordshire WS15 4PT
Tel: (01543) 490634
Head: Mrs C Georgeson
Type: Co-educational Boarding and
Day 5–19
No of pupils: 110 *No of Boarders:* F98
Special Needs: **AUT**
Independent
52-week care

HONORMEAD SCHOOL FOR CHILDREN WITH AUTISM*
Blithbury Road, Blithbury, Rugeley,
Staffordshire WS15 3JQ
Tel: (01889) 504400
Type: Co-educational Boarding and
Day 3–19
No of pupils: 110 *No of Boarders:* F98
Special Needs: **AUT**
Independent

MAPLE HAYES HALL DYSLEXIA SCHOOL*
Abnalls Lane, Lichfield, Staffordshire
WS13 8BL
Tel: (01543) 264387
Head: Dr E Neville Brown
Type: Co-educational Boarding and
Day 7–17 (Girls day only)
No of pupils: 120 *No of Boarders:* F22
W29
Special Needs: DYP **DYS** SPLD
Approved Independent

WESTWOOD*
Blithbury, Rugeley, Staffordshire
WS15 3JQ
Tel: (01889) 504353
Head: Miss S Hodge
Type: Co-educational Boarding and
Day 5–19
No of pupils: 57 *No of Boarders:* F56
Special Needs: AUT SLD
Approved Independent
52-week care

SUFFOLK

BRAMFIELD HOUSE
Walpole Road, Bramfield,
Halesworth, Suffolk IP19 9AB
Tel: (01986) 784235
Head: Mr M G Read
Type: Boys Boarding and Day 10–16
No of pupils: 40 *No of Boarders:* F35
Special Needs: EBD MLD
Approved Independent

**THE OLD RECTORY
SCHOOL**†
Brettenham, Ipswich, Suffolk
IP7 7QR
Tel: (01449) 736404
Head: Miss A Furlong
Type: Co-educational Boarding and
Day 7–13
No of pupils: B40 G10
No of Boarders: W39
Special Needs: **DYS**
Independent

THE RYES SCHOOL
Little Henny, Sudbury, Suffolk
CO10 7EA
Tel: (01787) 374998
Head: Mrs R Stamp
Type: Co-educational Boarding and
Day 7–16
No of pupils: B15 G10
Special Needs: AUT **EBD** MLD SLD
Approved Independent

SURREY

**GRAFHAM GRANGE
SCHOOL***
Grafham, Nr Bramley, Guildford,
Surrey GU5 0LH
Tel: (01483) 892214
Head: Mr R Norman
Type: Boys Boarding 10–16
No of pupils: 40
Special Needs: **EBD**
Non-Maintained

I CAN'S MEATH SCHOOL*
Brox Road, Ottershaw, Surrey
KT16 0LF
Tel: (01932) 872302
Head: Mr J Parrott
Type: Co-educational Boarding and
Day 5–12
No of pupils: B60 G15
Special Needs: **SP&LD**
Non-Maintained

THE KNOWL HILL SCHOOL†
School Lane, Pirbright, Surrey
GU24 0JN
Tel: (01483) 797032
Head: Mrs A J Bareford
Type: Co-educational Day 7–16
No of pupils: B38 G7
Special Needs: DYC DYP **DYS** SP&LD
SPLD
Approved Independent

THE LINK PRIMARY SCHOOL
138 Croydon Road, Beddington,
Croydon, Surrey CR0 4PG
Tel: (020) 8688 5239
Head: Mr G Stewart
Type: Co-educational Day 6–12
No of pupils: B27 G10
Special Needs: ASP AUT SP&LD
SPLD
Approved Independent

**THE LINK SECONDARY
SCHOOL**
82–86 Croydon Road, Beddington,
Surrey CR0 4PD
Tel: (020) 8688 7691
Head: Mr W E Fuller
Type: Co-educational Day Boys 11–16
Girls 8–16
No of pupils: B28 G9
Special Needs: MLD SP&LD
Approved Independent

MOON HALL SCHOOL*†
'Feldemore', Pasture Wood Lane,
Holmbury St Mary, Dorking, Surrey
RH5 6LQ
Tel: (01306) 731464
Head: Mrs J Lovett
Type: Co-educational Boarding and
Day 7–13
No of pupils: B66 G15
No of Boarders: W17
Special Needs: DYS SPLD
Independent

MOOR HOUSE SCHOOL
Hurst Green, Oxted, Surrey RH8 9AQ
Tel: (01883) 712271
Head: Mr A A Robertson
Type: Co-educational Boarding 7–16
No of pupils: B64 G20
No of Boarders: F84
Special Needs: DYC DYP DYS **SP&LD**
Non-Maintained

MORE HOUSE SCHOOL†
Moons Hill, Frensham, Farnham,
Surrey GU10 3AW
Tel: (01252) 792303
Head: Mr B G Huggett
Type: Boys Boarding and Day 9–16
No of pupils: 170 *No of Boarders:* F14
W40
Special Needs: DYS SPLD
Approved Independent

RUTHERFORD SCHOOL
1A Melville Avenue, South Croydon,
Surrey CR2 7HZ
Tel: (020) 8688 7560
Head: Mrs R G Hills
Type: Co-educational Day 2–12
No of pupils: 24
Special Needs: CP EPI HI PH PMLD
SLD VIS W
Approved Independent

ST DOMINIC'S SCHOOL*
Hambledon, Godalming, Surrey
GU8 4DX
Tel: (01428) 684693
Head: Mr I Leary
Type: Co-educational Boarding and
Day 7–16
No of pupils: B93 G11
No of Boarders: W78
Special Needs: ADD ADHD ASP DEL
DYC DYP DYS EPI SP&LD SPLD
Non-Maintained

ST JOSEPH'S SCHOOL
Amlets Lane, Cranleigh, Surrey
GU6 7DH
Tel: (01483) 272449
Head: Mr A Lowry
Type: Co-educational Boarding and
Day 7–19
No of pupils: B50 G20
No of Boarders: F40
Special Needs: AUT DOW DYC DYP
DYS MLD SLD SP&LD
Non-Maintained

ST MARGARET'S SCHOOL*
Tadworth Court, Tadworth, Surrey
KT20 5RU
Tel: (01737) 365810
Head: Mrs J Cunningham
Type: Co-educational Boarding and
Day 8–19
No of pupils: 37 *No of Boarders:* F30
Special Needs: CP EPI HI **PMLD**
VIS W
Approved Independent

ST PIERS*
St Piers Lane, Lingfield, Surrey
RH7 6PW
Tel: (01342) 832243
Head: Mr R S Haughton
Type: Co-educational Boarding and
Day 5–19
No of pupils: 207 *No of Boarders:* F185
Special Needs: **EPI** MLD SLD SP&LD
Non-Maintained

EAST SUSSEX

CHAILEY HERITAGE SCHOOL*
Haywards Heath Road, North
Chailey, East Sussex BN8 4EF
Tel: (01825) 724444
Head: Mr A C Bruce
Type: Co-educational Boarding and
Day 3–19
No of pupils: 100 *No of Boarders:* W27
Special Needs: CP MLD **PH** SLD
SP&LD VIS W
Non-Maintained

CORNERSTONES INDEPENDENT SCHOOL
110 Western Road, Brighton, East
Sussex BN1 2AA
Tel: (01273) 734164
Head: Ms M Rees
Type: Co-educational Day 7–16
No of pupils: 12
Special Needs: **EBD**
Independent

FREWEN COLLEGE*†
Brickwall, Northiam, Rye, East
Sussex TN31 6NL
Tel: (01797) 252494
Head: Mr S Horsley
Type: Boys Boarding and Day 9–17
No of pupils: 77 *No of Boarders:* W42
Special Needs: DYP **DYS**
Approved Independent

HAMILTON LODGE SCHOOL FOR DEAF CHILDREN
Walpole Road, Brighton, East Sussex
BN2 2ET
Tel: (01273) 682362
Head: Mrs A K Duffy
Type: Co-educational Boarding and
Day 5–18
No of pupils: 79 *No of Boarders:* W60
Special Needs: HI
Non-Maintained

KINGS MANOR EDUCATION CENTRE
Southdown Road, Seaford, East
Sussex BN25 4JS
Tel: (01323) 873400
Head: Mrs N Newman
Type: Co-educational Boarding 11–16
No of pupils: 42 *No of Boarders:* W6
Special Needs: **ADD** ADHD DEL **DYP**
DYS EBD EPI MLD PH
Independent

NORTHEASE MANOR†
Rodmell, Lewes, East Sussex
BN7 3EY
Tel: (01273) 472915
Head: Mr R J Dennien
Type: Co-educational Boarding and
Day 10–17
No of pupils: B68 G21
No of Boarders: W57
Special Needs: DYP DYS SPLD
Approved Independent

OVINGDEAN HALL SCHOOL
Greenways, Brighton, East Sussex
BN2 7BJ
Tel: (01273) 301929
Head: Mr M Bown
Type: Co-educational Boarding and
Day 10–19
No of pupils: B85 G50
No of Boarders: W115
Special Needs: ADHD CP DYS **HI**
MLD SP&LD SPLD VIS
Non-Maintained

OWLSWICK SCHOOL
Newhaven Road, Kingston, Lewes,
East Sussex BN7 3NF
Tel: (01273) 473078
Head: Mr & Mrs A K Harper
Type: Co-educational Boarding 10–18
No of pupils: B7 G4 *No of Boarders:* F11
Special Needs: ADD DYS EBD MLD
Approved Independent
52-week care

ST JOHN'S COLLEGE
Walpole Road, Brighton, East Sussex
BN2 2AF
Tel: (01273) 244000
Head: Mr M C Hudson
Type: Co-educational Boarding and
Day 6–19
No of pupils: 155 *No of Boarders:* F100
Special Needs: ADD ADHD ASP AUT
DOW EPI **MLD SLD** SP&LD
Independent

ST MARY'S SCHOOL*
Wrestwood Road, Bexhill-on-Sea,
East Sussex TN40 2LU
Tel: (01424) 730740
Head: Mr D Cassar
Type: Co-educational Boarding and
Day 7–19
No of pupils: 138 *No of Boarders:* F118
Special Needs: ASP AUT CP DEL
DOW DYP DYS EPI HI **MLD** PH
SP&LD SPLD TOU VIS W
Approved Independent

WEST SUSSEX

FARNEY CLOSE SCHOOL
Bolney Court, Bolney, Haywards
Heath, West Sussex RH17 5RD
Tel: (01444) 881811
Head: Mr B Robinson
Type: Co-educational Boarding and
Day 11–16
No of pupils: B53 G25
Special Needs: **EBD** SPLD
Independent

I CAN'S JOHN HORNIMAN
SCHOOL*
2 Park Road, Worthing, West Sussex
BN11 2AS
Tel: (01903) 200317
Head: Ms J Dunn
Type: Co-educational Boarding and
Day 4–11
No of pupils: B26 G6
No of Boarders: W14
Special Needs: **SP&LD**
Non-Maintained

INGFIELD MANOR SCHOOL*
Five Oaks, Billingshurst, West
Sussex RH14 9AX
Tel: (01403) 782294
Head: Mr C Jay
Type: Co-educational Boarding and
Day 3–11
No of pupils: 41 *No of Boarders:* W12
Special Needs: **CP**
Approved Independent

MUNTHAM HOUSE SCHOOL
Barns Green, Horsham, West Sussex
RH13 7NJ
Tel: (01403) 730302
Head: Mr R Boyle
Type: Boys Boarding 8–18
No of pupils: 56 *No of Boarders:* F48
Special Needs: ADD ADHD DYS EBD
Non-Maintained

PHILPOTS MANOR SCHOOL*
West Hoathly, East Grinstead, West
Sussex RH19 4PR
Tel: (01342) 811382
Head: Mrs S A Merrifield
Type: Co-educational Boarding and
Day 6–19
No of pupils: B45 G15
No of Boarders: F52
Special Needs: ADD ADHD ASP AUT
CP DEL DOW DYC DYP DYS EBD
EPI HI MLD SP&LD TOU
Approved Independent
52-week care

TYNE AND WEAR

NORTHERN COUNTIES
SCHOOL FOR THE DEAF
Great North Road, Newcastle-Upon-
Tyne, Tyne and Wear NE2 3BB
Tel: (0191) 281 5821
Head: Mr K J Lewis
Type: Co-educational Boarding and
Day 3–19
No of pupils: B56 G33
No of Boarders: W17
Special Needs: **HI** PH **PMLD VIS W**
Non-Maintained

PERCY HEDLEY SCHOOL
Station Road, Forest Hall,
Newcastle-upon-Tyne, Tyne and
Wear NE12 8YY
Tel: (0191) 266 5451
Head: Mr N Stromsoy
Type: Co-educational Boarding and
Day 3–18
No of pupils: B110 G54
No of Boarders: W18
Special Needs: CP SP&LD W
Non-Maintained

TALBOT HOUSE
INDEPENDENT SPECIAL
SCHOOL
Hexham Road, Walbottle,
Newcastle-upon-Tyne, Tyne and
Wear NE15 8HW
Tel: (0191) 229 0111
Head: Mr A P James
Type: Co-educational Day 11–16
No of pupils: 40
Special Needs: **EBD**
Approved Independent

THORNHILL PARK SCHOOL
21 Thornhill Park, Sunderland, Tyne
and Wear SR2 7LA
Tel: (0191) 514 0659
Head: Mr D Walke
Type: Co-educational Boarding and
Day 2–19
No of pupils: 87 *No of Boarders:* F44
Special Needs: ASP AUT
Approved Independent

WEST MIDLANDS

NATIONAL INSTITUTE OF CONDUCTIVE EDUCATION
Cannon Hill House, Russell Road, Moseley, Birmingham, West Midlands B13 8RD
Tel: (0121) 449 1569
Head: Mr C McGuigan
Type: Co-educational Day 1–11
No of pupils: 40
Special Needs: CP DYP PH W
Independent

SUNFIELD*
Clent Grove, Woodman Lane, Clent, Stourbridge, West Midlands DY9 9PB
Tel: (01562) 882253
Head: Professor B R Carpenter
Type: Co-educational Boarding 6–19
No of pupils: B60 G15
No of Boarders: F70
Special Needs: ADD ADHD ASP AUT DOW EBD PMLD SLD
Approved Independent
52-week care

WILTSHIRE

APPLEFORD SCHOOL†
Shrewton, Salisbury, Wiltshire SP3 4HL
Tel: (01980) 621020
Head: Mr P Stanley
Type: Co-educational Boarding and Day 7–13
No of pupils: B71 G18
No of Boarders: F59
Special Needs: ADD ADHD DYC DYP DYS SP&LD SPLD
Approved Independent

BELMONT SCHOOL
School Walk, Bedwin Street, Salisbury, Wiltshire
Tel: (01722) 421115
Head: Mr A E Thomas
Type: Co-educational Day
No of pupils: 25
Special Needs: **EBD**
Independent
52-week care

BURTON HILL SCHOOL
Malmesbury, Wiltshire SN16 0EG
Tel: (01666) 822685
Head: Mr P Drake
Type: Co-educational Boarding and Day 8–19
No of pupils: B22 G11
No of Boarders: F15 W7
Special Needs: CP MLD **PH** SLD W
Non-Maintained

CALDER HOUSE SCHOOL†
Thickwood Lane, Colerne, Chippenham, Wiltshire SN14 8BN
Tel: (01225) 742329
Head: Mrs S Agombar
Type: Co-educational Day 5–13
No of pupils: B23 G8
Special Needs: DEL DYC **DYP DYS** SPLD
Approved Independent

WORCESTERSHIRE

RNIB NEW COLLEGE
Whittington Road, Worcester, Worcestershire WR5 2JX
Tel: (01905) 763933
Head: Mr N Ratcliffe
Type: Co-educational Boarding and Day 11–19
No of pupils: 100 *No of Boarders:* F95 W4
Special Needs: **VIS** W
Non-Maintained

NORTH YORKSHIRE

BRECKENBROUGH SCHOOL*
Thirsk, North Yorkshire YO7 4EN
Tel: (01845) 587238
Head: Mr T G Bennett
Type: Boys Boarding and Day 9–17
No of pupils: 42 *No of Boarders:* F16
Special Needs: ADD ADHD ASP DEL
DYS EBD
Independent

**SPRING HILL SCHOOL
(BARNARDO'S)***
Palace Road, Ripon, North Yorkshire
HG4 3HN
Tel: (01765) 603320
Head: Mrs J E Clarke
Type: Co-educational Boarding and
Day 10–19
No of pupils: B21 G10
No of Boarders: F37
Special Needs: ADD ASP AUT CP DEL
DOW EBD EPI MLD SLD
Non-Maintained

SOUTH YORKSHIRE

FULLERTON HOUSE SCHOOL
off Tickhill Square, Denaby,
Doncaster, South Yorkshire
DN12 4AR
Tel: (01709) 861663
Head: Mr P Champion
Type: Co-educational Boarding 8–19
No of pupils: B27 G9
No of Boarders: F36
Special Needs: AUT EPI SLD SP&LD
Approved Independent
52-week care

**THE ROBERT OGDEN
SCHOOL**
Clayton Lane, Thurnscoe,
Rotherham, South Yorkshire S63 0BE
Tel: (01709) 874443
Head: Mrs A Hull
Type: Co-educational Boarding and
Day 4–19
No of pupils: 132 *No of Boarders:* F40
Special Needs: ASP AUT MLD SLD
Approved Independent

WILSIC HALL SCHOOL
Wadworth, Doncaster, South
Yorkshire DN11 9AG
Tel: (01302) 856382
Head: Mr M V Henderson
Type: Co-educational Boarding and
Day 9–19
No of pupils: 33 *No of Boarders:* F33
Special Needs: **AUT** DOW SLD
SP&LD SPLD
Independent
52-week care

**YORKSHIRE RESIDENTIAL
SCHOOL FOR THE DEAF***
Leger Way, Doncaster, South
Yorkshire DN2 6AY
Tel: (01302) 386700
Head: Mr H Heard
Type: Co-educational Boarding and
Day 5–16
No of pupils: B35 G25
No of Boarders: F4 W14
Special Needs: ASP CP DYC DYP DYS
EBD **HI** MLD PH SP&LD SPLD VIS
Non-Maintained

WEST YORKSHIRE

HOLLY BANK SCHOOL
Roe Head, Far Common Road,
Mirfield, West Yorkshire WF14 0DQ
Tel: (01924) 490833
Head: Mrs S Garland-Grimes
Type: Co-educational Boarding and
Day 5–19
No of pupils: B34 G22
No of Boarders: F25 W18
Special Needs: CP EPI MLD **PH PMLD
SLD** SP&LD W
Non-Maintained

**ST JOHN'S CATHOLIC
SCHOOL FOR THE DEAF***
Church Street, Boston Spa,
Wetherby, West Yorkshire LS23 6DF
Tel: (01937) 842144
Head: Mr T M Wrynne
Type: Co-educational Boarding and
Day 3–19
No of pupils: B34 G49
No of Boarders: F15 W51
Special Needs: DYP **HI** SP&LD W
Non-Maintained

**WILLIAM HENRY SMITH
SCHOOL**
Boothroyd, Brighouse, West
Yorkshire HD6 3JW
Tel: (01484) 710123
Head: Mr B J Heneghan
Type: Boys Boarding and Day 8–16
No of pupils: 64 *No of Boarders:* W56
Special Needs: **EBD**
Non-Maintained

NORTHERN IRELAND

COUNTY ANTRIM

JORDANSTOWN SCHOOLS
85 Jordanstown Road,
Newtownabbey, County Antrim
BT37 0QE
Tel: (028) 9086 3541
Head: Mr S L Clarke
Type: Co-educational Boarding and
Day 4–19
No of pupils: B59 G58
No of Boarders: W10
Special Needs: HI VIS W
Non-Maintained

SCOTLAND

ABERDEENSHIRE

THE CAMPHILL RUDOLF STEINER SCHOOLS
Central Office, Murtle Estate,
Bieldside, Aberdeenshire AB14 9EP
Tel: (01224) 867935
Head: Mr E Billet
Type: Co-educational Boarding and
Day 3–19
No of pupils: B61 G34
No of Boarders: F75 W10
Special Needs: ADD ADHD ASP AUT
CP DEL DOW DYP DYS EBD EPI HI
MLD PH PMLD SLD SP&LD SPLD
TOU VIS W
Independent
52-week care

LINN MOOR RESIDENTIAL SCHOOL
Peterculter, Aberdeen,
Aberdeenshire AB14 0PJ
Tel: (01224) 732246
Head: Mr J Davidson
Type: Co-educational Boarding 5–18
No of pupils: 30
Special Needs: ADHD AUT EBD MLD
PMLD SLD VIS
Independent
52-week care

OAKBANK SCHOOL*
Midstocket Road, Aberdeen,
Aberdeenshire AB15 5XP
Tel: (01224) 313347
Head: Mrs J C Arrowsmith
Type: Co-educational Boarding and
Day 12–18
No of pupils: B31 G10
No of Boarders: F41
Special Needs: ADHD **EBD**
Independent
52-week care

EAST AYRSHIRE

DALDORCH HOUSE SCHOOL
Thorn Road, Catrine, East Ayrshire
KA5 6NE
Tel: (01290) 551666
Head: Mrs S Pinkerton
Type: Co-educational Boarding and
Day 5–19
No of pupils: 40
Special Needs: **AUT**
Independent
52-week care

NORTH AYRSHIRE

GEILSLAND SCHOOL
Beith, North Ayrshire KA15 1HD
Tel: (01505) 504044
Head: Mr R Mair
Type: Boys Boarding and Day 15–18
No of pupils: 36 *No of Boarders:* F36
Special Needs: **EBD**
Independent

SEAFIELDS SCHOOL
86 Eglington Road, Ardrossan,
North Ayrshire KA22 8NL
Tel: (01294) 470355
Head: Mrs M Moran
Type: Co-educational Boarding and
Day 5–16
No of pupils: B63 *No of Boarders:* F28
Special Needs: **EBD**
Independent
52-week care

SOUTH AYRSHIRE

RED BRAE SCHOOL
24 Alloway Road, Maybole, South
Ayrshire KA19 8AA
Tel: (01655) 883104
Head: Dr R J Dalrymple
Type: Boys Day 12–16
No of pupils: 30
Special Needs: **EBD**
Independent
52-week care

CLACKMANNANSHIRE

STRUAN HOUSE SCHOOL
27 Claremont, Alloa,
Clackmannanshire FK10 2DF
Tel: (01259) 213435
Head: Mr J Taylor
Type: Co-educational Boarding and
Day 5–16
No of pupils: 30 *No of Boarders:* W22
Special Needs: **AUT**
Independent

DUMFRIES & GALLOWAY

WOODLANDS SCHOOL
Corsbie Road, Newton Stewart,
Dumfries & Galloway DG8 6JB
Tel: (01671) 402480
Head: Mr J White
Type: Boys Boarding 7–17
No of pupils: 24 *No of Boarders:* F24
Special Needs: ADD ADHD EBD MLD
SP&LD SPLD
Independent
52-week care

FIFE

HILLSIDE SCHOOL
Hillside, Aberdour, Fife KY3 0RH
Tel: (01383) 860731
Head: Mrs A Harvey
Type: Boys Boarding 11–16
No of pupils: 42 *No of Boarders:* F42
Special Needs: ADD ADHD DEL EBD
MLD SPLD
Independent

STARLEY HALL
Aberdour Road, Burntisland, Fife
KY3 0AG
Tel: (01383) 860314
Head: Mr A Pyle
Type: Co-educational Boarding and
Day 11–16
No of pupils: 44 *No of Boarders:* F32
W32
Special Needs: ADD ADHD ASP EBD
TOU
Independent
52-week care

GLASGOW

ST FRANCIS DAY BOY UNIT
1190 Edinburgh Road, Shettleston,
Glasgow G33 4EH
Tel: (0141) 774 4499
Head: Mrs L Johnson
Type: Boys Day 14–16
No of pupils: 34
Special Needs: EBD MLD
Independent

SPRINGBOIG ST JOHN'S
1190 Edinburgh Road, Glasgow
G2 6AH
Tel: (0141) 774 9791
Head: Mr W Fitzgerald
Type: Boys Boarding
No of pupils: 36 *No of Boarders:* F36
Special Needs: EBD MLD
Independent

HIGHLAND

RADDERY SCHOOL
Fortrose, Highland IV10 8SN
Tel: (01381) 620271
Head: Mr G Hurt
Type: Boys Boarding and Day
No of pupils: 28 *No of Boarders:* W22
Special Needs: ADD ADHD DYS **EBD**
Independent

NORTH LANARKSHIRE

ST PHILLIP'S SCHOOL
Plains, Airdrie, North Lanarkshire
ML6 7SF
Tel: (01236) 765407
Head: Mr P Hanrahan
Type: Boys Boarding and Day 10–16
No of pupils: 60 *No of Boarders:* F36
Special Needs: ADD ADHD **EBD** MLD
Independent
52-week care

SOUTH LANARKSHIRE

**STANMORE HOUSE
RESIDENTIAL SCHOOL**
Lanark, South Lanarkshire
ML11 7RR
Tel: (01555) 665041
Head: Mrs P Donnelly
Type: Co-educational Boarding and
Day 2–18
No of pupils: 76 *No of Boarders:* F31
Special Needs: **CP** EPI HI PH **PMLD**
SLD SP&LD VIS
Grant Aided

LOTHIAN

HARMENY SCHOOL
Balerno, Lothian EH14 7JY
Tel: (0131) 449 3938
Head: Mr P Webb
Type: Co-educational Boarding 6–13
No of pupils: 36 *No of Boarders:* F7
W24
Special Needs: ADD ADHD ASP DYS
EBD MLD SP&LD SPLD W
Independent
52-week care

MOORE HOUSE SCHOOL
Edinburgh Road, Bathgate, Lothian
EH48 1BX
Tel: (01506) 652312
Head: Mrs A Smith
Type: Co-educational Boarding
No of pupils: B20 G11
No of Boarders: F31
Special Needs: **EBD**
Independent
52-week care

ROYAL BLIND SCHOOL*
Craigmillar Park, Edinburgh,
Lothian EH16 5NA
Tel: (0131) 667 1100
Head: Mr K Tansley
Type: Co-educational Boarding and
Day 3–19
No of pupils: B60 G58
No of Boarders: W72
Special Needs: AUT CP EPI MLD
PMLD SLD SP&LD TOU **VIS** W
Grant Aided

PERTHSHIRE

**OCHIL TOWER (RUDOLF
STEINER) SCHOOL**
140 High Street, Auchterarder,
Perthshire PH3 1AD
Tel: (01764) 662416
Head: Mr U Ruprecht
Type: Co-educational Boarding and
Day 6–18
No of pupils: B25 G10
No of Boarders: W26
Special Needs: ASP AUT DEL EBD EPI
MLD PMLD SLD
Independent

PERTH AND KINROSS

BALNACRAIG SCHOOL
Fairmount Terrace, Perth, Perth and
Kinross PH2 7AR
Tel: (01738) 636456
Head: Mr E G Matthew
Type: Co-educational Boarding 12–16
No of pupils: B12 G12
No of Boarders: F24
Special Needs: **EBD**
Independent
52-week care

SEAMAB HOUSE SCHOOL
Rumbling Bridge, Kinross, Perth and
Kinross KY13 0PT
Tel: (01577) 840307
Head: Mrs A W Anderson
Type: Co-educational Boarding 7–12
No of pupils: 14 *No of Boarders:* W12
Special Needs: **EBD**
Independent

RENFREWSHIRE

GOOD SHEPHERD CENTRE
Greenock Road, Bishopton,
Renfrewshire PA7 5PF
Tel: (01505) 862814
Head: Mr F McCann
Type: Girls Boarding and Day 12–16
No of pupils: 59 *No of Boarders:* F30
Special Needs: **EBD** MLD
Independent

KIBBLE SCHOOL
Goudie Street, Paisley, Renfrewshire
PA3 2LG
Tel: (0141) 889 0044
Head: Mr G Bell
Type: Boys Boarding and Day 12–17
No of pupils: 84 *No of Boarders:* F50
Special Needs: **EBD MLD** PMLD
SP&LD SPLD
Independent

STIRLING

**BALLIKINRAIN RESIDENTIAL
SCHOOL**
Fintry Road, Balfron-by-Glasgow,
Stirling G63 0LL
Tel: (01360) 440244
Head: Mr C McKnott
Type: Boys Boarding and Day 8–16
No of pupils: 36 *No of Boarders:* F30
Special Needs: **EBD**
Independent
52-week care

**BARNARDO'S LECROPT
PROJECT**
Henderson Street, Bridge of Allan,
Stirling FK9 4NB
Tel: (01786) 834498
Head: Mr H Jones
Type: Co-educational Day 6–12
No of pupils: 18
Special Needs: ADHD EBD SP&LD
SPLD W
Independent

SNOWDON SCHOOL
31 Spittal Street, Stirling FK8 1DU
Tel: (01786) 464746
Head: Mr G Matthews
Type: Girls Boarding 12+
No of pupils: 18 *No of Boarders:* F18
Special Needs: **EBD** W
Independent
52-week care

STRATHCLYDE

CORSEFORD SCHOOL
Howood Road, Milliken Park,
Kilbarchan, Strathclyde PA10 2NT
Tel: (01505) 702141
Head: Mrs M Boyle
Type: Co-educational Day and
Boarding 0–19
No of pupils: 65 *No of Boarders:* F9
W21
Special Needs: **PH**
Independent

WALES

CARDIFF

CRAIG-Y-PARC SCHOOL*
Pentyrch, Cardiff CF15 9NB
Tel: (029) 2089 0397
Head: Mr N Harvey
Type: Co-educational Boarding and
Day 4–19
No of pupils: 52 *No of Boarders:* F9 W9
Special Needs: CP **PH PMLD**
SP&LD W
Independent

GWYNEDD

ARAN HALL SCHOOL*
Rhydymain, Dolgellau, Gwynedd
LL40 2AR
Tel: (01341) 450641
Head: Mr M Ferguson
Type: Co-educational Boarding 11–19
No of pupils: B19 G6
No of Boarders: F25
Special Needs: ADD ADHD ASP AUT
EPI **TOU**
Independent
52-week care

PEMBROKESHIRE

PORTFIELD SCHOOL
Portfield, Haverfordwest,
Pembrokeshire SA61 1BS
Tel: (01437) 762701
Head: Mr P Brayshaw
Type: Co-educational Day 2–19
No of pupils: 65
Special Needs: AUT CP EPI MLD
PMLD SLD SP&LD **VIS** W
Approved Independent

POWYS

**MACINTYRE SCHOOL
WOMASTON***
Womaston House, Walton,
Presteigne, Powys LD8 2PT
Tel: (01544) 230308
Head: Mr M J Bertulis
Type: Co-educational Boarding 11–19
No of pupils: B13 G3
No of Boarders: F16
Special Needs: AUT EBD EPI MLD
PMLD SLD
Approved Independent

VALE OF GLAMORGAN

**NCH ACTION FOR
CHILDREN**
Headlands School, 2 St Augustines
Road, Penarth, Vale of Glamorgan
CF64 1YY
Tel: (029) 2070 9771
Head: Mr P Carradice
Type: Co-educational Boarding and
Day 11–16
No of pupils: 30 *No of Boarders:* F24
Special Needs: ADD ADHD ASP DYP
DYS EBD EPI MLD SPLD TOU
Independent

2.2
Directory of Colleges and Other Provision at 16+

ENGLAND

BRISTOL

CINTRE COMMUNITY
54 St John's Road, Clifton, Bristol
BS8 2HG
Tel: (0117) 973 8546
Head: Ms C Twine
Type: Mixed Residential 16–35
No of pupils: B14 G7
No of Boarders: F13
Special Needs: AUT DOW DYS EBD
EPI MLD
Independent
52-week care

CAMBRIDGESHIRE

THE PAPWORTH TRUST*
Papworth Everard, Cambridge,
Cambridgeshire CB3 8RG
Tel: (01480) 830341
Head: Mr J Skipp
Type: Mixed Residential 19+
No of pupils: 120 *No of Boarders:* F110
Special Needs: CP DOW EPI MLD
PH W

SENSE EAST
72 Church Street, Market Deeping,
Peterborough, Cambridgeshire
PE6 8AL
Tel: (01778) 344921
Head: Mrs J McNeill
Type: Mixed Residential 16+
No of pupils: B45 G35
No of Boarders: F80
Special Needs: CP EBD EPI **HI** MLD
PH SLD **VIS** W
52-week care

CHESHIRE

BRIDGE COLLEGE
Curzon Road, Offerton, Stockport,
Cheshire SK2 5DG
Tel: (0161) 487 4293
Head: Mrs S Preece
Type: Mixed Day
No of pupils: B28 G25
Special Needs: CP DOW EPI MLD PH
PMLD SLD SP&LD W

CORNWALL

PEREDUR TRUST
Altarnun, Launceston, Cornwall
PL15 7RF
Tel: (01566) 86575
Head: Mr S W Rudel and Mrs J Rudel
Type: Male Residential 19+
No of pupils: 11 *No of Boarders:* F11
Special Needs: AUT EBD

CUMBRIA

LINDETH COLLEGE OF
FURTHER EDUCATION*
The Oaks, Lindeth, Bowness-on-
Windermere, Cumbria LA23 3NH
Tel: (01539) 446265
Head: Mrs N S Buckley
Type: Mixed Residential 16–25
No of pupils: 44 *No of Boarders:* F44
Special Needs: ADD ADHD ASP AUT
DOW DYS EPI HI **MLD** SP&LD
SPLD

DERBYSHIRE

DERBY COLLEGE FOR DEAF
PEOPLE
Ashbourne Road, Derby, Derbyshire
DE22 3BH
Tel: (01332) 297550
Head: Ms B Mullen
Type: Mixed Residential 16–25
No of pupils: B60 G40
No of Boarders: F94
Special Needs: **HI** MLD PH SLD SPLD
VIS W
Non-Maintained

GREEN LAUND F.E. CENTRE*
The Grange, Hospital Lane,
Mickleover, Derby, Derbyshire
DE3 5DR
Tel: (01332) 512855
Head: Mrs V Parkes
Type: Mixed Residential 19+
No of pupils: 7 *No of Boarders:* F7
Special Needs: ASP AUT MLD SLD
SP&LD SPLD
Independent
52-week care

DEVON

EXETER COLLEGE
Hele Road, Exeter, Devon EX4 4JS
Tel: (01392) 205443
Head: Ms B Jansson
Type: Mixed Day 16+
No of pupils: 13000
Special Needs: ADD ADHD ASP AUT
CP DOW DYC DYP DYS EBD EPI HI
MLD PH SLD SP&LD SPLD VIS W

OAKWOOD COURT
7–9 Oak Park Villas, Dawlish, Devon
EX7 0DE
Tel: (01626) 864066
Head: Mr J F Loft
Type: Mixed Residential 16–25
No of pupils: 30 *No of Boarders:* F30
Special Needs: ADHD ASP AUT CP
DEL DOW DYP DYS EBD EPI MLD
SLD SP&LD SPLD TOU W
Independent

RNIB MANOR HOUSE*
Middle Lincombe Road, Torquay,
Devon TQ1 2NG
Tel: (01803) 214523
Head: Mrs J Read
Type: Mixed Residential and Day 16+
No of pupils: 25
Special Needs: PH **VIS** W

ROYAL SCHOOL FOR THE DEAF
Further Education College, 50
Topsham Road, Exeter, Devon
EX2 4NF
Tel: (01392) 215179
Head: Mr J F Shaw
Type: Mixed 16+
No of pupils: 50
Special Needs: **HI**
Non-Maintained

ST LOYE'S COLLEGE
Fairfield House, Topsham Road,
Exeter, Devon EX2 6EP
Tel: (01392) 255428
Head: Miss M Peat
Type: Mixed Residential 18–63
No of pupils: 250 *No of Boarders:* F210
Special Needs: ASP DYS EPI HI PH
VIS W

THE WEST OF ENGLAND COLLEGE FOR STUDENTS WITH LITTLE OR NO SIGHT
Countess Wear, Exeter, Devon
EX2 6HA
Tel: (01392) 454245
Head: Mr H R T Dicks
Type: Mixed Residential and Day
16–22
No of pupils: B20 G25
No of Boarders: W45
Special Needs: DYS EPI HI **MLD** PH
SLD SP&LD **VIS** W
Non-Maintained

DORSET

FORTUNE CENTRE OF RIDING THERAPY
Avon Tyrrell, Bransgore,
Christchurch, Dorset BH23 8EE
Tel: (01425) 673297
Head: Mrs J Dixon-Clegg
Type: Mixed Residential 16–25
No of pupils: B8 G23
No of Boarders: F31
Special Needs: ADD ASP AUT CP
DOW DYC DYP DYS **EBD** EPI HI
MLD SLD SP&LD **SPLD** VIS
Independent

IVERS
Hains Lane, Marnhull, Sturminster
Newton, Dorset DT10 1JU
Tel: (01258) 820164
Head: Mrs H Heron
Type: Mixed Residential 16–25
No of pupils: 25 *No of Boarders:* F24
Special Needs: ASP AUT CP DOW
EBD EPI MLD SLD SP&LD
Independent
52-week care

COUNTY DURHAM

FINCHALE TRAINING COLLEGE*
Durham, County Durham DH1 5RX
Tel: (0191) 386 2634
Head: Dr D T Etheridge
Type: Mixed Residential 18–63
No of pupils: 180 *No of Boarders:* F120
Special Needs: ADD ADHD ASP CP
DEL DYP DYS EPI HI MLD PH VIS W
Independent

GLOUCESTERSHIRE

THE NATIONAL STAR CENTRE'S COLLEGE OF FURTHER EDUCATION
Ullenwood Manor, Cheltenham, Gloucestershire GL53 9QU
Tel: (01242) 527631
Head: Mrs H Sexton
Type: Mixed Residential and Day 16–25
No of pupils: 140 *No of Boarders:* F120
Special Needs: ASP CP DEL DYP EPI
PH PMLD SP&LD VIS W
Independent

STROUD COURT
Longfords, Minchinhampton, Stroud, Gloucestershire GL6 9AN
Tel: (01453) 834020
Head: Mr C Atkins
Type: Mixed Residential and Day 19+
No of pupils: 42 *No of Boarders:* F37
Special Needs: AUT EBD EPI MLD
SLD SP&LD

SOUTH GLOUCESTERSHIRE

THE HATCH
Camphill Community, St John's House, Kington Lane, Thornbury, South Gloucestershire BS35 1NA
Tel: (01454) 413010
Type: Mixed Residential 19–32
No of pupils: B12 G12
No of Boarders: F24
Special Needs: AUT CP DEL DOW
EPI HI MLD

HAMPSHIRE

THE ENHAM TRUST
Enham Alamein, Andover,
Hampshire SP11 6JS
Tel: (01264) 345800
Head: Ms D Lias
Type: Mixed Residential and Day 18+
Special Needs: DYS PH W
Independent

MINSTEAD TRAINING PROJECT
Minstead Lodge, Minstead,
Hampshire S043 7FU
Tel: (023) 8081 2254
Head: Mr M Lenaerts
Type: Mixed Residential and Day
16–30 (boarders from 18)
No of pupils: B43 G6
No of Boarders: F14
Special Needs: ADD ASP **DOW MLD**
Independent

YATELEY INDUSTRIES FOR THE DISABLED LTD
Mill Lane, Yateley, Hampshire
GU46 7TF
Tel: (01252) 872337
Head: Mrs L Robinson
Type: Mixed Residential and Day 18+
No of pupils: B26 G26
No of Boarders: F30
Special Needs: ADD ADHD ASP AUT
CP DOW DYP DYS EPI HI MLD PH
SP&LD SPLD W
52-week care

HEREFORDSHIRE

ROYAL NATIONAL COLLEGE FOR THE BLIND*
College Road, Hereford,
Herefordshire HR1 1EB
Tel: (01432) 265725
Head: Mrs R Burge
Type: Mixed Residential 16–60
No of pupils: 200
Special Needs: DYS HI SPLD **VIS** W
Independent

HERTFORDSHIRE

DELROW COLLEGE
Hilfield Lane, Aldenham, Watford,
Hertfordshire WD25 8DJ
Tel: (01923) 856006
Head: Ms L Has
Type: Mixed Residential 20–65
No of pupils: 50
Special Needs: AUT CP **HI** MLD
Independent

KENT

DORTON COLLEGE OF FURTHER EDUCATION
Seal Drive, Seal, Sevenoaks, Kent
TN15 0AH
Tel: (01732) 592602
Head: Mr M D Morris
Type: Mixed Residential and Day 16+
No of pupils: 65
Special Needs: EBD MLD **VIS**
Independent

NASH COLLEGE OF FURTHER EDUCATION
Croydon Road, Hayes, Bromley, Kent
BR2 7AG
Tel: (020) 8462 7419
Head: Mrs K Fletcher-Wright
Type: Mixed Residential and Day 16+
No of pupils: B41 G37
No of Boarders: F48
Special Needs: **CP** DOW DYP **EPI**
MLD **PH PMLD** SLD SPLD VIS W

WESTGATE COLLEGE
Westcliff House, 37 Sea Road,
Westgate, Kent CT8 8QP
Tel: (01843) 836300
Head: Mrs F Brown
Type: Mixed Residential and Day 16+
No of pupils: 70 *No of Boarders:* F70
Special Needs: EBD EPI HI MLD PH
PMLD SLD SP&LD SPLD VIS
Non-Maintained

LANCASHIRE

BEAUMONT COLLEGE OF FURTHER EDUCATION
Slyne Road, Lancaster, Lancashire
LA2 6AP
Tel: (01524) 64278
Head: Mr S Briggs
Type: Mixed Residential 16–25
No of pupils: B27 G50
No of Boarders: F77 W75
Special Needs: **CP** DOW DYC DYP
DYS MLD PH **PMLD** SLD SP&LD W
Independent

LEICESTERSHIRE

HOMEFIELD RESIDENTIAL COLLEGE
42 St Mary's Road, Sileby,
Loughborough, Leicestershire
LE12 7TL
Tel: (01509) 814827
Head: Mr K O'Brien
Type: Mixed Residential and Day 16+
No of pupils: 32 *No of Boarders:* W30
Special Needs: AUT HI MLD SLD
Independent

RNIB VOCATIONAL COLLEGE*
Radmoor Road, Loughborough,
Leicestershire LE11 3AB
Tel: (01509) 611077
Head: Mr K Connell
Type: Mixed Residential and Day
16–60
No of pupils: 80 *No of Boarders:* F74
Special Needs: DYS EPI HI PH **VIS** W
Independent

LINCOLNSHIRE

BROUGHTON HOUSE COLLEGE
Brant, Broughton, Lincolnshire
LN5 0SL
Tel: (01400) 272929
Head: Mr R Noble
Type: Mixed Residential 16–25
No of pupils: B15 G8
Special Needs: AUT SLD

LINKAGE FURTHER EDUCATION COLLEGE
Toynton All Saints, Spilsby,
Lincolnshire PE23 5AE
Tel: (01790) 752499
Head: Mrs J Blakeley
Type: Mixed Residential 16–26
No of pupils: 216 *No of Boarders:* F216
Special Needs: ADD ADHD ASP AUT
CP DEL DOW DYP DYS EPI HI MLD
PH SLD SP&LD SPLD TOU VIS W
Independent

NORTH EAST LINCOLNSHIRE

WEELSBY HALL FURTHER EDUCATION COLLEGE
Weelsby Road, Grimsby, North East
Lincolnshire DN32 9RU
Tel: (01472) 241044
Head: Mrs A Smith
Type: Mixed Residential 16+
No of pupils: B60 G40
Special Needs: ADHD ASP AUT CP
DEL DOW DYP DYS EPI HI MLD
SLD SP&LD SPLD
Independent

LONDON

LOVE WALK
10 Love Walk, Denmark Hill,
London SE5 8AE
Tel: (020) 7703 3632
Head: Mr M Green
Type: Mixed Residential 16+
No of pupils: 22 *No of Boarders:* F22
Special Needs: **PH**

GREATER MANCHESTER

FOURWAYS ASSESSMENT UNIT
Cleworth Hall Lane, off Manchester Lane, Tyldesley, Greater Manchester M29 8NT
Tel: (01942) 870841
Head: Mr I Earnshaw
Type: Mixed Residential 18–65
No of pupils: 30 *No of Boarders:* F15 W15
Special Needs: CP PH
52-week care

NORTHAMPTONSHIRE

HINWICK HALL COLLEGE OF FURTHER EDUCATION
Hinwick, Wellingborough, Northamptonshire NN29 7JD
Tel: (01933) 312470
Head: Mr E E Sinnott
Type: Mixed Residential and Day 16–25
No of pupils: B29 G20
No of Boarders: F45
Special Needs: CP DOW EPI HI MLD PH SLD SP&LD SPLD W
Independent
52-week care

SOLDEN HILL HOUSE
Banbury Road, Byfield, Daventry, Northamptonshire NN11 6UA
Tel: (01327) 260234
Head: Ms A O'Hare
Type: Mixed Residential 19+
No of pupils: 30 *No of Boarders:* F30
Special Needs: **MLD**

NORTHUMBERLAND

DILSTON COLLEGE OF FURTHER EDUCATION*
Dilston Hall, Corbridge, Northumberland NE45 5RJ
Tel: (01434) 632692
Head: Mr J A Jameson
Type: Mixed Residential and Day 16–25
No of pupils: 60 *No of Boarders:* F50
Special Needs: ASP AUT DOW EPI HI MLD SLD SP&LD SPLD
Independent

NOTTINGHAMSHIRE

PORTLAND COLLEGE
Nottingham Road, Mansfield,
Nottinghamshire NG18 4TJ
Tel: (01623) 499111
Head: Mr M E A Syms
Type: Mixed Residential and Day
16–60
No of pupils: 270 *No of Boarders:* F230
W40
Special Needs: CP DYC DYP DYS EPI
HI MLD PH SP&LD VIS W
Approved Independent

SHROPSHIRE

DERWEN COLLEGE
Oswestry, Shropshire SY11 3JA
Tel: (01691) 661234
Head: Mr D J Kendall
Type: Mixed Residential 16+
No of pupils: B111 G112
No of Boarders: F223
Special Needs: ASP CP DOW DYS EPI
HI MLD PH SLD SP&LD VIS W
Independent

**LOPPINGTON HOUSE
FURTHER EDUCATION &
ADULT CENTRE**
Loppington, Wem, Shropshire
SY4 5NF
Tel: (01939) 233926
Head: Mr P Harris
Type: Mixed Residential 16–25
No of pupils: B33 G10
No of Boarders: F43
Special Needs: AUT CP DOW EBD
EPI HI MLD SLD SP&LD SPLD VIS
52-week care

SOMERSET

LUFTON MANOR COLLEGE*
Yeovil, Somerset BA22 8ST
Tel: (01935) 423124
Head: Mr R Elliott
Type: Mixed Residential 16–25
No of pupils: B40 G32
No of Boarders: F72
Special Needs: MLD SLD SP&LD
Independent

NORTH EAST SOMERSET

RNID POOLEMEAD
Watery Lane, Twerton on Avon,
Bath, North East Somerset BA2 1RN
Tel: (01225) 332818
Head: Mr C Crowley
Type: Mixed Residential 18+
No of pupils: B18 G14
No of Boarders: F32
Special Needs: HI PH SP&LD **VIS** W
52-week care

STAFFORDSHIRE

**STRATHMORE HOUSE AND
FLORENCE VILLA**
27 Queens Park Avenue, Dresden,
Stoke on Trent, Staffordshire
Tel: (01782) 313508
Head: Ms K Smith & V A Heath
Type: Mixed Residential and Day 16+
No of pupils: 45 *No of Boarders:* F45
Special Needs: ASP AUT DOW EBD
EPI MLD SLD SPLD
Independent
52-week care

SURREY

**BANSTEAD PLACE BRAIN
INJURY REHABILITATION**
Centre, Park Road, Banstead, Surrey
SM7 3EE
Tel: (01737) 356222
Head: Mrs J E Oliver
Type: Mixed Residential 16–35
No of pupils: 28
Special Needs: EBD EPI MLD PH
SP&LD SPLD VIS W
Independent

**THE GRANGE CENTRE FOR
PEOPLE WITH DISABILITIES**
Rectory Lane, Bookham, Surrey
KT23 4DZ
Tel: (01372) 452608
Head: Mr P H Wood
Type: Mixed Residential and Day 19+
No of pupils: 50 *No of Boarders:* F50
Special Needs: CP DYS EPI HI MLD
PH W
Independent

**QUEEN ELIZABETH'S
TRAINING COLLEGE**
Leatherhead, Surrey KT22 0BN
Tel: (01372) 841100
Head: Mr R D Beckinsale
Type: Mixed Residential and Day
18–63
No of pupils: 205
Special Needs: CP DYS EBD EPI HI
MLD PH SPLD VIS W

RNIB REDHILL COLLEGE*
Philanthropic Road, Redhill, Surrey
RH1 4DG
Tel: (01737) 768935
Head: Mrs J Foot
Type: Mixed Residential and Day
16–59
No of pupils: B60 G40
No of Boarders: F90
Special Needs: **ASP** AUT CP DOW
DYS EPI HI **MLD** PH **SLD** SPLD
VIS W
Independent
52-week care

**SEEABILITY (FORMERLY
ROYAL SCHOOL FOR THE
BLIND)**
SeeABILITY House, Hook Road,
Epsom, Surrey KT19 8SQ
Tel: (01372) 755000
Head: Mr R M Perkins
Type: Mixed Residential and Day 18+
No of pupils: 200 *No of Boarders:* F150
Special Needs: CP EBD EPI HI MLD
PH PMLD SLD **VIS** W
Independent

EAST SUSSEX

THE MOUNT CAMPHILL COMMUNITY
Wadhurst, East Sussex TN5 6PT
Tel: (01892) 782025
Type: Mixed Residential 16–25
No of pupils: 35
Special Needs: ASP AUT DOW EBD MLD

WEST MIDLANDS

HEREWARD COLLEGE
Bramston Crescent, Tile Hill Lane,
Coventry, West Midlands CV4 9SW
Tel: (024) 7646 1231
Head: Ms C Cole
Type: Mixed Residential and Day 16+
No of pupils: B200 G200
No of Boarders: F85
Special Needs: ASP CP DEL DOW
DYC DYP DYS EPI HI MLD PH SLD
SP&LD SPLD TOU VIS W

QUEEN ALEXANDRA COLLEGE OF FURTHER EDUCATION
Court Oak Road, Harborne,
Birmingham, West Midlands
B17 9TG
Tel: (0121) 428 5050
Head: Ms S Wright
Type: Mixed Residential and Day
16–63
No of pupils: B80 G40
No of Boarders: F90
Special Needs: ASP CP EPI HI MLD
PH VIS W
Independent
52-week care

WILTSHIRE

FAIRFIELD OPPORTUNITY FARM
Dilton Marsh, Westbury, Wiltshire
BA13 4DL
Tel: (01373) 823028
Head: Ms J Kenward
Type: Mixed Residential and Day
16–30
No of pupils: 27 *No of Boarders:* F25
Special Needs: ASP AUT DOW DYP
EPI HI MLD SLD SP&LD SPLD
Independent

NORTH YORKSHIRE

HENSHAW'S COLLEGE
Bogs Lane, Harrogate, North
Yorkshire HG1 4ED
Tel: (01423) 886451
Head: Mrs J Cole
Type: Mixed Residential 16+
No of pupils: 64 *No of Boarders:* F64
Special Needs: CP DOW EPI HI MLD
PH SLD VIS W

SOUTH YORKSHIRE

**DONCASTER COLLEGE FOR
THE DEAF**
Leger Way, Doncaster, South
Yorkshire DN2 6AY
Tel: (01302) 386700
Head: Mr H Heard
Type: Mixed Residential and Day
16–63
No of pupils: B90 G50
No of Boarders: F120
Special Needs: ASP CP DYC DYP DYS
EBD HI MLD PH SP&LD SPLD VIS

HESLEY VILLAGE COLLEGE
Tickhill, Doncaster, South Yorkshire
DN11 9HH
Tel: (01302) 868313
Head: Mrs S Ekins
Type: Mixed Residential 16–25
No of pupils: B14 G2
Special Needs: ADHD AUT EBD
SLD W
Approved Independent

WEST YORKSHIRE

**PENNINE CAMPHILL
COMMUNITY**
Boyne Hill House, Chapelthorpe,
Wakefield, West Yorkshire WF4 3JH
Tel: (01924) 255281
Head: Mr S Hopewell
Type: Mixed Residential and Day
16–25
No of pupils: B20 G18
No of Boarders: F38
Special Needs: AUT CP DEL DYS EBD
EPI HI MLD SLD SP&LD SPLD VIS
Independent

SCOTLAND

ABERDEENSHIRE

**EASTER AUGUSTON
TRAINING FARM**
Peterculter, Aberdeen,
Aberdeenshire AB14 0PJ
Tel: (01224) 733627
Head: Mr G Phillips
Type: Mixed Residential 18+
No of pupils: 18 *No of Boarders:* F16
Special Needs: DOW MLD SP&LD
Independent
52-week care

FIFE

RNIB ALWYN HOUSE*
Alwyn House, 3 Wemysshall Road,
Ceres, Fife KY15 5LX
Tel: (01334) 828894
Head: Mrs M Lawrie
Type: Mixed Residential and Day
16–65
No of pupils: 16
Special Needs: CP EBD **VIS**

PERTHSHIRE

**CORBENIC CAMPHILL
COMMUNITY**
Trochry, Dunkeld, Perthshire
PH8 0DY
Tel: (01350) 723206
Head: Mrs Stolk
Type: Mixed Residential 25+
No of pupils: B26 G5
Special Needs: AUT DOW EPI HI
MLD SLD SP&LD SPLD VIS

STIRLING

**CAMPHILL BLAIR
DRUMMOND TRUST**
Blair Drummond House, Cuthil
Brae, Stirling FK9 4UT
Tel: (01786) 841573
Head: Mr G Allen
Type: Mixed Residential and Day
16–30
No of pupils: 37 *No of Boarders:* F30
Special Needs: AUT DOW EBD EPI HI
MLD PMLD SLD SP&LD SPLD

WALES

BRIDGEND

BRIDGEND COLLEGE*
Cowbridge Road, Bridgend
CF31 3DF
Tel: (01656) 302339
Head: Mr R Hampton
Type: Mixed Residential 16–25 (day age 16–40)
No of pupils: 308 *No of Boarders:* W26
Special Needs: DYS HI SPLD VIS

CARMARTHENSHIRE

COLEG ELIDYR*
Rhandirmwyn and Llangadog,
Llandovery, Carmarthenshire
SA20 0NL
Tel: (01550) 760400
Type: Mixed Residential 16+
No of pupils: B35 G30
No of Boarders: F65 W65
Special Needs: AUT EBD EPI MLD SLD
Non-Maintained

CONWY

FURZE MOUNT
Copthorne Road, Upper Colwyn Bay,
Conwy LL28 5YP
Tel: (01492) 532679
Head: Miss S Edwards
Type: Mixed Residential 16+
No of pupils: 19 *No of Boarders:* W19
Special Needs: CP EPI PH SLD W
Independent

DENBIGHSHIRE

PENGWERN COLLEGE*
Rhuddlan, Denbighshire LL18 5UH
Tel: (01745) 590281
Head: Mr M Booker
Type: Mixed Residential 16–25
No of pupils: 52 *No of Boarders:* F52
Special Needs: AUT CP DOW EPI
MLD PMLD SLD SP&LD W
Independent

GWYNEDD

BRYN MELYNGROUP
Llandderfel, Bala, Gwynedd
LL23 7RA
Tel: (01678) 530330
Head: Mrs S Hamilton
Type: Mixed Residential 12–19
No of pupils: 18 *No of Boarders:* F18
Special Needs: ADD DYP EBD EPI
MLD

CERRIG CAMU
Old Barmouth Road, Dolgellau,
Gwynedd LL40 2SP
Tel: (01341) 423075
Head: Mrs N McGrail
Type: Mixed Residential 18+
No of pupils: 21 *No of Boarders:* F21
Special Needs: EBD MLD PH SLD

2.3
Index of State Maintained Schools by Education Authority

State maintained schools are listed by Local Education Authority. Since 1996 a number of new unitary authorities have been created in addition to existing two-tier structures. The index below (for England) lists each local authority under the county of which it is deemed a part, and is designed to help you identify the local authorities responsible for schools in your area. Turn to the page number shown against each to find the schools within the authority. Schools in Northern Ireland, Scotland and Wales are listed by Local Education Authority only.

ENGLAND

NORTHERN IRELAND

SCOTLAND

WALES

2.4
Directory of State Maintained Schools by Education Authority

ENGLAND

BEDFORDSHIRE

Bedfordshire Education Authority

County Hall
Cauldwell Street
Bedford
Bedfordshire MK42 9AP
Tel: (01234) 363222

GLENWOOD SCHOOL
Beech Road, Dunstable, Bedfordshire
LU5 3LY
Tel: (01582) 667106
Head: Mrs J S Wadlow
Type: Co-educational Day 2–11
No of pupils: 132
Special Needs: **AUT** DOW **PMLD**
SLD W

HILLCREST SCHOOL
Ridgeway Avenue, Dunstable,
Bedfordshire LU5 4QL
Tel: (01582) 661983
Head: Mr P Skingley
Type: Co-educational Day 11–19
No of pupils: 89
Special Needs: **AUT PMLD SLD** W

OAK BANK SCHOOL
Sandy Lane, Leighton Buzzard,
Bedfordshire LU7 8BE
Tel: (01525) 374559
Head: Mr M Smith
Type: Boys Boarding 11–16
No of pupils: 40 *No of Boarders:* W24
Special Needs: **EBD**

RAINBOW SCHOOL
Chestnut Avenue, Bromham,
Bedford MK43 8HP
Tel: (01234) 822596
Head: Mrs J Mason
Type: Co-educational Day 2–19
No of pupils: 63
Special Needs: **AUT PMLD SLD** W

RIDGEWAY SCHOOL
Hill Rise, Kempston, Bedford,
Bedfordshire MK42 7EB
Tel: (01234) 853602
Head: Mr G Allard
Type: Co-educational Day 2–19
No of pupils: B46 G24
Special Needs: **PH** VIS

ST JOHNS SCHOOL
Austin Canons, Kempston, Bedford
MK42 8AA
Tel: (01234) 345565
Head: Mr R Babbage
Type: Co-educational Day 2–19
No of pupils: 130
Special Needs: **PMLD SLD** W

SUNNYSIDE SCHOOL
The Baulk, Biggleswade,
Bedfordshire SG18 0PT
Tel: (01767) 222662
Head: Mrs V G White
Type: Co-educational 2–19
No of pupils: B35 G15
Special Needs: **AUT PMLD SLD** W

WEATHERFIELD SCHOOL
Brewers Hill Road, Dunstable,
Bedfordshire LU6 1AF
Tel: (01582) 605632
Head: Mr C F Peters
Type: Co-educational Day
No of pupils: B82 G63
Special Needs: **MLD**

Luton Education Authority

Luton City Council
Unity House
111 Stuart Street
Luton
Bedfordshire LU1 5NP
Tel: (01582) 548000

FIVE SPRINGS SCHOOL
Northwell Drive, Luton,
Bedfordshire LU3 3SP
Tel: (01582) 572880
Head: Mrs H Hardie
Type: Co-educational Day 11–19
No of pupils: 152
Special Needs: **ADD ADHD ASP AUT
DYS HI MLD PMLD SLD SP&LD
VIS** W

LADY ZIA WERNER SCHOOL
Ashcroft Road, Luton, Bedfordshire
LU2 9AY
Tel: (01582) 28705
Head: Mrs J Jackson
Type: Co-educational Day 2–11
No of pupils: B41 G29
Special Needs: **CP DEL DOW PH
PMLD** W

RICHMOND HILL SCHOOL
Sunridge Avenue, Luton,
Bedfordshire LU2 7JL
Tel: (01582) 721019
Head: Mr M W Love
Type: Co-educational Day 5–16
No of pupils: 125
Special Needs: MLD

BERKSHIRE

Bracknell Forest Borough Council

Education Department
Edward Elgar House
Skimped Hill Lane
Bracknell
Berkshire RG12 1LY
Tel: (01344) 354000

KENNEL LANE SCHOOL
Kennel Lane, Bracknell, Berkshire
RG42 2EX
Tel: (01344) 483872
Head: Ms J Calcroft
Type: Co-educational Day 2–19
No of pupils: 155
Special Needs: AUT MLD PMLD
SLD W

Reading Borough Council

The Civic Centre
Reading
Berkshire RG1 7TD
Tel: (0118) 939 0923

THE AVENUE SCHOOL
Basingstoke Road, Reading,
Berkshire RG2 0EN
Tel: (0118) 901 5554
Head: Mrs V Brown
Type: Co-educational Day 2–19
No of pupils: 170
Special Needs: CP DEL EBD EPI MLD
PH PMLD SP&LD VIS W

READING ALTERNATIVE SCHOOL
40 Christchurch Road, Reading,
Berkshire RG2 7AY
Tel: (01734) 752095
Head: Ms J Kightley
Type: Co-educational Day 11–16
No of pupils: 84
Special Needs: EBD SPLD W

Slough Borough Council

Education Department
Toen Hall
Bath Road
Slough
Berkshire SL1 3UQ
Tel: (01753) 552288

ARBOUR VALE SCHOOL
Stoke Road, Slough, Berkshire
SL2 5AY
Tel: (01753) 525291
Head: Mr J Mansfield
Type: Co-educational Day 2–19
No of pupils: 300
Special Needs: AUT EPI HI MLD
PMLD SLD SP&LD SPLD VIS W

West Berkshire Council

Avonbank House
West Street
Newbury
Berkshire RG14 1BZ
Tel: (01635) 42400

BROOKFIELDS SCHOOL
Sage Road, Tilehurst, Reading,
Berkshire RG31 6SW
Tel: (0118) 942 1382
Head: Mr J Byrne
Type: Co-educational Day
No of pupils: B148 G73
Special Needs: AUT MLD PMLD
SLD W

THE CASTLE SCHOOL
Love Lane, Donnington, Newbury,
Berkshire RG13 2JG
Tel: (01635) 42976
Head: Mrs H Fernie
Type: Co-educational Day 2–19
No of pupils: B86 G54
Special Needs: AUT MLD PMLD SLD

Windsor & Maidenhead Education Authority

Education Directorate
Towen Hall
St Ives Road
Maidenhead
Berkshire SL6 1RF
Tel: (01628) 796367

HOLYPORT MANOR SCHOOL
Ascot Road, Holyport, Maidenhead,
Berkshire SL6 3LE
Tel: (01628) 623196
Head: Mr P Donkersloot
Type: Co-educational Day and
Boarding 2–16
No of pupils: B134 G66
No of Boarders: W17
Special Needs: AUT CP EPI HI MLD
PH PMLD SLD SP&LD

Wokingham District Council

Education and Cultural Services
Department
PO Box 156
Council Offices
Shute End
Wokingham
Berkshire RG40 1WQ
Tel: (0118) 974 6100

SINDLESHAM SCHOOL
Mole Road, Sindlesham,
Wokingham, Berkshire RG11 5DJ
Tel: (01734) 786900
Head: Mr J Urwin
Type: Boys Boarding 11–17
No of pupils: 56 *No of Boarders:* W56
Special Needs: ADHD ASP EBD SPLD

SOUTHFIELD SCHOOL
Gipsy Lane, Wokingham, Berkshire
RG40 2AR
Tel: (0118) 977 1293
Head: Mr K Bennett
Type: Co-educational 11–16
No of pupils: B69 *No of Boarders:* W20
Special Needs: EBD

BRISTOL

Bristol Education Authority

PO Box 57
Avon House
Bristol BS99 7EB
Tel: (0117) 903 7961

BRIARWOOD SCHOOL
Briar Way, Fishponds, Bristol
BS16 4EA
Tel: (0117) 965 7536
Head: Mr D Hussey
Type: Co-educational 2–19
No of pupils: B37 G31
Special Needs: AUT PMLD SLD W

CLAREMONT SCHOOL
Henleaze Park, Henleaze, Bristol
BS9 4LR
Tel: (0117) 924 7527
Head: Mr B Coburn
Type: Co-educational 2–11
No of pupils: 96
Special Needs: PMLD SLD

ELMFIELD SCHOOL
Greystoke Avenue, Westbury-on-
Trym, Bristol BS10 6AY
Tel: (0117) 903 0366
Head: Ms R Way
Type: Co-educational Day 3–16
No of pupils: 56
Special Needs: HI W

FLORENCE BROWN SCHOOL
Leinster Avenue, Knowle, Bristol
BS4 1NN
Tel: (0117) 966 8152
Head: Mr P Evans
Type: Co-educational Day 5–16
No of pupils: 200
Special Needs: EBD MLD PH
SP&LD W

KINGSDON MANOR SCHOOL
Kingsdon, Somerton, Bristol
TA11 7JZ
Tel: (01935) 840323
Head: Mr J Holliday
Type: Boys Boarding 10–16
No of pupils: 50
Special Needs: EBD MLD

KINGSWESTON SCHOOL
Napier Miles Road, Avonmouth,
Bristol BS11 0UT
Tel: (0117) 903 0400
Head: Mr D Capel
Type: Co-educational Day 3–19
No of pupils: B125 G65
Special Needs: ASP AUT MLD SLD

NEW FOSSEWAY SCHOOL
New Fosseway Road, Hengrove,
Bristol BS14 9LN
Tel: (01275) 839411
Head: Mr J Hiscox
Type: Co-educational Day 3–19
No of pupils: B52 G35
Special Needs: PMLD SLD W

NOTTON HOUSE
28 Notton, Lacock Nr Chippenham,
Wiltshire SN15 2NP
Tel: (01249) 730407
Head: Mr G M Gamble
Type: Boys Boarding 9–16
No of pupils: 55 *No of Boarders:* F55
Special Needs: EBD

WOODSTOCK SCHOOL
Courtney Road, Kingswood, Bristol
BS15 9RL
Tel: (0117) 967 1832
Head: Mr G Parsons
Type: Co-educational Day 7–11
No of pupils: 60
Special Needs: EBD

BUCKINGHAMSHIRE

Buckinghamshire Education Authority

County Hall
Aylesbury
Buckinghamshire HP20 1UZ
Tel: (01296) 383204

ALFRISTON SCHOOL
Penn Road, Beaconsfield,
Buckinghamshire HP9 2TS
Tel: (01494) 673740
Head: Mrs V Gordon
Type: Girls Day and Boarding 11–18
No of pupils: 120 *No of Boarders:* W32
Special Needs: MLD

CHILTERN GATE SCHOOL

Verney Avenue, High Wycombe,
Buckinghamshire HP12 3NE
Tel: (01494) 532621
Head: Mr W Marshall
Type: Day and Boarding
No of pupils: 125
Special Needs: ADHD ASP **AUT** DOW
DYP **EBD** EPI HI **MLD** SP&LD TOU
VIS W

FURZE DOWN SCHOOL

Verney Road, Winslow,
Buckinghamshire MK18 3BL
Tel: (01296) 713385
Head: Mr N Ward
Type: Co-educational Day 5–18
No of pupils: 140
Special Needs: ADHD ASP AUT DYC
DYP DYS EBD EPI HI **MLD** SLD
SP&LD SPLD

HERITAGE HOUSE SCHOOL

Cameron Road, Chesham,
Buckinghamshire HP5 3BP
Tel: (01494) 771445
Head: Mr M Barrie
Type: Co-educational Day 2–19
No of pupils: B50 G40
Special Needs: AUT **PMLD SLD W**

KYNASTON SCHOOL

Stoke Leys Close, Kynaston Avenue,
Aylesbury, Buckinghamshire
HP21 9ET
Tel: (01296) 427221
Head: Mr R Westwood
Type: Co-educational Day 5–11
No of pupils: 50
Special Needs: **EBD**

MAPLEWOOD SCHOOL

Cressex Road, High Wycombe,
Buckinghamshire HP12 4PR
Tel: (01494) 525728
Head: Mrs J Appleyard
Type: Co-educational Day 3–19
No of pupils: 87
Special Needs: **PMLD SLD**

PARK SCHOOL

Stocklake, Aylesbury,
Buckinghamshire HP20 1DP
Tel: (01296) 23507
Head: Mrs R Cutler
Type: Co-educational Day 3–19
No of pupils: 85
Special Needs: **AUT** CP DOW PH
PMLD SLD W

PEBBLE BROOK SCHOOL

Churchill Avenue, Aylesbury,
Buckinghamshire HP21 8LZ
Tel: (01296) 415761
Head: Mrs J Lloyd
Type: Day and Boarding
No of pupils: 62 *No of Boarders:* W28
Special Needs: **MLD**

PRESTWOOD LODGE SCHOOL FOR BOYS

Nairdwood Lane, Prestwood, Great
Missenden, Buckinghamshire
HP16 0QQ
Tel: (01494) 863514
Head: Mr M Rosner
Type: Boys Boarding 11–16
No of pupils: 44
Special Needs: **EBD**

STOKE LEYS SCHOOL

Claydon Path, Kynaston Avenue,
Aylesbury, Buckinghamshire
HP21 9EF
Tel: (01296) 427441
Head: Mr H Chapman
Type: Co-educational Day 4–12
No of pupils: 77
Special Needs: ADD ADHD CP DOW
DYS EPI MLD PH SP&LD VIS

STONY DEAN SCHOOL

Orchard End Avenue, off Pineapple
Road, Amersham, Buckinghamshire
HP7 9JW
Tel: (01494) 762538/762007
Head: Mr G Newsholme
Type: Co-educational Boarding and
Day 11–18
No of pupils: B105 G24
No of Boarders: W40
Special Needs: DYS **MLD** SP&LD
SPLD

VERNEY AVENUE SCHOOL

Verney Avenue, High Wycombe,
Buckinghamshire HP12 3NE
Tel: (01494) 530289
Head: Mr S Day
Type: Co-educational 11–18
No of pupils: 96
Special Needs: EBD **MLD** PH W

Milton Keynes Education Authority

PO Box 106
Saxon Court
502 Avebury Boulevard
Milton Keynes
Buckinghamshire MK9 3ZE
Tel: (01908) 253008

THE GATEHOUSE SCHOOL

Crosslands, Stantonbury,
Milton Keynes, Buckinghamshire
MK14 6AX
Tel: (01908) 313903
Head: Mrs J Park
Type: Boys Boarding and Day 12–16
No of pupils: 21 *No of Boarders:* W10
Special Needs: **EBD** W

THE REDWAY

Farmborough, Netherfield,
Milton Keynes, Buckinghamshire
MK6 4HG
Tel: (01908) 200000
Head: Mr R Fraser
Type: Co-educational Day
No of pupils: 120
Special Needs: AUT **PMLD SLD** W

ROMANS FIELD SCHOOL

Shenley Road, Bletchley,
Buckinghamshire MK3 7AW
Tel: (01908) 376011/2
Head: Mr J Thomas
Type: Co-educational Day and
Boarding 5–12
No of pupils: 60 *No of Boarders:* W25
Special Needs: **EBD**

SLATED ROW SCHOOL

Old Wolverton Road, Wolverton,
Milton Keynes, Buckinghamshire
MK12 5NJ
Tel: (01908) 316017
Head: Mr J O'Donnell
Type: Co-educational Day 5–19
No of pupils: B100 G55
Special Needs: **MLD**

THE WALNUTS SCHOOL

Simpson, Milton Keynes,
Buckinghamshire MK6 3AF
Tel: (01908) 670032
Head: Mrs P Ofield
Type: Co-educational Boarding and
Day
No of pupils: 43 *No of Boarders:* F11
Special Needs: **AUT**

CAMBRIDGESHIRE

Cambridgeshire Education Authority

Castle Court
Castle Hill
Cambridge
Cambridgeshire CB3 0AP
Tel: (01223) 717990

THE GREEN HEDGES SCHOOL
Bar Lane, Stapleford, Cambridge CB2 5BJ
Tel: (01223) 843872
Head: Mr G B Newell
Type: Co-educational Day
No of pupils: 50
Special Needs: AUT PMLD SLD

HIGHFIELD SCHOOL
Downham Road, Ely,
Cambridgeshire CB6 1BD
Tel: (01353) 662085
Head: Mrs V M Ashton
Type: Co-educational Day
No of pupils: 89
Special Needs: ADD ASP AUT CP DOW DYP EPI HI MLD PH PMLD SLD SP&LD TOU VIS W

THE LADY ADRIAN SCHOOL
Courtney Way, Cambridge CB4 2EE
Tel: (01223) 508793
Head: Mrs K Taylor
Type: Co-educational 7–16
No of pupils: 135
Special Needs: **MLD** W

LITTLETON HOUSE SCHOOL
Girton, Cambridge CB3 0QL
Tel: (01223) 277191
Head: Mr E Mash
Type: Boys Boarding and Day
No of pupils: 98 *No of Boarders:* W36
Special Needs: **EBD**

THE MANOR SCHOOL
Station Road, Wilburton, Ely,
Cambridgeshire CB6 3RR
Tel: (01353) 740229
Head: Mr T G Moran
Type: Co-educational Boarding and Day 5–11
No of pupils: 55
Special Needs: AUT DYS EBD MLD

MEADOWGATE SCHOOL
Meadowgate Lane, Wisbech,
Cambridgeshire PE13 2JH
Tel: (01945) 461836
Head: Mrs R M Blunt
Type: Co-educational Day 2–19
No of pupils: 107
Special Needs: MLD PMLD SLD

REES THOMAS SCHOOL
Downhams Lane, Cambridge CB4 1YB
Tel: (01223) 712100
Head: Mrs J Gawlinski
Type: Co-educational Day 2–19
No of pupils: B40 G20
Special Needs: ADHD **AUT** CP DOW HI **PMLD SLD** VIS W

SAMUEL PEPYS SCHOOL
Pepys Road, St Neots,
Cambridgeshire PE19 2EW
Tel: (01480) 375012
Head: Mr D C Baldry
Type: Co-educational 2–19
No of pupils: 95
Special Needs: AUT MLD PMLD SLD

SPRING COMMON SCHOOL
American Lane, Huntingdon,
Cambridgeshire PE18 7TY
Tel: (01480) 454396
Head: Mrs M Rawlings
Type: Co-educational Day
No of pupils: 147
Special Needs: AUT CP EPI HI MLD PMLD SLD VIS W

SPRINGFIELDS SCHOOL
Thames Road, Huntingdon,
Cambridgeshire PE18 7QW
Tel: (01480) 375106
Head: Mrs R S Keen
Type: Co-educational Day 2–11
No of pupils: 31
Special Needs: AUT MLD SLD SP&LD

THE WINDMILL SCHOOL
Fulbourn, Cambridge CB1 5EE
Tel: (01223) 880980
Head: Ms K Kemp
Type: Co-educational Day 2–19
No of pupils: 64
Special Needs: AUT CP DEL EPI HI PH **PMLD SLD** W

Peterborough City Council

Bayard Place
Broadway
Peterborough PE1 1FB
Tel: (01733) 748000

HELTWATE SCHOOL
North Bretton, Peterborough,
Cambridgeshire PE3 8RL
Tel: (01733) 262878
Head: Mr D R Smith
Type: Co-educational Day 4–16
No of pupils: 110
Special Needs: AUT HI MLD PH SLD W

ST GEORGE'S SCHOOL
Lawn Avenue, Peterborough,
Cambridgeshire PE1 3RB
Tel: (01733) 62058
Head: Mr A B Rudgley
Type: Co-educational Day
No of pupils: B18 G23
Special Needs: PMLD SLD

CHANNEL ISLANDS

Guernsey Education Authority

Education Department
Grange Road
St. Peter Port
Guernsey
Channel Islands GY1 1RQ
Tel: (01481) 710821

LONGFIELD CENTRE
Maurepas Road, St Peter Port,
Guernsey, Channel Islands GY1 2DS
Tel: (01481) 722339
Head: Mr R W Battye
Type: Co-educational Day 3–7
No of pupils: 32
Special Needs: MLD PH SP&LD W

MONT VAROUF SCHOOL
Le Neuf Chemin, St Saviours,
Guernsey, Channel Islands GY7 9FG
Tel: (01481) 63135
Head: Mr R W Battye
Type: Co-educational Day 3–19
No of pupils: B17 G19
Special Needs: AUT DOW EPI PMLD
SLD SP&LD VIS

OAKVALE SCHOOL
Collings Road, St Peter Port,
Guernsey, Channel Islands GY1 1FW
Tel: (01481) 723045
Head: Miss P Garthwaite
Type: Co-educational Day 7–16
No of pupils: B59 G40
Special Needs: EBD MLD W

D'HAUTREE HOUSE SCHOOL
St Saviour, Jersey, Channel Islands
JE2 4QP
Tel: (01534) 618042
Head: Mr R Matthews
Type: Co-educational Day 11–16
Special Needs: EBD

Jersey Education Authority

PO Box 142
Jersey
Channel Islands JE4 8QJ
Tel: (01534) 509500

MONT A L'ABBE SCHOOL
St Helier, Jersey, Channel Islands
JE2 3FN
Tel: (01534) 875801
Head: Mr J Grady
Type: Day
No of pupils: 86
Special Needs: AUT MLD PMLD
SLD W

CHESHIRE

Cheshire Education Authority

Education Department
County Hall
Chester
Cheshire CH1 1SQ
Tel: (01244) 602424

ADELAIDE SCHOOL
Adelaide Street, Crewe, Cheshire
CW1 3DT
Tel: (01270) 255661
Head: Mr L Willday
Type: Boys Day
No of pupils: 35
Special Needs: EBD

BROOK FARM SCHOOL
Brook Road, Tarporley, Cheshire
CW6 9HH
Tel: (01829) 732201
Head: Mrs C J Riley
Type: Co-educational Boarding
No of pupils: 45 No of Boarders: F45
Special Needs: EBD

CAPENHURST GRANGE SCHOOL
Chester Road, Great Sutton,
Cheshire CH66 2NA
Tel: (0151) 339 5141
Head: Mrs C Creasy
Type: Boys Boarding 11–16
No of pupils: 50
Special Needs: EBD

CLOUGHWOOD SCHOOL
Stones Manor Lane, Hartford,
Northwich, Cheshire CW8 1NU
Tel: (01606) 76671
Head: Mr D H Smith
Type: Boys Boarding
No of pupils: 65
Special Needs: EBD

DEE BANKS SCHOOL
Sandy Lane, Chester, Cheshire
CH3 5UX
Tel: (01244) 324012
Head: Mrs J Pendry
Type: Co-educational Day 2–19
No of pupils: 85
Special Needs: AUT CP DOW EPI
PMLD SLD W

DORIN PARK SCHOOL
Wealstone Lane, Upton-by-Chester,
Cheshire CH2 1HP
Tel: (01244) 381951
Head: Mr P Kidman
Type: Co-educational Day
No of pupils: 90
Special Needs: PH PMLD

GREENBANK SCHOOL
off Green Bank Lane, Hartford,
Northwich, Cheshire CW8 1LD
Tel: (01606) 76521
Head: Mr K D Boyle
Type: Co-educational Boarding 6–18
No of pupils: B68 G24
No of Boarders: F65 W27
Special Needs: AUT DEL EPI MLD
SLD SP&LD

HEBDEN GREEN SCHOOL
Woodford Lane West, Winsford,
Cheshire CW7 4EJ
Tel: (01606) 594221/2
Head: Mr A W Farren
Type: Co-educational Day and
Boarding 2–19
No of pupils: B80 G32
No of Boarders: W33
Special Needs: PH

HINDERTON SCHOOL
Capenhurst Lane, Whitby, Ellesmere Port, Cheshire CH65 7AQ
Tel: (0151) 355 2177
Head: Mr L McCallion
Type: Co-educational Day 3–7
No of pupils: 21
Special Needs: AUT SP&LD

OAKLANDS SCHOOL
Cheviot Square, Winsford, Cheshire CW7 1NU
Tel: (01606) 551048
Head: Mr I G Hopkins
Type: Co-educational Day 11–16
No of pupils: 106
Special Needs: **MLD**

PARK LANE SCHOOL
Park Lane, Macclesfield, Cheshire SK11 8JR
Tel: (01625) 423407
Head: Mr D Calvert
Type: Co-educational 2–19
No of pupils: B33 G37
Special Needs: PMLD SLD W

ROSEBANK SCHOOL
Townfield Lane, Barnton, Northwich, Cheshire CW8 4QP
Tel: (01606) 74975
Head: Ms C Newall
Type: Co-educational Day
No of pupils: 50
Special Needs: ADD ADHD ASP AUT DYS MLD SP&LD

THE RUSSETT SCHOOL
Middlehurst Avenue, Weaverham, Northwich, Cheshire CW8 3BW
Tel: (01606) 853005
Head: Mrs H M Watts
Type: Co-educational Day 2–19
No of pupils: 110
Special Needs: AUT DOW EPI HI PMLD **SLD** VIS W

ST JOHN'S WOOD COMMUNITY SCHOOL
Longridge, Knutsford, Cheshire WA16 8PA
Tel: (01565) 634578
Head: Mr A P Evans
Type: Co-educational Day
No of pupils: B31 G4
Special Needs: EBD

SPRINGFIELD SCHOOL
Crewe Green Road, Crewe, Cheshire CW1 5HS
Tel: (01270) 582446/582124
Head: Mr M Swaine
Type: Co-educational Day 3–19
No of pupils: B56 G50
Special Needs: AUT DOW **PMLD SLD**

Halton Borough Council

Education Directorate
Grosvenor House
Runcorn WA7 2WD
Tel: (0151) 424 2061

CAVENDISH SCHOOL
Lincoln Close, off Clifton Road, Runcorn, Cheshire WA7 4YX
Tel: (01928) 561706
Head: Mrs B E Fowler
Type: Co-educational Day 2–19
No of pupils: 81
Special Needs: ADHD AUT CP DEL DOW EPI **PMLD SLD** W

CHESNUT LODGE SCHOOL
Green Lane, Ditton, Widnes, Cheshire WA8 7HF
Tel: (0151) 424 0679
Head: Mrs A Westhead
Type: Co-educational Day 2–16
No of pupils: B45 G43
Special Needs: **PH** W

Warrington Borough Council

New Town House
Buttermarket Street
Warrington
Cheshire WA1 2NJ
Tel: (01925) 444400

GRAPPENHALL RESIDENTIAL SCHOOL
Church Lane, Grappenhall, Warrington, Cheshire WA4 3EU
Tel: (01925) 263895
Head: Mrs A Findlay
Type: Boys Boarding and Day
No of pupils: 123 *No of Boarders:* F30
Special Needs: **EBD** MLD

GREEN LANE SCHOOL
Green Lane, Padgate, Warrington, Cheshire WA1 4JL
Tel: (01925) 480128
Head: Mrs G Hunt
Type: Co-educational Day 4–16
No of pupils: 117
Special Needs: **MLD** SLD W

CORNWALL

Cornwall Education Authority

Education Department
County Hall
Truro
Cornwall TR1 3AY
Tel: (01872) 322000

CURNOW SCHOOL
Drump Road, Redruth, Cornwall TR15 1LU
Tel: (01209) 215432
Head: Mrs C Simpson
Type: Co-educational Day
No of pupils: B71 G48
Special Needs: **PMLD SLD**

DOUBLETREES SCHOOL
St Blazey Gate, St Blazey, Par, Cornwall PL24 2DS
Tel: (01726) 812757
Head: Ms C McCarthy
Type: Co-educational Boarding and Day 2–19
No of pupils: B57 G37
No of Boarders: W20
Special Needs: AUT HI PH PMLD SLD VIS W

NANCEALVERNE SCHOOL
Madron Road, Penzance, Cornwall
TR20 8TP
Tel: (01736) 365039
Head: Mrs F J Cock
Type: Co-educational Day 2–19
No of pupils: 90
Special Needs: PMLD SLD W

CUMBRIA

Cumbria Education Authority

5 Portland Square
Carlisle CA1 1PU
Tel: (01228) 606877

BALIOL SCHOOL
Sedbergh, Cumbria LA10 5LQ
Tel: 01539 620232
Head: Mr B J McArthur
Type: Boys Boarding 10–16
No of pupils: 48 *No of Boarders:* F48
Special Needs: EBD

GEORGE HASTWELL SCHOOL
Moor Tarn Lane, Walney, Barrow in Furness, Cumbria LA14 3LW
Tel: (01229) 475253
Head: Mr B J Gummett
Type: Co-educational Day 2–19
No of pupils: 50
Special Needs: AUT PMLD SLD W

JAMES RENNIE SCHOOL
Kingstown Road, Carlisle, Cumbria
CA3 0BU
Tel: (01228) 607559
Head: Mr S J Bowditch
Type: Co-educational Day 3–19
Special Needs: PMLD SLD W

MAYFIELD SCHOOL
Moresby, Whitehaven, Cumbria
CA28 8TU
Tel: (01946) 852676/7
Head: Ms S Leathers
Type: Co-educational Day
No of pupils: B50 G32
Special Needs: SLD

SANDGATE SCHOOL
Sandylands Road, Kendal, Cumbria
LA9 6JG
Tel: (01539) 773636
Head: Mrs W McManus
Type: Co-educational Day 2–19
No of pupils: B35 G15
Special Needs: AUT CP EBD EPI HI MLD PH **PMLD SLD** SPLD VIS W

SANDSIDE LODGE SCHOOL
Sandside Road, Ulverston, Cumbria
LA12 9EF
Tel: (01229) 894180
Head: Mrs J Billingham
Type: Co-educational Day 2–19
No of pupils: B39 G15
Special Needs: AUT EPI HI PH **PMLD SLD** SP&LD W

DERBYSHIRE

Derby City Council

Education Department
Middleton House
27 St Mary's Gate
Derby DE1 3NN
Tel: (01332) 293111

IVY HOUSE SCHOOL
249 Osmaston Road, Derby,
Derbyshire DE23 8LG
Tel: (01332) 344694
Head: Mrs P Sillitoe
Type: Co-educational Day 2–19
No of pupils: B48 G22
Special Needs: PMLD SLD W

ST ANDREW'S SCHOOL
St Andrew's View, Breadsall Hilltop,
Derby, Derbyshire DE2 4ET
Tel: (01332) 832746
Head: Mr M Dawes
Type: Co-educational Day and Boarding 2–19
No of pupils: 106 *No of Boarders:* W17
Special Needs: AUT PMLD **SLD**

ST CLARE'S SCHOOL
Rough Heanor Road, Mickleover,
Derby, Derbyshire DE3 5AZ
Tel: (01332) 511757
Head: Mrs M C McKenna
Type: Co-educational Day 11–16
No of pupils: 110
Special Needs: AUT EBD HI **MLD** SLD SP&LD

ST GILES SCHOOL
Hampshire Road, Chaddesden,
Derby, Derbyshire DE21 6BT
Tel: (01332) 343039
Head: Mr P J Walsh
Type: Co-educational 5–11
No of pupils: 75
Special Needs: AUT MLD **SLD** SP&LD

ST MARTIN'S SCHOOL
Wisgreaves Road, Alvaston, Derby,
Derbyshire DE2 8RQ
Tel: (01332) 571151
Head: Mr W G Jepson
Type: Co-educational Day 11–16
No of pupils: B60 G26
Special Needs: ADD DOW EBD
MLD W

Derbyshire Education Authority

County Hall
Matlock
Derbyshire DE4 3AG
Tel: (01629) 580000

ASHGATE CROFT SCHOOL
Ashgate Road, Chesterfield,
Derbyshire S40 4BN
Tel: (01246) 275111/237200
Head: Mr M J Meaton
Type: Co-educational Day 2–19
No of pupils: 191
Special Needs: AUT CP DEL DYS EBD
EPI HI MLD PH PMLD SLD SP&LD
VIS W

BENNERLEY FIELDS SCHOOL
Stratford Street, Ilkeston, Derbyshire
DE7 8QZ
Tel: (0115) 932 6374
Head: Mrs M Stirling
Type: Co-educational Day 3–16
No of pupils: 72
Special Needs: ASP AUT CP DOW
DYP EBD HI MLD PH SLD SP&LD W

BRACKENFIELD SCHOOL
Bracken Road, Long Eaton,
Nottingham, NG10 4DA
Tel: (0115) 973 3710
Head: Mrs S P Elkins
Type: Co-educational Day 5–16
No of pupils: B60 G18
Special Needs: EBD MLD

THE DELVES SCHOOL
Hayes Lane, Swanick, Derbyshire
DE55 1AR
Tel: (01773) 602198
Head: Mr I D Snodin
Type: Co-educational 5–16
No of pupils: 90
Special Needs: AUT EBD MLD SLD
SP&LD

HOLLY HOUSE SCHOOL
Church Street North, Old
Whittington, Chesterfield,
Derbyshire S41 9QR
Tel: (01246) 450530
Head: Mr G O'Neil
Type: Co-educational Day 4–11
No of pupils: 28
Special Needs: EBD

JOHN DUNCAN SCHOOL
Corbar Road, Buxton, Derbyshire
SK17 6RL
Tel: (01298) 23130
Head: Mrs S E Taylor
Type: Co-educational Boarding and
Day
No of pupils: B25 G15
No of Boarders: W10
Special Needs: DOW EPI MLD SLD
SP&LD

PARKWOOD COMMUNITY SPECIAL SCHOOL
Alfreton Park, Alfreton, Derbyshire
DE55 7AL
Tel: (01773) 832019
Head: Mrs R Mackenzie
Type: Co-educational Day 2–19
No of pupils: 60
Special Needs: PMLD SLD W

PEAK SCHOOL
Buxton Road, High Peak, Derbyshire
SK23 6ES
Tel: (01663) 751359
Head: Mrs L C Scowcroft
Type: Co-educational Boarding and
Day 2–19
No of pupils: 40 *No of Boarders:* W12
Special Needs: ASP AUT CP EPI PH
PMLD SLD W

STANTON VALE SCHOOL
Lower Stanton Road, Ilkeston,
Derbyshire DE7 4LR
Tel: (0115) 932 4783
Head: Mr M Emly
Type: Co-educational Day 2–19
No of pupils: B32 G33
Special Needs: PMLD SLD W

STUBBIN WOOD SCHOOL
Burlington Avenue, Langwith
Junction, Mansfield, Derbyshire
NG20 9AD
Tel: (01623) 742795
Head: Mr J M Youdan
Type: Co-educational Day 2–16
No of pupils: B94 G61
Special Needs: MLD PMLD SLD W

WESTBROOK SCHOOL
Thoresby Road, Long Eaton,
Nottingham, Derbyshire NG10 3NP
Tel: (0115) 972 9769
Head: Mr D J Ingham
Type: Co-educational Boarding and
Day 2–16
No of pupils: 92 *No of Boarders:* W20
Special Needs: CP PH W

DEVON

Devon Education Authority

County Hall
Topsham Road
Exeter
Devon EX2 4QG
Tel: (01392) 382000

BARLEY LANE SCHOOL
Barley Lane, St Thomas, Exeter,
Devon EX4 1TA
Tel: (01392) 430774
Head: Mr M S Davis
Type: Boys Day and Boarding 10–16
No of pupils: 40 *No of Boarders:* W8
Special Needs: EBD

BARNSTAPLE TUTORIAL UNIT (PRU)
St Johns Lane, Barnstaple, Devon
EX32 9DD
Tel: (01271) 376641
Head: Mr P Bowrey
Type: Co-educational Day
No of pupils: 12
Special Needs: EBD

BIDWELL BROOK SCHOOL
Shinner's Bridge, Dartington, Devon
TQ9 6JU
Tel: (01803) 864120
Head: Mrs S M Love
Type: Co-educational Day 3–17
No of pupils: 86
Special Needs: **PMLD SLD** W

ELLEN TINKHAM SCHOOL
Hollow Lane, Exeter, Devon
EX1 3RW
Tel: (01392) 467168
Head: Dr M Megee
Type: Co-educational Day 3–19
No of pupils: B48 G26
Special Needs: AUT CP **DOW** EPI HI
MLD PMLD SLD VIS W

HILL CREST SCHOOL
St John's Road, Exmouth, Devon
EX8 4ED
Tel: (01395) 263480
Head: Mr G Adler
Type: Co-educational Boarding and
Day 10–16
No of pupils: B40 *No of Boarders:* W36
Special Needs: ADD ADHD DYS **EBD**

THE LAMPARD-VACHELL SCHOOL
St John's Lane, Barnstaple, Devon
EX32 9DD
Tel: (01271) 345416
Head: Mrs M T Buckland
Type: Co-educational Day 5–16
No of pupils: 80
Special Needs: **MLD**

MARLAND SCHOOL
Petersmarland, Torrington, Devon
EX3 8QQ
Tel: (01805) 601324
Head: Mr A Bates
Type: Boys Boarding 11–16
No of pupils: 36 *No of Boarders:* F36
Special Needs: ADD ADHD EBD
SP&LD SPLD

OAKLANDS PARK SCHOOL
John Nash Drive, Dawlish, Devon
EX7 9SF
Tel: (01626) 862363
Head: Mr R W Pugh
Type: Co-educational Boarding and
Day 3–19
No of pupils: B35 G11
No of Boarders: W24
Special Needs: AUT CP EPI PMLD
SLD

RATCLIFFE SCHOOL
John Nash Drive, Dawlish, Devon
EX7 9RL
Tel: (01626) 862939
Head: Mr C Hackett
Type: Co-educational Boarding
No of pupils: B50 G15
No of Boarders: W65
Special Needs: **EBD**

SOUTHBROOK SCHOOL
Bishop Westall Road, Exeter, Devon
EX2 6JB
Tel: (01392) 58373
Head: Mr N G Glover
Type: Co-educational Day 7–16
No of pupils: 157
Special Needs: **MLD**

Plymouth City Council

Civic Centre
Armada Way
Plymouth PL1 2AA
Tel: (01752) 307400

COURTLANDS SCHOOL
Widey Court, Crownhill, Plymouth,
Devon PL6 5JS
Tel: (01752) 776848
Head: Mr G H J Dunkerley
Type: Day
No of pupils: 144
Special Needs: **EBD MLD SP&LD**

HILLSIDE SCHOOL
Bodmin Road, Whitleigh, Plymouth,
Devon PL5 4DZ
Tel: (01752) 773875
Head: Mr D Whitton
Type: Co-educational Day 11–19
No of pupils: 194
Special Needs: **MLD**

LONGCAUSE SCHOOL
Plympton, Plymouth, Devon PL7 3JB
Tel: (01752) 336881
Head: Mr M Jelly
Type: Co-educational
No of pupils: 92
Special Needs: **MLD**

MILL FORD SCHOOL
Rochford Crescent, Ernesettle,
Plymouth, Devon PL5 2PY
Tel: (01752) 300270
Head: Mr J Hill
Type: Co-educational Day 3–19
No of pupils: 110
Special Needs: AUT **PMLD SLD** W

WOODLANDS SCHOOL
Bodmin Road, Whitleigh, Plymouth,
Devon PL5 4DZ
Tel: (01752) 778229
Head: Miss M A Vatcher
Type: Co-educational Day and
Boarding 2–17
No of pupils: 85 *No of Boarders:* W12
Special Needs: **PH** W

Torbay Council

Education Services Directorate
Oldway Mansion
Torquay Road
Paignton
Devon TQ3 2TE
Tel: (01803) 208208

COMBE PAFFORD SCHOOL
Steps Lane, Watcombe, Torquay,
Devon TQ2 8NL
Tel: (01803) 327902
Head: Mr M E Lock
Type: Co-educational Day 5–16
No of pupils: B110 G57
Special Needs: **MLD**

MAYFIELD SCHOOL
Torquay Road, Paignton, Devon
TQ3 2AL
Tel: (01803) 557194
Head: Mrs J M Palmer
Type: Co-educational Day 2–19
No of pupils: 80
Special Needs: PMLD SLD W

MOUNT TAMAR SCHOOL
Row Lane, St Budeaux, Plymouth,
Devon PL5 2EF
Tel: (01752) 365128
Head: Mr I Weston
Type: Co-educational Day 5–16
No of pupils: 84
Special Needs: **EBD**

STEPS CROSS SCHOOL
Steps Lane, Watcombe, Torquay,
Devon TQ2 8NN
Tel: (01803) 328375
Head: Mr E R Blake
Type: Co-educational Day 4–16
No of pupils: 92
Special Needs: CP DEL EBD EPI MLD
PH SP&LD SPLD

DORSET

Bournemouth Borough Council

Education Department
Dorset House
20–22 Christchurch Road
Bournemouth BH1 3NL
Tel: (01202) 456219

THE BICKNELL FOUNDATION SCHOOL
Petersfield Road, Bournemouth,
Dorset BH7 6QP
Tel: (01202) 424361
Head: Mr B Hooper
Type: Boys Day and Boarding 7–16
No of pupils: 65
Special Needs: ADD ADHD ASP DYC
DYP DYS EBD SP&LD SPLD TOU

LINWOOD SCHOOL
Alma Road, Bournemouth, Dorset
BH9 1AJ
Tel: (01202) 525107
Head: Mr S D Brown
Type: Co-educational Day 3–19
No of pupils: 176
Special Needs: MLD PMLD SLD

SLADES FARM HOSTEL
Ensbury Avenue, Ensbury Park,
Bournemouth, Dorset
Tel: (01202) 518189
Head: Mr R A Humphries
Type: Co-educational Boarding 8–16
Special Needs: EBD MLD

Dorset Education Authority

County Hall
Dorchester
Dorset DT1 1XJ
Tel: (01305) 251000

BEAUCROFT GRANT MAINTAINED SCHOOL
Wimborne Road, Colehill,
Wimborne, Dorset BH21 2SS
Tel: (01202) 886083
Head: Mr A W Mears
Type: Co-educational Day
No of pupils: 127
Special Needs: AUT MLD

MOUNTJOY SCHOOL
Flood Lane, Bridport, Dorset
DT6 3QG
Tel: (01308) 422250
Head: Mrs S G Hosking
Type: Co-educational Day 2–19
No of pupils: B29 G11
Special Needs: AUT CP DEL DOW
EPI HI PMLD SLD SP&LD SPLD W

PENWITHEN SCHOOL
Winterborne Monkton, Dorchester,
Dorset DT2 9PS
Tel: (01305) 266842
Head: Mr J R Burton
Type: Co-educational Boarding and
Day 7–16
No of pupils: 55 No of Boarders: W25
Special Needs: EBD

THE PRINCE OF WALES UNIT
Maiden Castle Road, Dorchester,
Dorset DT1 2HH
Tel: (01305) 257120
Head: Mr P Farrington
Type: Co-educational Day 2–9
No of pupils: 21
Special Needs: CP PH W

WESTFIELD TECHNOLOGY COLLEGE
Littlemoor Road, Preston,
Weymouth, Dorset
Tel: (01305) 833518
Head: Mr P Silvester
Type: Co-educational 3–16
No of pupils: 174
Special Needs: AUT MLD W

WYVERN SCHOOL
307 Chickerell Road, Weymouth,
Dorset DT4 0QU
Tel: (01305) 783660
Head: Miss H Mackenzie
Type: Co-educational Day
No of pupils: 60
Special Needs: AUT PMLD SLD W

YEWSTOCK SCHOOL
Honeymead Lane, Sturminster
Newton, Dorset DT10 1EW
Tel: (01258) 472796
Head: Mrs J Davis
Type: Co-educational Day 2–19
No of pupils: 109
Special Needs: AUT MLD PMLD
SLD W

Poole Borough Council

Civic Centre
Poole BH15 2RU
Tel: (01202) 633202

LONGSPEE SCHOOL
Learoyd Road, Canford Heath,
Poole, Dorset BH17 8PJ
Tel: (01202) 380266
Head: Mr M T Amos
Type: Co-educational 4–11
No of pupils: 62
Special Needs: EBD

MONTACUTE SCHOOL
3 Canford Heath Road, Poole, Dorset
BH17 9NG
Tel: (01202) 693239
Head: Mrs M Sammons
Type: Co-educational Day 3–18
No of pupils: 75
Special Needs: AUT PMLD SLD

WINCHELSEA SCHOOL
Guernsey Road, Parkstone, Poole,
Dorset BH12 4LL
Tel: (01202) 746240
Head: Mr R Barnsley
Type: Co-educational Day 3–16
No of pupils: 150
Special Needs: MLD W

COUNTY DURHAM

Darlington Borough Council

Education Department
Town Hall
Darlington
County Durham DL1 5QT
Tel: (01325) 380651

BEAUMONT HILL TECHNOLOGY COLLEGE & PRIMARY SCHOOL

Glebe Road, Darlington, County
Durham DL1 3EB
Tel: (01325) 254000
Head: Mrs D Smith
Type: Co-educational Day 2–19
No of pupils: B149 G76
Special Needs: ADD ADHD AUT CP
DOW EBD EPI HI MLD PH PMLD
SLD SP&LD SPLD W

County Durham Education Authority

Education Offices
County Hall
Durham DH1 5UJ
Tel: (0191) 386 4411

DENE VIEW SCHOOL

Cotsford Park, Horden, Peterlee,
County Durham SR8 4SZ
Tel: (0191) 586 4166
Head: Mr A Dawson
Type: Co-educational Day 5–16
No of pupils: B47 G17
Special Needs: MLD W

DURHAM TRINITY SCHOOL

Aykley Heads, Durham, County
Durham DH1 5TS
Tel: (0191) 386 4612
Head: Miss J A Connolly
Type: Co-educational Day 2–19
No of pupils: B119 G64
Special Needs: AUT MLD PMLD SLD

ELEMORE HALL SCHOOL

Littletown, Sherburn, County
Durham DH6 1QD
Tel: (0191) 372 0275
Head: Mr M Davey
Type: Co-educational Boarding and
Day
No of pupils: 70 No of Boarders: W40
Special Needs: EBD

GLEN DENE SCHOOL

Crawlaw Road, Easington Colliery,
Peterlee, County Durham SR8 3BQ
Tel: (0191) 527 0304
Head: Mr E Baker
Type: Co-educational Day 2–19
No of pupils: B86 G50
Special Needs: AUT DYC DYP DYS
MLD PMLD SLD W

HARE LAW SCHOOL

Catchgate, Annfield Plain, Stanley,
County Durham DH9 8DT
Tel: (01207) 234547
Head: Mr P H Eagle
Type: Co-educational Day 5–16
No of pupils: B80 G40
Special Needs: AUT MLD SLD W

MURPHY CRESCENT SCHOOL

Murphy Crescent, Bishop Barrington
Campus, Woodhouse Lane, Bishop
Auckland, County Durham
DL14 6LA
Tel: (01388) 451199
Head: Mrs M Wilson
Type: Co-educational Day 3–19
No of pupils: 35
Special Needs: PMLD SLD W

ROSEBANK SCHOOL

Rutherford Terrace, Broom,
Ferryhill, County Durham DL17 8AN
Tel: (01740) 651555
Head: Mrs S Stubbs
Type: Co-educational Day 4–19
No of pupils: B21 G17
Special Needs: PMLD SLD W

VILLA REAL SCHOOL

Villa Real Road, Consett, County
Durham DH8 6BH
Tel: (01207) 503651
Head: Mrs F Wood
Type: Co-educational Day 2–19
No of pupils: 75
Special Needs: AUT PMLD SLD W

WALWORTH SCHOOL

Bluebell Way, Newton Aycliffe,
County Durham DL5 7LP
Tel: (01325) 300194
Head: Mr A Dawson
Type: Co-educational Day and
Boarding 5–11
No of pupils: 60 No of Boarders: W30
Special Needs: ADD ADHD ASP EBD
MLD SP&LD SPLD

WARWICK ROAD SCHOOL

Warwick Road, Bishop Auckland,
County Durham DL14 6LS
Tel: (01388) 602683
Head: Mr G Price
Type: Co-educational Day
No of pupils: 100
Special Needs: DYP DYS MLD

WINDLESTONE HALL SCHOOL

Rushyford, Chilton, Ferryhill,
County Durham DL17 0LX
Tel: (01388) 720337
Head: Mr P M Jonson
Type: Co-educational Boarding and
Day 11–16
No of pupils: 60 No of Boarders: F20
Special Needs: EBD

ESSEX

Essex Education Authority

PO Box 47
Chelmsford
Essex CM2 6WN
Tel: (01245) 436231

CASTLEDON SCHOOL
Bromfords Drive, Wickford, Essex
SS12 0PW
Tel: (01268) 761252
Head: Mr P B Webster
Type: Co-educational Day 4–16
No of pupils: 100
Special Needs: AUT **MLD**

CEDAR HALL SCHOOL
Hart Road, Thundersley, Benfleet,
Essex SS7 3UQ
Tel: (01268) 774723
Head: Mr C Bent
Type: Co-educational Day 4–16
No of pupils: B66 G31
Special Needs: HI **MLD** W

THE EDITH BORTHWICK SCHOOL
Fennes Road, Church Street,
Bocking, Braintree, Essex CM7 5LA
Tel: (01376) 326436
Head: Mr M Jelly
Type: Co-educational Day
No of pupils: 140
Special Needs: AUT MLD SLD

ELMBROOK SCHOOL
Church Road, Basildon, Essex
SS14 2EX
Tel: (01268) 521808
Acting Head: Mr S Horsted
Type: Co-educational Day 3–19
No of pupils: B62 G25
Special Needs: AUT CP EPI HI PH
PMLD SLD W

THE ENDEAVOUR SCHOOL
Hogarth Avenue, Brentwood, Essex
CM15 8BE
Tel: (01277) 217330
Head: Mr P L Pryke
Type: Co-educational Day 4–16
No of pupils: B53 G21
Special Needs: **MLD** W

GLENWOOD SCHOOL
Rushbottom Lane, New Thundersley,
Benfleet, Essex SS7 4LW
Tel: (01268) 792575
Head: Mrs J Salter
Type: Co-educational Day
No of pupils: B60 G20
Special Needs: AUT PMLD SLD W

HARLOW FIELDS SCHOOL
Tendring Road, Harlow, Essex
CM18 6RN
Tel: (01279) 423670
Head: Dr B Thomas
Type: Co-educational Day 3–19
No of pupils: 140
Special Needs: AUT MLD **PMLD SLD**

THE HAYWARD SCHOOL
Maltese Road, Chelmsford, Essex
CM1 2PA
Tel: (01245) 258667
Head: Mrs J Ragan
Type: Co-educational Day 5–16
No of pupils: B75 G35
Special Needs: ADD ADHD AUT
DOW DYP DYS **MLD**

THE HEATH SCHOOL
Winstree Road, Stanway, Colchester,
Essex CO3 5GE
Tel: (01206) 571379
Head: Mrs C F Creasy
Type: Boys Day and Boarding 11–16
No of pupils: 45
Special Needs: **EBD** W

HOMESTEAD SCHOOL
School Road, Langham, Colchester,
Essex CO4 5PA
Tel: (01206) 272303
Head: Mr W Campard
Type: Boys Boarding 11–18
No of pupils: 64
Special Needs: **EBD**

KINGSWODE HOE SCHOOL
Sussex Road, Colchester, Essex
CO3 3QJ
Tel: (01206) 576408
Head: Mrs E Drake
Type: Co-educational Day 5–16
No of pupils: B72 G30
Special Needs: **MLD**

THE LEAS SCHOOL
Leas Road, Clacton, Essex CO15 1DY
Tel: (01255) 426288
Head: Mr E A Barkley
Type: Co-educational Day 5–16
No of pupils: B64 G36
Special Needs: AUT MLD W

LEXDEN SPRINGS SCHOOL
Halstead Road, Colchester, Essex
CO3 5AB
Tel: (01206) 563321
Head: Mr S H Goldsmith
Type: Co-educational Day 3–19
No of pupils: B38 G27
Special Needs: AUT PMLD SLD W

MARKET FIELD SCHOOL
School Road, Elmstead Market,
Colchester, Essex CO7 7ET
Tel: (01206) 825195
Head: Mr G R Smith
Type: Co-educational Day 5–16
No of pupils: B70 G40
Special Needs: AUT DOW **EBD** EPI
MLD SLD SP&LD SPLD W

MOAT HOUSE SCHOOL
Church Road, Basildon, Essex
SS14 2NQ
Tel: (01268) 522077
Head: Mr S Horsted
Type: Co-educational 5–16
No of pupils: 70
Special Needs: MLD

OAKVIEW SCHOOL
Whitehills Road, Loughton, Essex
IG10 1TS
Tel: (020) 8508 4293
Head: Mr S P Armstrong
Type: Co-educational 2–19
No of pupils: 90
Special Needs: AUT MLD SLD
SP&LD

THE RAMSDEN HALL SCHOOL
Ramsden Heath, Billericay, Essex
CM11 1HN
Tel: (01277) 624580
Head: Mr S Grant
Type: Boarding
No of pupils: 55 *No of Boarders:* W30
Special Needs: **EBD**

THRIFTWOOD SCHOOL
Slades Lane, Galleywood,
Chelmsford, Essex CM2 8RW
Tel: (01245) 266880
Head: Mrs S Davies
Type: Co-educational Day 5–16
No of pupils: 126
Special Needs: AUT **MLD** SP&LD

WELLS PARK SCHOOL

Lambourne Road, Chigwell, Essex
IG7 6NN
Tel: (020) 8502 6442
Head: Mr D Wood
Type: Co-educational Day and
Boarding 5–12
No of pupils: 40 *No of Boarders:* F40
Special Needs: **EBD** W

WINDSOR SPECIAL SCHOOL

Ogilvie House, 114 Holland Road,
Clacton, Essex CO15 6HF
Tel: (01255) 424412
Head: Mrs J Hodges
Type: Co-educational Day 3–19
No of pupils: B38 G24
Special Needs: PMLD SLD W

WOODLANDS SCHOOL

Patching Hall Lane, Chelmsford,
Essex CM1 4BX
Tel: (01245) 355854
Head: Mr O Caviglioli
Type: Co-educational Day 3–19
No of pupils: 110
Special Needs: AUT DOW PH PMLD
SLD W

Southend-on-Sea Borough Council

Education and Library Services
PO Box 6
Civic Centre
Victoria Avenue
Southend-on-Sea SS2 6ER
Tel: (01702) 215921

KINGSDOWN SCHOOL

Snakes Lane, Southend-on-Sea,
Essex SS2 6XT
Tel: (01702) 527486
Head: Mr J F Hagyard
Type: Co-educational Day
No of pupils: B78 G37
Special Needs: CP DEL EPI PH W

LANCASTER SCHOOL

Prittlewell Chase, Westcliff-on-Sea,
Essex SS0 0RT
Tel: (01702) 342543
Acting Head: Mrs A Farrow
Type: Co-educational Day 2–19
No of pupils: B65 G45
Special Needs: AUT CP PMLD SLD

PRIORY SCHOOL

Burr Hill Chase, Southend-on-Sea,
Essex SS2 6PE
Tel: (01702) 347490
Head: Mrs V S Wathen
Type: Co-educational Day 8–16
No of pupils: 46
Special Needs: **EBD**

THE ST CHRISTOPHER SCHOOL

Mountdale Gardens, Leigh-on-Sea,
Essex SS9 4AW
Tel: (01702) 524193
Head: Mr T G Wilson
Type: Co-educational Day 3–16
No of pupils: 110
Special Needs: **ADD ADHD ASP** AUT
DOW DYP DYS EBD HI MLD SLD
SP&LD W

ST NICHOLAS SCHOOL

Philpott Avenue, Southend-on-Sea,
Essex SS2 4RL
Tel: (01702) 462322
Head: Mrs G M Houghton
Type: Co-educational Day 4–16
No of pupils: 95
Special Needs: **MLD**

Thurrock Council

Education Department
PO Box 118
Grays
Essex RM17 6GF
Tel: (01375) 652792

KNIGHTSMEAD SCHOOL

Fortin Close, South Ockendon,
Essex RM15 5NH
Tel: (01708) 852956
Head: Ms J Thomas
Type: Co-educational Day 3–12
No of pupils: B27 G14
Special Needs: **AUT PMLD SLD** W

TREETOPS SCHOOL

Dell Road, Grays, Essex RM17 5LH
Tel: (01375) 372723
Head: Mr P Smith
Type: Co-educational Day 5–16
No of pupils: 116
Special Needs: AUT MLD

WOODACRE SCHOOL

Erriff Drive, South Ockendon, Essex
RM15 5AY
Tel: (01708) 852006
Head: Mr J Stringer
Type: Co-educational Day 3–16
No of pupils: 100
Special Needs: CP DYP EPI MLD PH
PMLD SLD SP&LD W

GLOUCESTERSHIRE

Gloucestershire Education Authority

Shire Hall
Gloucester
Gloucestershire GL1 2TP
Tel: (01452) 425300

ALDERMAN KNIGHT SCHOOL
Ashchurch Road, Tewkesbury,
Gloucestershire GL20 8JJ
Tel: (01684) 295639
Head: Mr I T Walsh
Type: Co-educational Day 5–16
No of pupils: B58 G36
Special Needs: ASP AUT CP DEL DYS EBD EPI HI MLD PH SLD SP&LD SPLD VIS W

BATTLEDOWN CHILDREN'S CENTRE
Harp Hill, Battledown, Cheltenham,
Gloucestershire GL52 6PZ
Tel: (01242) 525472
Head: Mrs E M Rook
Type: Co-educational Day 2–7
No of pupils: 40
Special Needs: ASP AUT CP DOW EPI HI MLD PH SLD SP&LD VIS SLD W

BETTRIDGE SCHOOL
Warden Hill Road, Cheltenham,
Gloucestershire GL51 5AT
Tel: (01242) 514934
Head: Mrs M Saunders
Type: Co-educational Day 2–19
No of pupils: 90
Special Needs: AUT PMLD SLD VIS W

CAM HOUSE SCHOOL
Drake Lane, Dursley, Gloucestershire
GL11 5HD
Tel: (01453) 542130
Head: Mr T E Pascoe
Type: Boys Boarding and Day 11–16
No of pupils: 61
Special Needs: EBD

COLN HOUSE SCHOOL
Horcott Road, Fairford,
Gloucestershire GL7 4DB
Tel: (01285) 712308
Head: Mr J W Davidson
Type: Co-educational Boarding and Day 9–16
No of pupils: B51 G10
No of Boarders: W49
Special Needs: EBD MLD

DEAN HALL SCHOOL
Speech House Road, Coleford,
Gloucestershire GL16 7EJ
Tel: (01594) 822175
Head: Mr J N Haddock
Type: Co-educational Day 5–16
No of pupils: 90
Special Needs: EBD MLD

THE HAWTHORNS SCHOOL
Longford Lane, Gloucester,
Gloucestershire GL2 9EU
Tel: (01452) 500499
Head: Mr M T Musson
Type: Co-educational Day 2–16
No of pupils: B94 G48
Special Needs: PMLD SLD W

OAKDENE SCHOOL
Dockham Road, Cinderford,
Gloucestershire GL14 2AN
Tel: (01594) 822693
Acting Head: Mrs E Oates
Type: Co-educational Day
No of pupils: B17 G5
Special Needs: PMLD SLD

PATERNOSTER SCHOOL
Watermoor Road, Cirencester,
Gloucestershire GL7 1JS
Tel: (01285) 652480
Head: Mr P Barton
Type: Co-educational Day 2–16
No of pupils: 50
Special Needs: PMLD SLD W

SANDFORD SCHOOL
Seven Springs, Cheltenham,
Gloucestershire GL53 9NG
Tel: (01242) 870224
Head: Mr S Jones
Type: Co-educational Day 5–16
No of pupils: 105
Special Needs: EBD

THE SHRUBBERIES SCHOOL
Oldends Lane, Stonehouse,
Gloucestershire GL10 2DG
Tel: (01453) 822155
Head: Mr P J Morgan
Type: Co-educational Day 2–19
No of pupils: B44 G36
Special Needs: AUT PMLD SLD SP&LD

South Gloucestershire Education Authority

Bowling Hill
Chipping Sodbury
Bristol BS37 6JX
Tel: (01454) 868686

GRIMSBURY PARK SCHOOL
Tower Road North, Warmley, Bristol,
South Gloucestershire BS15 2XL
Tel: (0117) 967 3422
Head: Mr S Morris
No of pupils: 77
Special Needs: AUT PMLD SLD

NEW SIBLANDS SCHOOL
Easton Hill Road, Thornbury, South
Gloucestershire BS12 1AU
Tel: (01454) 414188
Head: Mr P Casson
Type: Co-educational Day 2–19
No of pupils: 55
Special Needs: PMLD SLD

HAMPSHIRE

Hampshire Education Authority

The Castle
Winchester
Hampshire SO23 8UG
Tel: (01962) 841841

BAYCROFT SCHOOL

Gosport Road, Stubbington,
Fareham, Hampshire PO14 2AE
Tel: (01329) 664151
Head: Mr R A Hendry
Type: Co-educational Day 11–16
No of pupils: 170
Special Needs: **ADD ADHD** AUT DYP
DYS EBD EPI HI **MLD**

THE CEDAR SPECIAL SCHOOL

Redbridge Lane, Nursling,
Southampton, Hampshire SO1 9XN
Tel: (023) 8073 4205
Head: Mr B G Hart
No of pupils: 90
Special Needs: **PH** W

DOVE HOUSE SPECIAL SCHOOL

Sutton Road, Basingstoke,
Hampshire RG21 5SU
Tel: (01256) 351555
Head: Mr C House
Type: Co-educational 11–16
No of pupils: 110
Special Needs: **MLD**

FOREST EDGE SPECIAL SCHOOL

Lydlynch Road, Totton,
Southampton, Hampshire SO40 3DW
Tel: (023) 8086 4949
Head: Mr P Hodgson
Type: Co-educational Day
No of pupils: B44 G13
Special Needs: ADD ADHD AUT HI
MLD SLD SP&LD VIS W

FOXBURY SPECIAL SCHOOL

Perth Road, Bridgemary, Gosport,
Hampshire PO13 0XX
Tel: (01329) 232998
Head: Mrs C Gedge
Type: Co-educational Day 3–11
No of pupils: 75
Special Needs: AUT EBD MLD
SP&LD

GLENWOOD SPECIAL SCHOOL

Washington Road, Evisworth,
Hampshire PO10 7NN
Tel: (01243) 373120
Head: Mrs C A Hill
Type: Co-educational Day 11–16
No of pupils: 92
Special Needs: **MLD**

GREENACRES SPECIAL SCHOOL

Andover Road, Winchester,
Hampshire SO22 6AU
Tel: (01962) 862450
Head: Mrs C Gayler
Type: Co-educational Day
No of pupils: B28 G15
Special Needs: AUT PMLD SLD W

HAWTHORNS SPECIAL SCHOOL

Pack Lane, Kempshott, Basingstoke,
Hampshire RG22 5TH
Tel: (01256) 336601
Head: Mr A K Beavan
Type: Co-educational Day and
Boarding 10–16
No of pupils: B46 G6
No of Boarders: W10
Special Needs: **EBD**

HEATHFIELD SPECIAL SCHOOL

Oldbury Way, Peak Lane, Fareham,
Hampshire PO14 3BN
Tel: (01329) 845150
Head: Mrs E Muirhead
Type: Co-educational Day 3–11
No of pupils: 142
Special Needs: **ADHD ASP** AUT CP
DYP EBD EPI HI MLD PH SP&LD
VIS W

HENRY TYNDALS SPECIAL SCHOOL

Croft Road, Church Lane East,
Aldershot, Hampshire GU11 3HR
Head: Mr C H Woodroffe
Type: Co-educational Day 5–16
Special Needs: ASP AUT MLD

ICKNIELD SPECIAL SCHOOL

River Way, Andover, Hampshire
SP11 6LT
Tel: (01264) 365297
Head: Mr S S Steer-Smith
Type: Co-educational Day 2–19
No of pupils: 66
Special Needs: AUT **PMLD SLD** W

LANKHILLS SPECIAL SCHOOL

Andover Road, Winchester,
Hampshire SO23 7BU
Tel: (01962) 854537
Head: Mr R J Wakelam
Type: Co-educational Boarding and
Day 11–19
No of pupils: 118 *No of Boarders:* W15
Special Needs: **MLD**

LIMINGTON HOUSE SPECIAL SCHOOL

St Andrew's Road, Basingstoke,
Hampshire RG22 6PS
Tel: (01256) 322148
Head: Mr M J C Balson
Type: Co-educational Day 2–19
No of pupils: 80
Special Needs: PMLD **SLD**

MAPLE RIDGE SPECIAL SCHOOL

Maple Crescent, Basingstoke,
Hampshire RG21 5SX
Tel: (01256) 323639
Head: Mrs J Martin
Type: Co-educational Day 4–11
No of pupils: B61 G21
Special Needs: AUT **MLD** W

THE MARK WAY SCHOOL

Bachelors Barn Road, Andover,
Hampshire SP10 1HR
Tel: (01264) 351835
Head: Mr T Oakley
Type: Co-educational Day 11–16
No of pupils: B40 G40
Special Needs: ASP AUT DYS HI **MLD**
SP&LD W

MEADOW SPECIAL SCHOOL

Mill Chase Road, Bordon,
Hampshire GU35 0HA
Tel: (01420) 474396
Head: Mr P Greenwood
Type: Co-educational Day 4–16
No of pupils: B78 G52
Special Needs: ADD ADHD AUT
DOW EPI MLD PH SPLD TOU W

NORMAN GATE SPECIAL SCHOOL

Vigo Road, Andover, Hampshire
SP10 1JZ
Tel: (01264) 323423
Head: Mrs J Sansome
Type: Co-educational 2–11
No of pupils: 58
Special Needs: AUT MLD W

OAK LODGE SCHOOL

Roman Road, Dibden Purlieu,
Southampton, Hampshire SO4 5RQ
Tel: (023) 8084 7213
Head: Mrs B A Hawker
Type: Co-educational Day 11–16
No of pupils: B82 G30
Special Needs: AUT **MLD**

RACHEL MADOCKS

Eagle Avenue, Cowplain,
Portsmouth, Hampshire PO8 9XP
Tel: (023) 9224 1818
Head: Mrs C A Browne
Type: Co-educational Day 2–19
No of pupils: B44 G34
Special Needs: **PMLD SLD**

ST FRANCIS SPECIAL SCHOOL

Oldbury Way, Fareham, Hampshire
PO14 3BN
Tel: (01329) 845730
Head: Mrs S Chalmers
Type: Co-educational Day 2–19
No of pupils: 98
Special Needs: AUT CP EPI PMLD
SLD W

SALTERNS SPECIAL SCHOOL

Commercial Road, Totton,
Southampton, Hampshire SO40 3AF
Tel: (023) 8086 4211
Head: Mrs Jackie Partridge
Type: Co-educational 4–19
No of pupils: 58
Special Needs: AUT CP EPI PMLD
SLD W

SAMUEL CODY SPECIAL SCHOOL

Lynchford Road, Farnborough,
Hampshire GU14 6BJ
Tel: (01252) 314720
Head: Mr L Bevan
Type: Co-educational Day 11–16
No of pupils: B57 G26
Special Needs: **MLD**

SAXON WOOD SPECIAL SCHOOL

Rooksdown, Barron Place,
Basingstoke, Hampshire RG24 9NH
Tel: (01256) 356635
Head: Mr P B Skinner
Type: Co-educational Day 2–11
No of pupils: B25 G25
Special Needs: CP DEL EPI HI **PH** W

SHEPHERDS DOWN SCHOOL

Shepherds Lane, Compton,
Winchester, Hampshire SO21 2AJ
Tel: (01962) 713445
Head: Mr A Gazzard
Type: Co-educational Day
No of pupils: 105
Special Needs: AUT DOW DYP EPI
MLD SP&LD

TANKERVILLE SPECIAL SCHOOL

Romsey Road, Eastleigh, Hampshire
SO50 9AJ
Tel: (023) 8061 2639
Head: Mrs G Clarke
Type: Co-educational Day 2–19
No of pupils: 56
Special Needs: **SLD** W

WATERLOO SPECIAL SCHOOL

Warfield Avenue, Waterlooville,
Hampshire PO7 7JJ
Tel: (023) 9225 5956
Head: Mr J E M Cahill
Type: Co-educational Day and
Boarding 4–11
No of pupils: 42 *No of Boarders:* W10
Special Needs: EBD

WHITEDOWN SCHOOL

Albert Road, Alton, Hampshire
GU34 1LP
Tel: (01420) 82201
Head: Mrs B Livings
Type: Co-educational Day 2–19
No of pupils: 48
Special Needs: AUT PMLD **SLD**

Portsmouth City Council

Education Department
Civic Offices
Guildhall Square
Portsmouth PO1 2EA
Tel: (023) 9284 1209

CLIFFDALE PRIMARY SCHOOL

Battenburg Avenue, North End,
Portsmouth, Hampshire PO2 0SN
Tel: (023) 9266 2601
Head: Mrs L Handford
Type: Co-educational Day 4–11
No of pupils: 124
Special Needs: AUT **MLD**

EAST SHORE SPECIAL SCHOOL

Eastern Road, Milton, Portsmouth,
Hampshire PO3 6EP
Tel: (023) 9283 9331
Head: P Clarke
Type: Co-educational Day 2–19
No of pupils: 80
Special Needs: AUT DOW EPI **PMLD**
SLD W

REDWOOD PARK SCHOOL

Wembley Grove, Highbury,
Portsmouth, Hampshire PO6 2RY
Tel: (023) 9237 7500
Head: Mrs E A Nye
Type: Co-educational 11–16
No of pupils: B89 G39
Special Needs: **MLD**

SUTCLIFFE HOUSE

76 Winchester Road, Portsmouth,
Hampshire PO2 7PT
Tel: (023) 9266 3894
Head: Mrs R Jenkins
No of pupils: 10
Special Needs: AUT CP EPI MLD SLD

WATERSIDE SCHOOL & UNIT

Tipner Lane, Tipner, Portsmouth,
Hampshire PO2 8RA
Tel: (023) 9222 1366
Head: Mr T Stokes
Type: Co-educational Boarding and
Day 11–16
No of pupils: B74 G3
No of Boarders: W10
Special Needs: ADD ADHD **EBD**
TOU W

THE WILLOWS NURSERY SPECIAL SCHOOL

Battenburg Avenue, North End,
Portsmouth, Hampshire PO2 0SN
Tel: (023) 9266 6918
Head: Mrs A M Swann
Type: Co-educational Day 2–5
No of pupils: 36
Special Needs: ADD ADHD ASP AUT
CP DEL DOW DYP DYS EBD EPI HI
MLD PH SLD SP&LD VIS

Southampton City Council

Education Department
Frobisher House
5th Floor
Nelson Gate
Southampton SO15 1BZ
Tel: (023) 8022 3855

NETLEY COURT SPECIAL SCHOOL

Victoria Road, Netley Abbey,
Southampton, Hampshire SO3 5DR
Tel: (023) 8045 3259
Head: Mr W R Ferry
Type: Co-educational 4–11
No of pupils: 80
Special Needs: AUT MLD SP&LD

THE POLYGON SPECIAL SCHOOL

Handel Terrace, The Polygon,
Southampton, Hampshire SO1 2FH
Tel: (023) 8063 6776
Head: Mr L M Gent
Type: Boys Day 11–16
No of pupils: 56
Special Needs: EBD

RED LODGE SCHOOL

Vermont Close, Winchester Road,
Southampton, Hampshire SO16 7LT
Tel: (023) 8076 7660
Head: Miss S P Mackie
Type: Co-educational Day 11–16
No of pupils: 155
Special Needs: MLD

RIDGEWAY HOUSE SPECIAL SCHOOL

Peartree Avenue, Bitterne,
Southampton, Hampshire SO19 7JL
Tel: (023) 8044 8897
Head: Mrs S J Savage
Type: Co-educational Day 3–19
No of pupils: 90
Special Needs: SLD

VERMONT SPECIAL SCHOOL

Vermont Close, off Winchester Road,
Southampton, Hampshire SO1 7LT
Tel: (023) 8076 7988
Head: Mr E Bell
Type: Boys Day 4–11
No of pupils: 42
Special Needs: EBD MLD SPLD

HARTLEPOOL

Hartlepool Education Authority

Level 4
Civic Centre
Hartlepool TS24 8AY
Tel: (01429) 523734

CATCOTE SCHOOL

Catcote Road, Hartlepool TS25 4EZ
Tel: (01429) 264036
Head: Mr N Carden
Type: Co-educational Day 11–19
No of pupils: 100
Special Needs: MLD PMLD SLD W

SPRINGWELL SCHOOL

Wiltshire Way, Hartlepool TS26 0TB
Tel: (01429) 280600
Head: Mr A J Lacey
Type: Co-educational 2–11
No of pupils: 66
Special Needs: ADD ADHD ASP AUT
CP DOW EPI HI PMLD SLD SP&LD
VIS W

THORNHILL SCHOOL

Elwick Road, Hartlepool TS26 0LQ
Tel: (01429) 276906
Head: Ms S Berwick
Type: Co-educational 2–19
No of pupils: 48
Special Needs: CP DEL EPI PH W

HEREFORDSHIRE

Herefordshire Education Authority

PO Box 185
Black Friars Street
Hereford HR4 9ZR
Tel: (01432) 260000

BARRS COURT SCHOOL

Barrs Court Road, Hereford,
Herefordshire HR1 1EQ
Tel: (01432) 265035
Head: Mrs S Ashley
Type: Co-educational Day 11–19
No of pupils: B22 G19
Special Needs: MLD PMLD SLD W

BLACKMARSTON SCHOOL

Honddu Close, Hereford,
Herefordshire HR2 7NX
Tel: (01432) 272376
Head: Mrs S Bailey
Type: Co-educational Day 2–11
No of pupils: 45
Special Needs: PMLD SLD W

WESTFIELD SCHOOL & LEOMINSTER EARLY YEARS CENTRE

Westfield Walk, Leominster,
Herefordshire HR6 8HD
Tel: (01568) 613147
Head: Mrs P Chesters
Type: Co-educational Day 3–19
No of pupils: 60
Special Needs: PMLD SLD W

HERTFORDSHIRE

Hertfordshire Education Authority

County Hall
Hertford
Hertfordshire SG13 8DF
Tel: (01992) 555827

AMWELL VIEW SCHOOL

St Margarets, Stanstead Abbotts,
Hertfordshire SG12 8EH
Tel: (01920) 870027
Head: Mrs J S Liversage
Type: Co-educational Day 2–19
No of pupils: B66 G32
Special Needs: **AUT** CP DOW EPI
PMLD SLD W

BATCHWOOD SCHOOL

Townsend Drive, St Albans,
Hertfordshire AL3 5RP
Tel: (01727) 765195
Head: Mr M E Hopkins
Type: Co-educational Day 11–16
No of pupils: 53
Special Needs: **EBD**

BOXMOOR HOUSE SCHOOL

Box Lane, Hemel Hempstead,
Hertfordshire HP3 0DF
Tel: (01442) 256915
Head: Mr J R Hooper
Type: Boys Day and Boarding 11–16
No of pupils: 62 No of Boarders: W37
Special Needs: **EBD**

THE COLLETT SCHOOL

Lockers Park Lane, Hemel
Hempstead, Hertfordshire HP1 1TQ
Tel: (01442) 398988
Head: Mrs M Lemarie
Type: Co-educational Day 5–16
No of pupils: B71 G52
Special Needs: **MLD**

COLNBROOK SCHOOL

Hayling Road, South Oxhey,
Watford, Hertfordshire WD1 6BN
Tel: (020) 8428 1281
Head: Mr R J Hill
Type: Co-educational Day 5–11
No of pupils: 88
Special Needs: AUT MLD W

FALCONER SCHOOL

Falconer Road, Bushey, Watford,
Hertfordshire WD2 3AT
Tel: (020) 8950 2505
Head: Mr J S B Page
Type: Boys Day and Boarding 11–16
No of pupils: 60 No of Boarders: W6
Special Needs: **EBD**

FOREST HOUSE EDUCATION CENTRE

Harperbury Hospital, Haper Lane,
Radlett, Hertfordshire WD7 9HQ
Tel: (01923) 427241
Head: Mr M R Ingham
Type: Co-educational Boarding and
Day 11–16
No of pupils: B8 G8 No of Boarders: F14
Special Needs: **EBD**

GARSTON MANOR SCHOOL

Horseshoe Lane, Garston, Watford,
Hertfordshire WD2 7HR
Tel: (01923) 673757
Head: Mr D N Harrison
Type: Co-educational Day 11–16
No of pupils: 115
Special Needs: **MLD**

GREENSIDE SCHOOL

Shephall Green, Stevenage,
Hertfordshire SG2 9XS
Tel: (01438) 315356
Head: Mrs A Biglands
Type: Co-educational Day 5–19
No of pupils: 100
Special Needs: AUT PMLD SLD W

HAILEY HALL SCHOOL

Hailey Lane, Hertford, Hertfordshire
SG13 7PB
Tel: (01992) 465208
Head: Mr B Evans
Type: Boys Boarding and Day 11–16
No of pupils: 55 No of Boarders: W30
Special Needs: **EBD**

HEATHLANDS SCHOOL

Heathlands Drive, St Albans,
Hertfordshire AL3 5AY
Tel: (01727) 868596
Head: Mr M Davis
Type: Co-educational Boarding and
Day 3–16
No of pupils: B57 G40
No of Boarders: W27
Special Needs: **HI** W

KNIGHTSFIELD SCHOOL

Knightsfield, Welwyn Garden City,
Hertfordshire AL8 7LW
Tel: (01707) 376874
Head: Mrs L M Lieth
Type: Co-educational Day and
Boarding 11–16
No of pupils: 50 No of Boarders: W20
Special Needs: **HI** W

LAKESIDE SCHOOL

Lemsford Lane, Welwyn Garden
City, Hertfordshire AL8 6YN
Tel: (01707) 327410
Head: Mrs J Chamberlain
Type: Co-educational Day
No of pupils: 63
Special Needs: PMLD SLD W

LARWOOD SCHOOL

Webb Rise, Stevenage, Hertfordshire
SG1 5QU
Tel: (01438) 236333
Head: Mr A K Whittaker
Type: Co-educational Day and
Boarding 4–11
No of pupils: B25 G26
Special Needs: **EBD**

LONSDALE SCHOOL

Webb Rise, Stevenage, Hertfordshire
SG1 5QU
Tel: (01438) 357631
Head: Mrs P M clark
Type: Co-educational Day and
Boarding 3–18
No of pupils: 84 No of Boarders: W28
Special Needs: **PH** W

MEADOW WOOD SCHOOL

Coldharbour Lane, Bushey, Watford,
Hertfordshire WD2 3NU
Tel: (020) 8420 4720
Head: Mr J Addison
Type: Co-educational 3–11
No of pupils: 32
Special Needs: **PH** W

MIDDLETON SCHOOL

Walnut Tree Walk, Ware,
Hertfordshire SG12 9PD
Tel: (01920) 485152
Head: Mr A Staras
Type: Co-educational 4–11
Special Needs: **MLD**

ST LUKE'S SCHOOL
Crouch Hall Lane, Redbourn,
Hertfordshire AL3 7ET
Tel: (01582) 626727
Head: Mr P Johnson
Type: Co-educational Day 9–16
No of pupils: 170
Special Needs: **MLD**

SOUTHFIELD SCHOOL
Travellers Lane, Hatfield,
Hertfordshire AL10 8TJ
Tel: (01707) 258259
Head: Mr M B Philp
Type: Co-educational Day 4–11
No of pupils: B54 G26
Special Needs: **MLD** W

THE VALLEY SCHOOL
Valley Way, Stevenage, Hertfordshire
SG2 9AB
Tel: (01438) 747274
Head: Mr R G Stabler
Type: Co-educational Day
No of pupils: B93 G79
Special Needs: **MLD**

WOODFIELD SCHOOL
Malmes Croft, Leverstock Green,
Hemel Hempstead, Hertfordshire
HP3 8RL
Tel: (01442) 253476
Head: Mrs J Johnson
Type: Co-educational Day 5–19
No of pupils: 78
Special Needs: AUT SLD W

WOOLGROVE SCHOOL
Pryor Way, Letchworth,
Hertfordshire SG6 2PT
Tel: (01462) 622422
Head: Mrs R V Tutt
Type: Co-educational Day 5–11
No of pupils: 108
Special Needs: AUT **MLD**

ISLE OF WIGHT

Isle of Wight Education Authority

County Hall
Newport
Isle of Wight PO30 1UD
Tel: (01983) 821000

MEDINA HOUSE SCHOOL
School Lane, Newport, Isle of Wight
PO30 2HS
Tel: (01983) 522917
Head: Mr D M Hughes
Type: Co-educational Day 2–19
No of pupils: 77
Special Needs: AUT CP DOW EPI
PMLD SLD W

WATERGATE SCHOOL
Watergate Road, Newport, Isle of
Wight PO30 1XW
Tel: (01983) 524634
Head: Mrs A E Munt-Davies
Type: Co-educational Day 3–18
No of pupils: 204
Special Needs: **MLD** W

KENT

Kent Education Authority

Sessions House
County Hall
Maidstone
Kent ME14 1XA
Tel: (01622) 671411

BOWER GROVE SCHOOL
Fant Lane, Maidstone, Kent
ME16 8NL
Tel: (01622) 726773
Head: Mr T N Phipps
Type: Co-educational Day 5–16
No of pupils: B93 G62
Special Needs: AUT CP DOW DYP
EBD EPI HI MLD PH SP&LD

BROOMHILL BANK SCHOOL
Broomhill Road, Rusthall, Tunbridge
Wells, Kent TN3 0TB
Tel: (01892) 522666
Head: Mr P Barnett
Type: Girls Boarding and Day 8–19
No of pupils: 90 *No of Boarders:* F28
Special Needs: **MLD** SP&LD

FIVE ACRE WOOD SCHOOL
Boughton Lane, Maidstone, Kent
ME15 9QL
Tel: (01622) 743925
Head: Ms J E Kratochvil
Type: Co-educational Day 5–19
No of pupils: 62
Special Needs: AUT PMLD **SLD** W

THE FORELAND SCHOOL
Lanthorne Road, Broadstairs, Kent
CT10 3NX
Tel: (01843) 863891
Head: Mr P S Hare
Type: Co-educational Day 2–19
No of pupils: 130
Special Needs: CP EPI HI PH **PMLD**
SLD VIS

FOXWOOD SCHOOL
Seabrook Road, Hythe, Kent
CT21 5QJ
Tel: (01303) 261155
Head: Mr C Soulsby
Type: Co-educational Boarding and
Day
No of pupils: B81 G41
No of Boarders: W23
Special Needs: AUT EBD PMLD SLD

FURNESS SCHOOL
Rowhill Road, Hextable, Swanley,
Kent BR8 7RP
Tel: (01322) 662937
Head: Mr R J Chapman
Type: Boys Day and Boarding 11–16
No of pupils: 72 *No of Boarders:* W52
Special Needs: **EBD**

GAP HOUSE SCHOOL
South Cliffe Parade, Broadstairs,
Kent CT10 1TJ
Tel: (01843) 861679
Head: Mr I P Cooke
Type: Co-educational Boarding and
Day
No of pupils: B53 G15
No of Boarders: W26
Special Needs: ASP DYS SP&LD SPLD

GRANGE PARK
Birling Road, Leybourne, Maidstone,
Kent ME19 5QA
Tel: (01732) 842144
Head: Mrs J Hanley
Type: Co-educational Day 11–19
No of pupils: 40
Special Needs: ASP **AUT** CP EBD EPI
HI **MLD** PH PMLD **SLD** SP&LD
VIS W

HALSTEAD PLACE SCHOOL
Church Road, Halstead, Sevenoaks,
Kent TN14 7HQ
Tel: (01959) 533294
Head: Mr N I Parkinson
Type: Co-educational
Special Needs: **EBD**

HARBOUR SCHOOL
Elms Vale Road, Dover, Kent
CT17 9PS
Tel: (01304) 201964
Head: Mr A Berresford
Type: Co-educational Day 5–16
No of pupils: 138
Special Needs: **MLD** W

HIGHVIEW SCHOOL
Moat Farm Road, Folkestone, Kent
CT19 5DJ
Tel: (01303) 258755
Head: Mr C J Hurling
Type: Co-educational Day 5–16
No of pupils: 141
Special Needs: MLD SLD SP&LD

IFIELD SCHOOL
Cedar Avenue, Gravesend, Kent
DA12 5JT
Tel: (01474) 365485
Head: Mr S M Harrison
Type: Co-educational Day
No of pupils: B111 G56
Special Needs: ASP AUT DOW DYS
MLD PH SP&LD SPLD

LALEHAM SCHOOL
Northdown Park Road, Margate,
Kent CT9 2TP
Tel: (01843) 221946
Head: Mr K Mileham
Type: Co-educational Boarding and
Day 11–16
No of pupils: B110 G15
No of Boarders: W60
Special Needs: DYC DYP **DYS** SP&LD
SPLD

MILESTONE SCHOOL
Ash Road, New Ash Green, Dartford,
Kent DA3 8JZ
Tel: (01474) 709420
Head: Miss E T Flanagan
Type: Co-educational Day 2–19
No of pupils: 150
Special Needs: AUT PMLD SLD VIS W

ORCHARD SCHOOL
Cambridge Road, Canterbury, Kent
CT1 3QQ
Tel: (01227) 769220
Head: Mr B S Shelley
Type: Co-educational Day 7–16
No of pupils: B80 G30
Special Needs: **MLD** W

PORTAL HOUSE SCHOOL
Sea Street, St Margaret's-at-Cliffe,
Dover, Kent CT15 6AR
Tel: (01304) 853033
Head: Mr L Sage
Type: Co-educational Boarding 8–13
No of pupils: 44 *No of Boarders:* W12
Special Needs: **EBD**

RIDGEVIEW SCHOOL
Cage Green Road, Tonbridge, Kent
TN10 4PT
Tel: (01732) 771384
Head: Mr A E Carver
Type: Co-educational Day 2–19
No of pupils: 95
Special Needs: AUT DOW **PMLD**
SLD W

ST ANTHONY'S SCHOOL
St Anthony's Way, Margate, Kent
CT9 3RA
Tel: (01843) 292015
Head: Mr R A O'Dell
Type: Co-educational Day 3–16
No of pupils: 170
Special Needs: EBD **MLD**

ST BARTHOLOMEW'S SCHOOL
Attlee Way, North Street, Milton
Regis, Sittingbourne, Kent
ME10 2HE
Tel: (01795) 477888
Head: Ms G M Hurstfield
Type: Co-educational 4–16
No of pupils: 78
Special Needs: AUT PMLD SLD W

ST GEORGE'S SCHOOL
Pembury Road, Tunbridge Wells,
Kent TN2 4NE
Tel: (01892) 823096
Head: Mr P J Carr
Type: Co-educational Day 5–19
No of pupils: 160
Special Needs: DYS HI MLD PH
SP&LD VIS

ST NICHOLAS' SCHOOL
Holme Oak Close, Nunnery Fields,
Canterbury, Kent CT1 3JJ
Tel: (01227) 464316
Head: Mr D Lewis
Type: Co-educational Day 4–19
No of pupils: B57 G35
Special Needs: AUT CP DOW PMLD
SLD W

ST THOMAS' SCHOOL
Swanstree Avenue, Sittingbourne,
Kent ME10 4NL
Tel: (01795) 477788
Head: Mr P J Rankin
Type: Co-educational 5–19
No of pupils: B85 G55
Special Needs: **MLD** W

STONE BAY SCHOOL
Stone Road, Broadstairs, Kent
CT10 1EB
Tel: (01843) 863421
Head: Mr R Edey
Type: Boarding and Day
No of pupils: 48 *No of Boarders:* F24
Special Needs: AUT DYP SLD

SWINFORD MANOR SCHOOL
Great Chart, Ashford, Kent
TN23 3BT
Tel: (01233) 622958
Head: Mr J L Davies
Type: Boys
No of pupils: 62 *No of Boarders:* W40
Special Needs: EBD

VALENCE SCHOOL
Westerham, Kent TN16 1QN
Tel: (01959) 562156
Head: Mr R Gooding
Type: Co-educational Boarding and
Day 5–19
No of pupils: B69 G36
No of Boarders: W56
Special Needs: CP EPI **PH** W

WAVENEY SCHOOL
Waveney Road, Tonbridge, Kent
TN10 3JU
Tel: (01732) 351917
Head: Mrs W Vaughan
Type: Co-educational Day 5–16
No of pupils: 70
Special Needs: SP&LD SPLD

WYVERN SCHOOL
Willesborough Site, Hythe Road,
Ashford, Kent TN24 0QF
Tel: (01223) 621468
Head: Mr D Spencer
Type: Co-educational Day 5–19
Special Needs: MLD SLD

Medway Council

Education Department
Compass Centre
Pembroke
Chatham Maritime
Chatham
Kent ME4 4YN
Tel: (01634) 306000

ABBEY COURT SCHOOL
Rede Court Road, Strood, Rochester,
Kent ME2 3SP
Tel: (01634) 718153/714600
Head: Ms K Joy
Type: Co-educational Day 5–19
No of pupils: B70 G38
Special Needs: PMLD **SLD**

BRADFIELDS SCHOOL
Churchill Avenue, Chatham, Kent
ME5 0LB
Tel: (01634) 683990
Head: Mr P J Harris
Type: Co-educational 11–19
No of pupils: B117 G68
Special Needs: AUT **MLD** PH W

DANECOURT SCHOOL
Hotel Road, Gillingham, Kent
ME8 6AA
Tel: (01634) 232589
Head: Mrs A Peters
Type: Co-educational Day 5–11
No of pupils: B67 G39
Special Needs: ADD ADHD AUT
DOW **MLD** W

LANCASHIRE

Blackburn with Darwen Borough Council

Town Hall
Joint Divisional Offices
Jubilee Street
Blackburn BB1 7DY
Tel: (01254) 585585

BANK HEY SCHOOL
Heys Lane, Blackburn, Lancashire
BB2 4NW
Tel: (01254) 261655
Head: Mr T Feely
Type: Co-educational Day 11–16
No of pupils: 40
Special Needs: **ADD ADHD EBD**

CROSSHILL SCHOOL
Shadsworth Road, Blackburn,
Lancashire BB1 2HR
Tel: (01254) 667713
Head: Mr M J Hatch
Type: Co-educational Day 5–16
No of pupils: B105 G53
Special Needs: **MLD**

TULLYALLAN SCHOOL
Salisbury Road, Darwen, Lancashire
BB3 1HZ
Tel: (01254) 702317
Head: Mrs J P Holman
Type: Co-educational Day 5–16
No of pupils: 50
Special Needs: **EBD**

Blackpool Borough Council

Progress House
Clifton Road
Blackpool FY4 4US
Tel: (01253) 476500

PARK SCHOOL
Whitegate Drive, Blackpool,
Lancashire FY3 9HF
Tel: (01253) 764130
Head: Mr E N M Parry
Type: Co-educational Day
No of pupils: 150
Special Needs: **MLD** W

WOODLANDS SCHOOL
Whitegate Drive, Blackpool,
Lancashire FY3 9HF
Tel: (01253) 316722
Head: Mr S J Forde
Type: Co-educational 2–19
No of pupils: B50 G26
Special Needs: PMLD SLD W

Lancashire Education Authority

PO Box 61
County Hall
Preston
Lancashire PR1 8RJ
Tel: (01772) 254868

ASTLEY PARK SCHOOL
Harrington Road, Chorley,
Lancashire PR7 1JZ
Tel: (01257) 262227
Head: Mr J McAndrew
Type: Co-educational Day 4–16
No of pupils: B80 G46
Special Needs: **MLD** W

BEACON SCHOOL
Tanhouse Road, Tanhouse,
Skelmersdale, Lancashire WN8 6BA
Tel: (01695) 721066
Head: Mr J H Taylor
Type: Co-educational Day 5–16
No of pupils: 72
Special Needs: **EBD**

BLACK MOSS SCHOOL
School Lane, Chapel House,
Skelmersdale, Lancashire WN8 8EH
Tel: (01695) 721487
Head: Mr P F Boycott
Type: Co-educational Day 4–18
No of pupils: 140
Special Needs: **MLD**

BLEASDALE HOUSE SCHOOL
Emesgate Lane, Silverdale,
Carnforth, Lancashire LA5 0RG
Tel: (01524) 701217
Head: Mrs L Ormrod
Type: Co-educational Boarding and
Day 2–19
No of pupils: 45 *No of Boarders:* F29
Special Needs: CP DEL EPI PH **PMLD**
SLD W

BROADFIELD SCHOOL
Fielding Lane, Oswaldtwistle,
Accrington, Lancashire BB5 3BE
Tel: (01254) 381782
Head: Mrs J White
Type: Co-educational Day
No of pupils: 100
Special Needs: **MLD**

BROUGHTON TOWER SCHOOL
Broughton-in-Furness, Lancashire
LA20 6AA
Tel: (01229) 716242
Head: Mr C Jones
Type: Boys Boarding 7–13
No of pupils: 44
Special Needs: ADD ADHD EBD SPLD

CALDER VIEW SCHOOL & EDUCATION SUPPORT CENTRE
March Street, Burnley, Lancashire
BB12 0BU
Tel: (01282) 433946
Head: Mr D Parkes
Type: Co-educational Day 4–16
No of pupils: B100 G50
Special Needs: MLD SLD W

THE COPPICE SCHOOL
Ash Grove, Bamber Bridge, Preston,
Lancashire PR5 6GY
Tel: (01772) 363342
Head: Mrs A Jenkins
Type: Co-educational Day 2–19
No of pupils: 58
Special Needs: PMLD SLD W

CRIBDEN HOUSE SCHOOL
Haslingden Road, Rawtenstall,
Rossendale, Lancashire BB4 6RX
Tel: (01706) 213048
Head: Mrs J Lord
Type: Co-educational Day 5–11
No of pupils: 50
Special Needs: **EBD**

ELMS SCHOOL
Moor Park, Blackpool Road, Preston,
Lancashire PR1 6AU
Tel: (01772) 792681
Head: Mr S Artis
Type: Co-educational Day 2–19
No of pupils: 70
Special Needs: PMLD SLD W

GREAT ARLEY SCHOOL
Holly Road, Thornton-Cleveleys,
Blackpool, Lancashire FY5 4HH
Tel: (01253) 821072
Head: Mrs J L Johns
Type: Co-educational 4–16
No of pupils: 90
Special Needs: **MLD**

HILLSIDE SCHOOL
Ribchester Road, Longridge, Preston,
Lancashire PR3 3XB
Tel: (01772) 782205
Head: Mrs C J Farmer
Type: Co-educational Day 2–16
No of pupils: B50 G10
Special Needs: **AUT**

LANCASTER PRIMARY PUPIL REFERRAL UNIT
Bowerham Road, Lancaster,
Lancashire LA1 4HT
Tel: (01524) 67164
Head: Mr D Ramsbottom
Type: Co-educational Day 4–11
No of pupils: 26
Special Needs: **EBD** W

THE LOYNE SCHOOL
Sefton Drive, Lancaster, Lancashire
LA1 2PZ
Tel: (01524) 64543
Head: Mrs C Murphy
Type: Co-educational Day 2–19
No of pupils: 51
Special Needs: PMLD SLD W

MASSEY HALL SCHOOL
Half Acre Lane, Thelwall,
Warrington, Cheshire WA4 3JQ
Tel: (01925) 752016
Head: Mr C Gleave
Type: Co-educational Boarding 11–19
No of pupils: 64 *No of Boarders:* W64
Special Needs: EBD EPI MLD

MAYFIELD SCHOOL
Gloucester Road, Chorley,
Lancashire PR7 3HN
Tel: (01257) 263063
Head: Mr P Monk
Type: Co-educational Day 2–19
No of pupils: B34 G26
Special Needs: **SLD** W

MINSTER LODGE PUPIL REFERRAL UNIT
Ruff Lane, Ormskirk, Lancashire
L39 4QX
Tel: (01695) 575486
Head: Mr G R Lucy
Type: Co-educational Day 11–15
No of pupils: 30
Special Needs: EBD SPLD

MOOR HEY SCHOOL
Far Croft, Lostock Hall, Preston,
Lancashire PR5 5SU
Tel: (01772) 336976
Head: Mr C W T Wilson
Type: Co-educational Day 5–16
No of pupils: B70 G38
Special Needs: **MLD**

MORECAMBE AND HEYSHAM ROAD SCHOOL
Morecambe Road, Morecambe,
Lancashire LA3 3AB
Tel: (01524) 414384/832074
Head: Mr T G Pickles
Type: Day
No of pupils: 181
Special Needs: AUT DOW EBD HI
MLD VIS

NORTH CLIFFE SCHOOL
Blackburn Old Road, Great
Harwood, Blackburn, Lancashire
BB6 7UW
Tel: (01254) 885245
Head: Mr R L Whitaker
Type: Co-educational Day 4–16
No of pupils: 110
Special Needs: **MLD**

PEAR TREE SCHOOL
29 Station Road, Kirkham,
Lancashire PR4 2HA
Tel: (01772) 683609
Head: Ms J Cook
Type: Co-educational Day 2–19
No of pupils: 60
Special Needs: PMLD **SLD** W

PRIMROSE HILL SCHOOL
Harrogate Crescent, Burnley,
Lancashire BB10 2NX
Tel: (01282) 424216
Head: Mr G McCabe
Type: Co-educational Day 3–16
No of pupils: B28 G19
Special Needs: CP DEL DYP DYS EBD
EPI HI MLD PH PMLD SLD SP&LD
SPLD VIS W

RED MARSH SCHOOL
Holly Road, Thornton Cleveleys,
Blackpool, Lancashire FY5 4HH
Tel: (01253) 868451
Head: Miss D Halpin
Type: Co-educational 2–19
No of pupils: 49
Special Needs: PMLD SLD

RED OAK
Child & Family Services, Piccadilly,
Lancaster, Lancashire LA1 4PW
Tel: (01524) 842266 Ex28
Head: Mr S Barraclough
Type: Co-educational
No of pupils: 16 *No of Boarders:* F12
Special Needs: ADD ADHD ASP AUT
DEL DYC DYP **DYS EBD** EPI MLD
SP&LD SPLD TOU W
52–week care

SHERBURN SCHOOL
Moor Park, Blackpool Road, Preston,
Lancashire PR1 6AA
Tel: (01772) 795749
Head: Mr M R Moss
Type: Co-educational Day 4–16
No of pupils: B67 G28
Special Needs: **MLD** W

TOR VIEW SCHOOL
Clod Lane, Haslingden, Lancashire
BB4 6LR
Tel: (01706) 214640
Head: Mr A J Squire
Type: Co-educational Day 4–19
No of pupils: 100
Special Needs: ASP **AUT** CP DOW
DYC DYP DYS EPI HI **MLD** PH
PMLD SLD VIS W

TOWNHOUSE SCHOOL
Townhouse Road, Nelson,
Lancashire BB9 8DG
Tel: (01282) 614013
Head: Mrs D E Morris
Type: Co-educational Day 2–19
No of pupils: B21 G14
Special Needs: PMLD **SLD** W

WENNINGTON HALL
Wennington, Lancashire LA2 8NS
Tel: (01524) 221333
Head: Mr J W N Prendergast
Type: Boys Boarding and Day
No of pupils: 70 *No of Boarders:* W46
Special Needs: **EBD**

WESTWAY SCHOOL
March Street, Burnley, Lancashire
BB12 0BU
Tel: (01282) 704499
Head: Mrs A C Stafford
Type: Co-educational 3–19
No of pupils: 30
Special Needs: PMLD **SLD** W

WHITE ASH SCHOOL
Thwaites Road, Oswaldtwistle,
Accrington, Lancashire BB5 4QG
Tel: (01254) 235772
Head: Mr B D Frew
Type: Co-educational Day 3–19
No of pupils: B24 G13
Special Needs: ASP AUT CP DOW EPI
PMLD SLD W

LEICESTERSHIRE

Leicester City Education Authority

Marlborough House
38 Welford Road
Leicester LE2 7AA
Tel: (0116) 252 7807

ASH FIELD SCHOOL
Broad Avenue, Leicester LE5 4PY
Tel: (0116) 273 7151
Head: Mr D Bateson
Type: Co-educational Day and
Boarding
No of pupils: B70 G50
No of Boarders: W18
Special Needs: CP HI PH SP&LD
VIS W

ELLESMERE COLLEGE
Ellesmere Road, Leicester,
Leicestershire LE3 1BE
Tel: (0116) 289 4242
Head: Mrs F Moir
Type: Co-educational Day 11–19
No of pupils: 250
Special Needs: **MLD** W

EMILY FORTEY SCHOOL
Glenfield Road, Leicester LE3 6DG
Tel: (0116) 285 7395
Head: Mr M W Thompson
Type: Co-educational Day
No of pupils: B48 G35
Special Needs: AUT CP EBD EPI HI
PH **PMLD SLD** SP&LD SPLD VIS

MILLGATE CENTRE
18 Scott Street, Leicester,
Leicestershire LE2 6DW
Tel: (0116) 270 4922
Head: Mrs K M Howells
Type: Boys Boarding and Day 11–16
No of pupils: 45 *No of Boarders:* W10
Special Needs: **EBD**

NETHER HALL SCHOOL
Netherhall Road, Leicester LE5 1DT
Tel: (0116) 241 7258
Acting Head: Mr P J Goodchild
Type: Co-educational Day 5–19
No of pupils: B43 G34
Special Needs: **PMLD SLD**

OAKLANDS SCHOOL
Whitehall Road, Evington, Leicester,
Leicestershire LE5 6GJ
Tel: (0116) 241 5921/2
Head: Mr P C Rowlands
Type: Co-educational Day 5–11
No of pupils: 80
Special Needs: **MLD** W

PIPER WAY SCHOOL
Grenfield Road, Leicester LE3 6DN
Tel: (0116) 285 6181
Head: Mrs A Standley
Type: Co-educational 5–11
No of pupils: 80
Special Needs: AUT **MLD** W

WESTERN PARK SCHOOL
Western Park, Leicester LE3 6HX
Tel: (01274) 687236
Head: Mr R D Gordon
Type: Day
No of pupils: 60
Special Needs: CP DEL EPI SP&LD

Leicestershire Education Authority
County Hall
Glenfield
Leicester
Leicestershire LE3 8RF
Tel: (0116) 232 3232

ASHMOUNT SCHOOL
Ashmount, Beacon Road,
Loughborough, Leicestershire
LE11 2BG
Tel: (01509) 268506
Head: Mrs K Waplington
Type: Co-educational Day 4–19
No of pupils: B35 G25
Special Needs: AUT CP DOW EPI PH
PMLD **SLD** W

CRAVEN LODGE SCHOOL
Burton Road, Melton Mowbray,
Leicestershire LE13 1DJ
Tel: (01664) 562246
Head: Mr P D Coopey
Type: Co-educational Day 4–11
No of pupils: 45
Special Needs: AUT **MLD** SP&LD

DOROTHY GOODMAN SCHOOL
Middlefield Lane, Hinckley,
Leicestershire LE10 0RB
Tel: (01455) 634582
Head: Mr T Smith
Type: Co-educational Day 3–19
No of pupils: 63
Special Needs: AUT DOW EPI PMLD
SLD W

FOREST WAY SCHOOL
Cropston Drive, Coalville, Leicester
LE67 4HS
Tel: (01530) 831899
Head: Ms L Slinger
Type: Co-educational Day 3–19
No of pupils: 80
Special Needs: AUT CP DEL DOW
EBD EPI HI PMLD **SLD** SP&LD
VIS W

MAPLEWELL HALL SCHOOL
Maplewell Road, Woodhouse Eaves,
Loughborough, Leicestershire
LE12 8QY
Tel: (01509) 890237
Head: Mrs P Jones
Type: Co-educational Day and
Boarding 11–16
No of pupils: B65 G50
No of Boarders: F17
Special Needs: **MLD**

LINCOLNSHIRE

Lincolnshire Education Authority
County Offices
Lincoln
Lincolnshire LN1 1YQ
Tel: (01522) 552222

AMBERGATE SCHOOL
Dysart Road, Grantham,
Lincolnshire NG31 7LP
Tel: (01476) 564957
Head: Mr D H Fuller
Type: Co-educational 5–16
No of pupils: 66
Special Needs: **MLD** W

THE ASH VILLA SPECIAL SCHOOL
Rauceby Hospital, Willoughby Road,
Sleaford, Lincolnshire NG34 8PP
Tel: (01529) 416046
Head: Mr D Robinson
Type: Co-educational Boarding and
Day 8–16
No of pupils: B12 G8
No of Boarders: F16
Special Needs: ADD ADHD ASP DEL
DYP DYS EBD EPI MLD TOU W

THE BECKETT SCHOOL
White's Wood Lane, Gainsborough,
Lincolnshire DN21 1TW
Tel: (01427) 612139
Head: Mrs S Hayter
Type: Co-educational Day 2–19
No of pupils: B20 G13
Special Needs: PMLD SLD W

THE ERESBY SCHOOL
Eresby Avenue, Spilsby, Lincolnshire
PE23 5HU
Tel: (01790) 752441
Head: Mr D J Middlehurst
Type: Co-educational Day 2–19
No of pupils: 41
Special Needs: PMLD SLD W

GARTH SCHOOL
Pinchbeck Road, Spalding,
Lincolnshire PE11 1QF
Tel: (01775) 725566
Head: Mrs L Dowson
Type: Co-educational Day 2–19
No of pupils: 26
Special Needs: PMLD **SLD** W

GOSBERTON HOUSE SCHOOL
Westhorpe Road, Gosberton, Spalding, Lincolnshire PE11 4EW
Tel: (01775) 840250
Head: Mr M R Allen
Type: Co-educational Day
No of pupils: 86
Special Needs: AUT MLD

JOHN FIELDING SCHOOL
Ashlawn Drive, Boston, Lincolnshire PE21 9PX
Tel: (01205) 363395
Head: Mrs S M Meakin
Type: Co-educational Day 2–19
No of pupils: B21 G8
Special Needs: PMLD **SLD** W

PRIORY SCHOOL
Neville Avenue, Spalding, Lincolnshire PE11 2EH
Tel: (01775) 724080
Head: Mr B J Howes
Type: Co-educational Day 11–16
No of pupils: 95
Special Needs: ADD **ADHD** ASP AUT DOW EBD **MLD** W

ST FRANCIS SPECIAL SCHOOL
Wickenby Crescent, Lincoln, Lincolnshire LN1 3TJ
Tel: (01522) 526498
Head: Mrs A Hoffman
Type: Co-educational Day and Boarding 2–19
No of pupils: 93 *No of Boarders:* W33
Special Needs: **CP** DEL DOW EPI MLD PH W

ST LAWRENCE SCHOOL
Bowl Alley Lane, Horncastle, Lincolnshire LN9 5EJ
Tel: (01507) 522563
Type: Co-educational Day and Boarding
No of pupils: 120 *No of Boarders:* W40
Special Needs: **MLD** W

SANDON SCHOOL
Sandon Close, Sandon Road, Grantham, Lincolnshire NG31 9AX
Tel: (01476) 564994
Head: Mrs S Gill
Type: Co-educational Day 2–19
No of pupils: B26 G19
Special Needs: AUT CP DOW EPI **PMLD SLD** W

STUBTON HALL SCHOOL
Stubton, Newark, Lincolnshire NG23 5DD
Tel: (01636) 626607
Head: Mr M Mihkelson
Type: Co-educational Boarding and Day 6–16
No of pupils: B50 G4
No of Boarders: W46
Special Needs: **EBD**

WILLIAM HARRISON SPECIAL SCHOOL
Middlefield Lane, Gainsborough, Lincolnshire DN21 1PU
Tel: (01427) 615498
Head: Dr M J Blackband
Type: Co-educational Day 3–16
No of pupils: B65 G35
Special Needs: ADD ADHD AUT DOW EPI HI MLD SP&LD W

THE WILLOUGHBY SCHOOL
South Road, Bourne, Lincolnshire PE10 9JE
Tel: (01778) 425203
Head: Mr P Pike
Type: Co-educational Day 2–19
No of pupils: 66
Special Needs: AUT CP DOW PMLD SLD W

North Lincolnshire Education Authority
Hewson House
PO Box 35
Station Road
Brigg DN20 8XJ
Tel: (01724) 297240

ST LUKE'S SCHOOL
Burghley Road, Scunthorpe, North Lincolnshire DN16 1JD
Tel: (01724) 844560
Head: Dr R W Ashdown
Type: Co-educational Day 3–16
No of pupils: 80
Special Needs: PMLD SLD W

North East Lincolnshire Education Authority
Eleanor Street
Grimsby DN32 9DU
Tel: (01472) 313131

CAMBRIDGE PARK SCHOOL
Cambridge Road, Grimsby, North East Lincolnshire DN34 5EB
Tel: (01472) 879282
Head: Mrs G Kendall
Type: Co-educational Day 3–16
No of pupils: 133
Special Needs: ADD **AUT** DOW DYP EBD EPI HI **MLD** SP&LD VIS W

HUMBERSTON PARK SCHOOL
St Thomas Close, Humberston, North East Lincolnshire DN36 4HS
Tel: (01472) 590645
Head: Mr A A Zielinski
Type: Co-educational Day 3–19
No of pupils: 75
Special Needs: PMLD SLD W

LONDON

Barnet Education Authority
The Old Town Hall
Friern Barnet Lane
London N11 3DL
Tel: (020) 8359 2000

MAPLEDOWN SCHOOL
Claremont Road, London NW2 1TR
Tel: (020) 8455 4111
Head: Mr J Feltham
Type: Co-educational Day 11–19
No of pupils: B29 G31
Special Needs: PMLD SLD

NORTHWAY SCHOOL
The Fairway, Mill Hill, London NW7 3HS
Tel: (020) 8959 4232
Head: Mrs L Burgess
Type: Co-educational 5–11
No of pupils: B46 G19
Special Needs: AUT **MLD** W

OAK LODGE SCHOOL
Heath View, off East End Road,
London N2 0QY
Tel: (020) 8444 6711
Head: Mrs L Walker
Type: Co-educational 11–19
No of pupils: B90 G60
Special Needs: AUT MLD

OAKLEIGH SCHOOL
Oakleigh Road North, Whetstone,
London N20 0DH
Tel: (020) 8368 5336
Head: Mrs J L Charlesworth
Type: Co-educational Day 2–11
No of pupils: B36 G28
Special Needs: AUT PMLD SLD W

Bexley Education Authority

Hill View
Hill View Drive
Welling
Kent DA16 3RY
Tel: (020) 8303 7777

MARLBOROUGH SCHOOL
Marlborough Park Avenue, Sidcup,
Kent DA15 9DP
Tel: (020) 8300 6896
Head: Mrs A Chamberlain
Type: Co-educational Day 11–19
No of pupils: B39 G25
Special Needs: PMLD SLD

OAKWOOD SCHOOL
Woodside Road, Bexleyheath, Kent
DA7 6LB
Tel: (01322) 529240
Head: Mr J Holliday
Type: Co-educational Day 11–16
No of pupils: 56
Special Needs: EBD

SHENSTONE SCHOOL
Old Road, Crayford, Kent DA1 4DZ
Tel: (01322) 524145
Head: Mrs L Aldcroft
Type: Co-educational Day 2–11
No of pupils: B37 G14
Special Needs: AUT CP DOW EPI HI
PH PMLD SLD VIS W

WESTBROOKE SCHOOL
South Gipsy Road, Welling, Kent
DA16 1JP
Tel: (020) 8304 1320
Head: Mrs C A Hance
Type: Co-educational Day 4–11
No of pupils: 40
Special Needs: EBD W

Brent Education Authority

PO Box 1
Chesterfield House
9 Park Lane
Wembley
Middlesex HA9 7RW
Tel: (020) 8937 3130

GROVE PARK SCHOOL
Grove Park, Kingsbury, London
NW9 0JY
Tel: (020) 8204 3293
Head: Ms J F Edwards
Type: Co-educational 2–19
No of pupils: B45 G45
Special Needs: CP DEL EPI PH W

HAY LANE SCHOOL
Grove Park, Kingsbury, London
NW9 0JY
Tel: (020) 8204 5396
Head: Mrs P M Theuma
Type: Co-educational Day 2–19
Special Needs: PMLD SLD W

MANOR SCHOOL
Chamberlayne Road, Kensal Rise,
London NW10 3NT
Tel: (020) 8968 3160
Head: Mrs J Drake
Type: Co-educational Day 4–11
No of pupils: 135
Special Needs: AUT DYP MLD SLD
SP&LD W

VERNON HOUSE SCHOOL
Drury Way, London NW10 0NQ
Tel: (020) 8451 6961
Head: Mr G S Davidson
Type: Co-educational 5–12
No of pupils: 50
Special Needs: EBD

WOODFIELD SCHOOL
Glenwood Avenue, Kingsbury,
London NW9 7LY
Tel: (020) 8205 1977
Head: Mr H Williams
Type: Co-educational Day 11–16
No of pupils: 100
Special Needs: MLD SP&LD

Bromley Education Authority

Civic Centre
Stockwell Close
Bromley
Kent BR1 3UH
Tel: (020) 8464 3333

GLEBE SCHOOL
Hawes Lane, West Wickham, Kent
BR4 9AE
Tel: (020) 8777 4540
Head: Mr K Seed
Type: Co-educational Day 11–16
No of pupils: 180
Special Needs: MLD

MARJORIE MCCLURE SCHOOL
Hawkwood Lane, Chislehurst, Kent
BR7 5PS
Tel: (020) 8467 0174
Head: Dr J W Wardle
Type: Co-educational Day 3–19
No of pupils: 80
Special Needs: CP DEL EPI PH W

RECTORY PADDOCK SCHOOL & RESEARCH UNIT
Main Road, Orpington, Kent
BR5 3HS
Tel: (01689) 870519
Head: Dr V I Hinchcliffe
Type: Co-educational Day 4–19
No of pupils: 75
Special Needs: PMLD SLD W

WOODBROOK SCHOOL
2 Hayne Road, Beckenham, Kent
BR3 4HY
Tel: (020) 8650 7205
Head: Mr S Gillow
Type: Co-educational 4–19
No of pupils: 67
Special Needs: PMLD SLD W

Camden Education Authority

Crowndale Centre
218–22– Eversholt Street
London NW1 1BD
Tel: (020) 7974 1525

CHALCOT SCHOOL
Harmood Street, London NW1 8DP
Tel: (020) 7485 2147
Head: Ms E Hales
Type: Boys Day
No of pupils: 54
Special Needs: **EBD**

FRANK BARNES SCHOOL
Harley Road, London NW3 3BY
Tel: (020) 7586 4665
Head: Ms K Simpson
Type: Co-educational 2–11
No of pupils: 45
Special Needs: **HI**

PENN SCHOOL
Church Road, Penn, High Wycombe,
Buckinghamshire HP10 8LZ
Tel: (01494) 812139
Head: Mr A Jones
Type: Boarding and Day
No of pupils: 22 *No of Boarders:* W13
Special Needs: **HI SP&LD W**

SWISS COTTAGE SCHOOL
Avenue Road, London NW8 6HX
Tel: (020) 7681 8080
Head: Ms K Bedford
Type: Co-educational Day
No of pupils: 125
Special Needs: **MLD PH PMLD SLD SP&LD W**

Croydon Education Authority

Taberner House
Park Lane
Croydon
Surrey CR9 1TP
Tel: (020) 8686 4433

BENSHAM MANOR SCHOOL
Ecclesbourne Road, Thornton
Heath, Surrey CR7 7BR
Tel: (020) 8684 0116
Head: Mrs E J Green
Type: Co-educational Day 11–16
No of pupils: B110 G51
Special Needs: AUT **MLD**

PRIORY SCHOOL
Tennison Road, South Norwood,
London SE25 5RR
Tel: (020) 8653 8222
Head: Mrs M A Simpson
Type: Co-educational Day 13–19
No of pupils: B23 G22
Special Needs: AUT SLD W

RED GATES SCHOOL
489 Purley Way, Croydon, Surrey
CR9 4RG
Tel: (020) 8688 1761
Head: Miss B A Fox
Type: Co-educational Day 3–14
No of pupils: 62
Special Needs: AUT PMLD SLD W

REDGATES
489 Purley Way, Croydon, Surrey
CR0 4RG
Tel: (020) 8688 8222
Head: Ms S Beaman
Special Needs: AUT SLD

ST GILES' SCHOOL
Pampisford Road, Croydon, Surrey
CR2 6DF
Tel: (020) 8680 2141
Head: Mrs J Thomas
Type: Co-educational Day 3–16
No of pupils: 106
Special Needs: **PH W**

ST NICHOLAS SCHOOL
Old Lodge Lane, Purley, Surrey
CR8 4DN
Tel: (020) 8660 4861
Head: Mrs J Melton
Type: Co-educational Day 4–11
No of pupils: 101
Special Needs: AUT MLD SP&LD

SOUTH NORWOOD PRIMARY
34 Crowther Road, London
SE25 5QP
Tel: (020) 8654 2983
Head: Mr A Rydzewski
Type: Co-educational Day
No of pupils: B10 G2
Special Needs: **MLD**

Ealing Education Authority

Percival House
14–16 Uxbridge Road
London W5 2HL
Tel: (020) 8579 2424

BELVUE SCHOOL
Rowdell Road, Northolt, Middlesex
UB5 6AG
Tel: (020) 8845 5766
Head: Mr D Whitton
Type: Co-educational Day 12–19
No of pupils: 124
Special Needs: **MLD**

CASTLEBAR SCHOOL
Hathaway Gardens, Ealing, London
W13 0DH
Tel: (020) 8998 3135
Head: Mr D J Perkins
Type: Co-educational Day 4–12
No of pupils: 118
Special Needs: **MLD W**

CAVENDISH SCHOOL
Compton Close, Cavendish Avenue,
Ealing, London W13 0JG
Tel: (020) 8998 6940
Head: Ms M Byrne
Type: Co-educational Day 7–12
No of pupils: 22
Special Needs: ADHD EBD MLD W

MANDEVILLE SCHOOL
Eastcote Lane, Northolt, Middlesex
UB5 4HW
Tel: (020) 8864 4921
Head: Mrs S Blee
Type: Co-educational Day 2–12
No of pupils: B50 G30
Special Needs: PMLD SLD W

ST ANN'S SCHOOL
Springfield Road, Hanwell, London
W7 3JP
Tel: (020) 8567 6291
Head: Mrs M Hughes
Type: Co-educational Day
No of pupils: 59
Special Needs: PMLD **SLD** W

SPRINGHALLOW SCHOOL
Compton Close, Cavendish Avenue,
Ealing, London W13 0JG
Tel: (020) 8998 2700
Head: Miss J E Birch
Type: Co-educational Day 3–16
No of pupils: B38 G12
Special Needs: AUT SP&LD W

Enfield Education Authority

PO Box 56
Civic Centre
Enfield EN1 3XQ
Tel: (020) 8366 6565

DURANTS SCHOOL
4 Pitfield Way, Enfield, Middlesex
EN3 5BY
Tel: (020) 8804 1980
Head: Mr K G Bovair
Type: Co-educational Day 5–19
No of pupils: 120
Special Needs: MLD W

OAKTREE SCHOOL
Chase Side, Southgate, London
N14 4HN
Tel: (020) 8440 3100
Head: Mr J H Harrison
Type: Co-educational Day 5–19
No of pupils: 120
Special Needs: MLD

RUSSET HOUSE
11 Autumn Close, Enfield,
Middlesex EN1 4JA
Tel: (020) 8350 0650
Head: Ms J Foster
Type: Co-educational Day 3–11
No of pupils: 60
Special Needs: ASP AUT SPLD

WAVERLEY SCHOOL
105 The Ride, Enfield, Middlesex
EN3 7DL
Tel: (020) 8805 1858
Head: Mrs L C Gibbs
Type: Co-educational Day 3–19
No of pupils: 115
Special Needs: PMLD SLD W

WEST LEA SCHOOL
Haslebury Road, Edmonton, London
N9 9TU
Tel: (020) 8807 2656
Head: Mrs A S Fox
Type: Co-educational Day
No of pupils: 120
Special Needs: ADD ASP CP DEL EPI
HI PH SP&LD W

Greenwich Education Authority

Riverside House
Woolwich High Street
London SE18 6DF
Tel: (020) 8854 8888

BRANTRIDGE SCHOOL
Staplefield Place, Staplefield,
Haywards Heath, West Sussex
RH17 6EQ
Tel: (01444) 400228
Head: Mr R Winn
Type: Boys Boarding 6–12
No of pupils: 36 *No of Boarders:* F36
Special Needs: EBD

CHARLTON PARK SCHOOL
Charlton Park Road, London
SE7 8HX
Tel: (020) 8854 6259
Head: Mr M Dale-Emberton
Type: Co-educational Boarding and
Day
No of pupils: B50 G35
Special Needs: CP EPI PH PMLD SLD
SP&LD W

CHURCHFIELD SCHOOL
Church Manorway, London SE2 0HY
Tel: (020) 8854 3739
Head: Mr P Goulden
No of pupils: 202
Special Needs: DEL MLD SPLD

GREENWOOD PRIMARY
SUPPORT N C SCHOOL
Swingate Lane, Plumstead, London
SE18 2JD
Tel: (020) 8854 5904
Head: Ms B Brammer
Type: Co-educational Day 2–11
No of pupils: 170
Special Needs: AUT CP DEL DYS EPI
MLD PH PMLD SLD SP&LD SPLD

GRIFFIN MANOR SCHOOL
Welton Road, Swingate Lane,
London SE18 2JD
Tel: (020) 8854 3905
Head: Mrs L Carroll
Type: Co-educational Day 5–18
No of pupils: B50 G12
Special Needs: AUT

MAZE HILL SCHOOL
Woodlands Crescent, London
SE10 9UP
Tel: (020) 8858 0265
Head: Ms P Hardaker
Type: Co-educational
No of pupils: B54 G38
Special Needs: PMLD SLD W

NINE ACRES SCHOOL
Robert Street, London SE18 7NB
Tel: (020) 8317 7659
Head: Mrs P Mathias
Type: Co-educational Day 5–19
No of pupils: 64
Special Needs: PMLD SLD W

Hackney Education Authority

Edith Cavell Building
Enfield Road
London N1 5BA
Tel: (020) 8356 8401

CRUSOE HOUSE SCHOOL
Nile Street, London N1 7DR
Tel: (020) 7251 3932
Head: Mrs I Flynn
Type: Boys Day
No of pupils: 55
Special Needs: EBD

DOWNSVIEW SCHOOL
Tiger Way, Downs Road, London
E5 8QP
Tel: (020) 8985 6833
Head: Mr W R Bulman
Type: Co-educational Day 5–16
No of pupils: 100
Special Needs: MLD

HORIZON SCHOOL
Wordsworth Road, London N16 8BZ
Tel: (020) 7254 8096
Head: Ms A Uhart
Type: Co-educational Day 5–16
No of pupils: 92
Special Needs: SPLD

ICKBURGH SCHOOL
Ickburgh Road, London E5 8AD
Tel: (020) 8806 4638
Head: Mr P Goss
Type: Co-educational Day 2–19
No of pupils: B59 G31
Special Needs: PMLD SLD

STORMONT HOUSE SCHOOL
Downs Park Road, London E5 8NP
Tel: (020) 8985 4245
Head: Ms A Murphy
Type: Co-educational 11–16
No of pupils: 100
Special Needs: DEL SP&LD

Hammersmith and Fulham Education Authority

Education Department
Cambridge House
Cambridge Grove
London W6 0LE
Tel: (020) 8576 5366

CAMBRIDGE SCHOOL
Cambridge Grove, London W6 0LB
Tel: (020) 8748 7585
Head: Ms J Barton
Type: Co-educational 11–16
No of pupils: 100
Special Needs: MLD

GIBBS GREEN SCHOOL
Mund Street, North End Road,
London W14 9LY
Tel: (020) 7385 3908
Head: Ms K Birchley
Type: Co-educational Day 4–11
No of pupils: 30
Special Needs: EBD

HEATHERMOUNT SCHOOL
Devenish Road, Ascot, Berkshire
SL5 9PG
Tel: (01344) 875101
Head: Ms S Lord
Type: Co-educational Boarding and
Day 7–19
No of pupils: 54 *No of Boarders:* W30
Special Needs: ASP

JACK TIZARD SCHOOL
Finlay Street, London SW6 6HB
Tel: (020) 7736 7949
Head: Mr T Baker
Type: Co-educational Day 2–19
No of pupils: 85
Special Needs: PMLD SLD W

QUEENSMILL SCHOOL
Clancarty Road, London SW6 3AA
Tel: (020) 7384 2330
Head: Mrs J Page
Type: Co-educational Day
No of pupils: B50 G12
Special Needs: AUT

WOODLANE HIGH SCHOOL
Du Cane Road, London W12 0TN
Tel: (020) 8743 5668
Head: Mr N Holt
Type: Co-educational Day 11–16
No of pupils: B30 G25
Special Needs: DEL VIS W

Haringey Education Authority

48 Station Road
Wood Green
London N22 7TY
Tel: (020) 8489 0000

BLANCHE NEVILE SCHOOL AND SERVICE
(Admin & Resources Centre),
Williams Grove, Wood Green,
London N22 5NR
Tel: (020) 8352 2100
Head: Mr P Makey
Type: Co-educational Day
No of pupils: B53 G44
Special Needs: HI

GREENFIELDS SCHOOL
Coppetts Road, London N10 1JP
Tel: (020) 8444 5366
Head: Ms S Wood
Type: Boys Day 7–16
No of pupils: 40
Special Needs: ADD ADHD EBD

MOSELLE SPECIAL SCHOOL
Adams Road, London N17 6HW
Tel: (020) 8808 8869
Head: Mr A Redpath
Type: Co-educational
No of pupils: 123
Special Needs: AUT DOW EPI MLD
SP&LD

VALE SPECIAL SCHOOL
c/o Northumberland Park
Community School, Trulock Road,
London N17 0PY
Tel: (020) 8801 6111
Head: Mr G Hill
Type: Day
No of pupils: 80
Special Needs: CP PH W

WILLIAM C HARVEY SPECIAL SCHOOL
Adams Road, London N17 6HW
Tel: (020) 8808 7120
Head: Ms M Sumner
Type: Co-educational
No of pupils: 75
Special Needs: PMLD SLD W

Harrow Education Authority

PO Box 22
Civic Centre
Harrow
Middlesex HA1 2UW
Tel: (020) 8863 5611

WHITTLESEA SCHOOL
Whittlesea Road, Harrow, Middlesex
HA3 6ND
Tel: (020) 8428 6968
Head: Ms A Carruthers
Type: Co-educational Day 2–19
No of pupils: B52 G39
Special Needs: PMLD SLD

Havering Education Authority

The Broxhill Centre
Broxhill Road
Harold Road
Romford
Essex RM4 1XN
Tel: (01708) 772222

CORBETS TEY SCHOOL
Harwood Hall Lane, Corbets Tey,
Upminster, Essex RM14 2YQ
Tel: (01708) 225888
Head: Mrs S D Gardiner
Type: Co-educational Day 4–16
No of pupils: 90
Special Needs: MLD

DYCORTS SCHOOL
Settle Road, Harold Hill, Romford,
Essex RM3 9YA
Tel: (01708) 343649
Head: Mr G Wroe
Type: Co-educational Day 3–16
No of pupils: 75
Special Needs: DYS EPI MLD PH
SP&LD SPLD W

RAVENSBOURNE SCHOOL
Neave Crescent, Farringdon Avenue,
Harold Hill, Romford, Essex
RM3 8HN
Tel: (01708) 341800
Head: Mrs M Cameron
Type: Co-educational Day 2–19
No of pupils: 75
Special Needs: AUT CP DEL DOW
DYS EBD VIS W

Hillingdon Education Authority

Civic Centre
Uxbridge
Middlesex UB8 1UW
Tel: (01895) 250529

CHANTRY SCHOOL
Falling Lane, Yiewsley, West
Drayton, Middlesex UB7 8AB
Tel: (01895) 446747
Head: Mr R Warnes
Type: Co-educational Day
No of pupils: B56 G4
Special Needs: ADD ADHD EBD EPI
HI

HEDGEWOOD SCHOOL
Weymouth Road, Hayes, Middlesex
UB4 8NF
Tel: (020) 8845 6756
Head: Mr M J Goddard
Type: Co-educational Day
No of pupils: 95
Special Needs: ASP AUT CP DOW
DYP HI MLD SP&LD SPLD SPLD
VIS W

MEADOW SCHOOL
Royal Lane, Hillingdon, Uxbridge,
Middlesex UB8 3QU
Tel: (01895) 443310
Head: Mr R Payne
Type: Co-educational Day 11–18
No of pupils: B124 G65
Special Needs: MLD W

MOORCROFT SCHOOL
Harlington Road, Hillingdon,
Uxbridge, Middlesex UB8 3HD
Tel: (01895) 236430
Head: Ms M J Geddes
Type: Co-educational Day
No of pupils: 67
Special Needs: AUT SLD W

THE WILLOWS SCHOOL
Stipularis Drive, Off Glencoe Road,
Hayes, Middlesex UB4 9QB
Tel: (020) 8841 7176
Head: Mrs F King
Type: Co-educational Day
No of pupils: 30
Special Needs: EBD

Hounslow Education Authority

Civic Centre
Lampton Road
Hounslow
Middlesex TW3 4DN
Tel: (020) 8862 5352

THE CEDARS PRIMARY SCHOOL
High Street, Cranford, Middlesex
TW5 9RU
Tel: (020) 8230 0015
Head: Mr A Costello
Type: Co-educational Day 4–11
No of pupils: 50
Special Needs: EBD

MARJORY KINNON SPECIAL SCHOOL
Hatton Road, Bedfont, Middlesex
TW14 9QZ
Tel: (020) 8890 2032
Head: Mr D J Harris
Type: Co-educational Day 5–16
No of pupils: 171
Special Needs: AUT MLD W

OAKLANDS SCHOOL
Woodlands Road, Isleworth,
Middlesex TW7 6HD
Tel: (020) 8560 3569
Head: Mrs E Felstead
Type: Co-educational Day 11–19
No of pupils: 72
Special Needs: PMLD SLD W

SYON PARK SCHOOL
Twickenham Road, Isleworth,
Middlesex TW7 6AU
Tel: (020) 8560 4300
Head: Mrs L Boys
Type: Co-educational 11–16
No of pupils: 50
Special Needs: EBD

Islington Education Authority

Education Offices
Laycock Street
London N1 1TH
Tel: (020) 7457 5566

HARBOROUGH SCHOOL
Elthorne Road, London N19 4AB
Tel: (020) 7272 5739
Type: Co-educational Day 2–19
No of pupils: B35 G8
Special Needs: AUT

RICHARD CLOUDESLEY SCHOOL
Golden Lane, London EC1Y 0TJ
Tel: (020) 7251 1161
Head: Ms A Corbett
Type: Co-educational Day 2–18
No of pupils: B35 G13
Special Needs: CP EPI PH SP&LD W

ROSEMARY SCHOOL
75 Prebend Street, London N1 8PW
Tel: (020) 7226 8223
Head: Mr J Wolger
Type: Co-educational Day
No of pupils: 76
Special Needs: PMLD SLD W

SAMUEL RHODES SCHOOL
Richmond Avenue, London N1
Tel: (020) 7837 9075
Head: Ms Jackie Blount
Type: Co-educational Day 5–16
No of pupils: 104
Special Needs: MLD

Kensington and Chelsea Education Authority

Town Hall
Hornton Street
London W8 7NX
Tel: (020) 7937 5464

PARKWOOD HALL SCHOOL
Beechenlea Lane, Swanley, Kent
BR8 8DR
Tel: (01322) 664441
Head: Mr R Lane
Type: Co-educational Boarding and
Day 8–17
No of pupils: B44 G35
No of Boarders: F59
Special Needs: EPI **MLD SLD SP&LD**

Kingston Upon Thames Education Authority

Guildhall 2
Kingston upon Thames
Surrey KT1 1EU
Tel: (020) 8546 2121

BEDELSFORD SCHOOL
Grange Road, Kingston upon
Thames, Surrey KT1 2QZ
Tel: (020) 8546 9838
Head: Mr J Murfitt
Type: Co-educational Day 2–16
No of pupils: B40 G21
Special Needs: **CP DEL EPI** HI MLD
PH VIS W

DYSART SPECIAL SCHOOL
Dukes Avenue, Kingston upon
Thames, Surrey KT2 5QY
Tel: (020) 8546 0610
Head: Ms P Smillie
Type: Co-educational Day 2–19
No of pupils: 65
Special Needs: ADHD AUT CP DOW
PH PMLD SLD TOU VIS

ST PHILIP'S SPECIAL SCHOOL
Harrow Close, Leatherhead Road,
Chessington, Surrey KT9 2HP
Tel: (020) 8397 2672
Head: Mrs H J Goodall
Type: Co-educational Day 5–16
No of pupils: B90 G54
Special Needs: DOW **MLD** SPLD

Lambeth Education Authority

International House
Canterbury Crescent
London SW9 7QE
Tel: (020) 7926 1000

CLAPHAM PARK SCHOOL
127 Park Hill, London SW4 9PA
Tel: (020) 8674 5639
Head: Ms B Raybould
Type: Co-educational Day 2–16
No of pupils: B11 G9
Special Needs: PH **VIS** W

ELM COURT SCHOOL
Elmcourt Road, West Norwood,
London SE27 9BZ
Tel: (020) 8670 6577
Head: Mr W Hutcheson
Type: Co-educational Day
No of pupils: 100
Special Needs: ADD CP DEL DOW
DYS EBD EPI MLD SP&LD SPLD W

GROVE HOUSE SCHOOL
Elmcourt Road, London SE27 2BZ
Tel: (020) 8670 9429
Head: Ms P Odlin
Type: Co-educational Day 2–11
No of pupils: B28 G12
Special Needs: **HI**

LANSDOWNE SCHOOL
Argyll Close, Dalyell Road, London
SW9 9QL
Tel: (020) 7737 3713
Head: Mrs G Bealing
Type: Co-educational Day 5–16
No of pupils: B47 G28
Special Needs: **MLD**

SHELLEY SCHOOL
Oakden Street, London SE11 4UG
Tel: (020) 7735 9081
Head: Mrs M Lozano-Luoma
Type: Co-educational Day 11–19
No of pupils: B20 G21
Special Needs: PMLD SLD W

THURLOW PARK SCHOOL
Elmcourt Road, London SE27 9DA
Tel: (020) 8670 3975
Head: Mr J Barrow
Type: Co-educational Day 2–16
No of pupils: 50
Special Needs: CP DEL EPI MLD PH
SP&LD W

TURNEY SCHOOL
Turney Road, West Dulwich, London
SE21 8LX
Tel: (020) 8670 7220
Head: Ms J Davis
Type: Co-educational 5–16
No of pupils: 164
Special Needs: ADD ADHD ASP AUT
DOW **MLD** SP&LD

WILLOWFIELD SCHOOL
Heron Road, Milkwood Road,
London SE24 0HY
Tel: (020) 7274 4372
Head: Ms J Loy
Type: Boys Day and Boarding 11–16
No of pupils: 48
Special Needs: **EBD**

WINDMILL SCHOOL
Mandrell Road, London SW2 5DW
Tel: (020) 7733 0681
Head: Mr P Steel
No of pupils: 45
Special Needs: PMLD SLD

Lewisham Education Authority

Directorate of Education
3rd Floor, Laurence House
1 Catford Road
Catford
London SE6 4RU
Tel: (020) 8314 6301

ANERLEY SCHOOL
Versailles Road, London SE20 8AX
Tel: (020) 8402 2929
Head: Mr E B Milner
Type: Boys Day and Boarding 11–16
No of pupils: 40
Special Needs: **EBD**

GREENVALE SCHOOL
69 Perry Rise, Forest Hill, London
SE23 2QU
Tel: (020) 8699 6515
Head: Mr P A Munro
Type: Co-educational Day 11–19
No of pupils: 60
Special Needs: PMLD SLD W

MEADOWGATE SCHOOL
Revelon Road, Brockley, London
SE4 2PR
Tel: (020) 7635 9022
Head: Mr R Leszczynski
Type: Co-educational Day 4–11
Special Needs: **MLD**

NEW WOODLANDS SCHOOL (JMI)

49 Shroffold Road, Bromley, Kent BR1 5PD
Tel: (020) 8314 9911
Head: Mr D H Harper
Type: Co-educational Day
No of pupils: 40
Special Needs: **EBD**

PENDRAGON SECONDARY SCHOOL

Pendragon Road, Downham, Bromley, Kent BR1 5LD
Tel: (020) 8698 9738
Head: Mr H Calthrop
Type: Co-educational Day 11–19
No of pupils: 132
Special Needs: **MLD**

WATERGATE SCHOOL

Church Grove, London SE13 7UU
Tel: (020) 8314 1751
Head: Ms A Youd
Type: Co-educational 2–11
No of pupils: 65
Special Needs: PMLD **SLD** W

Merton Education Authority

Civic Centre
London Road
Morden
Surrey SM4 5DX
Tel: (020) 8545 3268

CRICKET GREEN SCHOOL

Lower Green West, Mitcham, Surrey CR4 3AF
Tel: (020) 8640 1177
Head: Ms H Gannaway
Type: Co-educational Day 5–16
No of pupils: 120
Special Needs: **MLD** W

MELROSE SCHOOL

Church Road, Mitcham, Surrey CR4 3BE
Tel: (020) 8646 2620
Head: Mr D Eglin
Type: Co-educational Day 9–16
No of pupils: 60
Special Needs: **EBD**

ST ANN'S SCHOOL

Bordesley Road, Morden, Surrey SM4 5LT
Tel: (020) 8648 9737
Head: Ms T Harvey
Type: Co-educational Day 2–19
No of pupils: 81
Special Needs: PMLD SLD

Newham Education Authority

Broadway House
322 High Street
Stratford
London E15 1AJ
Tel: (020) 8555 5552

ELEANOR SMITH SCHOOL & PRIMARY SUPPORT SERVICE

North Street, London E13 9HN
Tel: (020) 8471 0018/9
Head: Mr M R Leaman
Type: Co-educational Day 5–11
No of pupils: 120
Special Needs: **EBD**

Redbridge Education Authority

Lynton House
255–259 High Road
Ilford
Essex IG1 1NN
Tel: (020) 8478 3020

ETHEL DAVIS SCHOOL

258 Barley Lane, Goodmayes, Ilford, Essex IG3 8XS
Tel: (020) 8599 1768
Head: Mr P Bouldstridge
Type: Co-educational 2–19
No of pupils: B30 G25
Special Needs: CP **MLD** PH PMLD **SLD** VIS W

HATTON SCHOOL

Roding Lane South, Woodford Green, Essex IG8 8EU
Tel: (020) 8551 4131
Head: Miss L Richardson
Type: Co-educational Day 5–11
No of pupils: 142
Special Needs: **ASP AUT** DOW DYP MLD **SP&LD** W

HYLEFORD SCHOOL

Loxford Lane, Ilford, Essex IG3 9AR
Tel: (020) 8590 7272
Head: Mrs G D Morgan
Type: Co-educational Day 3–19
No of pupils: 85
Special Needs: PMLD **SLD** W

LITTLE HEATH SCHOOL

Hainault Road, Little Heath, Romford, Essex RM6 5RX
Tel: (020) 8599 4864
Head: Mr P B Johnson
Type: Co-educational Day 11–19
No of pupils: 145
Special Needs: ADD ADHD ASP MLD SP&LD

NEW RUSH HALL SCHOOL

Fencepiece Road, Hainault, Essex IG6 2LJ
Tel: (020) 8501 3951
Head: Mr J V d'Abbro
Type: Co-educational Day 5–16
No of pupils: 60
Special Needs: **EBD**

Richmond upon Thames Education Authority

Regal House
London Road
Twickenham
Middlesex TW1 3QB
Tel: (020) 8891 1411

CLARENDON SCHOOL

Hanworth Road, Hampton, Middlesex TW12 3DH
Tel: (020) 8979 1165
Head: Mrs A Coward
Type: Co-educational Day 7–16
No of pupils: 100
Special Needs: **MLD** W

OLDFIELD HOUSE SCHOOL

Oldfield Road, Hampton, Middlesex TW12 2HP
Tel: (020) 8979 5102
Head: Mrs A Glenny
Type: Co-educational Day 5–11
No of pupils: 18
Special Needs: **EBD** W

RICHMOND HOUSE SCHOOL
Buckingham Road, Hampton,
Middlesex TW12 3LT
Tel: (020) 8941 2623
Head: Mr A Mitchell
Type: Co-educational Day
No of pupils: 20
Special Needs: EBD

STRATHMORE SCHOOL
Meadlands Drive, Petersham, Surrey
TW10 7ED
Tel: (020) 8948 0047
Head: Mr S Rosenberg
Type: Co-educational Day 3–19
No of pupils: 45
Special Needs: PMLD SLD W

Southwark Education Authority

1 Bradenham Close
Walworth
London SE17 2QA
Tel: (020) 7525 5001

BEORMUND SCHOOL
Crosby Row, Long Lane, London
SE1 3PS
Tel: (020) 7525 9027
Head: Mr D Hendrick
Type: Co-educational Day 5–11
No of pupils: 30
Special Needs: EBD W

BREDINGHURST SCHOOL
Stuart Road, London SE15 3AZ
Tel: (020) 7639 2541
Head: Ms J Anderson
Type: Boys Boarding and Day
No of pupils: 49 *No of Boarders:* W15
Special Needs: ADD ADHD EBD

CHERRY GARDEN SPECIAL PRIMARY SCHOOL
Macks Road, London SE16 3XU
Tel: (020) 7237 4050
Head: Ms M Trembath
Type: Co-educational Day 2–11
No of pupils: 46
Special Needs: AUT CP EPI HI PH
PMLD SLD SP&LD VIS W

HAYMERLE'S SCHOOL
Haymerle Road, London SE15 6SY
Tel: (020) 7639 6080
Head: Mr E M Nolan
Type: Co-educational Day 4–11
No of pupils: B57 G29
Special Needs: ADD ADHD AUT CP
DEL DOW DYP DYS EBD EPI MLD
PH SP&LD W

HIGHSHORE SPECIAL SCHOOL
Bellenden Road, London SE15 5BB
Tel: (020) 7639 7211
Head: Mrs Y Conlon
Type: Co-educational Day 11–17
No of pupils: 128
Special Needs: ADD ADHD DYC DYP
DYS MLD SP&LD

MAUDSLEY & BETHLEM SPECIAL SCHOOL
Royal Hospital School, Monks
Orchard Road, Beckenham, Kent
BR3 3BX
Tel: (020) 8777 1897
Head: Ms W French
Type: Co-educational Boarding
No of pupils: 25
Special Needs: ADD ADHD ASP AUT
EBD EPI MLD TOU

SPA SCHOOL
Monnow Road, London SE1 5RN
Tel: (020) 7237 3714
Head: Ms A Crispin
Type: Co-educational 11–16
No of pupils: 83
Special Needs: ASP AUT MLD

TUKE SCHOOL
4 Woods Road, London SE15 2PX
Tel: (020) 7639 5584
Head: Miss H Tully
Type: Co-educational Day 11–19
No of pupils: B34 G12
Special Needs: AUT PMLD SLD W

Sutton Education Authority

The Grove
Carshalton
Surrey SM5 3AL
Tel: (020) 8770 6568

CAREW MANOR SCHOOL
Church Road, Wallington, Surrey
SM6 7NH
Tel: (020) 8647 8349
Head: Mr M Midgley
Type: Co-educational Day 7–16
No of pupils: 125
Special Needs: ADD ADHD ASP AUT
CP DEL DOW DYP DYS EBD EPI HI
MLD SLD SP&LD SPLD VIS W

SHERWOOD PARK SCHOOL
Streeters Lane, Wallington, Surrey
SM6 7NP
Tel: (020) 8773 9930
Head: Mrs R Bezant
Type: Co-educational Day 2–19
No of pupils: 80
Special Needs: PMLD SLD W

WANDLE VALLEY SCHOOL
Welbeck Road, Carshalton, Surrey
SM5 1LP
Tel: (020) 8648 1365
Head: Mr D L Bone
Type: Co-educational Day 5–16
No of pupils: 80
Special Needs: EBD

Tower Hamlets Education Authority

Mulberry Place
5 Clove Crescent
London E14 2BG
Tel: (020) 7364 5000

BEATRICE TATE SCHOOL
St Jude's Road, London E2 9RW
Tel: (020) 7739 6249
Head: Mr A Black
Type: Co-educational Day 11–19
No of pupils: 75
Special Needs: PMLD SLD W

BOWDEN HOUSE
Firle Road, Seaford, East Sussex
BN25 2JB
Tel: (01323) 893138
Head: Mr M Price
Type: Boys Boarding 9–16
No of pupils: 47 *No of Boarders:* F47
Special Needs: EBD

BROMLEY HALL SCHOOL
Bromley Hall Road, London E14 0LF
Tel: (020) 7987 2563
Head: Mr J Earnshaw
Type: Co-educational Day 3–19
No of pupils: B13 G13
Special Needs: CP DEL EPI HI MLD
PH PMLD SLD SP&LD VIS W

GRENFELL SCHOOL
Myrdle Street, London E1 1HL
Tel: (020) 7247 9475
Head: Mr S Quilter
Type: Co-educational Day 3–11
No of pupils: 120
Special Needs: MLD SP&LD

HARPLEY SCHOOL
Globe Road, London E1 4DZ
Tel: (020) 7790 5170
Head: Mr A M Finch
Type: Co-educational Day 11–16
No of pupils: B60 G40
Special Needs: Supported National
Curriculum

PHOENIX SCHOOL
49 Bow Road, London E3 2AD
Tel: (020) 8980 4740
Head: Mr S Harris
Type: Co-educational Day
No of pupils: B101 G55
Special Needs: AUT MLD

STEPHEN HAWKING SCHOOL
Brunton Place, London E14 7LL
Tel: (020) 7423 9848
Head: Ms C Sibley
Type: Co-educational Day 2–11
No of pupils: 80
Special Needs: PMLD SLD

Waltham Forest Education Authority

Municipal Offices
High Road
Leyton
London E10 5QJ
Tel: (020) 8527 5544

BROOKFIELD HOUSE SCHOOL
Alders Avenue, Woodford Green,
Essex IG8 9PY
Tel: (020) 8527 2464
Head: Ms H Clasper
Type: Co-educational Day
No of pupils: 82
Special Needs: CP DEL PH

HAWKSWOOD SCHOOL AND CENTRE
Antlers Hill, London E4 7RT
Tel: (020) 8529 2561
Head: Ms K Khan
Type: Co-educational Day 2–16
No of pupils: 47
Special Needs: HI MLD SLD

JOSEPH CLARKE SCHOOL
Vincent Road, London E4 9PP
Tel: (020) 8527 8818
Head: Mr F Smith
Type: Co-educational Day 2–19
No of pupils: 120
Special Needs: VIS W

WHITEFIELD SCHOOL AND CENTRE
Macdonald Road, London E17 4AZ
Tel: (020) 8531 3426
Head: Mr N Chapman
Type: Co-educational Day and
Boarding 2–19
No of pupils: 310 *No of Boarders:* W10
Special Needs: ASP AUT CP DOW
DYP EPI HI MLD PMLD SLD SP&LD
SPLD VIS W

WILLIAM MORRIS SCHOOL
Folly Lane, London E17 5NT
Tel: (020) 8503 2225
Head: Miss M Woods
Type: Co-educational Day 11–19
No of pupils: 135
Special Needs: MLD PMLD SLD W

Wandsworth Education Authority

Town Hall
Wandsworth High Street
London SW18 2PU
Tel: (020) 8871 6000

BRADSTOW SCHOOL
34 Dumpton Park Drive, Broadstairs,
Kent CT10 1RG
Tel: (01843) 862123
Head: Mr B Furze
Type: Co-educational Boarding 6–19
No of pupils: 50 *No of Boarders:* W50
Special Needs: AUT EBD EPI SLD

BURROW HILL SCHOOL
St Catherines Road, Frimley,
Camberley, Surrey GU16 5NL
Tel: (01252) 835570
Head: Mr S Jones
Type: Boys Boarding 8–16
No of pupils: 65
Special Needs: EBD

CHARTFIELD DELICATE SCHOOL
St Margaret's Crescent, London
SW15 6HL
Tel: (020) 8788 7471
Head: Ms V Hand-Armitage
Type: Co-educational 11–16
No of pupils: B75 G25
Special Needs: ADD ADHD ASP CP
DEL DYC DYP DYS EPI MLD
SP&LD SPLD TOU W

GARRATT PARK SCHOOL
Waldron Road, London SW18 3SY
Tel: (020) 8946 5769
Head: Ms J Price
Type: Co-educational Day 11–17
No of pupils: B83 G42
Special Needs: ADHD AUT DYC DYS
MLD SP&LD

GREENMEAD SCHOOL
St Margaret's Crescent, London
SW15 6HL
Tel: (020) 8789 1466
Head: Miss A Laxton
Type: Co-educational Day 3–11
No of pupils: B22 G18
Special Needs: CP MLD PH PMLD
SLD SP&LD

LINDEN LODGE SCHOOL
61 Princes Way, London SW19 6JB
Tel: (020) 8788 0107
Head: Mr A Hudson
Type: Co-educational Day and
Boarding 5–18
No of pupils: 80
Special Needs: VIS

OAK LODGE SCHOOL
101 Nightingale Lane, London
SW12 8NA
Tel: (020) 8673 3453
Head: Mr P Merrifield
Type: Co-educational Boarding and
Day 11–19
No of pupils: B45 G42
No of Boarders: W17
Special Needs: HI

PADDOCK SCHOOL
Priory Lane, London SW15 5RT
Tel: (020) 8878 1521
Head: Mrs N Evans
Type: Co-educational Day 3–19
No of pupils: 92
Special Needs: PMLD SLD W

THE VINES
Forthbridge Road, London
SW11 5NX
Tel: (020) 7228 0602
Head: Ms J Hilary
Type: Co-educational 4–11
No of pupils: 100
Special Needs: MLD W

City of Westminster Education Authority

PO Box 240
Westminster City Hall
64 Victoria Street
London SW1E 6QP
Tel: (020) 7641 6000

COLLEGE PARK SCHOOL
Monmouth Road, London W2 4UT
Tel: (020) 7641 4460
Head: Ms A Anderson
Type: Co-educational 5–16
No of pupils: 80
Special Needs: MLD

QUEEN ELIZABETH II SCHOOL
Kennet Road, London W9 3LG
Tel: (020) 7641 5825
Head: Ms M Loughnan
Type: Co-educational Day 5–19
No of pupils: B33 G33
Special Needs: PMLD SLD W

GREATER MANCHESTER

Bolton Education Authority

PO Box 53
Paderborn House
Civic Centre
Bolton
Greater Manchester BL1 1JW
Tel: (01204) 333333

FIRWOOD SCHOOL
Crompton Way, Bolton, Greater
Manchester BL2 3AF
Tel: (01204) 303499
Head: Dr J Steele
Type: Co-educational 11–19
No of pupils: 82
Special Needs: PMLD SLD W

GREEN FOLD SCHOOL
Highfield Road, Farnworth, Greater
Manchester BL4 0RA
Tel: (01204) 572524
Head: Mrs C Chapman
Type: Day
No of pupils: 70
Special Needs: CP EPI **PMLD SLD W**

LADYWOOD SCHOOL
Masefield Road, Little Lever, Bolton,
Greater Manchester BL3 1NG
Tel: (01204) 840709
Head: Mrs S McFarlane
Type: Co-educational 4–11
No of pupils: B49 G22
Special Needs: AUT PMLD

LEVER PARK SCHOOL
Stocks Park Drive, Horwick, Bolton,
Greater Manchester BL6 6DE
Tel: (01204) 840321
Head: Mrs C A Hargreaves
Type: Co-educational Day 8–16
No of pupils: 50
Special Needs: ADD ADHD **EBD** W

THOMASSON MEMORIAL SCHOOL
Devonshire Road, Bolton, Greater
Manchester BL1 4PJ
Tel: (01204) 843063
Head: Mr W Wilson
Type: Co-educational Day 3–11
No of pupils: B25 G19
Special Needs: HI

WOODSIDE SENIOR SCHOOL
425 Chorley New Road, Bolton,
Greater Manchester BL1 5DH
Tel: (01204) 843637
Head: Mr A J Johns
Type: Co-educational Day
No of pupils: B83 G52
Special Needs: **MLD**

Bury Education Authority

Athenaeum House
Market Street
Bury
Greater Manchester BL9 0BN
Tel: (0161) 253 5000

ELMS BANK HIGH SCHOOL
Ripon Avenue, Whitefield,
Manchester M45 8PJ
Tel: (0161) 766 1597
Head: Ms L Lines
Type: Co-educational Day
No of pupils: B76 G56
Special Needs: AUT MLD PH PMLD
SLD W

MILLWOOD PRIMARY SPECIAL SCHOOL
Fletcher Fold Road, Bury, Greater
Manchester BL9 9RX
Tel: (0161) 253 6083
Head: Mr B J Emblem
Type: Co-educational Day 2–11
No of pupils: 86
Special Needs: MLD PMLD SLD W

Manchester Education Authority

Crown Square
Manchester M60 3BB
Tel: (0161) 234 7125

BUGLAWTON HALL SPECIAL SCHOOL
Buxton Road, Congleton, Cheshire
CW12 3PQ
Tel: (01260) 274492
Head: Mr A K Williams
Type: Boys Boarding
No of pupils: 46
Special Needs: EBD

EGERTON HIGH SCHOOL
Kingsway Park, Davy Hulme,
Manchester M41 7FZ
Tel: (0161) 749 7095
Head: Mr I Wright
Type: Co-educational Day 5–16
No of pupils: 60
Special Needs: EBD

EWING SCHOOL
Central Road, Manchester M20 4ZA
Tel: (0161) 445 0745
Head: Ms P Derbyshire
Type: Co-educational Day 5–16
No of pupils: 78
Special Needs: SP&LD

GORTON BROOK FIRST SCHOOL
Belle Vue Street, Manchester
M12 5PW
Tel: (0161) 223 1822
Head: Mr I John
Type: Co-educational Day 5–11
No of pupils: 100
Special Needs: **MLD** W

LEACROFT SPECIAL SCHOOL
Corelli Street, Manchester M40 8HX
Tel: (0161) 205 1839
Head: Mrs P A Vermes
Type: Co-educational 2–19
No of pupils: 60
Special Needs: PMLD SLD

MELLAND HIGH SCHOOL
Holmcroft Road, Gorton,
Manchester M18 7NG
Tel: (0161) 223 9915
Head: Mrs J D O'Kane
Type: Co-educational Day 11–19
No of pupils: B51 G51
Special Needs: PMLD **SLD** W

NORTH MANCHESTER SUPPORT SERVICE
Meade Hill Centre, Middleton Road,
Manchester M8 6NB
Tel: (0161) 795 8445
Head: Mr A J Farrell
Type: Co-educational Day 11–16
No of pupils: 70
Special Needs: ADD ADHD EBD W

PIPER HILL SPECIAL SCHOOL
200 Yew Tree Lane, Manchester
M23 0FF
Tel: (0161) 998 4068
Head: Ms J Andrews
Type: Co-educational Day 11–19
No of pupils: B40 G45
Special Needs: PMLD SLD W

RICHMOND PARK SCHOOL
Cochrane Avenue, Longsight,
Manchester M12 4FA
Tel: (0161) 273 4894
Head: Mrs J Holt
Type: Co-educational Day
No of pupils: B71 G39
Special Needs: **MLD**

RODNEY HOUSE SPECIAL SCHOOL
388 Slade Lane, Burnage,
Manchester M19 2TH
Tel: (0161) 224 2774
Head: Ms P H Stanier
Type: Co-educational Day 2–5
No of pupils: 45
Special Needs: ASP **AUT CP DEL**
DOW EBD EPI HI MLD PH PMLD
SLD SP&LD SPLD TOU VIS W

ROUNDWOOD SCHOOL
Roundwood Road, Northenden,
Manchester M22 4AB
Tel: (0161) 998 4138
Head: Ms S L Hibbert
Type: Day
No of pupils: 230
Special Needs: **MLD**

SHAWGROVE SCHOOL
Cavendish Road, Manchester
M20 1QB
Tel: (0161) 445 9435
Head: Mr H S Taylor
Type: Co-educational Day 3–11
No of pupils: 18
Special Needs: **VIS** W

TWO PORCHES SCHOOL
Gloucester Street, Atherton,
Manchester M46 0HX
Tel: (01942) 882012
Head: Mrs J Leach
Type: Co-educational
No of pupils: 45
Special Needs: PMLD SLD

WHITWORTH PARK SCHOOL
Monton Street, Moss Side,
Manchester M14 4GP
Tel: (0161) 226 2079
Head: Mr A T Barrand
Type: Co-educational 5–11
No of pupils: 100
Special Needs: **MLD**

WOODSIDE SPECIAL SCHOOL
Crossacres Road, Manchester
M22 5DR
Tel: (0161) 437 5697
Head: Mrs A M Stuart
Type: Co-educational Day
No of pupils: 76
Special Needs: **MLD**

Oldham Education Authority

Level 5
Civic Centre
West Street
Oldham
Greater Manchester OL1 1XJ
Tel: (0161) 911 4260

FERNEY FIELD SCHOOL
Hunt Lane, Chadderton, Greater
Manchester OL9 0LS
Tel: (0161) 624 9913
Head: Ms J Reid
Type: Co-educational Day
No of pupils: B35 G13
Special Needs: ADD ADHD DOW
EBD MLD SP&LD

FOXDENTON SCHOOL AND INTEGRATED NURSERY
Foxdenton Lane, Chadderton,
Greater Manchester OL9 9QR
Tel: (0161) 284 5335
Head: Mr M Farrar
Type: Co-educational Day 2–11
No of pupils: B65 G53
Special Needs: CP EPI **PH** SP&LD W

GORSE BANK SCHOOL
Foxdenton Lane, Chadderton,
Greater Manchester OL9 9QR
Tel: (0161) 284 5168
Head: Mrs A Greaves
Type: Co-educational Day 2–19
No of pupils: 52
Special Needs: AUT CP DEL DYS EBD
EPI HI PMLD SLD

HARDMAN FOLD SCHOOL
Dean Street, Failsworth, Greater
Manchester M35 0DQ
Tel: (0161) 688 7114
Head: Mr R Maycock
Type: Co-educational Boarding and
Day 11–16
No of pupils: 71 *No of Boarders:* W14
Special Needs: **EBD**

HILL TOP SCHOOL
Arncliffe Rise, Pennine Meadow,
Oldham, Greater Manchester
OL4 2LZ
Tel: (0161) 620 6070
Head: Mr G Quinn
Type: Co-educational Day 11–19
No of pupils: 75
Special Needs: ASP AUT DOW SLD W

PARK DEAN SCHOOL
St Martin's Road, Oldham, Greater
Manchester OL8 2PZ
Tel: (0161) 620 0231
Head: Mrs A Higgins
Type: Co-educational Day 2–19
No of pupils: 95
Special Needs: CP DEL HI PH VIS W

Rochdale Education Authority

PO Box 70
Municipal Offices
Smith Street
Rochdale
Greater Manchester
OL16 1YD
Tel: (01706) 647474

ALDERMAN KAY SPECIAL SCHOOL
Tintern Road, Hollin, Middleton,
Greater Manchester M24 6TQ
Tel: (0161) 643 4917
Head: Mrs J Clark
Type: Co-educational Day 5–16
No of pupils: 115
Special Needs: DOW DYS **EBD** EPI HI
MLD **SLD** SP&LD

ALF KAUFMAN SPECIAL SCHOOL
Highwood, Norden, Rochdale,
Greater Manchester OC11 5PX
Tel: (01706) 359153
Head: Mr P D Geldeart
Type: Co-educational Day 3–11
No of pupils: 37
Special Needs: **PH** W

INNES SPECIAL SCHOOL
Ings Lane, Rochdale, Greater
Manchester OL12 7DW
Tel: (01706) 646605
Head: Mr F Stanley
Type: Co-educational Day 3–19
No of pupils: B35 G29
Special Needs: CP EPI **PMLD SLD**
VIS **W**

RYDINGS SPECIAL SCHOOL
Great Howarth, Wardle Road,
Rochdale, Greater Manchester
OL12 9HJ
Tel: (01706) 57993
Head: Mr R A Jazwinski
Type: Co-educational Day 5–16
No of pupils: 100
Special Needs: **MLD** W

Salford Education Authority

Chapel Street
Salford
Greater Manchester M3 5LT
Tel: (0161) 832 9751

NEW CROFT HIGH SCHOOL
Seedley Road, Salford, Greater
Manchester M6 5NQ
Tel: (0161) 736 6415
Head: Mr J S Chapman
Type: Co-educational Day 11–19
No of pupils: 78
Special Needs: **PMLD SLD** W

NORTHUMBERLAND HIGH SCHOOL
Northumberland Street, Salford,
Greater Manchester M7 4RP
Tel: (0161) 792 8504
Head: Mrs A Kennedy
Type: Co-educational 11–16
No of pupils: 35
Special Needs: **EBD**

Stockport Education Authority

Stopford House
Stockport
Greater Manchester SK1 3XE
Tel: (0161) 480 4949

CASTLE HILL SCHOOL
Lapwing Lane, Brinnington,
Stockport, Greater Manchester
SK5 8LF
Tel: (01472) 879282
Head: Mr M Marra
Type: Co-educational Day 11–16
No of pupils: 168
Special Needs: **MLD**

HEATON SCHOOL
St James Road, Heaton Moor,
Stockport, Greater Manchester
SK4 4RE
Tel: (0161) 432 1931
Head: Ms E A Seers
Type: Co-educational Day 11–19
No of pupils: 50
Special Needs: **AUT PMLD SLD**

LISBURNE SCHOOL
Half Moon Lane, Offerton,
Stockport, Greater Manchester
SK2 5LB
Tel: (0161) 483 5045
Head: Mrs S Reid
Type: Co-educational Day
No of pupils: B30 G14
Special Needs: ADD ADHD ASP DOW
DYP EBD EPI HI MLD PH SP&LD
SPLD VIS

TAXAL LODGE SCHOOL
Linglongs Road, Whaley Bridge,
Greater Manchester SK12 7DU
Tel: (01663) 732613
Head: Mr M R Douglass
No of pupils: 30
Special Needs: **EBD**

VALLEY SCHOOL
Whitehaven Road, Bramhall,
Stockport, Greater Manchester
SK7 1EN
Tel: (0161) 439 7343
Head: Mrs C M Goodlet
Type: Co-educational Day 2–11
No of pupils: 70
Special Needs: **AUT CP PH PMLD
SLD** W

WINDLEHURST
Windlehurst Lane, Hawk Green,
Marple, Stockport, Cheshire
Head: Mr S G Woodgate
Type: Co-educational Day
No of pupils: 42
Special Needs: **EBD**

Tameside Education Authority

Council Offices
Wellington Road
Ashton-under-lyme
Lancashire OL6 6DL
Tel: (0161) 342 8355

CROMWELL SECONDARY SCHOOL
Thornley Lane South, Reddish,
Stockport, Greater Manchester
SK5 6QW
Tel: (0161) 320 8728
Head: Mr M Rogers
Type: Co-educational Day 11–19
No of pupils: B36 G36
Special Needs: PMLD **SLD** W

HAWTHORNS SCHOOL
Corporation Road, Audenshaw,
Greater Manchester M34 5LZ
Tel: (0161) 336 3389
Head: Mr J M Shore
Type: Co-educational Day 4–11
No of pupils: 80
Special Needs: **MLD**

OAKDALE SCHOOL & ACORN NURSERY
Cheetham Hill Road, Dukinfield,
Greater Manchester SK16 5LD
Tel: (0161) 367 9299
Head: Mrs I Howard
Type: Co-educational Day 2–11
No of pupils: 105
Special Needs: AUT **PMLD SLD** W

SAMUEL LAYCOCK SCHOOL
Mereside, Stalybridge, Cheshire
SK15 1JF
Tel: (0161) 303 1321
Head: Mr B Bradbury
Type: Co-educational Day 11–16
No of pupils: B77 G46
Special Needs: **MLD**

Trafford Education Authority

PO Box 19
Tatton Road
Sale
Cheshire M33 7YR
Tel: (0161) 912 1212

BRENTWOOD SCHOOL
Brentwood Avenue, Timperley,
Altrincham, Greater Manchester
WA14 1SR
Tel: (0161) 928 8109
Head: Mr C Oxley
Type: Co-educational Day
No of pupils: 70
Special Needs: **PMLD SLD** W

DELAMERE SCHOOL
Irlam Road, Flixton, Urmston,
Greater Manchester M41 6AP
Tel: (0161) 747 5893
Head: Ms S M Huddart
Type: Co-educational
No of pupils: 64
Special Needs: **PMLD SLD**

LONGFORD PARK SCHOOL

Longford Park, Stretford, Greater
Manchester M32 8PR
Tel: (0161) 881 2341
Head: Mr M G Coxe
Type: Co-educational Day 5–11
No of pupils: 56
Special Needs: ADD ADHD EBD **MLD**
SPLD

PICTOR SCHOOL

Harboro Road, Sale, Greater
Manchester M33 5AH
Tel: (0161) 962 5432
Head: Mrs J Spruce
Type: Co-educational Day 2–7
No of pupils: 65
Special Needs: ADD ADHD **ASP AUT
CP DOW** DYC DYS EBD **EPI HI MLD
PH SP&LD SPLD W**

Wigan Education Authority

Gateway House
Standishgate
Wigan
Lancashire WN1 1AE
Tel: (01942) 828891

BROOKFIELD HIGH

Park Road, Hindley, Wigan, Greater
Manchester WN2 3RY
Tel: (01942) 776142
Head: Mr J H Young
Type: Co-educational Day
No of pupils: B112 G53
Special Needs: **MLD**

GREEN HALL PRIMARY SCHOOL

Green Hall Close, Atherton, Greater
Manchester M46 9HP
Tel: (01942) 883928
Head: Mr Triska
Type: Co-educational Day 4–11
No of pupils: B65 G33
Special Needs: **MLD**

GREEN HALL SCHOOL

Green Hall Close, Atherton, Greater
Manchester M46 9HP
Tel: (01977) 722815
Head: Mr I A Triska
Type: Co-educational Day 4–16
No of pupils: 140
Special Needs: **MLD**

HIGHLEA SECONDARY SHOOL

294 Mosley Common Road, Worsley,
Greater Manchester M28 1DA
Tel: (0161) 790 2698
Head: Mr J Leamon
Type: Co-educational Boarding
No of pupils: B41 G2
No of Boarders: W12
Special Needs: EBD

HOPE SCHOOL

Kelvin Grove, Marus Bridge, Wigan,
Greater Manchester WN3 6SP
Tel: (01942) 824150
Head: Mr J P Dahlstrom
Type: Co-educational Day 2–19
No of pupils: 120
Special Needs: AUT PMLD SLD W

KINGSHILL SCHOOL

Elliot Street, Tyldesley, Greater
Manchester M29 8JE
Acting Head: M J Myerslough
Type: Co-educational Day
No of pupils: B53 G6
Special Needs: EBD

MERE OAKS SCHOOL

Boars Head, Standish, Wigan,
Greater Manchester WN1 2RF
Tel: (01942) 243481
Head: Mrs J Leach
Type: Co-educational Day 2–19
No of pupils: B58 G50
Special Needs: **PH** W

MONTROSE SCHOOL

Montrose Avenue, Pemberton,
Wigan, Greater Manchester
WN5 9XN
Tel: (01942) 223431
Head: Mr A Farmer
Type: Co-educational Day
No of pupils: 126
Special Needs: **MLD** W

WILLOW GROVE PRIMARY

Willow Grove, Ashton-in-Makefield,
Wigan, Greater Manchester
WN4 9HP
Tel: (01942) 727717
Head: V Pearson
Type: Co-educational Day
No of pupils: 56
Special Needs: EBD

MERSEYSIDE

Knowsley Education Authority

Huyton Hey Road
Huyton
Liverpool
Merseyside L36 5YH
Tel: (0151) 443 3232

ALT BRIDGE SECONDARY SUPPORT CENTRE

Wellcroft Road, Huyton, Knowsley,
Merseyside L36 7TA
Tel: (0151) 489 1050
Head: Mr I Chisnall
Type: Co-educational Day
No of pupils: 172
Special Needs: ASP EBD HI **MLD
SP&LD SPLD**

THE ELMS SPECIAL SCHOOL

Whitethorn Drive, Stockbridge
Village, Merseyside L28 1RX
Tel: (0151) 489 6517
Head: Mrs L Lowe
Type: Co-educational Day 2–19
No of pupils: 115
Special Needs: AUT DOW PMLD
SLD W

HIGHFIELD SCHOOL

Baileys Lane, Halewood, Merseyside
L26 0TY
Tel: (0151) 486 4787
Head: Mr A Macquarrie
Type: Co-educational Day 6–16
No of pupils: 48
Special Needs: EBD

KNOWSLEY NORTHERN PRIMARY SUPPORT CENTRE

Bramcote Walk, Northwood, Kirkby,
Merseyside L33 9UR
Tel: (0151) 546 2156
Head: Mrs B Twiss
Type: Co-educational Day
No of pupils: B43 G20
Special Needs: DYS **MLD** SP&LD
SPLD

KNOWSLEY SOUTHERN PRIMARY SUPPORT CENTRE

Arncliffe Road, Halewood,
Liverpool, Merseyside L25 9QE
Tel: (0151) 486 5514
Head: Mr E Smith
Type: Co-educational Day
No of pupils: 50
Special Needs: **MLD** W

PARKFIELD SCHOOL
Bracknell Avenue, Southdene,
Kirkby, Merseyside L32 9PW
Tel: (0151) 546 6355
Head: Ms J L Schofield-King
Type: Co-educational Day
No of pupils: 72
Special Needs: EBD SPLD

SPRINGFIELD SPECIAL SCHOOL
Cawthorne Close, Kirkby,
Merseyside L32 3XG
Tel: (0151) 549 1425
Head: Mr I Cordingley
Type: Co-educational Day
No of pupils: B45 G35
Special Needs: PH PMLD W

Liverpool Education Authority

14 Sir Thomas Street
Liverpool
Merseyside L1 6BJ
Tel: (0151) 225 2822

ABBOTS LEA SCHOOL
Beaconsfield Road, Liverpool,
Merseyside L25 6EE
Tel: (0151) 428 1161
Head: Mrs C A Boycott
Type: Co-educational Boarding and
Day 4–19
No of pupils: B46 G12
No of Boarders: W16
Special Needs: ASP AUT

ACORN NURSERY SCHOOL
Lowerson Road, Liverpool,
Merseyside L11 8LW
Tel: (0151) 226 0309
Head: Mrs L Wright
Type: Co-educational Day
No of pupils: 30
Special Needs: ASP AUT PMLD
SLD W

ASHFIELD SCHOOL
Childwall Abbey Road, Childwall,
Liverpool, Merseyside L16 5EY
Tel: (0151) 228 9500
Head: Mr J Ashley
Type: Co-educational Day 5–16
No of pupils: 150
Special Needs: ADD ASP AUT DYP
DYS EBD EPI MLD SP&LD SPLD

CLIFFORD HOLROYDE SPECIAL SCHOOL
Thingwall Lane, Liverpool,
Merseyside L14 7NX
Tel: (0151) 525 6943
Head: Mr M J Rees
Type: Co-educational Day 5–16
No of pupils: 55
Special Needs: EBD

ERNEST COOKSON SPECIAL SCHOOL
Mill Lane, Liverpool, Merseyside
L12 7JA
Tel: (0151) 220 1874
Head: Mr S W Roberts
Type: Co-educational Day
No of pupils: 50
Special Needs: EBD

FINCHLEA SCHOOL
Mill Lane, Old Swan, Liverpool,
Merseyside L13 5TF
Tel: (0151) 228 2578
Head: Mrs D Newman
Type: Co-educational 4–19
No of pupils: 36
Special Needs: AUT DOW EPI SLD

GRANTSIDE SPECIAL SCHOOL
Mill Road, Everton, Liverpool,
Merseyside L6 2AS
Tel: (0151) 263 6417
Head: Mr M H Horne
Type: Boys Day
No of pupils: 45
Special Needs: EBD

HAROLD MAGNAY SCHOOL
Woolton Hill Road, Liverpool,
Merseyside L25 6JA
Tel: (0151) 428 6305
Head: Mr M Little
Type: Co-educational Day and
Boarding 2–11
No of pupils: 70 *No of Boarders:* W24
Special Needs: PH W

LOWER LEE SPECIAL SCHOOL
Beaconsfield Road, Liverpool,
Merseyside L25 6EF
Tel: (0151) 428 4071
Head: Mr P Wright
Type: Boys Boarding 8–16
No of pupils: 45 *No of Boarders:* F36
Special Needs: EBD

MARGARET BEAVAN SCHOOL
Almonds Green, West Derby,
Liverpool, Merseyside L12 5HP
Tel: (0151) 226 1306
Head: Mr T B Flynn
Type: Co-educational Day 5–16
No of pupils: B80 G60
Special Needs: MLD

MEADOW BANK SPECIAL SCHOOL
Sherwoods Lane, Liverpool,
Merseyside L10 1LW
Tel: (0151) 525 3451
Head: Mrs C Clancy
Type: Co-educational Day 5–17
No of pupils: 145
Special Needs: ADD ASP AUT EPI
MLD SP&LD SPLD

MERSEY VIEW SCHOOL
Minehead Road, Liverpool,
Merseyside L17 6AX
Tel: (0151) 427 1863
Head: Mr C J Muscatelli
Type: Co-educational Day 5–16
No of pupils: B70 G20
Special Needs: MLD

MILLSTEAD SPECIAL NEEDS PRIMARY SCHOOL
Old Mill Lane, Wavertree, Liverpool,
Merseyside L15 8LW
Tel: (0151) 722 0974
Head: Mrs M Lucas
Type: Co-educational Day 2–11
No of pupils: B32 G18
Special Needs: AUT PMLD SLD W

PALMERSTON SCHOOL
Beaconsfield Road, Woolton,
Liverpool, Merseyside L25 6EE
Tel: (0151) 428 2128
Head: Mr J F Wright
Type: Co-educational Day 11–19
No of pupils: B48 G22
Special Needs: ADD ADHD ASP AUT
CP DEL DOW DYP EPI HI PH PMLD
SLD SP&LD VIS W

PRINCES SCHOOL
Selborne Street, Liverpool,
Merseyside L8 1YQ
Tel: (0151) 709 2602
Head: Mrs V Healy
Type: Co-educational Day 2–11
No of pupils: 50
Special Needs: AUT CP DOW HI
PMLD SLD SP&LD W

REDBRIDGE HIGH SCHOOL
Sherwoods Lane, Liverpool,
Merseyside L10 1LW
Tel: (0151) 525 5733
Head: Mrs S Coates
Type: Co-educational
No of pupils: 86
Special Needs: AUT PMLD **SLD** W

SANDFIELD PARK SCHOOL
Sandfield Walk, Liverpool,
Merseyside L12 1LH
Tel: (0151) 228 0324
Head: Mr J Hudson
Type: Co-educational Day 11–19
No of pupils: B47 G26
Special Needs: **CP EPI MLD** PH
PMLD W

WATERGATE SCHOOL
Speke Road, Liverpool, Merseyside
L25 8QA
Tel: (0151) 428 5812
Head: Mr P J Richardson
Type: Co-educational Day
No of pupils: 130
Special Needs: MLD SP&LD

WHEATHILL SCHOOL
Naylorsfield Drive, Liverpool,
Merseyside L27 0YD
Tel: (0151) 498 4811
Head: Mr D R Wade
Type: Co-educational Day 5–11
No of pupils: 30
Special Needs: ADHD **EBD** W

WHITE THORN SCHOOL (ASSESSMENT)
Ranworth Square, Liverpool,
Merseyside L11 3DQ
Tel: (0151) 233 4094
Head: Miss J Roberts
Type: Co-educational Day 3–7
No of pupils: 25
Special Needs: EBD MLD SLD
SP&LD W

St Helens Education Authority

The Rivington Centre
Rivington Road
St Helens
Merseyside WA10 4ND
Tel: (01744) 456000

HAMBLETT SCHOOL
Rainford Road, St Helens,
Merseyside WA10 6BX
Tel: (01744) 23078
Head: Mr R Brownlow
Type: Co-educational Day 2–19
No of pupils: 60
Special Needs: CP DEL DYP EPI **PH**
PMLD W

HURST SCHOOL
Hard Lane, St Helens, Merseyside
WA10 6PN
Tel: (01744) 25643
Head: Mr M J Carolan
Type: Co-educational Day
No of pupils: 170
Special Needs: MLD SP&LD

MILL GREEN SCHOOL
Mill Lane, Newton-le-Willows,
Merseyside WA12 8BG
Tel: (01925) 226213
Head: Mr G C Brown
Type: Co-educational Day 2–19
No of pupils: 88
Special Needs: PMLD SLD

PENKFORD SCHOOL
Wharf Road, Newton-le-Willows,
Merseyside WA12 9XZ
Tel: (01925) 224195
Acting Head: Mr D N Hartley
Type: Co-educational Day
No of pupils: B85 G40
Special Needs: **EBD MLD** W

Sefton Education Authority

Town Hall
Bootle
Merseyside L20 7AE
Tel: (0151) 922 4040

MEREFIELD SPECIAL SCHOOL
Westminster Drive, Southport,
Merseyside PR8 2QZ
Tel: (01704) 577163
Head: Ms A Foster
Type: Co-educational Day 2–19
No of pupils: 36
Special Needs: AUT PMLD **SLD** W

NEWFIELD SPECIAL SCHOOL
Edge Lane, Liverpool, Merseyside
L23 4TG
Tel: (0151) 931 3030
Head: Mr J Taylor
Type: Co-educational Day 5–16
No of pupils: B71 G3
Special Needs: ADD ADHD ASP DYP
DYS **EBD** EPI

PRESFIELD SPECIAL SCHOOL
Preston New Road, Southport,
Merseyside PR9 8PA
Tel: (01704) 227831
Head: Mr E T Powell
Type: Co-educational Day 5–16
No of pupils: 80
Special Needs: **MLD**

RONALD HOUSE SCHOOL
De Villiers Avenue, Crosby,
Merseyside L23 2TH
Tel: (0151) 924 3671
Head: Mrs B M Dornan
Type: Co-educational Day 5–16
No of pupils: B73 G52
Special Needs: ADHD ASP EBD **MLD**

ROWAN PARK SENIOR SCHOOL
Onell Road, Bootle, Merseyside
L20 6DU
Tel: (0151) 330 0528
Head: Mrs J A Kelly
Type: Co-educational Day
No of pupils: B69 G30
Special Needs: **AUT** CP DOW EBD
EPI HI PH **PMLD SLD** SP&LD VIS W

THE SCHOOL OF THE GOOD SHEPHERD
Sterrix Lane, Ford, Liverpool,
Merseyside L21 0DA
Tel: (0151) 928 6165
Head: Mr A M Sullivan
Type: Co-educational Day
No of pupils: 50
Special Needs: CP DEL EPI PH W

Wirral Education Authority

Hamilton Building
Conway Street
Birkenhead
Wirral
Merseyside CH41 4FD
Tel: (0151) 666 2121

CLARE MOUNT SCHOOL
Fender Lane, Moreton, Wirral,
Merseyside L46 9PA
Tel: (0151) 606 0274/9440
Head: Mrs L C Clare
Type: Co-educational 11–19
No of pupils: B145 G75
Special Needs: MLD

CLATTERBRIDGE SCHOOL
Wirral, Merseyside L63 4JY
Tel: (0151) 334 6120
Head: Mrs P Stewart
No of pupils: 59
Special Needs: CP PH PMLD SLD SP&LD W

ELLERAY PARK SCHOOL
Elleray Park Road, Wallasey,
Merseyside L45 0LH
Tel: (0151) 639 3594
Head: Mr D Quaife
Type: Co-educational Day 2–11
No of pupils: 82
Special Needs: ASP CP DEL DOW DYP DYS EPI MLD PH PMLD SLD SP&LD SPLD VIS W

FOXFIELD SCHOOL
Douglas Drive, Moreton, Wirral,
Merseyside L46 6BT
Tel: (0151) 677 8555
Head: Mr A M Baird
Type: Co-educational Day 11–19
No of pupils: B50 G40
Special Needs: AUT PMLD SLD W

GILBROOK SCHOOL
Pilgrim Street, Birkenhead,
Merseyside L41 5EH
Tel: (0151) 647 8411
Head: Mr K E Jackson
Type: Co-educational Day 5–11
No of pupils: 50
Special Needs: ADD ADHD EBD W

HAYFIELD SCHOOL
Manor Drive, Upton, Wirral,
Merseyside L49 4PJ
Tel: (0151) 677 9303
Head: Ms S A Lowy
Type: Co-educational
No of pupils: 120
Special Needs: AUT MLD SP&LD

KILGARTH SCHOOL
Cavendish Street, Birkenhead,
Merseyside CH41 8BA
Tel: (0151) 652 8071
Head: Miss J M Dawson
Type: Boys Day 11–16
No of pupils: 50
Special Needs: EBD

MEADOWSIDE SCHOOL
Pool Lane, Woodchurch,
Birkenhead, Merseyside CH49 5LA
Tel: (0151) 678 7711
Head: Ms L Kane
Type: Co-educational Day 11–19
No of pupils: B45 G25
Special Needs: ADD ADHD ASP AUT CP DEL DOW DYP DYS EPI HI MLD PH PMLD SLD SP&LD VIS W

ORRETS MEADOW SCHOOL
Chapelhill Road, Moreton,
Birkenhead, Merseyside L46 9QQ
Tel: (0151) 678 8070
Head: Mrs S E Blythe
Type: Co-educational Day 7–11
No of pupils: 66
Special Needs: DYS SPLD

STANLEY SCHOOL
Pensby Road, Thingwall, Heswall,
Merseyside L61 7UG
Tel: (0151) 648 3178
Head: Mr A Newman
Type: Co-educational Day 2–11
No of pupils: 90
Special Needs: SLD

MIDDLESBROUGH

Middlesbrough Borough Council

Education Department
PO Box 69
Vancouver House
Gurney Street
Middlesbrough TS1 1EL
Tel: (01642) 262001

BEVERLEY SCHOOL FOR THE DEAF
Beverley Road, Middlesbrough
TS4 3LQ
Tel: (01642) 815500
Head: Mrs E McBean
Type: Co-educational Day 4–19
No of pupils: B66 G29
Special Needs: AUT HI

HOLMWOOD SCHOOL
Saltersgill Avenue, Middlesbrough
TS4 3JS
Tel: (01642) 819157
Head: Mr D Johnson
Type: Co-educational Day
No of pupils: B60 G40
Special Needs: MLD

PRIORY WOODS SCHOOL
Tothill Avenue, Netherfields,
Middlesbrough TS3 0RH
Tel: (01642) 321212
Head: Mrs B Knill
Type: Co-educational Day 4–19
No of pupils: B83 G52
Special Needs: PMLD SLD W

TOLLESBY SCHOOL
Saltersgill Avenue, Middlesbrough
TS4 3JS
Tel: (01642) 815765
Head: Mr J Whittingham
Type: Co-educational Day 11–16
No of pupils: B100 G40
Special Needs: EBD MLD

NORFOLK

Norfolk Education Authority

County Hall
Norwich
Norfolk NR1 2DL
Tel: (01603) 222146

ALDERMAN JACKSON SPECIAL SCHOOL

Marsh Lane, Gaywood, King's Lynn,
Norfolk PE30 3AE
Tel: (01553) 672779/674281
Head: Mrs L F Tolfree
Type: Co-educational Day 2–19
No of pupils: B35 G28
Special Needs: **AUT CP PMLD** SLD W

THE CLARE SCHOOL

South Park Avenue, Norwich,
Norfolk NR4 7AU
Tel: (01603) 54199
Head: Mr C R Hocking
Type: Co-educational Day
No of pupils: 110
Special Needs: CP DYP EPI HI PH
SP&LD VIS W

EATON HALL SPECIAL SCHOOL

Pettus Road, Norwich, Norfolk
NR4 7BU
Tel: (01603) 457480
Head: Mr S T Lord
Type: Boys Boarding and Day 8–16
No of pupils: 48
Special Needs: **EBD**

EDINBURGH ROAD SPECIAL SCHOOL

Norwich Road, Holt, Norfolk
NR25 6SL
Tel: (01263) 713358
Head: Mrs G Measures
Type: Co-educational Day 2–19
No of pupils: 34
Special Needs: PMLD SLD W

FRED NICHOLSON SPECIAL SCHOOL

Westfield Road, Dereham, Norfolk
NR19 1BJ
Tel: (01362) 693915
Head: Mr M Clayton
Type: Co-educational Day and
Boarding 7–16
No of pupils: B60 G35
Special Needs: **MLD** W

HALL SPECIAL SCHOOL

St Faith's Road, Old Catton,
Norwich, Norfolk NR6 7AD
Tel: (01603) 466467
Head: Mrs A M Ruthven
Type: Co-educational Day 3–19
No of pupils: 80
Special Needs: AUT **CP DEL** DOW
EPI HI PH PMLD SLD VIS W

HARFORD MANOR SPECIAL SCHOOL

43 Ipswich Road, Norwich, Norfolk
NR2 2LN
Tel: (01603) 451809
Head: Mr G Kitchen
Type: Co-educational Day 3–19
No of pupils: 75
Special Needs: AUT PMLD SLD

JOHN GRANT SPECIAL SCHOOL

St George's Drive, Caistor-on-Sea,
Great Yarmouth, Norfolk NR30 5QW
Tel: (01493) 720158
Head: Mr G A Hampson
Type: Co-educational Day
No of pupils: B56 G37
Special Needs: PMLD **SLD** W

PARKSIDE SPECIAL SCHOOL

College Road, Norwich, Norfolk
NR2 3JA
Tel: (01603) 441126
Head: Mr B Payne
Type: Day
No of pupils: 145
Special Needs: MLD

SIDESTRAND HALL SPECIAL SCHOOL

Cromer Road, Sidestrand, Cromer,
Norfolk NR27 0NH
Tel: (01263) 578144
Head: Mr G R Scott
Type: Co-educational Boarding and
Day 7–16
No of pupils: 110 *No of Boarders:* W25
Special Needs: MLD

NORTHAMPTONSHIRE

Northamptonshire Education Authority

PO Box 216
John Dryden House
8–10 The Lakes
Northampton
Northamptonshire NN4 7DD
Tel: (01604) 236236

BILLING BROOK SCHOOL

Penistone Road, Lumbertubs,
Northampton NN3 8EZ
Tel: (01604) 773910
Head: Mr D Scott
Type: Co-educational Day 2–16
No of pupils: B95 G55
Special Needs: AUT **MLD SLD**

FAIRFIELDS SCHOOL

Trinity Avenue, Northampton
NN2 6JN
Tel: (01604) 714777
Head: Mrs C Murray
Type: Co-educational Day 3–11
No of pupils: 70
Special Needs: EPI **PH** PMLD SLD W

FRIARS SCHOOL
Friar's Close, Wellingborough,
Northamptonshire NN8 2LA
Tel: (01933) 304950
Head: Mrs P A Norton
Type: Co-educational Day
No of pupils: B98 G47
Special Needs: ASP AUT CP DEL
DOW DYS **MLD** SLD W

GREENFIELDS SCHOOL
Harborough Road, Northampton
NN2 8LR
Tel: (01604) 843657
Head: Mrs J Moralee
Type: Co-educational Day 11–16
No of pupils: 70
Special Needs: AUT PMLD SLD W

HIGHFIELD SCHOOL
273 Welford Road, Northampton,
Northamptonshire NN2 8PW
Tel: (01604) 846018
Head: Mr B Kettleborough
Type: Co-educational Day 4–11
Special Needs: **EBD**

ISEBROOK SCHOOL
Eastleigh Road, Kettering,
Northamptonshire NN15 6PT
Tel: (01536) 81606
Head: Mr K McHenry
Type: Co-educational Day 11–16
No of pupils: B63 G15
Special Needs: ASP AUT AUT MLD
PH W

NORTHGATE SCHOOL
Queens Park Parade, Northampton
NN2 6LR
Tel: (01604) 714098
Head: Mr T Clay
Type: Co-educational 7–16
No of pupils: 120
Special Needs: DYP **MLD** W

ORCHARD SCHOOL
Beatrice Road, Kettering,
Northamptonshire NN16 9QR
Tel: (01536) 513726
Head: Mrs V Payne
Type: Co-educational Day 11–16
No of pupils: 45
Special Needs: **EBD** W

RAEBURN SCHOOL
Raeburn Road, Northampton
NN2 7EU
Tel: (01604) 460017
Head: Mr D R Lloyd
Type: Co-educational Day 11–16
No of pupils: B45 G5
Special Needs: **EBD**

ROWANGATE PRIMARY SCHOOL
Finedon Road, Wellingborough,
Northamptonshire
Tel: (01933) 225280
Head: Mrs F Sutton
Type: Co-educational Day 3–11
No of pupils: B61 G40
Special Needs: ADD ADHD ASP AUT
CP DEL DOW DYP DYS EPI **MLD** PH
PMLD SLD SP&LD SPLD VIS W

NORTHUMBERLAND

Northumberland Education Authority

County Hall
Morpeth
Northumberland NE61 2EF
Tel: (01670) 533000

ATKINSON HOUSE SCHOOL
North Terrace, Seghill, Cramlington,
Northumberland NE23 7EB
Tel: (0191) 298 0838
Type: Boys Day
No of pupils: 40
Special Needs: **EBD**

BARNDALE HOUSE SCHOOL
Barndale House, Howling Lane,
Alnwick, Northumberland
NE66 1DQ
Tel: (01665) 602541
Head: Mr J P Chappells
Type: Co-educational Day and
Boarding 3–19
No of pupils: 35
Special Needs: SLD

CLEASWELL HILL SCHOOL
Guide Post, Choppington,
Northumberland NE62 5DJ
Tel: (01670) 823182
Head: Mr R J Hope
Type: Co-educational Day 4–16
No of pupils: B70 G35
Special Needs: **MLD**

COLLINGWOOD SCHOOL
Thingwall Lane, Morpeth,
Northumberland L14 7NX
Tel: (01670) 56374
Head: Ms C Hetherington
Type: Co-educational Day
No of pupils: 120
Special Needs: **MLD**

EAST HARTFORD SCHOOL
East Hartford, Cramlington,
Northumberland NE23 9AR
Tel: (01670) 713881
Head: Mr W K Telfer
Type: Co-educational 4–11
No of pupils: 53
Special Needs: **MLD**

THE GROVE SCHOOL
Grove Gardens, Tweedmouth,
Berwick Upon Tweed,
Northumberland TD15 2EN
Tel: (01289) 360390
Head: Mrs E E Brown
Type: Co-educational Day 3–19
No of pupils: 23
Special Needs: AUT DOW PMLD
SLD W

HACKWOOD PARK SCHOOL
Gallows Bank, Hexham,
Northumberland NE46 1AU
Tel: (01434) 604039
Head: Mr J Wells
Type: Co-educational Day
No of pupils: 86 *No of Boarders:* W12
Special Needs: **MLD**

PRIORY SCHOOL
Dene Park, Hexham,
Northumberland NE46 1HN
Tel: (01434) 605021
Head: Mr M Thompson
Type: Co-educational Day 3–18
No of pupils: B26 G14
Special Needs: **PMLD** SLD W

NOTTINGHAMSHIRE

Nottingham City Council

Education Department
Sandfield Centre
Sandfield Road
Lenton
Nottingham NG7 1QH
Tel: (0115) 915 0600

ASPLEY WOOD SCHOOL
Robins Wood Road, Aspley,
Nottingham NG8 3LD
Tel: (0115) 913 1400
Head: Mrs B Mole
Type: Co-educational Day 3–16
No of pupils: B25 G20
Special Needs: CP PH VIS W

NETHERGATE SCHOOL
Swansdowne Drive, Clifton Estate,
Nottingham NG11 8HX
Tel: (0115) 915 2959
Head: Mr S Johnson-Marshall
Type: Co-educational Day 5–16
No of pupils: B44 G21
Special Needs: ADHD AUT DOW
DYP DYS EBD EPI MLD SP&LD
SPLD VIS W

ROSEHILL SCHOOL
St Matthias Road, Nottingham
NG3 2FE
Tel: (0115) 950 2038
Head: Mr J Pearson
Type: Co-educational Day 3–19
No of pupils: B55 G15
Special Needs: ASP AUT

WESTBURY SCHOOL &
SUPPORT SERVICE
Chingford Road, Billingborough,
Nottingham NG8 3BT
Tel: (0115) 913 8005
Head: Mr J Haw
Type: Co-educational Day 10–16
No of pupils: 19
Special Needs: EBD

Nottinghamshire Education Authority

County Hall
West Bridgford
Nottingham
Nottinghamshire NG2 7QP
Tel: (0115) 982 3823

ASH LEA SCHOOL
Owthorpe Road, Cotgrave,
Nottingham NG12 3PA
Tel: (0115) 989 2744
Head: Mrs L Skillington
Type: Co-educational Day
No of pupils: B32 G31
Special Needs: SLD

BEECH HILL SCHOOL
Fairholme Drive, Mansfield,
Nottinghamshire NG19 6DX
Tel: (01623) 26008
Head: Mr M Sutton
Type: Co-educational 11–16
No of pupils: 70
Special Needs: AUT EBD MLD

BRACKEN HILL SCHOOL
Chartwell Road, Kirkby-in-Ashfield,
Nottinghamshire NG17 7HZ
Tel: (01623) 753068
Head: Mr A M Kawalek
Type: Co-educational Day
No of pupils: B45 G15
Special Needs: ADD ADHD ASP AUT
DEL MLD SLD SP&LD W

CARLTON DIGBY SCHOOL
Digby Avenue, Mapperley,
Nottinghamshire NG3 6DS
Tel: (0115) 956 8289
Head: Mrs G Clifton
Type: Co-educational Day 3–19
No of pupils: B47 G24
Special Needs: PMLD SLD W

DERRYMOUNT SCHOOL
Churchmoor Lane, Arnold,
Nottinghamshire NG5 8HN
Tel: (0115) 926 3355
Head: Mr E Thompson
Type: Co-educational Day 3–16
No of pupils: 60
Special Needs: AUT CP EBD EPI HI
MLD PH SLD SP&LD VIS

FOUNTAINDALE SCHOOL
Nottingham Road, Mansfield,
Nottinghamshire NG18 5BA
Tel: (01623) 792671
Head: Mr M Dengel
Type: Co-educational Boarding and
Day 3–19
No of pupils: B38 G40
No of Boarders: W8
Special Needs: CP DEL EPI PH
SP&LD VIS W

FOXWOOD SCHOOL
Derby Road, Bramcote Hills,
Beeston, Nottinghamshire NG9 3GE
Tel: (0115) 917 7202
Head: Ms J Baker
Type: Co-educational Day 3–19
No of pupils: B63 G32
Special Needs: ASP AUT DYS MLD
SP&LD SPLD W

REDGATE SCHOOL
Somersall Street, Mansfield,
Nottinghamshire NG19 6EL
Tel: (01623) 455955
Head: Mr K G Fallows
Type: Co-educational Day 3–11
No of pupils: B40 G10

ST GILES SCHOOL
North Road, Retford,
Nottinghamshire DN22 7XN
Tel: (01777) 703683
Head: Mrs C M Kirk
Type: Co-educational Day 3–19
No of pupils: 86
Special Needs: ADD ADHD ASP AUT
CP DOW EBD EPI HI MLD PH PMLD
SLD VIS W

SHEPHERD SCHOOL
Harvey Road, Off Beechdale Road,
Bilborough, Nottingham NG8 3BB
Tel: (0115) 929 1011
Head: Mr D S Stewart
Type: Co-educational 3–19
No of pupils: 160
Special Needs: AUT EPI MLD PMLD
SLD W

WOODLANDS SCHOOL
Beechdale Road, Aspley, Nottingham
NG8 3EZ
Tel: (0115) 929 5947
Acting Head: S D Fee
Type: Co-educational Day 3–16
No of pupils: 120
Special Needs: AUT EBD MLD SLD W

YEOMAN PARK SCHOOL
Park Hall Road, Mansfield
Woodhouse, Mansfield,
Nottinghamshire NG19 8PS
Tel: (01204) 840709
Head: Mr P Betts
Type: Co-educational Day 3–19
No of pupils: 73
Special Needs: SLD W

OXFORDSHIRE

Oxfordshire Education Authority

Macclesfield House
New Road
Oxford OX1 1NA
Tel: (01865) 792422

BARDWELL SCHOOL
Hendon Place, Sunderland Drive,
Bicester, Oxfordshire OX6 7RZ
Tel: (01869) 242182
Head: Mrs C Hughes
Type: Co-educational Day 2–16
No of pupils: 49
Special Needs: AUT CP EPI PMLD
SLD SP&LD VIS W

FITZWARYN SPECIAL SCHOOL
Denchworth Road, Wantage,
Oxfordshire OX12 9ET
Tel: (01235) 764504
Head: Mrs M Tighe
Type: Co-educational Day 3–16
No of pupils: B54 G22
Special Needs: MLD PMLD SLD W

FRANK WISE SCHOOL
Hornbeam Close, Banbury,
Oxfordshire OX16 9RL
Tel: (01295) 263520
Head: Mr K Griffiths
Type: Co-educational Day 2–16
No of pupils: 86
Special Needs: PMLD SLD W

IFFLEY MEAD SPECIAL SCHOOL
Iffley Turn, Oxford OX4 4DU
Tel: (01865) 747606
Head: Mr J Knox
Type: Day
No of pupils: 111
Special Needs: MLD

JOHN WATSON SPECIAL SCHOOL
Littleworth Road, Wheatley, Oxford
OX33 1NN
Tel: (01865) 872515
Head: Ms S Cook
Type: Co-educational Day
No of pupils: 68
Special Needs: PMLD SLD W

KINGFISHER SCHOOL
Radley Road, Abingdon, Oxfordshire
OX14 3RR
Tel: (01235) 523843
Head: Mrs A O'Meara
Type: Co-educational Day 2–16
No of pupils: 115
Special Needs: MLD PMLD SLD W

MABEL PRICHARD SPECIAL SCHOOL
St Nicholas Road, Littlemore,
Oxfordshire OX4 4PN
Tel: (01865) 777878
Head: Miss J Wallington
Type: Co-educational Day
No of pupils: 63
Special Needs: PMLD SLD W

NORTHERN HOUSE SPECIAL SCHOOL
South Parade, Summertown, Oxford
OX2 7JN
Tel: (01865) 557004
Head: Mr R Howarth
Type: Co-educational Day
No of pupils: B73 G5
Special Needs: EBD

NORTHFIELD SPECIAL SCHOOL
Knights Road, Blackbird Leys,
Oxford OX4 5HN
Tel: (01865) 771703
Head: Mr P Sheldon
Type: Co-educational Day
No of pupils: B88 *No of Boarders:* F7
W12
Special Needs: EBD

ORMEROD SPECIAL SCHOOL
Waynflete Road, Headington, Oxford
OX3 8DD
Tel: (01865) 744173
Head: Mr C Peters
Type: Co-educational Day 2–16
No of pupils: 57
Special Needs: PH

SPRINGFIELD SPECIAL SCHOOL
9 Moorland Close, Witney,
Oxfordshire OX8 5LN
Tel: (01993) 703963
Head: Mrs C Niner
Type: Co-educational Day 2–16
No of pupils: B64 G29
Special Needs: PMLD SLD W

WOODEATON MANOR SCHOOL
Woodeaton, Oxford OX3 9TS
Tel: (01865) 58722
Head: Miss C Greenhow
Type: Co-educational Boarding and
Day 7–16
No of pupils: 63 *No of Boarders:* W24
Special Needs: EBD EPI HI MLD VIS

REDCAR AND CLEVELAND

Redcar & Cleveland Education Authority

PO Box 83
Council Offices
Kirkleatham Street
Redcar TS10 1YA
Tel: (01642) 444000

KILTON THORPE SCHOOL

Marshall Drive, Brotton, Redcar and Cleveland TS12 2UW
Tel: (01287) 677265
Head: Mr J C Short
Type: Co-educational Day 3–19
No of pupils: 95
Special Needs: ADD ADHD AUT CP DOW DYP EBD EPI HI MLD PH PMLD SLD SP&LD SPLD VIS W

KIRKLEATHAM HALL SCHOOL

Kirkleatham, Redcar, Redcar and Cleveland TS10 4QR
Tel: (01642) 483009
Head: Mrs A G Naylor
Type: Co-educational Day 2–19
No of pupils: B75 G55
Special Needs: CP DOW EPI **MLD PMLD SLD** SP&LD W

RUTLAND

Rutland Education Authority

Catmose
Oakham
Leicestershire LE15 6HP
Tel: (01572) 772706

THE PARKS NURSERY SCHOOL

Barleythorpe Road, Oakham, Rutland LE15 6NR
Tel: (01572) 756747
Head: Mrs B Marchant
Type: Co-educational Day 2–6
No of pupils: 26
Special Needs: ASP AUT CP DEL DOW EBD EPI HI MLD PH PMLD SLD SP&LD SPLD VIS W

SHROPSHIRE

Shropshire Education Authority

Shirehall
Abbey Forgate
Shrewsbury
Shropshire SY2 6ND
Tel: (01473) 251000

THE CHARLES DARWIN SCHOOL

North Road, Wellington, Telford, Shropshire TF1 3ET
Tel: (01952) 242229
Head: Mr I Crawshaw
Type: Boys Day 13–16
No of pupils: 25
Special Needs: EBD

SEVERNDALE SCHOOL

Hearne Way, Monkmoor, Shrewsbury, Shropshire SY2 5SL
Tel: (01743) 281600
Head: Mr C Davies
Type: Co-educational Day
Special Needs: **AUT CP** DEL **DOW DYC DYP** EPI **HI MLD** PH **PMLD SLD SP&LD** SPLD VIS

SOUTHALL SCHOOL

off Rowan Road, Dawley, Telford, Shropshire TF4 3PN
Tel: (01952) 592485
Head: Mr A J Day
Type: Co-educational Day 5–16
No of pupils: B103 G52
Special Needs: **MLD**

TRENCH HALL SCHOOL

Tilley Green, Wem, Shrewsbury, Shropshire SY4 5PJ
Tel: (01939) 232372
Head: Mr B M Blakemore
Type: Co-educational Day 13–16
No of pupils: 35
Special Needs: ADD ADHD ASP DEL DYP DYS **EBD** EBD EPI SPLD

SOMERSET

Bath and North East Somerset Education Authority

PO Box 25
Riverside Temple Street
Keynsham
Bristol BS31 1DN
Tel: (01225) 394200

BARTLETT'S ELM SCHOOL
Field Road, Langport, Somerset
TA10 9SP
Tel: (01458) 252852
Head: Mrs J Bland
Type: Boys Day 10–16
No of pupils: 56
Special Needs: EBD

FOSSE WAY SCHOOL
Longfellow Road, Radstock, Bath,
North East Somerset BA3 3AL
Tel: (01761) 412198
Head: Mr D Gregory
Type: Co-educational Boarding and
Day 3–19
No of pupils: B77 G29
No of Boarders: W14
Special Needs: AUT MLD PMLD SLD

LIME GROVE SCHOOL
Pulteney Road, Bath, North East
Somerset BA2 4HE
Tel: (01225) 424732
Head: Mrs J Pulham
Type: Co-educational Day
No of pupils: B21 G24
Special Needs: PMLD SLD W

SUMMERFIELD SCHOOL
Weston Park East, Bath, North East
Somerset BA1 2UY
Tel: (01225) 423607
Head: Mr G Williams
Type: Co-educational Day 7–16
No of pupils: B60 G30
Special Needs: MLD

WANSDYKE SCHOOL
Frome Road, Odd Down, Bath,
North East Somerset BA2 5RF
Tel: (01225) 832212
Head: Mr J Ward
Type: Co-educational 11–16
No of pupils: 64 No of Boarders: W11
Special Needs: EBD

North Somerset Education Authority

PO Box 51
Town Hall
Weston-Super-Mare
Somerset BS23 1ZZ
Tel: (01934) 888888

BAYTREE SCHOOL
Baytree Road, Weston-Super-Mare,
North Somerset BS22 8HG
Tel: (01934) 625567
Head: Mrs C Penney
Type: Co-educational Day 3–19
No of pupils: 67
Special Needs: PMLD SLD W

RAVENSWOOD SCHOOL
Pound Lane, Nailsea, North
Somerset BS48 2NN
Tel: (01275) 854134
Head: Mrs G A Sawyer
Type: Co-educational Day 3–19
No of pupils: B76 G40
Special Needs: ASP AUT DYC DYP
DYS MLD SLD W

WESTHAVEN SCHOOL
Ellesmere Road, Uphill, Weston-
Super-Mare, North Somerset
BS23 4UT
Tel: (01934) 632171
Head: Mrs J Moss
Type: Co-educational Day 7–16
No of pupils: 75
Special Needs: MLD

Somerset Education Authority

County Hall
Taunton
Somerset TA1 4DY
Tel: (01823) 355455

AVALON SPECIAL SCHOOL
Brooks Road, Street, Somerset
BA16 0PS
Tel: (01458) 43081
Head: Mrs J M King
Type: Co-educational Day
No of pupils: B56 G29
Special Needs: ASP AUT CP DOW
DYP EPI MLD PH PMLD SLD SP&LD
VIS W

CRITCHILL SCHOOL & LEARNING SUPPORT CENTRE
Nunney Road, Frome, Somerset
BA11 4LB
Tel: (01373) 464148
Head: Mr L Rowsell
Type: Co-educational Day 4–16
No of pupils: B42 G30
Special Needs: ASP AUT MLD PMLD
SLD W

ELMWOOD SPECIAL SCHOOL
Hamp Avenue, Bridgwater, Somerset
TA6 6AP
Tel: (01278) 422866
Head: Mr C P Williams
Type: Co-educational Day 4–16
No of pupils: B60 G30
Special Needs: MLD

FAIRMEAD COMMUNITY SPECIAL SCHOOL
Mudford Road, Yeovil, Somerset
BA21 4NZ
Tel: (01935) 421295
Head: Mr R Hatt
Type: Co-educational Day 4–16
No of pupils: B70 G36
Special Needs: MLD W

FIVEWAYS SPECIAL SCHOOL
Victoria Road, Yeovil, Somerset
BA21 5AZ
Tel: (01935) 476227
Head: Mr M Collis
Type: Day
No of pupils: 67
Special Needs: PMLD SLD W

MONKTON PRIORS SPECIAL SCHOOL

Pickeridge Close, Taunton, Somerset
TA2 7HW
Tel: (01823) 275569
Head: Mr G Toller
Type: Boys Boarding and Day
No of pupils: 50 *No of Boarders:* W6
Special Needs: **EBD**

PENROSE SPECIAL SCHOOL

Albert Street, Bridgwater, Somerset
TA6 7ET
Tel: (01278) 423660
Head: Mrs S J Neale
Type: Co-educational Day 2–19
No of pupils: B32 G18
Special Needs: AUT CP DOW EPI
PMLD **SLD** W

SELWORTHY SPECIAL SCHOOL

Selworthy Road, Taunton, Somerset
TA2 8HD
Tel: (01823) 284970
Head: Mr D J Machell
Type: Co-educational Day 2–19
No of pupils: 65
Special Needs: ADD ADHD AUT CP
DOW EPI HI MLD PH PMLD SLD
VIS W

STAFFORDSHIRE

Staffordshire Education Authority

Tipping Street
Stafford
Staffordshire ST16 2DH
Tel: (01785) 223121

BITHAM SPECIAL SCHOOL

Bitham Lane, Stretton, Burton upon
Trent, Staffordshire DE13 0HB
Tel: (01283) 566988
Head: Ms P M Bullen
Type: Co-educational Day 4–18
No of pupils: 110
Special Needs: **MLD**

BLACKFRIARS SPECIAL SCHOOL

Priory Road, Newcastle under Lyme,
Staffordshire ST5 2TF
Tel: (01782) 297780
Head: Mr C E Lilley
Type: Co-educational 2–19
No of pupils: B100 G85
Special Needs: CP DEL EPI HI MLD
PH PMLD SP&LD VIS W

CHERRY TREES SPECIAL SCHOOL

Giggetty Lane, Wombourne,
Wolverhampton, West Midlands
WV5 0AX
Tel: (01902) 894484
Head: Mrs L J Allman
Type: Co-educational 2–19
Special Needs: PMLD SLD W

CICELY HAUGHTON SCHOOL

Westwood Manor, Westley Rocks,
Stoke on Trent, Staffordshire
ST9 0BX
Tel: (01782) 550202
Head: Mr N Phillips
Type: Boys Boarding and Day 5–11
No of pupils: 48 *No of Boarders:* F15
W30
Special Needs: **EBD**

COPPICE SPECIAL SCHOOL

Abbots Way, Westlands, Newcastle
under Lyme, Staffordshire ST5 2EY
Tel: (01782) 857030
Head: Mr J M Bevan
Type: Co-educational Day 3–16
No of pupils: 130
Special Needs: ASP MLD

CROWN SPECIAL SCHOOL

Bitham Lane, Stretton, Burton upon
Trent, Staffordshire DE13 0HB
Tel: (01283) 239700
Head: Mrs J M Harris
Type: Co-educational 2–19
No of pupils: B26 G52
Special Needs: PMLD **SLD** W

GREENHALL NURSERY SPECIAL SCHOOL

15 Lichfield Road, Stafford ST17 4JX
Tel: (01785) 246159
Head: Mrs S I Barlow
Type: Co-educational Day 2–6
No of pupils: 36
Special Needs: CP EPI HI PH PMLD
SLD VIS

HORTON LODGE SPECIAL SCHOOL

Rudyard, Leek, Staffordshire
ST13 8RB
Tel: (01538) 306214
Head: Ms C Coles
Type: Co-educational Day and
Boarding 2–11
No of pupils: 61 *No of Boarders:* W16
Special Needs: CP **PH** SP&LD VIS W

LOXLEY HALL SPECIAL SCHOOL

Stafford Road, Loxley, Uttoxeter,
Staffordshire ST14 8RS
Tel: (01889) 256390
Head: Mr W M Pearce
Type: Boys Boarding 10–16
No of pupils: 60 *No of Boarders:* W40
Special Needs: **EBD**

MARSHLANDS SPECIAL SCHOOL

Lansdowne Way, Wildwood,
Stafford, Staffordshire ST17 4RD
Tel: (01785) 664475
Head: Mr J P Kirkby
Type: Co-educational Day 2–19
No of pupils: 49
Special Needs: PMLD SLD

MEADOWS SPECIAL SCHOOL

Tunstall Road, Biddulph, Stoke on
Trent, Staffordshire ST8 7AB
Tel: (01782) 297920
Head: Mr C Fielding
Type: Co-educational Day
No of pupils: 120
Special Needs: ASP DOW **MLD** TOU

MERRYFIELDS SPECIAL SCHOOL
Hoon Avenue, Newcastle under Lyme, Staffordshire ST5 9NY
Tel: (01782) 296076
Head: Mrs A E Bird
Type: Co-educational Day
No of pupils: 84
Special Needs: PMLD SLD W

PARK SPECIAL SCHOOL
Solway Close, Wiggington Park, Tamworth, Staffordshire B79 8EB
Tel: (01827) 475690
Head: Mr F Bartlett
Type: Co-educational Day 4–16
No of pupils: 130
Special Needs: MLD

QUEEN'S CROFT COMMUNITY SCHOOL
Birmingham Road, Lichfield, Staffordshire WS13 6PJ
Tel: (01543) 510669
Head: Mrs A Hardman
Type: Co-educational Day 4–16
No of pupils: 150
Special Needs: MLD W

QUINCE TREE SPECIAL SCHOOL
Quince, Amington Heath, Tamworth, Staffordshire B77 4EN
Tel: (01827) 475740
Head: Mrs V A Vernon
Type: Co-educational Day 2–19
No of pupils: 84
Special Needs: PMLD SLD W

ROCKLANDS SPECIAL SCHOOL
Wissage Road, Lichfield, Staffordshire WS13 6SW
Tel: (01543) 510760
Head: Mr A Dooley
Type: Co-educational Day 2–19
No of pupils: 84
Special Needs: ASP AUT PMLD SLD

SAXON HILL SPECIAL SCHOOL
Kings Hill Road, Lichfield, Staffordshire WS14 9DE
Tel: (01543) 263231
Head: Mr D J Butcher
Type: Co-educational Day and Boarding 2–18
No of pupils: 112
Special Needs: PH W

SPRINGFIELD SPECIAL SCHOOL
Springfield Road, Leek, Staffordshire ST13 6LQ
Tel: (01538) 383558
Head: Ms I Corden
Type: Co-educational Day 2–19
No of pupils: 33
Special Needs: PMLD SLD W

WALTON HALL SPECIAL SCHOOL
Stafford Road, Eccleshall, Stafford ST21 6JR
Tel: (01785) 850420
Head: Mr R B Goldthorpe
No of pupils: 130 *No of Boarders:* W40
Special Needs: MLD W

WIGHTWICK HALL SPECIAL SCHOOL
Tinacre Hill, Wightwick, Wolverhampton, West Midlands WV6 8DA
Tel: (01902) 761889
Head: Mr P H Archer
Type: Co-educational Day and Boarding 2–16
No of pupils: 90 *No of Boarders:* F10
Special Needs: AUT MLD SP&LD W

WILLIAM BAXTER SPECIAL SCHOOL
Stanley Road, Hednesford, Cannock, Staffordshire WS12 4JS
Tel: (01543) 423714
Head: Mrs C M Allsop
Type: Co-educational Day 5–16
No of pupils: 130
Special Needs: MLD

Stoke-on-Trent Education Authority

Swann House
Boothen Road
Stoke-on-Trent ST4 4SY
Tel: (01782) 236100

ABBEY HILL SPECIAL SCHOOL
Greasley Road, Bucknall, Stoke on Trent, Staffordshire ST2 8LG
Tel: (01782) 534727
Head: Mrs M Coutouvidis
Type: Co-educational Day 2–19
No of pupils: B165 G57
Special Needs: AUT MLD SLD

AYNSLEY SPECIAL SCHOOL
Aynsley's Drive, Blythe Bridge, Staffordshire ST11 9HJ
Tel: (01782) 392071
Head: Mrs S Addis
Type: Co-educational Day
No of pupils: 120
Special Needs: MLD

HEATHFIELD SPECIAL SCHOOL
Chell Heath Road, Chell Heath, Stoke on Trent, Staffordshire ST6 6PD
Tel: (01782) 838938
Head: Mrs J Colesby
Type: Co-educational Day 2–19
No of pupils: 56
Special Needs: PMLD SLD

KEMBALL SPECIAL SCHOOL
Duke Street, Fenton, Stoke on Trent, Staffordshire ST4 3NR
Tel: (01782) 234879
Head: Mrs E Spooner
Type: Co-educational Day 2–19
No of pupils: 77
Special Needs: PMLD SLD

MIDDLEHURST SPECIAL SCHOOL
Turnhurst Road, Chell, Stoke on Trent, Staffordshire ST6 6NQ
Tel: (01782) 234612
Head: Mrs M Dutton
Type: Co-educational Day 5–16
No of pupils: B65 G35
Special Needs: EBD MLD SP&LD

MOUNT SPECIAL SCHOOL
The Mount, Penkhull, Stoke on Trent, Staffordshire ST4 7JU
Tel: (01782) 44313
Head: Mr B J Richards
Type: Co-educational Day 2–16
Special Needs: HI

STOCKTON-ON-TEES

Stockton-on-Tees Borough Council

Municipal Buildings
PO Box 228
Church Road
Stockton-on-Tees TS18 1XE
Tel: (01642) 393939

ABBEY HILL SCHOOL, TECHNOLOGY COLLEGE
Ketton Road, Hardwick, Stockton-on-Tees TS19 8BU
Tel: (01642) 677113
Head: Mr C M Vening
Type: Co-educational Day 11–19
No of pupils: 210
Special Needs: **ADHD AUT EBD MLD PMLD SLD** W

SUFFOLK

Suffolk Education Authority

St. Andrew House
County Hall
Ipswich
Suffolk IP4 1LJ
Tel: (01473) 583000

THE ASHLEY SCHOOL
Ashley Downs, Lowestoft, Suffolk
NR32 4EU
Tel: (01502) 574847
Head: Mr D Field
Type: Co-educational Day and Boarding 7–16
No of pupils: 115 *No of Boarders:* W29
Special Needs: **MLD**

BEACON HILL SCHOOL
Stone Lodge Lane West, Ipswich, Suffolk IP2 9HW
Tel: (01473) 601175
Head: Mr D Stewart
Type: Co-educational Day 5–16
No of pupils: B87 G68
Special Needs: **MLD** W

BELSTEAD SCHOOL
Sprites Lane, Belstead, Ipswich, Suffolk IP8 3ND
Tel: (01473) 556200
Head: Ms D Margerison
Type: Co-educational Day 11–19
No of pupils: B50 G26
Special Needs: **PMLD SLD** W

HAMPDEN HOUSE
Cats Lane, Great Cornard, Sudbury, Suffolk CO10 6SF
Tel: (01223) 843872
Head: Mr M W Charlton
Type: Boys Boarding and Day
No of pupils: 30 *No of Boarders:* F22
Special Needs: **ADD ADHD ASP EBD MLD SPLD TOU**

HEATHSIDE SCHOOL
Heath Road, Ipswich, Suffolk IP4 5SN
Tel: (01473) 725508
Head: Mr O Doran
Type: Co-educational Day
No of pupils: B35 G23
Special Needs: **PMLD SLD** W

HILLSIDE SCHOOL
Hitchcock Place, Sudbury, Suffolk CO10 1NN
Tel: (01787) 372808
Head: Miss J Freeman
Type: Co-educational Day 3–19
No of pupils: 52
Special Needs: **PMLD SLD** W

RIVERWALK SCHOOL
South Close, Bury St Edmunds, Suffolk IP33 3JZ
Tel: (01284) 764280
Head: Mr B Ellis
Type: Co-educational Day
No of pupils: 88
Special Needs: **PMLD SLD** W

WARREN SCHOOL
Clarkes Lane, Oulton Broad, Lowestoft, Suffolk NR33 8HT
Tel: (01502) 561893
Head: Mr C Moore
Type: Co-educational 3–19
No of pupils: B65 G42
Special Needs: **PMLD SLD** W

SURREY

Surrey Education Authority

Education Department
County Hall
Kingston upon Thames
Surrey KT1 2DJ
Tel: (020) 8541 9501

THE ABBEY SCHOOL
Menin Way, Farnham, Surrey GU9 8DY
Tel: (01252) 725059
Head: Ms A Scott
Type: Co-educational Day 7–16
No of pupils: 100
Special Needs: **MLD**

BROOKLANDS SCHOOL
27 Wray Park Road, Reigate, Surrey RH2 0DF
Tel: (01737) 249941
Head: Mrs S Wakenell
Type: Co-educational Day 2–10
No of pupils: 80
Special Needs: **PMLD SLD** W

CARWARDEN HOUSE COMMUNITY SCHOOL

118 Upper Chobham Road, Camberley, Surrey GU15 1EJ
Tel: (01276) 709080
Head: Mr J G Cope
Type: Co-educational Day 7–19
No of pupils: 140
Special Needs: **MLD**

CLIFTON HILL SCHOOL

Chaldon Road, Caterham, Surrey CR3 5PH
Tel: (01883) 347740
Head: Mr M Unsworth
Type: Co-educational Day 10–19
No of pupils: B46 G38
Special Needs: **SLD** W

FREEMANTLES SCHOOL

Pycroft Road, Chertsey, Surrey KT16 9ER
Tel: (01932) 563460
Head: Mrs R Buchan
Type: Co-educational Day 4–12
No of pupils: 66
Special Needs: **AUT** SP&LD W

GOSDEN HOUSE SCHOOL

Bramley, Guildford, Surrey GU5 0AH
Tel: (01483) 892008
Head: Mr J David
Type: Co-educational Boarding Boys 5–11 Girls 5–16
No of pupils: B30 G90
No of Boarders: W55
Special Needs: MLD SP&LD

LIMPSFIELD GRANGE SCHOOL

89 Blue House Lane, Limpsfield, Oxted, Surrey RH8 0RZ
Tel: (01883) 713928
Head: Mrs J A Humphreys
Type: Girls Boarding and Day 11–16
No of pupils: 56 *No of Boarders:* W36
Special Needs: DEL DYP DYS SP&LD SPLD

LINDEN BRIDGE SCHOOL

Grafton Road, Worcester Park, Surrey KT4 7JW
Tel: (020) 8330 3009
Head: Mrs R Smith
Type: Co-educational Boarding and Day 4–19
No of pupils: 107 *No of Boarders:* F33
Special Needs: AUT

MANOR MEAD SCHOOL

Laleham Road, Shepperton, Surrey TW17 8EL
Tel: (01932) 241834
Head: Mrs F Neal
Type: Co-educational Day
No of pupils: 60
Special Needs: CP EPI PMLD **SLD** W

THE PARK SCHOOL

Onslow Crescent, Woking, Surrey GU22 7AT
Tel: (01483) 772057
Head: Mrs J A Lonsdale
Type: Co-educational Day 8–16
No of pupils: 93
Special Needs: **MLD** SP&LD W

PHILIP SOUTHCOTE SCHOOL

Addlestonemoor, Addlestone, Surrey KT15 2QH
Tel: (01932) 562326
Head: Mr G L Rogers
Type: Co-educational Day 8–16
No of pupils: 115
Special Needs: HI **MLD**

POND MEADOW SCHOOL

Pond Meadow, Park Barn Estate, Guildford, Surrey GU2 6LG
Tel: (01483) 532239
Head: Miss A E Brighty
Type: Co-educational Day 2–19
Special Needs: PMLD SLD W

PORTESBERY SCHOOL

Portesbery Road, Camberley, Surrey GU15 3SZ
Tel: (01276) 63078
Head: Mrs J Nuthall
Type: Co-educational Day 2–19
No of pupils: B35 G30
Special Needs: **SLD**

THE RIDGEWAY SCHOOL

14 Frensham Road, Farnham, Surrey GU9 8HB
Tel: (01252) 724562
Head: Mrs M Hattey
Type: Co-educational Day 2–19
No of pupils: B50 G27
Special Needs: PMLD SLD

ST NICHOLAS SCHOOL

Taynton Drive, Merstham, Redhill, Surrey RH1 3PU
Tel: (01737) 215488
Head: Mr R Edey
Type: Co-educational Boarding and Day 11–19
No of pupils: 70 *No of Boarders:* W60
Special Needs: EBD MLD

SIDLOW BRIDGE CENTRE

Ironsbottom Lane, Reigate, Surrey RH2 8PP
Tel: (01737) 249079
Head: Mr D Davies
Type: Co-educational Day 14–16
No of pupils: 30
Special Needs: **EBD**

STARHURST SCHOOL

Chart Lane South, Dorking, Surrey RH5 4DB
Tel: (01306) 883763
Head: Mr H J Kiernan
Type: Boys Boarding and Day 11–16
No of pupils: 66 *No of Boarders:* W46
Special Needs: EBD

SUNNYDOWN SCHOOL†

Portley House, 152 Whyteleafe Road, Caterham, Surrey CR3 5ED
Tel: (01883) 342281/346502
Head: Mr T M Armstrong
Type: Boys Boarding and Day 11–16
No of pupils: 74 *No of Boarders:* W44
Special Needs: **DYS** SPLD

THORNCHACE SPECIAL SCHOOL

Grove Road, Merrow, Guildford, Surrey GU1 2HL
Tel: (01483) 573859
Head: Mr C Lodge
Type: Girls Boarding and Day 11–16
No of pupils: 24
Special Needs: **EBD**

WALTON LEIGH SCHOOL

Queens Road, Walton-on-Thames, Surrey KT12 5AB
Tel: (01932) 223243
Head: Mrs L Curtis
Type: Co-educational 12–19
No of pupils: 60
Special Needs: AUT **PMLD SLD** W

WEST HILL SCHOOL

Kingston Road, Leatherhead, Surrey KT22 7PW
Tel: (01372) 814714
Head: Ms M Goldie
Type: Co-educational Day 7–16
No of pupils: 140
Special Needs: **MLD**

WEY HOUSE SCHOOL

Bramley, Guildford, Surrey GU5 0BJ
Tel: (01483) 898130
Head: Mr M Keane
Type: Boys Day and Boarding 7–11
No of pupils: 48 *No of Boarders:* W21
Special Needs: **EBD**

WISHMORE CROSS SCHOOL
Alpha Road, Chobham, Surrey
GU24 8NE
Tel: (01276) 857555
Head: Mr J A Orr
Type: Boys Boarding 10–16
No of pupils: 60
Special Needs: **EBD**

WOODFIELD SCHOOL
Sunstone Grove, Merstham, Redhill,
Surrey RH1 3PR
Tel: (01737) 642623
Head: Miss S M Plant
Type: Co-educational Day 8–16
No of pupils: 140
Special Needs: **MLD** W

WOODLANDS SCHOOL
Fortyfoot Road, Leatherhead, Surrey
KT22 8RY
Tel: (01372) 377922
Head: Mrs H D J Taylor
Type: Co-educational Day 2–19
No of pupils: 80
Special Needs: **AUT DOW PMLD
SLD** W

EAST SUSSEX

Brighton & Hove Council

Education Services
PO Box 2503
Kings House
Grand Avenue
Hove BN3 2SU
Tel: (01273) 290000

THE ALTERNATIVE CENTRE FOR EDUCATION
St George's House, Dyke Road,
Brighton, East Sussex BN1 3JA
Tel: (01273) 327389
Type: Co-educational Day
Special Needs: **EBD**

CASTLEDEAN SCHOOL
Lynchet Close, Brighton, East Sussex
BN1 7PF
Tel: (01273) 702121
Head: Mrs V A Ellis
Type: Co-educational Day 4–11
No of pupils: 64
Special Needs: **MLD**

DOWNS PARK SCHOOL
Foredown Road, Portslade, Brighton,
East Sussex BN41 2FU
Tel: (01273) 417448
Head: Mr A S Jedras
Type: Co-educational Day 5–16
No of pupils: 121
Special Needs: **AUT MLD**

DOWNS VIEW SCHOOL
Warren Road, Brighton, East Sussex
BN2 6BB
Tel: (01273) 601680
Head: Mrs J Reed
Type: Co-educational Day 2–19
No of pupils: B76 G31
Special Needs: **AUT MLD PMLD
SLD** W

HILLSIDE SCHOOL
Foredown Road, Portslade, Brighton,
East Sussex BN41 2FU
Tel: (01273) 416979
Head: Mr R Wall
Type: Co-educational Day 3–19
No of pupils: B46 G26
Special Needs: **PMLD SLD** W

PATCHAM HOUSE SCHOOL
7 Old London Road, Patcham,
Brighton, East Sussex BN1 8XR
Tel: (01273) 551028
Head: Mr R L Humphrey
Type: Co-educational Day 3–16
No of pupils: 70
Special Needs: **ASP CP** DEL **DYP** EPI
EPI **PH SP&LD** SPLD W

UPLANDS SCHOOL
Lynchet Road, Brighton, East Sussex
BN1 7FP
Tel: (01273) 558622/3
Head: Mr P Atkins
Type: Co-educational Day
No of pupils: 110
Special Needs: **MLD**

East Sussex Education Authority

Education Department
PO Box 4
County Hall
St Annes Crescent
Lewes
East Sussex BN7 1SG
Tel: (01273) 481000

CUCKMERE HOUSE
Eastbourne Road, Seaford, East
Sussex BN25 4BA
Tel: (01323) 893319
Head: Mr F Stanford
Type: Boys Boarding and Day 9–16
No of pupils: 50 *No of Boarders:* W8
Special Needs: **EBD**

THE DOWNS SCHOOL
Beechy Avenue, Eastbourne, East
Sussex BN20 8NU
Tel: (01323) 730302
Head: Mrs E D Gidlow
Type: Co-educational Day 4–11
No of pupils: 88
Special Needs: **ADHD ASP AUT CP
DOW DYP EBD EPI MLD SP&LD**

GLYNE GAP SCHOOL
School Place, Hastings Road, Bexhill-
on-Sea, East Sussex TN40 2PU
Tel: (01424) 217720
Head: Mr J A Hassell
Type: Co-educational Day 2–19
No of pupils: 97
Special Needs: **AUT PMLD SLD**

GROVE PARK SCHOOL
Church Road, Crowborough, East
Sussex TN6 1BN
Tel: (01892) 663018
Head: Ms C A Moody
Type: Co-educational Day 2–19
No of pupils: 56
Special Needs: **AUT PMLD SLD** W

HAZEL COURT SCHOOL
Shinewater Lane, Milfoil Drive,
Eastbourne, East Sussex BN23 8AT
Tel: (01323) 761061
Head: Mr Peter Gordon
Type: Co-educational Day 2–19
No of pupils: 106
Special Needs: **PMLD SLD** W

INGLESEA SCHOOL
2 Tile Barn Road, St Leonards-on-
Sea, East Sussex TN38 9QU
Tel: (01424) 853232
Head: Mr L E Bush
Type: Boys Day 6–16
No of pupils: 42
Special Needs: **EBD**

THE LINDFIELD SCHOOL
Lindfield Road, Eastbourne, East
Sussex BN22 0BQ
Tel: (01323) 502988
Head: Ms Jane Oatey
Type: Co-educational Day 10–16
No of pupils: 88
Special Needs: ADD **ADHD ASP** AUT
DEL DOW DYC DYS EPI HI **MLD** PH
SP&LD SPLD VIS

ST ANNE'S SCHOOL
Rotten Row, Lewes, East Sussex
BN7 1LJ
Tel: (01273) 473018
Head: Ms J Arch
Type: Co-educational Day 4–16
No of pupils: B67 G30
Special Needs: ADHD **MLD** SP&LD

ST MARY'S SCHOOL
Horam, Heathfield, East Sussex
TN21 0BT
Tel: (01435) 812278
Head: Mr D F Bashford
Type: Co-educational Boarding and
Day 11–19
No of pupils: 61
Special Needs: EBD MLD

SAXON MOUNT SCHOOL
Edinburgh Road, St Leonards-on-
Sea, East Sussex TN38 8DA
Tel: (01424) 426303
Head: Mrs S Furey
Type: Co-educational Day 11–16
No of pupils: 120
Special Needs: AUT **MLD** SP&LD

TORFIELD SCHOOL
Croft Road, Hastings, East Sussex
TN34 3JT
Tel: (01424) 428228
Head: Mr C D Owen
Type: Co-educational Day 3–11
No of pupils: 120
Special Needs: AUT EBD MLD
SP&LD

WEST SUSSEX

**West Sussex Education
Authority**

County Hall
West Street
Chichester
West Sussex PO19 1RF
Tel: (01243) 777100

**ABBOTSFORD SPECIAL
SCHOOL**
Cuckfield Road, Burgess Hill, West
Sussex RH15 8RE
Tel: (01444) 235848
Head: Mr P Moxton
Type: Boys Boarding and Day 8–16
No of pupils: 64 *No of Boarders:* W34
Special Needs: ADD ADHD ASP AUT
DYS EBD

CORNFIELD
Cornfield Close, Littlehampton,
West Sussex BN17 6HY
Tel: (01903) 731277
Head: Mrs S Roberts
Type: Co-educational 10–16
No of pupils: 50
Special Needs: EBD

**COURT MEADOW SPECIAL
SCHOOL**
Hanlye Lane, Cuckfield, Haywards
Heath, West Sussex RH17 5HN
Tel: (01444) 454535
Head: Mrs J Hedges
Type: Co-educational Day 2–19
No of pupils: B42 G43
Special Needs: PMLD **SLD** W

DEERSWOOD SCHOOL
Ifield Green, Crawley, West Sussex
RH11 0GH
Tel: (01293) 520351
Head: Mr M R Turney
Type: Co-educational Day 5–16
No of pupils: 163
Special Needs: AUT MLD

**FORDWATER SPECIAL
SCHOOL**
Summersdale Road, Chichester,
West Sussex PO19 4PL
Tel: (01243) 782475
Head: Mr R Rendall
Type: Co-educational Day 2–19
No of pupils: B66 G41
Special Needs: DOW HI PMLD SLD
VIS W

**HERONS DALE SPECIAL
SCHOOL**
Hawkins Crescent, Shoreham-by-
Sea, West Sussex BN43 6TN
Tel: (01273) 596904
Head: Mrs S A Pritchard
No of pupils: 116
Special Needs: ASP **MLD**

HIGHDOWN SCHOOL
Durrington Lane, Worthing, West
Sussex BN13 2QQ
Tel: (01903) 249611
Head: Mr G Elliker
Type: Co-educational Day 3–19
No of pupils: 106
Special Needs: PMLD SLD

**LITTLEGREEN SPECIAL
SCHOOL**
Compton, Chichester, West Sussex
PO18 9NW
Tel: (023) 9263 1259
Head: Mr A R Bicknell
Type: Boys Boarding and Day 7–14
No of pupils: 42 *No of Boarders:* W12
Special Needs: ADD ADHD ASP EBD
MLD TOU

**NEWICK HOUSE SPECIAL
SCHOOL**
Birchwood Grove Road, Burgess Hill,
West Sussex RH15 0DP
Tel: (01444) 233550
Head: Mr A M Roberts
Type: Co-educational 5–16
No of pupils: 135
Special Needs: ADD ADHD DEL
DOW DYP DYS EBD EPI HI **MLD** PH
SLD SP&LD SPLD W

PALATINE SCHOOL
Palatine Road, Worthing, West
Sussex BN12 6JP
Tel: (01903) 242835
Head: Mr J D Clough
Type: Co-educational Day
No of pupils: B102 G50
Special Needs: **MLD** W

QUEEN ELIZABETH II SILVER JUBILEE SCHOOL
Comptons Lane, Horsham, West Sussex RH13 5NW
Tel: (01403) 266215
Head: Mrs L K Dyer
Type: Co-educational Day 2–19
No of pupils: 42
Special Needs: PMLD SLD W

ST ANTHONY'S SPECIAL SCHOOL
Woodlands Lane, off St Paul's Road, Chichester, West Sussex PO19 3PA
Tel: (01243) 785965
Head: Mr T Salt
Type: Co-educational Day 5–16
No of pupils: 154
Special Needs: **MLD**

TYNE AND WEAR

Gateshead Education Authority

Civic Centre
Regent Street
Gateshead
Tyne and Wear NE8 1HH
Tel: (0191) 477 1011

THE CEDARS SPECIAL SCHOOL
Ivy Lane, Low Fell, Gateshead, Tyne and Wear NE9 6QD
Tel: (0191) 487 7591/482 2993
Head: Mr E D Bartley
Type: Co-educational Day 2–16
No of pupils: 90
Special Needs: **PH SP&LD** W

DRYDEN SCHOOL
Shotley Gardens, Gateshead, Tyne and Wear NE9 5UR
Tel: (0191) 420 3811
Head: Mr G J Foster
Type: Co-educational Day
No of pupils: B34 G16
Special Needs: AUT CP DOW EPI HI PH **SLD** VIS W

FURROWFIELD SCHOOL
Senior Site, Whitehills Drive, Felling, Gateshead, Tyne and Wear NE10 9RZ
Tel: (0191) 469 9499
Head: Mr S Roberts
Type: Co-educational Day 7–11 (boys 11–16)
No of pupils: 79 *No of Boarders:* W14
Special Needs: EBD W

Newcastle upon Tyne Education Authority

Civic Centre
Barras Bridge
Newcastle upon Tyne
Tyne and Wear NE1 8PU
Tel: (0191) 232 8520

BRUNSWICK BEECH SPECIAL SCHOOL
Brunswick, Newcastle-Upon-Tyne, Tyne and Wear NE13 7DT
Tel: (0191) 236 2572
Head: Mrs E Turnbull
Type: Co-educational 3–11
No of pupils: B29 G18
Special Needs: **MLD PMLD SLD** W

HADRIAN SCHOOL
Bertram Crescent, Newcastle-Upon-Tyne, Tyne and Wear NE15 6PY
Tel: (0191) 273 4440
Head: Mrs E Turnbull
Type: Co-educational Day 2–11
No of pupils: B76 G47
Special Needs: PMLD SLD W

KENTON LODGE SPECIAL SCHOOL
Kenton Road, Newcastle-Upon-Tyne, Tyne and Wear NE3 4PD
Tel: (0191) 285 5392
Head: Mr D Tait
Type: Boys Boarding and Day 7–13
Special Needs: **EBD**

PARKWAY SCHOOL
Hillhead Parkway, Newcastle-Upon-Tyne, Tyne and Wear NE5 1DP
Tel: (0191) 267 4447
Head: Mrs M O Bell
Type: Co-educational Day 11–19
No of pupils: 140
Special Needs: EBD MLD PMLD SLD SP&LD

PENDOWER HALL SCHOOL
Bertram Crescent, Newcastle-Upon-Tyne, Tyne and Wear NE15 6PY
Tel: (0191) 273 4440
Head: Mr N O Stromsoy
Type: Co-educational Boarding and Day 2–19
No of pupils: 130 *No of Boarders:* W12
Special Needs: CP DEL EPI **PH** W

ST PETER'S SPECIAL SCHOOL
Freeman Road, Newcastle-Upon-Tyne, Tyne and Wear NE3 1SZ
Tel: (0191) 284 3533
Head: Mrs D Slater
Type: Co-educational Day 3–11
No of pupils: 70
Special Needs: AUT EBD MLD PMLD SLD

SIR CHARLES PARSONS SCHOOL
Westbourne Avenue, Newcastle-Upon-Tyne, Tyne and Wear NE6 4ED
Tel: (0191) 263 0261
Head: Mr J C Preston
Type: Co-educational
No of pupils: 140
Special Needs: EBD MLD **PMLD SLD** SP&LD W

North Tyneside Education Authority

Stephenson House
Stephenson Street
North Shields
Tyne and Wear NE30 1QA
Tel: (0191) 200 5151

ASHLEIGH SCHOOL
Charlotte Street, North Shields, Tyne and Wear NE30 1BP
Tel: (0191) 200 6339
Head: Mrs S Gibbon
Type: Co-educational Day 2–19
No of pupils: 78
Special Needs: AUT PMLD SLD W

GLEBE SCHOOL
Woodburn Drive, Whitley Bay,
Northumberland NE26 3HW
Tel: (0191) 251 2230
Head: Mrs L J Turner
Type: Co-educational Day 4–11
No of pupils: 100
Special Needs: AUT EBD **MLD**
SP&LD

PARKSIDE SCHOOL
Mullen Road, High Farm, Wallsend,
Tyne and Wear NE28 9HA
Tel: (0191) 262 3846
Head: Mrs H Jones
Type: Co-educational Day
Special Needs: AUT **SLD**

SOUTHLANDS SCHOOL
Beach Road, Tynemouth, North
Shields, Tyne and Wear NE30 2QR
Tel: (0191) 200 6348
Head: Mr D J Erskine
Type: Co-educational 11–17
No of pupils: 134
Special Needs: EBD **MLD**

WOODLAWN SCHOOL
Langley Avenue, Monkseaton,
Whitley Bay, Tyne and Wear
NE25 9DF
Tel: (0191) 200 8729
Head: Mr B Hickman
Type: Co-educational Day 2–16
No of pupils: B69 G25
Special Needs: CP DEL DYP HI PH
SPLD W

South Tyneside Education Authority

Town Hall and Civic Offices
South Shields
Tyne and Wear NE33 2RL
Tel: (0191) 427 1717

BAMBURGH SCHOOL
Cautley Road, South Shields, Tyne
and Wear NE34 7TD
Tel: (0191) 454 0671
Head: Mrs J M Fawcett
Type: Co-educational Day 2–17
No of pupils: 120
Special Needs: ASP CP DEL DYP EPI
HI PH W

EPINAY SCHOOL
Clervaux Terrace, Jarrow, Tyne and
Wear NE32 5UP
Tel: (0191) 489 8949
Head: Mrs H Harrison
Type: Co-educational Day
No of pupils: B64 G40
Special Needs: **MLD**

GREENFIELDS SCHOOL
Victoria Road East, Hebburn, Tyne
and Wear NE31 1YQ
Tel: (0191) 489 7480
Head: Miss M C Conway
Type: Co-educational Day 2–19
No of pupils: 47
Special Needs: CP DOW EPI HI PH
PMLD SLD VIS W

MARGARET SUTTON SCHOOL
Ashley Road, South Shields, Tyne
and Wear NE34 0PF
Tel: (0191) 455 3309
Head: Miss A Godfrey
Type: Co-educational Day
No of pupils: B59 G34
Special Needs: **MLD**

OAKLEIGH GARDENS SCHOOL
Oakleigh Gardens, Cleadon, Nr.
Sunderland, Tyne and Wear SR6 7PT
Tel: (0191) 536 2590
Head: Mrs M J Lockney
Type: Co-educational Day 2–19
No of pupils: B36 G19
Special Needs: **PMLD SLD** W

Sunderland Education Authority

Box 101
Civic Centre
Sunderland
Tyne and Wear SR2 7DN
Tel: (0191) 553 1000

BARBARA PRIESTMAN SCHOOL
Meadowside, Sunderland, Tyne and
Wear SR2 7QN
Tel: (0191) 553 6000
Head: Mr W F Hitchcock
Type: Co-educational Day
No of pupils: 140
Special Needs: EPI MLD PH SP&LD
SPLD W

DAVENPORT SCHOOL
Durham Road, Houghton-le-Spring,
Tyne and Wear DH5 8NF
Tel: (0191) 553 6572
Head: Mrs K Elliot
Type: Co-educational Day 3–13
No of pupils: B55 G26
Special Needs: AUT MLD PMLD SLD

FELSTEAD SCHOOL
Fordfield Road (North Side),
Sunderland, Tyne and Wear SR4 0DA
Tel: (0191) 567 4258
Head: Mr I Reed
Type: Co-educational Day 13–25
No of pupils: B182 G36
Special Needs: EBD MLD

MAPLEWOOD SCHOOL
Redcar Road, Sunderland, Tyne and
Wear SR5 5PA
Tel: (0191) 553 5587
Head: Mrs J Wilson
Type: Co-educational 5–13
No of pupils: B88 G2
Special Needs: ADD ADHD EBD W

PORTLAND SCHOOL
Portland Road, Sunderland, Tyne
and Wear SR3 1SS
Tel: (0191) 553 6050
Head: Mrs J Chart
Type: Co-educational Day 13–19
No of pupils: B67 G40
Special Needs: **PMLD SLD W**

SPRINGWELL DENE SCHOOL
Swindon Road, Sunderland, Tyne
and Wear SR3 4EE
Tel: (0191) 553 6067
Head: Mrs M D Mitchell
Type: Co-educational Day
No of pupils: B62 G3
Special Needs: **EBD**

SUNNINGDALE SCHOOL
Shaftoe Road, Sunderland, Tyne and
Wear SR3 4HA
Tel: (0191) 553 5880
Head: Mr J McKnight
Type: Co-educational Day 3–13
No of pupils: 175
Special Needs: MLD PMLD SLD W

WELLBANK SCHOOL
Wellbank Road, Washington, Tyne
and Wear NE37 1NL
Tel: (0191) 416 2514
Head: Mrs J Macleod
Type: Co-educational Day 3–13
No of pupils: 60
Special Needs: MLD PMLD SLD W

WARWICKSHIRE

Warwickshire Education Authority

22 Northgate Street
Warwick
Warwickshire CV34 4SP
Tel: (01926) 410410

BLYTHE SCHOOL

Packington Lane, Coleshill,
Birmingham, West Midlands B46 3JE
Tel: (01675) 463590
Head: Mrs G Simpson
Type: Co-educational Day 2–19
No of pupils: B61 G26
Special Needs: AUT **EBD** PMLD **SLD**

BROOKE SCHOOL

Merttens Drive, Rugby,
Warwickshire CV22 7AE
Tel: (01788) 576145
Head: Mrs S Cowen
Type: Co-educational Day 2–19
No of pupils: B93 G41
Special Needs: MLD PMLD SLD W

THE GRIFF SCHOOL

Coventry Road, Nuneaton,
Warwickshire CV10 7AX
Tel: (024) 7638 3315
Head: Mrs R M Scott
Type: Co-educational Day 5–16
No of pupils: 139
Special Needs: **MLD**

LAMBERT SCHOOL

Blue Cap Road, Stratford upon Avon,
Warwickshire CV37 6TQ
Tel: (01789) 266845
Head: Mrs S Franklin
Type: Co-educational Day 2–19
No of pupils: B54 G30
Special Needs: AUT DOW EPI PH
PMLD SLD W

MARIE CORELLI SCHOOL & SUPPORT SERVICE

Drayton Avenue, Stratford upon
Avon, Warwickshire CV37 9PT
Tel: (01789) 205992
Head: Mrs H Cobb
Type: Co-educational Day 5–16
No of pupils: 71
Special Needs: **MLD**

RIDGEWAY SCHOOL

Montague Road, Warwick,
Warwickshire CV34 5LW
Tel: (01926) 491987
Head: Mrs P A Flynn
Type: Co-educational Day 2–19
No of pupils: B62 G30
Special Needs: PMLD SLD W

RIVER HOUSE SCHOOL

Stratford Road, Henley-in-Arden,
Solihull, West Midlands B95 6AD
Tel: (01564) 792514
Head: Mr M J Turner
Type: Boys Day 11–16
No of pupils: 35
Special Needs: **EBD**

THE ROUND OAK SCHOOL

Pound Lane, Lillington, Leamington
Spa, Warwickshire CV32 7RT
Tel: (01926) 335566
Head: Mrs S Read
Type: Co-educational Day 5–16
No of pupils: B48 G32
Special Needs: **MLD**

SKILTS (RESIDENTIAL) SCHOOL

Gorcott Hill, Redditch, West
Midlands B98 9ET
Tel: (0152) 785 3851
Head: Miss M K Probert
Type: Boys Boarding and Day 4–12
No of pupils: 50 No of Boarders: W46
Special Needs: ADD ADHD ASP DYS
EBD MLD SPLD

SPARROWDALE SCHOOL

Spon Lane, Grendon, Atherstone,
Warwickshire CV9 2PD
Tel: (01827) 713436
Head: Mr B R Fitter
Type: Co-educational
No of pupils: 116
Special Needs: ASP AUT CP DOW
EBD EPI MLD

WEST MIDLANDS

Birmingham Education Authority

Margaret Street
Birmingham
West Midlands B3 3BU
Tel: (0121) 303 2590

BASKERVILLE SCHOOL

Fellows Lane, Birmingham, West
Midlands B17 9TS
Tel: (0121) 427 3191
Head: Mr G J Thornett
Type: Co-educational Boarding 11–19
No of pupils: B30 G6
No of Boarders: W20
Special Needs: **ASP AUT**

BEAUFORT SCHOOL

16 Coleshill Road, Birmingham,
West Midlands B36 8AA
Tel: (0121) 783 3886
Head: Ms S B Allen
Type: Co-educational 3–11
No of pupils: B20 G20
Special Needs: AUT PMLD **SLD** W

BRAIDWOOD SCHOOL

Perry Common Road, Birmingham,
West Midlands B23 7AT
Tel: (0121) 373 5558
Head: Mrs F Ison-Jacques
Type: Co-educational Day 11–19
No of pupils: B31 G35
Special Needs: **HI**

BRIDGE SCHOOL

290 Reservoir Road, Birmingham,
West Midlands B23 6DE
Tel: (0121) 373 8265
Head: Mr S White
Type: Co-educational 2–11
No of pupils: 37
Special Needs: PMLD SLD

CALTHORPE SCHOOL

Darwin Street, Birmingham, West
Midlands B12 0JJ
Tel: (0121) 773 4637
Head: Mr G Hardy
Type: Co-educational Day
No of pupils: B139 G99
Special Needs: ASP AUT CP DOW
EBD EPI HI PH PMLD SLD W

CHERRY OAK SCHOOL
60 Frederick Road, Birmingham,
West Midlands B29 6PB
Tel: (0121) 472 1263
Head: Mrs L Fowler
Type: Co-educational Day 2–11
No of pupils: B37 G11
Special Needs: PMLD **SLD** W

DAME ELLEN PINSENT SCHOOL
Ardencote Road, Birmingham, West
Midlands B13 0RW
Tel: (0121) 444 2487
Head: Mrs S Rodgers
Type: Co-educational 4–11
No of pupils: B108 G37
Special Needs: **MLD**

FOX HOLLIES SCHOOL AND PERFORMING ARTS COLLEGE
419 Fox Hollies Road, Birmingham,
West Midlands B27 7QA
Tel: (0121) 777 6566
Head: Ms K O'Leary
Type: Co-educational Day 11–19
No of pupils: 67
Special Needs: PMLD **SLD** W

HALLMOOR SCHOOL
Hallmoor Road, Birmingham, West
Midlands B33 9QY
Tel: (0121) 783 3972
Head: Mrs S Charvis
Type: Co-educational Day 4–19
No of pupils: 240
Special Needs: **MLD**

HAMILTON SCHOOL
Hamilton Road, Birmingham, West
Midlands B21 8AH
Tel: (0121) 554 1676
Head: Mr N P Carter
Type: Co-educational Day
No of pupils: B47 G28
Special Needs: ADHD DOW DYP HI
MLD SLD SP&LD

KINGSTANDING SCHOOL
Old Oscott Hill, Birmingham, West
Midlands B44 9SP
Tel: (0121) 360 8222
Head: Ms M C Pipe
Type: Co-educational Day 11–19
No of pupils: 83
Special Needs: AUT **PMLD SLD**
SP&LD W

LANGLEY SCHOOL
Lindridge Road, Sutton Coldfield,
West Midlands B75 7HU
Tel: (0121) 329 2929
Head: Mr A Reid
Type: Co-educational Day 3–11
No of pupils: 120
Special Needs: **MLD**

LONGMOOR SCHOOL
Coppice View Road, Sutton
Coldfield, West Midlands B7 6UE
Tel: (0121) 353 7833
Head: Mrs V Jenkins
Type: Co-educational Day and
Boarding 2–11
No of pupils: 40 *No of Boarders:* F12
W12
Special Needs: AUT PMLD **SLD**

LONGWILL SCHOOL
Bell Hill, Birmingham, West
Midlands B31 1LD
Tel: (0121) 475 3923
Head: Mr P Plant
Type: Co-educational Day 2–11
No of pupils: B37 G21
Special Needs: **HI**

MAYFIELD SCHOOL
Finch Road, Birmingham, West
Midlands B19 1HP
Tel: (0121) 554 3354
Head: Mr P Jenkins
Type: Co-educational Day 2–19
No of pupils: B65 G46
Special Needs: ADHD **AUT** CP DOW
EBD EPI HI **PMLD SLD** W

PINES SCHOOL
Dreghorn Road, Birmingham, West
Midlands B36 8LL
Tel: (0121) 747 6136
Head: Mr S G Tuft
Type: Co-educational Day
No of pupils: 100
Special Needs: AUT DEL **SP&LD** W

PRIESTLEY SMITH SCHOOL
Perry Common Road, Erdington,
Birmingham, West Midlands B23 7AT
Tel: (0121) 373 5493
Head: Mr C G Lewis
Type: Co-educational Day 2–17
No of pupils: B31 G30
Special Needs: DYS MLD **VIS** W

QUEENSBURY SCHOOL
Wood End Road, Birmingham, West
Midlands B24 8BL
Tel: (0121) 373 5731
Head: Mr W Warriner
Type: Day
No of pupils: 240
Special Needs: **MLD**

SPRINGFIELD HOUSE SCHOOL
Kenilworth Road, Knowle, Solihull,
West Midlands B93 0AJ
Tel: (01564) 775696
Head: Mrs P A Jacques
Type: Co-educational
No of pupils: B38 G12
No of Boarders: W40
Special Needs: **EBD**

UFFCULME SCHOOL
Queensbridge Road, Birmingham,
West Midlands B13 8QB
Tel: (0121) 449 1081
Head: Mr R J Williams
Type: Co-educational Day 3–11
No of pupils: 116
Special Needs: ASP AUT SP&LD

UNDERWOOD SCHOOL
Rowden Drive, Birmingham, West
Midlands B23 5UL
Tel: (0121) 373 5742
Head: Mr G Barratt
Type: Co-educational Day 11–16
No of pupils: 57
Special Needs: **EBD**

VICTORIA SCHOOL
Bell Hill, Birmingham, West
Midlands B31 1LD
Tel: (0121) 476 9478
Head: Mr I Glen
Type: Co-educational Day 2–19
No of pupils: B116 G100
Special Needs: CP EPI HI MLD PH
PMLD SLD VIS W

WILSON STUART SCHOOL
Perry Common Road, Birmingham,
West Midlands B23 7AT
Tel: (0121) 373 4475
Head: Mr J C Grantham
Type: Co-educational Day 3–19
No of pupils: 144
Special Needs: **PH** W

Coventry Education Authority

New Council Offices
Earl Street
Coventry
West Midlands CV1 5RS
Tel: (024) 7683 1511

ALICE STEVENS SCHOOL
Ashington Grove, Coventry, West
Midlands CV3 4DE
Tel: (024) 7630 3776
Head: Mr R I McAllister
Type: Co-educational Day 11–18
No of pupils: 200
Special Needs: MLD W

BAGINTON FIELDS
Sedgemoor Road, Coventry, West
Midlands CV3 4EA
Tel: (024) 7630 3854
Head: Mr R J Aird
Type: Co-educational
No of pupils: B60 G35
Special Needs: ADD ADHD ASP AUT
CP DOW DYP EBD EPI MLD PH
PMLD SLD SP&LD VIS W

CORLEY (COVENTRY) SCHOOL
Church Lane, Corley, Warwickshire
CV7 8AZ
Tel: (01676) 540218
Head: Mr R Nason
Type: Co-educational Day and
Boarding
No of pupils: 74 No of Boarders: F25
Special Needs: AUT MLD

DARTMOUTH SPECIAL SCHOOL
Tiverton Road, Coventry, West
Midlands CV2 3DN
Tel: (024) 7644 4141
Head: Mr P Davies
Type: Boys Day 11–16
No of pupils: 65
Special Needs: EBD W

DEEDMORE SPECIAL SCHOOL
Petitor Crescent, Coventry, West
Midlands CV2 1EW
Tel: (024) 7661 2271
Head: Mr G L Wilkinson
Type: Co-educational Day
No of pupils: 80
Special Needs: MLD

HAWKESBURY FIELDS SCHOOL
176/178 Aldermans Green Road,
Coventry, West Midlands CV2 1PL
Tel: (024) 7636 7075
Head: Ms H Bishton
Type: Co-educational Day 2–11
No of pupils: 58
Special Needs: PMLD SLD W

THE MEADOWS
Hawthorn Lane, Coventry, West
Midlands CV4 9PB
Tel: (024) 7646 2355/6
Head: Mr Robinson
Type: Boys Day and Boarding 11–16
No of pupils: 33
Special Needs: EBD

SHERBOURNE FIELDS SCHOOL
Rowington Close, off Kingsbury
Road, Coventry, West Midlands
CV6 1PS
Tel: (024) 7659 1501/2
Head: Mr D Southeard
Type: Co-educational Day
No of pupils: B80 G40
Special Needs: PH W

THREE SPIRES SCHOOL
Kingsbury Road, Coventry, West
Midlands CV6 1PJ
Tel: (024) 7659 4952
Head: Mr C Worrall
Type: Co-educational Day 3–11
No of pupils: B43 G25
Special Needs: MLD

TIVERTON SPECIAL SCHOOL
Rowington Close, off Kingsbury
Road, Coventry, West Midlands
CV6 1PS
Tel: (024) 7659 4954
Head: Mr A Chave
Type: Co-educational 3–11
No of pupils: 45
Special Needs: SLD W

WAINBODY WOOD SPECIAL SCHOOL
Stoneleigh Road, Coventry, West
Midlands CV4 7AB
Tel: (024) 7641 8755
Head: Mr J McGinty
Type: Co-educational Day
No of pupils: 55
Special Needs: EBD

Dudley Education Authority

Westox House
1 Trinity Road
Dudley
West Midlands DY1 1JQ
Tel: (01384) 818181

THE BRIER SPECIAL SCHOOL
Cottage Street, Brierley Hill, West
Midlands DY5 1RE
Tel: (01384) 816000
Head: Mr D K Postlethwaite
Type: Co-educational Day
No of pupils: B84 G47
Special Needs: MLD SP&LD

HALESBURY SPECIAL SCHOOL
Feldon Lane, Halesowen, West
Midlands B62 9DR
Tel: (01384) 818630
Head: Mr J Hackett
Type: Co-educational Day 5–16
No of pupils: 120
Special Needs: ASP MLD

PENS MEADOW SPECIAL SCHOOL
Ridge Hill, Brierley Hill Road,
Stourbridge, West Midlands DY8 5ST
Tel: (01384) 288201
Acting Head: Mrs K Grew
Type: Co-educational 3–19
No of pupils: 70
Special Needs: PMLD SLD

ROSEWOOD SCHOOL
Overfield Road, Russells Hall Estate,
Dudley, West Midlands DY1 2NX
Tel: (01384) 816800
Head: Mrs E M Williams
Type: Boys Day 11–16
No of pupils: 40
Special Needs: EBD W

THE WOODSETTON SPECIAL SCHOOL
Tipton Road, Woodsetton, Dudley,
West Midlands DY3 1BY
Tel: (01384) 818265
Head: Mr P A Rhind-Tutt
Type: Co-educational Day 4–11
No of pupils: B80 G20
Special Needs: MLD

Sandwell Education Authority

PO Box 41
Shaftesbury House
402 High Street
West Bromwich
West Midlands B70 9LT
Tel: (0121) 525 7366

SHENSTONE LODGE SCHOOL

Shenstone, Lichfield, Staffordshire
WS14 0LB
Tel: (01543) 263231
Head: Mr S P Butt
Type: Boys Boarding and Day
No of pupils: 28
Special Needs: AUT **EBD**

WHITTINGTON GRANGE SCHOOL

Burton Road, Whittington, Lichfield,
Staffordshire WS14 9NU
Tel: (01543) 432296
Head: Mr D J Winzor
Type: Boys Boarding and Day 11–16
No of pupils: 30 *No of Boarders:* F5
W25
Special Needs: **EBD**

Solihull Education Authority

PO Box 20
Council House
Solihull
West Midlands B91 3QU
Tel: (0121) 704 6656

FOREST OAK SCHOOL

Lanchester Way, Castle Bromwich,
Birmingham, West Midlands B36 9LF
Tel: (0121) 748 3411
Head: Mrs P L Sankey
Type: Co-educational Day 4–16
No of pupils: B76 G29
Special Needs: **MLD** W

HAZEL OAK SCHOOL

Hazel Oak Road, Shirley, Solihull,
West Midlands B90 2AZ
Tel: (0121) 744 4162
Head: Mr P Wright
Type: Co-educational Day 5–16
No of pupils: 100
Special Needs: ASP AUT **MLD**

MERSTONE SCHOOL

Exeter Drive, Marston Green,
Birmingham, West Midlands
B37 5NX
Tel: (0121) 788 8122
Head: Mrs A R Mordey
Type: Co-educational Day 2–18
No of pupils: 60
Special Needs: AUT CP DOW EPI PH
PMLD SLD W

REYNALDS CROSS SCHOOL

Kineton Green Road, Olton, Solihull,
West Midlands B92 7ER
Tel: (0121) 707 3012
Head: Ms M Daniels
Special Needs: PMLD SLD W

Walsall Education Authority

Civic Centre
Darwall Street
Walsall
West Midlands WS1 1DQ
Tel: (01922) 650000

BEACON SPECIAL SCHOOL

Beacon Street, Lichfield, West
Midlands WS13 7BG
Tel: (01543) 262043
Head: Mr R L Russon
Type: Co-educational Boarding
No of pupils: 24
Special Needs: **MLD**

CASTLE SPECIAL SCHOOL

Odell Road, Leamore, Walsall, West
Midlands WS3 2ED
Tel: (01922) 710129
Head: Mrs H J Whitehouse
Type: Co-educational Day 4–19
No of pupils: B79 G21
Special Needs: ASP **AUT MLD** SLD
SP&LD

DAW END SPECIAL SCHOOL

Floyds Lane, Rushall, Walsall, West
Midlands WS3 2ED
Tel: (01922) 721081
Head: Mr R Wilson
Type: Co-educational Day and
Boarding 5–16
No of pupils: 65 *No of Boarders:* W10
Special Needs: **EBD**

JANE LANE SCHOOL

Churchill Road, Bentley, Walsall,
West Midlands WS2 0JH
Tel: (01922) 721161
Head: Mrs H Lomas
Type: Co-educational Day 4–19
No of pupils: 135
Special Needs: **MLD** W

MARY ELLIOT SPECIAL SCHOOL

Brewer Street, Walsall, West
Midlands WS2 8BA
Tel: (01922) 720706
Head: Mrs E A Jordan
Type: Co-educational Day 13–19
No of pupils: B28 G23
Special Needs: **PMLD SLD** W

OAKWOOD SPECIAL SCHOOL

Druids Walk, Walsall Wood, Walsall,
West Midlands WS9 9JS
Tel: (01543) 452040
Head: Mrs K E Mills
Type: Co-educational Day 2–14
No of pupils: 60
Special Needs: AUT CP EPI HI PH
PMLD SLD VIS W

OLD HALL SPECIAL SCHOOL

Bentley Lane, Walsall, West
Midlands WS2 7LU
Tel: (01902) 368045
Head: Mr S W Jones-Eddie
Type: Co-educational Day 2–14
No of pupils: B55 G35
Special Needs: AUT **PMLD SLD** W

THREE CROWNS SPECIAL SCHOOL

Skip Lane, Walsall, West Midlands
WS5 3NB
Tel: (01922) 721119
Head: Mr P Nickless
Type: Co-educational Day 2–19
No of pupils: 57
Special Needs: PH

Wolverhampton Education Authority

Civic Centre
St Peter's Square
Wolverhampton
West Midlands WV1 1RR
Tel: (01902) 556556

BROADMEADOW NURSERY SPECIAL SCHOOL

Lansdowne Road, Wolverhampton,
West Midlands WV1 4AL
Tel: (01902) 558330
Head: Mrs A R Coates
Type: Co-educational Day 2–6
No of pupils: 40
Special Needs: PMLD SLD W

GREEN PARK SPECIAL SCHOOL
Green Park Avenue, Lumbertubs, Bilston, West Midlands WV14 6EH
Tel: (01902) 556429
Head: Mr M Partington
Type: Co-educational Day 5–19
No of pupils: 66
Special Needs: PMLD SLD W

PENN FIELDS SCHOOL
Birches Barn Road, Penn Fields, Wolverhampton, West Midlands WV3 7BJ
Tel: (01902) 831910
Head: Miss I C Turner
Type: Co-educational Day 5–16
No of pupils: 160
Special Needs: HI MLD SP&LD VIS W

PENN HALL SCHOOL
Vicarage Road, Penn, Wolverhampton, West Midlands WV4 5HP
Tel: (01902) 558355
Head: Mr A J Stoll
Type: Co-educational Day 3–19
No of pupils: B50 G30
No of Boarders: W6
Special Needs: PH VIS W

TETTENHALL WOOD SCHOOL
School Road, Tettenhall Wood, Wolverhampton, West Midlands WV6 8EJ
Tel: (01902) 758545
Head: Mr M Mahoney
Type: Co-educational Day 5–19
No of pupils: 50
Special Needs: ADD ADHD AUT CP DOW DYP EBD EPI HI **SLD** SP&LD SPLD VIS W

WESTCROFT SCHOOL
Greenacres Avenue, Underhill, Wolverhampton, West Midlands WV10 8NZ
Tel: (01902) 305970
Head: Mr A M Chilvers
Type: Co-educational Day 4–16
No of pupils: 180
Special Needs: **MLD** W

WILTSHIRE

Wiltshire Education Authority
County Hall
Bythesea Road
Trowbridge
Wiltshire BA14 8JB
Tel: (01225) 713000

DOWNLANDS SCHOOL
Downlands Road, Devizes, Wiltshire SN10 5EF
Tel: (01380) 724193
Head: Mr D Walsh
Type: Boys Boarding 10–16
No of pupils: 56
Special Needs: EBD SPLD

EXETER HOUSE SPECIAL SCHOOL
Somerset Road, Salisbury, Wiltshire SP1 3BL
Tel: (01722) 334168
Head: Mrs G Heather
Type: Co-educational Day 2–19
No of pupils: 69
Special Needs: AUT PMLD SLD W

LARKRISE SPECIAL SCHOOL
Ashton Street, Trowbridge, Wiltshire BA14 7EB
Tel: (01225) 761434
Head: Mr M Hull
Type: Co-educational Day 3–19
No of pupils: 53
Special Needs: PMLD SLD

ROWDEFORD SPECIAL SCHOOL
Rowde, Devizes, Wiltshire SN10 2QQ
Tel: (01380) 850309
Head: Mr G R Darnell
Type: Co-educational Day and Boarding 11–16
No of pupils: 90 *No of Boarders:* W25
Special Needs: **MLD**

ST NICHOLAS SCHOOL
Malmesbury Road, Chippenham, Wiltshire SN15 1QF
Tel: (01249) 650435
Head: Mr C Riches
Type: Co-educational Day 2–19
No of pupils: 63
Special Needs: PMLD SLD

SPRINGFIELDS SPECIAL SCHOOL
Curzon Street, Calne, Wiltshire SN11 0DS
Tel: (01249) 814125
Head: Mr R Nethercott
Type: Co-educational Boarding 10–17
No of pupils: 60
Special Needs: **EBD**

Swindon Borough Council
Sanford House
Sanford Street
Swindon SN1 1QH
Tel: (01793) 463000

THE CHALET SPECIAL SCHOOL
Queens Drive, Swindon, Wiltshire SN3 1AR
Tel: (01793) 534537
Head: Mrs M Topping
Type: Co-educational Day 2–7
No of pupils: 30
Special Needs: AUT EPI MLD PH SLD **SP&LD**

CROWDYS HILL SPECIAL SCHOOL
Jefferies Avenue, Cricklade Road, Swindon, Wiltshire SN2 6HJ
Tel: (01793) 332400
Head: Mr K Smith
Type: Co-educational Day 11–16
No of pupils: 160
Special Needs: ASP **MLD** W

NYLAND SPECIAL SCHOOL
Nyland Road, Nythe, Swindon,
Wiltshire SN3 3RD
Tel: (01793) 535023
Head: Mr P Sunners
Type: Co-educational Day 5–11
No of pupils: 60
Special Needs: AUT EBD EPI MLD
SP&LD

ST LUKE'S SPECIAL SCHOOL
Cricklade Road, Swindon, Wiltshire
SN2 5AH
Tel: (01793) 705566
Head: Mr I Wiltshire
Type: Co-educational Day 11–16
No of pupils: 64
Special Needs: **EBD** W

UPLANDS SPECIAL SCHOOL
Leigh Road, Penhill, Swindon,
Wiltshire SN2 5DE
Tel: (01793) 724751
Head: Miss M E Bishop
Type: Co-educational Day 11–19
No of pupils: B41 G29
Special Needs: AUT CP DOW **PMLD**
SLD W

WORCESTERSHIRE

Worcestershire Education Authority

Educational Services Department
PO Box 73
County Hall
Spetchley Road
Worcester WR5 2NP
Tel: (01905) 763763

THE ALEXANDER PATTERSON SCHOOL
Park Gate Road, Wolverley,
Kidderminster, Worcestershire
DY10 3PU
Tel: (01562) 851396
Head: Mrs M E Calvert
Type: Co-educational Day
No of pupils: 90
Special Needs: AUT EBD **MLD** PMLD
SP&LD W

BLAKEBROOK SPECIAL SCHOOL
Bewdley Road, Kidderminster,
Worcestershire DY11 6RL
Tel: (01562) 753066
Head: Mr M O G Russell
Type: Co-educational Day
No of pupils: B33 G19
Special Needs: ADD ADHD AUT CP
DOW DYP EPI HI PH PMLD SLD
VIS W

CHADSGROVE SPECIAL SCHOOL
Meadow Road, Catshill, Bromsgrove,
Worcestershire B61 0JL
Tel: (01527) 871511
Head: Mr R Aust
Type: Day
No of pupils: 110
Special Needs: CP DEL EPI **PH** PMLD
VIS W

CLIFFEY HOUSE SCHOOL
Hanley Castle, Worcester,
Worcestershire WR8 0AD
Tel: (01684) 310336
Head: Mr D Bishop-Rave
Type: Co-educational Day 11–16
No of pupils: B90 G42
Special Needs: ASP AUT **MLD**

MANOR PARK SPECIAL SCHOOL
Turnpike Close, Oldbury Road,
Worcester WR2 6AB
Tel: (01905) 423403
Head: Mr D C Palmer
Type: Co-educational Day 4–19
No of pupils: 75
Special Needs: PMLD **SLD** W

PITCHEROAK SPECIAL SCHOOL
Willow Way, Redditch,
Worcestershire B97 6PQ
Tel: (01527) 65576
Head: Ms K Earle
Type: Co-educational Day 2–18
No of pupils: 190
Special Needs: AUT MLD PMLD SLD

RIGBY HALL SPECIAL SCHOOL
Rigby Lane, Bromsgrove,
Worcestershire B60 2EP
Tel: (01527) 875475
Head: Mrs P A Griffiths
Type: Co-educational Day
No of pupils: 110
Special Needs: MLD SLD

ROSE HILL SPECIAL SCHOOL
Windermere Drive, Warndon,
Worcester, Worcestershire WR4 9JL
Tel: (01905) 454828
Head: Mr F W Steel
Type: Co-educational Day
No of pupils: B46 G33
Special Needs: **CP DEL PH** PMLD W

STOURMINSTER SPECIAL SCHOOL
Comberton Road, Kidderminster,
Worcestershire DY10 3DX
Tel: (01562) 823156
Head: Mr I D Hardicker
Type: Co-educational 7–16
No of pupils: B104 G53
Special Needs: **MLD** W

THORNTON HOUSE SPECIAL SCHOOL
Radley Road, Worcester,
Worcestershire OX14 3RR
Tel: (01905) 523843
Head: Mr H B Thomas
Type: Co-educational Day 2–11
No of pupils: 122
Special Needs: AUT MLD

VALE OF EVESHAM SPECIAL SCHOOL
Four Pools Lane, Evesham,
Worcestershire WR11 6DH
Tel: (01386) 443367
Head: Mr E P Matthews
Type: Co-educational Boarding and
Day 4–19
No of pupils: 143 *No of Boarders:* W15
Special Needs: **ADD** ADHD **ASP AUT**
CP DEL **DOW** DYP DYS EBD EPI HI
MLD PH **PMLD SLD** SP&LD SPLD
VIS W

EAST RIDING OF YORKSHIRE

East Riding of Yorkshire Education Authority

County Hall
Beverley HU17 9BA
Tel: (01482) 887700

GANTON SCHOOL

Springhead Lane, Willerby Road, Hull, East Riding of Yorkshire HU5 6YJ
Tel: (01482) 564646
Head: Mrs P J Glover
Type: Co-educational Day
No of pupils: 120
Special Needs: AUT CP DOW EPI PMLD SLD W

KING'S MILL SCHOOL

Victoria Road, Driffield, East Riding of Yorkshire YO25 7UG
Tel: (01377) 253375
Head: Ms S Young
Type: Co-educational Day and Boarding 2–16
No of pupils: 64 No of Boarders: W16
Special Needs: PMLD SLD W

ST ANNE'S SCHOOL

St Helen's Drive, Welton, Brough, East Riding of Yorkshire HU15 1NR
Tel: (01482) 667379
Head: Mr M Stubbins
Type: Co-educational Boarding and Day
No of pupils: 75
Special Needs: SLD

SOUTH WOLDS SCHOOL

Dalton Holme, Beverley, East Riding of Yorkshire HU17 7PB
Tel: (0191) 200 6348
Head: Mr L M Powell
Type: Co-educational Boarding and Day 8–16
No of pupils: 80 No of Boarders: W60
Special Needs: EBD W

Kingston upon Hull Education Authority

Education Services
Essex House
Manor Street
Kingston upon Hull HU1 1YD
Tel: (01482) 613161

FREDERICK HOLMES SCHOOL

Inglemire Lane, Kingston upon Hull, East Riding of Yorkshire HU6 8JJ
Tel: (01482) 804766
Head: Mr D Boyes
Type: Co-educational 2–19
No of pupils: 103
Special Needs: PH W

NORTHCOTT SCHOOL

Dulverton Close, Bransholme, Kingston upon Hull, East Riding of Yorkshire HU7 4EL
Tel: (01482) 825311
Head: Mr M Johnson
Type: Co-educational
No of pupils: 90
Special Needs: AUT DEL EBD EPI SP&LD

TWEENDYKES SCHOOL

Tweendykes Road, Sutton, Kingston upon Hull, East Riding of Yorkshire HU7 4XJ
Tel: (01482) 826508
Head: Mr K J Ogilvie
No of pupils: 79
Special Needs: PMLD SLD W

NORTH YORKSHIRE

North Yorkshire Education Authority

County Hall
Northallerton
North Yorkshire DL7 8AE
Tel: (01609) 780780

BROMPTON HALL SCHOOL

Brompton-by-Sawdon, Scarborough, North Yorkshire YO13 9BD
Tel: (01723) 859121
Acting Head: L Farn
Type: Boys Boarding
No of pupils: 38 No of Boarders: F38
Special Needs: ADHD EBD MLD

DALES SCHOOL

Moreton-on-Swale, Northallerton, North Yorkshire DL7 9QW
Tel: (01609) 772932
Head: Mr W F Rab
Type: Co-educational Day 2–19
No of pupils: 65
Special Needs: AUT PMLD SLD VIS

THE FOREST SCHOOL

Park Lane, Knaresborough, North Yorkshire HG5 0DQ
Tel: (01423) 864583
Head: Mrs S Wootton
Type: Co-educational Day 2–16
No of pupils: 122
Special Needs: MLD SP&LD W

MOWBRAY SCHOOL

Masham Road, Bedale, North Yorkshire DL8 2SD
Tel: (01677) 422446
Head: Mr A Burnett
Type: Co-educational Day 2–16
No of pupils: 150
Special Needs: AUT EBD MLD SLD SP&LD

NETHERSIDE HALL SCHOOL
Threshfield, Skipton, North
Yorkshire BD23 5PP
Tel: (01756) 752324
Head: Mr M E Hopkins
Type: Boys Boarding and Day 10–16
No of pupils: 45 *No of Boarders:* W37
Special Needs: DYS SPLD

SPRINGHEAD SCHOOL
Barry's Lane, Scarborough, North
Yorkshire YO12 4HA
Tel: (01723) 367829
Head: Mrs C D Wilson
Type: Co-educational Day 2–19
No of pupils: 46
Special Needs: PMLD SLD W

SPRINGWATER SCHOOL
High Street, Starbeck, Harrogate,
North Yorkshire HG2 7LW
Tel: (01423) 883214
Head: Mrs G M Cook
Type: Co-educational Day 2–19
No of pupils: 45
Special Needs: PMLD SLD

WELBURN HALL SCHOOL
Kirbymoorside, York, North
Yorkshire YO6 6HQ
Tel: (01751) 431218
Head: Mr J V Hall
Type: Co-educational Boarding and
Day 8–19
No of pupils: 70 *No of Boarders:* W35
Special Needs: CP EPI HI MLD PH
SLD SP&LD W

THE WOODLANDS SCHOOL
Woodlands Drive, Scarborough,
North Yorkshire YO12 6QN
Tel: (01723) 373260
Head: Mr C J Webley
No of pupils: 79 *No of Boarders:* F15
Special Needs: AUT MLD SLD W

York Education Authority
PO Box 404
10–12 George Hudson Street
York YO1 6ZG
Tel: (01904) 653219

FULFORD CROSS SCHOOL
Fulford Cross, York, North Yorkshire
YO1 4PB
Tel: (01904) 653219
Head: Mrs J Lock
No of pupils: 140
Special Needs: MLD

GALTRES SCHOOL
Bad Bargain Lane, York, North
Yorkshire YO31 0LW
Tel: (01904) 415924
Head: Mr G Gilmore
Type: Co-educational Day 11–19
No of pupils: B37 G28
Special Needs: PMLD SLD W

LIDGETT GROVE SCHOOL
Wheatlands Grove, Acomb, York,
North Yorkshire YO2 5NH
Tel: (01904) 791437
Head: Mr R Nicholls
Type: Co-educational Day 2–11
No of pupils: 70
Special Needs: AUT PMLD SLD

SOUTH YORKSHIRE

Doncaster Education Authority
PO Box 266
The Council House
College Road
Doncaster
South Yorkshire DN1 3AD
Tel: (01302) 737222

ANCHORAGE LOWER SCHOOL
Cusworth Lane, York Road,
Doncaster, South Yorkshire DN5 8JL
Tel: (01302) 391007
Head: Mr J Taylor
Type: Co-educational Day 4–12
No of pupils: B49 G21
Special Needs: MLD

ANCHORAGE UPPER SCHOOL
Barnsley Road, Scawsby, Doncaster,
South Yorkshire DN5 7UB
Tel: (01302) 391006
Head: Mr J Taylor
Type: Co-educational Day 13–16
Special Needs: MLD

ATHELSTANE SCHOOL
Old Road, Conisbrough, Doncaster,
South Yorkshire DN12 3LR
Tel: (01709) 864978
Head: Mr G Davies
Type: Co-educational Day 4–16
No of pupils: 130
Special Needs: MLD

CEDAR SCHOOL
Cedar Road, Balby, Doncaster, South
Yorkshire DN4 9HT
Tel: (01302) 853361
Head: Mr T M Kellett
Type: Co-educational 3–19
Special Needs: SLD

CHASE SCHOOL
Ash Hill, Hatfield, Doncaster, South
Yorkshire DN7 6JH
Tel: (01302) 844883
Head: Mr W J Evans
Type: Co-educational Day 3–19
No of pupils: 106
Special Needs: AUT PMLD SLD W

FERNBANK SCHOOL
Village Street, Adwick-le-Street,
Doncaster, South Yorkshire DN6 7AA
Tel: (01302) 723571
Head: Mr A R Bickerton
Type: Co-educational Day 2–19
No of pupils: 75
Special Needs: PMLD SLD

SANDALL WOOD SCHOOL

Leger Way, Doncaster, South
Yorkshire DN2 6HQ
Tel: (01302) 322044
Head: Mrs C M Ray
Type: Co-educational Day 3–19
No of pupils: 74
Special Needs: CP EPI PH PMLD
SP&LD W

Rotherham Education Authority

Norfolk House
Walker Place
Rotherham S65 1AS
Tel: (01709) 382121

ABBEY SCHOOL

Little Common Lane, Kimberworth,
Rotherham, South Yorkshire S61 2RA
Tel: (01709) 740074
Head: Mr J S Swain
Type: Co-educational Day 5–16
No of pupils: 143
Special Needs: **MLD**

GREEN ARBOUR SCHOOL

Locksley Drive, Thurncroft,
Rotherham, South Yorkshire S66 9NT
Tel: (01709) 542539
Head: Mr P Gawthorpe
Type: Co-educational Day 5–16
No of pupils: 140
Special Needs: AUT MLD SP&LD

HILLTOP SCHOOL

Larch Road, Maltby, Rotherham,
South Yorkshire S66 8AZ
Tel: (01709) 813386
Head: Mr P Leach
Type: Co-educational Day 2–19
No of pupils: 90
Special Needs: AUT CP DOW **PMLD**
SLD W

KELFORD SCHOOL

Oakdale Road, Kimberworth,
Rotherham, South Yorkshire
S61 2NU
Tel: (01709) 512088
Head: Mrs S Greenhough
Type: Co-educational Day 2–19
No of pupils: 90
Special Needs: PMLD SLD W

MILTON SCHOOL

Storey Street, Swinton, Mexborough,
South Yorkshire S64 8QG
Tel: (01709) 570246
Head: Mr C D Garford
Type: Co-educational Day 4–16
No of pupils: B83 G24
Special Needs: ASP AUT **MLD** W

NEWMAN SCHOOL

East Bawtry Road, Whiston,
Rotherham, South Yorkshire S60 2LX
Tel: (01709) 828262
Head: Mrs J Richards
Type: Co-educational Day 2–19
No of pupils: 90
Special Needs: CP PH W

WHISTON GRANGE SCHOOL

East Bawtry Road, Whiston,
Rotherham, South Yorkshire S60 3LX
Tel: (01709) 828838
Head: Mr B Wilcock
Type: Co-educational Day 11–14
No of pupils: B43
Special Needs: **EBD** W

Sheffield Education Authority

Leopold Street
Sheffield
South Yorkshire S1 1RJ
Tel: (0114) 272 6444

BENTS GREEN SECONDARY SCHOOL

Ringinglow Road, Sheffield, South
Yorkshire S11 7TB
Tel: (0114) 236 3545
Head: Mr R J Ellks
Type: Co-educational Day and
Boarding
No of pupils: 96 *No of Boarders:* F30
Special Needs: **AUT** DEL EBD HI
MLD VIS

EAST HILL PRIMARY SCHOOL

East Bank Road, Sheffield, South
Yorkshire S2 3PX
Tel: (0114) 272 9897
Head: Mr T Johnson
Type: Co-educational Day 4–11
No of pupils: 56
Special Needs: **MLD**

EAST HILL SECONDARY SCHOOL

East Bank Road, Sheffield, South
Yorkshire S2 3PX
Tel: (0114) 276 0245
Head: Mr K Jenkins
Type: Co-educational 11–16
No of pupils: 110
Special Needs: **MLD**

MOSSBROOK SCHOOL

Bochum Parkway, Sheffield, South
Yorkshire S8 8JR
Tel: (0114) 237 2768
Head: Mrs M Brough
Type: Co-educational Day and
Boarding
No of pupils: B54 G22
No of Boarders: W15
Special Needs: AUT DEL DOW EBD
EPI MLD SLD SP&LD W

OAKES PARK SCHOOL

Hemsworth Road, Sheffield, South
Yorkshire S8 8LN
Tel: (0114) 255 6754
Head: Mrs P Johnson
Type: Co-educational Day 2–19
No of pupils: 55
Special Needs: PH W

THE ROWAN SCHOOL

4 Durvale Court, Sheffield, South
Yorkshire S17 3PT
Tel: (0114) 235 0479
Head: Mr D R Quayle
Type: Co-educational Day 4–10
No of pupils: 60
Special Needs: ASP AUT SP&LD

WOOLLEY WOOD SCHOOL

Oaks Fold Road, Sheffield, South
Yorkshire S5 0TG
Tel: (0114) 245 6885
Head: Ms M J Holly
Type: Co-educational Day 3–10
No of pupils: 58
Special Needs: PMLD SLD W

WEST YORKSHIRE

Bradford Education Authority

Flockton House
Flockton Road
Bradford
West Yorkshire BD4 7RY
Tel: (01274) 751840

CHAPEL GRANGE SCHOOL
Rhodesway, Bradford, West
Yorkshire BD8 0DQ
Tel: (01274) 773307
Head: Mrs H Morrison
Type: Co-educational Day 11–19
No of pupils: 102
Special Needs: AUT MLD **SLD**

HAYCLIFFE SCHOOL
Haycliffe Lane, Bradford, West
Yorkshire BD5 9ET
Tel: (01274) 576123
Head: Mr K G Fair
Type: Co-educational Day 11–19
No of pupils: 120
Special Needs: **MLD** SLD W

HEATON ROYDS SCHOOL
Redburn Drive, Shipley, West
Yorkshire BD18 3AZ
Tel: (01274) 583759
Head: Mrs M Fowler
Type: Co-educational Day 2–11
No of pupils: B28 G17
Special Needs: EPI **MLD SLD** SP&LD

LISTER LANE SCHOOL
Lister Lane, Bradford, West
Yorkshire BD2 4LL
Tel: (01274) 777107/777108
Head: Mr W G Freeth
Type: Co-educational Day 2–13
No of pupils: 70
Special Needs: PH W

NETHERLANDS AVENUE SCHOOL
Netherlands Avenue, Bradford, West
Yorkshire BD6 1EA
Tel: (01274) 677711
Head: Mrs W Paley
Type: Co-educational 3–11
Special Needs: AUT CP EBD EPI HI
MLD PH SLD SP&LD

TEMPLE BANK SCHOOL
Daisy Hill Lane, Bradford, West
Yorkshire BD9 6BN
Tel: (01274) 776566/776588
Head: Mr R C Neal
Type: Co-educational Day 2–19
No of pupils: B31 G19
Special Needs: VIS W

THORN PARK SCHOOL
Thorn Lane, Bingley Road, Bradford,
West Yorkshire BD9 6RY
Tel: (01274) 773770
Head: Mr M A Gordon
Type: Co-educational Day 2–19
No of pupils: 82
Special Needs: HI

WEDGWOOD SCHOOL & COMMUNITY NURSERY
Landscove Avenue, Holmewood,
Bradford, West Yorkshire BD4 0NQ
Tel: (01274) 687236
Head: Mrs J Godward
Type: Co-educational Day 2–11
No of pupils: 81
Special Needs: CP MLD PH **PMLD**
SLD W

Calderdale Education Authority

Northgate House
Halifax
West Yorkshire HX1 1UN
Tel: (01422) 357257

HIGHBURY SCHOOL
Lower Edge Road, Rastrick,
Brighouse, West Yorkshire HD6 3LD
Tel: (01484) 716319
Head: Miss P J Sellers
Type: Co-educational Day
No of pupils: 40
Special Needs: AUT CP DOW EPI HI
PH PMLD SLD SP&LD VIS W

RAVENSCLIFFE HIGH SCHOOL
Skircoat Green, Halifax, West
Yorkshire HX3 0RZ
Tel: (01422) 358621
Head: Mr M D Hirst
Type: Co-educational Day 11–19
No of pupils: 115
Special Needs: AUT CP DYP DYS EPI
HI MLD PH PMLD SLD SP&LD
VIS W

WOOD BANK SPECIAL SCHOOL
Dene View, Luddendenfoot, Halifax,
West Yorkshire HX2 6PB
Tel: (01422) 884170
Head: Mrs J Ingham
Type: Co-educational Day 2–11
No of pupils: 40
Special Needs: AUT CP PMLD SLD W

Kirklees Education Authority

Oldgate House
2 Oldgate
Huddersfield
West Yorkshire HD1 6QW
Tel: (01484) 225000

FAIRFIELD SCHOOL
Dale Lane, Heckmondwike, West
Yorkshire WF16 9PA
Tel: (01924) 325700
Head: Mrs S L Williams
Type: Co-educational Day 3–19
No of pupils: B51 G36
Special Needs: PMLD SLD W

HIGHFIELDS SCHOOL
Cemetery Road, Edgerton,
Huddersfield, West Yorkshire
HD1 5NF
Tel: (01484) 226659
Head: Mr R T Ware
Type: Co-educational Day 3–19
No of pupils: B50 G27
Special Needs: PMLD SLD W

LONGLEY SCHOOL
Smithy Lane, Huddersfield, West
Yorkshire HD5 8JE
Tel: (01484) 223937
Head: Mr M Hogarth
Type: Co-educational Day 5–16
No of pupils: 135
Special Needs: ADD ADHD ASP AUT
CP DEL DOW DYP DYS EBD EPI HI
MLD SP&LD VIS W

LYDGATE SCHOOL
Kirkroyds Lane, New Mill,
Huddersfield, West Yorkshire
HD7 7LS
Tel: (01484) 222484
Head: Mr W Goler
Type: Co-educational Day 5–16
No of pupils: B52 G35
Special Needs: **MLD** W

NORTONTHORPE HALL SCHOOL
Busker Lane, Scissett, Huddersfield, West Yorkshire HD8 9JU
Tel: (01484) 222921
Head: Mr M Ironmonger
Type: Co-educational Boarding and Day 7–16
No of pupils: 70
Special Needs: **EBD**

RAVENSHALL SCHOOL
Ravensthorpe Road, Dewsbury, West Yorkshire WF12 9EE
Tel: (01924) 325234
Head: Mr C Newby
Type: Co-educational Day 11–16
No of pupils: 87
Special Needs: **MLD** W

TURNSHAWS SCHOOL
Turnshaws Avenue, Kirkburton, Huddersfield, West Yorkshire HD8 0TJ
Tel: (01484) 222760
Head: Ms G Taylor
Type: Co-educational Day
No of pupils: 50
Special Needs: PMLD SLD W

Leeds Education Authority
Selectapost 17
Merrion House
Leeds
West Yorkshire LS2 8DT
Tel: (0113) 247 5876

BROOMFIELD SCHOOL
Broom Place, Leeds, West Yorkshire LS10 3JP
Tel: (0113) 277 1603
Head: Mr D M Dewhirst
Type: Co-educational Day 2–19
No of pupils: B63 G31
Special Needs: **AUT** CP EBD EPI HI **MLD** PH **PMLD SLD** VIS **W**

ELMETE WOOD SCHOOL
Elmete Lane, Leeds, West Yorkshire LS8 2LJ
Tel: (0113) 265 5457
Head: Mr W J Chatloin
Type: Co-educational Day 11–19
No of pupils: 120
Special Needs: **MLD**

FEARNVILLE SCHOOL
Oakwood Lane, Leeds, West Yorkshire LS8 3LF
Tel: (0113) 293 0285
Head: Mr T R Hodgson
Type: Co-educational 3–11
No of pupils: 70
Special Needs: **MLD**

GRAFTON SCHOOL
Craven Road, Leeds, West Yorkshire LS6 2PW
Tel: (0113) 293 0323
Head: Mr K Purches
Type: Co-educational 3–11
No of pupils: 74
Special Needs: HI MLD

GREEN MEADOWS SCHOOL
Bradford Road, Guiseley, West Yorkshire LS20 8PP
Tel: (01943) 878536
Head: Mr P Isherwood
Type: Co-educational Day 2–19
No of pupils: B77 G40
Special Needs: **ADHD ASP AUT** CP DEL DOW DYP DYS EPI HI MLD PH PMLD SLD SP&LD SPLD TOU VIS W

JOHN JAMIESON SCHOOL
Hollin Hill Drive, Leeds, West Yorkshire LS8 2PW
Tel: (0113) 293 0236
Head: Mr P Hutchinson
Type: Co-educational Day
No of pupils: 100
Special Needs: CP DEL MLD PH W

MILESTONE SCHOOL
4 Town Street, Stanningley, West Yorkshire LS28 6HL
Tel: (0113) 214 6107
Head: Mr J C Tearle
Type: Co-educational Day 2–19
No of pupils: 64
Special Needs: **ADHD AUT** PMLD SLD W

NORTHWAYS SCHOOL
Willow Lane, Clifford, Wetherby, West Yorkshire LS23 6JN
Tel: (01937) 843766
Head: Mr J Boulton
Type: Boys Boarding and Day
No of pupils: 57
Special Needs: **EBD**

PENNY FIELD SCHOOL
Tongue Lane, Leeds, West Yorkshire LS6 4QE
Tel: (0113) 278 3577
Head: Mrs H M Barrett
Type: Co-educational Day 2–19
No of pupils: 75
Special Needs: CP EPI HI PH **PMLD SLD** VIS **W**

STONEGATE SCHOOL
Stonegate Road, Leeds, West Yorkshire LS6 4QJ
Tel: (0113) 278 6464
Head: Mr P Bailey
Type: Co-educational Day
No of pupils: 75
Special Needs: EBD

VICTORIA PARK SCHOOL
Victoria Park Grove, Leeds, West Yorkshire LS13 2RD
Tel: (0113) 278 3957
Head: Mr P J Miller
Type: Co-educational 11–19
No of pupils: 125
Special Needs: **MLD**

Wakefield Education Authority
County Hall
Wakefield
West Yorkshire WF1 2QL
Tel: (01924) 306090

THE FELKIRK SCHOOL
Highwell Hill Lane, South Hiendley, Barnsley, South Yorkshire S72 9DL
Tel: (01226) 718613
Head: Mr T R Howe
Type: Boys Boarding and Day 5–16
No of pupils: 80 *No of Boarders:* F30
Special Needs: **EBD**

HIGHFIELD SCHOOL
Gawthorpe Lane, Ossett, West Yorkshire WF5 9BS
Tel: (01924) 302980
Head: Mrs M Smith
Type: Co-educational Day 11–16
No of pupils: 120
Special Needs: ADD ADHD ASP AUT MLD PH SLD W

THE PARK SCHOOL
Lawefield Lane, Wakefield, West Yorkshire WF2 8SX
Tel: (01924) 303685
Head: Mrs N Wainwright
Type: Co-educational Day
No of pupils: 65
Special Needs: AUT **SLD** W

NORTHERN IRELAND

BELFAST

Belfast Area Education/ Library Board

40 Academy Street
Belfast
County Antrim BT1 2NQ
Tel: (028) 9056 4000

CEDAR LODGE SPECIAL SCHOOL
Gray's Lane, Newtownabbey, Belfast,
County Antrim BT36 7EB
Tel: (01232) 777292
Head: Mrs E G Bunting
Type: Co-educational Day
No of pupils: B100 G50
Special Needs: ADHD ASP CP **DEL**
EPI MLD SP&LD **W**

CLARAWOOD SCHOOL
Clarawood Park, Belfast, County
Antrim BT5 6FR
Tel: (01232) 472736
Head: Mr S McIntaggart
Type: Co-educational Day 8–13
No of pupils: 35
Special Needs: **EBD**

FLEMING FULTON SCHOOL
Upper Malone Road, Belfast, County
Antrim BT9 6TY
Tel: (01232) 613877
Head: Dr D Mehaffey
Type: Co-educational Day and
Boarding 2–19
No of pupils: B104 G66
Special Needs: **PH** W

GLENVEAGH SPECIAL SCHOOL
Harberton Park, Belfast, County
Antrim BT9 6TX
Tel: (01232) 669907
Head: Mrs K Murphy
Type: Co-educational Day
No of pupils: B98 G62
Special Needs: AUT CP PMLD SLD

GREENWOOD HOUSE ASSESSMENT CENTRE
Greenwood Avenue, Belfast, County
Antrim BT4 3JJ
Tel: (01232) 471000
Head: Mrs P E Scott
Type: Co-educational Day 4–7
No of pupils: 54
Special Needs: **ADD ADHD** ASP AUT
DEL DOW **DYP** DYS EBD HI MLD
PH SLD SP&LD SPLD VIS

JAFFE CENTRE
Craft Annex, Carolan Road, Belfast,
County Antrim BT7 3HE
Tel: (01232) 492601
Head: Mr D McConnell
Type: Co-educational Day 11–16
No of pupils: 45
Special Needs: **EBD**

LINDSAY SPECIAL SCHOOL
Foster Green Hospital, 110 Saintfield
Road, Belfast, County Antrim
BT8 4HD
Tel: (02890) 793681
Head: Mr P W Doherty
Type: Co-educational 3–14
No of pupils: 25 No of Boarders: W15
Special Needs: ADHD ASP AUT DYP
DYS EBD MLD SPLD

MITCHELL HOUSE SPECIAL SCHOOL
Marmont, 405 Holywood Road,
Belfast, County Antrim BT4 2GU
Tel: (01232) 768407
Head: Mrs P Grindle
Type: Co-educational Day 2–19
No of pupils: 75
Special Needs: CP PH W

OAKWOOD SCHOOL ASSESSMENT CENTRE
Harberton Park, Belfast, County
Antrim BT9 6TX
Tel: (01232) 605116
Head: Mrs M E Watson
Type: Co-educational 3–8
No of pupils: 77
Special Needs: AUT CP DEL DOW
EBD EPI HI PH PMLD SLD SP&LD
VIS W

PARK EDUCATION RESOURCE CENTRE
145 Ravenhill Road, Belfast, County
Antrim BT6 8GH
Tel: (01232) 450513
Head: Mr F Mitchell
Type: Co-educational Day 11–16
Special Needs: **MLD**

ST GERARD'S EDUCATION RESOURCE CENTRE
Upper Springfield Road, Belfast,
County Antrim BT12 7QP
Tel: (01232) 245593
Head: Mr R Rooney
Type: Co-educational Day 4–16
No of pupils: B160 G85
Special Needs: **MLD**

NORTH EASTERN AREA

North Eastern Area Education/Library Board

Board Offices
County Hall
182 Galgorm Road
Ballymena
Co. Antrim BT42 1HN
Tel: (028) 2565 3333

BEECHGROVE SCHOOL
91 Fry's Road, Ballymena, County
Antrim BT43 7EN
Tel: (0282) 564 8264
Acting Head: Mrs A Pinches
Type: Co-educational Day 3–11
No of pupils: 24
Special Needs: ADHD CP DEL EPI **PH**
VIS W

DUNFANE SCHOOL
91 Fry's Road, Ballymena, County
Antrim BT43 7EN
Tel: (01266) 48263
Head: Mr J Dixon
Type: Co-educational
No of pupils: B89 G53
Special Needs: ADD DOW DYP EBD
EPI MLD PH SP&LD VIS W

HILL CROFT SCHOOL
Abbot's Road, Newtownabbey,
County Antrim BT37 9RB
Tel: (01232) 863262
Head: Mr T Howard
Type: Co-educational Day
Special Needs: SLD W

KILRONAN SCHOOL
46 Ballyronan Road, Magherafelt,
County Londonderry BT45 6EN
Tel: (01648) 32168
Head: Mrs J Clarke
Type: Co-educational Day 3–19
No of pupils: 80
Special Needs: AUT CP DOW PMLD
SLD W

LOUGHAN SCHOOL
22 Old Ballymoney Road, Ballymena,
County Antrim BT43 6LX
Tel: (028) 2565 2944
Head: Miss M H Norris
Type: Co-educational Day 3–19
No of pupils: B48 G27
Special Needs: SLD W

RIVERSIDE SCHOOL
Fennel Road, Antrim, County
Antrim BT41 4PB
Tel: (028) 9442 8946
Head: Mrs R A Rankin
Type: Co-educational Day 3–19
No of pupils: B27 G18
Special Needs: AUT EPI PMLD SLD
SP&LD

RODDENSVALE SCHOOL
The Roddens, Larne, County Antrim
BT40 1PU
Tel: (01574) 272802
Head: Miss M Lynas
Type: Co-educational Day 3–19
No of pupils: 56
Special Needs: AUT CP DEL DOW
EBD EPI HI PH PMLD SLD SP&LD
SPLD VIS W

ROSSTULLA SCHOOL
2–6 Jordanstown Road,
Newtownabbey, County Antrim
BT37 0QF
Tel: (01232) 862743
Head: Mrs F Burke
Type: Co-educational 4–16
No of pupils: B99 G64
Special Needs: EBD EPI MLD

THORNFIELD SPECIAL SCHOOL
8–12 Jordanstown Road,
Newtownabbey, County Antrim
BT37 0QF
Tel: (01232) 851089
Head: Mrs A Ingram
Type: Co-educational Day
No of pupils: B68 G11
Special Needs: SP&LD

SOUTH EASTERN AREA

South Eastern Area Education/Library Board

Library Board
Grahamsbridge Road
Dundonald
Belfast BT16 2HS
Tel: (028) 9056 6200

ARDMORE HOUSE SCHOOL & SUPPORT SERVICE
95a Saul Street, Downpatrick,
County Down BT30 6NJ
Tel: (01396) 614881
Head: Mr W Dale
Type: Co-educational Day 11–16
No of pupils: 28
Special Needs: EBD

BEECHLAWN SCHOOL
3 Dromore Road, Hillsborough,
County Down BT26 6HY
Tel: (01846) 682302/682283
Head: Mr E S Gamble
Type: Boys Day 10–16
No of pupils: 250
Special Needs: DYP DYS MLD SPLD

CLIFTON SCHOOL
15 Ballyholme Road, Bangor, County
Down BT20 5JH
Tel: (01247) 270210
Head: Mrs J H Crowther
Type: Co-educational 3–19
No of pupils: 102
Special Needs: ADD ADHD AUT CP
DOW EBD EPI HI PH PMLD SLD
SP&LD VIS W

DONARD SPECIAL SCHOOL
Ballygowan Road, Banbridge,
County Down BT32 3EH
Tel: (01820) 662357
Head: Mrs F Wylie
Type: Co-educational Day
No of pupils: B23 G13
Special Needs: AUT CP EBD EPI PH
PMLD SLD W

KILLARD HOUSE SCHOOL
North Road, Newtownards, County
Down NT23 3AN
Tel: (01247) 813613
Head: Mr W J Haddick
Type: Girls Day and Boarding 4–16
(co-educational 4–11)
No of pupils: 205
Special Needs: MLD SP&LD

LONGSTONE SCHOOL
Millar's Lane, Dundonald, Belfast,
County Antrim BT16 0DA
Tel: (01232) 480071/484660
Head: Mr W J McLaughlin
Type: Co-educational Day 4–16
No of pupils: 200
Special Needs: EBD MLD SPLD W

SOUTHERN AREA

Southern Area Education/ Library Board

3 Charlemont Place
The Mall
Armagh
County Armagh BT61 9AX
Tel: (028) 3751 2200

RATHFRILAND HILL SPECIAL SCHOOL

Rathfriland Hill, Newry, County
Down BT34 1HU
Tel: (01693) 63068
Head: Mr R Cassidy
Type: Co-educational Day 3–19
No of pupils: B55 G34
Special Needs: PMLD **SLD**

SPERRINVIEW SPECIAL SCHOOL

8 Coalisland Road, Dungannon,
County Tyrone BT71 4AA
Tel: (028) 8772 2467
Head: Mr O Sherry
Type: Co-educational Day
No of pupils: B37 G20
Special Needs: SLD **W**

WESTERN AREA

Western Area Education/ Library Board

Headquarters Office
1 Hospital Road
Omagh
County Tyrone BT79 0AW
Tel: (028) 8241 1411

BELMONT HOUSE SCHOOL

Racecourse Road, Londonderry,
County Londonderry BT48 7RE
Tel: (01504) 351266
Head: Mr T McCully
Type: Co-educational Day 3–19
No of pupils: 219
Special Needs: EBD MLD SP&LD

CRANNY SPECIAL SCHOOL

4a Deverney Road, Cranny, Omagh,
County Tyrone BT79 0JJ
Tel: (01662) 242939
Head: Mrs K McGerty
Type: Co-educational Day
No of pupils: B21 G13
Special Needs: AUT CP DOW EPI HI
PH PMLD SLD SPLD VIS W

ELMBROOK

Derrygonnelly, Enniskillen, County
Fermanagh BT7 4AY
Tel: (01365) 329947
Head: Mrs H Lendrum
Type: Co-educational Day 4–19
No of pupils: 54
Special Needs: AUT CP DEL EBD EPI
PMLD SLD W

ENNISKILLEN MODEL PRIMARY SCHOOL

Special Unit (Language),
Enniskillen, Western Area BT74 6HZ
Tel: (01365) 324865
Head: Mrs S W Glass
Type: Co-educational 4–11
No of pupils: B13 G5
Special Needs: SP&LD W

ERNE SPECIAL SCHOOL

Derrygonnelly Road, Enniskillen,
County Fermanagh BT74 7EX
Tel: (01365) 323942
Head: Mrs K Turnbull
Type: Co-educational Day 4–16
No of pupils: 134
Special Needs: MLD W

FOYLE VIEW SCHOOL

15 Racecourse Road, Londonderry,
County Londonderry BT48 7RB
Tel: (02871) 263270
Head: Mr M Dobbins
Type: Co-educational Day 3–19
No of pupils: 108
Special Needs: AUT PMLD **SLD** W

GLASVEY SPECIAL SCHOOL

15 Loughermore Road, Ballykelly,
Limavady, County Londonderry
BT49 9PB
Tel: (01504) 762462
Head: Mrs L Wilson
Type: Co-educational Day 3–19
No of pupils: B22 G13
Special Needs: AUT CP DEL DYS EBD
EPI HI PH PMLD SLD SP&LD VIS W

GLENSIDE SCHOOL

45a Derry Road, Strabane, County
Tyrone BT82 8DY
Tel: (01504) 883319
Head: Ms C McCauley
Type: Co-educational Day 3–19
No of pupils: B21 G20
Special Needs: AUT CP DEL DOW
EBD EPI HI PH PMLD SLD SP&LD
SPLD VIS W

HEATHERBANK SCHOOL

17 Deverney Road, Omagh, County
Tyrone BT79 0ND
Tel: (01662) 249182
Head: Mr H McAteer
Type: Co-educational Day 4–19
No of pupils: 140
Special Needs: MLD

LIMEGROVE SCHOOL

2 Ballyquin Road, Limavady, County
Londonderry BT49 9ET
Tel: (028) 7776 2351
Head: Ms C O' Neil
Type: Co-educational Day 3–16
No of pupils: B70 G22
Special Needs: MLD

SCOTLAND

ABERDEENSHIRE

Aberdeen City Education Authority

Summerhill Education Centre
Stronsay Drive
Aberdeen AB15 6JA
Tel: (01224) 522000

ABERDEEN SCHOOL FOR THE DEAF

Regent Walk, Aberdeen,
Aberdeenshire AB24 1SX
Tel: (01224) 480303
Head: Mrs M Falconer
Type: Co-educational Day 2–12
No of pupils: B10 G8
Special Needs: HI SP&LD W

BEECHWOOD SCHOOL

Raeden Park Road, Aberdeen,
Aberdeenshire AB15 5PD
Tel: (01224) 323405
Head: Mr A Young
Type: Co-educational Day 5–18
No of pupils: 145
Special Needs: MLD SLD SP&LD W

CORDYCE RESIDENTIAL SCHOOL

Riverview Drive, Dyce, Aberdeen,
Aberdeenshire AB2 0NF
Tel: (01224) 724215
Head: Mr N Brown
No of pupils: 42
Special Needs: EBD

HAZLEWOOD SCHOOL

Fernielea Road, Aberdeen,
Aberdeenshire AB15 6JU
Tel: (01224) 321363
Head: Mrs R Jarvis
Type: Co-educational Day 4–18
No of pupils: 80
Special Needs: MLD PMLD SLD

LOIRSTON PRIMARY S.E.N BASE

Loirston Avenue, Cove Bay,
Aberdeen AB12 3HE
Tel: (01224) 897686
Head: Miss H Jamieson
Type: Co-educational
No of pupils: B6 G1
Special Needs: ADD ADHD CP DOW
DYS EPI HI MLD PH SLD SP&LD
SPLD W

MARLPOOL SCHOOL

Cloverfield Gardens, Bucksburn,
Aberdeen, Aberdeenshire AB2 9BE
Tel: (01224) 712735
Head: Mrs M Taylor
Special Needs: ADD ADHD ASP AUT
CP DEL DOW DYS EBD EPI HI MLD
PH PMLD SLD SP&LD TOU W

PITFODELS SCHOOL

North Deeside Road, Cults,
Aberdeen, Aberdeenshire AB15 9PN
Tel: (01224) 868480
Head: Mrs R Jarvis
Type: Co-educational Day 4–18
No of pupils: B10 G12
Special Needs: AUT CP EPI PMLD
SLD W

SEATON SCHOOL

Seaton Place East, Aberdeen,
Aberdeenshire AB2 1XE
Tel: (01224) 483414
Head: Ms C Harkess
Type: Co-educational Day
No of pupils: B6 G4
Special Needs: MLD SLD

SUNNYBANK HEARING IMPAIRED UNIT SCHOOL

Sunnybank Road, Aberdeen,
Aberdeenshire
Tel: (01224) 633363
Head: Mr A Mead
Type: Co-educational Day 3–11
No of pupils: 9
Special Needs: HI

WOODLANDS SCHOOL

Craigton Road, Cults, Aberdeen,
Aberdeenshire AB15 9PR
Tel: (01224) 868814
Head: Mr M Johnston
Type: Co-educational Day
No of pupils: 55
Special Needs: PMLD W

Aberdeenshire Education Authority

Woodhill House
Westburn Road
Aberdeen AB16 5GJ
Tel: (01224) 664630

CARRONHILL SCHOOL

Mill of Forest Road, Stonehaven,
Kincardineshire AB59 2GZ
Tel: (01569) 763886
Head: Mrs L Hawksfield
Type: Co-educational Day 5–17
No of pupils: B32 G15
Special Needs: AUT MLD PMLD SLD

CENTRAL PRIMARY SCHOOL

St Peter Street, Peterhead,
Aberdeenshire AB42 6QD
Tel: (01779) 72211
Head: Mr S Paul
Type: Co-educational Day
No of pupils: B7
Special Needs: SP&LD

CRIMOND SCHOOL

Logie Road, Crimond, Fraserburgh,
Aberdeenshire AB43 8QL
Tel: (01346) 532251
Head: Mrs H Ross
Type: Co-educational Day
No of pupils: 6
Special Needs: DYS

DALES PARK SCHOOL

Berryden Road, Peterhead,
Aberdeenshire AB42 6GD
Tel: (01779) 477133
Head: Miss D Mair
Type: Co-educational Day
No of pupils: B154 G131
Special Needs: HI SP&LD VIS W

ELLON PRIMARY SCHOOL

SEN Base, Modley Place, Ellon,
Aberdeenshire AB41 9BB
Tel: (01358) 720692
Head: Mrs J Buchan
Type: Co-educational Day
No of pupils: B10 G14
Special Needs: AUT CP DOW EBD
EPI MLD PMLD SLD SP&LD VIS W

KEMNAY ACADEMY
Bremner Way, Kemnay, Inverurie,
Aberdeenshire AB51 5FW
Tel: (01467) 643535
Type: Co-educational Day
No of pupils: 550
Special Needs: ADD ASP AUT CP DEL
DOW DYC DYP DYS EBD EPI HI
MLD PH SP&LD SPLD TOU VIS W

RAMSAY SCHOOL
Walker Avenue, Banff,
Aberdeenshire AB45 1AQ
Tel: (01261) 812598
Head: Mrs M Forsyth
Type: Co-educational Day 2–18
No of pupils: 45
Special Needs: ASP AUT CP DEL
DOW DYP DYS EBD EPI HI MLD PH
PMLD SLD SP&LD SPLD VIS W

ST ANDREW'S SCHOOL
St Andrew's Gardens, Inverurie,
Aberdeenshire AB51 3XT
Tel: (01467) 621215
Head: Mrs J Burnett
Type: Co-educational Day 3–16
No of pupils: 100
Special Needs: AUT CP EBD EPI HI
MLD PH PMLD SLD SP&LD VIS

THE STEVENSON CENTRE
Victoria Street, Fraserburgh,
Aberdeenshire AB43 9PJ
Head: Ms J A Kinnon
Type: Co-educational Day
No of pupils: B10 G8
Special Needs: ADD ADHD DYS **EBD**
EPI W

WESTFIELD SCHOOL
Argyll Road, Fraserburgh,
Aberdeenshire AB43 9BL
Tel: (01346) 28699
Head: Mr J Anderson
Type: Co-educational Day
No of pupils: B44 G16
Special Needs: AUT CP DEL DOW
DYS EBD EBD EPI HI MLD PH PMLD
SLD SP&LD VIS W

ARGYLL AND BUTE

Argyll and Bute Education Authority

Argyll House
Alexandra Parade
Dunoon
Argyll PA23 8AJ
Tel: (01369) 704000

BOWMER PRIMARY SCHOOL
Flora Street, Bowmore, Isle of Islay,
Argyll and Bute PA43 7JX
Tel: (01496) 810522
Head: Mr F MacDougall
Type: Co-educational Day
No of pupils: B1
Special Needs: AUT DYS EPI PMLD W

PARKLANDS SCHOOL
27 Charlotte Street, Helensburgh,
Argyll and Bute G84 7EZ
Tel: (01436) 673714
Head: Mrs L Downie
Type: Co-educational Day 5–18
No of pupils: 32
Special Needs: ASP AUT DOW MLD
PMLD SLD W

EAST AYRSHIRE

East Ayrshire Education Authority

Council Headquarters
London Road
Kilmarnock KA3 7BU
Tel: (01563) 576017

CROSSHOUSE COMMUNICATION CENTRE
Crosshouse Primary School,
Playingfield Road, Crosshouse,
Kilmarnock, KA2 0JJ
Tel: (01563) 521459
Head: Mr R Finleyson
Type: Co-educational Day 5–9
Special Needs: AUT SP&LD

HILLSIDE SCHOOL
Dalgleish Avenue, Cumnock, East
Ayrshire KA18 1QQ
Tel: (01290) 423239
Head: Mr M McCaffrey
Type: Co-educational Day 3–18
No of pupils: B20 G14
Special Needs: AUT CP DOW DYP
PMLD SLD W

PARK SCHOOL
Grassyards Road, Kilmarnock, East
Ayrshire KA3 7BB
Tel: (01563) 25316
Head: Mr G M Donnell
Special Needs: AUT CP DOW DYP
EBD EPI MLD PH SP&LD W

WITCHHILL SCHOOL
Witch Road, Kilmarnock, East
Ayrshire KA3 1JF
Tel: (01563) 33863
Head: Mrs N Lauchlan
Type: Co-educational Day
No of pupils: 20
Special Needs: **PMLD** W

WOODSTOCK SCHOOL
30 North Hamilton Street,
Kilmarnock, East Ayrshire KA1 2QJ
Tel: (01563) 533550
Head: Mrs L MacPhee
Type: Co-educational 5–18
No of pupils: B21 G9
Special Needs: **SLD** W

NORTH AYRSHIRE

North Ayrshire Education Authority

Department of Education
4th Floor, Cunninghame House
Irvine
Ayrshire KA12 8EE
Tel: (01294) 324400

JAMES MACFARLANE SCHOOL
Dalry Road, Ardrossan, North Ayrshire KA22 7DQ
Tel: (01294) 61370
Head: Mrs J Calvert
Type: Co-educational Day 2–18
No of pupils: 35
Special Needs: AUT CP EPI PH PMLD SLD W

JAMES REID SCHOOL
Primrose Place, Saltcoats, North Ayrshire KA21 6LH
Tel: (01294) 67105
Head: Mrs V Balatine
Type: Co-educational Day 5–18
No of pupils: 55
Special Needs: **ADD** ADHD ASP AUT CP DEL DOW DYP DYS **EBD** EPI HI **MLD** PH SP&LD SPLD VIS W

SOUTH AYRSHIRE

South Ayrshire Education Authority

Educational Services
County Buildings
Wellington Square
Ayr
Ayrshire KA7 1DR
Tel: (01292) 612201

CRAIGPARK SCHOOL
Belmont Avenue, Ayr, South Ayrshire KA7 2ND
Tel: (01292) 288982
Head: Miss L Stoddart
Type: Co-educational Day 2–19
No of pupils: B13 G10
Special Needs: CP DOW EPI **PMLD** VIS W

ROSEBANK SCHOOL
Belmont Avenue, Ayr, South Ayrshire KA7 2NA
Tel: (01292) 269422
Head: Ms M Muir
Type: Co-educational Day 5–11
No of pupils: B28 G5
Special Needs: AUT CP **DOW DYP** EBD EPI HI **MLD** PH SP&LD VIS W

CLACKMANNANSHIRE

Clackmannanshire Education Authority

Lime Tree House
Alloa FK10 1EX
Tel: (01259) 450000

CLACKMANNANSHIRE SECONDARY SCHOOL SUPPORT SERVICE
South School, Bedford Place, Alloa, Clackmannanshire FK10 1LJ
Tel: (01259) 724345
Head: Mr S Barrett
Type: Co-educational Day
No of pupils: 30
Special Needs: EBD

FAIRFIELD SCHOOL
Pompee Road, Sauchie, Alloa, Clackmannanshire FK10 3BX
Tel: (01259) 721660
Head: Mrs A H Morgan
Type: Co-educational
No of pupils: B13 G6
Special Needs: **SLD** W

LOCHIES SCHOOL
Gartmorn Road, Sauchie, Clackmannanshire FK10 3PB
Tel: (01259) 216928
Head: Mrs A H Morgan
Type: Co-educational Day 5–12
No of pupils: B24 G12
Special Needs: ADHD ASP AUT CP DOW **MLD** SLD SP&LD W

DUMFRIES AND GALLOWAY

Dumfries and Galloway Education Authority

30 Edinburgh Road
Dumfries
Dumfries & Galloway DG1 1NW
Tel: (01387) 260419

CALSIDE SCHOOL
Calside Road, Dumfries, Dumfries &
Galloway DG1 4HB
Tel: (01387) 68567
Head: Mr C R Ferguson
Type: Co-educational Day 5–12
No of pupils: 353
Special Needs: ASP AUT DOW MLD
SP&LD

ELM BANK SCHOOL
Lovers Walk, Dumfries, Dumfries &
Galloway DG1 1DP
Tel: (01387) 254438
Head: Mr W Maxwell
Type: Co-educational Day 12–16
No of pupils: B16 G4
Special Needs: **EBD** MLD SPLD

LANGLANDS SCHOOL
Loreburn Park, Dumfries, Dumfries
& Galloway DG1 1LS
Tel: (01387) 267834
Head: Mrs E Rae
Type: Co-educational Day 5–18
No of pupils: B11 G13
Special Needs: AUT CP PMLD SLD W

LOCHSIDE SCHOOL
Lochside Road, Dumfries, Dumfries
& Galloway DG2 0NF
Tel: (01387) 720318
Head: Ms M Farrell
Type: Co-educational Day
No of pupils: B186 G194
Special Needs: ADHD AUT CP DOW
DYP DYS EBD HI MLD PH SP&LD
SPLD VIS W

PENNINGHAME SCHOOL
Learning Centre, Auchendoon Road,
Newton Stewart, Dumfries &
Galloway DG8 6HD
Tel: (01671) 402386
Type: Co-educational Day 5–11
No of pupils: 6
Special Needs: **MLD**

STRANRAER ACADEMY
McMaster's Road, Stranraer,
Dumfries & Galloway DG9 8BW
Tel: (01776) 706484
Type: Co-educational Day
No of pupils: B569 G579
Special Needs: **ADHD ASP** CP DEL
DOW DYP DYS EBD EPI HI MLD PH
PMLD SLD SP&LD VIS W

EAST DUNBARTONSHIRE

East Dunbartonshire Education Authority

Education Department
Boclair House
100 Milngavie Road
Bearsden
Glasgow G61 2TQ
Tel: (0141) 578 8707

CAMPSIE VIEW SCHOOL
Boghead Road, Lenzie, East
Dunbartonshire G66 4DR
Tel: (0141) 777 6269
Head: Mrs C P Bowie
Type: Co-educational Day
No of pupils: B31 G25
Special Needs: **AUT** CP DOW EPI PH
PMLD SLD SP&LD VIS W

MERKLAND SCHOOL
Langmuir Road, Kirkintilloch, East
Dunbartonshire G66 2QF
Tel: (0141) 776 3454
Head: Mr J Simmons
Type: Co-educational Day 3–19
No of pupils: B54 G40
Special Needs: **MLD** W

WEST DUNBARTONSHIRE

West Dunbartonshire Education Authority

Garshake Road
Dunbarton G82 3PU
Tel: (01389) 737309

CUNARD SCHOOL
Whitecrook, Cochno Street,
Clydebank, West Dunbartonshire
G81 1RQ
Tel: (0141) 952 6614
Head: Mrs E Divers
Type: Co-educational Day 6–12
No of pupils: 27
Special Needs: **EBD**

KILPATRIC SCHOOL
Mountblow Road, Dalmuir,
Clydebank, West Dunbartonshire
G81 4SW
Tel: (01389) 872171
Head: Ms M Radcliffe
Type: Co-educational Day
No of pupils: B60 G30
Special Needs: MLD PMLD SLD W

MOUNT BLOW SCHOOL
Mountblow Road, Dalmuir,
Clydebank, West Dunbartonshire
G81 4SW
Tel: (01389) 72168
Head: Mrs G Shaw
Type: Co-educational Day 5–19
No of pupils: B30 G14
Special Needs: PMLD SLD SP&LD W

DUNDEE

Dundee Education Authority

Education Department
Tayside House
Dundee DD1 3RJ
Tel: (01382) 434000

KINGSPARK SCHOOL
Gillburn Road, Dundee DD3 0AB
Tel: (01382) 436284
Head: Mr S H Johnston
Type: Co-educational Day 5–18
No of pupils: B91 G74
Special Needs: AUT CP EPI MLD PH
PMLD SLD SP&LD W

EDINBURGH

Edinburgh Education Authority

Wellington Court
8–10 Waterloo Place
Edinburgh EH1 3BY
Tel: (0131) 469 3000

CAIRNPARK SCHOOL
Redhall House Drive, Edinburgh
EH14 1JE
Tel: (0131) 443 0903
Head: Mrs H Heslop
Type: Co-educational Day 14–16
No of pupils: 35
Special Needs: **EBD**

CANNONMILLS SCHOOL
Rodney Street, Edinburgh, Lothian
EH7 4EL
Tel: (0131) 556 6000
Head: Ms M Wilson
Type: Co-educational Day 12–16
No of pupils: B41 G13
Special Needs: **EBD**

DONALDSON'S COLLEGE FOR THE DEAF
West Coates, Edinburgh, Lothian
EH12 5JJ
Tel: (0131) 337 9911
Head: Mrs J L Allan
Type: Co-educational Boarding and Day 3–19
No of pupils: B40 G25
No of Boarders: W20
Special Needs: **HI** SP&LD W

DRYLAW SPECIAL SCHOOL
Easter Drylaw Drive, Edinburgh,
Lothian EH4 2RY
Tel: (0131) 343 6116
Head: Mrs J Perry
Type: Co-educational Day 5–12
No of pupils: B54 G6
Special Needs: **EBD** W

GRAYSMILL SCHOOL
1 Redhall House Drive, Edinburgh,
Lothian EH14 1JE
Tel: (0131) 443 8096
Head: Mr I H Elfick
Type: Co-educational Day 3–18
No of pupils: B45 G40
Special Needs: **PH** W

KAIMES SPECIAL SCHOOL
140 Lasswade Road, Edinburgh,
Lothian EH16 6RT
Tel: (0131) 664 8241
Head: Mrs C Mumford
Type: Co-educational Day 5–18
No of pupils: B70 G13
Special Needs: **ASP AUT** DYS EBD
SP&LD W

KINGSINCH SPECIAL SCHOOL
233 Gilmerton Road, Edinburgh,
Lothian EH16 5UD
Tel: (0131) 664 1911
Head: Mrs M Price
Type: Co-educational Day 5–18
No of pupils: 106
Special Needs: ADHD AUT DOW
MLD SP&LD SPLD

OAKLANDS SPECIAL SCHOOL
Broomhouse Crescent, Edinburgh,
Lothian EH11 3UB
Tel: (0131) 455 7311
Head: Mrs S Harland
Type: Co-educational Day 5–18
No of pupils: 33
Special Needs: **PMLD**
52–week care

PIERSHILL SPECIAL SCHOOL
70 Willowbrae Road, Edinburgh,
Lothian EH8 7HA
Tel: (0131) 661 1488
Head: Mr E Simpson
Type: Co-educational Day 8–12
No of pupils: B24
Special Needs: **EBD** W

PILRIG PARK SCHOOL
Balfour Place, Edinburgh, Lothian
EH6 5DW
Tel: (0131) 467 7960
Head: Mrs J H Mudie
Type: Co-educational Day 11–18
No of pupils: 80
Special Needs: ADD ADHD CP DOW
DYP DYS EBD EPI HI **MLD** SP&LD

PROSPECT BANK
81 Restalrig Road, Edinburgh,
Lothian EH6 8BQ
Tel: (0131) 553 2239
Head: Mrs M E Donaldson
Type: Co-educational Day 5–12
No of pupils: B35 G25
Special Needs: **MLD** SP&LD

ST CRISPIN'S SCHOOL
Watertoun Road, Edinburgh
EH9 3HZ
Tel: (0131) 667 4831
Head: Mr S Pinkerton
Type: Co-educational Day 5–18
No of pupils: B51 G18
Special Needs: **AUT** CP DOW EBD
EPI PH **SLD** SP&LD W

ST NICHOLAS SPECIAL SCHOOL
Gorgie Road, Edinburgh, Lothian
EH11 2RG
Tel: (0131) 337 6077
Head: Mrs C McLaren
Type: Co-educational Day
No of pupils: B49 G31
Special Needs: **MLD**

WILLOWPARK SPECIAL SCHOOL
Gorgie Road, Edinburgh, Lothian
EH11 2RG
Tel: (0131) 337 1622
Head: Mr D J Strathdee
Type: Co-educational Day 5–17
No of pupils: 84
Special Needs: DYP EPI PH SP&LD
SPLD

FIFE

Fife Education Authority

Council Headquarters
Fife House
North Street
Glenrothes
Fife KY7 5LT
Tel: (01592) 414141

BALWEARIE HIGH SCHOOL
Department of Special Education,
Balwearie Gardens, Kirkcaldy, Fife
KY2 5LX
Tel: (01592) 412262
Head: Mrs L McMurchie
Type: Co-educational Day 5–16
No of pupils: B60 G35
Special Needs: **MLD** SLD SP&LD

BENARTY PRIMARY SCHOOL
Lochleven Road, Lochure, Lochgelly,
Fife KY5 8HU
Tel: (01592) 414375
Head: Miss A S Howitt
Type: Co-educational Day
No of pupils: 520
Special Needs: **MLD**

HEADWELL SPECIAL SCHOOL
Headwell Avenue, Dunfermline, Fife
KY12 0JU
Tel: (01383) 721589
Head: Mrs G Franklin
Type: Co-educational 5–18
No of pupils: B23 G11
Special Needs: AUT EBD EPI HI SLD
SP&LD VIS

HYNDHEAD SCHOOL
Barncraig Street, Buckhaven, Leven,
Fife KY8 1JE
Tel: (01592) 414499
Head: Mrs M Bendex
Type: Co-educational Day 3–19
No of pupils: B14 G9
Special Needs: PMLD SLD W

JOHN FERGUS SCHOOL
Erskine Place, Glenrothes, Fife
KY7 4EF
Tel: (01592) 415335
Head: Mrs M A Sankey
Type: Co-educational Day
No of pupils: B12 G4
Special Needs: ADD ASP AUT CP
DOW EBD EPI HI PH PMLD SLD
VIS W

KILMARON SPECIAL SCHOOL
Balgarvie Road, Cupar, Fife
KY15 4PE
Tel: (01334) 53125
Head: Ms W Lawson
Type: Co-educational
Special Needs: ASP DOW PMLD
SLD W

LOCHGELLY HIGH SCHOOL
Department of Special Education,
Station Road, Lochgelly, Fife
KY5 8LZ
Tel: (01592) 418000
Head: Ms S Auras
Type: Co-educational Day
No of pupils: B20 G24
Special Needs: ADD ADHD AUT CP
DEL DYP DYS EBD EPI **MLD** SLD
SPLD W

LOCHGELLY NORTH SPECIAL SCHOOL
McGregor Avenue, Lochgelly, Fife
KY5 9PE
Tel: (01592) 418110
Head: Mrs H Farmer
Type: Co-educational Day 4–19
No of pupils: 22
Special Needs: MLD PMLD SLD W

LUMPHINNANS PRIMARY SCHOOL
Main Street, Lumphinnans,
Cowdenbeath, Fife KY4 9HG
Tel: (01383) 511360
Head: Mr H J Hamilton
Type: Co-educational Day
Special Needs: EBD W

MELVILLE HOUSE SPECIAL SCHOOL
Monimail, Cupar, Fife KY7 7RJ
Tel: (0133) 7810343
Head: Mr J Cocker
Type: Boys Boarding and Day 12–16
No of pupils: 40 *No of Boarders:* W24
Special Needs: **EBD**

OVENSTONE SCHOOL
Pittenweem, Anstruther, Fife
KY10 2RR
Tel: (01333) 311330
Head: Mr G McDonnell
Type: Boys Day
No of pupils: 11
Special Needs: ADD ADHD ASP EBD
SPLD

ROBERT HENRYSON SCHOOL
Linburn Road, Dunfermline Road,
Fife KY11 4LD
Tel: (01383) 728004
Head: Ms M Lorimer
Type: Co-educational Day 2–19
No of pupils: B25 G26
Special Needs: AUT CP EPI PMLD
SLD VIS W

FALKIRK

Falkirk Education Authority
Education Services
McLaren House
Polmont
Falkirk
Stirlingshire FK2 0NZ
Tel: (01324) 506600

CARRONGRANGE SCHOOL
Corrongrange Avenue,
Stenhousemuir, Larbert, Falkirk
FK5 3BH
Tel: (01324) 555266
Head: Mr K O'Hagan
Type: Co-educational Day 5–18
No of pupils: 250
Special Needs: **MLD**

MORAY DAY UNIT
Moray Place, Grangemouth, Falkirk
FK3 9DL
Tel: (01324) 474884
Head: Mr D G Bell
Type: Co-educational Day
Special Needs: **EBD**

ROSSVAIL SCHOOL
108 Glasgow Road, Camelon,
Falkirk FK1 4HS
Tel: (01324) 508660
Head: Mrs H Fitzpatrick
Type: Co-educational Day
No of pupils: B17 G10
Special Needs: PMLD SLD W

TORWOOD SCHOOL
Stirling Road, Larbert, Falkirk
FK5 4SR
Tel: (01324) 503970
Head: Ms J Stewart
Type: Co-educational Day 0–12
No of pupils: B13 G12
Special Needs: AUT CP DEL DOW
EPI PH SLD SP&LD W

WEEDINGSHALL EDUCATION UNIT
Polmont, Falkirk FK2 0XS
Tel: (01324) 506770
Head: Mrs M Kydd
Type: Co-educational Day 12–16
No of pupils: 30
Special Needs: **EBD**

WINDSOR PARK SCHOOL
Bantaskine Road, Falkirk FK1 5HT
Tel: (01324) 508640
Head: Mrs C Finestone
Type: Co-educational Day 4–18
No of pupils: B8 G10
Special Needs: **HI** VIS

GLASGOW

Glasgow City Education Authority
Education Department
Nye Bevan House
20 India Street
Glasgow G2 4PF
Tel: (0141) 287 2000

ABERCORN SCHOOL
195 Garscube Road, Glasgow
G4 9QH
Tel: (0141) 332 6212
Head: Mrs P Smith
Type: Co-educational Day 11–18
No of pupils: B98 G34
Special Needs: **MLD** W

ASHCRAIG SCHOOL
100 Avenue End Road, Glasgow
G33 3SW
Tel: (0141) 774 3428
Head: Ms M McGeever
Type: Co-educational Day 12–19
No of pupils: B91 G53
Special Needs: CP EPI PH VIS W

BROOMLEA SCHOOL
168 Broomhill Drive, Glasgow
G11 7NH
Tel: (0141) 339 6494
Head: Mrs L Rankin
Type: Co-educational Day 2–12
No of pupils: 36
Special Needs: **PMLD**

CARTVALE SCHOOL
80 Vicarfield Street, Glasgow
G51 2DF
Tel: (0141) 445 5272
Head: Miss M Castle
Type: Boys Day 11–16
No of pupils: 30
Special Needs: **EBD**

CROFTCROIGHN SCHOOL
180 Findochty Street, Glasgow
G33 5EP
Tel: (0141) 774 7777
Head: Mrs W Craig
Type: Co-educational Day 2–11
No of pupils: 65
Special Needs: CP DOW EPI **PMLD**
SLD W

DRUMMORE SCHOOL
129 Drummore Road, Glasgow
G15 7NH
Tel: (0141) 944 1323
Head: Mrs M Wallace
Type: Co-educational Day 5–12
No of pupils: 68
Special Needs: **MLD**

EASTMUIR SCHOOL
211 Hallhill Road, Glasgow G33 4QL
Tel: (0141) 771 3464
Head: Mrs A Conway
Type: Co-educational Day 4–11
No of pupils: B50 G20
Special Needs: DYC DYP DYS **MLD**

GADBURN SCHOOL
70 Rockfield Road, Glasgow
G21 3DZ
Tel: (0141) 558 5373
Head: Mr G Hercus
Type: Co-educational Day 5–12
No of pupils: B50 G10
Special Needs: **MLD** W

HAMPDEN SCHOOL
80 Ardnahoe Avenue, Glasgow
G42 0DL
Tel: (0141) 647 7720
Head: Mrs M Cloughley
Type: Day
No of pupils: 35
Special Needs: AUT DOW EPI PMLD
SLD SP&LD W

HOLLYBROOK SCHOOL
135 Hollybrook Street, Glasgow
G42 7HU
Tel: (0141) 423 5937
Head: Mrs M Horn
Type: Co-educational Day 12–19
No of pupils: 128
Special Needs: **MLD**

HOWFORD SCHOOL
487 Crookston Road, Pollok,
Glasgow, Strathclyde G53 7TX
Tel: (0141) 882 2605
Head: Mrs M Barwell
Type: Co-educational Day
No of pupils: B42 G36
Special Needs: AUT **MLD** W

KELBOURNE SCHOOL
109 Hotspur Street, Glasgow
G20 8LH
Tel: (0141) 946 1405
Head: Mrs M McIntosh
Type: Co-educational Day 2–12
No of pupils: B25 G27
Special Needs: CP EPI MLD **PH**
SP&LD SPLD VIS W

KENNYHILL SCHOOL
375 Cumbernauld Road, Glasgow
G31 3LP
Tel: (0141) 554 2765
Head: Miss I Orr
Type: Co-educational Day
No of pupils: 120
Special Needs: **MLD**

LINBURN SCHOOL
77 Linburn Road, Penilee, Glasgow
G52 4EX
Tel: (0141) 883 2082
Head: Mrs M Hardie
Type: Co-educational Day 12–18
No of pupils: B28 G16
Special Needs: PMLD SLD W

MIDDLEFIELD SCHOOL
26 Partickhill Road, Glasgow
G11 5BP
Tel: (0141) 334 0159
Head: Mr C Crawford
Type: Co-educational Day and
Boarding 5–16
No of pupils: 24
Special Needs: ASP AUT

NEWHILLS SCHOOL
Newhills Road, Glasgow G33 4HJ
Tel: (0141) 773 1296
Head: Mrs M Mimnagh
Type: Co-educational Day 12–18
No of pupils: B26 G24
Special Needs: PMLD SLD W

RICHMOND PARK SCHOOL
30 Logan Street, Glasgow G5 0HP
Tel: (0141) 429 6095
Head: Mrs M Pollard
Type: Co-educational Day 4–11
No of pupils: 100
Special Needs: CP EPI MLD PH
SP&LD

ST JOAN OF ARC SCHOOL
722 Balmore Road, Glasgow G22 6QS
Tel: (0141) 336 6885
Head: Miss M McCusker
Type: Co educational Day 12–19
No of pupils: B44 G56
Special Needs: **MLD** SPLD

ST KEVIN'S SCHOOL
25 Fountainwell Road, Glasgow
G21 1TN
Tel: (0141) 557 3722
Head: Miss M T Gallagher
Type: Co-educational Day 5–12
No of pupils: 70
Special Needs: **MLD** W

ST OSWALD'S SCHOOL
83 Brunton Street, Glasgow G44 3NF
Tel: (0141) 637 3952
Head: Mr G McDonnell
Type: Co-educational Day
No of pupils: B70 G58
Special Needs: DYS **MLD**

ST RAYMOND'S SCHOOL
384 Drakemire Drive, Glasgow
G45 9SR
Tel: (0141) 634 1551
Head: Mrs E Muchan
Type: Co-educational
No of pupils: B41 G28
Special Needs: ADD ADHD AUT
DOW DYP DYS EBD EPI HI **MLD** PH
SP&LD SPLD W

ST VINCENT'S (TOLLCROSS) SCHOOL
30 Fullarton Avenue, Tollcross,
Glasgow G32 8NJ
Tel: (0141) 778 2254
Head: Mrs A Crilly
No of pupils: 40
Special Needs: HI W

HIGHLAND

Highland Education Authority

Education Service
Glenurquhart Road
Inverness IV3 5NX
Tel: (01463) 702000

DALNEIGH PRIMARY SCHOOL

St Ninian's Drive, Inverness,
Highland IV3 5AU
Tel: (01463) 232636
Head: Mr J Sutherland
Type: Day
No of pupils: 6
Special Needs: SP&LD

DRUMMOND SCHOOL

Drummond Road, Inverness,
Highland IV2 4NZ
Tel: (01463) 233091
Head: Mr M Butler
Type: Co-educational Day 2–19
No of pupils: 122
Special Needs: AUT MLD PMLD
SLD W

ST CLEMENT'S SCHOOL

Old Academy, Dingwall, Highland
IV15 9JZ
Tel: (01349) 63284
Head: Mrs J Livingstone
Type: Co-educational Day 3–19
No of pupils: B21 G14
Special Needs: AUT CP DOW EBD
EPI PMLD SLD SP&LD W

ST DUTHUS SCHOOL

Old Academy, Tain, Highland
IV19 1ED
Tel: (01862) 894407
Head: Mrs M MacKenzie
Type: Co-educational Day 3–19
No of pupils: B9 G5
Special Needs: ASP AUT DOW EBD
PMLD SLD W

THURSO HIGH SCHOOL

Ormlie Road, Thurso, Highland
KW14 7DS
Tel: (01847) 893822
Type: Co-educational Day 11–18
No of pupils: 1000
Special Needs: DYC DYS MLD PMLD
SLD SPLD

INVERCLYDE

Inverclyde Education Authority

105 Dalrymple Street
Greenock
Renfrewshire PA15 1HT
Tel: (01475) 712824

GARVEL SCHOOL

Chester Road, Larkfield, Greenock,
Inverclyde PA16 0TT
Tel: (01475) 635477
Acting Head: Ms C Tulloch
Type: Co-educational Day 2–11
No of pupils: B2 G1
Special Needs: HI

GLENBURN SCHOOL

Inverkip Road, Greenock, Inverclyde
PA16 0QG
Tel: (01475) 715400
Head: Mrs E McGeer
Type: Co-educational Day
No of pupils: B59 G32
Special Needs: MLD SP&LD W

HIGHLANDERS ACADEMY PRIMARY SCHOOL

24 Mount Pleasant Street, Greenock,
Inverclyde PA15 4DP
Tel: (01475) 745121
Head: Mr C McConnachie
Type: Co-educational Day 5–11
No of pupils: 12
Special Needs: SP&LD

LILYBANK SCHOOL

Birkmyre Avenue, Port Glasgow,
Inverclyde PA14 5AN
Tel: (01475) 715703
Head: Ms E Stewart
Type: Co-educational Day
No of pupils: B40 G13
Special Needs: AUT CP DOW EPI
PMLD SLD W

NORTH LANARKSHIRE

North Lanarkshire Education Authority

Department of Education
Municipal Buildings
Kildonan Street
Coatbridge ML5 3BT
Tel: (01236) 812222

DRUMPARK SCHOOL

Coatbridge Road, Bargeddie, North
Lanarkshire G69 7TW
Tel: (01236) 423955
Head: Mrs M Sutherland
Type: Co-educational
No of pupils: B92 G80
Special Needs: ASP DOW MLD SLD
SP&LD W

FIRPARK SCHOOL

Firpark Street, Motherwell, North
Lanarkshire ML1 2PR
Tel: (01698) 251313
Head: Mr J Connelly
Type: Co-educational Day 3–18
No of pupils: 210
Special Needs: AUT CP DOW DYP
DYS EBD EPI HI MLD PH SLD
SP&LD SPLD VIS W

GLENCAIRN PRIMARY SCHOOL
Glencairn Street, Motherwell, North Lanarkshire ML1 1TT
Tel: (01698) 300281
Head: Ms M Johnstone
Type: Day
No of pupils: 29
Special Needs: HI

GLENCRYAN SCHOOL
Greenfaulds Ring Road, Cumbernauld, North Lanarkshire G67 2XJ
Tel: (01236) 724125
Head: Mrs A B Irvine
Type: Co-educational Day 3–18
No of pupils: 142
Special Needs: ADD ASP DEL DOW DYC DYP DYS HI MLD PH SP&LD SPLD TOU VIS W

MAVISBANK SCHOOL
Mitchell Street, Airdrie, North Lanarkshire ML6 0EB
Tel: (01236) 752725
Head: Ms Sally Cunningham
Type: Co-educational 2–19
No of pupils: B18 G15
Special Needs: PMLD W

MOSSKNOWE SCHOOL
Ring Road, Kildrum, Cumbernauld, North Lanarkshire G67 2EL
Tel: (01236) 736904
Head: Mrs J Winnick
Type: Co-educational Day 2–19
No of pupils: B41 G24
Special Needs: AUT CP DOW EPI PH PMLD SPLD TOU VIS W

PENTLAND SCHOOL
Pentland Road, Chryston, North Lanarkshire G69 9DL
Tel: (0141) 779 3351
Head: Mr I Porteous
Type: Co-educational Day
No of pupils: B13 G2
Special Needs: EBD

REDBURN
Mossknowe Building, Kildrum Ring Road, Cumbernauld, North Lanarkshire G67 2EL
Tel: (01236) 736904
Head: Ms M H O'Brien
Type: Co-educational Day 2–19
No of pupils: B34 G18
Special Needs: AUT CP DOW EBD EPI PH PMLD SLD SP&LD VIS W

SCOT CENTRE FOR CHILDREN WITH MOTOR IMPAIRMENTS
1 Craighalbert Way, Cumbernauld, Glasgow G68 0LS
Tel: (01236) 456100
Head: Dr L Jernquist
Type: Co-educational Day 0–8
No of pupils: 40
Special Needs: CP EPI MLD PH W

VIEWPARK SUPPORT CENTRE
Viewpark Community Centre, Old Edinburgh Road, Uddingston, Lanarkshire G71 6HL
Tel: (01698) 811215
Head: Mr V Jack
Type: Co-educational Day
No of pupils: 25
Special Needs: EBD

WILLOWBANK SCHOOL
299 Bank Street, Coatbridge, North Lanarkshire ML5 1EG
Tel: (01236) 421911
Head: Mr V Jack
Type: Co-educational Day 11–17
No of pupils: 55
Special Needs: EBD

SOUTH LANARKSHIRE

South Lanarkshire Education Authority
Council Offices
Almada Street
Hamilton ML3 0AE
Tel: (01698) 454379

CRAIGHEAD SCHOOL
Whistleberry Road, Hamilton, South Lanarkshire ML3 0EG
Tel: (01698) 285678
Head: Mr J McEnaney
Type: Co-educational Day 5–18
No of pupils: B156 G74
Special Needs: ASP AUT DYP MLD PH SLD W

EARLY LEARNING UNIT
Avon School, Carlisle Road, Hamilton, South Lanarkshire ML3 7EW
Tel: (01698) 281228
Head: Mrs C Young
Type: Co-educational Day 3–5
No of pupils: B22 G8
Special Needs: ADD ASP AUT CP DOW EPI HI MLD PH SP&LD VIS W

HAMILTON SCHOOL FOR THE DEAF
Wellhall Road, Hamilton, South Lanarkshire ML3 9UE
Tel: (01698) 286618
Head: Ms J Gorman
Type: Co-educational Day 3–11
No of pupils: B13 G6
Special Needs: HI W

SANDERSON HIGH SCHOOL
High Common Road, St Leonards's, East Kilbride, South Lanarkshire G74 2LX
Tel: (01355) 249073
Head: Ms M McLullich
Type: Co-educational Day 11–18
No of pupils: B34 G19
Special Needs: ADHD ASP AUT CP DOW DYP EPI HI MLD PMLD SLD SP&LD VIS W

UDDINGSTON GRAMMAR SCHOOL
Station Road, Uddingston, Glasgow G71 7BS
Tel: (01698) 327400
Head: Mr D Greenshields
Type: Co-educational Day
No of pupils: B605 G645
Special Needs: SPLD VIS

VICTORIA PARK SCHOOL
Market Road, Carluke, South
Lanarkshire ML8 4BE
Tel: (01555) 750591
Head: Mrs M Constable
Type: Co-educational Day 3–18
No of pupils: 65
Special Needs: AUT CP DOW EBD
EPI PH PMLD SLD SP&LD SPLD
VIS W

WEST MAINS SCHOOL
Logie Park, East Kilbride, South
Lanarkshire G74 4BU
Tel: (01355) 249938
Head: Mrs M Campbell
Type: Co-educational Day 5–9
No of pupils: B14 G5
Special Needs: **SP&LD**

EAST LOTHIAN

**East Lothian Education
Authority**

John Muir House
Haddington
East Lothian EH41 3HA
Tel: (01620) 827361

ST JOSEPH'S SCHOOL
Tranent, East Lothian EH33 1DT
Tel: (01875) 610794
Head: Mr J Taig
Type: Co-educational Boarding and
Day 11–16
Special Needs: EBD MLD

MIDLOTHIAN

**Midlothian Education
Authority**

Fairfield House
8 Lotham Road
Dalkeith
Midlothian EH22 3ZG
Tel: (0131) 270 7500

**GARDEN HOUSE SUPPORT
CENTRE**
Lugton Brae, Dalkeith, Midlothian
EH22 1JX
Tel: (0131) 440 2022
Head: Sister G Keating
Type: Boys Day
No of pupils: 5
Special Needs: **PMLD** W

LUGTON SPECIAL SCHOOL
Lugton Brae, Dalkeith, Midlothian
EH22 1JX
Tel: (0131) 663 7146
Head: Mrs L Walker
Type: Co-educational Day 5–18
No of pupils: B80 G30
Special Needs: **ADD AUT DEL DOW
DYS EBD EPI MLD SLD SP&LD
SPLD** W

WEST LOTHIAN

**West Lothian Education
Authority**

Lindsay House
South Bridge Street
Bathgate
EH48 1TS
Tel: (01506) 776000

BATHGATE ACADEMY
Edinburgh Road, Bathgate, West
Lothian EH48 1LF
Tel: (01506) 653725
Type: Co-educational Day 11–16
No of pupils: B7 G3
Special Needs: **MLD**

MORAYSHIRE

Moray Education Authority

County Offices
High Street
Elgin IV30 1BX
Tel: (01343) 563097

KINLOSS SCHOOL
Burghead Road, Kinloss, Morayshire
IV36 3SX
Tel: (01309) 690376
Head: Mr I Brodie
Type: Co-educational Day
No of pupils: B2 G1
Special Needs: ASP AUT
52–week care

ORKNEY

Orkney Education Authority

Council Offices
Kirkwall
Orkney KW15 1NY
Tel: (01856) 873535

GLAITNESS AURRIDA SPECIAL SCHOOL
Pickaquoy Road, Kirkwall, Orkney
KW15 1RP
Tel: (01856) 870330
Head: Mr T Delaney
Type: Co-educational Day and
Boarding 2–18
No of pupils: B14 G7
Special Needs: MLD PMLD SLD W

PERTH AND KINROSS

Perth and Kinross Education Authority

Blackfriars
Perth PH1 5LU
Tel: (01738) 476200

CHERRYBANK SCHOOL
Viewlands Terrace, Perth, Perth and
Kinross PH2 0LZ
Tel: (01738) 622147
Head: Mr G Hutchison
Type: Co-educational Day
No of pupils: 25
Special Needs: AUT PMLD SLD W

THE GLEBE SCHOOL
Abbey Road, Scone, Perth, Perth and
Kinross PH2 6LW
Tel: (01738) 551493
Head: Mrs N Guthrie
Type: Co-educational Day and
Boarding 10–18
No of pupils: B15 G6
No of Boarders: W12
Special Needs: CP EPI MLD PMLD
SP&LD VIS

ROBERT DOUGLAS MEMORIAL P.S
Spoutwells Road, Scone, Perth, Perth
and Kinross PH2 6RS
Tel: (01738) 551136
Head: Mr D F Campbell
Type: Co-educational Day
No of pupils: B8 G2
Special Needs: AUT

RENFREWSHIRE

Renfrewshire Education Authority

South Building
Cotton Street
Paisley PA1 1LE
Tel: (0141) 8425663

CLIPPENS SCHOOL

Brediland Road, Linwood,
Renfrewshire PA3 3RX
Tel: (01505) 325333
Head: Mrs O Clark
Type: Co-educational Day 5–19
No of pupils: 46
Special Needs: AUT PMLD SLD W

GATESIDE SCHOOL SENSORY IMPAIRMENT SERVICE

Craigelinn Avenue, Paisley,
Renfrewshire PA2 8RH
Tel: (0141) 884 2090
Head: Mrs E Quinn
Type: Co-educational Day 5–18
No of pupils: B65 G56
Special Needs: HI VIS

HUNTERHILL TUTORIAL CENTRE

Cartha Crescent, Paisley,
Renfrewshire PA2 7EL
Tel: (0141) 889 6876
Head: Mrs R Campbell
Type: Boys Day 5–11
No of pupils: 21
Special Needs: ADD ADHD DYS EBD

KERSLAND SCHOOL

Ben Nevis Road, Paisley,
Renfrewshire PA2 7BU
Tel: (0141) 889 8251
Head: Mrs C Jackson
Type: Co-educational Day 5–18
No of pupils: B33 G30
Special Needs: AUT SLD W

SCOTTISH BORDERS

Scottish Borders Education Authority

Education Department
Council Headquarters
Newton St. Boswells
Melrose TD6 0SA
Tel: (01835) 824000

BERWICKSHIRE HIGH SCHOOL SPECIAL UNIT

Duns, Scottish Borders TD11 3QQ
Tel: (01361) 883710
Head: Mr R F Kelly
Type: Co-educational Day
Special Needs: DOW MLD PH SLD SPLD W

COLDSTREAM PRIMARY SCHOOL

Coldstream, Berwickshire, Scottish Borders TD12 4DT
Tel: (01890) 882189
Head: Mr M Kerr
Type: Co-educational Day
No of pupils: B92 G92
Special Needs: SP&LD

EARLSTON PRIMARY SCHOOL

Earlston, Berwickshire, Scottish Borders TD4 6JQ
Tel: (01896) 848851
Head: Mr C Maclean
Type: Co-educational Day
No of pupils: B105 G100
Special Needs: HI W

KELSO HIGH SCHOOL SPECIAL UNIT

Bowmont Street, Kelso, Scottish Borders TD5 7EG
Tel: (01573) 224444
Head: Mr A Johnston
Type: Co-educational Day
Special Needs: ADHD CP DYS EBD EPI MLD SP&LD SPLD

PHILLIPHAUGH COMMUNITY SCHOOL

2 Linglie Road, Selkirk, Scottish Borders TD7 5JJ
Tel: (01750) 21774
Head: Mr S Vannan
Type: Co-educational Day
No of pupils: 18
Special Needs: SP&LD W

WILTON PRIMARY SCHOOL SPECIAL SCHOOL

Wellfield Road, Hawick, Scottish Borders TD9 7EN
Tel: (01450) 272075
Head: Mr I Topping
Type: Co-educational Day 5–13
No of pupils: 27
Special Needs: CP DYS EBD EPI MLD PH PMLD SLD W

STIRLING

Stirling Education Authority

Viewforth
Stirling
Central FK8 2ET
Tel: (01786) 443322

CALLANDER PRIMARY SCHOOL

Bridgend, Callander, Stirling
FK17 8AG
Tel: (01877) 331576
Type: Co-educational Day
No of pupils: B12 G2
Special Needs: ADD AUT DOW DYP DYS EBD MLD SP&LD SPLD

CHARLES BROWN SCHOOL

Fallin Primary School, Lamont Crescent, Fallin, Stirling FK7 7EJ
Tel: (01786) 816756
Head: Mrs J Smith
Type: Co-educational Day
No of pupils: B6 G5
Special Needs: PH W

WESTERN ISLES

Western Isles Education Authority

Stornoway
Isle of Lewis
Western Isles HS1 2BW
Tel: (01851) 703773

STORNOWAY PRIMARY SCHOOL SPECIAL CLASS

Stornoway, Western Isles HS1 2LF
Tel: (01851) 704700
Head: Mrs G L Veals
Type: Co-educational Day
No of pupils: B6 G2
Special Needs: AUT CP DEL DOW EPI PMLD SLD SP&LD W

WALES

ANGLESEY

Isle of Anglesey City Council

Education Department
Fforddd
Glanhfa
Anglesey LL77 7EY
Tel: (01248) 752900

YSGOL Y BONT
The Industrial Estate, Llangefni,
Anglesey LL77 7JA
Tel: (01248) 750151
Head: Mr D Hughes
Type: Co-educational Day 3–19
Special Needs: MLD PMLD SLD

BLAENAY GWENT

Blaenau Gwent County Borough

Victoria House
Victoria Business Park
Victoria
Ebbw Vale NP3 6ER
Tel: (01495) 355347

PEN Y CWM SCHOOL
Beaufort Hill, Ebbw Vale, Gwent
NP3 5OG
Tel: (01495) 304031
Head: Mr R Dickenson
Type: Co-educational Day
No of pupils: B35 G25
Special Needs: PMLD SLD W

BRIDGEND

Bridgend County Borough

Sunnyside
Bridgend CF31 4AR
Tel: (01656) 642643

HERONSBRIDGE SCHOOL
Ewenny Road, Bridgend CF31 3HT
Tel: (01656) 653974
Head: Mr C D Major
Type: Co-educational Boarding and
Day 3–19
No of pupils: B110 G55
No of Boarders: W7
Special Needs: ASP AUT CP DOW EPI
PMLD SLD VIS W

YSGOL BRYN CASTELL
Llangewydd Road, Cefn Glas,
Bridgend CF31 4JP
Tel: (01656) 767517
Head: Mr G Le Page
Type: Co-educational Boarding and
Day 8–16
No of pupils: 187 *No of Boarders:* W26
Special Needs: ADHD ASP **EBD** MLD
SLD SP&LD

YSGOL CEFN GLAS
Llangewydd Road, Bridgend
CF31 4JP
Tel: (01656) 766221
Head: Mrs A R Bolton
Type: Co-educational Day
No of pupils: 158
Special Needs: EBD HI SP&LD SPLD

CAERPHILLY

Caerphilly County Borough

Caerphilly Road
Ystrad Mynach
Hengoed CF82 7EP
Tel: (01443) 864956

TRINITY FIELDS SCHOOL & RESOURCE CENTRE
Caerphilly Road, Ystrad Mynach,
Hengoed, Caerphilly CF82 7XW
Tel: (01443) 866000
Head: Mr M Hughes
Type: Co-educational Day
No of pupils: 133
Special Needs: PMLD SLD

CARDIFF

Cardiff Education Authority

County Hall
Atlantic Wharf
Cardiff CF1 5UW
Tel: (029) 2087 2000

THE COURT SCHOOL
96a Station Road, Llanishen, Cardiff
CF4 5UX
Tel: (029) 2075 2713
Head: Mrs G Unwin
Type: Co-educational Day 5–11
No of pupils: 35
Special Needs: ADD ADHD DYP **EBD**
MLD

GREENHILL SCHOOL
Heol Brynglas, Rhiwbina, Cardiff
CF4 6UJ
Tel: (029) 2069 3786
Head: Mr A R Lewis
Type: Co-educational Day 11–16
No of pupils: B55 G1
Special Needs: EBD

THE HOLLIES SCHOOL
Pentwyn Drive, Pentwyn, Cardiff
CF2 7XG
Tel: (029) 2073 4411
Head: Mrs C M Matthews
Type: Co-educational Day 3–11
No of pupils: 92
Special Needs: ADD ADHD ASP AUT
CP **PH** SP&LD SPLD W

MEADOWBANK SCHOOL
Colwill Road, Gabalfa, Cardiff
CF14 2QQ
Tel: (029) 2061 6018
Head: Mrs C Arthurs
Type: Co-educational Day 5–16
No of pupils: 36
Special Needs: **SP&LD**

RIVERBANK SCHOOL
Vincent Road, Ely, Cardiff CF5 5AQ
Tel: (029) 2056 3860
Head: Mrs G A Evans
Type: Co-educational Day 4–11
No of pupils: 70
Special Needs: ADHD AUT CP DOW
DYP EBD EPI HI **MLD** PH **SLD**
SP&LD

TY GWYN SCHOOL
Ty Gwyn Road, Penylan, Cardiff
CF23 5JG
Tel: (029) 2048 5570
Head: Mr D Dwyer
Type: Co-educational Day 3–19
No of pupils: B41 G41
Special Needs: **PMLD** SLD W

CARMARTHENSHIRE

Carmarthenshire County Council

Education Headquarters
Pibwrlwyd
Carmarthen SA31 2NH
Tel: (01267) 234567

YSGOL HEOL GOFFA
Heol Goffa, Llanelli,
Carmarthenshire SA15 3LS
Tel: (01554) 759465
Head: Mr R A Davies
Type: Co-educational Day 2–19
No of pupils: 73
Special Needs: CP EPI **PMLD** SLD W

CONWY

Conwy County Borough

Government Buildings
Dinerth Road
Colwyn Bay LL28 4UL
Tel: (01492) 575001

CANOLFAN ADDYSG Y GOGARTH

Ffordd Nant y Gamar, Llandudno,
Conwy LL30 1YF
Tel: (01492) 860077
Head: Mr I G Jones
Type: Co-educational Boarding and
Day 3–19
No of pupils: B73 G48
No of Boarders: F17 W11
Special Needs: ADHD ASP AUT CP
DOW EPI HI **MLD PH** PMLD SLD
SP&LD VIS W

CEDAR COURT SCHOOL

65 Victoria Park, Colwyn Bay,
Conwy LL29 7AJ
Tel: (01492) 533199
Head: Mrs P M Stanley
Type: Co-educational Boarding and
Day 11–18
No of pupils: B12 G6
No of Boarders: W12
Special Needs: **EBD**

YSGOL GOGARTH

Nant y Gamar Road, Llandudno,
Conwy LL30 1YF
Tel: (01492) 860077
Head: Mr I G Jones
Type: Co-educational Day and
Boarding
No of pupils: B64 G41
No of Boarders: F26
Special Needs: CP EPI HI MLD PH
SP&LD VIS

YSGOL Y GRAIG

Penrhos Avenue, Colwyn Bay,
Conwy LL29 9HW
Tel: (01492) 516838
Head: Mr J Hewitt
Type: Co-educational Boarding 3–19
Special Needs: AUT CP EBD EPI HI
PH PMLD SLD SP&LD SPLD VIS

DENBIGHSHIRE

Denbighshire Education Authority

Education Department
C/o Phase 4
County Hall
Moldn CH7 6GR
Tel: (01824) 706777

RHUALLT SCHOOL

Rhuallt, St Asaph, Denbighshire
LL18 0TD
Tel: (01745) 583375
Head: Mr D H O Messum
Type: Co-educational Day
No of pupils: B54 G15
Special Needs: **EBD**

YSGOL PLAS BRONDYFFRYN

Ystrad Road, Denbigh, Denbighshire
LL11 4RH
Tel: (01745) 813841
Head: Dr M Toman
Type: Co-educational Boarding and
Day 3–19
No of pupils: B79 G16
No of Boarders: W30
Special Needs: **ASP AUT** EPI SP&LD

YSGOL TIRMORFA

Ffordd Derwen, Rhyl, Denbighshire
LL18 2RN
Tel: (01745) 350388
Head: Mr S Murphy
Type: Co-educational Day 3–19
No of pupils: 175
Special Needs: ADD DOW **EBD** EPI
HI **MLD** PH **SLD** SP&LD VIS W

FLINTSHIRE

Flintshire Education Authority

County Hall
Mold CH7 6ND
Tel: (01352) 704010

YSGOL BELMONT

Windmill Road, Buckley, Flintshire
CH7 3HA
Tel: (01244) 543971/546358
Head: Mr D G Jones
Type: Co-educational Day
No of pupils: B100 G56
Special Needs: CP EPI MLD PH SLD

YSGOL DELYN
Alexandra Road, Mold, Flintshire
CH7 1HJ
Tel: (01352) 755701
Head: Mrs V Newman
Type: Co-educational Day 2–19
No of pupils: 50
Special Needs: ADD ADHD ASP AUT
CP DEL DEL DOW DYP DYS EBD
EPI EPI HI MLD PH PMLD SLD
SP&LD SPLD VIS W

YSGOL Y BRYN
King George Street, Shotton,
Flintshire CH5 1EA
Tel: (01244) 830281
Head: Mrs S A Taylor
Type: Co-educational Day 2–19
No of pupils: B41 G18
Special Needs: AUT PMLD **SLD** W

GWYNEDD

Gwynedd Education Authority

Shirehall Street
Caernarfon LL55 1SH
Tel: (01286) 672255

YSGOL COEDMENAI
Bangor, Gwynedd LL57 2RX
Tel: (01248) 353527
Head: Mr J O Grisdale
Type: Co-educational Boarding 9–16
No of pupils: 45 *No of Boarders:* W23
Special Needs: **EBD**

YSGOL HAFOD LON
Y Ffor, Pwllheli, Gwynedd
Tel: (01766) 810626
Head: Mrs D R Davies
Type: Co-educational Day 4–19
No of pupils: 25
Special Needs: **ADHD AUT CP DOW**
EPI PH **PMLD SLD** SP&LD **SPLD** W

YSGOL PENDALAR
Victoria Road, Caernarfon, Gwynedd
LL55 2RN
Tel: (01286) 672141
Head: Mr E Jones
Type: Co-educational Day 2–19
No of pupils: B40 G25
Special Needs: AUT EPI MLD PMLD
SLD SP&LD SPLD W

MERTHYR TYDFIL

Merthyr Tydfil Education Authority

Education Directorate
Ty Keir Hardie
Riverside Close
Avenue de Clichy
Merthyr Tydfil CF47 8XD
Tel: (01685) 724600

GREENFIELD SPECIAL SCHOOL
Duffryn Road, Pentrebach, Merthyr
Tydfil CF48 4BJ
Tel: (01443) 690468
Head: Mr A Blake
Type: Co-educational Day 2–19
No of pupils: 145
Special Needs: **MLD** PH **PMLD SLD**
SP&LD W

MONMOUTHSHIRE

Monmouthshire County Council

County Hall
Cwmbran NP44 2XH
Tel: (01633) 644487

MOUNTON HOUSE SCHOOL
Pwyllmeyric, Chepstow,
Monmouthshire NP6 6LA
Tel: (01291) 622014
Head: Mr R A Hughes
Special Needs: EBD MLD

NEATH PORT TALBOT

Neath Port Talbot Education Authority

Civic Centre
Port Talbot SA13 1PJ
Tel: (01639) 763298

BRITON FERRY SPECIAL SCHOOL

Ynysmaerdy Road, Briton Ferry,
Neath Port Talbot SA11 2TL
Tel: (01639) 813100
Head: Mrs M Scales
Type: Co-educational Day 2–19
No of pupils: B14 G14
Special Needs: PMLD SLD W

YSGOL HENDRE SPECIAL SCHOOL

Main Road, Bryncoch, Neath, Neath
Port Talbot SA10 7TY
Tel: (01639) 642786
Head: Mr P H Smith
Type: Co-educational Boarding
No of pupils: B70 G20
No of Boarders: W10
Special Needs: ADD ADHD DOW DYS
EBD EPI **MLD** SLD

NEWPORT

Newport Education Authority

Civic Centre
Newport NP9 4UR
Tel: (01633) 232431

WESTFIELD LOWER SCHOOL

Westfield Way, Malpas, Newport
NP9 6EW
Tel: (01633) 855170
Head: Mr E Smith
Type: Co-educational Day 3–13
No of pupils: 54
Special Needs: PMLD SLD

POWYS

Powys City Council

County Hall
Llandrindod Wells
Powys LD1 5LG
Tel: (01597) 826000

BRYNLLYWARCH HALL SCHOOL

Kerry, Newtown, Powys SY16 4PB
Tel: (01686) 670276
Head: Mr D C Williams
Type: Co-educational Boarding and
Day
No of pupils: B31 G15
No of Boarders: W28
Special Needs: ADD ASP EBD MLD

YSGOL CEDEWAIN

Maesyrhandir, Newtown, Powys
SY16 1LH
Tel: (01686) 627454
Head: Mr P A Tudor
Type: Co-educational Day 2–19
No of pupils: 40
Special Needs: PMLD **SLD** SP&LD
VIS W

YSGOL PENMAES

Canal Road, Brecon, Powys LD3 7HL
Tel: (01874) 623508
Head: Mr I Elliott
Type: Co-educational Day 2–19
No of pupils: 46
Special Needs: AUT PMLD SLD W

RHONDDA CYNON TAFF

Rhondda Cynon Taff Education Authority

The Education Centre
Grawen Street
Porth CF39 0BU
Tel: (01443) 687666

PARK LANE SPECIAL SCHOOL

Park Lane, Trecynon, Aberdare,
Rhondda Cynon Taff CF44 8HN
Tel: (01685) 874489
Head: Mr C R Jones
Type: Co-educational
No of pupils: 53
Special Needs: AUT CP DOW EBD
EPI HI PMLD **SLD** SP&LD VIS W

RHONDDA SPECIAL SCHOOL

Brithweunydd Road, Trealaw,
Tonypandy, Rhondda Cynon Taff
CF40 2UH
Tel: (01443) 433046
Head: Mrs H Dando
Type: Co-educational
No of pupils: B47 G21
Special Needs: PMLD SLD W

YSGOL TY COCH

Lansdale Drive, Tonteg, Pontypridd,
Rhondda Cynon Taff CF38 1PG
Tel: (01443) 203471
Head: Mr H Hodges
Type: Co-educational Boarding 3–19
No of pupils: B47 G31
No of Boarders: W11
Special Needs: ASP AUT CP DOW
EBD EPI HI PMLD SLD VIS W

SWANSEA

Swansea City and County Council

County Hall
Swansea SA1 3SN
Tel: (01792) 636000

PENBRYN SPECIAL SCHOOL

Glasbury Road, Morriston, Swansea
SA6 7PA
Tel: (01792) 799064
Head: Mr A Williams
Type: Co-educational Day and
Boarding 4–19
No of pupils: 115 *No of Boarders:* W13
Special Needs: AUT **MLD** SLD

YSGOL CRUG GLAS

Croft Street, Swansea SA1 1QA
Tel: (01792) 652388
Head: Mrs E Jones
Type: Co-educational 2–19
No of pupils: B27 G23
Special Needs: **PMLD** W

TORFAEN

Torfaen County Borough

County Hall
Cwmbran NP44 2WN
Tel: (01633) 648610

CROWNBRIDGE SCHOOL

Greenhill Road, Sebaslopol,
Pontypool, Torfaen NP4 5YW
Tel: (01782) 857030
Head: Mr R Phillips
Type: Co-educational Day 3–19
No of pupils: B47 G28
Special Needs: AUT DOW PMLD SLD
SP&LD W

VALE OF GLAMORGAN

Vale of Glamorgan Education Authority

Education Department
Civic Offices
Holton Road
Barry CF63 4RU
Tel: (01446) 709138

ASHGROVE SCHOOL

Sully Road, Penarth, Vale of Glamorgan CF64 2TP
Tel: (029) 2070 4212
Head: Mr B Brayford
Type: Day and Boarding
No of pupils: 77 No of Boarders: W16
Special Needs: ADD **ASP AUT HI** W

YSGOL ERW'R DELYN

St Cyres Road, Penarth, Vale of Glamorgan CF64 1WR
Tel: (029) 2070 7225
Head: Mr M Farrell
Type: Co-educational Boarding and Day 3–19
No of pupils: 57 No of Boarders: W6
Special Needs: PH PMLD

YSGOL MAES DYFAN

Gibbonsdown Rise, Barry, Vale of Glamorgan CF6 7QZ
Tel: (01446) 732112
Head: Mr J A Aubrey
Type: Co-educational Day
No of pupils: 98
Special Needs: AUT **CP DOW** EPI HI **MLD SLD** VIS W

WREXHAM

Wrexham Education Authority

Education and Leisure Services
Roxburgh House
Hill Street
Wrexham LL11 1SN
Tel: (01978) 297400

ST CHRISTOPHER SCHOOL

Stockwell Grove, Wrexham LL13 7BW
Tel: (01978) 346910
Head: Mrs M P Grant
Type: Co-educational Day
No of pupils: 238
Special Needs: ADD ADHD ASP AUT CP DOW DYP DYS EBD EPI HI MLD PH PMLD SLD SP&LD SPLD VIS W

SPECIAL EDUCATION CENTRE

Park Avenue, Wrexham LL12 7AQ
Tel: (01978) 290101
Head: Mrs P A Pumford
Type: Co-educational Day 3–11
No of pupils: 113
Special Needs: ADD ADHD ASP AUT CP DOW DYP EBD EPI HI MLD PH SP&LD VIS VIS

PART THREE: PROFILES OF SPECIAL SCHOOLS AND COLLEGES

3.1
Profiles of Independent and Non-maintained Special Schools

Annie Lawson School

Ravenswood Village, Nine Mile Ride, Crowthorne, Berkshire RG45 6BQ
Tel: 01344 755508   Fax: 01344 762317
E-mail: lynnemorris@annielawson.org.uk   Website: www.nwrw.org

Founded 1954
Religious denomination Jewish faith, students also welcome from all cultural and ethnical backgrounds
School status DfEE approved independent co-educational boarding and day
Special needs provision PMLD, SLD
Other needs catered for Complex learning difficulties
Age range 11–19
Boarding from 11
No of pupils 23
Boarders (full) 20 (some day pupils)

Set in 126 acres of Berkshire countryside, the Annie Lawson School offers freedom of movement within a safe and varied natural environment.

The School aims to meet the needs of students with severe and profound learning difficulties. Many of our students have additional physical disabilities or sensory impairments or have difficulties understanding and managing their own behaviour, which gives rise to problems accessing the wider curriculum.

The Annie Lawson School is committed to meeting the individual needs of students, through a holistic approach, with priority being given to their physical and emotional well-being, communication skills and access to motivating learning experiences. Individual development is the focus of our school. Access to the National Curriculum is supported by a programme of Personal, Social and Health Education (PSHE) which puts an emphasis on individual self-esteem and personal communication.

We aim to make students feel valued by engaging them in interaction at their level, by entering into their world if they are unable or unwilling to enter ours.

Students benefit from a wide range of facilities:

- Three sensory rooms offering activities ranging from relaxation and aromatherapy to choice making and interactive environmental control
- A wide variety of IT equipment, access devices and software to support the curriculum
- Gym, with integral trampoline
- Wheelchair accessible adventure playground
- Access to onsite swimming/hydrotherapy pool and to horse riding and carting

Therapists are an integral part of our team including speech, language, music and physiotherapy.

Aran Hall School

Rhydymain, Dolgellau, Gwynedd LL40 2AR
Tel: 01341 450641   Fax: 01341 450637
E-mail: Mferguson@aranhall.demon.com   Website: www.aranhall.demon.co.uk

Head M Ferguson BEd, DipSpEd
Founded 1980
School status Co-educational independent
boarding
Accredited by DfEE and National Assembly for
Wales
Special needs provision ADD, ADHD, ASP, AUT,
EPI, SLD
Other needs catered for Challenging behaviour
Age range 11–19
Boarding from 11
No of pupils 25
Girls 6   *Boys* 19

Aran Hall benefits from being within the picturesque and relaxing environment of Snowdonia National Park. It is situated within easy reach of the sea, mountains and Bala Lake. Full use is made of all these natural resources in addition to local libraries, leisure centres, riding clubs, shops and cafes to encourage integration within the community.

Individual programmes, based upon each pupil's statement of special educational needs, are implemented consistently within educational and care environments. Each pupil is a member of a small family group with a high staff ratio. There is a homely environment for twenty-five pupils.

The quality of relationships between pupils and staff is central to all our work.

Teachers and care staff work in close partnership to realise individual objectives for each pupil. These individual plans are agreed with the pupil, parents, carers, local education, health and social services departments.

Recent, very positive Ofsted inspection report is available, together with Social Services and Investors in People reports.

Barnardo's

High Close School

Wiltshire Road, Wokingham, Berkshire RG40 1TT
Tel: 0118 978 5767   Fax: 0118 989 4220

Principal Rose Mahony
School status Co-educational non-maintained
boarding and day
Special needs provision EBD, MLD, W
Age range 6–16   *Boarding from* 10
No of pupils 64
Girls 17   *Boys* 47
Fees per annum (boarding) £42,277 *(day)*
£21,138

High Close is a co-educational, non-maintained special school for pupils with emotional, social, behavioural and associated learning difficulties. The school has purpose-built education facilities with four on-site residential units. There are places for 44 boarders (aged 10–16) and 24 day pupils (aged 6–16). There is also a field social work team, which supports families and provides after-care to pupils when they leave at age 16.

Meadows School

London Road, Tunbridge Wells, Kent TN4 0RJ
Tel: 01892 529144   Fax: 01892 527787

Principal Sandy Paterson
Founded 1950
School status Co-educational non-maintained
boarding and day
Special needs provision EBD, MLD, W
Age range 11–16   *Boarding from* 11
No of pupils 46
Girls 10   *Boys* 36
Fees per annum (boarding) £46,000 *(day)*
£23,000

Meadows is a co-educational, non-maintained special school for pupils with social, emotional, behavioural and associated learning difficulties. The school has new purpose-built education facilities with two on-site and two off-site residential units. There are places for 40 boarders and 18 day pupils.

Spring Hill School

Palace Road, Ripon, North Yorkshire HG4 3HN
Tel: 01765 603320

Principal Janet Clarke
Founded 1950
School status Co-educational non-maintained
boarding and day
Special needs provision DEL, DOW, EBD, EPI,
MLD, SLD, W
Other needs catered for AUT, ASP, ADD
Age range 8–19   *Boarding from* 10
No of pupils 31
Girls 10   *Boys* 21
Fees per annum (boarding) £43,000

Spring Hill is a residential co-educational, non-maintained special school for pupils aged 8–19 who have moderate to severe learning difficulties and challenging behaviour. Some pupils have medical, emotional and psychiatric conditions with mild sensory deficits, physical disabilities, autism and specific medical neurological conditions. Accommodation is for 44 pupils in four purpose-built cottages around an administrative and teaching resource block. The post-16 curriculum follows EQUALS, ASDAN, OCR key skills as well as NPTC accreditation in horticulture, catering and retail.

Bessels Leigh School

Bessels Leigh, Abingdon, Oxfordshire OX13 5QB
Tel: 01865 390436   Fax: 01865 390688

Principal Mr J Boulton DipPsych, BEd (Hons), MEd
Founded 1962
Special needs provision ADHD, DYS, EBD, SPLD
School status Boys DfEE registered non-maintained boarding
Religious denomination All
Age range 11–16
No of pupils 38
Fees per annum £41,655 *(38 weeks)*; £71,790 *(52 weeks)*

Curriculum: the school aims to provide a warm, caring and supportive environment so that each boy can develop to his full potential. The school follows a curriculum which is sympathetic to the needs of the boys and is closely allied to the National Curriculum.

Entry requirements: all boys have a specific statement of special educational needs and are generally referred to the school by local education authorities or social service departments.

Examinations offered: GCSE, City and Guilds, AEB Basic Tests and Achievement tests are offered as well as vocational courses including TRIDENT, work experience and Duke of Edinburgh Awards.

Academic and leisure facilities: there are four general-purpose classrooms as well as rooms for art, science, home economics and workshop crafts. A sports hall and swimming pool complement the 23-acre site.

Special approaches: an SPLD department is growing and the school caters for dyslexic children with associated behaviour problems. An increasing number of boys have been diagnosed as being ADD/ADHD.

Birkdale School for Hearing Impaired Children

40 Lancaster Road, Birkdale, Southport, Merseyside PR8 2JY
Tel: 01704 567220   Fax: 01704 568342
E-mail: admin@birkdale-school.merseyside.org   Website: www.birkdale-school.merseyside.org

Principal Mrs Anne Wood BA (Hons)
Founded 1825
Special needs provision ASP, DYS, DYP, HI, MLD. SP&LD
School status Non-maintained co-educational boarding and day
Religious denomination Non-denominational
Member of NASS
Age range 5–19
No of pupils 44
Senior 30   *Sixth Form* 2   *FE dept* 12
Boys 21   *Girls* 23
No of boarders (termly) 4   *(weekly)* 17
Fees per annum on application

Birkdale School for Hearing Impaired Children is a non-maintained school which provides an oral education for primary and secondary aged children who have a moderate, severe or profound hearing-impairment. The school provides a broad and balanced curriculum, giving the pupils the opportunity to achieve excellent results in a wide range of GCSEs, Certificates of Achievement and GNVQ. Students are achieving 100% pass rates at A–G. Pupils are taught by qualified Teachers of the Deaf in acoustically treated classrooms. We also cater for hearing-impaired children who may have additional special needs. The audiological needs of pupils are reviewed regularly in a well-resourced Audiology Department. The Language Department works in conjunction with a Speech and Language Therapist to enhance pupils' language development. Our Further Education Support Service supports post 16 hearing-impaired students in local mainstream colleges of Further Education. Resident pupils are looked after by dedicated Care Officers.

Birtenshaw Hall School

Darwen Road, Bromley Cross, Bolton, Lancashire BL7 9AB
Tel: 01204 304230   Fax: 01204 597995   E-mail: enquiries@birtenshawhall.bolton.sch.uk
Website: www.birtenshawhall.bolton.sch.uk

Principal Mr C D Jamieson
School status Co-educational non-maintained boarding and day
Member of NAIMS, NASS   *Accredited by* DfEE
Special needs provision CP, DEL, EPI, MLD, PH, PMLD, SLD, W
Age range 3–19   *Boarding from* 7
No of pupils (boarding) 22 *(day)* 8
Fees per annum (boarding) (full) £45,000; *(weekly)* £28,258–£33,990; *(day)* £18,654–£23,204

Birtenshaw Hall offers day and residential education for pupils with physical disabilities and associated learning difficulties. Individual programmes provide a full, varied, balanced and relevant curriculum, including access to the National Curriculum, suitably differentiated to meet individual needs.

A high staff/pupil ratio is provided by our multi-disciplinary team of teaching, physiotherapy, occupational therapy, speech and language therapy, nursing and care staff.

Specialist facilities include swimming/hydrotherapy pool, dark room, multi-sensory room, MOVE groups and a wide variety of extra-curricular activities. Our accommodation provides a variety of recreational, dining and bedroom facilities. Some bedrooms are equipped with overhead tracking giving direct access to purpose designed en-suite bathrooms.

Blossom House School

8, The Drive, Wimbledon, London SW20 8TG
Tel: 020 8946 7348   Fax: 020 8944 5848
E-mail: blossom.house@appleonline.net

Principal Mrs J Burgess
School status Co-educational independent day only
Special needs provision SP&LD
Age range 3–12
No of pupils 90
Boys 76   *Girls* 14
Fees per annum £11,475–£11,895

Blossom House is a specialist school in Wimbledon for children (3–12 years) with speech and language problems. Although many of the children have some associated difficulties, such as fine motor problems or poor organisational skills, they are all within the normal range of intelligence. Our aim is that in the course of time as many children as possible will return to a mainstream education.

Blossom House provides an integrated programme of learning in a caring and highly supportive environment with physiotherapy, occupational therapy and music therapy as part of the curriculum. Self-esteem and confidence are crucial to success, so each child is valued as an individual with his or her specific strengths acknowledged and weaknesses supported. A positive behavioural approach encompasses every part of school life.

Breckenbrough School

Thirsk, North Yorkshire YO7 4EN
Tel: 01845 587238   Fax: 01845 587385

Head Mr T G Bennett
Founded 1934
School status DfEE approved independent Boys
boarding and day
Religious denomination Society of Friends
Special needs provision ADD, ADHD, ASP, DEL,
DYS, EBD
Other needs catered for Emotional and
behavioural difficulties
Age range 9–17   *Boarding from* 9
No of pupils 42   *boarding* 16
Fees per annum Available on request

Breckenbrough is a residential special school,
which specialises in the care and education of
boys of high academic potential who have emotional and behavioural difficulties (EBD).

The school has small teaching groups (up to a
maximum of seven) and has enjoyed much
success in achieving very good public examination results and re-socialisation of pupils to
take an equal place in society.

The school has an individual approach to help
each pupil build strong foundations upon
which to base their future. We offer all National
Curriculum subjects and a range of up to 12
different GCSE options.

Brewood Education Centre

86 London Road, Deal, Kent CT14 9TR
Tel: 01304 363000   Fax: 01304 363099

Head Miss Chris Simcox BSc, PGCE
Founded 1995
School status Co-educational independent
Religious denomination Non-denominational
Special needs provision ADD, ADHD, ASP, DYC,
DYP, DYS, EBD, HI, MLD, SP&LD, TOU, VIS
Age range 7–14 (Key stages 2 & 3)
Fees per term from £6,656

The school offers provision for children being
looked after either in residential settings or in
foster care, but we are also willing to consider
other children, for whom mainstream education is not immediately appropriate. The ethos
of the school is that although the children have
been assessed as EBD/MLD, they can achieve

and ultimately be considered for inclusion into
mainstream schools. The school is proud that
several of its pupils have not only been reinte-
grated into mainstream schools but have gone
on to be successful. Emphasis is placed on
praising the success of the individual and therefore promoting self-esteem. Children in the
school experience full National Curriculum
with use of a science laboratory, ICT equipment
and DT studio. The average class size is four or
less and the ratio for staff to pupils is 2:1; in
some instances 1:1 provision is offered. All the
staff are aware of the nature of problems experienced by the children and are able to provide
the therapeutic atmosphere required to achieve
positive outcomes.

Bruern Abbey School

Chesterton, Oxfordshire OX26 1UY
Tel: 01869 242448   Fax: 01869 243949

Head Mr J S Stover
Founded 1996
School status Boys independent boarding and day
Religious denomination Church of England
Special needs provision DYS, DYP, SP&LD
Age range 8–13 Boarding from 8
No of pupils 36   *(weekly boarding/boarding)* 30
Fees per term (boarding/weekly boarding) £4,516
(day) £3,488

An independent day, weekly boarding, and boarding school for boys aged 8–13 with specific learning difficulties. Bruern Abbey is the only preparatory school in the country to have as its main purpose the preparation of dyslexic and dyspraxic boys for Common Entrance and other entrance examinations to mainstream independent senior schools.

During the past two years, pupils have successfully gained entry to a wide number of mainstream senior schools, including Stowe, Bryanston, Wellington, Ampleforth, Shiplake and Milton Abbey. The school is located in 21 acres of wooded countryside near junction 9 of the M40, only an hour from either London or Birmingham and 15 minutes from Oxford.

Centre Academy

92 St John's Hill, Battersea, London SW11 1SH
Tel: 020 7738 2344   Fax: 020 7738 9862
E-mail: ukadmin@centreacademy   Website: www.centreacademy.com

Head Mr F J O'Regan
Founded 1974
School status Independent co-educational day
Accredited by Crested
Religious denomination Non-denominational
Special needs provision DYS
Other needs ADD, ADHD, DYC, DYP, DYS, SP&LD
Age range 8–18
No of pupils 55
Girls 15   *Boys* 30
Junior 10   *Senior* 45
Fees per annum £8,500–£15,000

Centre Academy is a full day school for children with learning difficulties such as dyslexia and ADHD. Our students have normal or above-average intelligence, but they demonstrate specific deficiencies because of problems with motivation, maturing or learning. Whilst teaching them how to overcome their learning difficulties we also teach the standard curriculum so that they can stay abreast of their peers. Older students are preparing for GCSEs or the US High School Graduation Certificate.

Centre Academy is a Category A CReSTeD approved school.

Admission is by evaluation of ability, learning style and achievement levels at the school.

Centre Academy offers the following GCSEs: English, English Literature, Maths, Dual Science, History, Geography, Spanish, IT and Art. American students sit the SAT and PSAT tests.

A complete programme of activities and athletics is offered at the nearby Wandsworth Common and the Latchmere and Battersea Sports Centres.

Chailey Heritage School

Haywards Heath Road, North Chailey, East Sussex BN8 4EF
Tel: 01825 724444   Fax: 01825 723773
E-mail: chailey@pavilion.co.uk   Website: www.chs.org.uk

Head A C Bruce MA
Founded 1903
School status Non-maintained co-educational
boarding and day
Member of NAIMS, NASS
Accredited by DfEE
Special needs provision CP, MLD, PH, SLD,
SP&LD, VIS
Age range 3–19   *Boarding from* 8
No of pupils 99
Fees per annum (boarding) (weekly) £19,080–
£27,081   *(day)* £14,898–£17,898

Chailey Heritage School is a nationally recognised non-maintained residential special school
catering for children of all ages, who have a
wide range of physical and learning difficulties.
The children we cater for may have:

- severe, complex, and multiple physical disabilities
- speech and language impairment
- communication difficulties
- a range of learning difficulties

The provision includes:
- health cover, provided by South Downs
Health (NHS) Trust, working in close conjunction with school staff
- on-site Rehabilitation and Engineering Unit,
making and maintaining special postural
equipment.

The Charmandean Dyslexia Centre

Lillingstone Dayrell, Buckingham MK18 5AN
Tel: 01280 860182

Principal W H Wilcox
Founded 1998
School status Co-educational independent day
Religious denomination Non-denominational
Age range 8–16
Girls 8   *Boys* 40
Fees per annum Tuition fees £5,970

The Charmandean Dyslexia Centre, which opened in September 1998, offers a comprehensive education for pupils aged from 8 to 16 who are held back by Dyslexia and certain other learning difficulties.

Curriculum: All pupils have an Individual Education Plan outlining their needs and targets for each term. Teaching is in small classes with additional periods of intensive specialised tuition directed at overcoming specific difficulties. The main emphasis for the younger children is on English and Mathematics, using a multisensory approach. Science, French (mainly oral), History, Geography, Scripture, Art, Design, Music, Drama, Computing (including keyboard skills) and Study Skills all feature in the curriculum.

The mainstream curriculum is followed wherever possible, but it is presented in ways best suited to individual learning patterns.

Physical education: Pupils are able to take part in a varied programme of Physical Education and Games. In the winter terms the main sports for boys are rugby and football; in the summer term the main sports are cricket and athletics. For girls the winter sports are netball and hockey, with rounders, athletics and tennis in the summer. Charmandean has its own covered and heated swimming pool for use throughout the year. There is a full programme of competitive fixtures with other schools.

Drama and Music: Both Drama and Music are an integral part of the Dyslexia Centre curriculum. In addition, individual tuition can be arranged with our peripatetic teachers on a wide variety of musical instruments.

Computing: Benefiting from an up-to-date facility, the pupils are taught keyboard skills and basic computing. Those pupils for whom a laptop computer is an essential classroom aid are thus able to use it to best advantage.

Mrs Hawkins is the Head Teacher and in charge of organising and supervising the work. Every term there is a more formal parents' evening to review pupils' achievements and a detailed written report is sent home.

Entry is by interview, test and a psychological assessment arranged by the school.

Chelfham Senior School

Bere Alston, Yelverton, Devon PL20 7EX   Tel: 01822 840379   Fax: 01822 841489
Kilworthy House, Tavistock, Devon PL19 0JN   Tel: 01822 618515   Fax: 01822 618703

Principal Ms Julia Marks
School status Boys residential DfEE approved
independent
Religious denomination Multi-faith
Special needs provision ASP, EBD, MLD, TOU
Age range 11–16 (Bere Alston site) 15–19
(Tavistock site)
No of pupils 37 (Bere Alston site) 26 (Tavistock
site)
Fees per annum Individually costed from
£16,000 per term

The students who attend Chelfham Senior
School have a range of emotional and behavioural difficulties with associated learning difficulties. Many of the students will have
experienced failure, disappointment and criticism, resulting in feelings of inadequacy and
poor self-image. They require a sensitive and
supportive environment in which they can gain
confidence and enhance their self-esteem. The
school specialises in working with vulnerable
students exhibiting bizarre and obsessive behaviours and those who have difficulty with
acquiring appropriate social communication
skills.

Some of our young people will also have other
complicating conditions and syndromes, eg,
Asperger's Syndrome, Gilles de la Tourette's
Syndrome and Obsessive Compulsive Disorder.
Others may have experienced deprivation or
abuse. We offer either 38 or 52-week provision,
a broad and balanced 24-hour curriculum
including the National Curriculum for 11–16,
and courses which focus on communication
skills, social competence, and vocational awareness for 15–19. High staff/pupil ratio, individual
bedrooms and a keyworker system. The main
therapeutic approach is the use of positive
behavioural techniques, eg token economy
and individual programmes. Please telephone
for a prospectus. Informal visits welcome.

Cotswold Chine School

Box, Near Stroud, Gloucestershire GL6 9AG
Tel: 01453 837550   Fax: 01453 837555
E-mail: mail@cotswold-chine.org.uk

Head Ms Silla Rieser
Founded 1953
School status Co-educational DfEE approved
independent boarding
Religious denomination Non-denominational
Christian
Special needs provision ADD, ADHD, ASP, AUT,
EBD, EPI, MLD, SLD, SP&LD, SPLD, TOU,
Emotional and behavioural
Age range 10–16 (and exceptionally 8–18
years)   *Boarding from* 10
No of pupils 42
Fees per annum Individual based on pupil need

The school has recently had a successful
OFSTED Inspection. The following statements
are taken from the report: (dated January 2001)

'Teamwork is of a very high standard. The
quality of the residential care is high and the
ethos of the school is distinctive and very positive. The pupils trust and respect adults in the
school and turn to them readily if they need
support. The quality of teaching has improved
greatly since the last inspection: 69% of the
lessons seen were good or very good. This high
quality of teaching is reflected in the good
quality of learning across the school. The
School's procedures for ensuring pupils' welfare
and support are excellent. The pupils are happy
and feel safe and secure: they enjoy the education, the care and the therapies provided.'
The school caters for children who need a high
staff ratio and also pupils with a wide range of
learning difficulties. Specific medical needs can

be catered for. The placements are available for term and holiday time. Respite care is also available.

The school offers a modern approach to Rudolf Steiner curriculum linked to the National Curriculum where appropriate. The children are taught in small groups and all have access to individual tuition in certain areas. The therapeutic curriculum includes pottery, music, horse riding, drama, woodwork, sailing, biking and computer skills. Children are encouraged to develop their full potential through many varied activities with a strong emphasis on arts, crafts and sciences.

Teaching staff meet DfEE requirements and many are Rudolf Steiner trained or experts in their own fields. All pupils study for examinations in numeracy and literacy. The school also offers Certificate of Education and GCSE courses.

The children have eurythmy movement therapy, art and speech therapy. Informal counselling is offered and the school has access to the county's psychiatric advisors.

The houses operate upon the therapeutic guidelines taken from the caring insights of Rudolf Steiner, and are situated on the main school site and in detached houses close by.

The school is set amidst rolling hills and is adjacent to National Trust common land in the heart of the Cotswolds. Parents/carers can visit any time by arrangement. Regular interviews are held where parents/carers and other professionals connected to the child discuss the child's progress with school staff.

Crowthorn School

Broadhead Road, Edgworth, Bolton, Lancashire BL7 0JS
Tel: 01204 852143   Fax: 01204 853682
E-mail: NWCS@mail.nch.org.uk

Director Mr S Forster MBA, Dip-Ed, Cert-Ed, T.Cert
School status Non-maintained co-educational boarding and day
Religious denomination Methodist
Member of NCH   *Accredited by* DfEE registered
Special needs provision EBD, MLD
Age range 8–16   *Boarding from* 8
No of pupils 56
Fees per annum On application

Crowthorn is a residential school for children whose emotional and behavioural problems are exacerbated by moderate learning and communication difficulties.

Pupils reside in five separate houses that are staffed by well-qualified and experienced residential social work staff. We are committed to working towards a fully qualified workforce.

The teaching team has specialist and good quality resources. The Sportsmark Award was achieved for a quality programme of physical education and after-school activities.

The National Curriculum is offered in all academic subjects and Crowthorn offers: Northern Partnership of Records of Achievement, Youth Award School (Asdan), Certificate of Educational Achievement and GCSE's.

The school works within the framework of NCH standards and guidelines, and is committed to high quality of education and care.

Dame Hannah Rogers School

Woodland Road, Ivybridge, Devon PL21 9HQ
Tel: 01752 892461   Fax: 01752 892461
E-mail: dhrs@iname.com   Website: dame-hannah.virtualave.net

Principal Mr W R Evans
Founded 1766
School status Co-educational non-maintained boarding and day
Religious denomination Multi-faith
Member of NAIMS, NASS
Accredited by DfEE (878/7082)
Special needs provision CP, DEL, EPI, MLD, PH, PMLD, SLD, SP&LD, W
Age range 8–19   *Boarding from* 8
No of pupils 47 (boarding) (full) 30 (weekly) 20 (day) 5
Girls 21   *Boys* 34
Fees per annum (boarding) £31,730–£64,955

'Dame Hannah Rogers School is a very good school with some outstanding features . . . and provides very good value for money' (OFSTED, 1997). It was also one of only 19 special schools mentioned by Chris Woodhead, the former Chief Inspector, as worthy of special praise'.

Dame Hannah Rogers School is a recognised centre of excellence meeting the needs of young people with physical disabilities and learning difficulties. Its duty is to ensure that the young people in its care are valued as individuals and treated with dignity and respect. It encourages self-esteem and develops individual's self-dependence in a variety of settings.

Independence training and augmentative communication are, along with therapeutic aims, reinforced throughout each student's waking hours so that skills can become an integral part of each student's life. Independence bungalows enable students in the Further Education department to develop their own quality of life.

Eden Grove School

Bolton, Appleby, Cumbria CA16 6AJ
Tel: 017683 61346   Fax: 017683 61356
E-mail: generalenquiries@eden18.freeserve.co.uk   Website: www.prioryhealthcare.co.uk

Head Mr I G McCready
Founded 1955
School status Boys DfEE approved independent boarding and day
Religious denomination Non-denominational
Member of Priory Services for Young People
Special needs provision ADD, ADHD, ASP, DYS, EBD, MLD, SP&LD, TOU, W
Age range 8–19
Boarding from 8
No of pupils 96
Fees per annum (boarding) (38 week) £32,271; *(51 week)* £43,837; *(day)* £23,642

Eden Grove is situated two miles from the A66 at the edge of a small village called Bolton, in the heart of the Eden Valley. It is two hours from Glasgow, Manchester, Liverpool and Newcastle-upon-Tyne by road via the A66 or the M6. The nearest mainline rail station is Penrith, 20 minutes from the school.

The school offers flexible placement packages to local authorities for young people aged between 8 and 19. Current placement facilities are as follows:

- 51 week placements
- 38 week placements
- day pupil placements
- 16+ placements
- 38 week placements with holiday care
- 1:1 placements

Most of the young people referred to Eden Grove have a Statement of Special Educational Needs which has been prepared by their placing authority. Some also come with the label of having Learning Difficulties. A significant amount of these children are diagnosed as having a 'syndrome' such as Attention Deficit Disorder, Tourettes, Language Delay, Fragile X and Autistic Spectrum Disorder.

The school has a full comprehensive education package which is regularly inspected by OFSTED. The subjects on the curriculum include: English, Maths, Science, History, Geography, Art, IT, Home Economics, PE, Religious and Moral Education, Outdoor Pursuits and Careers. In terms of nationally accredited courses, the school operates the National Curriculum, ASDAN Award Scheme, Certificate of Achievement, CLAIT and COA Unit awards and GCSE. All of the above are supported by the school Learning Support Department. There is also an extensive Work Experience and College Placement Programme in operation.

Eden Grove was founded on the principles of family values and the ethos of structure, content and purpose. This remains the case to this day. All of our young people are part of a particular Unit, which is age-associated. Within this Unit there are routines and expectations which would apply to any household. There is also an opportunity for young people to engage with adults in a positive/trusting way and an opportunity to participate in a wide range of activities. An opportunity is also there to address any specific difficulty.

All young people have a Care Plan, which is addressed through their own Unit staff.

The school has a thriving Cadets Programme, which has been described by a Senior Army Officer as 'the best Detachment in Cumbria'. All young people involved participate in a variety of activities/skill-training exercises. These include an annual skiing trip, hillcraft and Army-Base related activities at the Warcop camp.

The 16+ Initiative is based in a completely refurbished Unit that can accommodate, in single bedrooms, up to seven young people. These young people still require a great deal of support.

The Unit provides Life-Skills, Work Experience, College Placements, Careers Advice and many other individual packages that suit the needs and aspirations of the young people involved.

The school employs the services of a counsellor, an educational psychologist, a speech/language therapist and a play therapist. These services allow the school to address specific difficulties with young people in a very personal way.

All enquiries regarding admissions should be made to: Miss Susan Mullen, Senior Administrator.

Fairley House School

30 Causton Street, London SW1P 4AU
Tel: 020 7976 5456   Fax: 020 7976 5905
E-mail: office@fairleyhouse.westminster.sch.uk

Principal Mrs J Ferman
Founded 1982
School status Co-educational independent day
Religious denomination Inter-denominational
Special needs provision ADD, ADHD, DYS, DYP, SPLD
Age range 6–12
No of pupils 95
Girls 26 *Boys* 69
Fees per annum £15,600

Curriculum: the prime aim is to improve the basic literacy and numeracy skills and to establish the self-confidence of dyslexic children. There is a 1:3 staff-pupil ratio with small group and individual teaching, and a structured, multi-sensory approach. The National Curriculum is followed throughout the school with emphasis on ICT, Science, and DT. Children normally remain for two to three years and are carefully prepared for appropriate onward placement.

The multi-disciplinary team includes full-time speech and language and occupational therapists. An educational psychologist spends one day a week in school. All class teachers and special provision staff are fully qualified and experienced in teaching SPLD children.

Entry requirements: Fairley House School assessment.

Frewen College

Brickwall, Northiam, Near Rye, East Sussex, TN31 6NL
Tel: 01797 252494   Fax: 01797 252567

Head S C Horsley B.A. (Hons)
Founded 1947
School status Boys DfEE approved independent weekly boarding and day
Religious denomination Non-denominational
Supporting Corporate member of British Dyslexia Association
Accredited by CReSTeD Category A(SP); ISA
Special needs provision DYS
Other needs catered for DYP
Age range 9–17   *Weekly boarding from* 10
No of pupils 77 (*boarding*) (*weekly*) 42
Junior 7   *Senior* 70
Fees per annum (*weekly boarding*) from £15,660 (*day*) from £8,910

Frewen College is a specialist school for the education of dyslexic boys. We believe not only in tackling the difficulties which each boy has but also in establishing the strengths and talents of each individual so that success is experienced at every level.

There are 77 boys and 22 teaching staff. All boys go on to further and/or higher education. The full National Curriculum is offered within a small class environment which allows for a whole school approach to the problems of specific learning difficulites. Each boy has an individual education plan which allows for the tackling of his dyslexic problems and for the development of his strengths. Literacy problems are tackled using a range of programmes including THRASS and the Dyslexic Institute

Literacy Programme. A wide range of GCSEs are offered.

There is a particular emphasis on Technology, Art and Design with fully equipped Design and Technology workshops, Motor Mechanics workshop, pottery, art studio and food technology area. Music facilities allow for teaching up to GCSE as well as individual lessons in instruments of the pupil's choice.

Information Technology is at the heart of our educational programmes. A 'state of the art' computer network runs through the main teaching areas with a pupil computer ratio of 1:4. Pupils have access to the network throughout the working day and during prep sessions both in classrooms and in the open access study centre.

Our unique sixth form offers City and Guilds courses in Professional Cookery and Motor Vehicle Repair and Maintenance as well as GCSE retakes and a structured introduction to the adult world.

Dyspraxia provision includes specialist tuition within a fully equipped fitness studio. All programmes are developed in consultation with our visiting Occupational Therapist. There is also a Speech and Language Therapist on the staff.

Boarding provision features en-suite bedrooms, a full range of supervised recreational activities and transport to and from London on Friday and Sunday evenings. Day placements are also available.

Grafham Grange School

Grafham Grange, Bramley, Guildford, Surrey GU5 0LH
Tel: 01483 892214   Fax: 01483 894297
E-mail: dggrafham@aol.com

Head Mr R Norman
Founded 1946
School status Boys non-maintained boarding
Special needs provision EBD
Age range 10–16   *Boarding from* 10
No of pupils 40
Fees per annum £37,000

Grafham Grange provides residential education for boys aged 10–16 within the average range of cognitive ability, who may be under-functioning as a result of emotional and behavioural disorder.

Set in 40 acres with four self-contained living groups and an independence living group, the school provides a wide range of facilities. We offer an intensive programme of remediation, high staff to pupil ratio, external examinations in Years 10 and 11, independence training, FE links and post-16 support.

We use a range of adaptable techniques to achieve each pupil's potential; a keyworker provides individual support and counselling, and monitors progress. The school provides expert support to pupils and their families, recognising the importance of the family unit whilst allowing pupils to develop towards independence at their own pace.

We also offer specialist family support work which is carried out by our own Social Work Department, consultant psychiatrist and specialist counsellors.

HONORMEAD

SCHOOLS

HONORMEAD SCHOOLS LIMITED
THE GRANGE, HOSPITAL LANE, MICKELOVER, DERBY, DE3 5DR
Telephone: Derby (01332) 523951
Facsimile: Derby (01332) 523995
E-mail: schooladmissions@honormead.btinternet.com

Since 1976 Honormead schools have specialised in the provision of therapeutic education for boys and girls with speech and language impairment, profound communication disorders and autism. We have always considered the total needs of the pupils when developing individual programmes in education, speech and language therapy, physical therapy, independence and life and social skills training.

Alderwasley Hall School
Alderwasley Hall, Belper
Derbyshire DE56 2SR
Tel: (01629) 822586 / 822919 / 825765
Fax: (01629) 826661
E-mail: alderwasleyhallschool@btinternet.com
DfEE Registration No: 830\6016

Children and students aged 5 to 19 years who are potentially of average intelligence, but have severe speech and language disorders. Places available for 146 residential pupils and 30 day pupils. Day and termly boarding placements are available.

Bladon House School
Newton Solney, Burton on Trent
Staffordshire DE15 0TA
Tel: (01283) 563787 / 565220
Fax: (01283) 510980
E-mail: bladonhouseschool@btinternet.com
DfEE Registration No: 830\6009

Children and students aged 5 to 19 years who have speech and language disorders and moderate/severe learning difficulties. Places are available for 132 residential pupils and 15 day pupils. Day, termly boarding and 52 week placements are available. 14 to 19 provision and vocational training are available on the other school sites ie The Grange and Abbey Lodge Annexes.

Pegasus School
Main Street, Caldwell, Swadlincote
Derbyshire DE12 6RS
Tel: (01283) 761352
Fax: (01283) 761312
E-mail: caldwellhallschool@btinternet.com

Children aged 5 to 19 years who need highly specialised education and who present challenging behaviour and learning difficulties due to their inability both to communicate and to take in information from the outside world. Centre staffed on a 1:1 basis for 24 hours per day. Day, termly boarding and 52 week placements are available. Available to LEAs for independent assessments.

FUTURE DEVELOPMENTS
Honormead continues to be at the forefront of research and developments in the area of residential special needs education and care. We continue to work in collaboration with local authority professionals to maintain and improve the level and quality of our services. Individual school brochures and school videos are available on request.

HONORMEAD

SCHOOLS

MISSION STATEMENT
Honormead's objective is to realise the full potential of children and young people with special educational needs through the provision of high quality education in a caring and supportive environment.

Westwood School
Blithbury, Rugeley
Staffordshire WS15 3JQ
Tel: (01889) 504353
Fax: (01889) 504361
E-mail: westwoodschool@btinternet.com
DfEE Registration No: 860\6002

Children and students aged 5 to 19 years who exhibit severe learning difficulties which may be associated with the autistic continuum, including intentional communication deficit, fine and gross motor problems and behaviour difficulties. Places are available for 48 residential and 6 day pupils. Day, termly boarding and 52 week placements are available.

Honormead School
For Children with Autism
Blithbury Road, Blithbury, Rugeley
Staffordshire WS15 3JQ
Tel: (01889) 504400
Fax: (01889) 504010
E-mail: autism@btinternet.com
DfEE Registration No: 860/6024

The Honormead School offers both day and residential places for students aged 3 to 19 years who exhibit learning difficulties within the spectrum of autism. Day and termly boarding (44 weeks) are available. Under the auspices of an agreement between Boston Higashi School and the Honormead Group the new educational centre will benefit from staff training and curriculum enhancement based on Daily Life Therapy from Boston Higashi School.

Green Laund,
Hospital Lane, Mickleover
Derby DE3 5DR
Tel: (01332) 512855

Young people aged 19 and over who need further independent/life/social skills and vocational training. It offers them home based residential care and a realistic work training environment in preparation for semi-independent living. Inspected and approved by the FEFC.

EXTRA CURRICULAR ACTIVITIES
All pupils enjoy a wide and varied range of extra curricular activities including riding therapy at the three equestrian centres and on the Honormead narrowboat which gives them an opportunity to explore the local inland waterways.

I CAN

4 Dyer's Buildings, Holborn, London EC1N 2QP
Tel: 0870 010 4066   Fax: 0870 010 4067
E-mail: ican@ican.org.uk   Website: www.ican.org.uk

Helps Children Communicate
registered charity 210031

I CAN is the national educational charity for children with speech and language difficulties. In addition to three special schools (Dawn House, John Horniman and Meath) the charity runs other programmes for Early Years, Training and Information and Mainstream Support for mainstream schools via partnership projects.

I CAN's Dawn House School

Helmsley Road, Rainworth, Nottinghamshire NG21 0DQ
Tel: 01623 795361   Fax: 01623 491173

Helps Children Communicate
registered charity 210031

Head Ms M Uden
Founded 1974
School status Co-educational non-maintained boarding and day
Special needs provision Speech and language impairment
Age range 5–16   *Boarding from* 6
No of pupils (day) 30 *(boarding)* 47
Girls 18   *Boys* 59
Fees per annum (boarding) £23,556–£26,352 *(day)* £14,493

Dawn House School is known nationally as a centre of excellence, which specialises in meeting the needs of pupils with speech and language problems from 5–16. The OFSTED Inspection Team praised Dawn House for providing "high quality teaching and good value for money". The pupils are offered access to the National Curriculum through courses leading to external accreditation at the end of Key Stage 4. The school aims to support the pupil's development in speech and language, thinking and reasoning, self-confidence and independence. Integrated education, therapy and care programmes are tailored to meet the needs of each pupil. Joint planning by our highly qualified and experienced staff ensures that the school provides a fully integrated language environment. Teaching and therapy are supported by up-to-date technology and Paget Gorman Signed Speech.

Pupils are encouraged to develop their independence throughout the 24-hour curriculum the school works in close partnership with parents.

I CAN's John Horniman School

2 Park Road, Worthing, West Sussex BN11 2AS
Tel: 01903 200317   Fax: 01903 214151

Helps Children Communicate
registered charity 210031

Head Ms J Dunn
School status Co-educational non-maintained boarding and day
Accredited by DfEE
Age range 4–11   *Boarding from* 4
No of pupils (day) 18 *(boarding) (weekly)* 14
Girls 6   *Boys* 26
Fees per annum (boarding) £29,616 *(day)* £19,158

John Horniman School works with children where speech and language impairment is their primary area of need. Multi-disciplinary teams of teaching staff, care workers and speech and language therapists work together to provide a specialised and innovative approach to teaching and learning, integrating education and therapy. OFSTED inspectors noted the school offers "a wealth of expertise in speech and language disorders".

Intensive individual and small group speech and language therapy programmes are delivered flexibly in order to meet each child's specific needs. Key Stages 1 and 2 of the National Curriculum including the National Literacy and Numeracy Strategies are followed at the appropriate level for each child and Paget Gorman Signing is incorporated into the learning environment.

I CAN's Meath School

Brox Road, Ottershaw, Surrey KT16 0LF
Tel: 01932 872302   Fax: 01932 875180

Helps Children Communicate
registered charity 210031

Head Mr John Parrott
School status Co-educational non-maintained boarding and day
Age range 5–12   *Boarding from* 5
No of Pupils (day) 55 *(boarding) (weekly)* 20
Girls 15   *Boys* 60
Fees per annum (boarding) £28,460–£33,497; *day* £17,410–£19,508

Pupils at Meath School show language impairment which severely affects their communication and learning; many also have speech, literacy and co-ordination difficulties.

Children within the average or below average range of non-verbal ability benefit from the school's integrated multi-professional approach to delivering a curriculum, which includes many practical and experience based activities. Meath School is cited as being "particularly successful in developing pupils' self confidence and self esteem and in securing their good progress in English" and the pupils' levels of attainment in this area is the "result of skilled teaching and management ... and the effective work of teams of teachers, therapists and support staff".

The National Curriculum is adapted to the specific needs of the children and delivered through subject specific teaching and cross curricular topic work. Individual programmes of speech and language therapy are integrated into the curriculum leading to a strong emphasis on the development of the children's communication skills throughout class and residential groups. Augmentative communication systems are used as appropriate, eg Paget Gorman Signing Cued Articulation and individual communication aids.

Ingfield Manor School

Five Oaks, Billingshurst, West Sussex RH14 9AX
Tel: 01403 782294   Fax: 01403 785066

Head Mr Christopher Jay
Founded 1961
School status DfEE approved independent (supported by Scope)
Special needs provision CP
Age range 3–11   *Boarding from* 3
No of pupils (day) 29   *(boarding) (weekly)* 12
Girls 22   *Boys* 19
Fees per annum On application

Ingfield Manor is a day and weekly boarding school for children with cerebral palsy with learning abilities in the average range. The school is at the forefront of the development of Conductive Education in the UK and is advised and supported by the Peto Institute in Budapest. Staff work in inter-disciplinary teams responsible for the needs of the children throughout the day.

The latest OFSTED report concluded that, 'The work in Conductive Education by pupils and staff is outstanding. This is a centre of excellence for an alternative approach to the education of children with cerebral palsy'.

Children follow National Curriculum core and foundation subjects. The curriculum is based on a holistic view of children and their intellectual, emotional and social needs. Information technology features strongly and is used to support the children as they extend their repertoire of skills. The school has a national reputation for the development of computer assisted communication.

Kisimul School

The Old Vicarage, High Street, Swinderby, Lincolnshire LN6 9LU
Tel: 01522 868279   Fax: 01522 866000
E-mail: sueshaw@kisimul.co.uk   Website: www.kisimul.co.uk

Head Mrs S J Shaw
Founded 1977
School status Co-educational DfEE approved
boarding and day
Religious denomination Non-denominational
Special needs provision AUT, DOW, EPI, SLD,
SP&LD, SPLD
Age range 10–19   *Boarding from* 10
No of pupils 28
Girls 7   *Boys* 21
Junior 1   *Senior* 11   *Sixth Form* 16
Fees per annum On application

Access to both the National Curriculum and our own developmental curriculum based upon individual needs. We aim to provide a warm, caring environment in which a child can flourish and be able to develop skills to his or her full potential. We provide a consistent 24-hour approach with house and school staff working together as a team. Each child has an individual programme based on an assessment of his or her needs in which parental views are considered to be an important contribution.

We have a very high staff/pupil ratio that enables us to fully utilise facilities within the community. The school has its own soft play, adventure playground, heated indoor swimming pool and multi-sensory room. Speech, physio and music therapy are available together with external support agencies. The school also has a consultant educational psychologist.

MACINTYRE CARE

602 South Seventh Street, Milton Keynes, Buckinghamshire, MK9 2JA
Tel: 01908 230100   Fax: 01908 234379

MacIntyre Care is a national charity which has been providing support to children and adults with learning disabilities across the UK for the last thirty years. Current services include residential accommodation, supported living, and adult education and training opportunities, as well as its schools at Wingrave and Womaston.

MacIntyre School Wingrave

Leighton Road, Wingrave, Nr Aylesbury, Buckinghamshire HP22 4PD
Tel: 01296 681274   Fax: 01296 681091
E-mail: wingrave@macintyre-care.org

Head Mrs H Willdridge
School status Co-educational boarding only
Special needs provision SLD
Other needs catered for AUT, EPI, PMLD, SLD, SP&LD, SPLD
Member of NASS
Age range 10–19   *Boarding from* 10
No of boarders (full) 34
Girls 12   *Boys* 20
Senior 18 sixth form 12
Fees per annum (boarding) (full) £75,000

MacIntyre School Wingrave, is located in rural Buckinghamshire five miles from the towns of Aylesbury and Leighton Buzzard. Students live in purpose-built houses and are taught in small classes by specialist staff. Our Individual Education and Care Plans are based on Person Centred Planning and reflect the needs and aspirations of each person in a caring and supportive environment.

We work in partnership with parents and other professionals to support the young people to acquire the skills and experience to enable them to take their rightful place as valued and contributing members of society.

MacIntyre School Womaston

Walton, Presteigne, Powys LD8 2PT   Tel: 01544 230308
Fax: 01544 231317   E-mail: womaston@macintyre-care.org

Head Mr M J Bertulis
Founded 1986
School status DfEE approved independent co-educational voluntary boarding only
Special needs provision AUT, MLD, SLD
Other needs catered for AUT, EBD, EPI
Age range 11–19   *Boarding from* 11
No of boarders (full) 16
Girls 3   *Boys* 13
Fees per annum (boarding) (full) £81,047

A 52 week boarding school providing education and care for children who need a '24 hour approach'. The school has consistently provided good quality education for young people who have suffered exclusion from schools and/or have found it difficult to live at home. The school has recently achieved a successful ESTYN inspection report. The school is set in 20 acres of grounds.

Philosophy and Approaches: The school employs an empathetic, person-centred approach aiming to understand, develop and extend each student. Positive behavioural standards are set whilst maintaining an understanding of the communication intended by the behaviour.

Curriculum and Resources: Students follow individual curricula with an emphasis on physical, creative and environmental activities to complement and aid delivery of the key skills. Students are expected to play an active part in the choice of activities and programmes selected. Womaston has positive links with Coleg Powys. Specialist support is available to the school in psychiatry, psychology, sexuality, speech therapy and physiotherapy.

Well equipped residential houses and classrooms for up to five students, potter, craft workshop, training kitchen, multisensory room and individual session rooms.

The Marchant-Holliday School

North Cheriton, Templecombe, Somerset BA8 0AH
Tel: 01963 33234   Fax: 01963 33432
E-mail: mhs@ncheriton.freeserve.co.uk

Head Mr J M Robertson BEd (Hons), DipEd
Founded 1950
School status Boys DfEE approved independent boarding and day
Religious denomination Non-denominational
Member of AWCEBD, NASEN, NASS
Special needs provision ADD, ADHD, ASP, DYS, EBD, SPLD
Age range 7–12 *Boarding from* 7
No of pupils 38 (day) 5 (boarding) 33
Junior 38
Fees per annum (boarding) £26,000 *(day)* £12,750

This is a charity-based independent residential school for junior aged boys who have emotional and behavioural difficulties. Associated learning difficulties and dyslexia can also be catered for. Pupils follow the National Curriculum, but at a level appropriate to their needs. Classes are of no more than eight pupils and facilities and resources are of the highest standard. Children are encouraged to fulfil their potential for social and academic growth and often make sufficient progress to allow a return to mainstream schooling. We are accredited by Somerset Social Services and had a very successful OFSTED inspection in February 1998.

Mark College

Blackford Road, Mark, Highbridge, Somerset TA9 4NP
Tel: 01278 641632   Fax: 01278 641426
E-mail: post@markcollege.somerset.sch.uk   Website: www.markcollege.somerset.sch.uk

Principal Dr S J Chinn
Founded 1986
School status Boys DfEE approved independent boarding and day
Religious denomination Non affiliated
Member of ISA   *Accredited by* ISC, DfEE, (CReSTeD)
Special needs provision DYC, DYS
Age range 10–16 *Boarding from* 10
No of pupils 80   *Boarders* 60
Senior 80
Fees per annum (boarding) (full) £14,343–£15,771 *(day)* £9,960–£11,061 *(weekly)* £14,130–£15,447

Mark College is a specialist secondary school for dyslexic boys. Founded in 1986, it has established an international reputation for its expertise. Its success has been recognised in the UK by achieving approval from the DfEE followed by an outstanding Ofsted report, which led to Beacon status. The college offers superb facilities for sport, boarding and academic work. It has been at the forefront of using ITC for English and for teaching mathematics to dyslexics. The college runs teacher-training courses for both these areas.

GCSE results in 2000 were excellent with 87 per cent of grades at C and above and with 75 per cent of Year 11 boys obtaining 5 or more grades at C and above. These results were achieved by boys whose dyslexic problems were at the severe end of the spectrum.

Maple Hayes School

Abnall's Lane, Lichfield, Staffordshire WS13 8BL
Tel: 01543 264387   Fax: 01543 262022
Website: www.dyslexia.gb.com

Principal Dr E N Brown
Founded 1982
School status Co-educational DfEE approved independent boarding and day
Religious denomination Church of England
Member of ISIS, ISA, ISC, ECIS
Special needs provision ADD, ADHD, DYS, SPLD
Age range 7–17   *Boarding (Boys) from* 7
No of pupils (day) 59 *(boarding)* 50
Pupils 120 Girls day only
Fees per annum *(boarding)* £13,020–£16,245 *(day)* £9,045–£12,255

Maple Hayes School is one of the select few schools for dyslexics and underachievers which is inspected and approved by the Department for Education. The school is set in extensive grounds near Lichfield and caters for up to 120 children from 7 to 17 years. We have a world-wide reputation for our unique and effective teaching methods and for our examination results. After taking GCSEs with us, most students go on to higher education at college or university. Excellent OFSTED report.

We provide a good all-round education without the stigma of withdrawal to a special unit and our youngsters compete well in the Midland and National Independent School sports championships. Children's learning is under the supervision of a chartered psychologist and an assessment service is available. Private and LEA placements are welcome. In addition to bursaries for private placements, there is a bursary scheme for children of very high intelligence. Admission is by interview and psychologist's report.

Moon Hall School for Dyslexic Children

Feldemore, Holmbury St Mary, Nr Dorking, Surrey RH5 6LQ
Tel: 01306 731464   Fax: 01306 731504
E-mail: enquiries@moonhall.surrey.sch.uk   Website: www.moonhall.surrey.sch.uk

Head Mrs J Lovett
Founded 1985
School status Co-educational independent boarding and day
Religious denomination Church of England
Member of BDA, IAPS   *Accredited by* CReSTeD "A"   *Special needs provision* DYS, SPLD
Age range 7–13
Boarding from 7   *No of pupils (day)* 64 *(boarding at Belmont)* 17
Girls 15 *Boys* 66   *Fees per annum (boarding) (weekly)* £13,416 *(day)* £10,440

Moon Hall has a special relationship with Belmont Preparatory (3–13 year olds). Together they provide unrivalled opportunities for intelligent dyslexic children:
- Purpose-built Moon Hall school house
- Full-time specialist teaching (7–11 year olds)
- English and Maths groups: normal maximum six pupils

- Other subjects: normal maximum – 12 pupils
- One-to-one as needed
- Vast array of materials/equipment
- Well-equipped computer room – additional machines in form rooms
- Every child taught touch-typing. OCR examinations taken where appropriate
- 60-acre site – heated swimming pool, all-weather pitches etc
- Games/PE – taught by Preparatory School – pupils play in joint school teams
- Regular cross-site dramatic/musical productions
- Uniform common to both schools. Assemblies/lunches/playtimes together
- Dyslexic pupils move into Belmont classes when ready – returning for ongoing support as required up to age 13
- Personal tutors for all.

Mulberry Bush School

Abingdon Road, Standlake, Witney, Oxfordshire OX29 7RW
Tel: 01865 300202   Fax: 01865 300084
E-mail: director@mulberrybushschool.fsnet.co.uk

Director Richard R Rollinson
Founded 1948
School status Co-educational non-maintained boarding
Religious denomination Non-denominational
Member of Charterhouse Group, AWCEBD
Accredited by DfEE
Special needs provision EBD
Other needs catered for Severe emotional/behavioural problems
Age range 5–12   *Boarding from* 5
No of pupils 36
Girls 14   *Boys* 22
Fees per annum £71,880

The Mulberry Bush School provides therapeutic education and treatment for emotionally troubled children of primary school age, who have failed to develop secure ego integration and identity in early childhood, which conse-quently led to serious emotional and beha-vioural problems which disrupt their education.

Curriculum: all children have access to learning programmes, incorporating an Early Years cur-riculum and Key Stages 1 & 2 of the National Curriculum, in a setting where educational and group living experiences are carefully inte-grated. Staff pay heed to emotional ages and stages as much as to children's chronological ages and academic abilities. Children have experiences of, and opportunities for: good quality primary child care; an environment/ther-apeutic education for 'learning to live and living to learn'; development of healthy relationships with mature adults; development of trust in people and a belief that needs may be satisfied.

Assessment involves: written reports; interviews with professionals, parents and child; visits to the school.

Nugent House

Carr Mill Road, Billinge, Wigan, St Helens WN5 7TT
Tel: 01744 892551   Fax: 01744 895697
E-mail: HEAD@NugentWiganSch.uk

Head Mrs J L G Bienias
Founded 1983
School status Boys DfEE approved independent boarding and day
Religious denomination Catholic, although referrals are accepted of all faiths
Special needs provision ADD, ADHD, ASP, AUT, DYS, SPLD, TOU, EBD and associated mental needs
Age range 7–19   *Boarding from* 7
No of pupils 92 (day) 30 (boarding) 62
Junior 16   *Senior* 76
Fees per annum (boarding) from £26,721 *(day) from* £20,043

Nugent House is a residential special school for boys experiencing behavioural and emotional problems. It seeks to meet the educational, spiritual, social and welfare needs of its children in a supportive and caring environment including, where possible, the encouragement and facilitation of their integration into mainstream education.

A range of educational abilities exists within the school population. For some, therefore, specialised support is available. A full public examination programme is offered. Unless a student's ability warrants being taught at a different level, all children are grouped according to National Curriculum age with the nature and presentation of work reflecting this.

We make provision for primary and secondary aged pupils. Education is provided in three buildings which have specialist departments. The school enjoys its own large and superbly equipped sports hall accommodating PE, gymnastics, indoor games and a climbing wall. Full use is made of the extensive playing fields, athletics track and tennis courts. The school has fully-equipped classrooms and therapy rooms. The school employs a multi-disciplinary team including psychiatrist, clinical and educational psychologists, family therapists (on a sessional basis), and also complementary therapists including music, art, play and horticulture.

Close contact with home is maintained through telephone, visits and regular home leave wherever possible. Boys in the school reside in one of nine houses. The senior boys' provision is one of four houses, three of which are smaller houses catering for boys with specific needs. Within this provision boys have the opportunity to live semi-independently. Pinnington House is a specialist provision for young people who have socially challenging behaviours and associated mental health problems.

The school is situated in a pleasant rural district of south-west Lancashire, midway between Liverpool and Manchester and with easy access to national motorway and rail links.

The teaching staff are encouraged and expected to pursue programmes of advanced qualification in special education for which financial support is granted. Residential social work staff, nursing staff and teaching staff have access to the training department of the Nugent Care Society, which is responsible for the implementation of the NVQ scheme throughout the school. Productive and well-established relationships exist with a number of universities throughout the UK and overseas. The school provides a balanced and broadly-based curriculum which seeks to promote the spiritual, moral, cultural, mental and physical development of the pupils and prepares them for opportunities, and responsibilities of adult life. The facilitation of a normal pattern of development is central in the organisation of the school curriculum which enables the children to acquire separate bodies of knowledge and skills, and also creates an enjoyable learning environment where the individual potential of each child may be fulfilled to its maximum.

Well placed

Finding the right school for children and young people with special needs is a major responsibility. You'll want to have total confidence in the quality of the services and care offered by the provider. Here at the Hesley Group, we have been providing residential education, care and therapy for children and young adults since 1975. Today, we are the largest group of independent residential special schools in the UK.

Our expertise and experience is focused around care and provision for those who present significant challenges due to:-

- Complex learning and social problems
- Autism
- Asperger Syndrome
- Severe learning difficulties

We are wholly committed to providing a high quality lifestyle in our specialist homes, schools and colleges. In all Hesley Group establishments, there is a culture of positive developments and support. Above all, we aim to ensure that each and every person in our care is given the opportunity to achieve their full potential.

The Hesley Group comprises:

Dorset
The Forum School (AUT)
Purbeck View School (AUT)

Hampshire
Grateley House School (ASP, ADD, TOU)
Hill House School (AUT/SLD)
Southlands School (boys, ASP)

S Yorkshire
Fullerton House School (AUT/SLD)
Wilsic Hall School (AUT/SLD)

for AUT/SLD 16-Adult:
S Yorkshire
Hesley Village College

Lincolnshire
Broughton House College

see individual entries for contact details

We don't just provide - we care. For more information contact one of our regional offices

 The Hesley Group
Enabling people with special needs to achieve their full potential.

INVESTORS IN PEOPLE

The Hesley Group Head Office
The Coach House, Hesley Hall,
Tickhill, Doncaster DN11 9HH
Telephone: 01302 866906.

The Hesley Group Southern Office
Brock House, Grigg Lane,
Brockenhurst, Hampshire SO42 7RE
Telephone: 01590 624484

Hesley Group
establishments have
achieved ISO 9002.
Investors In People and
NVQs in care.

Oakbank School

Midstocket Road, Aberdeen AB15 5XP
Tel: 01224 313347   Fax: 01224 312017   E-mail: oakbankschool@hotmail.com

Head Mrs J C Arrowsmith
Founded 1870
School status Co-educational independent
boarding and day
Religious denomination Non-denominational
Special needs provision ADHD, EBD
Age range 12–18   *Boarding from* 12
No of pupils (boarding) (full) 41
Girls 10   *Boys* 31
Fees (boarding per annum) £69,598–£101,835
(boarding per week) £1,335–£1,953 *(day)* on
application

Oakbank offers a high quality care and education service to young people displaying social, emotional and behavioural difficulites.

Oakbank aims to facilitate the holistic development of each young person through an unconditional, caring, child-centred approach. The environment within Oakbank strives to nurture the young person and assist them in developing the ability to form trusting relationships with adults, to raise their self-esteem, and generally to provide a secure framework for each young person. The School endeavours at every opportunity to work in partnership with parents, carers, and local authorities. Through responsible stewardship, we work with young people on the underlying difficulties in their lives, and the presenting behaviour they display, via individual counselling, groupwork and family work. We provide support and understanding to enable young people to get through difficult periods without being labelled as disruptive.

The full curriculum is offered, providing the opportunity to pursue nationally recognised courses, which encompass compensatory and enriching experiences. Every young person has an individualised educational plan which promotes the partnership between the teacher and learner.

Parayhouse School

(Old Ellerslie Site) South Africa Road, Shepherd's Bush, London W12 7BP
Tel: 020 8740 6333   Fax: 020 8740 6333
E-mail: slj@parayhouse.demon.co.uk

Head Mrs Sarah Jackson
Founded 1964
School status Co-educational independent day
Religious denomination Non-denominational
Special needs provision ADD, ADHD, ASP, CP
(mild), DEL, DOW, DYP, EPI, HI, MLD,
SP&LD
Other needs catered for Moderate learning
difficulties and speech, language and
communication problems
Age range 8–16
No of pupils 30
Girls 3 *Boys* 27
Junior 10   *Senior* 20
Fees per annum £10,650–£12,450

Parayhouse provides a safe, structured and nurturing environment for pupils with moderate learning difficulties and speech, language and communication delay/disorder.

All pupils have an IEP, targeted within a structured class framework. Each programme encompasses the National Curriculum subjects taught at differentiated individual levels. Qualified, experienced SEN teachers are supported by full and part-time speech and language therapists, learning support assistants, a paediatric physiotherapist and specialist teachers of music, art and swimming.

Parayhouse currently caters for pupils between the ages of 8–16 years. Prospective pupils attend for an observation day, or for an assessment where no LEA statement of SEN is available.

Interested families and professionals are welcome to attend one of the school's regular visitors' afternoons, details of which can be found in our informative prospectus, available on request from the school.

Penhurst School

New Street, Chipping Norton, Oxfordshire OX7 5LN
Tel: 01608 647020   Fax: 01608 647029

Head Richard Aird
Founded 1903
School status Non-maintained DfEE approved
independent
Religious denomination Methodist
Member of NASEN, NAIMS, NASS
Special needs provision CP, EPI, HI, PH, PMLD,
SP&LD, VIS, W
Age range 5–19
No of pupils 24
Fees per annum available on request

Pupils at Penhurst School have full access to the
National Curriculum, but delivery and cover-
age is differentiated to match pupils' individual
abilities. Teaching and learning is further
enhanced by the provision of a specialist curriculum that relates directly to the special educational needs of the children on roll. This
specialist curriculum, together with priorities
taken from the care plans of individual pupils,
is used to help minimise the handicapping
effects of profound and multiple disability and
enable pupils to reach their full potential.
Penhurst School is a residential, multi-agency
school in which professionals from different
disciplines work together in partnership with
parents. The work of teachers, care workers,
therapists, nurses and classroom assistants is
fully integrated to ensure that the holistic needs
of pupils are fully accommodated and that their
education, care and treatment is delivered in a
dynamic, caring environment over a 24 hour
period.

Philip Green Memorial School

Boveridge House, Cranborne, Wimborne, Dorset BH21 5RU
Tel: 01725 517218   Fax: 01725 517968

Head Mrs L M Walter
Founded 1964
School status Co-educational independent
boarding and day
Religious denomination Non-denominational
Member of NASEN
Accredited by OCR, WGEC, SEG
Special needs provision ADD, ASP, DEL, DOW,
DYP, MLD, SLD, SP&LD
Age range 11–19 *Boarding from* 11
No of pupils 24 *(day)* 4 *(boarding)* *(full)* 19
(weekly) 3
Girls 11   *Boys* 13   *Senior* 14   *Sixth Form* 10
Fees per annum (boarding) (full) £18,900
(weekly) £16,800 *(day)* £7,800

The Philip Green Memorial School (formerly
Boveridge House) is a school which caters for
children with moderate/severe learning difficulties and/or speech and language disorders.
The age range is from 11 to 19 and boarders are
accepted from the age of eleven.
The students follow the National Curriculum
prior to a modified GCSE or equivalent
curriculum. Older pupils follow a life skills
programme in addition to the academic curriculum. Extra-curricular activities include
sports, drama, craft, visits etc.
The Philip Green Memorial School is an elegant
Georgian mansion offering the highest standards of education, care and accommodation
to students.

Philpots Manor School and Further Training Centre

West Hoathly, East Grinstead, West Sussex RH19 4PR
Tel: 01342 811382/810268   Fax: 01342 811363

Administrator Simon Blaxland-de Lange
Founded 1959
School status Co-educational DfEE approved
independent boarding and day
Religious denomination Christian (non-
denominational)
Member of Committee for Steiner Special
Schools
Accredited by OFSTED, DfEE
Special needs provision ADD, ADHD, ASP, AUT,
CP(mild), DEL, DOW, DYC, DYS, DYP, EBD,
EPI(mild), HI(mild), MLD, SP&LD, SPLD,
TOU
Age range 6–19 *Boarding from* 6
No of pupils (day) 8 *(boarding) (full)* 52
Girls 15   *Boys* 45
Junior 35   *Senior* 13   *Training Course* 12
Fees per annum (boarding) £32,940 *(day)*
£24,705

Philpots Manor School is a residential school and training centre based on the education principles of Rudolf Steiner. It was founded in 1959 to offer care and education to children with special needs who, because of their particular difficulties, have been unable to learn and develop in an ordinary school.

The school admits children who present a broad range of emotional and behavioural difficulties. Most, but not all, are of below average ability and have moderate learning difficulties. These may stem from social deprivation, abuse and a recognised clinical condition such as epilepsy, a developmental disorder or mild autism. Children are eligible providing they have the potential to function in a classroom situation where children are helped to reach their full potential within the Steiner curriculum. It is our aim that by the time pupils leave, they have acquired a sense of self-respect, self-control and personal responsibility in order to give them confidence to go out into the community.

Pontville School

Black Moss Lane, Ormskirk, Lancashire L39 4TW
Tel: 01695 578734   Fax: 01695 579224
E-mail:pontville.office@virgin.net

Head Mr R Farbon
School status Co-educational independent
boarding and day
Religious denomination Non-denominational
Special needs provision ADD, ASP, MLD, TOU
Other needs catered for Social and emotional
problems
Age range 9–19   *Boarding from* 11
No of pupils 51 *(boarding) (full)* 21
Girls 12   *Boys* 39
Fees per annum (boarding) £24,786 *(day)*
£17,901

The full National Curriculum is offered by specialist teachers in specialised accommodation.

Pontville also has a Transition Unit offering a vocational curriculum for students aged 16–19. Courses include basic education, social and life skills, woodwork, ceramics, catering, vehicle maintenance, animal husbandry, horticultural studies and IT.

Staff at Pontville are committed to providing high quality care, education and support to pupils and parents at all times.

Pontville School hopes the transfer to the Witherslack Group of Schools will be confirmed during April 2001. The school caters for young people aged 9–19 years with moderate learning difficulties and social, emotional problems.

Prior's Court School

Hermitage, Thatcham, Berkshire RG18 9NU
Tel: 01635 247202   Fax: 01635 247203
Email: mail@priorscourt.org.uk

Principal Mr R G Hubbard
Chair of Governors Sir Derek Hornby
School status Co-educational independent
boarding and day (boarding 38 weeks/weekly)
Registered Charity Number 1070227
Religious denomination Multi-denominational
Special needs provision AUT, ASP,
DfEE Number 869/6014
Age range 3–19
Fees per annum available on request

Prior's Court School is a specialist residential school for children diagnosed as Autistic who have moderate to severe learning difficulties. Prior's Court School is particularly appropriate for pupils who require a coordinated programme of education and care.

The strengths of Daily Life Therapy, TEACCH and the best practices from other approaches have been adapted, incorporated with a clear contemporary knowledge of Autism.

The Curriculum includes the National Curriculum, sensory curriculum and Information-Communication Technology. There is strong emphasis on physical activities, music and the arts.

Staff are available to discuss the school with parents, Local Authorities and visits can be arranged.

RNIB Condover Hall School

Condover, Near Shrewsbury, Shropshire SY5 7AH
Tel: 01743 872320   Fax: 01743 873310
E-mail: Tony.Best@rnib.org.uk

Head Dr A Best
Special needs provision PMLD, SLD, VIS, visual impairment and multiple disabilities
Age range 5–19
No of pupils 60
Fees per annum (boarding) from £31,103

The school provides for pupils aged 5–19 years who have a visual disability with one or more additional impairment. The Pathways Service provides education for deaf-blind pupils. A Further Education Centre for young people aged 18–24 years is attached to the school.

The school curriculum covers National Curriculum areas concentrating on work at levels 1 and 2. Our additional curriculum includes specialist areas such as mobility, use of residual vision and social skills development. Many aspects of the curriculum are delivered through practical activities using the extensive school campus and facilities in the community.

Residential accommodation is in small family groups, with qualified child care staff. Accommodation is available at the school for parents/families. The residential service is available for 52 weeks.

Support staff includes physiotherapists, speech therapists, mobility teacher and educational psychologist.

Admissions: A member of staff is available to discuss the school with parents and local authorities, and arrange visits to the school.

RNIB Rushton Hall School

Rushton, Kettering, Northamptonshire NN14 1RR
Tel: 01536 710506   Fax: 01536 418506

Head Mrs Rita Kirkwood
Founded 1961
Needs for which school offers provision CP, EPI, MLD, PH, PMLD, SLD, SP&LD, VIS, W
Other needs Children with a visual impairment and multiple disabilities
School status Non-maintained – DfEE Registered 931/7026
Registered Charity Number 226227
Age range 4–19
No of pupils (boarding) 35   *(day)* 10
Fees per annum Available on request

Rushton provides education and care for pupils who are aged 4 to 19 years with visual impairment and additional disabilities of a learning, physical, medical, social or emotional nature. Rushton aims to give each child a high quality of life and the opportunity to maximise their independence. Each child has a thorough assessment to ensure the development of an individual educational programme suited to their needs and potential. This is delivered within an environment designed to allow them to make sense of the world around them and to encourage them to explore and learn. The curriculum aims to help pupils acquire the knowledge and skills that will enable them to be as independent as possible. Access to the National Curriculum ensures breadth and balance for all pupils. Outreach services include assessment, training, pre-school group and specialist 52 week care for children and young people. Rushton Hall School will be moving from its present site to relocate with an LEA special school at Exhall in Warwickshire.

Rowden House School

Rowden, Bromyard, Herefordshire HR7 4LS
Tel: 01885 488096   Fax: 01885 483361
E-mail: info@rowden.co.uk   Website: www.rowden.co.uk

Head Mrs H Hardy
Founded 1986
School status Co-educational DfEE approved
independent boarding
Member of BILD, SCA
Special needs provision AUT, DOW, EPI, PMLD,
SLD, TOU, W
Other needs catered for Severe learning
difficulties, challenging behaviour
Age range 11–19   *Boarding from* 11
No of pupils (boarding) (full) 28
Girls 6   *Boys* 22
Fees per annum £75,000–£110,000

Rowden House School is pleased to announce the completion of the final phase of a £1.5m redevelopment programme which now enables the school to offer all its residents single bedrooms in purpose-built, single-storey accommodation.

The Coppice, The Glade, The Spinney and The Grove are high-specification homes each offering single-occupancy rooms for seven residents in a courtyard setting. Each unit has generously proportioned communal living spaces with fully equipped kitchen, dining room and lounge. Each private room has built-in bedroom furniture and has facilities to enable residents to use TV, sound systems and computers as appropriate. There are washrooms, bathrooms and showers on each wing of the buildings.

Each home has a Unit Manager with a dedicated team of fifteen Support Staff. Waking night staff are available to the children throughout the night, supported by sleep-in staff with whom they are connected by radio handset.

The homes have been designed within a courtyard setting at the edge of the woodland which borders the Rowden site. These units therefore offer an unrivalled situation within an outstanding natural environment. New purpose-built play facilities adjoin the homes.

We believe these new facilities will enable each of our client youngsters to develop skills towards independence in an appropriate domestic and social setting.

For further information regarding these developments and our education offer, visit our website at www.rowden.co.uk

The Royal Blind School, Edinburgh

Craigmillar Park, Edinburgh EH16 5NA
Tel: 0131 667 1100   Fax: 0131 662 9700
E-mail: office@royalblindschool.org.uk   Website: www.royalblindschool.org.uk

Head Mr K Tansley
Religious denomination Non-denominational
School status Grant aided co-educational
boarding and day
Member of Scottish Council of Independent
Schools (SCIS) Headteachers' Association of
Scotland (HAS)
Accredited by Scottish Executives
Special needs provision AUT, CP, DEL, DYP, EPI,
MLD, PH, PMLD, SLD, SP&LD, SPLD, TOU,
VIS, W
Age range 5–14   *Boarding from*
No of pupils 118   *Junior* 22   *Senior* 47
Nursery 8   *PMLD* 41
Fees per annum On application

The Royal Blind School is a national centre of
expertise, providing high quality education and
care, for blind and partially sighted young people. Throughout this day/residential school the
children are provided with individual
programmes of study and guidance, they have
access to the latest technology, small classes,
mobility training and the availability of physiotherapists, speech & language therapists and OT.
The school is organised into four departments:
Nursery – consists of the Pre School Unit, play
group and toy library. Primary & Secondary
Departments – follow the full 5–14 programme,
Standard Grade, Higher Still courses and work
experience. Canaan Lodge caters for visually
impaired pupils in the 5–19 age range who have
additional disabilities.
The school has been completely refurbished
and provides a wide range of additional services
for parents and professionals, these include: a
multi-professional assessment service, outreach
support for children in mainstream school, in
service training, advice and support for families
provided by our parent counsellor.

Royal School for the Deaf Derby

Ashbourne Road, Derby DE22 3BH
Tel/Minicom: 01332 362512   Fax: 01332 299708
E-mail: admin.rsdd@virgin.net   Website: www.rsd-derby.org.uk

Head Mr T Silvester
Founded 1893
School status Co-educational non-maintained
boarding and day
Religious denomination Non-denominational
Member of NASS   *Special needs provision* HI
Age range 3–16   *Boarding from* 5
No of pupils (day) 47   *(boarding) (weekly)* 52
Girls 49   *Boys* 50
Junior 24   *Senior* 75
Fees per annum (boarding) (weekly) £21,420
(day) £15,090

RSD Derby meets the communicative, academic and social needs of deaf children within
a bilingual environment.
Weekly boarders and day pupils access a curriculum best suited to their needs. The school's
bilingual approach using British Sign Language,
written and spoken English aims to produce
independent individuals confident of their ability to integrate into the community. Dedicated
staff, both deaf and hearing ensure that pupils
fulfil their potential in a supportive environment. Commitment to academic achievement is
combined with excellent facilities for sport and
outdoor education.
The nursery offers free places to deaf children
from the ages of three to five. Primary curriculum is designed to develop skills at every level
and follows the framework and guidelines of
the National Curriculum. In secondary school
all National Curriculum subjects are taught by
specialist teachers and offered for GCSE. The
Certificate of Achievement is offered for pupils
who may not achieve GCSE.

Royal School for the Deaf (Manchester)

Stanley Road, Cheadle Hulme, Cheadle, Cheshire SK8 6RQ
Tel: 0161 610 0100   Fax: 0161 610 0101
E-mail: headmaster.sec@rsd.manchester.btinternet.com
Website: www.rsdmanchester.org

INVESTOR IN PEOPLE

Head Mr L Reed, MSc, BEd, DipVI, Cert HI
Founded 1823
School status Independent non-maintained co-educational boarding and day
Accredited by DfEE
Special needs provision AUT, CP, HI, MLD, PH, PMLD, SLD, SPLD, VIS, W
Other needs catered for severe/complex learning difficulties
Age range 5–19+   *Boarding from* 5
No of pupils (day) 38   *(boarding) (full)* 8
(weekly) 32
Girls 29   *Boys* 44
Fees per annum On application

Specialist provision for pupils/students with complex communication difficulties arising from sensory loss, severe learning difficulties, autistic spectrum disorders or behaviours that challenge services.

High staff/pupil ratio (1:1 in our deafblind department) ensure learning opportunities are appropriately constructed and are supported by our specialist assessment centre staff.

Our curriculum takes account of the individual's communication difficulties and encompasses needs-related teaching/care programmes designed to meet present and future needs.

Our total communication approach includes the use of sign-supported English, together with pictorial system creating and communicating environment across both the school and residential care.

Leisure and recreational activities support the pupils needs and include a swimming and hydrotherapy pool, outdoor sensory gardens, recreational areas, multi-sensory rooms, together with a variety of youth clubs.

Rutland House School

Elm Bank, Mapperley Road, Nottingham NG5 3AJ
Tel: 0115 962 1315   Fax: 0115 962 2867
E-mail: caroleoviatt-ham113674.2000@compuserve.com

Head Mrs C Oviatt-Ham
Founded 1979
School status DfEE approved independent
Special needs provision CP, EPI, HI, PH, PMLD, SP&LD, VIS, W
Age range 5–19   *Boarding from* 5
No of pupils (day) 6 *(boarding) (full)* 18 *(weekly)* 6
Girls 13   *Boys* 17
Junior 16   *Senior* 10   *Sixth Form* 4
Fees per annum £31,112–£65,057

Rutland House School is managed by Scope. This school is staffed with specialist teachers, therapists, conductors, nurses, qualified support staff and access to a qualified advocate. A comprehensive team of medical specialists oversees the medical and health needs of the children.

The education philosophy of the school is founded on the teaching and principles of Conductive Education. The school has successfully combined the Conductive Education system with the National Curriculum. The curriculum is designed to promote the child's physical, cognitive, communication, social, emotional and independence skills.

The school has four departments:

The School For Parents is designed for parents of pre-school children to provide support, information and a comprehensive education programme. The primary school curriculum is designed to promote the child's physical skills, social awareness, communication and growing independence.

The Secondary School and 16–19 Unit occupy a separate site. All students live in specially adapted and resourced bungalows in the local community. The aim of the secondary school is to consolidate skills and knowledge in a wider environment. The aim of the 16–19 programme is to prepare the students for adult life by maintaining, developing and transferring skills in a range of settings.

SCOPE

Meldreth Manor School

Fenny Lane, Meldreth, Nr Royston, Hertfordshire SG8 6LG
Tel: 01763 260771   Fax: 01763 263316   Website: www.meldrethmanor.com

Head Eric Nash
Founded 1966
School status Co-educational DfEE approved
No. 873/6008, Independent voluntary
boarding, *(day, week and termly boarding)*
Member of NAIMS, SCOPE
Religious denomination Non-denominational

Special needs provision AUT, CP, EPI, HI, PH,
PMLD, SLD, SP&LD, VIS, W
Age range 5–19 *Boarding from* 5
No of pupils (day) 3 *(boarding) (full)* 74
Girls 30 *Boys* 47
Junior 41 *Senior* 31 *Sixth Form* 5
Fees per annum On application

Craig-y-Parc School

Pentyrch, Cardiff CF15 9NB
Tel: 029 2089 0397   Fax: 029 2089 1404

Head Mr Neil Harvey
Founded 1955
School status Co-educational DfEE approved
independent boarding and day *(day, week and
termly boarding)*
Member of NASS, SCOPE

Religious denomination Non-denominational
Accredited by DfEE, National Assembly for
Wales
Special needs provision CP, PH, PMLD
Age range 4–19
Fees per annum On application

Sheiling School, Camphill Community Thornbury

Thornbury Park, Park Road, Thornbury, Bristol BS35 1HP
Tel: 01454 412194   Fax: 01454 411860
E-mail: mail@sheilingschool.org.uk   Website: www.sheilingschool.org.uk

Contact Point Admissions Co-ordinator
Founded 1952
School status Independent co-educational
boarding and day
Member of Association of Camphill
Communities
Special needs provision AUT, DOW, EBD, EPI,
MLD, PMLD, SLD, SP&LD
Age range 6–19 *Boarding from* 6
No of pupils (boarding) (full) 28   *(weekly)* 7
(day) 4   *(boarding)* 41
Girls 12   *Boys* 23
Fees per annum (boarding) (full) from £33,000
(weekly) £26,000   *(day)* £22,000

A caring, residential environment in a beautiful
parkland close to the historic town of Thorn-

bury is offered for pupils with a wide range of
learning difficulties. The school curriculum is
based on Rudolf Steiner's Waldorf Curriculum.
There are small classes where the needs of each
child are assessed. Swimming, eurythmy, weav-
ing, pottery, woodwork, gymnastics, gardening
and farming are available. Individual therapies
are prescribed where needed, including speech
thereapy, eurythmy therapy and art therapy.
The home life in family settings provides education and life skills to enhance individual
development.
A varied social life is provided both within the
school setting and in the locality.
There is high staff:pupil ratio.
Recent HMI and Social Services inspection
reports available on request.

The Sheiling School, Ringwood

Horton Road, Ashley, Near Ringwood, Hampshire BH24 2EB
Tel: 01425 477488   Fax: 01425 479536
E-mail: sheilingco@aol.com   Website: www.sheilingschool.co.uk

Contact point Admissions co-ordinator
Founded 1951
School status Independent co-educational boarding and day
Special needs provision MLD/SLD, FragileX, Williams Syndrome and others
Member of Association of Camphill Communities
Age range 6–19   *Boarding from* 6
No of students 51   *Junior* 32   *Senior* 19
Boys 31   *Girls* 20
No of boarders (full) 49   *(weekly)* 1   *(day)* 1
Fees per annum (boarding) (full) from £21,000
(weekly) from £17,450 *(day)* from £12,000

The Sheiling School is an independent Camphill Rudolf Steiner School for children aged between 6 and 19 years.

The School is situated close to Ringwood in the New Forest and within 10 miles of the coast. It encompasses a 58-acre semi-rural site of fields, gardens and woodlands, with family sized houses, classrooms, multi-purpose hall, gymnasium, swimming pool, therapy centre, workshops, a chapel and multi-purpose play areas. The Sheiling provides a fully integrated school and house life in a community village setting. It offers residential care [38 weeks], education and special therapies for up to 55 children and adolescents with moderate to severe learning difficulties. Education is based on the Waldorf Curriculum.

Senior's Programme is a three year provision for up to 20 students. The Programme offers formal training and education in classroom and workshop settings, on-site integrated activities with other local organisations, and a strong, round-the-clock social and cultural programme. Outward bound activities take a central role within this programme.

St Catherine's School

Grove Road, Ventnor, Isle of Wight PO38 1TT
Tel: 01983 852722   Fax: 01983 857219
E-mail: stcaths@onthepc.co.uk   Website: www.stcatherines.org.uk

Principal Mr G E Shipley
Founded 1879
School status Co-educational non-maintained boarding and day
Religious denomination Church of England
Member of NASS
Accredited by Investors in People, Basic Skills Agency   *Special needs provision* SP&LD
Other needs catered for Speech and language difficulties   *Age range* 7–18   *Boarding from* 7
No of pupils 74 *(day)* 4   *(boarding) (full)* 56 *(weekly)* 5   *Girls* 12   *Boys* 55
Junior 6   *Senior* 39   *Sixth Form* 17
Fees per annum (boarding) (full) £25,170 *(weekly)* £23,373 *(day)* £18,877

Special needs catered for: Specific speech and language disorder plus associated learning difficulties.
Specialist facilities: Speech and language therapy delivered across the curriculum with teachers and therapists working together.
Education: The curriculum is broad, balanced and relevant to the needs of each student. Our basic skills curriculum has been awarded a quality mark by the Basic Skills Agency. Students have access to mainstream education and work experience.
Support services: School nurse, occupational therapy.
Home/school links: Frequent communication by letter and telephone. Parents always encouraged to visit. Regular annual review other events.
General environment: Residentially divided into five separate Houses. Access to many local community activities.
Aims and philosophy: To provide, through a multi-disciplinary approach, a programme of education and language remediation that meets the individual needs of each student.

St Christopher's School

Carisbrooke Lodge, Westbury Park, Bristol BS6 7JE
Tel: 0117 973 3301/ 973 6875   Fax: 0117 974 3665

Head Ms Orna Matz
Founded 1945
School status Co-educational independent boarding
Religious denomination Christian non-denominational
Special needs provision AUT, CP, EPI, PMLD, SLD, SP&LD, W
Age range 6–19   *Boarding from* 6
No of pupils 45–49
Girls 22   *Boys* 27
Fees per annum Available on request

St Christopher's is a residential school for pupils aged 6–19 with severe and complex, profound and multiple learning difficulties. Many of our pupils have autism. The curriculum is guided by the educational principles of Rudolf Steiner and includes relevant aspects of the National Curriculum. Emphasis on developing skills is done through individual care and education plans for each pupil. Residential provision is available for up to 52 weeks.

Therapeutic support is provided from an occupational therapist, physiotherapist, speech and language therapist, educational psychologist, Steiner-trained therapists and regular qualified nursing support. Staff in houses and classes work with no more than two pupils; some pupils have one-to-one support. Each house has waking night staff.

The school is situated in spacious, attractive grounds, with a heated indoor swimming pool and other facilities on site.

For further information contact the Educational Registrar.

St Dominic's School

Hambledon, Godalming, Surrey GU8 4DX
Tel: 01428 684693   Fax: 01428 685018

Head Mr I Leary
Founded 1929
School status Co-educational non-maintained weekly boarding and day
Religious denomination Roman Catholic
Special needs provision Speech and language difficulties, Medical conditions, ADD, ADHD, ASP, DEL, DYC, DYS, DYP, EPI, SP&LD, SPLD
Other needs catered for Social communication difficulties
Age range 7–16   *Boarding from* 8
No of pupils 104   *No of boarders (weekly)* 78
Girls 11   *Boys* 93
Fees per annum (boarding) (weekly) £24,042–£26,898   *(day)* £16,029–£18,885

St Dominic's provides residential and day placements for pupils of average intelligence but with special needs. These include impaired physical health, specific learning, speech and language and social communication difficulties. Pupils may also be emotionally vulnerable and have motor planning, co-ordination and perceptual difficulties.

The School offers a caring environment where pupils do not miss out on educational opportunities as they are given access to a curriculum similar to that found in mainstream schools leading to GCSE examinations.

Pupils are taught in small class groups with help from learning support teachers. A modern and customised therapy suite meets the needs of physiotherapy, sensory integration therapy, occupational and speech and language therapy. There is a fully equipped surgery with 24-hour nursing cover to meet the needs of children with medical problems, including asthma and epilepsy.

Admission is usually arranged through the Local Education Authority in whose area the child's family reside.

St Edward's School

Melchet Court, Sherfield English, Romsey, Hampshire SO51 6ZR
Tel: 01794 884271   Fax: 01794 884762

Headteacher Mr L P Bartel BEd (Hons)
Founded 1963
School status Boys independent
Religious denomination Non-denominational
Special needs provision ADD, DYS, EBD, MLD
Age range 10–17   *Boarding from* 10
No of pupils (boarding) (full) 68
Junior 34   *Senior* 34
Fees per annum (boarding) £40,320

Special needs catered for: A residential special school for emotionally and behaviourally disturbed boys, including those whose condition may be complicated by mild, moderate and specific learning difficulties.

Specialist facilities: The full National Curriculum is followed at all levels. Specialist learning support for a wide range of learning difficulties. Emphasis upon vocational preparation in Years 10 and 11. Options are matched to individual interests and aptitudes. The school is organised into three year groups for education and care. Separate accommodation allows distinct arrangements reflecting the age and maturity of the pupils. Lower school (ages 10–14) Year 6–9 have a very wide variety of learning experiences covering 11 subjects. Emphasis is placed on core subjects with specialist assistance for boys with learning difficulties. Middle school (ages 14–15) Year 10 are taught within a broad curriculum including Science, Information Technology, Physical Education, Personal and Social Education, Design Technology, Games and Humanities. Mathematics and English are given very full and specialist treatment. Senior school (ages 15–16) Year 11. Within the National Curriculum framework GCSE courses are followed in English, Mathematics. Vocational courses are followed in carpentry and joinery, painting and decorating, brickwork and horticulture, taken to pre-NVQ and NVQ level.

Support services provided: A comprehensive educational and personality assessment can be offered by our consultant child and educational psychologist.

General environment: The school offers a wide range of sporting and social activities, which take place at weekends and evenings throughout the year. The activities are too numerous to list in full, but they include: motorcycling, quad biking, motor mechanics, sub-aqua club, horse riding, canoeing, food technology, model-making, weight training, computers, swimming, roller hockey, gymnastics, football, badminton, basketball, art and multigym. An extensive summer expedition programme complements the leisure activities. The week long camps include outward bound activities in Devon; cycling, canoeing and hiking on the Isle of Wight; pony riding in the New Forest; and fishing on our own lakes.

Aims and philosophy: St Edward's School Charitable Trust aims to foster each boy's personal and social growth.

St Elizabeth's School

Much Hadham, Hertfordshire SG10 6EW
Tel: 01279 844270   Fax: 01279 843903

School status Non-maintained boarding and day
Religious denomination Roman Catholic
Special needs provision AUT, DOW, DYS, DYP, EPI, MLD, PH, SLD, SP&LD, TOU, VIS, W
Age range 5–19+
Registered (boarders) 53
Fees per annum (boarding) £47,400–£72,966

Curriculum: St Elizabeth's offers a 24-hour curriculum, which embraces all areas of the National Curriculum. French is the modern foreign language. A high ratio of teaching and support staff alongside well-resourced specialist subject rooms support truly differentiated programmes of study. Senior pupils and students have the opportunity to take part in enterprise projects, work experience and community service. There is a stress on self-help and independence training at all levels. Link programmes of study are available in local colleges.

Entry requirements: Pupils are formally referred through their LEA – possible joint funding with social services and health. Students 16–19 are placed through their specialist careers service. The options of informal visits, interview, overnight stays are all possible. Admission forms to be completed before formal interview. The school welcomes children from all or no faiths.

External Accreditation: All school leavers and students, work towards their achievements being accredited by one or more of the following national schemes: OCR Accreditation for Life and Living or the National Skills profile; WJEC First Skills Award; ASDAN Towards Independence, alternatively the Bronze and Silver (NVQ Level II) Youth Award Schemes; City and Guild; Numberpower, Wordpower or Communication Skills; Young Enterprise – Team Enterprise award and the Duke of Edinburgh Award. Every young person has their own individual programme and full review meetings are held annually.

Academic and leisure facilities: Academic and residential areas are light, airy, comfortably furnished and well equipped. Situated within a 68-acre site, there are many areas for sport and leisure. Excellent use is made of local leisure facilities. The school has on-site medical/nursing support with staff on nightly duty. Speech and language, physiotherapy and occupational therapy are available on site. The school's educational psychologist and counsellor are available in both residential and academic settings. Families may stay in self-catering accommodation on site.

Religious activities: St Elizabeth's is administered by the Congregation of the Daughters of The Cross of Liege (RC). It admits children of any or no faith. Dignity and privacy are key words in helping each child and family to a better quality of life through improved seizure control and independence. St Elizabeth's is committed to an equal opportunities policy and welcomes the opportunity to work with families. There is parental representation on the governing body and regular parent/staff contact to guarantee the degree of contact, commitment and service. Daughters of The Cross (St Elizabeth's), a registered charity, exists to provide education, training and care for children and students who have epilepsy and associated disabilities.

Our 1998 OFSTED Inspection said:

- "Teaching is very good or better in one out of every three lessons"
- "The Curriculum is broad and highly relevant to pupils"
- "Provision for pupils' spiritual development is outstanding"
- "Particular strengths of teaching are the management of pupils and the quality of lesson planning"
- "The school provides good value for money"
- "The good team work between teachers, learning support assistants and care staff ensures that pupils and students are actively and meaningfully involved in all areas of school life"
- "Parents ... speak highly of the patience of care staff and the quality of medical support available to pupils".

St John's Catholic School for the Deaf

Church Street, Boston Spa, West Yorkshire LS23 6DF
Tel: 01937 842144   Fax: 01937 541471
E-mail: info@stjohns.org.uk   Website: www.stjohns.org.uk

Head Mr T M Wrynne, BEd (Hons), MA, TOD
Founded 1870
School status Co-educational non-maintained
boarding and day
Religious denomination Roman Catholic
catering for pupils of all denominations
Special needs provision DYP, HI, SP&LD, W
Age range 3–19   *Boarding from* 7
No of pupils (boarding) (full) 15   *(weekly)* 51
Girls 49   *Boys* 34
Junior 23   *Senior* 49   *Sixth Form* 11
Fees per annum On application

St John's is a non-maintained residential and
day school offering a first class oral education
for children aged from 3 to 19 years of age. A
strong Christian ethos permeates all aspects of
school life and children of all denominations
are welcomed. The curriculum is broad and
balanced and provides the opportunity for
pupils to take GCSEs, Certificates of Achievement and a wide range of vocationally oriented
courses. In addition to 20 qualified teachers of
the deaf, support is available from our speech
and language therapists, audiologist, and
school nurse. The OFSTED inspectors who
visited our school said, *St John's is a very good
school ... the clear progress made by pupils
means that some are reaching levels of attainment
comparable to or exceeding national
expectations ... parents hold the school in high
esteem ... the school's ethos is excellent ... there
is an atmosphere of security in which pupils and
staff flourish.*

St Margaret's School

The Children's Trust, Tadworth Court, Tadworth, Surrey KT20 5RU
Tel: 01737 365810   Fax: 01737 365819

Head Mrs J E Cunningham
Founded 1985
School status Co-educational DfEE approved
independent boarding and day
Member of NAIMS, NASS
Special needs provision CP, EPI, HI, PMLD, VIS
Other needs catered for Complex care and
medical needs
Age range 8–19   *Boarding from* 8
No of pupils 37 (capacity 40)
Girls 23   *Boys* 14
Fees per annum On application

Curriculum: St Margaret's School provides education and care and therapy, and accesses for all
pupils a broad, balanced curriculum designed
to be relevant to individual needs, which is
delivered to a 24-hour model. The curriculum
emphasises sensory awareness, the importance
of developing precursors to learning, intentional communication and interactions. It also
promotes the integration of all therapy procedures in order to facilitate a holistic delivery.
Entry requirements: Informal visits, followed by
request for assessment to establish individual
special needs. LEA sponsorship.
Open for 48 weeks a year, the school has its
own doctor, small team of nurses and provides
24 hour medical cover.
The Children's Trust is a registered charity,
exists to offer care, treatment and education
to children with exceptional needs and profound disabilities, and to give support to their
families.

St Mary's School

Wrestwood Road, Bexhill-on-Sea, East Sussex TN40 2LU
Tel: 01424 730740   Fax: 01424 733575   E-mail: stmarys@wrestwood.freeserve.co.uk

Principal and C.E.O. Mr David Cassar MA, MIMgt
Founded 1922
School status Co-educational DfEE approved independent voluntary boarding and day
Religious denomination Christian Foundation
Member of NASS
Special needs provision ASP, AUT, CP, DEL, DOW, DYP, DYS, EPI, HI, MLD, PH, SP&LD, SPLD, VIS, W
Other needs catered for Complex medical conditions
Age range 7–19
No of pupils (day) 20 *(boarding)* 118
Fees per annum Contact school for information

Curriculum: We follow the National Curriculum, differentiated where necessary, plus individual learning programmes and a comprehensive life skills programme. We have a team of speech and language therapists, an art thera-

pist, physiotherapists, occupational therapists, specialist teacher for the hearing impaired and a high ratio of qualified and experienced care and nursing staff.

Entry requirements: Formal assessments and interview. Referrals are normally made through local education departments. Private referrals are also considered.

St Mary's is a DfEE approved school, situated in a semi-rural location in Sussex near the sea. It is set in attractive buildings in woodland on the outskirts of Bexhill. Children are referred from all parts of the country and abroad.

St Mary's Wrestwood Educational Trust is a registered charity which exists to provide high quality education, therapy and care in a residential setting, for boys and girls with special educational needs, which can include quite complex and unique conditions and syndromes.

St Piers

St Piers Lane, Lingfield, Surrey RH7 6PW
Tel: 01342 832243   Fax: 01342 834639
Website: www.stpiers.org.uk

Chief Executive Mr R S Haughton BA(psych), BSW
Founded 1895
School status DfEE approved independent co-educational non-maintained boarding and day
Special needs provision EPI, MLD, SLD, SP&LD
Age range 5–19+   *Boarding from 5*
No of students (boarding and day) (School, aged 5–16) 85 *(Further Education Centre, aged 16–19+)* 122

St Piers is a national centre providing education, care and medical supervision for students aged 5–19+ with epilepsy, learning difficulties and other special needs.

St Piers provides integrated education and care with residential and day attendance at its school and brand new further education college opened in September 2000. An Epilepsy Resource Centre provides information and edu-

cation which includes seminars and tailormade training. There is also a fully staffed medical centre with excellent EEG facilities. St Piers works in close partnership with Great Ormond Street Hospital for Children NHS Trust. Programmes are individually tailored with wide-ranging support services. An assessment service is available.

For further information please contact The Admissions Co-ordinator on 01342 831243.

St Rose's School

Stratford Lawn, Stroud, Gloucestershire GL5 4AP
Tel: 01453 763793   Fax: 01453 752617
Website: www.stroses.gloucs.sch.uk

Head Sister M Quentin OP, BA
Founded 1912
School status Non-maintained boarding and day
Religious denomination Catholic
Member of NAIMS, NASS, NCSE
Special needs provision ASP, CP, DEL, DYP, EPI, MLD, PH, SLD, SP&LD, VIS, W
Age range 2–18   *Boarding from* 5
No of pupils 70 *(day)* 37 *(boarding)* *(full)* 33
Girls 31   *Boys* 39
Fees per annum Available on request

Curriculum: The curriculum includes all National Curriculum subjects, and GCSE is available for those who are able. For the less able a broad-based curriculum is available with accreditation through ASDAN, C&G and the Basic Skills Agency. To suit the needs of the children, this would include social skills, therapy, creative skills etc.

Entry requirements: All children have a physical disabilities and other associated impairments. St Rose's School exists to provide high quality education and care for children with special needs, and is part of the English Dominican Sisters of St Catherine of Siena Charitable Trust.

St Vincent's School for Blind and Partially Sighted Children

Yew Tree Lane, West Derby, Liverpool L12 9HN   Tel: 0151 228 9968   Fax: 0151 252 0216
Website: www.ourworld.compuserve.com/homepages/STVINCENTS/

Head Mr A MacQuarrie
Founded 1850
School status Co-educational non-maintained weekly boarding and day
Member of OPSIS, NASS, CES
Accredited by DfEE, Registered Charity 526756
Special needs provision VIS
Age range 4–17 *Boarding from* 4 *No of pupils* 93

What we provide:
- Academic, vocational, personal and social education. Access to National Curriculum, tailored to individual need, leading to GCSE, NVQ, AEB, Basic and Certificates of Education, Bronze Level Youth Award Scheme.
- High staff to pupil ratio. Specialist staff supported by a qualified team of learning support assistants and nursery nurses.
- Independence training by mobility officers and care staff.
- Access to physiotherapist, speech therapist, optician, ophthalmologist, dentist and doctor.

Facilities at St Vincent's:
- Well-equipped classrooms with appropriate lighting and blinds, computers with speech synthesizers and large print facility.
- Specialist rooms for science, art, information/ design and food technology.
- Multi-gym, indoor swimming pool, canoes, all-weather pitch and soft play room.

Extra-curricular activities include:
- Educational visits and field trips, Duke of Edinburgh Awards.
- Tandem riding, cricket, snooker, karaoke, make-up and beauty.

Pupils are expected to, and do, work hard. The staff are committed to serving the needs of the pupils.

Applications should be made to the Head by the LEA, who are also responsible for the fees.

Sunfield

Clent Grove, Woodman Lane, Clent, Stourbridge, West Midlands DY9 9PB
Tel: 01562 882253   Fax: 01562 883856
E-mail: sunfield@sunfield.worcs.sch.uk   Website: www.sunfieldsch.u-net.com

Head Professor B Carpenter OBE
Founded 1930
School status DfEE approved independent co-educational boarding, registered charity
Religious denomination Non-denominational
Member of NAIMS, NASS, Association of West Midlands and Non-maintained Special Schools
Accredited by DfEE
Special needs provision ADD, ADHD, ASP, AUT, DOW, EBD, PMLD, SLD
Other needs catered for Severe and complex learning needs and challenging behaviour
Age range 6–19   *Boarding from* 6
No of pupils 75
Girls 15   *Boys* 60
Fees per annum Available on application

Sunfield offers education and 52-week residential care. Our integrated care and education based curriculum encompasses National Curriculum and individual needs. Students are supported by OTs, speech therapists and psychologists.

Sunfield offers specialist provision for children with severe autistic spectrum disorders.

Eleven houses each provide homes for 6–9 children. The school buildings comprise classrooms, theatre, games, craft, soft play and sensory rooms, kitchen, library and shop.

In preparation for citizenship, we use community facilities, eg, swimming pools, leisure centres, local clubs and shops. Our grounds, shop and farm offer meaningful accredited work experience for older students.

At Sunfield we recognise each child as a learner and communicator with a unique contribution to make. The principles of dignity and respect inform all aspects of our practice.

Swalcliffe Park School

Swalcliffe, Banbury, Oxfordshire OX15 5EP
Tel: 01295 780302   Fax: 01295 780006
E-mail: admin@swalcliffepark.co.uk

Principal Ray Hooper
Founded 1965
School status DfEE approved non-maintained 931/7007
Religious denomination Non-denominational
Member of NAES, NAS(Corp), NASS, SERSS
Special needs provision EBD, ASP, ADHD, ADD, MLD
Age range 11–19
No of pupils Boys 62   *(boarding)* 57
Fees per annum from £29,700 *(day) to* £45,975

Facilities include purpose-built educational and residential accommodation, set in 20 acres with lake, adventure playground, motorbikes, go-karts and swimming pool.

High quality education and care is offered to young people who have previously failed in a variety of educational establishments. We offer provision for a range of developmental, learning, behavioural and emotional difficulties.

A wide range of recreational activities are available. There is special provision for young people with Asperger Syndrome. Pupils follow the National Curriculum with emphasis on literacy, numeracy, practical curriculum (where appropriate) and a range of external examinations including GCSEs, City & Guilds and CoAs.

A well qualified co-ordinator gives individual help with severe literacy difficulties. Support is provided by a Psychiatrist, Educational Psychologist. Counselling can be facilitated at an additional cost.

Trengweath School

Hartley Road, Plymouth, Devon PL3 5LW
Tel: 01752 771975   Fax: 01752 793388

Head Mrs G B Pratchett MEd, BA
School status Co-educational DfEE approved
independent boarding and day
Religious denomination Non-denominational
Member of Scope
Special needs provision PMLD
Other needs catered for Multiply-disabled
visually impaired, multi-sensory impairment
Age range 2–19
No of pupils 30
Girls 12   *Boys* 8
Junior 12   *Senior* 8
Fees per annum (boarding) (full) £45,000–
£50,000 *(weekly)* £35,000 *(day)* £27,000

Trengweath is set in a residential district within
easy reach of Plymouth City. It is a centre of
advice and help for the community, keeping
close links with local families.

School: Day and boarding pupils aged 2–19
years, including a nursery. Mainstream children
learn alongside those with special needs in our
Integrated Nursery. Opportunities for integration in mainstream are available.
Therapy: We provide physiotherapy, music,
occupational and speech and language therapy.
Facilities include a gym, hydrotherapy pool,
sensory room, sand and water room, soft play
area and sensory garden.
Family Support: Working directly with parent
and child in-group sessions. Children attend
from three years old or from their first diagnosis. There is an Outreach Service in Cornwall.
Respite care: Operates in partnership with local
authorities. Open seven days a week, fifty
weeks of the year, on a 24-hour basis with an
Emergency Service available.

Treloar School

Upper Froyle, Alton, Hampshire GU34 4LA
Tel: 01420 526400   Fax: 01420 526426
E-mail: admissions@treloar.org.uk   Website: www.treloar.org.uk

Head Mr Neil Clark
Founded 1908
School status Co-educational non-maintained boarding and day
Religious denomination Non-denominational
Member of ISIS, NAIMS, NASS
Special needs provision CP, DEL, DYC, DYP, EPI, HI, MLD, PH, SP&LD, SPLD, VIS, W
Other needs catered for Physical disability with or without associated communication impairment or learning difficulties
Age range 5–16+   *Boarding from* 7
No of pupils 140
Girls 55   *Boys* 85
Fees per annum (boarding) £19,989–£51,300 *(day)* £14,991–£33,345

What do we offer and for whom?

Treloar School provides education, independence training and care for young people with physical disabilities. Many also have communication, hearing or visual impairment, or a degree of learning difficulty.

We aim to provide each individual with the support, confidence and skills to achieve in all aspects of daily living. Emphasis, as far as possible, is on independence, on taking control of one's own life.

Our approach

Our teaching, care, therapy and counselling staff work together as a multi-disciplinary team to develop a detailed 24-hour curriculum for each student. This close, caring co-operation seeks to address the academic, emotional, social, physical and medical needs of each individual.

Parents or carers are closely involved with this extended team. We aim to work with parents, social workers, and others, as appropriate, to help every student reach his or her potential.

Curriculum

The school provides a curriculum based on the individual needs and abilities of each student. We cater for a broad spectrum, offering all National Curriculum subjects and a range of certificated courses at Key Stage 4, including 12 subjects at GCSE.

We have small classes (six to eight students) with a large team of dedicated learning support assistants to help teachers in the classroom.

Entry requirements

Each potential student is considered individually.

Medical and therapy

The school has its own medical centre with full night cover. The medical team consists of a doctor and over 30 nurses and physio-, occupational and speech and language therapists. Our therapists routinely integrate their treatment with classroom activity. If an individual requires separate therapy session their timetable is arranged to accommodate this, which minimises the disruption to a student's education.

Residential and care

The school has three boarding houses, to which students are admitted according to their age. Day-to-day responsibility falls to the care co-ordinator. He or she works with other house staff and those in the wider school community to develop a warm, supportive environment. This helps students to grow into mature individuals who value their independence and the freedom to make responsible choices. Building a good relationship between the house and each child and his or her family is regarded as crucial.

Underley Garden School

Kirkby Lonsdale, Carnforth, Lancashire LA6 2DZ
Tel: 01524 271569   Fax: 01524 272581

Head Mrs Pam Redican
Founded 1990
School status Co-educational DfEE approved
independent boarding
Religious denomination Non-denominational
Special needs provision ADD, ADHD, ASP, EBD,
MLD, SPLD
Age range 9–16 Boarding from 9
No of pupils 49
Girls 28   *Boys* 21
Fees per annum Available on application

Curriculum: 24-hour care and education curriculum for boys and girls who have special educational needs that leave them vulnerable and troubled, and need help to develop confidence and relationships.
Entry requirements and procedures: Referrals by local education authorities and/or social services, resident and consultant staff available for assessment.
Examinations offered: GCSEs, Certificates of Achievement, AEB Basic Tests, AQA (NPRA) Units of Accreditation, CLAIT.
Academic and leisure facilities: Classrooms, residential accommodation, vocational workshops, laboratory, sports hall and playing fields, permanent camp site.
Special approaches: Small classes (7–8 pupils), individual education programmes of study, specialist and class teachers with a learning support assistant, special needs department (educational psychologist and learning support co-ordinator), consultant child psychiatrist, careers programme and work experience.
Boarding facilities: Residence in modern bungalows with domestic routines for seven pupils. Progression towards independence.

Underley Hall School

Kirkby Lonsdale, Carnforth, Lancashire LA6 2HE
Tel: 01524 271206   Fax: 01524 272581

Head Ms L Rosehr
Founded 1976
School status Boys DfEE approved independent
boarding
Religious denomination Non-denominational
Special needs provision ADD, ADHD, EBD,
MLD, SPLD
Age range 9–16   Boarding from 9
No of pupils 70
Fees per annum Available on application

Curriculum: 24-hour care and education curriculum for boys who are unable to make or hold good relationships, may have learning difficulties and who often cause problems or anxiety at home.
Entry requirements and procedures: Referrals by local education authorities and/or social services, resident and consultant staff available for assessment.
Examinations offered: GCSEs, Certificates of Achievement, AEB Basic Tests, AQA (NPRA) Units of Accreditation.
Academic and leisure facilities: Classrooms, residential accommodation, vocational workshops, laboratory, sports hall and playing fields, permanent camp site.
Special approaches: Small classes (7–8 pupils), individual education programmes of study, specialist and class teachers with a learning support assistant, special needs department (educational psychologist and learning support co-ordinator), consultant child psychiatrist, careers programme and work experience.
Boarding facilities: Residence in living areas with domestic routines. Progression towards independence with a town house for school leavers.

The Unicorn School

Stroud Court, Oxford Road, Eynsham, Oxfordshire OX8 1BY
Tel: 01865 881820   Fax: 01865 881820
E-mail: unicorndyslexia@hotmail.com

Head Mrs E Christie
Founded 1991
School status Co-educational independent day
Religious denomination Non-denominational
Special needs provision ADD, ADHD, DYC, DYP, DYS, W
Age range 6–12
No of pupils 30
Boys 30
Fees per annum £7,650

Aims and philosophy
To provide specialist education for dyslexic children, from both independent and maintained sector, and to teach strategies and skills to enable them to return to mainstream education as soon as possible.

The Unicorn caters for dyslexic children who often also have difficulties stemming from ADD, ADHD, dyspraxia and dyscalculia. Pupils are taught by specialist teachers in small classes of 8–10, with a daily half-hour of individual tuition, including Phonographix.

A structured, multi-sensory programme, including an appropriately differentiated national curriculum is followed with extensive use of word processors and encouragement to develop creative talents.

Educational and emotional needs are met on an individual basis as well as through a friendly atmosphere and community spirit.

Close liaison is maintained with the local education authority; parents are supported throughout the time they are associated with the Unicorn and helped to find suitable schools for their children to move on to.

Westwood School (NCH)

479 Margate Road, Broadstairs, Kent CT10 2QA
Tel: 01843 600820   Fax: 01843 600827

Head Mr C L Walter
Founded 1995
School status Co-educational independent day
Religious denomination Methodist
Member of NCH
Special needs provision ADHD, EBD, MLD
Age range 11–16
No of pupils 21
Girls 3   *Boys* 18
Junior 10   *Senior* 11
Fees per annum £19,570–£20,900

Westwood School is situated on the outskirts of Broadstairs – one of Kent's premier seaside towns. The School is managed by NCH, one of Britain's leading child care charities.

Westwood School currently caters for up to 30 young people between the ages of 11 and 16, whose primary special needs are concerned with Emotional and Behavioural Difficulties (EBD). Pupils may also experience delay with their academic progress and consequently require additional support accordingly.

Children benefit from an excellent teacher-pupil ratio, enabling us to deliver a tailored curriculum to meet the needs of the individual. Our team of experienced staff is able to offer pastoral care, in addition to delivering the National Curriculum up to GCSE level in a number of subjects. A discrete Vocational Programme also provides vital independence skills and knowledge for later life. This programme includes units on citizenship, careers education, and work experience.

"We wish to be a special, happy and caring school, expecting all users to be valued and expecting them to value the school."

Willoughby Hall Dyslexia Centre

1 Willoughby Road, London NW3 1RP
Tel: 020 7794 3538   Fax: 020 7435 2872

Principal W H Wilcox
Founded September 1998
School status Co-educational independent day
Religious denomination Non-denominational
Age range 6–12
Girls 7   *Boys* 26
Fees per annum £11,550

Willoughby Hall Dyslexia Centre offers a complete course of education for pupils aged from 6 to 12 years, who are held back by dyslexia and other learning difficulties. The Centre is a development of work done over the last twenty years at North Bridge House School, culminating in the opening of this special facility, itself based on a pilot scheme at our Parkway premises.

The teaching is based on a two year full-time course which aims to provide the pupils with a thorough knowledge of the skills required in Secondary Education, enabling pupils to return to the mainstream. As dyslexic children can have a very limited span of concentration, the intensive work in therapy can only be maintained for very short periods. This means that other activities such as Art, Music and CDT must be simultaneously available so that they can relax, whenever necessary. The children are taught in a small group from which individuals are drawn out to concentrate on building the skills they have failed to develop earlier and overcoming their specific difficulties.

Each pupil works to an Individual Education Plan. The main emphasis is on English and Mathematics, using a multi-sensory approach. Science, History, Geography, Scripture, Art, Design, Music, Drama, Computing (including keyboarding skills) and Study Skills all feature in the curriculum. We keep as close as possible to the mainstream syllabus.

Pupils are able to take part in a varied programme of Physical education at Willoughby Hall.

Dyslexia Centre pupils are taught keyboard skills and basic computing. Those pupils for whom a laptop computer is an essential classroom aid will thus be able to use it to best advantage.

At the Dyslexia Centre it is understood that parents will want to be very closely involved with their child's education and the Head Teacher and her Deputy will always make time to see parents, even at short notice.

Should you wish to discuss the work of the Willoughby Hall Dyslexia Centre further, please telephone the secretary on 020 7794 3538. Entry to the department is by interview and test. The parent is also required to arrange for an assessment by an Educational Psychologist recommended by the school.

Woodcroft School

Whitakers Way, Loughton, Essex IG10 1SQ
Tel: 020 8508 1369   Fax: 020 8502 4855

Head Mrs Margaret Newton
Founded 1963
School status DfEE approved independent
Special needs provision ADD, ADHD, ASP, AUT,
CP, DEL, DOW, DYS, DYP, EBD, EPI, HI, MLD,
PH, PMLD, SLD, SPLD, SP&LD, VIS, W
Age range 2–11   *No of pupils (day)* 24
Fees per annum On application

Woodcroft School provides child-centred educational and therapeutic interventions for children who have been referred from local education authorities for a variety of reasons. These include uneven developmental progress; 'failing in school'; being under educational, emotional or social stress; and having varying degrees of communication, sensory and physical disorders. A broad and balanced curriculum, including the National Curriculum, is fostered by providing a high ratio of qualified and experienced staff to pupils; a flexible structure, which can adapt to the pupils' abilities and aptitudes; and a setting which is secure, friendly and pleasant. Close co-operation is maintained with sending authorities and parents. Our on-site mainstream nursery for children from the local area provides a unique resource for children to integrate appropriately with others, and links with local mainstream schools offer similar opportunities. Our aim is to help children to make the most of their abilities and to prepare them to enter or to continue their schooling under their LEA's statutory provision.

Yorkshire Residential School for the Deaf

(incorporating Doncaster College for the Deaf)
Leger Way, Doncaster, South Yorkshire DN2 6AY
Tel: 01302 386700 Fax: 01302 361808
E-mail: enquiries@yrsd-dcd.org.uk   Website: www.yrsd-dcd.org.uk

Director Mr H Heard, MA, FCollP
Founded 1829
School status Co-educational DfEE approved independent boarding and day
Special needs provision ASP, CP, DYC, DYS, DYP, EBD, HI, MLD, PH, SP&LD, SPLD, VIS
Age range 5–16 *Boarding from* 5
No of pupils 60   *Girls* 25   *Boys* 35
School year 190 days
Fees per annum Available on request

The school provides high quality education and training for deaf and hearing-impaired young people. Registered Charity No. 529410.
Curriculum: Pupils receive a balanced education following the National Curriculum guidelines. The main aim is to help each child reach his or her full potential intellectually, physically, emotionally and socially.

Examinations offered: GCSE qualifications, unit accreditation and Communicative use of English examinations.
Academic and leisure facilities: All classrooms and workshops are designed to provide ideal acoustic conditions and have the latest auditory equipment.
The teaching staff are skilled and experienced, and are qualified Teachers of the Deaf.
There are superb sports and recreational facilities, including a sports hall, a heated indoor swimming pool, and extensive playing fields.
Educational Management Unit: The Educational Management Unit is for pupils with significant behavioural problems. The aim of the unit is to help the pupils remediate their behaviour until they can be fully integrated into normal classes.

3.2
Profiles of Colleges and Other Provision at 16+

Bridgend College

Cowbridge Road, Bridgend, CF31 3DH
Tel: 01656 302302   Fax: 01656 663912
E-mail: KMjones@bridgend.ac.uk   Website: www.bridgend.ac.uk

Principal Mr Roger Hampton
Founded 1929
College Status Co-educational, FEFCW
maintained
Special needs provision DYS, HI, SPLD, VIS
Member of NFAC
Accredited by National Federation of Access
Centres
Age range 16–25
No of resident places 23

The College has a long established provision for students with special needs and this continues to evolve to meet the needs of our students. The college's SEN provision has two modes of attendance. Students may attend specialist and mainstream courses on a day or residential basis.

School of Pre-Vocational Education
Classroom accommodation is at the centre of the college with safe and easy access to the main college facilities. The department has an Access Centre for technical assessment and support as well as specialist service for students with Dyslexia, hearing and visual impairments.
Weston House
This purpose-built facility has been developed to provide opportunities for young people with learning difficulties and/or disabilities to access further education, enhancing their career prospects and quality of life. The students are offered a 24-hour curriculum, which is individually negotiated in conjunction with the student's chosen college course. The residential unit operates from Sunday to Friday afternoons.

Coleg Elidyr

Rhandirmwyn, Llandovery, Carmarthenshire SA20 0NL
Tel: 01550 760400   Fax: 01550 760331

Contact Admissions Group
Founded 1973
College of Further Education status Co-educational Non-maintained boarding
Special needs provision AUT, EBD, EPI, MLD, SLD
Age range 16+
No of pupils (boarding) 65
Fees per annum (boarding) from £20,000
(reviewed every August)

Coleg Elidyr is a Camphill Community College and a registered charity for further education and training for young people with learning difficulties. It is set on three sites, in the beautiful Towy Valley. The residential houses are run as family units, for up to 10 students.

We offer a 3-year residential programme of learning for the post-16 age group, which includes opportunities to develop and improve the following: independent living skills, basic/key skills (literacy, numeracy and IT), arts/crafts, personal and social skills, as well as work experience in a range of vocational areas. The extended curriculum allows for learning throughout a student's individual programme. Where relevant, students can continue with a 2-year vocational apprenticeship. Nationally recognised courses are accredited through LCCIEB, NPTC and SWWOCN. Students may also have the opportunity of progressing to our more adult setting at Glasallt Fawr, or to the more independent household in the village of Llangadog.

Finchale Training College

Durham, DH1 5RX
Tel: 0191 386 2634   Fax: 0191 386 4962
E-mail: finchale.college@mailbox.as   Website: www.finchalecollege.co.uk

Head Dr D T Etheridge
Founded 1943
School status N/A
Religious denomination Non-denominational
Member of NCVO   *Accredited by* ISO9002; lip
Special needs provision ADD, ADHD, ASP, CP,
DEL, DYS, DYP, EPI, HI (limited provision),
MLD, PH, VIS (limited provision), W
Age range 18+
No of students (boarding) approx. 120
(day) approx. 60
Fees per annum N/A

Finchale Training College offers integrated programmes of vocational training and individual specialist support to disabled adults who have a wide range of impairments, ranging from physical to stress-related conditions. Our students come to us having shared experiences of unemployment and the barriers, as a result of their condition, faced in gaining employment. It is our aim and focus to enable the individual to gain the skills necessary to make the transition from welfare dependency to work. This is achieved through varied means, for some it involves short courses that build confidence and personal skills and others undertake full time vocational training programmes leading to employment in the related industry.

Personal support, including counselling, is tailored to meet individual needs with qualified nursing staff and wardens on duty 24 hours a day. Finchale also has a Learning Support Unit, which enables the development of literacy, communication and numerical skills to providing dyslexia support.

**At Finchale We actively promote Equal
Opportunities for All**

Lindeth College of Further Education

The Oaks, Lindeth, Bowness-on-Windermere, Cumbria LA23 3NH
Tel: 015394 46265   Fax: 015394 88840
E-mail: lindeth.college@nbol.co.uk

Head Mrs N S Buckley
Founded 1985
School status Co-educational independent
boarding only
Religious denomination Non-denominational
Member of NATSPEC, ARC
Special needs provision ADD, ADHD, ASP, AUT,
DOW, DYS, EPI, HI, MLD, SP&LD, SPLD
Age range 16–25   *Boarding from* 16
No of boarders (full) 44
Fees per annum (boarding) (full) £14,000–
£30,000

The College provides residential education courses for up to a 3-year period within a caring, supportive and inclusive learning residential environment. Individual Programmes are negotiated and formulated according to student needs.

The 24-hour curriculum offers courses in independent living and community skills, vocational training, IT, literacy and numeracy and work placement opportunities. The aim is that on leaving the College the student will be able to live more independently, and access the local community, further education, training or employment opportunities as appropriate.

The atmosphere is happy and purposeful, within a structured and disciplined framework. Initial accommodation is provided in the main house, which is homely, colourfully decorated and well maintained. When confident and ready for further independence, students are able to move to the training cottages.

The students are supported by a high ratio of staff who offer guidance and encouragement in their continued development in academic, social and recreational skills.

Mencap National College

mencap
making the most of life

Dilston College of Further Education

Dilston Hall, Corbridge, Northumberland NE45 5RJ
Tel: 01434 632692   Fax: 01434 633721

Head Mr J A Jameson BA, PGCE
Founded 1971
College status Co-educational independent

Member of NATSPEC, Skill
No of students   50 *Boarding from* 16
Fees per annum (boarding) On application

Lufton Manor College

Lufton, Yeovil, Somerset BA22 8ST
Tel: 01935 403120   Fax: 01935 403126

Principal Mr Rupert Elliot
School status Residential specialist college,
boarding and day
Special needs provision MLD, SLD, SP&LD

Age range 16–25   *Boarding from* 16
No of students 70
Female 30   *Male* 40
Fees per annum (boarding) On application

Pengwern College

Sarn Road, Rhuddlan, Denbighshire LL18 5UH
Tel: 01745 590281   Fax: 01745 591735
E-mail: mencap.pengwern.college@campus.bt.com
Website: www.campus.com/campusworld/orgs/org/12021

Principal Mr Melvyn Booker BA, Dip TMHA,
Dip TA
Founded 1966
School status Independent specialist college for
learning disabilities
Member of ARC, NATSPEC, Skill

Accredited by Open College, City & Guilds,
NVQ awarding bodies
Age range 16–25   *Boarding from* 16
No of students 47
Fees per annum (boarding) On application

Going to a residential college or university is an opportunity which many young people take advantage of, but it can prove an even more valuable experience for school leavers with a learning disability.

That's why Mencap National College has been created – to give young people with learning disabilities the same access to residential further education as their non-disabled peers. In addition to gaining vital qualifications and skills for employment – including National Vocational Qualifications, City & Guilds and Open College accreditation – students learn to socialise and to take responsibility for themselves. Meanwhile, their parents and carers have the space and time to adapt to their son's or daughter's developing independence and maturity.

Because it is run by the UK's largest charity for people with a learning disability, Mencap National College is able to draw on a vast store of experience, knowledge and services from across the country. Courses are tailored to the individual, and each student is encouraged to experience as many different subjects, occupations, leisure pursuits and hobbies as possible during their time at college. This enables them to make appropriate choices about their future and to work towards the occupation, which they feel suits them best.

The College incorporates three separate sites, in Northumberland, North Wales and Somerset. While all three operate within the same framework and according to the same principles and objectives, each has its own particular features and specialisms.

The Papworth Trust

Papworth Everard, Cambridge CB3 8RG
Tel: 01480 830341   Fax: 01480 830781
E-mail: jeffrey_SKIPP@papworth.org.uk

Chief Executive Mr Gordon Lister
Special needs provision CP, DOW, EPI, MLD, PH, W
Age range 19+

Papworth Trust provides a range of individually tailored programmes designed to maximise independence and enable people with disabilities aged 19+ to live and work independently. Our services include supported accommodation, registered care homes, Progression programmes, supported employment as well as early rehab and assessment services. We also provide fully accessible housing across the East Anglia region.

Our vocational programmes give people the opportunity to achieve NVQ and Open College qualifications in a variety of topics. We are also able to access other educational, employment, social and leisure facilities within the wider community. This enables The Papworth Trust to offer a wider and truly individualised programme to the people accessing our services. Experienced care, welfare and supported housing staff, together with a physiotherapy service, provide comprehensive support to residents and tenants. The support offered works within an ethos of enabling independence and autonomy through the development of social and independent living skills.

Portland College

Nottingham Road, Mansfield, Nottinghamshire NG18 4TJ
Tel: 01623 499111   Fax: 01623 499134
E-mail: college@portland.org.uk Website: www.portland.org.uk

Head M E A Syms OBE
Founded 1950
School status Co-educational DfEE approved independent
Religious denomination Non-denominational
Member of NATSPEC
Inspected by FEFC
Special needs provision CP, DYC, DYS, DYP, EPI, HI, MLD, PH, SP&LD, VIS, W
Other needs catered for Physical disabilities and associated learning difficulties
Age range 16–60
No of pupils (boarding) (full) 230 *(weekly)* 40
Fees per annum (boarding) £14,000–£50,000

Portland College provides first class education and training in a caring residential environment for students with disabilities age 16–60. Portland is able to offer individual customised programmes of education and training, allowing each student to develop their potential. A wide programme of activity and learning takes place throughout the day placing great emphasis on a complete 'living' experience for all students.

Vocational programmes lead to occupation in the fields of business and information technology, electronics, engineering and horticulture, and to the achievement of National Vocational Qualifications.

Accommodation on campus is purpose built with easy access for those with mobility problems. Students live in comfortable residences, each with single study bedrooms. All meals are provided and the catering service is able to offer any type of diet.

Experienced care and welfare staff, together with 24 hour medical cover and the disciplines of physiotherapy, occupational and speech and language therapy, provide a comprehensive student support service.

The recreation and leisure facilities are excellent providing a wide range of activity.

RNIB Redhill College

Philanthropic Road, Redhill, Surrey RH1 4DG
Tel: 01737 768935   Fax: 01737 778776   E-mail: liliffe@rnib.org.uk

Head Mrs Judith Foot
Founded 1958
School status Co-educational independent
voluntary
Member of NATSPEC
Accredited by FEFC
Special needs provision ASP, AUT, CP, DOW,
DYS, EPI, HI, MLD, PH, SLD, SPLD, VIS, W
Age range 16–60   *Boarding from* 16
No of pupils 100
Fees per annum Various

RNIB Redhill College provides further education and vocational training courses for visually impaired school leavers and adult trainees. Programmes range from a course to develop skills for independent living through to vocational training courses. The College fosters a holistic and developmental approach to learning, with programmes tailored to meet the learning needs of each student.

The College has a wide range of specialist equipment designed to meet the needs of students of differing abilities and needs, supported by staff with appropriate specialist qualifications. A new fitness centre with adapted equipment was opened in January 2000.

Redhill College has close links with local mainstream FE colleges, as well as providing link courses for several schools. Students are encouraged, if appropriate, to access mainstream courses on a part-time basis, and are supported by experienced staff from Redhill College.

A range of specialist support staff, including a physiotherapist and speech therapist, provide a comprehensive student support service.

The College is situated on a 13-acre campus close to Redhill with good rail links with London, Reading and the south coast. It is also close to the M25, M23 and Gatwick Airport.

Royal National College for the Blind (RNC)

College Road, Hereford HR1 1EB
Tel: 01432 265725   Fax: 01432 353478
E-mail: reg@rncb.ac.uk   Website: www.rncb.ac.uk

Head Mrs R Burge
Founded 1872
School status Co-educational DfEE approved
boarding and day
Religious denomination Non-denominational
Member of National Federation of Access
Centres, NATSPEC, OPSIS
Special needs provision DYS, HI, VIS
Age range 16–56
No of pupils 200
Fees per annum On application

RNC offers a wide range of academic and vocational programmes to school leavers from across the UK and overseas. Learning takes place in a friendly, supportive and professional atmosphere. At an initial assessment, students have an opportunity to discuss their career

objectives and the support they will need to achieve their goals. This forms the basis for an *Action Plan* aimed at promoting personal development with an emphasis on personal responsibility, learning and transition to independence. All students have open access to RNC's unique 'Flexible Learning Centre'. Classrooms are bright, modern and fully equipped with the latest technology. RNC's teaching staff are professionally qualified and experienced in providing education to people who are blind or partially sighted. The College has a fully qualified counselling team, a Welfare/Benefits Counsellor and a fully equipped medical centre providing 24-hour care. RNC has the services of two GPs and an Ophthalmologist as well as links with the local Eye Hospital.

RNIB Skills Development Centres   Charity number 226227

RNIB Alwyn House

3 Wemyshall Road, Ceres, Fife KY15 5LX
Tel: 01334 828894   Fax: 01334 828911
E-mail: mlawrie@rnib.org.uk

College status Co-educational boarding and day
Special needs provision CP, EBD, VIS
Age range 16+

No of boarders up to 60
Fees per annum Contact each centre

RNIB Manor House

Middle Lincombe Road, Torquay, Devon TQ1 2NG
Tel: 01803 214523   Fax: 01803 214143
E-mail: manorhouse@rnib.org.uk   Website: www.rnib.org.uk/services/manorpro.htm

College status Co-educational boarding and day
Special needs provision PH, VIS, W
Age range 16+
No of boarders up to 30
Fees per annum Contact each centre

RNIB Alwyn House and RNIB Manor House cater for adults and young people over 16 who have visual impairment, including those with additional disabilities and health problems. These centres enable people to gain the skills and confidence needed to cope independently at home, college, work and within the community. The centres provide specialist assessment and a wide range of rehabilitation, training and work preparation programmes.

Programmes and courses are tailored according to an individual's needs and both centres offer residential, non-residential, part time or full time programmes.

For further details contact the appropriate centre manager (addresses above).

RNIB Vocational College

Radmoor Road, Loughborough, Leicestershire LE11 3AB
Tel: 01509 611077   Fax: 01509 232013
E-mail: enquiries@rnibvocoll.ac.uk   Website: www.rnibvocoll.ac.uk

Head Mr K Connell
Founded 1989
Status Co-educational boarding and day
Member of NATSPEC
Special needs provision VIS-primarily, DYS, EPI,
HI, PH, W-secondary
Age range 16–60   *Boarding from* 16
No of students 80   *No of boarders* 74
Fees per annum Upon application

The RNIB Vocational College Loughborough is a residential college for people who are blind or partially sighted, sometimes with additional disabilities or moderate learning difficulties. The college is situated on the same campus and works in close partnership with Loughborough College to provide students with an unrivalled range of specialist and mainstream courses, in a superb location with all the support they need.

Staff are experienced at supporting students. A wide range of adapted materials and specialist equipment can be provided, based upon the student's particular needs. The Residential Support team provides counselling and training in a variety of independent living skills. A dedicated Employment Placement Officer helps students to prepare for work or continuing education upon leaving.

The College and Residential Centre are purpose built and modern.

Students have access to all the clubs and facilities provided by Loughborough Students Union and the college has a busy social life.

PART FOUR: INDEPENDENT MAINSTREAM SCHOOLS WITH SPECIALIST PROVISION

4.1

Provision for special educational needs in independent mainstream schools: An Introduction

As a parent, you have the best knowledge of your child's individual needs. You will want to consider whether he or she would be happy and able to thrive with appropriate help in a mainstream school, or whether a special school, with highly specialist facilities and resources, is more appropriate. You may feel that a special school will be best able to meet his or her needs. Alternatively, you may prefer your child to learn in a mainstream school environment if the right support is available.

Many independent mainstream schools offer help for pupils with SEN, most often with specific learning difficulties such as dyslexia. However, most will not accept children with Statements of SEN and the vast majority are unlikely to be able to cater for children with severe emotional and behavioural difficulties. The specialist teaching expertise and facilities in school, and the extent of help available, varies widely from one school to another. Some have extensive experience in providing SEN support. A few have a significant proportion of students with SEN and a dedicated unit in school staffed by qualified specialist teachers. Pupils may be withdrawn from certain lessons during the school day, during which time they receive specialist support. Some may offer differentiated work within the normal classroom. Others may be sympathetic to special needs but may not have the facilities to make any special provision. It is important to remember that in most cases schools will expect your child to meet the normal entry requirements for the school and to be able to cope in an ordinary school setting.

If you are considering mainstream schools, it is important to find out exactly how these would meet your child's individual needs. To help you find out which schools in the directory are appropriate for your child, the help available at each school for each type of need listed is shown in one of three different categories (see page 361). If you are looking for schools which make provision for dyslexia, you may also find it helpful to consult the register of schools produced by CReSTeD (Council for the Registration of Schools Teaching Dyslexic pupils) on page 520.

When contacting or visiting schools which interest you, you may wish to ask about the following points to help you make an assessment of the school's suitability:

Academic pace
Finding the right academic environment for your child is every bit as essential as finding a school that will provide the right level of SEN support. Ask to see examples of children's work. Where do leavers go? Is the school's overall thrust and ethos suitable for your child?

Experience and expertise in managing SEN
- How much experience has the school had of teaching children with needs or a spectrum of needs similar to your child's?
- How many such students are currently enrolled? What help do these students receive?
- What proportion of pupils in the school have SEN?
- Are staff qualified in SEN teaching?
- Does the school have full-time SEN teaching specialists or is teaching done on a part-time basis?
- What have been the destinations of recent leavers with SEN?

Meeting the needs of your child
- What strategy would the school suggest for meeting your child's needs? How many special lessons would your child have per week? How big are the groups for these lessons? Will your child have to give up another subject in order to have special lessons or will these be given outside normal lesson times? What will the lessons cover? Will there be additional support in class? If so, from whom?
- If Information Technology facilities are an important resource for your child, what can the school offer? Is there a dedicated area available? Are computers and laptops freely available for use?
- Will the school arrange for special arrangements during GCSE and/or A Level examinations, if appropriate?

Communication with teachers and parents
- How will those in school, who are responsible for teaching and caring for your child, be kept informed of his or her needs and progress by the Special Needs department?
- How, and how often, will parents be kept in touch with progress and plans?

Wider needs
- It is equally important to check that your child's strengths and interests outside the classroom can be catered for. If he or she is good at music, sport, drama or has a special interest in, for example, outdoor pursuits or debating, will the school offer the right levels of encouragement and opportunities to develop these, either now or at a later stage?
- Similarly, what help and advice is given to senior school pupils about university entry and careers?
- Does your child have particular medical or dietary needs that must be provided for in school?
- Are there any religious considerations? If your family is of a faith different from that of the school, how will your child's faith be accommodated? Will he/she find it difficult to play a full part in school life?
- Does the school share your values as a parent? What are its policies with reference to discipline, bullying and drugs and the extent of guidance given on Personal & Social Education (PSE)?

For information on individual schools, see the profiles in this section (pages 423–428) If you would like more personal help to find suitable mainstream schools for your child, contact Gabbitas, who can assist with independent educational assessment and make a personal selection of schools.

Gabbitas Educational Consultants
Carrington House, 126–130 Regent Street, London W1B 5EE
Tel: 020 7734 0161   Fax: 020 7437 1764
Email: admin@gabbitas.co.uk   Website: www.gabbitas.co.uk

Independent Mainstream Schools with Specialist Provision
Note on information given in the directory section

Type of school

This directory comprises schools listed within the Department for Education and Employment Register of Independent Schools which replied to our request for information. These schools offer varying levels of help for students with special needs, from additional tuition on a limited withdrawal basis, to specialist units and teaching programmes (see below). For specific details parents should contact individual schools direct.

Each school is given a brief description, which explains whether the school is single-sex or co-educational. In some cases schools take small numbers of the opposite sex within a specified age range. These are indicated where appropriate, eg: Boys boarding and day 3–18 (Day girls 16–18).

Schools are described as 'boarding' (which indicates boarding pupils only), 'boarding and day', 'day and boarding' (indicating a predominance of day pupils) or 'day' only.

Number of boarders

Where necessary these are divided into full boarders (F) and weekly boarders (W). Weekly boarding arrangements vary according to individual school policy.

Fees

All fees are given annually from September 2000 unless otherwise stated. It should be remembered, however, that some schools increase fees during the year and the figures shown may therefore be subject to change after September 2000. Where the date is other than September 2000, the information provided is the latest available from the school. Figures are shown for full boarding (FB), weekly boarding (WB) and day fees. In some instances the fees for full and weekly boarding are the same (F/WB). A minimum and a maximum fee are given for each range. These figures are intended as a guide only. For more precise information schools should be contacted direct.

Symbols

* denotes that the school has a profile later in this section
† denotes that the school is registered with CReSTeD (see Part 5.2)

Levels of Provision

The schools in this section are mainstream independent schools which offer levels of varying provision for students with special needs. In some cases help may be extensive; in others it may be more limited. In order to offer a guide to the level of provision, each school is asked to classify its provision for each type of need at one of three levels:

Level 1

The school has a dedicated special needs unit with suitably qualified staff to provide for this type of special need or provides teaching by suitably qualified staff in special classes for pupils with this type of need.

Level 2

Pupils with this type of special need are withdrawn from certain lessons during the school day, during which time they receive extra support from suitably qualified staff, or are given differentiated work within the normal classroom environment.

Level 3

Pupils with this type of special need are treated sympathetically but there is no specialist support available.

Unspecified

Special needs for which the school makes provision but has not given a classification are listed as 'Unspecified'.

Key to abbreviations

Abbreviations used to denote Special Needs provision in this section are as follows:

ADD	Attention Deficit Disorder	EPI	Epilepsy
ADHD	Attention Deficit/Hyperactivity Disorder	HI	Hearing Impairment
		MLD	Moderate Learning Difficulties
ASP	Asperger Syndrome	PH	Physical Impairment
AUT	Autism	PMLD	Profound and Multiple
CP	Cerebral Palsy		Learning Difficulties
DEL	Delicate	SLD	Severe Learning Difficulties
DOW	Down's Syndrome	SP&LD	Speech and Language
DYC	Dyscalculia		Difficulties
DYP	Dyspraxia	SPLD	Specific Learning Difficulties
DYS	Dyslexia	TOU	Tourette's Syndrome
EBD	Emotional and Behavioural Difficulties	VIS	Visual Impairment
		W	Wheelchair access

4.2
Directory of Independent Mainstream Schools with Specialist Provision

ENGLAND

BEDFORDSHIRE

BEDFORD SCHOOL
De Parys Avenue, Bedford,
Bedfordshire MK40 2TU
Tel: (01234) 362200
Head: Dr I P Evans
Type: Boys Day and Boarding 13–18
No of pupils: B649 *No of Boarders:* F160
W49
Fees: (September 00) FB £14460 WB
£14070 Day £9120
Special Needs: Level 2: ADD DYC
DYP DYS

BEDFORD SCHOOL STUDY CENTRE
67 De Parys Avenue, Bedford,
Bedfordshire MK40 2TR
Tel: (01234) 362300
Head: Mrs O Heffill
Type: Co-educational Boarding 11–17
No of pupils: B18 G12
No of Boarders: F30
Fees: (September 00) FB £18960
Special Needs: Level 2: DYC DYP DYS

BROADMEAD SCHOOL
Tennyson Road, Luton, Bedfordshire
LU1 3RR
Tel: (01582) 722570
Head: Mr A F Compton
Type: Co-educational Day 2–11
No of pupils: B65 G65
Fees: (September 00) Day £3090
Special Needs: Level 2: DYC DYS
SP&LD

MOORLANDS SCHOOL
Leagrave Hall, Luton, Bedfordshire
LU4 9LE
Tel: (01582) 573376
Head: Mr A Cook
Type: Co-educational Day 2–11
No of pupils: B178 G180
Fees: (September 00) Day £3654 –
£3894
Special Needs: Unspecified: DYS

BERKSHIRE

BRADFIELD COLLEGE
Bradfield, Reading, Berkshire
RG7 6AR
Tel: (0118) 964 4500
Head: Mr P B Smith
Type: Boys Boarding and Day 13–18
(Co-ed VIth Form)
No of pupils: B460 G120
No of Boarders: F550
Fees: (September 00) FB £14160 –
£15105 Day £10620 – £11328
Special Needs: Level 1: DYS

THE BRIGIDINE SCHOOL
Queensmead, Kings Road, Windsor,
Berkshire SL4 2AX
Tel: (01753) 863779
Head: Mrs M B Cairns
Type: Girls Day 3–18 (Boys 3–7)
No of pupils: 280
Fees: (September 00) Day £4425 –
£6405
Special Needs: Level 1: DYP DYS
SPLD

CHEAM SCHOOL
Headley, Newbury, Berkshire
RG19 8LD
Tel: (01635) 268381
Head: Mr M R Johnson
Type: Co-educational Boarding and
Day 3–13
No of pupils: B202 G126
No of Boarders: F50 W35
Fees: (September 00) FB £12120 Day
£5130 – £8970
Special Needs: Level 2: DYP DYS
SPLD

EAGLE HOUSE
Sandhurst, Berkshire GU47 8PH
Tel: (01344) 772134
Head: Mr S J Carder
Type: Co-educational Day and
Boarding 3–13
No of pupils: B246 G62
No of Boarders: F17 W16
Fees: (September 00) F/WB £10600
Day £4830 – £8100
Special Needs: Level 2: DYS

ELSTREE SCHOOL
Woolhampton, Reading, Berkshire
RG7 5TD
Tel: (0118) 971 3302
Head: Mr S M Hill
Type: Boys Boarding and Day 3–13
(Girls 3–7)
No of pupils: B240 G20
No of Boarders: F100 W10
Fees: (September 00) FB £11700 Day
£4950 – £8400
Special Needs: Level 1: DYS Level 2:
DYC Level 3: DEL

ETON COLLEGE
Windsor, Berkshire SL4 6DW
Tel: (01753) 671000
Head: Mr J E Lewis
Type: Boys Boarding 13–18
No of pupils: 1283
No of Boarders: F1283
Fees: (September 00) FB £16488
Special Needs: Level 1: DYP DYS

ETON END PNEU
35 Eton Road, Datchet, Slough,
Berkshire SL3 9AX
Tel: (01753) 541075
Head: Mrs B E Ottley
Type: Girls Day 3–11 (Boys 3–7)
No of pupils: B70 G165
Fees: (September 00) Day £3105 –
£4755
Special Needs: Level 2: DYP DYS

HOLME GRANGE SCHOOL
Heathlands Road, Wokingham,
Berkshire RG40 3AL
Tel: (0118) 978 1566
Head: Mr N J Brodrick
Type: Co-educational Day 3–13
No of pupils: B176 G140
Fees: (September 00) Day £2328 –
£5952
Special Needs: Level 2: DYS SPLD

HURST LODGE†
Bagshot Road, Ascot, Berkshire
SL5 9JU
Tel: (01344) 622154
Head: Mrs A M Smit
Type: Girls Day and Boarding 2–18
(Boys 2–11)
No of pupils: B41 G210
No of Boarders: F12 W12
Fees: (September 00) FB £12600 Day
£2340 – £7530
Special Needs: Level 2: ADD DYC
DYP DYS SPLD Level 3: EPI PH

LICENSED VICTUALLERS' SCHOOL
London Road, Ascot, Berkshire
SL5 8DR
Tel: (01344) 882770
Head: Mr I A Mullins
Type: Co-educational Boarding and
Day 4–18
No of pupils: 720 *No of Boarders:* F70
W120
Fees: (September 00) FB £11007 –
£11595 WB £11008 – £11595 Day
£3994 – £6573
Special Needs: Unspecified: DYS PH

LONG CLOSE SCHOOL
Upton Court Road, Slough,
Berkshire SL3 7LU
Tel: (01753) 520095
Head: Mr M H Kneath
Type: Co-educational Day 2–13
No of pupils: B172 G64
Fees: (September 00) Day £3228 –
£6426
Special Needs: Level 1: ADD ADHD
DYC DYS SPLD Level 2: DYP PH
SP&LD Unspecified: W

LUCKLEY-OAKFIELD SCHOOL
Luckley Road, Wokingham,
Berkshire RG40 3EU
Tel: (0118) 978 4175
Head: Mr R C Blake
Type: Girls Day and Boarding 11–18
No of pupils: 280 *No of Boarders:* F25
W38
Fees: (September 00) FB £12102 WB
£11169 Day £7092
Special Needs: Level 2: DYP DYS
Level 3: ADD EPI HI

THE ORATORY PREPARATORY SCHOOL
Goring Heath, Reading, Berkshire
RG8 7SF
Tel: (0118) 984 4511
Head: Mr D L Sexon
Type: Co-educational Day and
Boarding 3–13
No of pupils: B272 G83
No of Boarders: F53
Fees: (September 00) FB £10080 Day
£2025 – £7290
Special Needs: Level 2: DYP DYS MLD
SPLD Unspecified: W

OUR LADY'S PREPARATORY SCHOOL
The Avenue, Crowthorne, Berkshire
RG45 6PB
Tel: (01344) 773394
Head: Mrs E A Rhodes
Type: Co-educational Day 3–11
No of pupils: B55 G55
Fees: (September 00) Day £1900 –
£3100
Special Needs: Level 2: ADD ADHD
DYC Unspecified: DYS

PRESENTATION COLLEGE
63 Bath Road, Reading, Berkshire
RG30 2BB
Tel: (0118) 957 2861
Head: Mr F Loveder
Type: Boys Day 4–18 (Co-ed VIth
Form)
No of pupils: 384
Fees: (September 00) Day £3450 –
£4566
Special Needs: Unspecified: DYS

ST BERNARD'S PREPARATORY SCHOOL
Hawtrey Close, Slough, Berkshire
SL1 1TB
Tel: (01753) 521821
Head: Mrs M F Casey
Type: Co-educational Day 3–11
No of pupils: B120 G90
Fees: (September 00) Day £4050 –
£4335
Special Needs: Unspecified: DYS

ST GABRIEL'S SCHOOL
Sandleford Priory, Newbury,
Berkshire RG20 9BD
Tel: (01635) 40663
Head: Mr D Cobb
Type: Girls Day 3–18 (Boys 3–8)
No of pupils: B18 G414
Fees: (September 00) Day £4800 –
£6687
Special Needs: Level 2: DYS Level 3:
DEL

ST JOSEPH'S CONVENT SCHOOL

64 Upper Redlands Road, Reading, Berkshire RG1 5JT
Tel: (0118) 966 1000
Head: Mrs V Brookes
Type: Girls Day 3–18
No of pupils: B17 G448
Fees: (September 00) Day £2100 – £5595
Special Needs: Unspecified: DYS

ST PIRAN'S PREPARATORY SCHOOL

Gringer Hill, Maidenhead, Berkshire SL6 7LZ
Tel: (01628) 627316
Head: Mr A P Blumer
Type: Co-educational Day 3–13
No of pupils: B260 G80
Fees: (September 00) Day £3555 – £6450
Special Needs: Level 2: DYP DYS SPLD

UPTON HOUSE SCHOOL

115 St Leonard's Road, Windsor, Berkshire SL4 3DF
Tel: (01753) 862610
Head: Mrs M Collins
Type: Girls Day 3–11 (Boys 3–7)
No of pupils: B50 G148
Fees: (September 00) Day £2265 – £5475
Special Needs: Level 2: DYP DYS MLD Level 3: ASP CP HI SP&LD SPLD

WAVERLEY SCHOOL

Waverley Way, Finchampstead, Wokingham, Berkshire RG40 4YD
Tel: (0118) 973 1121
Head: Mr S G Melton
Type: Co-educational Day 3–11
No of pupils: B75 G75
Fees: (September 00) Day £1848 – £5058
Special Needs: Level 2: DYP DYS MLD SPLD

WELLINGTON COLLEGE

Crowthorne, Berkshire RG45 7PU
Tel: (01344) 444 012
Head: Mr A H Monro
Type: Boys Boarding and Day 13–18 (Co-ed VIth Form)
No of pupils: B749 G55
No of Boarders: F664
Fees: (September 00) FB £16380 Day £12285
Special Needs: Unspecified: DYS

WHITE HOUSE PREPARATORY SCHOOL

Finchampstead Road, Wokingham, Berkshire RG40 3HD
Tel: (0118) 978 5151
Head: Mrs M L Blake
Type: Co-educational Day Boys 3–4 Girls 3–11
No of pupils: B7 G138
Fees: (September 00) Day £4236 – £4740
Special Needs: Level 2: DYS

BRISTOL

BRISTOL GRAMMAR SCHOOL

University Road, Bristol BS8 1SR
Tel: (0117) 973 6006
Head: Dr D J Mascord
Type: Co-educational Day 7–18
No of pupils: B856 G407
Fees: (September 00) Day £3030 – £5160
Special Needs: Level 3: DYP DYS EPI

CLEVE HOUSE SCHOOL

254 Wells Road, Bristol BS4 2PN
Tel: (0117) 977 7218
Head: Mr D Lawson and Mrs E Lawson
Type: Co-educational Day 3–11
No of pupils: B66 G76
Fees: (September 00) Day £2685
Special Needs: Level 2: DYS

CLIFTON COLLEGE

32 College Road, Bristol BS8 3JH
Tel: (0117) 315 7000
Head: Dr M S Spurr
Type: Co-educational Boarding and Day 13–18
No of pupils: B430 G240
No of Boarders: F430
Fees: (September 00) FB £15675 Day £10740
Special Needs: Level 1: DYC DYP DYS Level 2: MLD Level 3: ADD

CLIFTON COLLEGE PREPARATORY SCHOOL†

The Avenue, Clifton, Bristol BS8 3HE
Tel: (0117) 315 7502
Head: Dr R J Acheson
Type: Co-educational Boarding and Day 3–13
No of pupils: B332 G139
No of Boarders: F61 W19
Fees: (September 00) FB £11145 – £11595 WB £10665 – £11115 Day £3495 – £7950
Special Needs: Unspecified: DYP DYS

MOUNT ZION (CHRISTIAN PRIMARY) SCHOOL

Christchurch, Redland Road, Cotham, Bristol BS6 6AG
Tel: (0117) 942 5686
Head: Mrs C L S Vooght
Type: Co-educational Day
No of pupils: B8 G9
Fees: (September 00) On application
Special Needs: Level 3: DYS SPLD Unspecified: MLD

QUEEN ELIZABETH'S HOSPITAL

Berkeley Place, Bristol BS8 1JX
Tel: (0117) 929 1856
Head: Mr S W Holliday
Type: Boys Day and Boarding 11–18
No of pupils: B540 *No of Boarders:* F50 W15
Fees: (September 00) FB £9525 WB £8658 Day £5127
Special Needs: Level 2: DYS

SACRED HEART PREPARATORY SCHOOL

Winford Road, Chew Magna, Bristol BS40 8QY
Tel: (01275) 332470
Head: Mrs B Huntley
Type: Co-educational Day 3–11
No of pupils: B59 G68
Fees: (September 00) Day £600 – £3390
Special Needs: Unspecified: DYC DYP DYS SPLD

ST URSULA'S HIGH SCHOOL
Brecon Road, Westbury-on-Trym,
Bristol BS9 4DT
Tel: (01179) 622616
Head: Mrs M A Macnaughton
Type: Co-educational Day 3–16
No of pupils: B174 G131
Fees: (September 00) Day £1620 –
£4545
Special Needs: Level 2: ADD ADHD
ASP CP DYP DYS EPI MLD SPLD
TOU Level 3: HI

TOCKINGTON MANOR SCHOOL
Tockington, Bristol BS32 4NY
Tel: (01454) 613229
Head: Mr R G Tovey
Type: Co-educational Day and
Boarding 2–14
No of pupils: B157 G90
No of Boarders: F28
Fees: (September 00) FB £9390 –
£10440 Day £4170 – £6930
Special Needs: Level 2: DYP DYS

BUCKINGHAMSHIRE

AKELEY WOOD SCHOOL*
Akeley Wood, Buckingham
MK18 3AE
Tel: (01280) 814110
Head: Mr W H Wilcox
Type: Co-educational Day 2–18
No of pupils: 699
Fees: (September 00) Day £3870–
£5700
Special Needs: Unspecified: DYS

CALDICOTT
Crown Lane, Farnham Royal,
Buckinghamshire SL2 3SL
Tel: (01753) 644457
Head: Mr S J G Doggart
Type: Boys Boarding and Day 7–13
No of pupils: 247 *No of Boarders:* F119
Fees: (September 00) FB £11295 Day
£8475
Special Needs: Level 2: DYS

DAVENIES SCHOOL
Beaconsfield, Buckinghamshire
HP9 1AA
Tel: (01494) 685400
Head: Mr A J P Nott
Type: Boys Day 4–13
No of pupils: 300
Fees: (September 00) Day £5250 –
£6255
Special Needs: Unspecified: ADD
ADHD DYP DYS EPI HI

FILGRAVE SCHOOL
Filgrave, Newport Pagnell,
Buckinghamshire MK16 9ET
Tel: (01234) 711534
Head: Mrs S Marriott
Type: Co-educational Day 2–11
No of pupils: B28 G32
Fees: (September 00) Day £3600
Special Needs: Unspecified: DYP DYS
SPLD

GATEWAY SCHOOL
1 High Street, Great Missenden,
Buckinghamshire HP16 9AA
Tel: (01494) 862407
Head: J H Wade and J L Wade
Type: Co-educational Day 2–12
No of pupils: B203 G162
Fees: (September 00) Day £4950
Special Needs: Level 2: DYP DYS EBD
SPLD

GODSTOWE PREPARATORY SCHOOL
Shrubbery Road, High Wycombe,
Buckinghamshire HP13 6PR
Tel: (01494) 529273
Head: Mrs F J Henson
Type: Girls Day and Boarding 3–13
(Boys 3–8)
No of pupils: B14 G443
No of Boarders: F92 W36
Fees: (September 00) F/WB £11580
Day £2100 – £7395
Special Needs: Unspecified: DYP DYS
SPLD

HIGH MARCH SCHOOL
23 Ledborough Lane, Beaconsfield,
Buckinghamshire HP9 2PZ
Tel: (01494) 675186
Head: Mrs P A Forsyth
Type: Girls Day 3–12 (Boys 3–7)
No of pupils: B16 G290
Fees: (September 00) Day £1830 –
£5700
Special Needs: Unspecified: DYP DYS
HI PH SP&LD SPLD

LADYMEDE
Little Kimble, Aylesbury,
Buckinghamshire HP17 0XP
Tel: (01844) 346154
Head: Mr A Witte
Type: Co-educational Day 3–11
No of pupils: B51 G99
Fees: (September 00) Day £2400 –
£5025
Special Needs: Level 2: DYP DYS EBD
HI MLD SP&LD SPLD VIS Level 3:
ADHD EPI

ST MARY'S SCHOOL
Packhorse Road, Gerrards Cross,
Buckinghamshire SL9 8JQ
Tel: (01753) 883370
Head: Mrs F Balcombe
Type: Girls Day 3–18
No of pupils: G290
Fees: (September 00) Day £3495 –
£6695
Special Needs: Level 3: DYS

STOWE SCHOOL
Buckingham, Buckinghamshire
MK18 5EH
Tel: (01280) 818000
Head: Mr J G L Nichols
Type: Boys Boarding and Day 13–18
(Co-ed VIth Form)
No of pupils: B490 G100
No of Boarders: F530
Fees: (September 00) FB £16545 Day
£12405
Special Needs: Unspecified: DYP DYS
MLD SPLD

THORNTON COLLEGE CONVENT OF JESUS AND MARY

Thornton, Milton Keynes,
Buckinghamshire MK17 0HJ
Tel: (01280) 812610
Head: Miss A Williams
Type: Girls Day and Boarding 2–16
(Boys 2–7+)
No of pupils: B20 G330
No of Boarders: F30 W16
Fees: (September 00) FB £8850 –
£10200 WB £8040 – £9270 Day
£4200 – £6030
Special Needs: Level 1: DEL DYP EPI
PH Level 2: DYS SPLD

THORPE HOUSE SCHOOL

Oval Way, Gerrards Cross,
Buckinghamshire SL9 8PZ
Tel: (01753) 882474
Head: Mr A F Lock
Type: Boys Day 3–13
No of pupils: 260
Fees: (September 00) Day £4704 –
£6300
Special Needs: Level 2: DYP DYS MLD
SPLD Level 3: ADD ASP

CAMBRIDGESHIRE

CAMBRIDGE ARTS & SCIENCES (CATS)

Round Church Street, Cambridge
CB5 8AD
Tel: (01223) 314431
Head: Miss E R Armstrong and Mr P
McLaughlin
Type: Co-educational Day and
Boarding 14–19
No of pupils: B104 G75
No of Boarders: F123 W5
Fees: (September 00) F/WB £7500 –
£18000 Day £3600 – £10500
Special Needs: Level 1: ADD ADHD
DYC DYP DYS EBD EPI MLD

CAMBRIDGE CENTRE FOR VITH FORM STUDIES (CCSS)

1 Salisbury Villas, Station Road,
Cambridge CB1 2JF
Tel: (01223) 716890
Head: Mr P C Redhead
Type: Co-educational Boarding and
Day 15–19
No of pupils: B95 G85
No of Boarders: F130 W5
Fees: (September 00) FB £10578 –
£17619 Day £4338 – £11379
Special Needs: Level 2: ASP DYP DYS
MLD

OUNDLE SCHOOL LAXTON JUNIOR

North Street, Oundle, Peterborough,
Cambridgeshire PE8 4AL
Tel: (01832) 273673
Head: Miss S C Thomas
Type: Co-educational Day 4–11
No of pupils: B69 G70
Fees: (September 00) Day £4845
Special Needs: Unspecified: ADD
ADHD DYP DYS MLD SPLD

ST FAITHS SCHOOL

Trumpington Road, Cambridge
CB2 2AG
Tel: (01223) 352073
Head: Mr R A Dyson
Type: Co-educational Day 4–13
No of pupils: B340 G165
Fees: (September 00) Day £5130 –
£6465
Special Needs: Level 2: DYP DYS
Level 3: HI

ST MARY'S SCHOOL

Bateman Street, Cambridge CB2 1LY
Tel: (01223) 353253
Head: Dr A H Jackson
Type: Girls Day and Boarding 11–18
No of pupils: G500 *No of Boarders:* F25
W25
Fees: (September 00) FB £13650 WB
£11070 Day £6180
Special Needs: Level 2: DYS Level 3:
ASP CP DEL EPI SPLD

SANCTON WOOD SCHOOL

2 St Paul's Road, Cambridge CB1 2EZ
Tel: (01223) 359488
Head: Mrs J Avis
Type: Co-educational Day 3–16
No of pupils: B85 G80
Fees: (September 00) Day £2475 –
£5085
Special Needs: Level 2: DYS HI
SP&LD SPLD Level 3: ADD DEL DYP
PH

WHITEHALL SCHOOL

117 High Street, Somersham,
Huntingdon, Cambridgeshire
PE28 3EH
Tel: (01487) 840966
Head: Mrs D Hutley
Type: Co-educational Day 3–11
No of pupils: B52 G57
Fees: (September 00) Day £2916 –
£3600
Special Needs: Level 2: DYP DYS MLD
SP&LD SPLD Level 3: EBD

CHESHIRE

ABBEY GATE SCHOOL
Victoria Road, Chester, Cheshire
CH2 2AY
Tel: (01244) 380552
Head: Mrs S Fisher
Type: Co-educational Day 3–11
No of pupils: B60 G60
Fees: (September 00) Day £2280 –
£2445
Special Needs: Level 2: DYS

BEECH HALL SCHOOL
Beech Hall Drive, Tytherington,
Macclesfield, Cheshire SK10 2EG
Tel: (01625) 422192
Head: Mr J S Fitz-Gerald
Type: Co-educational Day 4–13
(Kindergarten 1–5)
No of pupils: B130 G62
Fees: (September 00) Day £3375 –
£5295
Special Needs: Level 2: ADD ASP DYC
DYP EBD HI MLD PH SLD SP&LD
SPLD VIS Unspecified: DYS

CRANSLEY SCHOOL
Belmont Hall, Great Budworth,
Northwich, Cheshire CW9 6NQ
Tel: (01606) 891747
Head: Mrs H P Laidler
Type: Girls Day 3–16 (Boys 3–11)
No of pupils: B27 G176
Fees: (September 00) Day £2970 –
£5130
Special Needs: Unspecified: ASP DYC
DYS

THE FIRS SCHOOL
45 Newton Lane, Chester, Cheshire
CH2 2HJ
Tel: (01244) 322443
Head: Mrs M Denton
Type: Co-educational Day 4–11
No of pupils: B118 G97
Fees: (September 00) Day £2955 –
£3255
Special Needs: Level 2: DYC DYP DYS
PH SP&LD SPLD

GREENBANK
Heathbank Road, Cheadle Hulme,
Cheadle, Cheshire SK8 6HU
Tel: (0161) 485 3724
Head: Mr K Phillips
Type: Co-educational Day 3–11
No of pupils: B100 G68
Fees: (September 00) Day £2085 –
£3630
Special Needs: Level 2: DYC DYP DYS
SPLD

THE KING'S SCHOOL
Macclesfield, Cheshire SK10 1DA
Tel: (01625) 260000
Head: Dr S Coyne
Type: Co-educational Day 3–18
(Single sex education 11–16)
No of pupils: B886 G449
Fees: (September 00) Day £3555 –
£5340
Special Needs: Level 2: DYP DYS
Level 3: ADD ADHD

LADY BARN HOUSE SCHOOL
Langlands, Schools Hill, Cheadle
Hulme, Cheadle, Cheshire SK8 1JE
Tel: (0161) 428 2912
Head: Mr E J Bonner
Type: Co-educational Day 3–11
No of pupils: B309 G210
Fees: (September 00) Day £3150 –
£3600
Special Needs: Level 2: DYP DYS

MOSTYN HOUSE SCHOOL
Parkgate, South Wirral, Cheshire
CH64 6SG
Tel: (0151) 336 1010
Head: Mr A D J Grenfell
Type: Co-educational Day 4–18
No of pupils: 310
Fees: (September 00) Day £3903 –
£6075
Special Needs: Level 1: DYP DYS
Level 3: ADD ADHD DOW DYC
SPLD

NORTH CESTRIAN GRAMMAR SCHOOL
Dunham Road, Altrincham,
Cheshire WA14 4AJ
Tel: (0161) 928 1856
Head: Mr D G Vanstone
Type: Boys Day 11–18
No of pupils: 320
Fees: (September 00) Day £4416
Special Needs: Level 2: DYP DYS
Level 3: ADD ADHD AUT DEL

ORIEL BANK HIGH SCHOOL
Devonshire Park Road, Davenport,
Stockport, Cheshire SK2 6JP
Tel: (0161) 483 2935
Head: Mr R A Bye
Type: Girls Day 3–16
No of pupils: 180
Fees: (September 00) Day £1930 –
£4620
Special Needs: Level 2: DYP DYS MLD
SP&LD SPLD Level 3: EBD PH

RAMILLIES HALL SCHOOL
Cheadle Hulme, Cheadle, Cheshire
SK8 7AJ
Tel: (0161) 485 3804
Head: Mrs A L Poole & Miss D M
Patterson
Type: Co-educational Boarding and
Day 0–13
No of pupils: B114 G71
No of Boarders: F17 W4
Fees: (September 00) FB £8820 WB
£7800 Day £3630 – £4740
Special Needs: Level 2: DYC DYP DYS
SPLD Level 3: ADD ADHD

THE RYLEYS
Ryleys Lane, Alderley Edge,
Cheshire SK9 7UY
Tel: (01625) 583241
Head: Mr P G Barrett
Type: Boys Day 3–13
No of pupils: 284
Fees: (September 00) Day £4410 –
£5052
Special Needs: Level 2: DYC DYP DYS
SPLD Level 3: ADD ADHD ASP AUT
DEL EBD EPI HI PH SP&LD TOU
VIS

TERRA NOVA SCHOOL
Jodrell Bank, Holmes Chapel,
Cheshire CW4 8BT
Tel: (01477) 571251
Head: Mr N Johnson
Type: Co-educational Boarding and
Day 3–13
No of pupils: B120 G74
No of Boarders: F25
Fees: (September 00) F/WB £6855 –
£9570 Day £5025 – £7770
Special Needs: Unspecified: DYP DYS

WOODFORD PREP & NURSERY SCHOOL
Chester Road, Woodford, Stockport,
Cheshire SK7 1PS
Tel: (0161) 439 9302
Head: Mrs V E Blundell
Type: Co-educational Day 2–11
No of pupils: B48 G40
Fees: (September 00) Day £1500 –
£3375
Special Needs: Level 3: ASP DYP DYS
MLD

CORNWALL

ST IA SCHOOL
St Ives Road, Carbis Bay, St Ives,
Cornwall TR26 2SF
Tel: (01736) 796963
Head: Mr D M P Bennett
Type: Co-educational Day 4–12
No of pupils: B23 G14
Fees: (September 00) Day £975 –
£1155
Special Needs: Level 2: DYP MLD

ST PIRAN'S SCHOOL
Trelissick Road, Hayle, Truro,
Cornwall TR27 4HY
Tel: (01736) 752612
Head: Mr D G Jones
Type: Co-educational Day 3–12
No of pupils: B45 G45
Fees: (September 00) Day £2130 –
£2250
Special Needs: Level 2: DYP DYS EBD
MLD

WHEELGATE HOUSE SCHOOL
Trevowah Road, Crantock, Newquay,
Cornwall TR8 5RU
Tel: (01637) 830680
Head: Mrs G Wilson
Type: Co-educational Day 2–12
No of pupils: B20 G20
Fees: (September 00) Day £2000 –
£2700
Special Needs: Level 2: DYC DYS MLD
SP&LD Level 3: ADD ADHD
DEL DYP EBD HI Unspecified: VIS W

CUMBRIA

AUSTIN FRIARS SCHOOL
Etterby Scaur, Carlisle, Cumbria
CA3 9PB
Tel: (01228) 528042
Head: Mr N J B O'Sullivan
Type: Co-educational Day 11–18
No of pupils: B163 G127
Fees: (September 00) Day £5814
Special Needs: Level 2: DYS

CASTERTON SCHOOL
Kirkby Lonsdale, Carnforth,
Cumbria LA6 2SG
Tel: (01524) 279200
Head: Mr A F Thomas
Type: Girls Boarding and Day 4–18
(Day boys 4–11)
No of pupils: B17 G345
No of Boarders: F215 W5
Fees: (September 01) FB £10287 –
£12870 WB £10017 Day £3654 –
£7920
Special Needs: Level 2: DYS
Level 3: HI

HARECROFT HALL SCHOOL
Gosforth, Seascale, Cumbria CA20
1HS
Tel: (01946) 725220
Head: Mr D G Hoddy
Type: Co-educational Boarding and
Day 2–16
No of pupils: B48 G49
No of Boarders: F11 W4
Fees: (September 00) FB £8475 –
£9294 WB £8085 – £8925 Day £4185
– £5910
Special Needs: Level 2: DYP DYS MLD

ST BEES SCHOOL†
St Bees, Cumbria CA27 0DS
Tel: (01946) 822263
Head: Mr P J Capes
Type: Co-educational Boarding and
Day 11–18
No of pupils: B182 G119
No of Boarders: F67 W49
Fees: (September 00) FB £10611 –
£14499 WB £9372 – £13308 Day
£7719 – £9528
Special Needs: Level 1: DYC DYS
SPLD Level 2: ADD ASP DYP HI VIS

SEDBERGH SCHOOL
Sedbergh, Cumbria LA10 5HG
Tel: (01539) 620535
Head: Mr C H Hirst
Type: Co-educational Boarding and
Day 8–18
No of pupils: 325 *No of Boarders:* F320
Fees: (September 00) FB £9690 –
£15495 Day £6600 – £11460
Special Needs: Unspecified: DYS

WELLSPRING CHRISTIAN SCHOOL
Cotehill, Carlisle, Cumbria CA4 0EA
Tel: (01228) 562023
Head: Mr A G Field
Type: Co-educational Day 3–18
No of pupils: B12 G8
Fees: (September 00) Day £1300 –
£1820
Special Needs: Level 3: DYS

DERBYSHIRE

ASHBOURNE PNEU SCHOOL
St Monica's House, Windmill Lane,
Ashbourne, Derbyshire DE6 1EY
Tel: (01335) 343294
Head: Mr M A Broadbent
Type: Co-educational Day 0–13
No of pupils: 60
Fees: (September 00) Day £720 –
£4050
Special Needs: Level 2: ADD ADHD
ASP CP DYC DYP DYS EBD HI MLD
PH SP&LD SPLD

BARLBOROUGH HALL
SCHOOL
Barlborough, Chesterfield,
Derbyshire S43 4TJ
Tel: (01246) 810511
Head: Mrs W Parkinson
Type: Co-educational Day 3–11
No of pupils: B100 G81
Fees: (September 00) Day £3315 –
£5025
Special Needs: Level 2: DYS

DERBY INDEPENDENT
GRAMMAR SCHOOL
Rykneld Road, Littleover, Derby,
Derbyshire DE23 7BH
Tel: (01332) 523027
Head: Mr R D Waller
Type: Boys Day 7–18
No of pupils: B260
Fees: (September 00) Day £5460
Special Needs: Level 2: DYS PH
Level 3: ADD ADHD ASP DYC DYP
EBD EPI HI MLD VIS

FOREMARKE HALL
Milton, Derby, Derbyshire DE65 6EJ
Tel: (01283) 703269
Head: Mr P Brewster
Type: Co-educational Boarding and
Day 3–13
No of pupils: B225 G123
No of Boarders: F48 W34
Fees: (September 00) F/WB £9870
Day £4515 – £7380
Special Needs: Unspecified: DYP DYS
HI MLD

MOUNT ST MARY'S COLLEGE
Spinkhill, Derbyshire S21 3YL
Tel: (01246) 433388
Head: Mr P G MacDonald
Type: Co-educational Boarding and
Day 11–18
No of pupils: B169 G80
No of Boarders: F84 W20
Fees: (September 00) FB £8505 –
£11580 WB £7530 – £10260 Day
£5700 – £6585
Special Needs: Level 2: ADD DYP DYS

THE OLD VICARAGE
SCHOOL
11 Church Lane, Darley Abbey,
Derby, Derbyshire DE22 1EW
Tel: (01332) 557130
Head: Mr G C Holbrow and Mrs M
Holbrow
Type: Co-educational Day 3–11
No of pupils: B44 G44
Fees: (September 00) Day £3990 –
£4275
Special Needs: Unspecified: DYS

ST ANSELM'S
Bakewell, Derbyshire DE45 1DP
Tel: (01629) 812734
Head: Mr R J Foster
Type: Co-educational Boarding and
Day 7–13
No of pupils: B110 G75
No of Boarders: F105
Fees: (September 00) FB £10200 Day
£4500 – £8700
Special Needs: Level 1: DYS SPLD
Level 2: DYC DYP Level 3: ADD
ADHD ASP

ST JOSEPH'S CONVENT
42 Newbold Road, Chesterfield,
Derbyshire S41 7PL
Tel: (01246) 232392
Head: Mrs B Deane
Type: Co-educational Day 2–11
No of pupils: B69 G66
Fees: (September 00) Day £2580 –
£3150
Special Needs: Level 1: CP Level 2:
ADD ADHD DYC DYP DYS

ST PETER & ST PAUL
SCHOOL
Brambling House, Hady Hill,
Chesterfield, Derbyshire S41 0EF
Tel: (01246) 278522
Head: Mrs B Beet
Type: Co-educational Day 3–11
No of pupils: B82 G91
Fees: (September 00) Day £2745 –
£3108
Special Needs: Level 2: ASP DYS MLD
SP&LD SPLD Level 3: ADD ADHD
DYP EBD

DEVON

BLUNDELL'S SCHOOL
Tiverton, Devon EX16 4DN
Tel: (01884) 252543
Head: Mr J Leigh
Type: Co-educational Boarding and
Day 11–18
No of pupils: B330 G189
No of Boarders: F115 W255
Fees: (September 00) FB £10005 –
£15060 WB £6225 – £10080 Day
£5310 – £9180
Special Needs: Level 2: DYS

EMMANUEL SCHOOL
36–38 Blackboy Road, Exeter, Devon
EX4 6SZ
Tel: (01392) 258150
Head: Mr P J Gedye
Type: Co-educational Day 4–16
No of pupils: B28 G25
Fees: (September 00) Day £1824
Special Needs: Level 1: DYC DYP DYS
MLD SPLD Level 2: SP&LD Level 3:
DOW

EXETER TUTORIAL COLLEGE
44/46 Magdalen Road, Exeter, Devon
EX2 4TE
Tel: (01392) 278101
Head: Mr K D Jack
Type: Co-educational Day 15+
No of pupils: B30 G35
Fees: (September 00) Day £1550 –
£7200
Special Needs: Unspecified: DYS

GRENVILLE COLLEGE*†
Bideford, Devon EX39 3JR
Tel: (01237) 472212
Head: Dr M C V Cane
Type: Co-educational Boarding and
Day 3–18
No of pupils: B212 G158
No of Boarders: F85 W10
Fees: (September 00) FB £10149 –
£13071 WB £7608 – £9801 Day
£2715 – £6471
Special Needs: Level 1: DYS

HYLTON KINDERGARTEN &
PRE-PREPARATORY SCHOOL
13A Lyndhurst Road, Exeter, Devon
EX2 4PA
Tel: (01392) 254755
Head: Mrs R C Leveridge
Type: Co-educational Day 2–8
No of pupils: 75
Fees: (September 00) Day £236 –
£2475
Special Needs: Level 2: DYS

KELLY COLLEGE
Tavistock, Devon PL19 0HZ
Tel: (01822) 813127
Head: Mr M Turner
Type: Co-educational Boarding and
Day 11–18
No of pupils: B210 G160
No of Boarders: F110 W70
Fees: (September 00) FB £12195 –
£14580 WB £11100 – £13965 Day
£6150 – £9165
Special Needs: Level 1: ADD ADHD
Level 2: DYC DYP Level 3: DYS
Unspecified: EPI

KELLY COLLEGE JUNIOR
SCHOOL
Hazeldon House, Parkwood Road,
Tavistock, Devon PL19 0JS
Tel: (01822) 612919
Head: Mr R P Jeynes
Type: Co-educational Boarding and
Day 2–11
No of pupils: B64 G62
No of Boarders: W1
Fees: (September 00) FB £10170 WB
£9075 Day £3075 – £4125
Special Needs: Unspecified: DYS

KING'S SCHOOL
Hartley Road, Mannamead,
Plymouth, Devon PL3 5LW
Tel: (01752) 771789
Head: Mrs J Lee
Type: Co-educational Day 3–11
No of pupils: B98 G74
Fees: (September 00) Day £2505 –
£2835
Special Needs: Unspecified: ADD DYP
DYS MLD SP&LD SPLD

MAGDALEN COURT SCHOOL
Mulberry House, Victoria Park Road,
Exeter, Devon EX2 4NU
Tel: (01392) 494919
Head: Mr J G Bushrod
Type: Co-educational Day 2–18
No of pupils: B75 G70
Fees: (September 00) Day £2625 –
£6000
Special Needs: Level 1: DYC DYS MLD
SP&LD SPLD VIS

MANOR HOUSE SCHOOL
Springfield House, Honiton, Devon
EX14 9TL
Tel: (01404) 42026
Head: Mr S J Bage
Type: Co-educational Day 3–11
No of pupils: B65 G65
Fees: (September 00) Day £2820 –
£3885
Special Needs: Level 2: DYP DYS MLD
SP&LD SPLD

MOUNT HOUSE SCHOOL
Tavistock, Devon PL19 9JL
Tel: (01822) 612244
Head: Mr C D Price
Type: Co-educational Boarding and
Day 3–13
No of pupils: B175 G75
No of Boarders: F102
Fees: (September 00) FB £10284 Day
£3657 – £7701
Special Needs: Unspecified: DYP DYS
HI

OSHO KO HSUAN SCHOOL
Chawleigh, Chulmleigh, Devon
EX18 7EX
Tel: (01769) 580896
Head: Mr K Bartlam
Type: Co-educational Boarding 7–16
No of pupils: B14 G15
No of Boarders: F29
Fees: (September 00) FB £7200 WB
£5850 Day £4050
Special Needs: Level 2: DYP DYS

ST AUBYN'S SCHOOL
Milestones House, Blundell's Road,
Tiverton, Devon EX16 4NA
Tel: (01884) 252393
Head: Mr B J McDowell
Type: Co-educational Day 0–11
No of pupils: B152 G107
No of Boarders: F3 W2
Fees: (September 00) Day £648 –
£5295
Special Needs: Level 2: DYC DYS MLD
SPLD Level 3: ADD ADHD EBD

ST JOHN'S SCHOOL
Broadway, Sidmouth, Devon EX10
8RG
Tel: (01395) 513984
Head: Mr N R Pockett
Type: Co-educational Day and
Boarding 2–13
No of pupils: B140 G110
No of Boarders: F50 W10
Fees: (September 00) FB £9078 WB
£8499 Day £1431 – £5040
Special Needs: Level 1: DYC DYP
Level 2: DYS MLD

ST MARGARET'S SCHOOL
147 Magdalen Road, Exeter, Devon
EX2 4TS
Tel: (01392) 273197
Head: Mrs M D'Albertanson
Type: Girls Day 7–18
No of pupils: 430
Fees: (September 00) Day £2592 –
£5472
Special Needs: Level 2: DYS SPLD
Level 3: VIS Unspecified: HI

ST MICHAEL'S
Tawstock Court, Barnstaple, Devon
EX31 3HY
Tel: (01271) 343242
Head: Mr J W Pratt
Type: Co-educational Boarding and
Day 0–13
No of pupils: B128 G75
No of Boarders: F5
Fees: (September 00) F/WB £9705 –
£10005 Day £2985 – £6375
Special Needs: Level 2: ADD ADHD
DYC DYP DYS MLD SP&LD SPLD

SHEBBEAR COLLEGE
Shebbear, Beaworthy, Devon
EX21 5HJ
Tel: (01409) 281228
Head: Mr L D Clark
Type: Co-educational Boarding and
Day 3–18
No of pupils: B116 G88
No of Boarders: F60 W14
Fees: (September 00) FB £7935 –
£11985 WB £6525 – £9630 Day
£2070 – £6420
Special Needs: Level 2: ADD ADHD
DYC DYP DYS EBD MLD SPLD
Level 3: EPI HI SP&LD Unspecified:
DEL

WEST BUCKLAND PREPARATORY SCHOOL

West Buckland, Barnstaple, Devon EX32 0SX
Tel: (01598) 760545
Head: Mr A Moore
Type: Co-educational Day and Boarding 3–11
No of pupils: B109 G82
No of Boarders: F8 W2
Fees: (September 00) FB £7545 – £8820 Day £2880 – £5250
Special Needs: Level 2: DYP DYS Level 3: ADD ADHD Unspecified: W

WEST BUCKLAND SCHOOL

Barnstaple, Devon EX32 0SX
Tel: (01598) 760281
Head: Mr J Vick
Type: Co-educational Boarding and Day 3–18
No of pupils: B371 G260
No of Boarders: F118
Fees: (September 00) FB £7545 – £11745 Day £2880 – £6630
Special Needs: Level 3: ADD ADHD DYC DYP DYS EBD HI SPLD TOU

DORSET

CANFORD SCHOOL

Wimborne, Dorset BH21 3AD
Tel: (01202) 841254
Head: Mr J D Lever
Type: Co-educational Boarding and Day 13–18
No of pupils: B389 G204
No of Boarders: F389
Fees: (September 00) FB £16170 Day £12135
Special Needs: Level 1: DYS EPI Unspecified: W

CLAYESMORE PREPARATORY SCHOOL†

Iwerne Minster, Blandford Forum, Dorset DT11 8PH
Tel: (01747) 811707
Head: Mr A Roberts-Wray
Type: Co-educational Boarding and Day 2–13
No of pupils: B185 G111
No of Boarders: F62 W22
Fees: (September 00) F/WB £9888 – £10836 Day £3702 – £7740
Special Needs: Level 2: DYC DYP DYS EPI HI SP&LD SPLD

DORCHESTER PREPARATORY SCHOOL

25/26 Icen Way, Dorchester, Dorset DT1 1EP
Tel: (01305) 264925
Head: Mr J. de B. Miller
Type: Co-educational Day 3–13
No of pupils: B43 G45
Fees: (September 01) Day £1464 – £3990
Special Needs: Level 2: ADD ADHD ASP DEL DYC HI MLD SP&LD SPLD VIS Level 3: AUT CP DOW EPI PH TOU Unspecified: DYS

KNIGHTON HOUSE

Durweston, Blandford Forum, Dorset DT11 0PY
Tel: (01258) 452065
Head: Mrs M Willson
Type: Girls Day and Boarding 2–13 (Day boys 2–7)
No of pupils: B14 G136
No of Boarders: F24 W27
Fees: (September 00) F/WB £11010 Day £1800 – £8040
Special Needs: Level 2: DYS MLD SPLD

MILTON ABBEY SCHOOL

Blandford Forum, Dorset DT11 0BZ
Tel: (01258) 880484
Head: Mr J Hughes-D'Aeth
Type: Boys Boarding and Day 13–18
No of pupils: 224 No of Boarders: F190
Fees: (September 00) FB £14955 Day £11220
Special Needs: Unspecified: ADD ADHD ASP DYC DYP DYS

PORT REGIS

Motcombe Park, Shaftesbury, Dorset SP7 9QA
Tel: (01747) 852566
Head: Mr P A E Dix
Type: Co-educational Boarding and Day 3–13
No of pupils: B225 G173
No of Boarders: F150 W105
Fees: (September 00) F/WB £13185 Day £4050 – £9885
Special Needs: Level 2: DYC DYP DYS MLD SP&LD SPLD Level 3: HI PH

ST ANTONY'S-LEWESTON SCHOOL

Sherborne, Dorset DT9 6EN
Tel: (01963) 210691
Head: Mr H MacDonald
Type: Girls Boarding and Day 11–18
No of pupils: G245 No of Boarders: F100
Fees: (September 00) FB £13539 Day £8919
Special Needs: Level 2: DYC DYP DYS Unspecified: SPLD

ST MARY'S SCHOOL

Shaftesbury, Dorset SP7 9LP
Tel: (01747) 854005
Head: Mrs S Pennington
Type: Girls Boarding and Day 9–18
No of pupils: G326 No of Boarders: F223
Fees: (September 00) FB £12450 – £13125 Day £8100 – £8520
Special Needs: Level 2: DYC DYS

SHERBORNE SCHOOL

Abbey Road, Sherborne, Dorset DT9 3AP
Tel: (01935) 812249
Head: Mr S F Eliot
Type: Boys Boarding 13–18
No of pupils: 520 No of Boarders: F490
Fees: (September 00) FB £16350 Day £12255
Special Needs: Unspecified: DYS PH

TALBOT HEATH
Rothesay Road, Bournemouth,
Dorset BH4 9NJ
Tel: (01202) 761881
Head: Mrs C Dipple
Type: Girls Day and Boarding 3–18
(Boys 3–7)
No of pupils: B6 G652
No of Boarders: F29 W5
Fees: (September 00) FB £11805 WB
£11505 Day £2175 – £6885
Special Needs: Level 2: DYS Level 3:
ADD ADHD DEL DYC DYP EPI PH
SPLD

THORNLOW PREPARATORY SCHOOL†
Connaught Road, Weymouth, Dorset
DT4 0SA
Tel: (01305) 785703
Head: Mr R A Fowke
Type: Co-educational Day 3–13
No of pupils: B43 G35
Fees: (September 00) Day £2100
Special Needs: Level 1: DYP DYS
SP&LD SPLD

WENTWORTH COLLEGE
College Road, Bournemouth, Dorset
BH5 2DY
Tel: (01202) 423266
Head: Miss S Coe
Type: Girls Boarding and Day 11–18
No of pupils: 200 *No of Boarders:* F35
W25
Fees: (September 00) F/WB £10950
Day £6885
Special Needs: Level 2: DYS Level 3:
ADD DYP EPI HI PH SP&LD SPLD
TOU VIS Unspecified: DEL

YARRELLS SCHOOL
Yarrells House, Upton, Poole, Dorset
BH16 5EU
Tel: (01202) 622229
Head: Mrs Covell
Type: Co-educational Day 2–13
No of pupils: B103 G137
Fees: (September 00) Day £1109 –
£5786
Special Needs: Level 2: ASP DYP DYS
SP&LD Level 3: ADD EPI HI

COUNTY DURHAM

BARNARD CASTLE SCHOOL
Barnard Castle, County Durham
DL12 8UN
Tel: (01833) 690222
Head: Mr M D Featherstone
Type: Co-educational Boarding and
Day 4–18
No of pupils: B430 G207
No of Boarders: F176
Fees: (September 00) FB £8568 –
£11181 Day £2892 – £6618
Special Needs: Level 2: DYP DYS

BOW SCHOOL
South Road, Durham, County
Durham DH1 3LS
Tel: (0191) 384 8233
Head: Mr R N Baird
Type: Boys Day 3–13
No of pupils: 157
Fees: (September 00) Day £3135 –
£5868
Special Needs: Level 2: DYS MLD
Level 3: ADD ADHD ASP

DURHAM HIGH SCHOOL FOR GIRLS
Farewell Hall, Durham, County
Durham DH1 3TB
Tel: (0191) 384 3226
Head: Mrs A J Templeman
Type: Girls Day 3–18
No of pupils: 520
Fees: (September 00) Day £3780 –
£5790
Special Needs: Level 2: DYS

DURHAM SCHOOL
Durham, County Durham DH1 4SZ
Tel: (0191) 384 7977
Head: Mr M N G Kern
Type: Co-educational Boarding and
Day 11–18
No of pupils: B276 G51
No of Boarders: F91
Fees: (September 00) FB £11589 –
£13614 Day £6156 – £8910
Special Needs: Level 2: ADD DYS
Level 3: PH

HURWORTH HOUSE SCHOOL
The Green, Hurworth-on-Tees,
Darlington, County Durham
DL2 2AD
Tel: (01325) 720645
Head: Mr C R T Fenwick
Type: Boys Day 3–18
No of pupils: 172
Fees: (September 00) Day £3675 –
£5694
Special Needs: Level 2: DYS MLD
Level 3: DYP PH VIS W

POLAM HALL
Darlington, County Durham
DL1 5PA
Tel: (01325) 463383
Head: Mrs H C Hamilton
Type: Girls Boarding and Day 4–18
No of pupils: 463 *No of Boarders:* F38
W10
Fees: (September 00) FB £10047 –
£12285 WB £9972 – £12210 Day
£2703 – £5715
Special Needs: Level 2: ASP CP DEL
DYC DYP DYS EPI HI MLD PH SPLD
VIS Level 3: SP&LD

RAVENTHORPE PREPARATORY SCHOOL
96 Carmel Road North, Darlington, County Durham DL3 8JB
Tel: (01325) 463373
Head: Mrs D A Procter
Type: Co-educational Day 3–11
No of pupils: B55 G56
Fees: (September 00) Day £1923 – £2232
Special Needs: Level 2: DYS MLD SPLD

ESSEX

AVON HOUSE
490 High Road, Woodford Green, Essex IG8 0PN
Tel: (020) 8504 1749
Head: Mrs S Ferrari
Type: Co-educational Day 3–11
No of pupils: B132 G111
Fees: (September 00) Day £3300 – £4425
Special Needs: Level 1: DYC DYS SPLD Level 2: ASP DYP Level 3: ADD ADHD AUT CP DEL DOW EBD EPI MLD SP&LD

BRENTWOOD SCHOOL
Ingrave Road, Brentwood, Essex CM15 8AS
Tel: (01277) 243243
Head: Mr J A B Kelsall
Type: Co-educational Boarding and Day 3–18
No of pupils: B854 G546
No of Boarders: F75
Fees: (September 00) FB £13515 Day £7785
Special Needs: Unspecified: ADD DYP DYS MLD

COLCHESTER HIGH SCHOOL
Wellesley Road, Colchester, Essex CO3 3HD
Tel: (01206) 573389
Head: Mr A T Moore
Type: Boys Day 3–16 (Girls 3–11)
No of pupils: B330 G35
Fees: (September 00) Day £1230 – £4770
Special Needs: Level 2: DYP DYS SPLD Level 3: PH

COLLEGE SAINT-PIERRE
16 Leigh Road, Leigh-on-Sea, Essex SS9 1LE
Tel: (01702) 474164
Head: Mr G Bragard
Type: Co-educational Day 3–11
No of pupils: B70 G40
Fees: (April 01) Day £1740 – £3681
Special Needs: Unspecified: DYS MLD

DAME JOHANE BRADBURY'S SCHOOL
Ashdon Road, Saffron Walden, Essex CB10 2AL
Tel: (01799) 522348
Head: Mrs R M Rainey
Type: Co-educational Day 3–11
No of pupils: B145 G164
Fees: (September 00) Day £3513 – £4653
Special Needs: Unspecified: DYS

FELSTED SCHOOL
Felsted, Dunmow, Essex CM6 3LL
Tel: (01371) 821594
Head: Mr S C Roberts
Type: Co-educational Boarding and Day 13–18
No of pupils: B254 G153
No of Boarders: F272
Fees: (September 00) FB £15720 Day £11490 – £12390
Special Needs: Level 1: ADD DYS Unspecified: EPI HI MLD

FRIENDS' SCHOOL
Mount Pleasant Road, Saffron Walden, Essex CB11 3EB
Tel: (01799) 525351
Head: Ms J E Laing
Type: Co-educational Boarding and Day 3–18
No of pupils: B183 G143
No of Boarders: F81 W5
Fees: (January 01) F/WB £8919 – £13614 Day £4542 – £8205
Special Needs: Level 2: ASP DEL DYP DYS Level 3: EPI HI

HEATHCOTE SCHOOL
Eves Corner, Danbury, Chelmsford, Essex CM3 4QB
Tel: (01245) 223131
Head: Mrs L Mitchell-Hall
Type: Co-educational Day 2–11
No of pupils: B93 G87
Fees: (September 00) Day £3780
Special Needs: Level 2: ADD ADHD ASP DYP DYS SPLD Level 3: EPI PH Unspecified: W

HOLMWOOD HOUSE†
Chitts Hill, Lexden, Colchester, Essex CO3 5ST
Tel: (01206) 574305
Head: Mr H S Thackrah
Type: Co-educational Day and Boarding 4–14
No of pupils: B228 G138
No of Boarders: W30
Fees: (September 00) WB £9795 – £10968 Day £4764 – £8481
Special Needs: Level 2: DYC DYP DYS

LITTLEGARTH SCHOOL
Horkesley Park, Nayland,
Colchester, Essex CO6 4JR
Tel: (01206) 262332
Head: Mrs E P Coley
Type: Co-educational Day 2–11
No of pupils: B153 G140
Fees: (September 00) Day £960 –
£4176
Special Needs: Level 2: DYP DYS
SPLD

MALDON COURT PREPARATORY SCHOOL
Silver Street, Maldon, Essex
CM9 4QE
Tel: (01621) 853529
Head: Mr A G Webb
Type: Co-educational Day 4–11
No of pupils: B66 G58
Fees: (September 00) Day £3615 –
£3765
Special Needs: Level 2: DYS VIS

NEW HALL SCHOOL†
Chelmsford, Essex CM3 3HT
Tel: (01245) 467588
Head: Sister Anne-Marie
Type: Girls Boarding and Day 4–18
(Boys day 4–11)
No of pupils: B89 G543
No of Boarders: F74 W39
Fees: (September 00) FB £13410 –
£13680 WB £12990 – £13260 Day
£8700 – £8910
Special Needs: Level 1: DYS SPLD
Level 2: ADD DYC Level 3: ADHD CP
DEL DYP EPI PH SP&LD VIS
Unspecified: W

ST AUBYN'S SCHOOL
Bunces Lane, Woodford Green,
Essex IG8 9DU
Tel: (020) 8504 1577
Head: Mr G James
Type: Co-educational Day 3–13
No of pupils: B275 G165
Fees: (September 00) Day £1944 –
£5436
Special Needs: Level 3: DYC DYP DYS

ST HILDA'S SCHOOL
15 Imperial Avenue, Westcliff-on-
Sea, Essex SSO 8NE
Tel: (01702) 344542
Head: Mrs S O'Riordan
Type: Girls Day 2–16 (Boys 2–7)
No of pupils: B1 G180
Fees: (September 00) Day £2994 –
£4149
Special Needs: Level 2: DYS Level 3:
ADD ASP DYC DYP SPLD

ST JOHN'S SCHOOL
Stock Road, Billericay, Essex
CM12 0AR
Tel: (01277) 623070
Head: Mrs S Hillier and Mrs F S
Armour
Type: Co-educational Day 3–16
No of pupils: B238 G164
Fees: (September 00) Day £2640 –
£4980
Special Needs: Level 2: DYS Level 3:
ADD ADHD

ST MARGARET'S SCHOOL
Gosfield Hall Park, Gosfield,
Halstead, Essex CO9 1SE
Tel: (01787) 472134
Head: Mrs B Y Boyton
Type: Co-educational Day 2–11
No of pupils: B70 G80
Fees: (September 00) Day £3375 –
£4800
Special Needs: Level 3: ADD DEL DYP
DYS HI MLD Unspecified: PH W

WIDFORD LODGE
Widford Road, Chelmsford, Essex
CM2 9AN
Tel: (01245) 352581
Head: Mr S C Trowell
Type: Co-educational Day 2–11
No of pupils: B130 G65
Fees: (September 00) Day £3405 –
£4575
Special Needs: Level 3: DYS MLD

GLOUCESTERSHIRE

THE ABBEY SCHOOL
Church Street, Tewkesbury,
Gloucestershire GL20 5PD
Tel: (01684) 294460
Head: Mr J H Milton
Type: Co-educational Day and
Boarding 2–13
No of pupils: B67 G38
No of Boarders: W8
Fees: (September 00) WB £7845 –
£9015 Day £1080 – £6495
Special Needs: Level 2: DYC DYP DYS
SPLD

ACORN SCHOOL
Church Street, Nailsworth,
Gloucestershire GL6 0BP
Tel: (01453) 836508
Head: Mr G E B Whiting
Type: Co-educational Day and
Boarding 3–19
No of pupils: B41 G44
No of Boarders: F2 W2
Fees: (September 00) FB £1980 –
£2700 Day £1650 – £4080
Special Needs: Level 2: DYS

AIRTHRIE SCHOOL
29 Christ Church Road,
Cheltenham, Gloucestershire GL50
2NY
Tel: (01242) 512837
Head: Mrs A E Sullivan
Type: Co-educational Day 3–11
No of pupils: B90 G90
Fees: (September 00) Day £3060 –
£3882
Special Needs: Level 1: CP DYC DYS
SPLD Unspecified: DYP

BREDON SCHOOL*

Pull Court, Bushley, Tewkesbury,
Gloucestershire GL20 6AH
Tel: (01684) 293156
Head: Mr M Newby
Type: Co-educational Boarding and
Day 8–18
No of pupils: B137 G580
No of Boarders: F175 W20
Fees: (September 01) FB £10275 –
£14850 WB £9975 – £14550 Day
£5250 – £10125
Special Needs: Level 1: ADD DYC
DYP DYS MLD SPLD Level 2: SP&LD

DEAN CLOSE PREPARATORY SCHOOL

Lansdown Road, Cheltenham,
Gloucestershire GL51 6QS
Tel: (01242) 512217
Head: Mr S W Baird
Type: Co-educational Boarding and
Day 2–13
No of pupils: B175 G138
No of Boarders: F72
Fees: (September 00) FB £11640 Day
£3750 – £7950
Special Needs: Unspecified: DYS

DEAN CLOSE SCHOOL

Cheltenham, Gloucestershire
GL51 6HE
Tel: (01242) 522640
Head: The Revd T M Hastie-Smith
Type: Co-educational Boarding and
Day 13–18
No of pupils: B242 G188
No of Boarders: F262
Fees: (September 00) FB £15930 Day
£11130
Special Needs: Level 2: DYP DYS
SPLD

THE DORMER HOUSE PNEU SCHOOL

High Street, Moreton-in-Marsh,
Gloucestershire GL56 0AD
Tel: (01608) 650758
Head: Ms D A Trembath
Type: Co-educational Day 2–11
No of pupils: B60 G62
Fees: (September 00) Day £2125 –
£3130
Special Needs: Level 2: DYS
Unspecified: ASP

HATHEROP CASTLE SCHOOL

Hatherop, Cirencester,
Gloucestershire GL7 3NB
Tel: (01285) 750206
Head: Mr P Easterbrook
Type: Co-educational Boarding and
Day 4–13
No of pupils: B111 G98
No of Boarders: F28
Fees: (September 00) F/WB £8970 –
£9450 Day £3630 – £6105
Special Needs: Unspecified: ADD
ADHD DYC DYP DYS

INGLESIDE PNEU SCHOOL

Beeches Road, Cirencester,
Gloucestershire GL7 1BN
Tel: (01285) 654046
Head: Mrs F M M Blades
Type: Co-educational Day 4–11
No of pupils: B41 G33
Fees: (September 00) Day £2580 –
£2835
Special Needs: Unspecified: MLD

THE KING'S SCHOOL

Pitt Street, Gloucester,
Gloucestershire GL1 2BG
Tel: (01452) 337337
Head: Mr P R Lacey
Type: Co-educational Boarding and
Day 4–19
No of pupils: B286 G185
No of Boarders: F10
Fees: (January 01) FB £14055 WB
£13155 Day £4185 – £8775
Special Needs: Level 2: DYP DYS
SPLD

THE QUERNS SCHOOL

Querns Lane, Cirencester,
Gloucestershire GL7 1RL
Tel: (01285) 652953
Head: Mr C Whytehead
Type: Co-educational Day 4–11
No of pupils: B45 G70
Fees: (September 00) Day £2985 –
£4065
Special Needs: Level 2: DYS

WYCLIFFE JUNIOR SCHOOL

Ryeford Hall, Stonehouse,
Gloucestershire GL10 2LD
Tel: (01453) 823233
Head: Mr R Outwin-Flinders
Type: Co-educational Boarding and
Day 2–13
No of pupils: B215 G160
No of Boarders: F40
Fees: (September 00) F/WB £7995 –
£10035 Day £3585 – £7125
Special Needs: Level 2: DYC DYP DYS
MLD SP&LD SPLD Level 3: ADD
ADHD CP DEL EPI HI PH VIS

WYCLIFFE COLLEGE*

Stonehouse, Gloucestershire
GL10 2JQ
Tel: (01453) 822432
Head: Dr R A Collins
Type: Co-educational Boarding and
Day 13–18
No of pupils: B255 G58
No of Boarders: 264
Fees: FB £11160 – £18600 Day
£10755 – £14400
Boarding 264
Special Needs: Mild ADHD, ASP, DYS,
MLD

HAMPSHIRE

BALLARD PREPARATORY SCHOOL
Fernhill Lane, New Milton,
Hampshire BH25 5SU
Tel: (01425) 611153
Head: Mr S P Duckitt
Type: Co-educational Day 2–13
No of pupils: B150 G140
Fees: (September 00) Day £3870 –
£6705
Special Needs: Level 2: DYC DYP DYS
SPLD Level 3: ADD ASP SP&LD

BALLARD SCHOOL
New Milton, Hampshire BH25 5SU
Tel: (01425) 611153
Head: Mr P Stockdale
Type: Co-educational Day 13–18
No of pupils: B49 G27
Fees: (September 00) Day £6990
Special Needs: Level 2: DYS
Unspecified: W

CHILTERN TUTORIAL UNIT
c/o Otterbourne Village Hall,
Cranbourne Drive, Otterbourne,
Winchester, Hampshire SO21 2ET
Tel: (01962) 860482
Head: Mrs J Gaudie
Type: Co-educational Day 8–11
No of pupils: B12 G4
Fees: (September 00) Day £4470
Special Needs: Level 1: DYS

CHURCHERS COLLEGE
Portsmouth Road, Petersfield,
Hampshire GU31 4AS
Tel: (01730) 263033
Head: Mr G W Buttle
Type: Co-educational Day 4–18
No of pupils: B435 G280
Fees: (September 00) Day £3495 –
£6555
Special Needs: Level 2: DYS
Unspecified: W

DITCHAM PARK SCHOOL
Ditcham Park, Petersfield,
Hampshire GU31 5RN
Tel: (01730) 825659
Head: Mrs K S Morton
Type: Co-educational Day 4–16
No of pupils: B203 G110
Fees: (September 00) Day £3930 –
£6570
Special Needs: Level 1: DYS

DUNHURST (BEDALES JUNIOR SCHOOL)
Alton Road, Steep, Petersfield,
Hampshire GU32 2DP
Tel: (01730) 300200
Head: Mr M Piercy
Type: Co-educational Boarding and
Day 8–13
No of pupils: B101 G90
No of Boarders: F61
Fees: (September 00) FB £11400 Day
£8280
Special Needs: Level 2: DYP DYS
SPLD

DURLSTON COURT
Becton Lane, Barton-on-Sea, New
Milton, Hampshire BH25 7AQ
Tel: (01425) 610010
Head: Mr D C Wansey
Type: Co-educational Day 2–13
No of pupils: B150 G110
Fees: (September 00) Day £2115 –
£7238
Special Needs: Level 2: DYC DYS
SPLD Level 3: ADD ADHD DYP HI

FARLEIGH SCHOOL
Red Rice, Andover, Hampshire
SP11 7PW
Tel: (01264) 710766
Head: Mr J A Allcott
Type: Co-educational Day and
Boarding 3–13
No of pupils: B254 G147
No of Boarders: F99
Fees: F/WB £11520 Day £2331 –
£8640
Special Needs: Level 2: DYS

FORRES SANDLE MANOR
Fordingbridge, Hampshire SP6 1NS
Tel: (01425) 653181
Head: Mr R P Moore
Type: Co-educational Boarding and
Day 3–13
No of pupils: B136 G115
No of Boarders: F50 W35
Fees: (September 00) F/WB £11220
Day £2415 – £8325
Special Needs: Level 2: ADD ADHD
DYC DYP DYS MLD SPLD

HIGHFIELD SCHOOL
Liphook, Hampshire GU30 7LQ
Tel: (01428) 728000
Head: Mr P G S Evitt
Type: Co-educational Boarding and
Day 7–13
No of pupils: B111 G84
No of Boarders: F94
Fees: (September 00) FB £9975 –
£11400 Day £7560 – £10050
Special Needs: Unspecified: DYP DYS

HORDLE WALHAMPTON SCHOOL†
Walhampton, Lymington,
Hampshire SO41 5ZG
Tel: (01590) 672013
Head: Mr R H C Phillips
Type: Co-educational Boarding and
Day 2–13
No of pupils: B183 G163
No of Boarders: F35 W34
Fees: (September 00) F/WB £10050
Day £3930 – £8100
Special Needs: Level 2: ADD ADHD
CP DYC DYP DYS MLD Level 3: HI

THE KING'S SCHOOL SENIOR
Lakesmere House, Allington Lane,
Fair Oak, Eastleigh, Hampshire
SO50 7DB
Tel: (023) 8060 0956
Head: Mr D Greenwood
Type: Co-educational Day 11–16
No of pupils: B55 G53
Fees: (September 00) Day £3284
Special Needs: Level 3: DYS HI

LITTLEFIELD SCHOOL
Midhurst Road, Liphook, Hampshire
GU30 7HT
Tel: (01428) 723187
Head: Mr S M Lewis
Type: Co-educational Day 3–11
No of pupils: B56 G79
Fees: (January 01) Day £1680 –
£4785
Special Needs: Unspecified: ASP DYS

LORD WANDSWORTH COLLEGE

Long Sutton, Hook, Hampshire RG29 1TB
Tel: (01256) 862482
Head: Mr I G Power
Type: Co-educational Boarding and Day 11–18
No of pupils: B391 G84
No of Boarders: F52 W210
Fees: (September 00) F/WB £12945 – £13650 Day £9750 – £10260
Special Needs: Level 2: DYS Unspecified: W

MAYVILLE HIGH SCHOOL†

35 St Simon's Road, Southsea, Hampshire PO5 2PE
Tel: (023) 9273 4847
Head: Mrs L Owens
Type: Girls Day 2–16 (Boys 2–11, co-ed from 2002)
No of pupils: B101 G222
Fees: (September 00) Day £3075 – £4605
Special Needs: Level 1: DYS SPLD

ST ANNE'S NURSERY & PRE-PREPARATORY SCHOOL

13 Milvil Road, Lee-on-the-Solent, Hampshire PO13 9LU
Tel: (023) 9255 0820
Head: Mrs A M Whitting
Type: Co-educational Day 3–8
No of pupils: B11 G12
Fees: (September 00) Day £2295 – £2610
Special Needs: Level 1: DYC DYP DYS MLD SLD Level 3: ADD ADHD EBD EPI PH Unspecified: W

ST SWITHUN'S SCHOOL

Winchester, Hampshire SO21 1HA
Tel: (01962) 835700
Head: Dr H L Harvey
Type: Girls Boarding and Day 11–18
No of pupils: 470 *No of Boarders:* F42 W178
Fees: (September 00) F/WB £14505 Day £8790
Special Needs: Level 1: DYS Unspecified: W

SHERBORNE HOUSE SCHOOL

Lakewood Road, Chandler's Ford, Eastleigh, Hampshire SO53 1EU
Tel: (023) 8025 2440
Head: Mrs L M Clewer
Type: Co-educational Day 3–11
No of pupils: B102 G168
Fees: (September 00) Day £3390 – £4365
Special Needs: Unspecified: DYS

STANBRIDGE EARLS SCHOOL*†

Stanbridge Lane, Romsey, Hampshire SO51 0ZS
Tel: (01794) 516777
Head: Mr N R Hall
Type: Co-educational Boarding and Day 11–18
No of pupils: B148 G42
No of Boarders: F167
Fees: (September 00) FB £13650 – £15000 Day £10200 – £11100
Special Needs: Level 1: ASP DEL DYC DYP DYS SP&LD SPLD Level 2: ADD ADHD HI VIS Unspecified: W

HARTLEPOOL

WILTON GRANGE SCHOOL

Wilton Grange, Grange Road, Hartlepool TS26 8LX
Tel: (01429) 264976
Head: Mrs S Bruce
Type: Co-educational Day 5–11
No of pupils: B10 G10
Fees: (September 00) Day £2000
Special Needs: Level 2: ASP AUT DEL DYS EBD EPI HI MLD SP&LD SPLD VIS Unspecified: W

HEREFORDSHIRE

LUCTON PIERREPONT SCHOOL

Leominster, Herefordshire HR6 9PN
Tel: (01568) 780686
Head: Mr R Cusworth
Type: Co-educational Boarding and Day 3–16
No of pupils: B65 G55
No of Boarders: F36 W14
Fees: (September 00) FB £8526 – £9735 WB £7299 – £8526 Day £3141 – £5325
Special Needs: Unspecified: DYS

THE MARGARET ALLEN SCHOOL

32 Broomy Hill, Hereford, Herefordshire HR4 0LH
Tel: (01432) 273594
Head: Mrs A Evans
Type: Girls Day 2–11
No of pupils: 102
Fees: (September 00) Day £3180 – £3870
Special Needs: Level 2: ASP DYC DYP DYS EPI HI SP&LD SPLD VIS Unspecified: PH

ST RICHARD'S

Bredenbury Court, Bromyard, Herefordshire HR7 4TD
Tel: (01885) 482491
Head: Mr R E Coghlan
Type: Co-educational Boarding and Day 3–13
No of pupils: B76 G61
No of Boarders: F31 W30
Fees: (September 00) FB £9345 WB £8745 Day £2310 – £6375
Special Needs: Level 2: DYS

HERTFORDSHIRE

ALDENHAM SCHOOL
Elstree, Hertfordshire WD6 3AJ
Tel: (01923) 858122
Head: Mr R S Harman
Type: Boys Boarding and Day 11–18
(Co-ed VIth Form)
No of pupils: B416 G17
No of Boarders: F110 W29
Fees: (September 00) FB £10275 –
£14490 WB £8565 – £12000 Day
£6825 – £10215
Special Needs: Level 2: ASP DYC DYP
DYS SPLD

DUNCOMBE SCHOOL
4 Warren Park Road, Bengeo,
Hertford, Hertfordshire SG14 3JA
Tel: (01992) 414100
Head: Mr D Baldwin
Type: Co-educational Day 2–11
No of pupils: B153 G163
Fees: (September 00) Day £332 –
£5715
Special Needs: Level 2: DYS SPLD
Level 3: ADD ASP DYC DYP EPI HI
MLD VIS

EGERTON-ROTHESAY
SCHOOL
Durrants Lane, Berkhamsted,
Hertfordshire HP4 3UJ
Tel: (01442) 865275
Head: Mrs N Boddam-Whetham
Type: Co-educational Day 2–18
No of pupils: B324 G167
Fees: (January 01) Day £3435 –
£7620
Special Needs: Unspecified: DYP DYS
MLD SPLD

FIRST IMPRESSIONS
MONTESSORI SCHOOLS
Norfolk Lodge School, Dancers Hill
Road, Barnet, Hertfordshire EN5 4RP
Tel: (020) 8447 1565
Head: Mrs L Beirne
Type: Co-educational Day 2–11
No of pupils: B60 G65
Fees: (September 00) Day £402 –
£1470
Special Needs: Unspecified: ASP DEL
DOW DYP DYS SP&LD SPLD

HABERDASHERS' ASKE'S
SCHOOL
Butterfly Lane, Elstree, Hertfordshire
WD6 3AF
Tel: (020) 8266 1700
Head: Mr J W R Goulding
Type: Boys Day 7–18
No of pupils: 1300
Fees: (September 00) Day £7050 –
£7650
Special Needs: Level 3: DYP DYS

HAILEYBURY
Hertford, Hertfordshire SG13 7NU
Tel: (01992) 463353
Head: Mr S A Westley
Type: Co-educational Boarding and
Day 11–18
No of pupils: B456 G224
No of Boarders: F410
Fees: (September 00) FB £10530 –
£16440 Day £7785 – £11895
Special Needs: Level 1: DYP DYS
SPLD Level 3: DYC

HARESFOOT PREPARATORY
SCHOOL
Chesham Road, Berkhamsted,
Hertfordshire HP4 2SZ
Tel: (01442) 872742
Head: Mrs G R Waterhouse
Type: Co-educational Day 3–11
No of pupils: B108 G117
Fees: (September 00) Day £1425 –
£4320
Special Needs: Level 2: DYP DYS
SPLD Unspecified: SP&LD

HARPENDEN PREPARATORY
SCHOOL
53 Luton Road, Harpenden,
Hertfordshire AL5 2UE
Tel: (01582) 712361
Head: Mrs E R Broughton
Type: Co-educational Day 2–11
No of pupils: B77 G64
Fees: (September 00) Day £1743 –
£4305
Special Needs: Level 3: ADD DYP DYS
Unspecified: MLD

HEATH MOUNT SCHOOL
Woodhall Park, Watton-at-Stone,
Hertford, Hertfordshire SG14 3NG
Tel: (01920) 830230
Head: Rev H J Matthews
Type: Co-educational Boarding and
Day 3–13
No of pupils: B213 G139
No of Boarders: W56
Fees: (September 00) WB £9015 –
£10575 Day £2190 – £7590
Special Needs: Unspecified: DYS

HOMEWOOD INDEPENDENT
SCHOOL
Hazel Road, Park Street, St Albans,
Hertfordshire AL2 2AH
Tel: (01727) 873542
Head: Mrs S King
Type: Co-educational Day 3–8
No of pupils: B38 G34
Fees: (September 00) Day £182 –
£4035
Special Needs: Level 3: MLD
Unspecified: W

KINGSHOTT
St Ippolyts, Hitchin, Hertfordshire
SG4 7JX
Tel: (01462) 432009
Head: Mr P R Ilott
Type: Co-educational Day 4–13
No of pupils: B215 G116
Fees: (September 00) Day £4080 –
£5460
Special Needs: Level 2: DYS

LOCHINVER HOUSE SCHOOL
Heath Road, Little Heath, Potters
Bar, Hertfordshire EN6 1LW
Tel: (01707) 653064
Head: Mr P C E Atkinson
Type: Boys Day 4–13
No of pupils: 340
Fees: (September 00) Day £5013 –
£6540
Special Needs: Level 2: DEL DYC DYP
DYS HI SP&LD SPLD Level 3: ADD
ADHD ASP AUT CP DOW EBD EPI
MLD PH PMLD SLD TOU VIS

LONGWOOD SCHOOL
Bushey Hall Drive, Bushey,
Hertfordshire WD23 2QG
Tel: (01923) 253715
Head: Mr M Livesey
Type: Co-educational Day 3–9
No of pupils: B49 G47
Fees: (September 01) Day £2250 –
£3450
Special Needs: Level 3: DYC DYP DYS
EBD EPI HI MLD PH SP&LD SPLD
VIS Unspecified: W

MARLIN MONTESSORI SCHOOL
1 Park View Road, Berkhamsted,
Hertfordshire HP4 3EY
Tel: (01442) 866290
Head: Mrs J Harrison-Sills
Type: Co-educational Day 0–5
No of pupils: B24 G24
Fees: (September 00) Day £350 –
£6800
Special Needs: Unspecified: ADD ASP
CP DEL DOW DYP DYS MLD
SP&LD

NORFOLK LODGE NURSERY & PREPARATORY SCHOOL
Dancers Hill Road, Barnet,
Hertfordshire EN5 4RP
Tel: (020) 8447 1565
Head: Mrs L Beirne
Type: Co-educational Day 2–11
No of pupils: B90 G85
Fees: (September 00) Day £700 –
£4230
Special Needs: Unspecified: ADD
ADHD ASP AUT DEL DOW DYP DYS
EBD EPI SP&LD

ST ANDREW'S MONTESSORI SCHOOL
Garston Manor, High Elms Lane,
Watford, Hertfordshire WD25 0JX
Tel: (01923) 663875
Head: Mrs S O'Neill
Type: Co-educational Day 0–12
No of pupils: B30 G30
Fees: (September 00) Day £1872 –
£4500
Special Needs: Level 2: ASP DOW DYS
MLD SP&LD SPLD Level 3: DEL DYP
HI PH VIS Unspecified: W

ST COLUMBA'S COLLEGE
King Harry Lane, St Albans,
Hertfordshire AL3 4AW
Tel: (01727) 855185
Head: Dom S Darlington
Type: Boys Day 11–18
No of pupils: 550
Fees: (September 00) Day £5610
Special Needs: Level 2: ADD ADHD
DYC DYP DYS SP&LD SPLD Level 3:
ASP TOU

ST JOSEPH'S IN THE PARK
St Mary's, Hertingfordbury, Hertford,
Hertfordshire SG14 2LX
Tel: (01992) 581378
Head: Mrs J King
Type: Co-educational Day 3–11
No of pupils: B90 G90
Fees: (September 00) Day £1500
Special Needs: Level 1: DYC DYP DYS
MLD PH SLD SP&LD SPLD Level 2:
ADD HI VIS Level 3: ASP DEL

ST NICHOLAS HOUSE
Bunkers Lane, Hemel Hempstead,
Hertfordshire HP3 8RP
Tel: (01442) 211156
Head: Mrs B B Vaughan
Type: Girls Day 3–11 (Boys 3–7)
No of pupils: B38 G165
Fees: (September 00) Day £1525 –
£1895
Special Needs: Unspecified: DEL DYC
DYP DYS

WESTWOOD
6 Hartsbourne Road, Bushey Heath,
Hertfordshire WD2 1JH
Tel: (020) 8950 1138
Head: Mrs J Hill
Type: Co-educational Day 4–8
No of pupils: B36 G36
Fees: (September 00) Day £3885
Special Needs: Level 3: DYP DYS HI
PH VIS

YORK HOUSE SCHOOL
Redheath, Croxley Green,
Rickmansworth, Hertfordshire
WD3 4LW
Tel: (01923) 772395
Head: Mr P B Moore
Type: Boys Day 4–13 (Co-ed 2–5)
No of pupils: B255 G12
Fees: (September 00) Day £3578 –
£5628
Special Needs: Unspecified: DYP DYS
HI

ISLE OF MAN

KING WILLIAM'S COLLEGE
Castletown, Isle of Man IM9 1TP
Tel: (01624) 822551
Head: Mr P D John
Type: Co-educational Boarding and
Day 11–18
No of pupils: B156 G119
No of Boarders: F61
Fees: (September 00) FB £11430 –
£14175 Day £7335 – £10080
Special Needs: Level 2: ADD ADHD
ASP DYS EBD MLD Level 3: CP PH

ISLE OF WIGHT

PRIORY SCHOOL
The Broadway, Sandown, Isle of
Wight PO36 9BY
Tel: (01983) 406866
Head: Mrs E J Goldthorpe
Type: Co-educational Day 2–18
No of pupils: B56 G53
Fees: (September 00) Day £382 –
£2550
Special Needs: Unspecified: ADD
ADHD DYC DYS MLD SPLD

RYDE SCHOOL
Queen's Road, Ryde, Isle of Wight
PO33 3BE
Tel: (01983) 562229
Head: Dr N J England
Type: Co-educational Day and
Boarding 3–18
No of pupils: B394 G305
No of Boarders: F26 W19
Fees: (January 01) FB £10680 –
£12015 WB £10065 – £11295 Day
£2385 – £5700
Special Needs: Unspecified: DYC DYP
DYS

WESTMONT SCHOOL
82/88 Carisbrooke Road, Newport,
Isle of Wight PO30 1BY
Tel: (01983) 523051
Head: Mr D Reading
Type: Co-educational Day 0–19
No of pupils: B53 G49
Fees: (September 00) Day £300 –
£3600
Special Needs: Level 2: ASP DYS SPLD
Level 3: DYC

KENT

ASHGROVE SCHOOL
116 Widmore Road, Bromley, Kent
BR1 3BE
Tel: (020) 8460 4143
Head: Dr P Ash
Type: Co-educational Day 3–11
No of pupils: B51 G49
Fees: (September 00) Day £4485
Special Needs: Level 3: ADD DYC
DYP DYS

BASTON SCHOOL
Baston Road, Hayes, Bromley, Kent
BR2 7AB
Tel: (020) 8462 1010
Head: Mr C R C Wimble
Type: Girls Day 2–18
No of pupils: 135
Fees: (September 00) Day £1278 –
£5970
Special Needs: Level 2: DYS

BEDGEBURY SCHOOL
Bedgebury Park, Goudhurst,
Cranbrook, Kent TN17 2SH
Tel: (01580) 211221
Head: Mrs H Moriarty
Type: Girls Boarding and Day 2–18
(Boys Day 2–7)
No of pupils: B10 G375
No of Boarders: F78 W79
Fees: (September 00) F/WB £9240 –
£14010 Day £2220 – £8700
Special Needs: Level 2: ADD ADHD
DYC DYP DYS SP&LD SPLD VIS

BETHANY SCHOOL†
Goudhurst, Cranbrook, Kent
TN17 1LB
Tel: (01580) 211273
Head: Mr N Dorey
Type: Co-educational Boarding and
Day 11–18
No of pupils: B268 G60
No of Boarders: F140
Fees: (September 00) F/WB £12513 –
£13365 Day £8040 – £8890
Special Needs: Unspecified: DYS HI

COBHAM HALL†
Cobham, Gravesend, Kent DA12 3BL
Tel: (01474) 823371
Head: Mrs R McCarthy
Type: Girls Boarding and Day 11–18
No of pupils: G200 *No of Boarders:* F104
W16
Fees: (September 00) F/WB £13500 –
£14985 Day £8100 – £10005
Special Needs: Unspecified: DYP DYS
SP&LD

DARUL ULOOM LONDON
Foxbury Avenue, Perry Street,
Chislehurst, Kent BR7 6SD
Tel: (020) 8295 0637
Head: Mr M Musa
Type: Boys Boarding 11+
No of pupils: B170 *No of Boarders:* F30
W140
Fees: (September 00) FB £1500 –
£1800
Special Needs: Unspecified: W

DOVER COLLEGE
Effingham Crescent, Dover, Kent
CT17 9RH
Tel: (01304) 205969
Head: Mr H W Blackett
Type: Co-educational Boarding and
Day 11–18
No of pupils: B150 G100
No of Boarders: F100
Fees: (September 00) FB £10350 –
£13185 WB £9750 – £10485 Day
£5250 – £7785
Special Needs: Level 2: ADD ADHD
DYC DYP DYS MLD SPLD
Unspecified: W

DUKE OF YORK'S ROYAL
MILITARY SCHOOL
Dover, Kent CT15 5EQ
Tel: (01304) 245029
Head: Mr J A Cummings
Type: Co-educational Boarding 11–18
No of pupils: B348 G152
No of Boarders: F500
Fees: (September 00) FB £975
Special Needs: Level 2: DYS Level 3:
ADD

DULWICH PREPARATORY SCHOOL, CRANBROOK
Coursehorn, Cranbrook, Kent
TN17 3NP
Tel: (01580) 712179
Head: Mr M C Wagstaffe
Type: Co-educational Day and
Boarding 3–13
No of pupils: B299 G246
No of Boarders: F20 W26
Fees: (September 00) F/WB £11205 –
£11505 Day £2625 – £7635
Special Needs: Level 1: DYS
Unspecified: W

GAD'S HILL SCHOOL
Higham, Rochester, Kent ME3 7AA
Tel: (01474) 822366
Head: Mr D Craggs
Type: Co-educational Day 3–18
No of pupils: B80 G140
Fees: (September 00) Day £1638 –
£3624
Special Needs: Level 2: DYP DYS

HILDEN GRANGE SCHOOL
62 Dry Hill Park Road, Tonbridge,
Kent TN10 3BX
Tel: (01732) 352706
Head: Mr J Withers
Type: Co-educational Day 3–13
No of pupils: B204 G100
Fees: (September 00) Day £3750 –
£6000
Special Needs: Unspecified: DYS

HOLMEWOOD HOUSE
Langton Green, Tunbridge Wells,
Kent TN3 0EB
Tel: (01892) 860000
Head: Mr A S R Corbett
Type: Co-educational Boarding and
Day 3–13
No of pupils: B290 G216
No of Boarders: W19
Fees: (September 00) WB £13335 Day
£2475 – £9165
Special Needs: Level 2: DYP DYS

THE JUNIOR SCHOOL, ST LAWRENCE COLLEGE
Ramsgate, Kent CT11 7AF
Tel: (01843) 591788
Head: Mr R Tunnicliffe
Type: Co-educational Boarding and
Day 3–13
No of pupils: B73 G83
No of Boarders: F55
Fees: (September 00) FB £11700 Day
£3400 – £7268
Special Needs: Unspecified: ADD
ADHD DYC DYP DYS MLD

KENT COLLEGE
Canterbury, Kent CT2 9DT
Tel: (01227) 763231
Head: Mr E B Halse
Type: Co-educational Boarding and
Day 3–18
No of pupils: 690 *No of Boarders:* F150
Fees: (September 00) FB £14400 Day
£8100
Special Needs: Unspecified: DYS

KENT COLLEGE PEMBURY
Tunbridge Wells, Kent TN2 4AX
Tel: (01892) 822006
Head: Miss B J Crompton
Type: Girls Boarding and Day 3–18
No of pupils: 520 *No of Boarders:* F40
W30
Fees: (September 00) FB £10920 –
£14220 WB £10080 – £13860 Day
£4020 – £8790
Special Needs: Level 2: DYP DYS

THE KING'S SCHOOL
Canterbury, Kent CT1 2ES
Tel: (01227) 595501
Head: Rev Canon K H Wilkinson
Type: Co-educational Boarding and
Day 13–18
No of pupils: B423 G339
No of Boarders: F612
Fees: (September 00) FB £16800 Day
£11730
Special Needs: Level 3: DYP DYS

THE NEW BEACON
Brittains Lane, Sevenoaks, Kent
TN13 2PB
Tel: (01732) 452131
Head: Mr R Constantine
Type: Boys Day and Boarding 5–13
No of pupils: 400 *No of Boarders:* W25
Fees: (September 00) WB £7755 –
£9480 Day £4500 – £6225
Special Needs: Level 2: DYC DYS
Level 3: ADD

NORTHBOURNE PARK SCHOOL
Betteshanger, Deal, Kent CT14 0NW
Tel: (01304) 611215/8
Head: Mr S Sides
Type: Co-educational Day and
Boarding 3–13
No of pupils: 211 *No of Boarders:* F49
Fees: (September 00) FB £9555 –
£11730 Day £4740 – £7515
Special Needs: Level 2: ADD ADHD
DYC DYP DYS SPLD Unspecified: HI

ST ANDREW'S SCHOOL
24–28 Watts Avenue, Rochester,
Kent ME1 1SA
Tel: (01634) 843479
Head: Mr N D Kynaston
Type: Co-educational Day 4–11
No of pupils: B150 G160
Fees: (September 00) Day £2865 –
£3030
Special Needs: Level 3: ADD ADHD
ASP AUT CP DEL DOW DYC DYP
DYS EBD EPI HI MLD PH PMLD SLD
SP&LD SPLD TOU VIS

ST EDMUND'S JUNIOR SCHOOL
Canterbury, Kent CT2 8HU
Tel: (01227) 475600
Head: Mr R G Bacon
Type: Co-educational Day and
Boarding 3–13
No of pupils: B168 G90
No of Boarders: F44
Fees: (September 00) FB £10935 Day
£1650 – £7695
Special Needs: Level 1: EPI Level 2:
ADD ASP DYC DYP DYS SPLD

ST EDMUND'S SCHOOL
Canterbury, Kent CT2 8HU
Tel: (01227) 475600
Head: Mr A N Ridley
Type: Co-educational Day and
Boarding 3–18
No of pupils: B313 G214
No of Boarders: F121
Fees: (September 00) FB £10755 –
£15642 Day £3099 – £10095
Special Needs: Unspecified: ASP DYS
SPLD

ST LAWRENCE COLLEGE
Ramsgate, Kent CT11 7AE
Tel: (01843) 592680
Head: Mr M Slater
Type: Co-educational Boarding and
Day 3–18
No of pupils: B267 G185
No of Boarders: F179 W5
Fees: (September 00) F/WB £11715 –
£15540 Day £4185 – £9975
Special Needs: Unspecified: DYC DYP
DYS MLD

ST MARY'S WESTBROOK

Ravenlea Road, Folkestone, Kent
CT20 2JU
Tel: (01303) 851222
Head: Mrs L A Watson
Type: Co-educational Boarding and
Day 2–16
No of pupils: B170 G122
No of Boarders: F47
Fees: (September 00) FB £9975 –
£10995 Day £4710 – £7320
Special Needs: Level 1: ASP AUT DYS
Level 2: ADD ADHD SPLD Level 3:
SP&LD Unspecified: DYP MLD

ST MICHAEL'S SCHOOL

Otford Court, Otford, Sevenoaks,
Kent TN14 5SA
Tel: (01959) 522137
Head: Dr P Roots
Type: Co-educational Day 2–13
No of pupils: B223 G196
Fees: (September 00) Day £2340 –
£6210
Special Needs: Level 1: SP&LD
Level 2: ADD ASP MLD Level 3: DYC
DYP DYS SPLD

ST RONAN'S

St Ronan's Road, Hawkhurst, Kent
TN18 5DJ
Tel: (01580) 752271
Head: Mr E Yeats-Brown
Type: Co-educational Boarding and
Day 3–13
No of pupils: B100 G50
No of Boarders: F16 W25
Fees: (September 00) F/WB £10434
Day £7689
Special Needs: Unspecified: DEL

SEVENOAKS PREPARATORY SCHOOL

Fawke Cottage, Godden Green,
Sevenoaks, Kent TN15 0JU
Tel: (01732) 762336
Head: Mr E H Oatley
Type: Co-educational Day 3–13
No of pupils: B230 G90
Fees: (September 00) Day £4050 –
£5730
Special Needs: Level 2: MLD
Unspecified: DYS W

STEEPHILL SCHOOL

Castle Hill, Fawkham, Longfield,
Kent DA3 7BG
Tel: (01474) 702107
Head: Mr P D Stradling
Type: Co-educational Day 3–11
No of pupils: B50 G49
Fees: (September 00) Day £2742
Special Needs: Level 2: ADD ADHD
DYC DYP DYS EBD MLD SP&LD

UNDERHILL – JUNIOR SCHOOL TO SUTTON VALENCE

Chart Sutton, Maidstone, Kent
ME17 3RF
Tel: (01622) 842117
Head: Mr A M Brooke
Type: Co-educational Day 3–11
No of pupils: B169 G151
Fees: (September 00) Day £4155 –
£5805
Special Needs: Level 2: DYP DYS

WALTHAMSTOW HALL

Hollybush Lane, Sevenoaks, Kent
TN13 3UL
Tel: (01732) 451334
Head: Mrs J S Lang
Type: Girls Day 3–18
No of pupils: 435
Fees: (September 00) Day £696 –
£8580
Special Needs: Level 2: DYS
Unspecified: W

LANCASHIRE

ARNOLD SCHOOL

Lytham Road, Blackpool, Lancashire
FY4 1JG
Tel: (01253) 346391
Head: Mr W T Gillen
Type: Co-educational Day 11–18
No of pupils: B374 G400
Fees: (September 00) Day £4950
Special Needs: Level 2: ADD ADHD
DYC DYP DYS SPLD

BENTHAM GRAMMAR SCHOOL

Low Bentham, Lancaster, Lancashire
LA2 7DB
Tel: (01524) 261275
Head: Miss R E Colman
Type: Co-educational Boarding and
Day 4–18
No of pupils: B107 G70
No of Boarders: F65 W7
Fees: (September 00) FB £9705 –
£11490 WB £8490 – £9705 Day
£3615 – £5820
Special Needs: Level 2: ADD ADHD
ASP DYS SPLD Level 3: DYC DYP PH
SP&LD

BOLTON SCHOOL (GIRLS' DIVISION)

Chorley New Road, Bolton,
Lancashire BL1 4PB
Tel: (01204) 840201
Head: Miss E J Panton
Type: Girls Day 4–18 (Boys 4–8)
No of pupils: B100 G1063
Fees: (September 00) Day £4188 –
£5664
Special Needs: Level 3: DYS EPI HI PH
VIS

HIGHFIELD PRIORY SCHOOL
Fulwood Row, Fulwood, Preston,
Lancashire PR2 6SL
Tel: (01772) 709624
Head: Mr B C Duckett
Type: Co-educational Day 2–11
No of pupils: B151 G157
Fees: (September 00) Day £3120 –
£3420
Special Needs: Level 2: DYC MLD
SPLD

KING EDWARD VII AND QUEEN MARY SCHOOL
Clifton Drive South, Lytham St
Annes, Lancashire FY8 1DS
Tel: (01253) 723246
Head: Mr P J Wilde
Type: Co-educational Day 3–18
(Single sex education 13–16)
No of pupils: B536 G448
Fees: (September 00) Day £3285 –
£4770
Special Needs: Level 2: DYS SP&LD
SPLD Level 3: ADHD PH
Unspecified: HI

KINGSWOOD COLLEGE AT SCARISBRICK HALL
Southport Road, Ormskirk,
Lancashire L40 9RQ
Tel: (01704) 880200
Head: Mr E J Borowski
Type: Co-educational Day 2–18
No of pupils: B333 G241
Fees: (September 00) Day £1920 –
£4050
Special Needs: Level 2: ADD ADHD
DYC DYP DYS

OAKHILL COLLEGE
Wiswell Lane, Whalley, Clitheroe,
Lancashire BB7 9AF
Tel: (01254) 823546
Head: Mr P S Mahon
Type: Co-educational Day 2–16
No of pupils: B124 G90
Fees: (September 00) Day £3585 –
£5574
Special Needs: Level 1: PH Level 2:
ADD DYC DYS SPLD

QUEEN ELIZABETH'S GRAMMAR SCHOOL
Blackburn, Lancashire BB2 6DF
Tel: (01254) 686300
Head: Dr D S Hempsall
Type: Boys Day 7–18 (Co-ed VIth
Form)
No of pupils: B783 G20
Fees: (September 00) Day £4290 –
£5454
Special Needs: Level 3: DYP DYS

ROSSALL SCHOOL
Fleetwood, Lancashire FY7 8JW
Tel: (01253) 774201
Head: Mr G S H Pengelley
Type: Co-educational Boarding and
Day 11–18
No of pupils: B239 G175
No of Boarders: F174
Fees: (September 00) FB £9750 –
£14985 Day £4875 – £5685
Special Needs: Level 1: ADD ADHD
DYP DYS

WESTHOLME SCHOOL
Wilmar Lodge, Meins Road,
Blackburn, Lancashire BB2 6QU
Tel: (01254) 53447
Head: Mrs L Croston
Type: Girls Day 3–18 (Boys 3–7)
No of pupils: B70 G1035
Fees: (September 00) Day £3255 –
£4545
Special Needs: Level 3: HI VIS
Unspecified: DYS W

LEICESTERSHIRE

FAIRFIELD SCHOOL
Leicester Road, Loughborough,
Leicestershire LE11 2AE
Tel: (01509) 215172
Head: Mr T A Eadon
Type: Co-educational Day 4–11
No of pupils: B245 G213
Fees: (September 00) Day £4293
Special Needs: Unspecified: DYS

GRACE DIEU MANOR SCHOOL
Grace Dieu, Thringstone, Leicester
LE67 5UG
Tel: (01530) 222276
Head: Mr D Hare
Type: Co-educational Day 3–13
No of pupils: B209 G111
Fees: (September 00) Day £3621 –
£5865
Special Needs: Unspecified: DYS

LEICESTER GRAMMAR JUNIOR SCHOOL
Evington Hall, Spencefield Lane,
Leicester LE5 6HN
Tel: (0116) 210 1299
Head: Mr H McFaul
Type: Co-educational Day 3–11
No of pupils: B134 G115
Fees: (September 00) Day £4320
Special Needs: Level 2: ADD DYC
DYP DYS

LEICESTER GRAMMAR SCHOOL
8 Peacock Lane, Leicester LE1 5PX
Tel: (0116) 222 0400
Head: Mr J B Sugden
Type: Co-educational Day 10–18
No of pupils: B402 G292
Fees: (September 01) Day £5985
Special Needs: Level 3: DYS

MANOR HOUSE SCHOOL
South Street, Ashby-de-la-Zouch,
Leicestershire LE65 1BR
Tel: (01530) 412932
Head: Mr R J Sill
Type: Co-educational Day 3–14
No of pupils: B117 G90
Fees: (September 00) Day £3195 –
£4260
Special Needs: Level 2: DYP DYS MLD

ST CRISPIN'S SCHOOL
St Mary's Road, Leicester,
Leicestershire LE2 1XA
Tel: (0116) 270 7648
Head: Mrs D Lofthouse
Type: Co-educational Day 2–16
No of pupils: B160 G40
Fees: (September 00) Day £1620 –
£4785
Special Needs: Level 2: ADD DYC
DYP DYS MLD SPLD Unspecified:
SP&LD

LINCOLNSHIRE

**CONWAY PREPARATORY
SCHOOL**
Tunnard Street, Boston, Lincolnshire
PE21 6PL
Tel: (01205) 363150
Head: Mr S P McElwain
Type: Co-educational Day 2–11
No of pupils: B70 G70
Fees: (September 00) Day £1380 –
£2715
Special Needs: Level 2: DYS

COPTHILL SCHOOL
Barnack Road, Uffington, Stamford,
Lincolnshire PE9 4TD
Tel: (01780) 757506
Head: Mr J A Teesdale
Type: Co-educational Day 2–11
No of pupils: B137 G142
Fees: (September 00) Day £810 –
£4050
Special Needs: Level 3: ASP DYP HI
MLD PH SPLD VIS Unspecified:
DYS W

**THE FEN PREPARATORY
SCHOOL**
Side Bar Lane, Heckington Fen,
Sleaford, Lincolnshire NG34 9LY
Tel: (01529) 460966
Head: Mrs J M Dunkley
Type: Co-educational Day 2–16
No of pupils: B14 G16
Fees: (September 00) Day £1860 –
£4095
Special Needs: Level 2: ADD ADHD
CP DEL DOW DYP DYS EBD EPI
MLD PH SP&LD VIS Unspecified: W

**THE GRANTHAM
PREPARATORY SCHOOL**
Gorse Lane, Grantham, Lincolnshire
NG31 7UF
Tel: (01476) 593293
Head: Mrs D J Wand
Type: Co-educational Day 3–11
No of pupils: B76 G80
Fees: (September 00) Day £3120 –
£3900
Special Needs: Level 2: DYS MLD

**ST MARY'S PREPARATORY
SCHOOL**
5 Pottergate, Lincoln LN2 1PH
Tel: (01522) 524622
Head: Mr M Upton
Type: Co-educational Day 2–11
No of pupils: B150 G141
Fees: (September 00) Day £3450 –
£5220
Special Needs: Level 2: DYS SPLD

NORTH EAST LINCOLNSHIRE

**ST MARTIN'S PREPARATORY
SCHOOL**
63 Bargate, Grimsby, North East
Lincolnshire DN34 5AA
Tel: (01472) 878907
Head: Mrs M Preston
Type: Co-educational Day 3–11
No of pupils: B109 G125
Fees: (April 00) Day £1620 – £2985
Special Needs: Level 2: DYC DYP DYS

NORTH LINCOLNSHIRE

TRENTVALE PREPARATORY SCHOOL
Trentside, Keadby, North Lincolnshire DN17 3EF
Tel: (01724) 782904
Head: Mr P Wright
Type: Co-educational Day 3–11
No of pupils: B45 G45
Fees: (September 00) Day £1575
Special Needs: Level 3: DYS

LONDON

EC1

DALLINGTON SCHOOL
8 Dallington Street, London EC1V 0BW
Tel: (020) 7251 2284
Head: Mrs M C Hercules
Type: Co-educational Day 3–11
No of pupils: B102 G110
Fees: (September 00) Day £3940 – £5265
Special Needs: Level 2: DYP DYS SPLD Level 3: SP&LD

N2

THE KEREM SCHOOL
Norrice Lea, London N2 0RE
Tel: (020) 8455 0909
Head: Mrs R Goulden
Type: Co-educational Day 4–11
No of pupils: B79 G81
Fees: (September 00) Day £4500
Special Needs: Unspecified: DYP DYS

N3

AKIVA SCHOOL
Levy House, The Sternberg Centre, 80 East End Road, London N3 2SY
Tel: (020) 8349 4980
Head: Mrs L Bayfield
Type: Co-educational Day 4–11
No of pupils: B81 G73
Fees: (September 00) Day £4410
Special Needs: Level 2: DYP DYS EBD HI MLD SP&LD SPLD VIS

N5

PRIMROSE MONTESSORI SCHOOL
Congregational Church, Highbury, London N5 2TE
Tel: (020) 7359 8985
Head: Mrs L Grandson
Type: Co-educational Day 2–11
No of pupils: 110
Fees: (September 00) Day £4680
Special Needs: Level 2: DYS MLD SPLD

N6

RAINBOW MONTESSORI NURSERY SCHOOL
Highgate URC, Pond Square, London N6 6BA
Tel: (020) 7328 8986
Head: Mrs L Madden
Type: Co-educational Day 2–5
No of pupils: B18 G18
Fees: (January 01) Day £2805 – £4365
Special Needs: Level 3: DOW DYS EPI MLD

N11

WOODSIDE PARK INTERNATIONAL SCHOOL
Friern Barnet Road, London N11 3DR
Tel: (020) 8368 3777
Head: Mr R F Metters
Type: Co-educational Day 2–18
No of pupils: B376 G184
Fees: (September 00) Day £2730 – £9000
Special Needs: Level 1: ADD ASP AUT DYC DYP MLD SP&LD SPLD Level 3: DYS

N16

LUBAVITCH HOUSE SENIOR SCHOOL FOR GIRLS
107–115 Stamford Hill, Hackney, London N16 5RP
Tel: (020) 8800 0022
Head: Rabbi S Lew
Type: Girls Day 11–18
No of pupils: G80
Fees: (September 00) On application
Special Needs: Level 2: MLD Level 3: ADD DYS EBD HI

NW1

NORTH BRIDGE HOUSE SCHOOL*
1 Gloucester Avenue, London NW1 7AB
Tel: (020) 7267 6266
Head: Mr W H Wilcox
Type: Co-educational Day 2–18
No of pupils: B463 G397
Fees: (September 00) Day £6900
Special Needs: Unspecified: DYS

NW3

THE HALL SCHOOL
23 Crossfield Road, Hampstead,
London NW3 4NU
Tel: (020) 7722 1700
Head: Mr P F Ramage
Type: Boys Day 4–13
No of pupils: 420
Fees: (September 00) Day £6000 –
£7350
Special Needs: Level 2: DYP DYS

HAMPSTEAD HILL PRE-PREPARATORY & NURSERY SCHOOL
St Stephen's Hall, Pond Street,
Hampstead, London NW3 2PP
Tel: (020) 7435 6262
Head: Mrs A Taylor
Type: Co-educational Day Boys 2–8
Girls 2–7
No of pupils: B150 G100
Fees: (September 00) Day £4500 –
£8250
Special Needs: Level 2: CP DYC DYS
MLD SP&LD SPLD Level 3: ADD
ADHD AUT DOW DYP EPI HI
Unspecified: W

SOUTHBANK INTERNATIONAL SCHOOL, HAMPSTEAD
16 Netherhall Gardens, Hampstead,
London NW3 5TH
Tel: (020) 7431 1200
Head: Mrs J Treftz
Type: Co-educational Day 3–14
No of pupils: B90 G94
Fees: (September 00) Day £3600 –
£12000
Special Needs: Level 2: DYP DYS
SPLD

NW4

HENDON PREPARATORY SCHOOL
20 Tenterden Grove, Hendon,
London NW4 1TD
Tel: (020) 8203 7727
Head: Mr J Gear
Type: Co-educational Day 2–13
No of pupils: B184 G88
Fees: (September 00) Day £5700 –
£7140
Special Needs: Level 2: DYP DYS

THE TUITION CENTRE
Lodge House, Lodge Road, London
NW4 4DQ
Tel: (020) 8203 5025
Head: Mr B Canetti
Type: Co-educational Day 15+
No of pupils: B129 G103
Fees: (September 00) Day £2145 –
£9850
Special Needs: Unspecified: ADD ASP
DYP DYS MLD

NW7

BELMONT (MILL HILL JUNIOR SCHOOL)
Mill Hill, London NW7 4ED
Tel: (020) 8959 1431
Head: Mr J R Hawkins
Type: Co-educational Day 7–13
No of pupils: B278 G105
Fees: (September 00) Day £7779
Special Needs: Level 1: DYS Level 2:
ADD ADHD DYP EBD SPLD Level 3:
HI SP&LD

THE MOUNT SCHOOL
Milespit Hill, Mill Hill, London
NW7 2RX
Tel: (020) 8959 3403
Head: Mrs J K Jackson
Type: Girls Day 4–18
No of pupils: G400
Fees: (January 01) Day £4920 –
£5820
Special Needs: Level 3: ADD ADHD
ASP CP DEL DYP DYS HI PH SPLD
VIS

ST MARTIN'S
22 Goodwyn Avenue, Mill Hill,
London NW7 3RG
Tel: (020) 8959 1965
Head: Mrs A Wilson
Type: Co-educational Day 3–11
No of pupils: B50 G85
Fees: (September 00) Day £2760 –
£2970
Special Needs: Level 2: DYS

NW8

ARNOLD HOUSE SCHOOL
1, Loudoun Road, St John's Wood,
London NW8 0LH
Tel: (020) 7266 4840
Head: Mr N M Allen
Type: Boys Day 5–13
No of pupils: 250
Fees: (September 00) Day £7380
Special Needs: Level 2: DYP DYS MLD
Level 3: EBD HI

NW10

WELSH SCHOOL OF LONDON
Welsh School of London, c/o
Stonebridge Primary School,
Shakespeare Avenue, London NW10
8NG
Tel: (020) 8965 3585
Head: Miss S Edwards
Type: Co-educational Day 4–11
No of pupils: 28
Fees: (September 00) Day £1500
Special Needs: Unspecified: MLD

SE1

THE SCHILLER ACADEMY
Royal Waterloo House, 51–55
Waterloo Road, London SE1 8TX
Tel: (020) 7928 1372
Head: Mr G Selby
Type: Co-educational Day 14–18
No of pupils: 35
Fees: (September 00) Day £8800 –
£9170
Special Needs: Level 2: ADD ADHD
DYC DYS SPLD Level 3: DYP

SE9

ELTHAM COLLEGE
Grove Park Road, Mottingham,
London SE9 4QF
Tel: (020) 8857 1455
Head: Mr P J Henderson
Type: Boys Day and Boarding 7–18
(Co-ed VIth Form)
No of pupils: B741 G42
No of Boarders: F5 W5
Fees: (September 00) FB £15282 WB
£14682 Day £6384 – £7398
Special Needs: Level 3: DYP DYS

SE21

DULWICH COLLEGE
Dulwich Common, London
SE21 7LD
Tel: (020) 8299 9263
Head: Mr G G Able
Type: Boys Day and Boarding 7–18
No of pupils: 1400 *No of Boarders:* F80
W20
Fees: (September 00) FB £15975 WB
£15345 Day £8175
Special Needs: Level 2: ADD ASP DEL
DYC DYP DYS MLD SPLD Level 3:
ADHD EPI HI PH Unspecified: W

SW1

EATON HOUSE SCHOOL
3 and 5 Eaton Gate, Eaton Square, London SW1W 9BA
Tel: (020) 7730 9343
Head: Miss L Watts
Type: Boys Day 4–9
No of pupils: 250
Fees: (September 00) Day £5850
Special Needs: Level 2: MLD SPLD

FRANCIS HOLLAND SCHOOL
39 Graham Terrace, London SW1W 8JF
Tel: (020) 7730 2971
Head: Miss S Pattenden
Type: Girls Day 4–18
No of pupils: 410
Fees: (September 00) Day £8130
Special Needs: Level 3: DYS HI

HELLENIC COLLEGE OF LONDON
67 Pont Street, London SW1X 0BD
Tel: (020) 7581 5044
Head: Mr J Wardrobe
Type: Co-educational Day 2–18
No of pupils: B95 G95
Fees: (September 01) Day £6099 – £7632
Special Needs: Unspecified: DYP DYS HI

WESTMINSTER CATHEDRAL CHOIR SCHOOL
Ambrosden Avenue, London SW1P 1QH
Tel: (020) 7798 9081
Head: Mr C Foulds
Type: Boys Boarding and Day 8–13
No of pupils: 100 *No of Boarders:* F30
Fees: (September 00) FB £4170 Day £7950
Special Needs: Level 1: DYP DYS

SW3

CAMERON HOUSE
4 The Vale, Chelsea, London SW3 6AH
Tel: (020) 7352 4040
Head: Mrs F M Stack
Type: Co-educational Day 4–11
No of pupils: B52 G60
Fees: (September 00) Day £6960 – £7350
Special Needs: Level 1: DYP DYS

SW5

COLLINGHAM
23 Collingham Gardens, London SW5 0HL
Tel: (020) 7244 7414
Head: Mr G Hattee
Type: Co-educational Day 14–20
No of pupils: B125 G115
Fees: (September 00) Day £10050 – £11850
Special Needs: Level 2: DYC DYP DYS VIS Level 3: ADD ASP DEL EPI HI

SW7

FALKNER HOUSE
19 Brechin Place, London SW7 4QB
Tel: (020) 7373 4501
Head: Mrs A Griggs
Type: Girls Day 3–11 (Co-ed 3–4)
No of pupils: B10 G160
Fees: (September 00) Day £7800
Special Needs: Level 3: HI

THE HAMPSHIRE SCHOOLS (KNIGHTSBRIDGE UNDER SCHOOL)
5 Wetherby Place, London SW7 4NX
Tel: (020) 7584 3297
Head: Mr A G Bray
Type: Co-educational Day 3–6
No of pupils: B45 G45
Fees: (September 00) Day £2820 – £5820
Special Needs: Level 2: DYP DYS Level 3: ADD ADHD

THE HAMPSHIRE SCHOOLS (KNIGHTSBRIDGE UPPER SCHOOL)
63 Ennismore Gardens, London SW7 1NH
Tel: (020) 7584 3297
Head: Mr A G Bray
Type: Co-educational Day 6–11
No of pupils: B56 G56
Fees: (September 00) Day £6180 – £8085
Special Needs: Level 2: DYP DYS Level 3: ADD ADHD

ST PHILIP'S SCHOOL
6 Wetherby Place, London SW7 4ND
Tel: (020) 7373 3944
Head: Mr H Biggs-Davison
Type: Boys Day 7–13
No of pupils: 111
Fees: (September 00) Day £6450
Special Needs: Level 2: DYS

THE VALE SCHOOL
2 Elvaston Place, London SW7 5QH
Tel: (020) 7924 6000
Head: Miss S Calder
Type: Co-educational Day Boys 4–9 Girls 4–11
No of pupils: B40 G60
Fees: (September 00) Day £6150
Special Needs: Unspecified: DYS

SW11

THE DOMINIE†
142 Battersea Park Road, London SW11 4NB
Tel: (020) 7720 8783
Head: Mrs L Robertson
Type: Co-educational Day 6–13
No of pupils: B22 G10
Fees: (September 00) Day £11100
Special Needs: Level 1: DYP DYS SP&LD Unspecified: SPLD

NORTHCOTE LODGE
26 Bolingbroke Grove, London SW11 6EL
Tel: (020) 7924 7170
Head: Mr P Cheeseman
Type: Boys Day 8–13
No of pupils: 150
Fees: (September 00) Day £7320 – £7680
Special Needs: Level 2: ADD ADHD DYC DYP DYS

SW12

HORNSBY HOUSE SCHOOL
Hearnville Road, London SW12 8RS
Tel: (020) 8673 7573
Head: Mrs J Strong
Type: Co-educational Day 3–11
No of pupils: B122 G112
Fees: (September 00) Day £2385 – £5880
Special Needs: Level 3: DYS Unspecified: W

SW15

IBSTOCK PLACE SCHOOL
Clarence Lane, Roehampton, London SW15 5PY
Tel: (020) 8876 9991
Head: Mrs A Sylvester Johnson
Type: Co-educational Day 3–16
No of pupils: B284 G332
Fees: (September 00) Day £2610 – £7140
Special Needs: Level 3: DYS SPLD

SW17

EVELINE DAY SCHOOL
14 Trinity Crescent, Upper Tooting, London SW17 7AE
Tel: (020) 8672 4673
Head: Ms E Drut
Type: Co-educational Day 3–11
No of pupils: B34 G41
Fees: (September 00) Day £7956
Special Needs: Level 3: ASP DYS SP&LD SPLD

SW19

PLAYDAYS NURSERY/ SCHOOL AND MONTESSORI COLLEGE
58 Queens Road, Wimbledon, London SW19 8LR
Tel: (020) 8946 8139
Head: Ms F Baxter-Warman
Type: Co-educational Day 0–5
No of pupils: B25 G25
Fees: (September 00) Day £8839 – £10087
Special Needs: Level 2: HI Level 3: ADD ADHD ASP AUT CP DEL DOW DYC DYP DYS EBD EPI MLD PH PMLD SLD SP&LD SPLD TOU VIS Unspecified: W

WIMBLEDON COLLEGE PREP SCHOOL
Donhead Lodge, 33 Edge Hill, Wimbledon, London SW19 4NP
Tel: (020) 8946 7000
Head: Mr G C McGrath
Type: Boys Day 7–13
No of pupils: 295
Fees: (September 00) Day £3990
Special Needs: Level 2: DYP DYS HI MLD PH SP&LD SPLD

W1

PORTLAND PLACE SCHOOL
56–58 Portland Place, London W1B 1NJ
Tel: (020) 7307 8700
Head: Mr R Walker
Type: Co-educational Day 11–18
No of pupils: B120 G80
Fees: (September 00) Day £7320 – £7650
Special Needs: Unspecified: DYS

W2

CONNAUGHT HOUSE
47 Connaught Square, London W2 2HL
Tel: (020) 7262 8830
Head: Mr F Hampton and Mrs J A Hampton
Type: Co-educational Day 4–11
No of pupils: B35 G36
Fees: (September 00) On application
Special Needs: Level 2: DYC DYP DYS

THE HAMPSHIRE SCHOOLS (KENSINGTON GARDENS)
9 Queensborough Terrace, London W2 3TB
Tel: (020) 7229 7065
Head: Mr A G Bray
Type: Co-educational Day 4–13
No of pupils: B80 G80
Fees: (September 00) Day £5145 – £7830
Special Needs: Level 2: DYC DYP DYS Level 3: ADD ADHD Unspecified: MLD

LANSDOWNE SIXTH FORM COLLEGE
40–44 Bark Place, London W2 4AT
Tel: (020) 7616 4400
Head: Mr H Templeton
Type: Co-educational Day 15+
No of pupils: B110 G95
Fees: (January 01) Day £1890 – £10500
Special Needs: Level 3: DYS

WETHERBY SCHOOL
11 Pembridge Square, London W2 4ED
Tel: (020) 7727 9581
Head: Mrs J Aviss
Type: Boys Day 4–8
No of pupils: 150
Fees: (September 00) Day £6900
Special Needs: Unspecified: SPLD

W3

EALING MONTESSORI SCHOOL
St Martins Church Hall, Hale Gardens, London W3 9SQ
Tel: (020) 8992 4513
Head: Mrs P Jaffer
Type: Co-educational Day 2–6
No of pupils: B10 G21
Fees: (September 00) Day £2145 – £3165
Special Needs: Level 1: AUT DEL Level 2: DYC DYS

THE JAPANESE SCHOOL
87 Creffield Road, Acton, London W3 9PU
Tel: (020) 8993 7145
Head: Mr K Yamada
Type: Co-educational Day 6–15
No of pupils: B320 G260
Fees: (January 01) Day £1560
Special Needs: Level 1: AUT DOW Level 2: HI MLD

W4

CHISWICK AND BEDFORD PARK PREPARATORY SCHOOL
Priory House, Priory Avenue, Bedford Park, London W4 1TX
Tel: (020) 8994 1804
Head: Mrs M B Morrow
Type: Co-educational Day Boys 4–8 Girls 4–11
No of pupils: B70 G115
Fees: (September 00) Day £4290 – £5160
Special Needs: Level 2: DYS SPLD

ELMWOOD MONTESSORI SCHOOL
St Michaels Centre, Elmwood Road, London W4 3DY
Tel: (020) 8994 8177
Head: Mrs S Herbert
Type: Co-educational Day 2–5
No of pupils: B20 G20
Fees: (September 00) Day £2550
Special Needs: Level 3: ADD ADHD ASP AUT CP DEL DOW DYC DYP DYS EBD EPI HI MLD PH PMLD SLD SP&LD SPLD TOU VIS Unspecified: W

ORCHARD HOUSE SCHOOL
16 Newton Grove, Bedford Park, London W4 1LB
Tel: (020) 8742 8544
Head: Mrs S A B Hobbs
Type: Co-educational Day Boys 3–8 Girls 3–11
No of pupils: B80 G140
Fees: (September 00) Day £3150 – £6300
Special Needs: Level 2: DYS Level 3: ASP AUT DYC DYP SPLD

W5

HARVINGTON SCHOOL

20 Castlebar Road, Ealing, London
W5 2DS
Tel: (020) 8997 1583
Head: Dr F Meek
Type: Girls Day 3–16 (Boys 3–5)
No of pupils: B9 G187
Fees: (September 00) Day £3840 –
£4905
Special Needs: Level 2: DYC DYP DYS

W6

BUTE HOUSE PREPARATORY SCHOOL FOR GIRLS

Luxemburg Gardens, London
W6 7EA
Tel: (020) 7603 7381
Head: Mrs S Salvidant
Type: Girls Day 4–11
No of pupils: 306
Fees: (September 00) Day £6330
Special Needs: Unspecified: W

THE JORDANS NURSERY SCHOOL

Lower Hall, Holy Innocents Church,
Paddenswick Road, London W6 0UB
Tel: (020) 8741 3230
Head: Mrs S Jordan
Type: Co-educational Day 2–5
No of pupils: 50
Fees: (September 01) Day £2250 –
£2715
Special Needs: Level 3: MLD SP&LD

LE HERISSON

c/o The Methodist Church,
Rivercourt Road, Hammersmith,
London W6 9JT
Tel: (020) 8563 7664
Head: Ms B Rios
Type: Co-educational Day 2–6
No of pupils: 64
Fees: (September 00) Day £2850 –
£3960
Special Needs: Unspecified: EBD HI
MLD W

W8

HAWKESDOWN HOUSE SCHOOL

27 Edge Street, Kensington, London
W8 7PN
Tel: (020) 7727 9090
Head: Mrs C J Leslie
Type: Boys Day 3–8
No of pupils: 160
Fees: (September 00) Day £6375 –
£7185
Special Needs: Unspecified: DYS

GREATER MANCHESTER

CLARENDON COTTAGE SCHOOL

Ivy Bank House, Half Edge Lane,
Eccles, Greater Manchester M30 9BJ
Tel: (0161) 950 7868
Head: Mrs E Bagnall
Type: Co-educational Day 1–11
No of pupils: B100 G100
Fees: (September 00) Day £1000 –
£4150
Special Needs: Level 2: DYS
Level 3: HI

TASHBAR PRIMARY SCHOOL

20 Upper Park Rd, Salford, Greater
Manchester M7 4HL
Tel: (0161) 720 8254
Head: Rabbi C S Roberts
Type: Boys Day 3–11
No of pupils: B250
Fees: (September 00) Day £1020 –
£1620
Special Needs: Level 2: ASP Level 3:
EBD

WILLIAM HULME'S GRAMMAR SCHOOL

Spring Bridge Road, Manchester
M16 8PR
Tel: (0161) 226 2054
Head: Mr S R Patriarca
Type: Co-educational Day 3–18
No of pupils: B546 G271
Fees: (September 00) Day £2745 –
£5121
Special Needs: Level 1: DYP DYS

WITHINGTON GIRLS' SCHOOL

Wellington Road, Fallowfield,
Manchester, Greater Manchester
M14 6BL
Tel: (0161) 224 1077
Head: Mrs J D Pickering
Type: Girls Day 7–18
No of pupils: 635
Fees: (September 00) Day £3525 –
£5040
Special Needs: Level 3: DYS

MERSEYSIDE

THE BELVEDERE SCHOOL GDST
17 Belvidere Road, Princes Park, Liverpool, Merseyside L8 3TF
Tel: (0151) 727 1284
Head: Mrs G Richards
Type: Girls Day 3–18
No of pupils: G600
Fees: (September 00) Day £2940 – £5040
Special Needs: Level 3: DYP DYS

CARLETON HOUSE PREPARATORY SCHOOL
Lyndhurst Road, Mossley Hill, Liverpool, Merseyside L18 8AQ
Tel: (0151) 724 4880
Head: Mrs C Line
Type: Co-educational Day 4–11
No of pupils: B88 G55
Fees: (September 00) Day £3225
Special Needs: Level 2: DYP DYS
SPLD Level 3: ADD ASP

HESWALL PREPARATORY SCHOOL
Carberry, Quarry Road East, Heswall, Wirral, Merseyside CH60 6RB
Tel: (0151) 342 7851
Head: Mrs M Hannaford
Type: Co-educational Day 3–11
No of pupils: B25 G25
Fees: (September 00) Day £1575 – £2700
Special Needs: Level 2: DYP DYS
SP&LD Unspecified: MLD

KINGSMEAD SCHOOL
Bertram Drive, Hoylake, Wirral, Merseyside CH47 0LL
Tel: (0151) 632 3156
Head: Mr E H Bradby
Type: Co-educational Boarding and Day 2–16
No of pupils: B148 G88
No of Boarders: F27 W11
Fees: (September 00) FB £7575 – £8205 WB £7275 – £7905 Day £3480 – £5205
Special Needs: Level 2: ADD ASP DYP DYS SPLD Unspecified: EPI MLD

MARYMOUNT CONVENT SCHOOL
Love Lane, Wallasey, Merseyside CH44 5SB
Tel: (0151) 638 8467
Head: Sister C O'Reilly
Type: Co-educational Day 3–11
No of pupils: B44 G146
Fees: (September 00) Day £2025
Special Needs: Level 2: DYS

MERCHANT TAYLORS' SCHOOL
Crosby, Liverpool, Merseyside L23 0QP
Tel: (0151) 928 3308
Head: Mr S J R Dawkins
Type: Boys Day 7–18
No of pupils: 890
Fees: (September 00) Day £3564 – £4968
Special Needs: Level 2: DYS

MIDDLESEX

EILMAR MONTESSORI SCHOOL & NURSERY
Sidmouth Drive, Ruislip Gardens, Ruislip, Middlesex HA4 0BY
Tel: (01895) 635796
Head: Ms M A Portland
Type: Co-educational Day 2–5
No of pupils: B34 G34
Fees: (September 00) Day £2791 – £5016
Special Needs: Unspecified: MLD PH SPLD W

HARROW SCHOOL
Harrow on the Hill, Middlesex HA1 3HW
Tel: (020) 8872 8000
Head: Mr B J Lenon
Type: Boys Boarding 13–18
No of pupils: 790 *No of Boarders:* F790
Fees: (January 01) FB £16860
Special Needs: Level 2: DYS

NORTHWOOD COLLEGE
Maxwell Road, Northwood, Middlesex HA6 2YE
Tel: (01923) 825446
Head: Mrs A Mayou
Type: Girls Day 3–18
No of pupils: 782
Fees: (September 00) Day £3660 – £6567
Special Needs: Level 2: DYS

ST DAVID'S SCHOOL
Church Road, Ashford, Middlesex TW15 3DZ
Tel: (01784) 252494
Head: Ms P Bristow
Type: Girls Day and Boarding 3–18
No of pupils: 400 *No of Boarders:* F25 W6
Fees: (September 00) FB £11850 WB £11040 Day £5070 – £6750
Special Needs: Level 2: DYP DYS SP&LD SPLD Level 3: DEL EPI HI PH VIS

ST HELEN'S COLLEGE
Parkway, Hillingdon, Uxbridge, Middlesex UB10 9JX
Tel: (01895) 234371
Head: Mr D A Crehan
Type: Co-educational Day 3–11
No of pupils: B130 G156
Fees: (September 00) Day £2040 – £4185
Special Needs: Level 1: DYP Level 2: ASP DYS

ST JAMES INDEPENDENT SCHOOL FOR BOYS (SENIOR)
Pope's Villa, 19 Cross Deep, Twickenham, Middlesex TW1 4QG
Tel: (020) 8892 2002
Head: Mr N Debenham
Type: Boys Day 10–18
No of pupils: 240 *No of Boarders:* W32
Fees: (September 00) WB £7055 Day £6180 – £6375
Special Needs: Level 2: DYC DYP DYS EPI MLD SP&LD SPLD

ST MARTIN'S SCHOOL
40 Moor Park Road, Northwood,
Middlesex HA6 2DJ
Tel: (01923) 825740
Head: Mr M J Hodgson
Type: Boys Day 3–13
No of pupils: B400
Fees: (September 00) Day £1935 –
£6375
Special Needs: Level 2: SPLD

STAINES PREPARATORY SCHOOL TRUST
3 Gresham Road, Staines, Middlesex
TW18 2BT
Tel: (01784) 452916/450909
Head: Mr P Roberts
Type: Co-educational Day 3–11
No of pupils: B250 G150
Fees: (September 00) Day £3630 –
£4185
Special Needs: Level 1: DYS Level 3:
ADD ADHD DYP

NORFOLK

ALL SAINTS SCHOOL
School Road, Lessingham, Norwich,
Norfolk NR12 0DJ
Tel: (01692) 582083
Head: Mrs J Gardiner
Type: Co-educational Day 2–16
No of pupils: B35 G35
Fees: (September 00) Day £1650 –
£2700
Special Needs: Level 2: ASP DYP DYS
MLD SPLD Level 3: DOW

GRESHAM'S PREPARATORY SCHOOL
Cromer Road, Holt, Norfolk
NR25 6EY
Tel: (01263) 712227
Head: Mr A H Cuff
Type: Co-educational Day and
Boarding 4–13
No of pupils: B127 G96
No of Boarders: F28 W43
Fees: (September 00) FB £11340 WB
£10500 Day £8610
Special Needs: Unspecified: DYC DYP
DYS HI SPLD

HETHERSETT OLD HALL SCHOOL
Hethersett, Norwich, Norfolk
NR9 3DW
Tel: (01603) 810390
Head: Mrs J M Mark
Type: Girls Boarding and Day 4–18
(Boys 4–7 years)
No of pupils: B1 G271
No of Boarders: F47
Fees: (September 00) FB £9855 –
£12255 Day £3900 – £6150
Special Needs: Level 2: ADD CP DYP
DYS SPLD

LANGLEY PREPARATORY SCHOOL & NURSERY
Beech Hill, 11 Yarmouth Road,
Thorpe St Andrew, Norwich, Norfolk
NR7 0EA
Tel: (01603) 433861
Head: Mr P J Weeks
Type: Co-educational Day 2–11
No of pupils: B95 G55
Fees: (September 00) Day £3450 –
£5070
Special Needs: Level 2: DYC DYP DYS
EBD MLD SP&LD SPLD Unspecified:
EPI

LANGLEY SCHOOL
Langley Park, Loddon, Norwich,
Norfolk NR14 6BJ
Tel: (01508) 520210
Head: Mr J G Malcolm
Type: Co-educational Boarding and
Day 10–18
No of pupils: B220 G85
No of Boarders: F72 W11
Fees: (September 00) FB £10845 –
£13140 WB £10125 – £12285 Day
£5580 – £6825
Special Needs: Level 2: ADD AUT
DEL DYC DYP DYS EPI SPLD
Unspecified: W

THE NORWICH HIGH SCHOOL FOR GIRLS GDST
95 Newmarket Road, Norwich,
Norfolk NR2 2HU
Tel: (01603) 453265
Head: Mrs V C Bidwell
Type: Girls Day 4–18
No of pupils: 900
Fees: (September 00) Day £3660 –
£5040
Special Needs: Level 2: DYS

NOTRE DAME PREPARATORY SCHOOL
147 Dereham Road, Norwich,
Norfolk NR2 3TA
Tel: (01603) 625593
Head: Mrs A E Mancini
Type: Co-educational Day 3–11
No of pupils: B67 G100
Fees: (January 01) Day £2280 –
£2760
Special Needs: Unspecified: ADD
ADHD DEL DYC DYP DYS EBD EPI
HI MLD PH SP&LD SPLD

TAVERHAM HALL
Taverham, Norwich, Norfolk
NR8 6HU
Tel: (01603) 868206
Head: Mr W D Lawton
Type: Co-educational Boarding and
Day 3–13
No of pupils: B131 G78
No of Boarders: F4 W20
Fees: (September 00) FB £7005 –
£9405 Day £1500 – £7785
Special Needs: Unspecified: ADD
ADHD DYP DYS MLD

NORTHAMPTONSHIRE

BOSWORTH INDEPENDENT COLLEGE
Nazareth House, Barrack Road,
Northampton NN2 6AF
Tel: (01604) 239995
Head: Mr M McQuin
Type: Co-educational Boarding and
Day 14–21
No of pupils: 200 *No of Boarders:* F150
Fees: (September 00) FB £12600 Day
£6600
Special Needs: Level 2: DYS Level 3:
DYP

NORTHAMPTON CHRISTIAN SCHOOL
The Parish Rooms, Park Avenue
North, Northampton,
Northamptonshire NN3 2HT
Tel: (01604) 715900
Head: Mrs Z Blakeman
Type: Co-educational Day 4–16
No of pupils: B8 G7
Fees: (January 01) Day £1986 –
£2216
Special Needs: Level 1: ADD ADHD
DYC DYP DYS MLD SP&LD
Unspecified: EBD EPI

NORTHAMPTON PREPARATORY SCHOOL
Great Houghton Hall, Northampton,
Northamptonshire NN4 7AG
Tel: (01604) 761907
Head: Mr M T E Street
Type: Co-educational Day 4–13
No of pupils: B183 G69
Fees: (September 01) Day £3435 –
£6600
Special Needs: Level 1: DYS SPLD
Level 2: DYC MLD SP&LD Level 3:
DYP

OUR LADY'S CONVENT PREPARATORY SCHOOL
Hall Lane, Kettering,
Northamptonshire NN15 7LJ
Tel: (01536) 513882
Head: Mrs L Burgess
Type: Co-educational Day 2–11
No of pupils: B83 G66
Fees: (September 00) Day £3195
Special Needs: Level 2: DYS Level 3:
MLD

WELLINGBOROUGH SCHOOL
Wellingborough, Northamptonshire
NN8 2BX
Tel: (01933) 222427
Head: Mr F R Ullmann
Type: Co-educational Day 3–18
No of pupils: B470 G280
Fees: (September 00) Day £3810 –
£6870
Special Needs: Level 2: DYP DYS

NOTTINGHAMSHIRE

ATTENBOROUGH PREPARATORY SCHOOL
The Strand, Attenborough, Beeston,
Nottingham, Nottinghamshire
NG9 6AU
Tel: (0115) 943 6725
Head: Mrs M Cahill
Type: Co-educational Day 4–11
No of pupils: B59 G28
Fees: (September 00) Day £1680 –
£2265
Special Needs: Level 2: DYP DYS
Level 3: ADD ADHD HI
Unspecified: W

DAGFA HOUSE SCHOOL
Broadgate, Beeston, Nottingham
NG9 2FU
Tel: (0115) 913 8330
Head: Mr A Oatway
Type: Co-educational Day 3–16
No of pupils: B165 G115
Fees: (September 00) Day £2535 –
£4275
Special Needs: Level 2: DYS Level 3:
ADD ADHD ASP AUT DYC DYP EPI
SPLD

HOLLYGIRT SCHOOL
Elm Avenue, Nottingham,
Nottinghamshire NG3 4GF
Tel: (0115) 958 0596
Head: Mrs M Connolly
Type: Girls Day 4–16
No of pupils: 340
Fees: (September 00) Day £3465 –
£4584
Special Needs: Level 2: DYC DYP DYS

THE KING'S SCHOOL
Collygate Road, The Meadows,
Nottingham, Nottinghamshire
NG2 2EJ
Tel: (0115) 953 9194
Head: Mr R Southey
Type: Co-educational Day 4–16
No of pupils: B71 G71
Fees: (September 00) Day £2340
Special Needs: Level 2: DYS Level 3:
ADD ASP AUT DEL DYP EBD MLD

MANSFIELD PREPARATORY SCHOOL
Welbeck Road, Mansfield,
Nottinghamshire NG19 9LA
Tel: (01623) 420940
Head: Mrs S Mills
Type: Co-educational Day 3–11
No of pupils: B25 G16
Fees: (September 01) Day £1695
Special Needs: Level 2: ADD ADHD
AUT CP DEL DOW DYS EBD EPI HI
MLD PH SP&LD SPLD VIS

NOTTINGHAM HIGH SCHOOL

Waverley Mount, Nottingham, Nottinghamshire NG7 4ED
Tel: (0115) 978 6056
Head: Mr C S Parker
Type: Boys Day 11–18
No of pupils: 806
Fees: (September 00) Day £5994
Special Needs: Level 2: ADHD DYC DYP DYS MLD SPLD Level 3: EPI HI PH VIS

NOTTINGHAM HIGH SCHOOL PREPARATORY SCHOOL

Waverley Mount, Nottingham, Nottinghamshire NG7 4ED
Tel: (0115) 845 2214
Head: Mr P M Pallant
Type: Boys Day 7–11
No of pupils: 170
Fees: (September 00) Day £5007
Special Needs: Level 3: DYS EPI

PLUMTREE SCHOOL

Church Hill, Plumtree, Nottingham, Nottinghamshire NG12 5ND
Tel: (0115) 937 5859
Head: Mr N White
Type: Co-educational Day 3–11
No of pupils: B76 G51
Fees: (September 00) Day £2985
Special Needs: Level 2: DYS

ST JOSEPH'S SCHOOL

33 Derby Road, Nottingham, Nottinghamshire NG1 5AW
Tel: (0115) 941 8356
Head: Mr J Crawley
Type: Co-educational Day 1–11
No of pupils: B122 G89
Fees: (September 00) Day £3720
Special Needs: Unspecified: DYS MLD W

SALTERFORD HOUSE SCHOOL

Salterford Lane, Calverton, Nottingham NG14 6NZ
Tel: (0115) 965 2127
Head: Mrs M Venables
Type: Co-educational Day 2–11
No of pupils: B118 G107
Fees: (September 00) Day £2700 – £2910
Special Needs: Level 2: DYS MLD VIS Unspecified: SP&LD

TRENT COLLEGE

Long Eaton, Nottingham, Nottinghamshire NG10 4AD
Tel: (0115) 849 4949
Head: Mr J S Lee
Type: Co-educational Boarding and Day 3–18
No of pupils: B490 G300
No of Boarders: F60 W105
Fees: (September 00) FB £12382 WB £8477 – £11422 Day £3700 – £7650
Special Needs: Level 2: DYC DYP DYS MLD SPLD

WORKSOP COLLEGE

Worksop, Nottinghamshire S80 3AP
Tel: (01909) 537127
Head: Mr R A Collard
Type: Co-educational Boarding and Day 13–18
No of pupils: B255 G125
No of Boarders: F120 W95
Fees: (September 00) F/WB £13575 Day £9300
Special Needs: Level 1: DYS Level 2: SPLD Level 3: ADD ADHD ASP CP DYP

OXFORDSHIRE

CHERWELL COLLEGE

Greyfriars, Paradise Street, Oxford OX1 1LD
Tel: (01865) 242670
Head: Mr P J Gordon
Type: Co-educational Day and Boarding 16+
No of pupils: B90 G80
No of Boarders: F90 W10
Fees: (September 00) F/WB £15000 Day £10000
Special Needs: Unspecified: ADD ADHD DYC DYP DYS

COKETHORPE SCHOOL*

Witney, Oxfordshire OX8 7PU
Tel: (01993) 703921
Head: Mr P J S Cantwell
Type: Co-educational Boarding and Day 7–18 (Day girls only)
No of pupils: B320 G160
No of Boarders: F30 W30
Fees: (September 00) F/WB £9810 – £14700 Day £4950 – £8850
Special Needs: Level 2: DEL DYC DYP DYS MLD PH SP&LD SPLD

CRANFORD HOUSE SCHOOL

Moulsford, Wallingford, Oxfordshire OX10 9HT
Tel: (01491) 651218
Head: Mrs A B Gray
Type: Girls Day 3–16 (Boys 3–7)
No of pupils: B44 G220
Fees: (September 00) Day £4075 – £6750
Special Needs: Unspecified: CP DEL DYP DYS MLD SPLD

D'OVERBROECK'S COLLEGE

1 Park Town, Oxford OX2 6SN
Tel: (01865) 310000
Head: Mr S Cohen and Dr R K Knowles
Type: Co-educational Day and Boarding 13–19 (Day only 13–16)
No of pupils: 260 *No of Boarders:* F100
Fees: (September 00) FB £10650 – £14175 Day £7050 – £10575
Special Needs: Unspecified: ADD ADHD DYC DYP DYS EBD HI SPLD

EDWARD GREENE'S TUTORIAL ESTABLISHMENT
45 Pembroke Street, Oxford OX1 1BP
Tel: (01865) 248308
Head: Mr E P C Greene
Type: Co-educational Day 15–19
No of pupils: B31 G23
No of Boarders: F8
Fees: (September 01) Day £600 –
£5850
Special Needs: Level 2: DYC DYS MLD
SPLD VIS Level 3: DEL DYP EBD EPI
HI PH TOU

JOSCA'S PREPARATORY SCHOOL
Frilford, Abingdon, Oxfordshire
OX13 5NX
Tel: (01865) 391570
Head: Mr C J Davies
Type: Boys Day 4–13 (Girls 4–7)
No of pupils: B179 G1
Fees: (September 00) Day £4674 –
£6024
Special Needs: Level 2: DYS

MANOR PREPARATORY SCHOOL
Faringdon Road, Abingdon,
Oxfordshire OX13 6LN
Tel: (01235) 523789
Head: Mrs D A Robinson
Type: Co-educational Day Boys 3–7
Girls 3–11
No of pupils: B38 G322
Fees: (September 00) Day £2520 –
£5460
Special Needs: Level 2: ADD ASP DEL
DYC DYP DYS PH SPLD

OUR LADY'S CONVENT JUNIOR SCHOOL
St John's Road, Abingdon,
Oxfordshire OX14 2HB
Tel: (01235) 523147
Head: Sister J Frances
Type: Co-educational Day 4–11
No of pupils: B55 G75
Fees: (September 00) Day £3300 –
£3390
Special Needs: Level 2: DYS MLD

OXFORD HIGH SCHOOL GDST
Belbroughton Road, Oxford
OX2 6XA
Tel: (01865) 559888
Head: Miss O F S Lusk
Type: Girls Day 3–18 (Boys 3–7)
No of pupils: B45 G874
Fees: (September 00) Day £1470 –
£5040
Special Needs: Unspecified: DYS

OXFORD TUTORIAL COLLEGE
12 King Edward Street, Oxford
OX1 4HT
Tel: (01865) 793333
Head: Mrs J Palmer
Type: Co-educational Day 16+
No of pupils: B57 G53
Fees: (September 00) Day £11934 –
£16062
Special Needs: Level 2: ADD ASP DYC
DYP DYS PH SPLD VIS

RUPERT HOUSE
90 Bell Street, Henley-on-Thames,
Oxfordshire RG9 2BN
Tel: (01491) 574263
Head: Mrs G M Crane
Type: Co-educational Day Boys 4–7
Girls 4–11
No of pupils: B54 G173
Fees: (September 00) Day £2295 –
£5565
Special Needs: Level 2: DYC DYP DYS
Level 3: HI SP&LD

ST CLARE'S, OXFORD
139 Banbury Road, Oxford OX2 7AL
Tel: (01865) 552031
Head: Mr Boyd Roberts
Type: Co-educational Boarding and
Day 16–20
No of pupils: B231 G119
No of Boarders: F319
Fees: (September 00) FB £16360 –
£16635 Day £10235
Special Needs: Level 3: ADHD DYS HI
PH VIS Unspecified: EPI

ST EDWARD'S SCHOOL
Woodstock Road, Oxford OX2 7NN
Tel: (01865) 319200
Head: Mr D Christie
Type: Co-educational Boarding and
Day 13–18
No of pupils: B412 G198
No of Boarders: F422
Fees: (September 00) FB £16230 Day
£11885 – £11985
Special Needs: Level 1: DYP DYS
SPLD

ST HUGH'S SCHOOL
Carswell Manor, Faringdon,
Oxfordshire SN7 8PT
Tel: (01367) 870223
Head: Mr D Cannon
Type: Co-educational Boarding and
Day 4–13
No of pupils: B168 G110
No of Boarders: W40
Fees: (September 00) F/WB £9405 –
£10020 Day £4635 – £8220
Special Needs: Unspecified: DYC DYP
DYS MLD SPLD

ST MARY'S SCHOOL*
Newbury Street, Wantage,
Oxfordshire OX12 8BZ
Tel: (01235) 763571
Head: Mrs S Sowden
Type: Girls Boarding and Day 11–18
No of pupils: 191 *No of Boarders:* F174
Fees: (September 00) FB £15075 Day
£10050
Special Needs: Unspecified: DYC DYS
DYP MLD EPI SPLD

SCHOOL OF ST HELEN & ST KATHARINE
Faringdon Road, Abingdon,
Oxfordshire OX14 1BE
Tel: (01235) 520173
Head: Mrs C Hall
Type: Girls Day 9–18
No of pupils: 592
Fees: (September 00) Day £5937
Special Needs: Level 3: DYS EPI HI
VIS

SHIPLAKE COLLEGE
Henley-on-Thames, Oxfordshire
RG9 4BW
Tel: (0118) 940 2455
Head: Mr N V Bevan
Type: Boys Day and Boarding 13–18
(Day Girls 16–18)
No of pupils: B270 G9
No of Boarders: F120 W100
Fees: (September 00) FB £13590 Day
£9165
Special Needs: Level 1: DYS MLD
Level 3: DYP EPI

SUMMER FIELDS
Oxford, Oxfordshire OX2 7EN
Tel: (01865) 454433
Head: Mr R Badham-Thornhill
Type: Boys Boarding and Day 8–13
No of pupils: 255 *No of Boarders:* F244
Fees: (September 00) FB £12450 Day
£8100 – £8910
Special Needs: Level 3: MLD
Unspecified: W

WYCHWOOD SCHOOL
74 Banbury Road, Oxford OX2 6JR
Tel: (01865) 557976
Head: Mrs S M P Wingfield Digby
Type: Girls Boarding and Day 11–18
No of pupils: 150 *No of Boarders:* F25
W35
Fees: (September 00) FB £9540 WB
£9240 Day £5985
Special Needs: Level 3: ADD CP DYP
DYS HI

SHROPSHIRE

BELLAN HOUSE PREPARATORY SCHOOL
Bellan House, Church Street,
Oswestry, Shropshire SY11 2ST
Tel: (01691) 653453
Head: Mrs S L Durham
Type: Co-educational Day 2–9
No of pupils: B91 G92
Fees: (September 00) On application
Special Needs: Level 1: SP&LD
Level 2: DYP DYS EPI MLD Level 3:
CP DEL PH

CASTLE HOUSE SCHOOL
Chetwynd End, Newport, Shropshire
TF10 7JE
Tel: (01952) 811035
Head: Mr R M Walden
Type: Co-educational Day 3–11
No of pupils: B55 G55
Fees: (September 00) Day £1260 –
£3720
Special Needs: Level 2: DYC DYS MLD
SPLD

ELLESMERE COLLEGE*†
Ellesmere, Shropshire SY12 9AB
Tel: (01691) 622321
Head: Mr B J Wignall
Type: Co-educational Boarding and
Day 9–18
No of pupils: B325 G145
No of Boarders: F190
Fees: (September 00) FB £13800 Day
£9141
Special Needs: Level 1: ADD ADHD
DYP DYS Level 2: DYC Unspecified:
SPLD

KINGSLAND GRANGE
Old Roman Road, Shrewsbury,
Shropshire SY3 9AH
Tel: (01743) 232132
Head: Mr M C James
Type: Boys Day 4–13
No of pupils: B150
Fees: (September 00) Day £3570 –
£5790
Special Needs: Level 2: DYP DYS MLD
SPLD VIS

MORETON HALL
Weston Rhyn, Oswestry, Shropshire
SY11 3EW
Tel: (01691) 773671
Head: Mr J Forster
Type: Girls Boarding and Day 9–18
No of pupils: 270 *No of Boarders:* F230
Fees: (September 00) FB £14850 Day
£10200
Special Needs: Level 1: DYC DYS
SPLD Level 3: CP DYP EPI HI

OSWESTRY SCHOOL
Upper Brook Street, Oswestry,
Shropshire SY11 2TL
Tel: (01691) 655711
Head: Mr P K Smith
Type: Co-educational Boarding and
Day 9–18
No of pupils: B170 G145
No of Boarders: F101 W30
Fees: (September 00) FB £12120 –
£12726 Day £6915 – £7560
Special Needs: Level 1: DYC DYP DYS
MLD Level 2: ADD ADHD Level 3:
ASP

PRESTFELDE PREPARATORY SCHOOL
London Road, Shrewsbury,
Shropshire SY2 6NZ
Tel: (01743) 356500
Head: Mr J R Bridgeland
Type: Co-educational Day and
Boarding 3–13
No of pupils: B244 G66
No of Boarders: F25
Fees: (January 01) FB £8550 Day
£2130 – £6750
Special Needs: Level 1: DYP DYS
SPLD Unspecified: HI SP&LD

WREKIN COLLEGE
Wellington, Telford, Shropshire
TF1 3BH
Tel: (01952) 240131/242305
Head: Mr S G Drew
Type: Co-educational Boarding and
Day 11–19
No of pupils: B191 G149
No of Boarders: F120
Fees: (September 00) FB £12480 –
£14340 Day £7170 – £8670
Special Needs: Level 1: DYS

SOMERSET

ALL HALLOWS
Cranmore Hall, East Cranmore,
Shepton Mallet, Somerset BA4 4SF
Tel: (01749) 880227
Head: Mr C J Bird
Type: Co-educational Boarding and
Day 4–13
No of pupils: B149 G112
No of Boarders: F60
Fees: (September 00) F/WB £10305
Day £3435 – £7005
Special Needs: Level 2: ADD ADHD
ASP DEL DYP DYS EPI HI MLD PH
SP&LD SPLD VIS

CHARD SCHOOL
Fore Street, Chard, Somerset TA20
1QA
Tel: (01460) 63234
Head: Mr J G Stotesbury
Type: Co-educational Day 2–11
No of pupils: B60 G60
Fees: (September 00) Day £2490 –
£2679
Special Needs: Level 2: DYS

CHILTON CANTELO SCHOOL
Chilton Cantelo, Yeovil, Somerset
BA22 8BG
Tel: (01935) 850555
Head: Mr D S von Zeffman
Type: Co-educational Boarding and
Day 7–18
No of pupils: B120 G70
No of Boarders: F120
Fees: (September 00) FB £8490 –
£10050 Day £4290 – £5490
Special Needs: Unspecified: ADD DYP
DYS SPLD

HAZLEGROVE (KING'S BRUTON PREPARATORY SCHOOL)

Hazlegrove House, Sparkford, Yeovil, Somerset BA22 7JA
Tel: (01963) 440314
Head: Rev B Bearcroft
Type: Co-educational Day and Boarding 3–13
No of pupils: B300 G120
No of Boarders: F85
Fees: (September 00) FB £9660 – £11010 Day £3855 – £7890
Special Needs: Level 1: DYC DYP DYS SPLD Level 3: ADD ASP HI PH SP&LD

KING'S HALL SCHOOL

Pyrland, Kingston Road, Taunton, Somerset TA2 8AA
Tel: (01823) 285920
Head: Mr J K Macpherson
Type: Co-educational Boarding and Day 3–13
No of pupils: B215 G165
No of Boarders: F50 W25
Fees: (September 00) FB £6105 – £10260 WB £5760 – £9885 Day £2415 – £7275
Special Needs: Unspecified: DYC DYS

KING'S SCHOOL

Bruton, Somerset BA10 0ED
Tel: (01749) 814200
Head: Mr R I Smyth
Type: Co-educational Boarding and Day 13–18
No of pupils: B285 G80
No of Boarders: F245
Fees: (September 00) FB £13860 Day £10050
Special Needs: Level 1: DYP DYS SPLD Level 2: ASP DYC SP&LD Level 3: ADD ADHD HI PH VIS

MILLFIELD PREPARATORY SCHOOL

Glastonbury, Somerset BA6 8LD
Tel: (01458) 832446
Head: Mr K Cheney
Type: Co-educational Boarding and Day 7–13
No of pupils: B270 G190
No of Boarders: F218
Fees: (September 00) FB £12270 Day £8295
Special Needs: Level 1: DYS MLD SPLD Level 2: DYC

THE PARK SCHOOL

Yeovil, Somerset BA20 1DH
Tel: (01935) 423514
Head: Mr P W Bate
Type: Co-educational Day and Boarding 3–16
No of pupils: B99 G136
No of Boarders: F26 W8
Fees: (September 01) FB £9240 – £10300 WB £8610 – £9660 Day £2850 – £5640
Special Needs: Level 3: ADD CP DYP DYS MLD PH TOU

QUEEN'S COLLEGE JUNIOR AND PRE-PREPARATORY SCHOOLS

Trull Road, Taunton, Somerset TA1 4QR
Tel: (01823) 272990
Head: Mr P N Lee-Smith and Mrs E Gibbs
Type: Co-educational Day and Boarding 2–11
No of pupils: B104 G105
No of Boarders: F33
Fees: (September 00) FB £5904 – £8535 Day £2556 – £5863
Special Needs: Level 2: DYS Level 3: DYC DYP

ROSSHOLME SCHOOL

East Brent, Highbridge, Somerset TA9 4JA
Tel: (01278) 760219
Head: Mrs S J Webb
Type: Girls Boarding and Day 3–16 (Co-ed 3–7)
No of pupils: B4 G72 *No of Boarders:* F8 W4
Fees: (September 00) FB £6960 – £8670 WB £6750 – £8460 Day £2520 – £5940
Special Needs: Level 2: DYC DYP DYS MLD SPLD Level 3: ASP

ST BRANDON'S SCHOOL

Elton Road, Clevedon, Somerset BS21 7SD
Tel: (01275) 875092
Head: Mrs S Vesey
Type: Co-educational Day 3–11
No of pupils: B70 G70
Fees: (January 01) Day £625 – £3600
Special Needs: Level 1: DYS MLD Level 3: DYP Unspecified: ASP

TAUNTON SCHOOL

Taunton, Somerset TA2 6AD
Tel: (01823) 349200/349223
Head: Mr J P Whiteley
Type: Co-educational Boarding and Day 13–18
No of pupils: B260 G185
No of Boarders: F177
Fees: (September 00) FB £13995 Day £8985
Special Needs: Level 2: DYC DYS MLD Level 3: ADD ADHD ASP AUT CP DEL DOW DYP EBD EPI HI PH

WELLINGTON SCHOOL

South Street, Wellington, Somerset TA21 8NT
Tel: (01823) 668800
Head: Mr A J Rogers
Type: Co-educational Boarding and Day 10–18
No of pupils: B439 G412
No of Boarders: F153
Fees: (September 00) FB £9405 – £10515 Day £4653 – £5763
Special Needs: Level 2: DYS

WELLS CATHEDRAL JUNIOR SCHOOL

8 New Street, Wells, Somerset BA5 2LQ
Tel: (01749) 672291
Head: Mr N M Wilson
Type: Co-educational Boarding and Day 3–11
No of pupils: B106 G89
No of Boarders: F9 W4
Fees: (September 00) FB £11265 Day £3612 – £6948
Special Needs: Level 3: DYP DYS

WELLS CATHEDRAL SCHOOL

Wells, Somerset BA5 2ST
Tel: (01749) 672117
Head: Mrs E C Cairncross
Type: Co-educational Boarding and Day 3–18
No of pupils: B392 G345
No of Boarders: F244 W2
Fees: (September 00) FB £11265 – £13353 Day £3612 – £7929
Special Needs: Level 2: DYS Level 3: DYP

NORTH EAST SOMERSET

DOWNSIDE SCHOOL
Stratton-on-the-Fosse, Radstock,
Bath, North East Somerset BA3 4RJ
Tel: (01761) 235100
Head: Dom Antony Sutch
Type: Boys Boarding and Day 9–18
No of pupils: B330 *No of Boarders:* F296
Fees: (September 00) FB £11256 –
£14172 Day £6528 – £7260
Special Needs: Level 2: DYP DYS
SP&LD SPLD Level 3: DYC PH

MONKTON COMBE SCHOOL
Bath, North East Somerset BA2 7HG
Tel: (01225) 721102
Head: Mr M J Cuthbertson
Type: Co-educational Boarding and
Day 7–19
No of pupils: B387 G230
No of Boarders: F254
Fees: (September 00) FB £12960 –
£15405 Day £6660 – £10512
Special Needs: Level 2: DYP DYS
Level 3: ADD ADHD EPI

PRIOR PARK COLLEGE
Ralph Allen Drive, Bath, North East
Somerset BA2 5AH
Tel: (01225) 831000
Head: Dr G Mercer
Type: Co-educational Boarding and
Day 11–18
No of pupils: B292 G219
No of Boarders: F102 W32
Fees: (September 00) FB £13485 Day
£7185 – £7485
Special Needs: Unspecified: DYC DYP
DYS HI MLD PH

THE ROYAL HIGH SCHOOL
Lansdown, Bath, North East
Somerset BA1 5SZ
Tel: (01225) 313877
Head: Mr J Graham-Brown
Type: Girls Boarding and Day 3–18
No of pupils: 925 *No of Boarders:* F100
Fees: (September 00) FB £9900 Day
£3660 – £5040
Special Needs: Level 1: DYP DYS
Level 2: DYC Level 3: ADD ADHD
ASP AUT DEL EBD EPI HI PH VIS

STAFFORDSHIRE

ABBOTSHOLME SCHOOL†
Rocester, Uttoxeter, Staffordshire
ST14 5BS
Tel: (01889) 590217
Head: Dr S D Tommis
Type: Co-educational Boarding and
Day 7–18 (Boarders from 11)
No of pupils: B149 G103
No of Boarders: F63 W27
Fees: (September 00) F/WB £13764 –
£14520 Day £5688 – £9720
Special Needs: Level 1: DYC DYP DYS
Level 2: ADD

BROOKLANDS SCHOOL
167 Eccleshall Road, Stafford,
Staffordshire ST16 1PD
Tel: (01785) 251399
Head: Mr C T O'Donnell
Type: Co-educational Day 3–11
No of pupils: B79 G74
Fees: (January 01) Day £2724 –
£4959
Special Needs: Level 2: DYC DYP DYS
MLD SP&LD

CHASE ACADEMY
St John's Road, Cannock,
Staffordshire WS11 3UR
Tel: (01543) 501800
Head: Mr M D Ellse
Type: Co-educational Day and
Boarding 3–18
No of pupils: B115 G74
No of Boarders: F42
Fees: (September 00) FB £9900 Day
£2544 – £5496
Special Needs: Level 2: DYP DYS
Level 3: DEL

EDENHURST SCHOOL
Westlands Avenue, Newcastle-under-
Lyme, Staffordshire ST5 2PU
Tel: (01782) 619348
Head: Mr N H F Copestick
Type: Co-educational Day 3–14
No of pupils: B118 G122
Fees: (September 00) Day £2895 –
£4700
Special Needs: Level 2: DYS Level 3:
DYC DYP Unspecified: MLD

ST DOMINIC'S PRIORY
SCHOOL
21 Station Road, Stone, Staffordshire
ST15 8EN
Tel: (01785) 814181
Head: Mrs J Hildreth
Type: Girls Day 3–18 (Boys 3–11)
No of pupils: B20 G300
Fees: (September 00) Day £2994 –
£4596
Special Needs: Unspecified: EPI

ST DOMINIC'S SCHOOL
32 Bargate Street, Brewood, Stafford,
Staffordshire ST19 9BA
Tel: (01902) 850248
Head: Mrs M E K Peakman
Type: Girls Day 2–16 (Co-ed 2–7)
No of pupils: B15 G240
Fees: (September 00) Day £3363 –
£6900
Special Needs: Level 2: DEL DYC DYP
DYS MLD

SCHOOL OF ST MARY AND ST ANNE
Abbots Bromley, Staffordshire
WS15 3BW
Tel: (01283) 840232
Head: Mrs M Steel
Type: Girls Boarding and Day 5–18
No of pupils: 240 *No of Boarders:* F58 W29
Fees: (September 00) FB £11082 – £12975 Day £3057 – £8226
Special Needs: Level 2: DYC DYS MLD SPLD Unspecified: SP&LD

VERNON LODGE PREPARATORY SCHOOL
School Lane, Stretton, Stafford, Staffordshire ST19 9LJ
Tel: (01902) 850568
Head: Mrs P Sills
Type: Co-educational Day 2–11
No of pupils: B67 G38
Fees: (September 00) Day £3390
Special Needs: Level 2: CP DYS Level 3: ASP Unspecified: DYP

STOCKTON-ON-TEES

TEESSIDE HIGH SCHOOL
The Avenue, Eaglescliffe, Stockton-on-Tees TS16 9AT
Tel: (01642) 782095
Head: Mrs H J French
Type: Girls Day 3–18
No of pupils: 470
Fees: (September 00) Day £3510 – £5250
Special Needs: Level 2: DYS Level 3: DYP HI VIS

SUFFOLK

THE ABBEY
The Prep School of Woodbridge School, Woodbridge, Suffolk IP12 1DS
Tel: (01394) 382673
Head: Mr N J Garrett
Type: Co-educational Day 4–11
No of pupils: B144 G131
Fees: (September 00) Day £3960 – £5994
Special Needs: Level 2: DYS

AMBERFIELD SCHOOL
Nacton, Ipswich, Suffolk IP10 0HL
Tel: (01473) 659265
Head: Mrs L Amphlett Lewis
Type: Girls Day 3–16 (Boys 3–7)
No of pupils: B19 G267
Fees: (September 00) Day £3435 – £5130
Special Needs: Level 2: DYC DYS MLD SPLD Level 3: HI

BARNARDISTON HALL PREPARATORY SCHOOL
Barnardiston, Haverhill, Suffolk CB9 7TG
Tel: (01440) 786316
Head: Lt Col K A Boulter
Type: Co-educational Day and Boarding 2–13
No of pupils: B154 G106
No of Boarders: F57 W4
Fees: (September 00) FB £9750 WB £8850 Day £4740 – £5955
Special Needs: Unspecified: AUT DYC DYP DYS EBD MLD SPLD

CULFORD SCHOOL
Bury St Edmunds, Suffolk IP28 6TX
Tel: (01284) 728615
Head: Mr J Richardson
Type: Co-educational Boarding and Day 2–18
No of pupils: B382 G265
No of Boarders: F175 W25
Fees: (September 00) FB £10956 – £14211 WB £9750 – £14211 Day £7038 – £9249
Special Needs: Level 2: DYS Level 3: ADD CP DYP EPI SPLD TOU

FAIRSTEAD HOUSE SCHOOL
Fordham Road, Newmarket, Suffolk CB8 7AA
Tel: (01638) 662318
Head: Mrs D J Buckenham
Type: Co-educational Day 3–11
No of pupils: B78 G65
Fees: (September 00) Day £2910 – £3630
Special Needs: Unspecified: DYS MLD

FINBOROUGH SCHOOL
The Hall, Great Finborough,
Stowmarket, Suffolk IP14 3EF
Tel: (01449) 773600
Head: Mr J Sinclair
Type: Co-educational Boarding and
Day 2–18
No of pupils: B93 G92
No of Boarders: F109 W9
Fees: (September 00) FB £9300 –
£10875 WB £6930 – £8475 Day
£3150 – £5550
Special Needs: Unspecified: DYS

FRAMLINGHAM COLLEGE JUNIOR SCHOOL
Brandeston Hall, Woodbridge,
Suffolk IP13 7AH
Tel: (01728) 685331
Head: Mr S Player
Type: Co-educational Boarding and
Day 4–13
No of pupils: B164 G103
No of Boarders: F50 W10
Fees: (September 00) FB £10221 Day
£3630 – £6342
Special Needs: Level 2: DYS

HILLCROFT PREPARATORY SCHOOL
Walnutree Manor, Haughley Green,
Stowmarket, Suffolk IP14 3RQ
Tel: (01449) 673003
Head: Mr F Rapsey and Mrs G Rapsey
Type: Co-educational Day 2–13
No of pupils: B59 G52
Fees: (September 00) Day £1203 –
£5670
Special Needs: Level 2: DYC DYP DYS
SP&LD SPLD Level 3: ADD ASP DEL
HI MLD Unspecified: VIS

IPSWICH SCHOOL
Henley Road, Ipswich, Suffolk
IP1 3SG
Tel: (01473) 408300
Head: Mr I G Galbraith
Type: Co-educational Day and
Boarding 11–18
No of pupils: B490 G141
No of Boarders: F27 W22
Fees: (September 00) FB £9636 –
£11274 WB £9261 – £10701 Day
£5796 – £6507
Special Needs: Level 3: DEL DYS EPI
HI

MORETON HALL PREPARATORY SCHOOL
Mount Road, Bury St Edmunds,
Suffolk IP32 7BJ
Tel: (01284) 753532
Head: Mr N Higham
Type: Co-educational Boarding and
Day 3–13
No of pupils: B73 G48
No of Boarders: F12 W13
Fees: (September 00) FB £10110 WB
£9003 Day £4380 – £7335
Special Needs: Level 2: DYS MLD

ORWELL PARK
Nacton, Ipswich, Suffolk IP10 0ER
Tel: (01473) 659225
Head: Mr A H Auster
Type: Co-educational Boarding and
Day 3–13
No of pupils: B170 G90
No of Boarders: F135
Fees: (September 00) FB £10515 –
£11820 Day £3150 – £8835
Special Needs: Unspecified: DYP DYS
MLD SPLD

ST GEORGE'S SCHOOL
Southwold, Suffolk IP18 6SD
Tel: (01502) 723314
Head: Mrs W H Holland
Type: Co-educational Day 2–11
No of pupils: B90 G85
Fees: (September 00) Day £2880 –
£5400
Special Needs: Level 1: EPI HI Level 2:
DYP DYS MLD PH SPLD TOU
Level 3: SLD SP&LD Unspecified: W

ST JOSEPH'S COLLEGE
Belstead Road, Birkfield, Ipswich,
Suffolk IP2 9DR
Tel: (01473) 690281
Type: Co-educational Day and
Boarding 3–18
No of pupils: 620
Fees: (September 00) FB £10056 –
£10971 WB £9597 – £10503 Day
£5607 – £6276
Special Needs: Level 2: DYP DYS

STOKE COLLEGE
Stoke by Clare, Sudbury, Suffolk
CO10 8JE
Tel: (01787) 278141
Head: Mr J Gibson
Type: Co-educational Day and
Boarding 3–16
No of pupils: B155 G90
No of Boarders: W25
Fees: (September 00) WB £9795 –
£10905 Day £4485 – £6480
Special Needs: Level 2: DYS
Unspecified: MLD

SURREY

BARFIELD SCHOOL
Runfold, Farnham, Surrey GU10 1PB
Tel: (01252) 782271
Head: Mr B Hoar
Type: Co-educational Day 3–13
No of pupils: B185 G125
Fees: (September 00) Day £4524 –
£6900
Special Needs: Level 2: DYS MLD
SPLD Level 3: DYP

BOX HILL SCHOOL†
Mickleham, Dorking, Surrey
RH5 6EA
Tel: (01372) 373382
Head: Dr R A S Atwood
Type: Co-educational Boarding and
Day 11–18
No of pupils: B208 G115
No of Boarders: F104 W55
Fees: (September 00) FB £12894 WB
£11115 Day £5685 – £7527
Special Needs: Level 2: DYS

BRAMLEY SCHOOL
Chequers Lane, Walton-on-the-Hill,
Tadworth, Surrey KT20 7ST
Tel: (01737) 812004
Head: Mrs B Johns
Type: Girls Day 3–11
No of pupils: 130
Fees: (September 00) Day £2100 –
£5040
Special Needs: Level 3: DYS

CAMBRIDGE TUTORS COLLEGE
Water Tower Hill, Croydon, Surrey CR0 5SX
Tel: (020) 8688 5284
Head: Mr D A Lowe
Type: Co-educational Day 16–21
No of pupils: B130 G120
Fees: (September 00) Day £4400 – £9250
Special Needs: Unspecified: DEL DYS EBD HI

CANBURY SCHOOL
Kingston Hill, Kingston-upon-Thames, Surrey KT2 7LN
Tel: (020) 8549 8622
Head: Mr C Y Harben
Type: Co-educational Day 10–17
No of pupils: B40 G20
Fees: (September 00) Day £6000
Special Needs: Unspecified: ADD ADHD ASP CP DYS EPI MLD SP&LD

CATERHAM SCHOOL
Harestone Valley Road, Caterham, Surrey CR3 6YA
Tel: (01883) 343028
Head: Mr R A E Davey
Type: Co-educational Day and Boarding 11–18
No of pupils: B478 G254
No of Boarders: F136
Fees: (September 00) FB £14058 – £14817 Day £7746 – £7944
Special Needs: Level 2: DYS SPLD

CHARTERHOUSE
Godalming, Surrey GU7 2DJ
Tel: (01483) 291501
Head: Rev J S Witheridge
Type: Boys Boarding and Day 13–18 (Co-ed VIth Form)
No of pupils: B605 G95
No of Boarders: F670
Fees: (September 00) FB £16446 Day £13590
Special Needs: Level 3: DYP DYS

CHINTHURST SCHOOL
Tadworth Street, Tadworth, Surrey KT20 5QZ
Tel: (01737) 812011
Head: Mr T J Egan
Type: Boys Day 3–13
No of pupils: B390
Fees: (September 00) Day £1800 – £5184
Special Needs: Level 2: ADD ASP DYC DYP DYS Level 3: ADHD PH SPLD

CLEWBOROUGH HOUSE SCHOOL AT CHESWYCKS
Guildford Road, Frimley Green, Camberley, Surrey GU16 6PB
Tel: (01252) 835669
Head: Mr S C Emmerson
Type: Co-educational Day 2–11
No of pupils: B187 G97
Fees: (September 00) Day £840 – £1820
Special Needs: Level 2: DYS

COLLINGWOOD SCHOOL
3 Springfield Road, Wallington, Surrey SM6 0BD
Tel: (020) 8647 4607
Head: Mr G M Barham
Type: Co-educational Day 2–11
No of pupils: B112 G64
Fees: (September 00) Day £1080 – £3765
Special Needs: Unspecified: DYS

COWORTH PARK SCHOOL
Valley End, Chobham, Woking, Surrey GU24 8TE
Tel: (01276) 855707
Head: Mrs C Fairbairn
Type: Co-educational Day Boys 3–7 Girls 3–11
No of pupils: B26 G136
Fees: (September 00) Day £2340 – £5580
Special Needs: Level 2: DYS

DANES HILL PREPARATORY SCHOOL
Leatherhead Road, Oxshott, Leatherhead, Surrey KT22 0JG
Tel: (01372) 842509
Head: Mr R Parfitt
Type: Co-educational Day 3–13
No of pupils: B467 G361
Fees: (September 00) Day £1020 – £6855
Special Needs: Level 1: ASP AUT CP DYC SP&LD SPLD Level 3: ADD EPI HI MLD VIS Unspecified: DYP DYS W

DUKE OF KENT SCHOOL
Peaslake Road, Ewhurst, Surrey GU6 7NS
Tel: (01483) 277313
Head: Dr A Cameron
Type: Co-educational Boarding and Day 4–13
No of pupils: B117 G88
No of Boarders: F40 W20
Fees: (September 00) FB £8820 – £10590 Day £3210 – £7785
Special Needs: Level 2: DYS

EPSOM COLLEGE
Epsom, Surrey KT17 4JQ
Tel: (01372) 821004
Head: Mr S R Borthwick
Type: Co-educational Boarding and Day 13–18
No of pupils: B517 G160
No of Boarders: F168 W157
Fees: (September 00) FB £15423 WB £15216 Day £11362
Special Needs: Level 2: DYS

ESSENDENE LODGE SCHOOL
Essendene Road, Caterham, Surrey CR3 5PB
Tel: (01883) 348349
Head: Mrs S A Haydock
Type: Co-educational Day 2–11
No of pupils: B89 G110
Fees: (September 00) Day £990 – £2955
Special Needs: Level 2: ADD ADHD ASP DYC DYP DYS SP&LD

FLEXLANDS SCHOOL
Station Road, Chobham, Woking, Surrey GU24 8AG
Tel: (01276) 858841
Head: Mrs A Vincent
Type: Girls Day 3–11
No of pupils: G160
Fees: (September 00) Day £2335 – £5355
Special Needs: Level 2: DEL DYP DYS PH VIS Unspecified: W

FRENSHAM HEIGHTS
Rowledge, Farnham, Surrey GU10 4EA
Tel: (01252) 792134
Head: Mr P M de Voil
Type: Co-educational Boarding and Day 3–18
No of pupils: B184 G216
No of Boarders: F116
Fees: (September 00) FB £13860 – £14985 WB £13200 – £14490 Day £9000 – £10080
Special Needs: Unspecified: DYC DYP DYS

GRANTCHESTER HOUSE
5 Hinchley Way, Hinchley Wood, Esher, Surrey KT10 0BD
Tel: (020) 8398 1157
Head: Mrs A E Fry
Type: Co-educational Day 3–7
No of pupils: B44 G48
Fees: (September 00) Day £2280 – £3900
Special Needs: Unspecified: DYS

GREENFIELD SCHOOL

Brooklyn Road, Woking, Surrey
GU22 7TP
Tel: (01483) 772525
Head: Mrs J S Becker
Type: Co-educational Day 3–11
No of pupils: B96 G100
Fees: (September 00) Day £2460 –
£4185
Special Needs: Level 2: ADD DYP DYS

HALSTEAD PREPARATORY SCHOOL

Woodham Rise, Woking, Surrey
GU21 4EE
Tel: (01483) 772682
Head: Mrs A Hancock
Type: Girls Day 3–11
No of pupils: 209
Fees: (September 00) Day £2100 –
£5970
Special Needs: Level 2: ADD ADHD
DYP DYS SPLD

HAWLEY PLACE SCHOOL

Fernhill Road, Blackwater,
Camberley, Surrey GU17 9HU
Tel: (01276) 32028
Head: Mr and Mrs T G Pipe
Type: Girls Day 2–16 (Boys 2–11)
No of pupils: B110 G170
Fees: (September 00) Day £4140 –
£5190
Special Needs: Level 2: DYS MLD
Level 3: DYP

KINGSWOOD HOUSE SCHOOL

56 West Hill, Epsom, Surrey
KT19 8LG
Tel: (01372) 723590
Head: Mr P Brooks
Type: Boys Day 3–13
No of pupils: 210
Fees: (September 00) Day £4200 –
£5775
Special Needs: Level 1: DYC DYP DYS
SPLD Unspecified: SP&LD

LANESBOROUGH

Maori Road, Guildford, Surrey
GU1 2EL
Tel: (01483) 880650
Head: Mr K S Crombie
Type: Boys Day 3–13
No of pupils: 340
Fees: (September 00) Day £1755 –
£6036
Special Needs: Level 2: DYS Level 3:
HI

LAVEROCK SCHOOL

19 Bluehouse Lane, Oxted, Surrey
RH8 0AA
Tel: (01883) 714171
Head: Mrs A C Paterson
Type: Girls Day 3–11
No of pupils: 150
Fees: (September 00) Day £2025 –
£5250
Special Needs: Level 2: DYP DYS
SPLD Level 3: ADD CP PH

LYNDHURST SCHOOL

36 The Avenue, Camberley, Surrey
GU15 3NE
Tel: (01276) 22895
Head: Mr R L Cunliffe
Type: Co-educational Day 2–12
No of pupils: B121 G70
Fees: (September 00) Day £1920 –
£4620
Special Needs: Level 2: DYS Level 3:
EPI HI VIS

MARYMOUNT INTERNATIONAL SCHOOL

George Road, Kingston-upon-
Thames, Surrey KT2 7PE
Tel: (020) 8949 0571
Head: Sister R Sheridan
Type: Girls Day and Boarding 11–18
No of pupils: 198 *No of Boarders:* F73
W13
Fees: (September 00) FB £16165 –
£17165 WB £15945 – £16945 Day
£9000 – £10000
Special Needs: Level 2: ADD DYS
SPLD

MICKLEFIELD SCHOOL

10/12 Somers Road, Reigate, Surrey
RH2 9DU
Tel: (01737) 242615
Head: Mrs C Belton
Type: Co-educational Day 2–11
No of pupils: B76 G205
Fees: (September 00) Day £990 –
£4890
Special Needs: Unspecified: DYS HI
MLD PH

NOTRE DAME PREPARATORY SCHOOL

Burwood House, Cobham, Surrey
KT11 1HA
Tel: (01932) 862152
Head: Mrs E Brook
Type: Girls Day 2–11 (Boys 2–5)
No of pupils: B30 G340
Fees: (September 00) Day £600 –
£1750
Special Needs: Level 2: DEL DYP
Level 3: EBD HI SP&LD SPLD
Unspecified: DYS

OAKHYRST GRANGE SCHOOL

160 Stanstead Road, Caterham,
Surrey CR3 6AF
Tel: (01883) 343344
Head: Mr N J E Jones
Type: Co-educational Day 2–11
No of pupils: B115 G31
Fees: (September 00) Day £705 –
£3795
Special Needs: Level 2: DYP DYS
SP&LD

PARSONS MEAD

Ottways Lane, Ashtead, Surrey
KT21 2PE
Tel: (01372) 276401
Head: Mrs P M Taylor
Type: Girls Day and Boarding 3–18
No of pupils: G300 *No of Boarders:* W2
Fees: (September 00) WB £9261 –
£11934 Day £4173 – £6846
Special Needs: Unspecified: DYS HI

PRIOR'S FIELD SCHOOL

Priorsfield Road, Godalming, Surrey
GU7 2RH
Tel: (01483) 810551
Head: Mrs J Dwyer
Type: Girls Boarding and Day 11–18
No of pupils: G260 *No of Boarders:* F38
W52
Fees: (September 00) F/WB £13188
Day £8820
Special Needs: Level 1: DYS

ROYAL ALEXANDRA AND ALBERT SCHOOL

Gatton Park, Reigate, Surrey
RH2 0TW
Tel: (01737) 645835
Head: Mr R Bushin
Type: Co-educational Boarding and
Day 7–18
No of pupils: B328 G258
No of Boarders: F410 W32
Fees: (September 00) FB £6600 WB
£6450 Day £825
Special Needs: Level 2: ADD ADHD
ASP AUT DYP DYS EPI HI MLD PH
PMLD SLD SP&LD SPLD Level 3:
EBD TOU VIS

ROYAL SCHOOL HASLEMERE
Farnham Lane, Haslemere, Surrey
GU27 1HQ
Tel: (01428) 605805
Head: Mrs L Taylor-Gooby
Type: Girls Day and Boarding 2–18
(Boys 2–4)
No of pupils: B4 G288
No of Boarders: F47 W13
Fees: (September 00) FB £9981 –
£12672 Day £4716 – £8073
Special Needs: Level 2: DYP DYS EPI
SPLD Level 3: ASP DEL HI VIS

RYDES HILL PREPARATORY
SCHOOL
Aldershot Road, Guildford, Surrey
GU2 6BP
Tel: (01483) 563160
Head: Mrs J Lenahan
Type: Girls Day 3–11 (Boys 3–7)
No of pupils: B10 G150
Fees: (September 00) Day £2175 –
£5160
Special Needs: Level 2: ADD DYP DYS

ST ANDREW'S SCHOOL
Church Hill House, Wilson Way,
Horsell, Woking, Surrey GU21 4QW
Tel: (01483) 760943
Head: Mr B Pretorius
Type: Co-educational Day 3–13
No of pupils: 235
Fees: (September 00) Day £3540 –
£7365
Special Needs: Level 2: DYS MLD
SP&LD

ST CATHERINE'S SCHOOL
Station Road, Bramley, Guildford,
Surrey GU5 0DF
Tel: (01483) 893363
Head: Mrs A M Phillips
Type: Girls Day and Boarding 4–18
No of pupils: 710 *No of Boarders:* F58
W59
Fees: (September 00) F/WB £11220 –
£12465 Day £3795 – £9795
Special Needs: Level 2: DYS

ST GEORGE'S COLLEGE
Weybridge Road, Addlestone,
Weybridge, Surrey KT15 2QS
Tel: (01932) 839300
Head: Mr J A Peake
Type: Co-educational Day 11–18
No of pupils: B550 G350
Fees: (September 00) Day £6900 –
£7950
Special Needs: Level 2: ASP DYP DYS

ST HILARY'S SCHOOL
Holloway Hill, Godalming, Surrey
GU7 1RZ
Tel: (01428) 416551
Head: Mrs S Bailes
Type: Co-educational Day Boys 2–8
Girls 2–11
No of pupils: B110 G298
Fees: (September 00) Day £3900 –
£5850
Special Needs: Level 2: ADD DYP DYS
SP&LD

ST IVES SCHOOL
Three Gates Lane, Haslemere, Surrey
GU27 2ES
Tel: (01428) 643734
Head: Mrs M S Greenway
Type: Girls Day 3–11 (Boys 3–5)
No of pupils: B8 G137
Fees: (September 00) Day £4605 –
£6450
Special Needs: Level 2: DYS SPLD

ST TERESA'S PREPARATORY
SCHOOL
Grove House, Guildford Road,
Effingham, Surrey KT24 5QA
Tel: (01372) 453456
Head: Mrs M Head
Type: Girls Day and Boarding 2–11
No of pupils: G200 *No of Boarders:* F6
W2
Fees: (September 00) F/WB £11250
Day £1810
Special Needs: Unspecified: ADD DEL
DYP DYS HI MLD PH

SEATON HOUSE
67 Banstead Road South, Sutton,
Surrey SM2 5LH
Tel: (020) 8642 2332
Head: Mrs V A Richards
Type: Girls Day 3–11 (Boys 3–5)
No of pupils: B20 G180
Fees: (September 00) Day £1260 –
£3750
Special Needs: Level 3: ADD DYP DYS

SHREWSBURY HOUSE
SCHOOL
107 Ditton Road, Surbiton, Surrey
KT6 6RL
Tel: (020) 8399 3066
Head: Mr C M Ross
Type: Boys Day 7–13
No of pupils: B280
Fees: (September 00) Day £7050
Special Needs: Level 3: HI MLD VIS

SIR WILLIAM PERKINS'S
SCHOOL
Guildford Road, Chertsey, Surrey
KT16 9BN
Tel: (01932) 562161
Head: Miss S Ross
Type: Girls Day 11–18
No of pupils: G580
Fees: (September 00) Day £6120
Special Needs: Level 3: CP DYS HI

STANWAY SCHOOL
Chichester Road, Dorking, Surrey
RH4 1LR
Tel: (01306) 882151
Head: Mr P H Rushforth
Type: Girls Day 3–11 (Boys 3–8)
No of pupils: B45 G123
Fees: (September 00) Day £1200 –
£5310
Special Needs: Unspecified: DYS

SURBITON PREPARATORY
SCHOOL
3 Avenue Elmers, Surbiton, Surrey
KT6 4SP
Tel: (020) 8546 5245
Head: Mr S J Pryce
Type: Boys Day 4–11
No of pupils: B140
Fees: (September 00) Day £3402 –
£5664
Special Needs: Level 2: DYS

SURREY COLLEGE
Administration Centre, Abbot
House, Sydenham Road, Guildford,
Surrey GU1 3RL
Tel: (01483) 565887
Head: Ms L Cody
Type: Co-educational Day and
Boarding 14+
No of pupils: B60 G50
No of Boarders: F20
Fees: (September 00) Day £1575 –
£8850
Special Needs: Unspecified: DYS

SUTTON HIGH SCHOOL
GDST
55 Cheam Road, Sutton, Surrey
SM1 2AX
Tel: (020) 8642 0594
Head: Mrs A J Coutts
Type: Girls Day 4–18
No of pupils: 742
Fees: (September 00) Day £4764 –
£6132
Special Needs: Level 3: DYS VIS

TORMEAD SCHOOL

27 Cranley Road, Guildford, Surrey
GUI 2JD
Tel: (01483) 575101
Head: Mrs H E M Alleyne
Type: Girls Day 4–18
No of pupils: 680
Fees: (September 00) Day £3180 –
£6750
Special Needs: Level 2: DYS

TRINITY SCHOOL

Shirley Park, Croydon, Surrey
CR9 7AT
Tel: (020) 8656 9541
Head: Mr C J Tarrant
Type: Boys Day 10–18
No of pupils: 860
Fees: (September 00) Day £7305
Special Needs: Level 3: DYS PH
Unspecified: W

UNICORN SCHOOL

238 Kew Road, Richmond, Surrey
TW9 3JX
Tel: (020) 8948 3926
Head: Mrs F Timmis
Type: Co-educational Day 3–11
No of pupils: B84 G84
Fees: (September 00) Day £3000 –
£5520
Special Needs: Level 2: DYS

WARLINGHAM PARK SCHOOL

Chelsham Common, Warlingham,
Croydon, Surrey CR6 9PB
Tel: (01883) 626844
Head: Mr M R Donald
Type: Co-educational Day 2–11
No of pupils: B66 G64
Fees: (September 00) Day £2100 –
£3750
Special Needs: Level 2: DYS SP&LD
Unspecified: W

WEST DENE SCHOOL

167 Brighton Road, Purley, Surrey
CR8 4HE
Tel: (020) 8660 2404
Head: Mrs S Topp
Type: Co-educational Day 2–11
No of pupils: B52 G77
Fees: (September 00) Day £3540 –
£3570
Special Needs: Level 3: DEL HI VIS

WOODCOTE HOUSE SCHOOL

Snows Ride, Windlesham, Surrey
GU20 6PF
Tel: (01276) 472115
Head: Mr N H K Paterson
Type: Boys Boarding and Day 7–14
No of pupils: 105 *No of Boarders:* F90
Fees: (September 00) FB £9825 Day
£6870
Special Needs: Level 2: ADD ADHD
DYP DYS

YEHUDI MENUHIN SCHOOL

Stoke D'Abernon, Cobham, Surrey
KT11 3QQ
Tel: (01932) 864739
Head: Mr N Chisholm
Type: Co-educational Boarding 8–18
No of pupils: B24 G36
No of Boarders: F57
Fees: (September 00) On application
Special Needs: Level 3: DYS

EAST SUSSEX

ASHDOWN HOUSE SCHOOL

Forest Row, East Sussex RH18 5JY
Tel: (01342) 822574
Head: Mr A J Fowler-Watt
Type: Co-educational Boarding and
Day 8–13
No of pupils: B163 G57
No of Boarders: F215
Fees: (September 00) FB £11985 Day
£10005
Special Needs: Level 3: DYC DYS

BATTLE ABBEY SCHOOL

Battle, East Sussex TN33 0AD
Tel: (01424) 772385
Head: Mr R Clark
Type: Co-educational Boarding and
Day 2–18
No of pupils: B116 G142
No of Boarders: F60 W3
Fees: (September 00) F/WB £9630 –
£11910 Day £4050 – £7380
Special Needs: Level 2: DYC DYP DYS
SPLD

BODIAM MANOR SCHOOL†

Bodiam, Robertsbridge, East Sussex
TN32 5UJ
Tel: (01580) 830225
Head: Mr C Moore
Type: Co-educational Day 2–13
No of pupils: B89 G94
Fees: (September 00) Day £2904 –
£5994
Special Needs: Level 2: DYS

BRIGHTON COLLEGE PREP SCHOOL

Walpole Lodge, Walpole Road,
Brighton, East Sussex BN2 2EU
Tel: (01273) 704210
Head: Mr B Melia and Mrs H Beeby
Type: Co-educational Boarding and
Day 3–13
No of pupils: B274 G130
No of Boarders: W2
Fees: (September 00) WB £7932 –
£9741 Day £6405 – £8214
Special Needs: Level 2: DYS

CLAREMONT SCHOOL

Baldslow, St Leonards-on-Sea, East
Sussex TN37 7PW
Tel: (01424) 751555
Head: Mr I Culley
Type: Co-educational Day 2–14
No of pupils: B175 G175
Fees: (September 00) Day £3135 –
£5400
Special Needs: Level 2: DYS SP&LD

EASTBOURNE COLLEGE

Old Wish Road, Eastbourne, East
Sussex BN21 4JY
Tel: (01323) 452300
Head: Mr C M P Bush
Type: Co-educational Boarding and
Day 13–18
No of pupils: B262 G60
No of Boarders: F57 W100
Fees: (September 00) FB £15450 Day
£9990
Special Needs: Level 2: DYS

MOIRA HOUSE GIRLS' SCHOOL

Upper Carlisle Road, Eastbourne, East Sussex BN20 7TE
Tel: (01323) 644144
Head: Mrs A Harris
Type: Girls Boarding and Day 11–18
No of pupils: 220 *No of Boarders:* F100
Fees: (September 00) FB £12300 –
£14400 WB £10200 – £12900 Day
£7380 – £8700
Special Needs: Level 1: EBD Level 2:
DYP DYS

NEWLANDS MANOR SCHOOL

Sutton Place, Seaford, East Sussex
BN25 3PL
Tel: (01323) 892334 / 490000
Head: Mr O T Price
Type: Co-educational Boarding and
Day 13–18
No of pupils: 208 *No of Boarders:* F91
W1
Fees: (September 00) FB £11700 –
£13050 WB £11550 – £12900 Day
£7350 – £7650
Special Needs: Level 2: DYC DYP DYS
SPLD

NEWLANDS PREPARATORY SCHOOL†

Eastbourne Road, Seaford, East
Sussex BN25 4NP
Tel: (01323) 892334 / 490000
Head: Mr O T Price
Type: Co-educational Boarding and
Day 2–13
No of pupils: 489 *No of Boarders:* F160
W3
Fees: (September 00) FB £8850 –
£13050 WB £8700 – £11350 Day
£3300 – £7350
Special Needs: Level 2: DYC DYP DYS
SPLD

ST ANDREW'S SCHOOL

Meads, Eastbourne, East Sussex
BN20 7RP
Tel: (01323) 733203
Head: Mr F Roche
Type: Co-educational Boarding and
Day 3–13
No of pupils: B294 G193
No of Boarders: F44 W12
Fees: (September 00) FB £11100 WB
£9680 – £10950 Day £2525 – £7630
Special Needs: Level 2: DYS SP&LD
SPLD Level 3: ADD ADHD CP DEL
DYC DYP EPI HI

ST AUBYN'S

High Street, Rottingdean, Brighton,
East Sussex BNZ 7JN
Tel: (01273) 302170
Head: Mr A G Gobat
Type: Co-educational Boarding and
Day 4–13
No of pupils: B123 G37
No of Boarders: F16 W18
Fees: (September 00) FB £11295 Day
£3420 – £8400
Special Needs: Level 2: ADD DYC
DYP DYS SP&LD SPLD

ST BEDE'S SCHOOL

The Dicker, Hailsham, East Sussex
BN27 3QH
Tel: (01323) 843252
Head: Mr R A Perrin
Type: Co-educational Boarding and
Day 2–19
No of pupils: B580 G386
No of Boarders: F340 W20
Fees: (September 00) F/WB £14475
Day £8820
Special Needs: Unspecified: DYP DYS

ST MARY'S HALL

Eastern Road, Brighton, East Sussex
BN2 5JF
Tel: (01273) 606061
Head: Mrs S M Meek
Type: Girls Day and Boarding 3–18
(Boys 3–8)
No of pupils: B6 G376
No of Boarders: F62 W4
Fees: (September 00) FB £8658 –
£11709 WB £8598 – £11223 Day
£1515 – £7428
Special Needs: Unspecified: DYS

STONELANDS SCHOOL OF BALLET & THEATRE ARTS

170A Church Road, Hove, East
Sussex BN3 2DJ
Tel: (01273) 770445
Head: Mrs D Carteur
Type: Co-educational Boarding and
Day 6–16
No of pupils: B6 G36
No of Boarders: F10 W10
Fees: (September 00) FB £9600 Day
£5385
Special Needs: Unspecified: DYS

WEST SUSSEX

ARUNDALE PREPARATORY SCHOOL

Lower Street, Pulborough, West
Sussex RH20 2BX
Tel: (01798) 872520
Head: Miss K Lovejoy
Type: Co-educational Day Boys 2–8
Girls 2–12
No of pupils: B24 G84
Fees: (September 00) Day £1725 –
£5370
Special Needs: Unspecified: DYS

BRAMBLETYE SCHOOL

Brambletye, East Grinstead, West
Sussex RH19 3PD
Tel: (01342) 321004
Head: Mr H D Cocke
Type: Co-educational Boarding and
Day 3–13
No of pupils: B163 G22
No of Boarders: F84
Fees: (September 00) FB £11685 Day
£2550 – £8835
Special Needs: Level 2: DYC DYP DYS

BROADWATER MANOR SCHOOL

Broadwater Road, Worthing, West
Sussex BN14 8HU
Tel: (01903) 201123
Head: Mrs E K Woodley
Type: Co-educational Day 2–13
No of pupils: B186 G182
Fees: (September 00) Day £375 –
£4500
Special Needs: Level 2: ADD ADHD
ASP DYP DYS

BURGESS HILL SCHOOL FOR GIRLS
Keymer Road, Burgess Hill, West Sussex RH15 0EG
Tel: (01444) 241050
Head: Mrs R Lewis
Type: Girls Day and Boarding 3–18 (Co-ed nursery)
No of pupils: 700 *No of Boarders:* F45
Fees: (September 00) FB £11865 WB £10485 Day £3345 – £7020
Special Needs: Level 2: VIS Level 3: DYP DYS EPI HI PH

COPTHORNE SCHOOL
Effingham Lane, Crawley, West Sussex RH10 3HR
Tel: (01342) 712311
Head: Mr G C Allen
Type: Co-educational Day and Boarding 2–13
No of pupils: B160 G104
No of Boarders: W10
Fees: (September 00) WB £8685 Day £4128 – £7488
Special Needs: Level 2: DYC DYP DYS Level 3: ADD ADHD HI MLD SPLD

COTTESMORE SCHOOL
Buchan Hill, Pease Pottage, West Sussex RH11 9AU
Tel: (01293) 520648
Head: Mr M A Rogerson
Type: Co-educational Boarding 7–13
No of pupils: B100 G50
No of Boarders: F150
Fees: (September 00) FB £11400
Special Needs: Unspecified: DYP DYS MLD

CUMNOR HOUSE SCHOOL
Danehill, Haywards Heath, West Sussex RH17 7HT
Tel: (01825) 790347
Head: Mr P Wigan
Type: Co-educational Boarding and Day 4–13
No of pupils: B152 G117
No of Boarders: F28
Fees: (September 00) FB £11400 Day £4800 – £8895
Special Needs: Unspecified: ADD DYP DYS SP&LD SPLD

DORSET HOUSE SCHOOL
The Manor, Bury, Pulborough, West Sussex RH20 1PB
Tel: (01798) 831456
Head: Mr A L James
Type: Boys Boarding and Day 4–13
No of pupils: 152 *No of Boarders:* W43
Fees: (September 00) F/WB £9315 – £10500 Day £4350 – £8775
Special Needs: Level 2: DYS

FARLINGTON SCHOOL
Strood Park, Horsham, West Sussex RH12 3PN
Tel: (01403) 254967
Head: Mrs P M Mawer
Type: Girls Day and Boarding 4–18
No of pupils: G410 *No of Boarders:* F25 W15
Fees: (September 00) FB £10020 – £12315 WB £9765 – £12060 Day £3660 – £7635
Special Needs: Level 2: DYS Level 3: DYP SPLD

FONTHILL LODGE
Coombe Hill Road, East Grinstead, West Sussex RH9 4LY
Tel: (01342) 321635
Head: Mrs J Griffiths
Type: Co-educational Day 2–11 (Single sex education 8–11)
No of pupils: 190
Fees: (September 00) Day £2160 – £6195
Special Needs: Level 2: DYS Unspecified: W

GREAT BALLARD SCHOOL
Eartham, Chichester, West Sussex PO18 0LR
Tel: (01243) 814236
Head: Mr R E Jennings
Type: Co-educational Boarding and Day 2–13
No of pupils: B102 G83
No of Boarders: F5 W29
Fees: (September 00) F/WB £9063 Day £1623 – £6804
Special Needs: Level 2: DYC DYP DYS Unspecified: ADD MLD PH SPLD

NEW WEST PRESTON MANOR NURSERY SCHOOL
39 Park Drive, Rustington, Littlehampton, West Sussex BN16 3DY
Tel: (01903) 784282
Head: Mrs J M Drury
Type: Co-educational Day 2–5
No of pupils: 38
Fees: (September 00) On application
Special Needs: Level 3: ADD DEL DYP SP&LD Unspecified: HI

OAKWOOD SCHOOL
Oakwood, Chichester, West Sussex PO18 9AN
Tel: (01243) 575209
Head: Mr A H Cowell
Type: Co-educational Boarding and Day 2–11
No of pupils: B102 G88
No of Boarders: W15
Fees: (September 00) WB £8580 Day £2100 – £6426
Special Needs: Unspecified: DYC DYP DYS

ST MARGARET'S JUNIOR SCHOOL CONVENT OF MERCY
Petersfield Road, Midhurst, West Sussex GU29 9JN
Tel: (01730) 813956
Head: Sister M Martina
Type: Co-educational Day 3–11
No of pupils: B125 G205
Fees: (September 00) Day £1650 – £3210
Special Needs: Level 1: ADD ADHD DEL EPI HI PH VIS Level 2: DYP MLD SP&LD Level 3: DYS SPLD

ST PETER'S SCHOOL
Upper St John's Road, Burgess Hill, West Sussex RH15 8HB
Tel: (01444) 235880
Head: Mr H G Stevens
Type: Co-educational Day 2–8
No of pupils: B98 G84
Fees: (September 00) Day £513 – £3434
Special Needs: Level 2: DEL Level 3: ASP DYC DYP DYS EPI HI MLD SP&LD SPLD

SANDHURST SCHOOL
101 Brighton Road, Worthing, West Sussex BN11 2EL
Tel: (01903) 201933
Head: Mrs A B Glover
Type: Co-educational Day 2–13
No of pupils: B85 G94
Fees: (September 00) Day £1944 – £2268
Special Needs: Level 2: DYS

SEAFORD COLLEGE
Lavington Park, Petworth, West
Sussex GU28 0NB
Tel: (01798) 867392
Head: Mr T J Mullins
Type: Co-educational Boarding and
Day 10–18
No of pupils: B262 G60
No of Boarders: F57 W100
Fees: (September 00) F/WB £10890 –
£14100 Day £7500 – £9390
Special Needs: Level 1: DYC DYS
Level 3: ADD ADHD DYP EBD MLD

SLINDON COLLEGE
Slindon House, Slindon, Arundel,
West Sussex BN18 0RH
Tel: (01243) 814320
Head: Mr I P Graham
Type: Boys Boarding and Day 9–16
No of pupils: B100 *No of Boarders:* F20
W30
Fees: (September 00) F/WB £11880
Day £7215
Special Needs: Level 2: ADD ADHD
DYC DYS SPLD Level 3: DEL DYP
EPI

STOKE BRUNSWICK
Ashurstwood, East Grinstead, West
Sussex RH19 3PF
Tel: (01342) 828200
Head: Mr W M Ellerton
Type: Co-educational Boarding and
Day 3–13
No of pupils: B100 G55
No of Boarders: W10
Fees: (September 00) WB £9555 Day
£2085 – £7875
Special Needs: Unspecified: DYP DYS

WORTH SCHOOL
Turners Hill, West Sussex RH10 4SD
Tel: (01342) 710200
Head: Fr C Jamison
Type: Boys Boarding and Day 11–18
No of pupils: B428 *No of Boarders:* F269
Fees: (September 00) FB £13327 –
£14808 Day £9689 – £10767
Special Needs: Level 2: ADD ADHD
DYP DYS Unspecified: MLD

TYNE AND WEAR

ASCHAM HOUSE SCHOOL
30 West Avenue, Gosforth,
Newcastle upon Tyne, Tyne and
Wear NE3 4ES
Tel: (0191) 285 1619
Head: Mr S H Reid
Type: Boys Day 4–13
No of pupils: 270
Fees: (September 00) Day £4575
Special Needs: Level 2: DYC DYP DYS

NEWLANDS SCHOOL
34 The Grove, Gosforth, Newcastle
upon Tyne, Tyne and Wear NE3 1NH
Tel: (0191) 285 2208
Head: Mr R McDuff
Type: Boys Day 3–13
No of pupils: 220
Fees: (September 00) Day £3750 –
£4815
Special Needs: Level 2: DYS Level 3:
ADD Unspecified: ADHD ASP AUT
CP DEL DOW

WARWICKSHIRE

BILTON GRANGE
Dunchurch, Rugby, Warwickshire
CV22 6QU
Tel: (01788) 810217
Head: Mr Q G Edwards
Type: Co-educational Boarding and
Day 4–13
No of pupils: B267 G150
No of Boarders: F34 W39
Fees: (September 00) F/WB £10854
Day £7509 – £8580
Special Needs: Level 2: DYP DYS

EMSCOTE HOUSE SCHOOL
AND NURSERY
46 Warwick Place, Leamington Spa,
Warwickshire CV32 5DE
Tel: (01926) 425067
Head: Mrs G J Andrews
Type: Co-educational Day 2–7
No of pupils: B53 G42
Fees: (September 00) Day £600 –
£3600
Special Needs: Unspecified: DYS

PRINCETHORPE COLLEGE
Leamington Road, Princethorpe,
Rugby, Warwickshire CV23 9PX
Tel: (01926) 634200
Head: Mr J M Shinkwin
Type: Co-educational Day and
Boarding 11–18 (Girls day only 11–
16)
No of pupils: B404 G156
No of Boarders: F38 W12
Fees: (September 00) FB £11265 WB
£10470 Day £5175
Special Needs: Level 1: DYS Level 3:
ADD HI Unspecified: DYP

RUGBY SCHOOL
Rugby, Warwickshire CV22 5EH
Tel: (01788) 556274
Head: Mr P Derhan
Type: Co-educational Boarding and
Day 11–18
No of pupils: B496 G282
No of Boarders: F610
Fees: (September 00) FB £15375 Day
£5520 – £12300
Special Needs: Level 2: DYP DYS

WEST MIDLANDS

ARDEN LAWN
Henley-in-Arden, Solihull, West
Midlands B95 6AB
Tel: (01564) 796800
Head: Mrs J Thomas
Type: Co-educational Day 3–18
No of pupils: B270 G200
Fees: (January 01) Day £4245 –
£6150
Special Needs: Level 3: DYC DYP DYS
Unspecified: W

COVENTRY PREPARATORY SCHOOL
Kenilworth Road, Coventry, West
Midlands CV3 6PT
Tel: (024) 7667 5289
Head: Mr D Clark
Type: Co-educational Day 3–13
No of pupils: B112 G68
Fees: (September 00) Day £4299 –
£5820
Special Needs: Level 2: DYC DYP DYS
SPLD

EVERSFIELD PREPARATORY SCHOOL
Warwick Road, Solihull, West
Midlands B91 1AT
Tel: (0121) 705 0354
Head: Mr K U Madden
Type: Co-educational Day 2–11
No of pupils: B161 G15
Fees: (September 00) Day £4275 –
£5925
Special Needs: Level 2: DYC DYS
Level 3: ADD ADHD DYP HI PH

KINGSLEY PREPARATORY SCHOOL
53 Hanbury Road, Dorridge,
Solihull, West Midlands B93 8DW
Tel: (01564) 774144
Head: Mrs J A Scott
Type: Co-educational Day 3–11
No of pupils: B20 G20
Fees: (September 00) On application
Special Needs: Level 1: ADD ASP DYP
DYS MLD SP&LD SPLD TOU Level 3:
DEL HI PH Unspecified: W

MANDER PORTMAN WOODWARD
38 Highfield Road, Edgbaston,
Birmingham, West Midlands
B15 3ED
Tel: (0121) 454 9637
Head: Mr M Lloyd
Type: Co-educational Day 14+
No of pupils: B60 G60
Fees: (September 00) Day £5370 –
£9456
Special Needs: Level 3: DYS

THE ROYAL WOLVERHAMPTON SCHOOL
Penn Road, Wolverhampton, West
Midlands WV3 0EG
Tel: (01902) 341230
Head: Mr T J Brooker
Type: Co-educational Boarding and
Day 11–18
No of pupils: B193 G108
No of Boarders: F160 W20
Fees: (September 00) FB £13560 WB
£12300 – £12660 Day £6210 – £6615
Special Needs: Level 2: DYS

RUCKLEIGH SCHOOL
17 Lode Lane, Solihull, West
Midlands B91 2AB
Tel: (0121) 705 2773
Head: Mr D N Carr-Smith
Type: Co-educational Day 3–11
No of pupils: B119 G101
Fees: (September 00) Day £2430 –
£4761
Special Needs: Unspecified: DYS

ST GEORGE'S SCHOOL, EDGBASTON
31 Calthorpe Road, Birmingham,
West Midlands B15 1RX
Tel: (0121) 625 0398
Head: Miss H J Phillips
Type: Co-educational Day 3–18
No of pupils: B120 G180
Fees: (September 00) Day £2700 –
£5325
Special Needs: Level 3: ADD ADHD
DYC DYP DYS EPI HI PH VIS

ST MARTIN'S SCHOOL
Malvern Hall, Brueton Avenue,
Solihull, West Midlands B91 3EN
Tel: (0121) 705 1265
Head: Mrs S J Williams
Type: Girls Day 3–18
No of pupils: 540
Fees: (September 00) Day £1965 –
£5490
Special Needs: Level 3: DYS EPI PH

TETTENHALL COLLEGE
Wood Road, Wolverhampton, West Midlands WV6 8QX
Tel: (01902) 751119
Head: Dr P C Bodkin
Type: Co-educational Boarding and Day 7–18
No of pupils: B223 G121
No of Boarders: F75 W11
Fees: (September 00) FB £9444 – £11502 WB £7662 – £9570 Day £5568 – £6957
Special Needs: Level 2: DYC DYP DYS SPLD

WEST HOUSE SCHOOL
24 St James's Road, Edgbaston, Birmingham, West Midlands B15 2NX
Tel: (0121) 440 4097
Head: Mr G K Duce
Type: Boys Day 1–11 (Girls 1–4)
No of pupils: B205 G16
Fees: (September 00) Day £2947 – £6015
Special Needs: Level 2: MLD
Unspecified: DYS

WOLVERHAMPTON GRAMMAR SCHOOL
Compton Road, Wolverhampton, West Midlands WV3 9RB
Tel: (01902) 421326
Head: Dr B Trafford
Type: Co-educational Day 11–18
No of pupils: B481 G274
Fees: (September 00) Day £6420
Special Needs: Level 1: DYS Level 3: DYP HI

WYLDE GREEN COLLEGE
245 Birmingham Road, Sutton Coldfield, West Midlands B72 1EA
Tel: (0121) 354 1505
Head: Mr P J Burd
Type: Co-educational Day 1–11
No of pupils: B120 G40
Fees: (September 00) Day £2976 – £4032
Special Needs: Level 2: DYS SP&LD

WILTSHIRE

LEADEN HALL
70 The Close, Salisbury, Wiltshire SP1 2EP
Tel: (01722) 334700
Head: Mrs D Watkins
Type: Girls Day and Boarding 3–13 (Boys 3–4)
No of pupils: B4 G248
No of Boarders: F40
Fees: (September 00) FB £7550 – £8550 Day £4035 – £5400
Special Needs: Unspecified: DYS MLD PH

MEADOWPARK NURSERY & PRE-PREP
Calcutt Street, Cricklade, Wiltshire SN6 6BB
Tel: (01793) 752600
Head: Mrs R Kular and Mrs S Hanbury
Type: Co-educational Day 1–7
No of pupils: B51 G39
Fees: On application
Special Needs: Level 2: DYS

NORMAN COURT PREPARATORY SCHOOL
West Tytherley, Salisbury, Wiltshire SP5 1NH
Tel: (01980) 862345
Head: Mr K N Foyle
Type: Co-educational Boarding and Day 3–13
No of pupils: B118 G172
No of Boarders: F26 W39
Fees: (September 00) F/WB £10563 Day £3972 – £7896
Special Needs: Unspecified: DYC DYP DYS MLD SPLD

PINEWOOD SCHOOL
Bourton, Swindon, Wiltshire SN6 8HZ
Tel: (01793) 782205
Head: Mr J Croysdale
Type: Co-educational Boarding and Day 3–13
No of pupils: B143 G107
No of Boarders: W26
Fees: (September 00) FB £10185 Day £3975 – £6768
Special Needs: Level 2: DYC DYP DYS MLD SPLD

PRIOR PARK PREPARATORY SCHOOL
Calcutt Street, Cricklade, Wiltshire SN6 6BB
Tel: (01793) 750275
Head: Mr G B Hobern
Type: Co-educational Boarding and Day 7–13
No of pupils: B134 G73
No of Boarders: F34 W39
Fees: (September 00) F/WB £9156 – £9234 Day £6294 – £6639
Special Needs: Level 2: DYC DYP DYS MLD Level 3: ADD TOU

SANDROYD
Tollard Royal, Salisbury, Wiltshire SP5 5QD
Tel: (01725) 516264
Head: Mr M J Hatch
Type: Boys Boarding 7–13 (A few day places 7–11)
No of pupils: 145 *No of Boarders:* F110
Fees: (September 00) FB £9300 – £11475 Day £6750 – £9450
Special Needs: Level 2: DYP DYS SPLD

SOUTH HILLS SCHOOL
Home Farm Road, Salisbury,
Wiltshire SP2 8PJ
Tel: (01722) 744971
Head: Mrs A Proctor
Type: Co-educational Day 0–8
No of pupils: B30 G30
Fees: (September 00) Day £778 –
£3402
Special Needs: Level 2: DYP DYS
Level 3: ADD ADHD ASP AUT CP
DEL DOW EBD EPI HI MLD
Unspecified: PMLD SLD W

STONAR SCHOOL
Melksham, Wiltshire SN12 8NT
Tel: (01225) 702795/702309
Head: Mrs S Hopkinson
Type: Girls Boarding and Day 4–18
No of pupils: 400 *No of Boarders:* F150
W20
Fees: (September 00) F/WB £10881 –
£11880 Day £2931 – £6600
Special Needs: Level 2: DYS HI Level 3:
DEL EPI PH SPLD VIS

STOURBRIDGE HOUSE SCHOOL
Castle Street, Mere, Warminster,
Wiltshire BA12 6JQ
Tel: (01747) 860165
Head: Mrs E Coward
Type: Co-educational Day 2–9
No of pupils: B25 G25
Fees: (September 00) Day £2955 –
£3102
Special Needs: Level 2: DYS

WORCESTERSHIRE

THE ALICE OTTLEY SCHOOL
Upper Tything, Worcester,
Worcestershire WR1 1HW
Tel: (01905) 27061
Head: Mrs M Chapman
Type: Girls Day 3–19
No of pupils: 640
Fees: (September 00) Day £2970 –
£6381
Special Needs: Level 2: DYS SPLD

BROMSGROVE SCHOOL
Worcester Road, Bromsgrove,
Worcestershire B61 7DU
Tel: (01527) 579679
Head: Mr T M Taylor
Type: Co-educational Boarding and
Day 13–18
No of pupils: B408 G283
No of Boarders: F305
Fees: (January 01) FB £13755 Day
£8400
Special Needs: Level 2: DYS SPLD
Level 3: ADD DYC DYP

THE ELMS
Colwall, Malvern, Worcestershire
WR13 6EF
Tel: (01684) 540344
Head: Mr L A C Ashby
Type: Co-educational Boarding and
Day 3–13
No of pupils: B96 G74
No of Boarders: F83
Fees: (September 00) FB £10560 Day
£3900 – £9240
Special Needs: Level 2: ADD ASP AUT
DYP DYS MLD

THE GRANGE
Royal Grammar School Worcester
Pre-Prep, Grange Lane, Claines,
Worcester, Worcestershire WR3 7RR
Tel: (01905) 451205
Head: Miss A Gleave
Type: Co-educational Day 3–8
No of pupils: B130 G70
Fees: (September 00) Day £954 –
£1212
Special Needs: Level 1: EBD Level 2:
DYP DYS HI MLD SP&LD SPLD VIS
Unspecified: W

GREEN HILL SCHOOL
Evesham, Worcestershire WR11 4NG
Tel: (01386) 442364
Head: Mr O Lister
Type: Co-educational Day 3–13
No of pupils: B55 G50
Fees: (September 00) Day £2640 –
£3840
Special Needs: Level 2: ADD ADHD
ASP DYC DYP DYS SP&LD SPLD
Level 3: CP EPI VIS

HARTLEBURY SCHOOL
Hartlebury, Kidderminster,
Worcestershire DY11 7TE
Tel: (01299) 250258
Head: Mr D R Bolam
Type: Co-educational Day 4–16
No of pupils: B52 G31
Fees: (September 00) Day £1950 –
£6300
Special Needs: Level 3: DYC DYS PH
TOU Unspecified: W

THE KING'S SCHOOL
Worcester, Worcestershire WR1 2LH
Tel: (01905) 721700
Head: Mr T H Keyes
Type: Co-educational Day 7–18
No of pupils: B581 G376
Fees: (September 00) Day £4305 –
£6681
Special Needs: Level 2: DYS

MALVERN COLLEGE
College Road, Malvern,
Worcestershire WR14 3DF
Tel: (01684) 581500
Head: Mr H C K Carson
Type: Co-educational Boarding and
Day 13–18
No of pupils: B365 G183
No of Boarders: F448
Fees: (September 00) FB £15930 Day
£10095 – £11580
Special Needs: Level 2: DYC DYP DYS
SPLD Level 3: ADD

MALVERN GIRLS' COLLEGE
Avenue Road, Malvern,
Worcestershire WR14 3BA
Tel: (01684) 892288
Head: Mrs P M C Leggate
Type: Girls Boarding and Day 11–18
No of pupils: G420 *No of Boarders:* F350
Fees: (September 00) FB £15900 Day
£10575
Special Needs: Level 2: DYS MLD
SPLD

MOUNT SCHOOL
Birmingham Road, Bromsgrove,
Worcestershire B61 0EP
Tel: (01527) 877772
Head: Mr S A Robinson
Type: Co-educational Day 3–11
No of pupils: B82 G68
Fees: (September 00) Day £2970 –
£4260
Special Needs: Level 2: DYS

ST JAMES'S SCHOOL
West Malvern, Malvern,
Worcestershire WR14 4DF
Tel: (01684) 560851
Head: Mrs S Kershaw
Type: Girls Boarding and Day 10–18
No of pupils: G150 *No of Boarders:* F50
W50
Fees: (September 00) FB £13965 –
£14865 Day £6750 – £9150
Special Needs: Level 1: DYP DYS
SPLD Level 3: DEL EPI

WHITFORD HALL & DODDERHILL SCHOOL
Crutch Lane, Droitwich,
Worcestershire WR9 0BE
Tel: (01905) 778290
Head: Mrs J Mumby
Type: Girls Day 3–16 (Boys 3–9)
No of pupils: B20 G180
Fees: (September 00) Day £1800 –
£5625
Special Needs: Unspecified: DYS HI
MLD

WINTERFOLD HOUSE
Chaddesley Corbett, Kidderminster,
Worcestershire DY10 4PL
Tel: (01562) 777234
Head: Mr W C R Ibbetson-Price
Type: Co-educational Day 3–13
No of pupils: B220 G90
Fees: (September 00) Day £3195 –
£6000
Special Needs: Level 1: DYC DYP DYS
SPLD Unspecified: DEL

EAST RIDING OF YORKSHIRE

HULL GRAMMAR SCHOOL
Cottingham Road, Kingston-Upon-
Hull, East Riding of Yorkshire
HU5 2DL
Tel: (01482) 440144
Head: Mr R Haworth
Type: Co-educational Boarding and
Day 2–18
No of pupils: B279 G168
No of Boarders: F3
Fees: (September 00) FB £10860 –
£13860 WB £9660 – £10290 Day
£2580 – £4935
Special Needs: Level 2: DYS Level 3:
ADHD

POCKLINGTON MONTESSORI SCHOOL
Bielby Lane, Pocklington, East
Riding of Yorkshire YO42 1NT
Tel: (01759) 305436
Head: Ms R Pressland
Type: Co-educational Day 2–7
No of pupils: B82 G83
Fees: (September 00) Day £1327
Special Needs: Level 2: AUT DOW
DYP DYS MLD Level 3: ADD ADHD

NORTH YORKSHIRE

AMPLEFORTH COLLEGE
York, North Yorkshire YO62 4ER
Tel: (01439) 766000
Head: Rev G F L Chamberlain
Type: Boys Boarding 13–18
No of pupils: B501 G6
No of Boarders: F461
Fees: (September 00) FB £15765 Day
£7644 – £8145
Special Needs: Level 1: DYC Level 2:
ADD DYP DYS MLD SPLD

ASHVILLE COLLEGE
Harrogate, North Yorkshire HG2 9JP
Tel: (01423) 566358
Head: Mr M H Crosby
Type: Co-educational Day and
Boarding 4–18
No of pupils: B487 G339
No of Boarders: F120 W30
Fees: (September 00) F/WB £9837 –
£11781 Day £3513 – £6330
Special Needs: Unspecified: DYP DYS
EPI PH

BELMONT GROSVENOR SCHOOL
Swarcliffe Hall, Birstwith, Harrogate,
North Yorkshire HG3 2JG
Tel: (01423) 771029
Head: Mrs R Innocent
Type: Co-educational Day 2–13
No of pupils: 325
Fees: (April 01) Day £633 – £5250
Special Needs: Level 2: DYC DYS MLD
Level 3: ADD DYP HI

BOOTHAM SCHOOL
Bootham, York, North Yorkshire
YO30 7BU
Tel: (01904) 623636
Head: Mr I M Small
Type: Co-educational Boarding and
Day 11–18
No of pupils: B245 G175
No of Boarders: F80 W40
Fees: (September 00) F/WB £12825
Day £8395
Special Needs: Unspecified: DYP DYS
HI PH

BRACKENFIELD SCHOOL
128 Duchy Road, Harrogate, North
Yorkshire HG1 2HE
Tel: (01423) 508558
Head: Mrs M Sutcliffe
Type: Co-educational Day 3–11
No of pupils: B75 G85
Fees: (September 00) On application
Special Needs: Level 1: ADD ADHD
SP&LD Level 2: HI Level 3: DYP DYS
MLD SPLD

BRAMCOTE SCHOOL
Filey Road, Scarborough, North
Yorkshire YO11 2TT
Tel: (01723) 373086
Head: Mr J P Kirk
Type: Co-educational Boarding and
Day 7–13
No of pupils: B60 G26
No of Boarders: F70
Fees: (September 00) FB £10710 Day
£7260 – £7680
Special Needs: Level 1: DYS MLD
SPLD Level 2: SP&LD Level 3: DYC
DYP

CATTERAL HALL
Giggleswick, Settle, North Yorkshire
BD24 0DG
Tel: (01729) 893100
Head: Mr R Hunter
Type: Co-educational Boarding and
Day 3–13
No of pupils: B100 G70
No of Boarders: F50
Fees: (September 00) FB £11700 –
£12570 Day £3850 – £8600
Special Needs: Level 2: ADD ADHD
DYC DYS SPLD Level 3: ASP
Unspecified: DYP

FYLING HALL SCHOOL
Robin Hood's Bay, Whitby, North
Yorkshire YO22 4QD
Tel: (01947) 880353
Head: Mr M D Bayes
Type: Co-educational Boarding and
Day 4–19
No of pupils: B120 G110
No of Boarders: F146 W11
Fees: (September 00) FB £7300 –
£8950 WB £7300 Day £3600 – £4400
Special Needs: Level 2: DYS

GIGGLESWICK SCHOOL
Giggleswick, Settle, North Yorkshire
BD24 0DE
Tel: (01729) 893000
Head: Mr A P Millard
Type: Co-educational Boarding and
Day 11–18
No of pupils: B214 G103
No of Boarders: F255
Fees: (September 00) FB £11700 –
£15402 Day £7800 – £10251
Special Needs: Level 2: DYC DYP DYS
MLD SPLD Level 3: ADD ADHD PH

MALSIS SCHOOL
Cross Hills, Skipton, North
Yorkshire BD20 8DT
Tel: (01535) 633027
Head: Mr J Elder
Type: Co-educational Boarding and
Day 3–13
No of pupils: B125 G45
No of Boarders: F60
Fees: (September 00) FB £10395 Day
£4158 – £7638
Special Needs: Unspecified: DYP DYS
EPI HI MLD PH SP&LD SPLD VIS

THE MOUNT JUNIOR SCHOOL
Dalton Terrace, York, North
Yorkshire YO24 4DD
Tel: (01904) 667513
Head: Miss J Wilson
Type: Co-educational Day 3–11
No of pupils: B52 G116
Fees: (September 00) Day £3180 –
£4890
Special Needs: Level 2: DYS

THE MOUNT SENIOR SCHOOL
Dalton Terrace, York, North
Yorkshire YO24 4DD
Tel: (01904) 667500
Head: Mrs D J Gant
Type: Girls Boarding and Day 11–18
No of pupils: G423 *No of Boarders:* F91
Fees: (September 01) F/WB £12795
Day £3180 – £8025
Special Needs: Unspecified: DYS

RIPON CATHEDRAL CHOIR SCHOOL
Whitcliffe Lane, Ripon, North
Yorkshire HG4 2LA
Tel: (01765) 602134
Head: Mr C R G Western
Type: Co-educational Boarding and
Day 4–13
No of pupils: B71 G49
No of Boarders: F18 W5
Fees: (September 00) FB £8520 WB
£7890 Day £4170 – £6255
Special Needs: Level 2: DYS

SCARBOROUGH COLLEGE
Filey Road, Scarborough, North
Yorkshire YO11 3BA
Tel: (01723) 360621
Head: Mr T L Kirkup
Type: Co-educational Boarding and
Day 11–18
No of pupils: B183 G148
No of Boarders: F21 W8
Fees: (September 00) FB £8681 WB
£8631 Day £6240
Special Needs: Unspecified: DYP DYS
SPLD

SCARBOROUGH COLLEGE JUNIOR SCHOOL
Filey Road, Scarborough, North
Yorkshire YO11 3BA
Tel: (01723) 380606
Head: Mr R G Costin
Type: Co-educational Day 3–11
No of pupils: 145 *No of Boarders:* W2
Fees: (September 00) Day £3240 –
£4434
Special Needs: Unspecified: DYP
DYS W

TERRINGTON HALL
Terrington, York, North Yorkshire
YO60 6PR
Tel: (01653) 648227
Head: Mr J Glen
Type: Co-educational Boarding and
Day 3–13
No of pupils: B110 G70
No of Boarders: F32 W10
Fees: (September 00) F/WB £9150
Day £2600 – £6100
Special Needs: Level 2: DYC DYP DYS
SPLD

WOODLEIGH SCHOOL
Langton, Malton, North Yorkshire
YO17 9QN
Tel: (01653) 658215
Head: Mr D M England
Type: Co-educational Boarding and
Day 3–13
No of pupils: B64 G39
No of Boarders: F10 W25
Fees: (September 00) F/WB £6090 –
£7350 Day £2000 – £5610
Special Needs: Level 2: DYP DYS
SP&LD

SOUTH YORKSHIRE

**ASHDELL PREPARATORY
SCHOOL**
266 Fulwood Road, Sheffield, South
Yorkshire S10 3BL
Tel: (0114) 266 3835
Head: Mrs J Upton
Type: Girls Day 4–11
No of pupils: G115
Fees: (September 00) Day £4425 –
£5025
Special Needs: Level 2: DYS SPLD

BIRKDALE SCHOOL
Oakholme Road, Sheffield, South
Yorkshire S10 3DH
Tel: (0114) 266 8409
Head: Mr R J Court
Type: Boys Day 4–18 (Co-ed VIth
Form)
No of pupils: B800 G28
Fees: (September 00) Day £4056 –
£5766
Special Needs: Level 2: ADD DYP DYS
SPLD

WEST YORKSHIRE

ACKWORTH SCHOOL
Ackworth, Pontefract, West
Yorkshire WF7 7LT
Tel: (01977) 611401
Head: Mr M J Dickinson
Type: Co-educational Boarding and
Day 4–18
No of pupils: 450 No of Boarders: F100
W10
Fees: (September 00) F/WB £12033
Day £3684 – £6843
Special Needs: Level 1: AUT Level 2:
DYS

ALCUIN SCHOOL
64 Woodland Lane, Leeds, West
Yorkshire LS7 4PD
Tel: (0113) 269 1173
Head: Mr J Hipshon
Type: Co-educational Day 4–11
No of pupils: B20 G31
Fees: (September 00) Day £1500
Special Needs: Level 2: ADD CP DYP
DYS MLD PH Unspecified: W

**BRADFORD GRAMMAR
SCHOOL**
Keighley Road, Bradford, West
Yorkshire BD9 4JP
Tel: (01274) 542492
Head: Mr S R Davidson
Type: Co-educational Day 7–18
No of pupils: B970 G63
Fees: (September 00) Day £4725 –
£5960
Special Needs: Level 3: ADHD DYP
DYS EPI TOU

BRONTE HOUSE SCHOOL†
Apperley Bridge, Bradford, West
Yorkshire BD10 0PQ
Tel: (0113) 250 2811
Head: Mr C B F Hall
Type: Co-educational Boarding and
Day 3–11
No of pupils: B200 G110
No of Boarders: F6
Fees: (September 00) F/WB £10380 –
£10575 Day £3990 – £5850
Special Needs: Level 2: DYS Level 3:
DYC DYP MLD

CLIFF SCHOOL
St John's Lodge, 2 Leeds Road,
Wakefield, West Yorkshire WF1 3JT
Tel: (01924) 373597
Head: Mrs K M Wallace
Type: Co-educational Day Boys 2–9
Girls 2–11
No of pupils: B64 G111
Fees: (September 00) Day £3495
Special Needs: Level 2: ASP DYP DYS
HI MLD PH SP&LD SPLD VIS
Level 3: ADD DEL EPI Unspecified:
ADHD

THE FROEBELIAN SCHOOL
Clarence Road, Horsforth, Leeds,
West Yorkshire LS18 4LB
Tel: (0113) 258 3047
Head: Mr J Tranmer
Type: Co-educational Day 3–11
No of pupils: B93 G97
Fees: (September 00) Day £2280 –
£3450
Special Needs: Level 2: DYP DYS MLD
Level 3: ASP SP&LD

GLEN HOUSE MONTESSORI SCHOOL
Cragg Vale, Hebden Bridge, West Yorkshire HX7 5SQ
Tel: (01422) 884682
Head: Ms M Scaife
Type: Co-educational Day 2–15
No of pupils: B11 G21
Fees: (September 00) Day £555 – £2775
Special Needs: Level 2: CP DYC DYP DYS EPI HI MLD PH SP&LD SPLD VIS

HUDDERSFIELD GRAMMAR SCHOOL
Royds Mount, Luck Lane, Marsh, Huddersfield, West Yorkshire HD1 4QX
Tel: (01484) 424549
Head: Mrs E J Jackson and Mrs J L Straughan
Type: Co-educational Day 3–16
No of pupils: B190 G145
Fees: (September 00) Day £2070 – £4305
Special Needs: Level 3: DYC DYP DYS SPLD

LEEDS GIRLS' HIGH SCHOOL
Headingley Lane, Leeds, West Yorkshire LS6 1BN
Tel: (0113) 274 4000
Head: Ms S Fishburn
Type: Girls Day 3–19
No of pupils: 959
Fees: (September 00) Day £3927 – £5871
Special Needs: Level 2: CP Unspecified: DYS

LEEDS ISLAMIA GIRLS' SCHOOL
Newton Hill House, Newton Hill Road, Leeds, West Yorkshire LS7 4JE
Tel: (0113) 262 4001
Head: Mrs Z Arshad
Type: Girls Day 11–16
No of pupils: 85
Fees: (September 00) Day £400 – £600
Special Needs: Unspecified: MLD

MOORFIELD SCHOOL
Wharfedale Lodge, Ben Rhydding Road, Ilkley, West Yorkshire LS29 8RL
Tel: (01943) 607285
Head: Mrs P Burton
Type: Girls Day 2–11
No of pupils: 160
Fees: (September 00) Day £645 – £3750
Special Needs: Level 2: DYS MLD SPLD Level 3: HI

MOUNT SCHOOL
3 Binham Road, Edgerton, Huddersfield, West Yorkshire HD2 2AP
Tel: (01484) 426432
Head: Mr N M Smith
Type: Co-educational Day 3–11
No of pupils: B75 G77
Fees: (September 00) Day £3045 – £3300
Special Needs: Level 2: DYS

ST AGNES PNEU SCHOOL
25 Burton Crescent, Leeds, West Yorkshire LS6 4DN
Tel: (0113) 278 6722
Head: Mrs S McMeeking
Type: Co-educational Day 2–7
No of pupils: B35 G19
Fees: (September 00) Day £2145 – £3915
Special Needs: Level 2: DYS Level 3: HI

ST HILDA'S SCHOOL
Dovecote Lane, Horbury, Wakefield, West Yorkshire WF4 6BB
Tel: (01924) 260706
Head: Mrs A R Mackenzie
Type: Co-educational Day Boys 3–7 Girls 3–11
No of pupils: B60 G95
Fees: (September 00) Day £3360 – £3516
Special Needs: Level 2: DYS

SHAW HOUSE SCHOOL
150–152 Wilmer Road, Heaton, Bradford, West Yorkshire BD9 4AH
Tel: (01274) 496299
Head: Mr R C Williams
Type: Co-educational Day 9–18
No of pupils: B57 G55
Fees: (September 00) Day £3000 – £4500
Special Needs: Unspecified: DYS MLD

WOODHOUSE GROVE SCHOOL†
Apperley Bridge, West Yorkshire BD10 0NR
Tel: (0113) 250 2477
Head: Mr D C Humphreys
Type: Co-educational Boarding and Day 11–18
No of pupils: B385 G229
No of Boarders: F80 W15
Fees: (September 00) FB £11610 – £11700 Day £6690 – £6795
Special Needs: Unspecified: DYS MLD

NORTHERN IRELAND

COUNTY ANTRIM

BELFAST ROYAL ACADEMY
7 Cliftonville Road, Belfast, County
Antrim BT14 6JL
Tel: (028) 9074 0423
Head: Mr W S F Young
Type: Co-educational Day 4–19
No of pupils: B781 G813
Fees: (September 00) On application
Special Needs: Level 2: DYS
Unspecified: VIS

COUNTY DOWN

BANGOR GRAMMAR SCHOOL
13 College Avenue, Bangor, County
Down BT20 5HJ
Tel: (028) 9147 3734
Head: Dr N D Argent
Type: Boys Day 11–18
No of pupils: 913
Fees: (September 00) Day £80 – £450
Special Needs: Level 2: DYS Level 3:
EBD EPI HI PH VIS

SCOTLAND

ABERDEENSHIRE

ABERDEEN WALDORF SCHOOL
Craigton Road, Cults, Aberdeen,
Aberdeenshire AB15 9QD
Tel: (01224) 869932
Head: Mr P Hausmann
Type: Co-educational Day 3–16
No of pupils: B79 G58
Fees: (September 00) Day £1000 –
£5265
Special Needs: Level 2: DYP DYS
Level 3: EBD EPI HI MLD
Unspecified: SPLD

ST MARGARET'S SCHOOL FOR GIRLS
17 Albyn Place, Aberdeen AB10 1RU
Tel: (01224) 584466
Head: Miss F E G Carey
Type: Girls Day 3–18 (Boys 3–5)
No of pupils: B2 G388
Fees: (September 00) Day £1614 –
£5316
Special Needs: Level 2: ADD ADHD
ASP CP DYC DYP DYS EBD HI SPLD
Level 3: EPI SP&LD

THE HIGH SCHOOL OF DUNDEE
Euclid Crescent, Dundee, London
DD1 1HU
Tel: (01382) 202921
Head: Mr A M Duncan
Type: Co-educational Day 5–18
No of pupils: B575 G521
Fees: (September 00) Day £3744 –
£5325
Special Needs: Level 2: ADHD DYC
DYP DYS SPLD

ANGUS

LATHALLAN SCHOOL
Brotherton Castle, Johnshaven,
Montrose, Angus DD10 0HN
Tel: (01561) 362220
Head: Mr P Platts-Martin
Type: Co-educational Boarding and
Day 3–13
No of pupils: B90 G60
No of Boarders: F6 W38
Fees: (September 00) FB £10869 WB
£10626 Day £4794
Special Needs: Unspecified: DYS EPI
SPLD

ARGYLL AND BUTE

LOMOND SCHOOL
10 Stafford Street, Helensburgh,
Argyll and Bute G84 9JX
Tel: (01436) 672476
Head: Mr A D Macdonald
Type: Co-educational Day and
Boarding 3–19
No of pupils: B247 G223
No of Boarders: F60 W10
Fees: (September 00) FB £11550 –
£12420 WB £11430 – £12360 Day
£1845 – £5820
Special Needs: Unspecified: DYC DYS
PH SPLD

SOUTH AYRSHIRE

WELLINGTON SCHOOL
Carleton Turrets, Ayr, South Ayrshire
KA7 2XH
Tel: (01292) 269321
Head: Mrs D A Gardner
Type: Co-educational Day 3–18
No of pupils: B250 G270
Fees: (September 00) Day £1800 –
£6060
Special Needs: Level 2: DYS MLD
Level 3: DYP

BANFFSHIRE

ABERLOUR HOUSE
Aberlour, Banffshire AB38 9LJ
Tel: (01340) 871267
Head: Mr N W Gardner and Mrs C E
Gardner
Type: Co-educational Boarding and
Day 8–13
No of pupils: B46 G40
No of Boarders: F60
Fees: (September 00) FB £10836 Day
£7560
Special Needs: Level 2: DYS

CLACKMANNANSHIRE

DOLLAR ACADEMY
Dollar, Clackmannanshire FK14 7DU
Tel: (01259) 742511
Head: Mr J S Robertson
Type: Co-educational Day and
Boarding 5–18
No of pupils: B607 G536
No of Boarders: F86 W15
Fees: (September 00) FB £10656 –
£11988 WB £10026 – £11358 Day
£4068 – £5400
Special Needs: Unspecified: ADD
ADHD ASP DYC DYP DYS EBD SPLD
TOU

FIFE

ST KATHARINES PREPARATORY SCHOOL

The Pends, St Andrews, Fife
KY16 9RB
Tel: (01334) 460470
Head: Mrs J Gibson
Type: Co-educational Boarding and
Day 3–12
No of pupils: B22 G49
No of Boarders: F7
Fees: (September 00) FB £11490 WB
£10950 Day £1815 – £6525
Special Needs: Level 2: DYS SPLD

ST LEONARDS SCHOOL & ST LEONARDS VITH FORM COLLEGE

St Andrews, Fife KY16 9QJ
Tel: (01334) 472126
Head: Mrs W A Bellars
Type: Co-educational Boarding and
Day 12–19
No of pupils: B15 G212
No of Boarders: F148
Fees: (September 00) FB £15150 Day
£8490
Special Needs: Level 2: DYS

GLASGOW

CRAIGHOLME SCHOOL

72 St Andrews Drive, Glasgow
G41 4HS
Tel: (0141) 427 0375
Head: Mrs G Burt
Type: Girls Day 3–18 (Boys 3–5)
No of pupils: B13 G485
Fees: (September 00) Day £2250 –
£5235
Special Needs: Level 2: DYS

THE GLASGOW ACADEMY

Colebrooke Street, Glasgow G12 8HE
Tel: (0141) 334 8558
Head: Mr D Comins
Type: Co-educational Day 2–18
No of pupils: B651 G454
Fees: (September 00) Day £3321 –
£5424
Special Needs: Unspecified: DYS

LANARKSHIRE

HAMILTON COLLEGE

Bothwell Road, Hamilton,
Lanarkshire ML3 0AY
Tel: (01698) 282700
Head: Mr A J Leach
Type: Co-educational Day 3–18
No of pupils: B439 G342
Fees: (September 00) Day £2994 –
£3972
Special Needs: Level 2: ASP DEL DYC
DYP DYS MLD SP&LD SPLD

SOUTH LANARKSHIRE

FERNHILL SCHOOL
Fernbrae Avenue, Rutherglen, South
Lanarkshire G73 4SG
Tel: (0141) 634 2674
Head: Mrs L M McLay
Type: Girls Day 4–18 (Boys 4–11)
No of pupils: B50 G260
Fees: (September 00) Day £3390 –
£4095
Special Needs: Unspecified: DYS MLD

LOTHIAN

**BASIL PATERSON TUTORIAL
COLLEGE**
Dugdale-McAdam House, 23
Abercromby Place, Edinburgh,
Lothian EH3 6QE
Tel: (0131) 556 7698
Head: Mrs I P Shewan
Type: Co-educational Day 14+
No of pupils: 35
Fees: (September 00) Day £4455 –
£9900
Special Needs: Level 2: DYP DYS
Level 3: ADD ASP HI VIS

CLIFTON HALL
Newbridge, Lothian EH28 8LQ
Tel: (0131) 333 1359
Head: Mr M Adams
Type: Co-educational Day 3–11
No of pupils: B74 G70
Fees: (September 00) Day £320 –
£5820
Special Needs: Level 2: DYS SP&LD
Level 3: HI

THE COMPASS SCHOOL
West Road, Haddington, Lothian
EH41 3RD
Tel: (01620) 822642
Head: Mr M Becher
Type: Co-educational Day 4–11
No of pupils: B57 G49
Fees: (September 00) Day £2610 –
£4245
Special Needs: Level 2: DYS MLD

DUNEDIN SCHOOL
5 Gilmerton Road, Edinburgh,
Lothian EH16 5TY
Tel: (0131) 664 1328
Head: Mrs J Foulner
Type: Co-educational Day 7–17
No of pupils: B14 G6
Fees: (September 00) Day £7000 –
£7700
Special Needs: Level 3: ASP DEL DYP
EBD MLD SPLD Unspecified: W

GEORGE HERIOT'S SCHOOL
Lauriston Place, Edinburgh, Lothian
EH3 9EQ
Tel: (0131) 229 7263
Head: Mr A G Hector
Type: Co-educational Day 4–18
No of pupils: B912 G606
Fees: (September 00) Day £3378 –
£5106
Special Needs: Level 2: DYP DYS
SPLD

LORETTO JUNIOR SCHOOL
North Esk Lodge, Musselburgh,
Lothian EH21 6JA
Tel: (0131) 653 4570
Head: Mr M Mavor
Type: Co-educational Boarding and
Day 5–13
No of pupils: B50 G50
No of Boarders: F30
Fees: (September 00) Day £1195 –
£3200
Special Needs: Level 2: DYS SPLD
Unspecified: HI

**MERCHISTON CASTLE
SCHOOL†**
Colinton, Edinburgh, Lothian
EH13 0PU
Tel: (0131) 312 2200
Head: Mr A R Hunter
Type: Boys Boarding and Day 10–18
No of pupils: 380 *No of Boarders:* F260
Fees: (September 00) FB £10500 –
£15300 Day £6900 – £10350
Special Needs: Level 1: DYS HI MLD
SPLD Level 3: VIS Unspecified: DYP

ST MARGARET'S SCHOOL
East Suffolk Road, Edinburgh,
Lothian EH16 5PJ
Tel: (0131) 668 1986
Head: Miss A Mitchell
Type: Girls Day and Boarding 3–18
(Boys 3–8)
No of pupils: B21 G620
No of Boarders: F25 W10
Fees: (September 00) FB £9225 –
£11085 WB £8260 – £11085 Day
£2065 – £5310
Special Needs: Level 1: DYP DYS EBD
EPI HI MLD PH PMLD SLD SPLD VIS

**STEWART'S MELVILLE
COLLEGE**
Queensferry Road, Edinburgh,
Lothian EH4 3EZ
Tel: (0131) 332 7925
Head: Mr J N D Gray
Type: Boys Day and Boarding 12–18
No of pupils: B748 *No of Boarders:* F13
Fees: (September 00) FB £11424 Day
£5454 – £5775
Special Needs: Level 2: DYS

PERTHSHIRE

CRAIGCLOWAN PREPARATORY SCHOOL
Edinburgh Road, Perth, Perthshire
PH2 8PS
Tel: (01738) 626310
Head: Mr M E Beale
Type: Co-educational Day 4–13
No of pupils: B130 G130
Fees: (September 00) Day £5400
Special Needs: Level 1: DYS SPLD
Level 2: ADD ASP

KILGRASTON (A SACRED HEART SCHOOL)
Bridge of Earn, Perth, Perthshire
PH2 9BQ
Tel: (01738) 812257
Head: Mrs J L Austin
Type: Girls Boarding and Day 5–18
(Boys day 2–8)
No of pupils: B15 G219
No of Boarders: F109
Fees: (September 00) F/WB £11310 –
£13560 Day £4605 – £7995
Special Needs: Level 2: ADD ADHD
ASP DEL DYC DYP DYS PH SPLD
Level 3: EBD EPI

QUEEN VICTORIA SCHOOL
Dunblane, Perthshire FK15 0JY
Tel: (01786) 822288
Head: Mr B Raine
Type: Co-educational Boarding 11–18
No of pupils: B182 G91
No of Boarders: F273
Fees: (September 00) FB £603 – £669
Special Needs: Level 2: ADD ADHD
DYC DYP DYS EBD HI PH SPLD

STRATHALLAN SCHOOL
Forgandenny, Perth, Perthshire
PH2 9EG
Tel: (01738) 812546
Head: Mr B K Thompson
Type: Co-educational Boarding 10–18
No of pupils: B269 G166
No of Boarders: F353
Fees: (September 00) FB £11010 –
£15024 Day £7290 – £10350
Special Needs: Level 2: DYS SPLD
Level 3: ADD ASP DYP EBD EPI HI
SP&LD

ROXBURGHSHIRE

ST MARY'S PREPARATORY SCHOOL
Abbey Park, Melrose, Roxburghshire
TD6 9LN
Tel: (01896) 822517
Head: Mr J Brett
Type: Co-educational Boarding and
Day 4–13
No of pupils: B56 G60
No of Boarders: W6
Fees: (September 00) FB £10230 WB
£10050 Day £4725 – £7110
Special Needs: Level 2: DYC DYP DYS
SPLD Level 3: ADD ADHD
Unspecified: MLD

WALES

CARDIFF

THE CATHEDRAL SCHOOL
Llandaff, Cardiff CF5 2YH
Tel: (029) 2056 3179
Head: Mr P L Gray
Type: Co-educational Day 3–16
No of pupils: B296 G100
Fees: (September 00) Day £3870 –
£5835
Special Needs: Level 2: DYS

**HOWELL'S SCHOOL,
LLANDAFF GDST**
Cardiff Road, Llandaff, Cardiff
CF5 2YD
Tel: (029) 2056 2019
Head: Mrs J Fitz
Type: Girls Day 3–18
No of pupils: 729
Fees: (September 00) Day £2940 –
£5040
Special Needs: Level 2: DYS

CARMARTHENSHIRE

LLANDOVERY COLLEGE†
Llandovery, Carmarthenshire
SA20 0EE
Tel: (01550) 723000
Head: Mr P A Hogan
Type: Co-educational Boarding and
Day 11–18
No of pupils: B132 G68
No of Boarders: F82 W31
Fees: (September 00) F/WB £12468
Day £8280
Special Needs: Level 1: DYC DYP DYS
SPLD Level 3: MLD

CONWY

LYNDON SCHOOL
Grosvenor Road, Colwyn Bay,
Conwy LL29 7YF
Tel: (01492) 532347
Head: Mr M B Collins
Type: Co-educational Day 2–11
No of pupils: B37 G50
Fees: (January 01) Day £1830 –
£3810
Special Needs: Level 2: ADD ADHD
DYC DYP DYS MLD SP&LD SPLD
VIS Unspecified: PH

ST DAVID'S COLLEGE†
Llandudno, Conwy LL30 1RD
Tel: (01492) 875974
Head: Mr W Seymour
Type: Co-educational Boarding and
Day 11–18
No of pupils: B200 G50
No of Boarders: F160
Fees: (September 00) FB £11505 –
£13638 Day £7482 – £9273
Special Needs: Level 1: ASP DYC DYP
DYS SPLD

DENBIGHSHIRE

HOWELL'S SCHOOL
Denbigh, Denbighshire LL16 3EN
Tel: (01745) 813631
Head: Mrs L Robinson
Type: Girls Boarding and Day 3–18
No of pupils: G330 *No of Boarders:* F90
W20
Fees: (September 00) FB £7095 –
£11085 Day £2925 – £7485
Special Needs: Level 2: DYS HI TOU
Unspecified: VIS

PEMBROKESHIRE

**HAYLETT GRANGE
PREPARATORY SCHOOL**
Merlin's Bridge, Haverfordwest,
Pembrokeshire SA62 4LA
Tel: (01437) 762472
Head: Mr M J Gilbert
Type: Co-educational Day 2–12
No of pupils: B50 G50
Fees: (September 00) Day £1995 –
£2595
Special Needs: Level 2: ADD ADHD
DYC DYS

POWYS

CHRIST COLLEGE
Brecon, Powys LD3 8AG
Tel: (01874) 623359
Head: Mr D P Jones
Type: Co-educational Boarding and
Day 11–18
No of pupils: B220 G90
No of Boarders: F190 W44
Fees: (September 00) F/WB £9999 –
£12798 Day £7500 – £9918
Special Needs: Level 2: DYP DYS
SPLD Level 3: EPI HI

SWANSEA

CRAIG-Y-NOS SCHOOL
Clyne Common, Bishopston,
Swansea SA3 3JB
Tel: (01792) 234288
Head: Mr G W Fursland
Type: Co-educational Day 2–11
No of pupils: B85 G62
Fees: (September 00) On application
Special Needs: Level 2: DYS

4.3
Profiles of Independent Mainstream Schools with Specialist Provision

The schools in this section offer varying levels of help for students with special needs, from additional tuition on a limited withdrawal basis to specialist units and teaching programmes. For specific details parents should contact individual schools direct.

Akeley Wood School

Akeley Wood, Buckingham MK18 3AE
Tel: 01280 814110

Principal W H Wilcox
Religious denomination Non-denominational
Special needs provision DYS
Age range 2½–18
Girls 258   *Boys* 441
Fees per annum £3,870–£5,700

Akeley Wood School has always helped children with dyslexia and related problems.
The pupils are withdrawn from the mainstream timetable for a few hours per week to attend these comprehensive sessions following individual education plans to include study skills, cross curriculum teaching, spelling programmes, reading strategies and writing skills.

Although the school bears much of the cost of employing the experienced staff, an extra charge has to be made for this specialised work. For the more seriously handicapped we have now opened the Charmandean Dyslexia Centre which tackles problems met by children more seriously affected by dyslexia and related learning problems.
Mrs Hawkins is the Head Teacher in charge of organising and supervising the work.
Details of our facilities are available from the school secretary.

Bredon School

Pull Court, Bushley, Tewkesbury, Gloucestershire GL20 6AH
Tel: 01684 293156   Fax: 01684 298008
E-mail: enquiries@bredonschool.worcs.sch.uk   enquiries@bredonschool.co.uk
Website: www.bredonschool.ik.org   www.boardingschools.com

Head Mr M J Newby
Founded 1962
School status DfEE approved independent
Religious denomination Church of England
Member of ISA, BSA, DYS
Special needs provision DYC, DYP, DYS, SP&LD, SPLD
Age range 8–18   *Boarding from* 8–18
No of pupils (day) 78   *boarding (full)* 75
(weekly) 42
Girls 58   *Boys* 137
Junior 30   *Senior* 131   *Sixth Form* 34
Fees per annum (boarding) (full) £10,275–£14,850   *(weekly)* £9,975–£14,550   *(day)* £5,250–£10,125

Bredon is a co-educational independent school for 200 pupils with full and weekly boarders

and day pupils. The school stands in attractive rural surroundings near the River Severn, on the Worcestershire and Gloucestershire borders in an estate of 85 acres, which includes a school farm. Bredon follows the National Curriculum at all Key Stages and students will sit the national assessment tests at the appropriate stages. In addition Bredon offers GNVQ vocational programmes at Foundation, Intermediate and Advanced level. Some pupils are able to benefit from the experience of the Learning Support Centre staff and the school is CReSTeD registered.

Cokethorpe School

Witney, Oxfordshire OX29 7PU
Tel: (01993) 703921   Fax: (01993) 773499
E-mail: admin@cokethorpe.org   Website: www.cokethorpe.org

Head P J S Cantwell
Founded 1957
School status Co-educational independent boarding and day
Religious denomination Inter-denominational
Member of SHMIS, GBA; *accredited by* DfEE, ISC
Special needs provision DEL, DYC, DYS, DYP, MLD, PH, SP&LD, SPLD
Age range 7–18; *boarders from* 10 (boys only)
No of pupils (day) 420; *(boarding)* 60
Girls 160; *boys* 320
Junior 160; *Senior* 260; *Sixth Form* 60
Fees per annum (full and weekly boarding) £9,810–£14,700; *(day)* £4,950–£8,850

A broad academic and vocational curriculum is followed to GCSE. Traditional A Levels and GNVQs are available to the Sixth Form. Small classes provide everyone with the opportunity to fulfil their potential. Extra help is available in the learning support department. Entry requirements are interview and headteacher's report at the age of 7 and 9, interview and assessment at 11, 13 and 16 years.
Examinations: GCSE, A/S Level, A2 and GNVQ level 2 and 3. New buildings house the library, art and ceramics, information technology and design and technology. There are also modern laboratories, Music School and Sixth Form facilities. The new Sports Hall provides for a wide range of indoor sports. There is a wide range of extra-curricular activities within 50 acres of grounds, and a new network of 200 PCs are controlled from the Learning and Resource Centre.

Scholarships are awarded on entrance assessment. Bursaries are available on application for details.

Ellesmere College

Ellesmere, Shropshire SY12 9AB
Tel: 01691 622321   Fax: 01691 623286
E-mail: admin@ellesmere.biblio.net

Head Mr B J Wignall MA MIMgt
Founded 1884
School status Independent co-educational boarding and day
Religious denomination Church of England
Member of HMC Woodard Corporation and corporate member of BDA
Accredited by CreSTeD
Special needs provision ADD, ADHD, DYC, DYP, DYS, SPLD
Age range 9–18 Boarding from 11
No of pupils 465 *(boarding) (full)* 164
Junior 150   *Senior* 315   *Sixth Form* 105
Boys 317   *Girls* 148
Fees per annum (boarding) (full) £13,800; *(day)* £9,141

Ellesmere College is a school of 465 boys and girls set in its own grounds of 70 acres of rural North Shropshire. There are approximately 150 children in the Lower School (9–13). There are 315 in the 13–18 range of whom 164 are boarders. Boarding accommodation has benefited from a recent multi-million pound refurbishment programme and is of the highest quality. There are 105 pupils in the Sixth Form. The college has provided high quality dyslexia support for 30 years; it is a CreSTeD category B school and is in corporate membership of the British Dyslexia Association.

Grenville College

Bideford, Devon EX39 3JR
Tel: 01237 472212   Fax: 01237 477020
E-mail: info@grenville.devon.sch.uk   Website: www.grenville.devon.sch.uk

Head Dr Michael Cane BSc, PhD, MRSC
Founded 1954
Needs for which school offers provision DYS
School status Independent
Religious denomination Church of England
Members of GBA, SHMIS, ISA, CReSTeD
Age range 2½–19   *Boarders from* 8
No of pupils (day) 275   *(boarding)* 95
Girls 158   *Boys* 212
Junior 98   *Senior* 272   *Sixth Form* 73
Fees per annum (boarding) (full) £10,149–
£13,071 *(weekly)* £7,608–£9,801 *(day)*
£2,715–£6,471

Pupils are taught in small groups with their own individual learning programmes, leading to GCSE, GNVQ or A level. The Dyslexia Unit, established in 1969, aims to provide specialist teaching support and to encourage pupils to fulfil their potential.

Entry at all levels is by report and interview. Scholarship and bursary enquiries are welcomed.

The boarding houses stand in 40 acres of gardens and parkland providing excellent opportunities for sporting and extra-curricular activities. The school's coastal location and proximity to Dartmoor and Exmoor make watersports and outdoor pursuits particularly popular.

Grenville College provide high quality education in a caring Christian community.

North Bridge House School

1 Gloucester Avenue, London NW1 7AB
Tel: 020 7267 6266   Fax: 020 7267 0071

Principal W H Wilcox
Founded 1939
School status Co-educational independent day
Religious denomination Non-denominational
Special needs provision DYS
Age range 2 yrs 9 mts–18
Sixth Form opens in September 2001
No of pupils 950
Junior 720   *Senior* 230
Girls 397   *Boys* 463
Fees per annum Tuition fees £6,900 plus
Dyslexia tuition, lunch and extras

North Bridge House School offers withdrawal tuition for pupils between 7 and 16 years who have special educational needs or who have been classified as dyslexic by educational psychologists.

The pupils are withdrawn from the mainstream timetable for a few hours each week to attend these comprehensive sessions following individual educational plans to include study skills, cross curriculum teaching, spelling programmes, reading strategies and writing skills.

The pupils are taught by a dedicated teacher in a purpose-built department fully equipped with excellent computer facilities.

Mrs Hawkins is the Head Teacher in charge of organising and supervising the work.

Although the school bears much of the cost of employing the experienced staff, an extra charge has to be made – in addition to the school fees – for this specialised work.

St Mary's School, Wantage

Newbury Street, Wantage, Oxfordshire OX12 8BZ
Tel: (01235) 763571   Fax: (01235) 760467
E-mail: stmarysw@rmplc.co.uk

Head Mrs S Sowden BSc, AKC
Founded 1873
Type Girls' independent senior boarding and day
Religious denomination Church of England
Special needs provision DYC, DYS, DYP, MLD, EPI, SPLD
Age range 11–18; *boarders from* 11
No of pupils (day) 17; *(boarding)* 174
Senior 134; *Sixth Form* 57
Fees per annum (full boarding) £15,075; *(day)* £10,050

As a Christian foundation, we aim to give each girl a stable set of values, ensuring the best possible preparation for life beyond the School. Strong academic results are achieved without excessive pressure. Particular strengths are in Art, Music and ICT. A new wireless computer system means that the girls use their laptops anywhere on the 13 acre campus to contact their tutors, central printers, or their parents via the internet. A specialist support unit provides for all special needs including the gifted child and those with dyslexia and other specific learning difficulties.

We take weekends seriously. Girls are full-time boarders or local day girls (who may sleep any number of nights on a regular or occasional basis).

Stanbridge Earls

Romsey, Hampshire SO51 0ZS
Tel: (01794) 516777   Fax: (01794) 511201
E-mail: stanbridgesec@aol.com

Head N R Hall BSc (London)
Founded 1952
Type Co-educational senior boarding and day
Religious denomination Inter-denominational
Special needs provision DYS, DYC, DYP, SP&LD, ASP, DEL, ADD, ADHD
Member of GBA, SHMIS, BSA; *corporate member* British Dyslexia Association, CReSTeD
Age range 11–18; *boarders from* 11
No of pupils (day) 21; *(boarding)* 167
Girls 42; *boys* 148
Junior 39; *Senior* 120; *Sixth Form* 34
Fees per annum (boarding) £13,650–£15,000; *(day)* £10,200–£11,100
Average size of class: 10
Teacher:pupil ratio: 1:6

Curriculum: all the traditional subjects are offered up to GCSE level but there is a great variety of alternatives designed to develop the strengths and interest of every pupil, such as Drama, Craft, Design and Technology, Motor Vehicle Studies, and Photography. Thirteen subjects are available at A Level. Many pupils are dyslexic but everyone takes GCSE.

Entry requirements and procedures: by interview, school report and where appropriate educational psychologists' report.

Academic and leisure facilities available: the School has excellent facilities for all academic subjects. Accelerated learning centre, with 16 experienced specialist teachers, for those with dyslexia. Maths skills centre, with 5 specialist staff, for those with dyscalculia. There is a wide choice of games and the School has a large sports hall, indoor swimming pool, squash courts, floodlit tennis courts, vehicle engineering workshops and playing fields. Sailing is done from Lymington.

The School is registered charity number 307342.

Wycliffe College

Stonehouse, Gloucestershire GL10 2JQ
Tel: (01453) 822432   Fax: (01453) 827634
E-mail: senior@wycliffe.co.uk   Web site: www.gabbitas.net

Head Dr R A Collins MA, DPhil
Founded 1882
Type Co-educational independent senior boarding and day
Religious denomination Inter-denominational
Member of HMC, ISIS, GBA
Special needs provision Mild ADHD, ASP, DYS, MLD
Age range 13–18; *boarders from* 13
No of pupils (day) 132; *(boarding)* 264
Girls 141; *boys* 255
Sixth Form 209
Fees per annum (boarding) £11,160–£14,400; *(day)* £10,755 *Sixth form (boarding)* £15,495–£18,600 *(day)* £11,160–£14,400

Aims and objectives of special educational needs provision: to provide a continuum of special educational needs in mainstream education for children with mild and moderate learning difficulties. To achieve this, we maintain close consultation and partnership with parents and pupils, evaluating and taking into account pupils preferred learning styles and strengths, as well as their learning difficulties.

SEN Specialists and Facilities
We provide a range of facilities, these include:
- Individual Learning Plans, focusing on learning styles, strategies and target setting
- Individual Education Plans to address the specific needs and difficulties of students with SENs
- Differentiated work for students with SpLDs
- Specialist in-class support where needed
- Extra tuition by specialist teachers, in small groups or on a one to one basis, to improve literacy/numeracy skills
- Specialist tuition to improve study skills, organisation and examination technique
- A flexible approach to the curriculum at GCSE
- Small class sizes

Assessment and Screening
All students are screened for dyslexia in Years R, 3, 7, 9, FY, and D6. Pupils joining the school in other years are screened upon entry. These results are analysed and pupils showing signs of special educational needs are placed on the SEN register. The school then adopts a two-staged approach to intervention. Their progress is closely monitored and reviewed by both teachers and the Special Educational Needs Co-ordinator (SENCO). Students whose difficulties persist are assessed by educational psychologist.

Admission Arrangements
The school does not operate a selective admissions policy and has a broad ability intake. Admission is by Common Entrance or by Wycliffe Entrance exam. However, in order to ensure that our SEN provision can match the child's need, the SENCO will normally meet parents of prospective entrants to the school, where the child has, or may have, special educational needs. The child's difficulties will be discussed at this meeting, and they may be assessed to determine their ability to cope with the mainstream education offered at Wycliffe. Previous school records are used in the pre-entry assessment. In some cases, the school may require an Educational Psychologist's assessment, before an offer of a place at the school can be confirmed.

Wycliffe College incorporated is a Registered Charity No 311714

4.4
Index of Independent Mainstream Schools with Specialist Provision Classified by Special Need

Note: Schools in London are identified by postal areas.

Asperger's Syndrome

Level 1

Danes Hill Preparatory School, Surrey
Kingsley Preparatory School,
  West Midlands
St David's College, Conwy

St Mary's Westbrook, Kent
Stanbridge Earls School, Hampshire
Woodside Park International School,
  N11

Level 2

Aldenham School, Hertfordshire
All Hallows, Somerset
All Saints School, Norfolk
Ashbourne PNEU School, Derbyshire
Avon House, Essex
Beech Hall School, Cheshire
Bentham Grammar School, Lancashire
Broadwater Manor School, West Sussex
Cambridge Centre for VIth Form Studies
  (CCSS), Cambridgeshire
Chinthurst School, Surrey
Cliff School, West Yorkshire
Craigclowan Preparatory School,
  Perthshire
Dorchester Preparatory School, Dorset
Dulwich College, SE21
The Elms, Worcestershire
Essendene Lodge School, Surrey
Friends' School, Essex
Green Hill School, Worcestershire

Hamilton College, Lanarkshire
Heathcote School, Essex
Kilgraston (A Sacred Heart School),
  Perthshire
King William's College, Isle of Man
King's School, Somerset
Kingsmead School, Merseyside
Manor Preparatory School, Oxfordshire
The Margaret Allen School,
  Herefordshire
Oxford Tutorial College, Oxfordshire
Polam Hall, County Durham
Royal Alexandra and Albert School,
  Surrey
St Andrew's Montessori School,
  Hertfordshire
St Bees School, Cumbria
St Edmund's Junior School, Kent
St George's College, Surrey
St Helen's College, Middlesex

St Margaret's School for Girls, Aberdeenshire
St Michael's School, Kent
St Peter & St Paul School, Derbyshire
St Ursula's High School, Bristol

Tashbar Primary School, Greater Manchester
Westmont School, Isle of Wight
Wilton Grange School, Hartlepool
Yarrells School, Dorset

Level 3

Ballard Preparatory School, Hampshire
Basil Paterson Tutorial College, Lothian
Bow School, County Durham
Carleton House Preparatory School, Merseyside
Catteral Hall, North Yorkshire
Collingham, SW5
Copthill School, Lincolnshire
Dagfa House School, Nottinghamshire
Derby Independent Grammar School, Derbyshire
Duncombe School, Hertfordshire
Dunedin School, Lothian
Elmwood Montessori School, W4
Eveline Day School, SW17
The Froebelian School, West Yorkshire
Hazlegrove (King's Bruton Preparatory School), Somerset
Hillcroft Preparatory School, Suffolk
The King's School, Nottinghamshire
Lochinver House School, Hertfordshire
The Mount School, NW7
Orchard House School, W4
Oswestry School, Shropshire

Playdays Nursery/School and Montessori College, SW19
Rossholme School, Somerset
The Royal High School, North East Somerset
Royal School Haslemere, Surrey
The Ryleys, Cheshire
St Andrew's School, Kent
St Anselm's, Derbyshire
St Columba's College, Hertfordshire
St Hilda's School, Essex
St Joseph's in the Park, Hertfordshire
St Mary's School, Cambridgeshire
St Peter's School, West Sussex
South Hills School, Wiltshire
Strathallan School, Perthshire
Taunton School, Somerset
Thorpe House School, Buckinghamshire
Upton House School, Berkshire
Vernon Lodge Preparatory School, Staffordshire
Woodford Prep & Nursery School, Cheshire
Worksop College, Nottinghamshire

Unspecified

Canbury School, Surrey
Cransley School, Cheshire
Dollar Academy, Clackmannanshire
The Dormer House PNEU School, Gloucestershire
First Impressions Montessori Schools, Hertfordshire
Littlefield School, Hampshire

Marlin Montessori School, Hertfordshire
Milton Abbey School, Dorset
Newlands School, Tyne and Wear
Norfolk Lodge Nursery & Preparatory School, Hertfordshire
St Brandon's School, Somerset
St Edmund's School, Kent
The Tuition Centre, NW4
Wycliffe College, Gloucestershire

Attention Deficit Disorder

Level 1

Brackenfield School, North Yorkshire
Bredon School, Gloucestershire
Cambridge Arts & Sciences (CATS),
    Cambridgeshire
Ellesmere College, Shropshire
Felsted School, Essex
Kelly College, Devon
Kingsley Preparatory School,
    West Midlands
Long Close School, Berkshire
Northampton Christian School,
    Northamptonshire
Rossall School, Lancashire
St Margaret's Junior School Convent of
    Mercy, West Sussex
Woodside Park International School,
    N11

Level 2

Abbotsholme School, Staffordshire
Alcuin School, West Yorkshire
All Hallows, Somerset
Ampleforth College, North Yorkshire
Arnold School, Lancashire
Ashbourne PNEU School, Derbyshire
Bedford School, Bedfordshire
Bedgebury School, Kent
Beech Hall School, Cheshire
Belmont (Mill Hill Junior School), NW7
Bentham Grammar School, Lancashire
Birkdale School, South Yorkshire
Broadwater Manor School, West Sussex
Catteral Hall, North Yorkshire
Chinthurst School, Surrey
Craigclowan Preparatory School,
    Perthshire
Dorchester Preparatory School, Dorset
Dover College, Kent
Dulwich College, SE21
Durham School, County Durham
The Elms, Worcestershire
Essendene Lodge School, Surrey
The Fen Preparatory School, Lincolnshire
Forres Sandle Manor, Hampshire
Green Hill School, Worcestershire
Greenfield School, Surrey
Halstead Preparatory School, Surrey
Haylett Grange Preparatory School,
    Pembrokeshire
Heathcote School, Essex
Hethersett Old Hall School, Norfolk
Hordle Walhampton School, Hampshire
Hurst Lodge, Berkshire
Kilgraston (A Sacred Heart School),
    Perthshire
King William's College, Isle of Man
Kingsmead School, Merseyside
Kingswood College at Scarisbrick Hall,
    Lancashire
Langley School, Norfolk
Leicester Grammar Junior School,
    Leicestershire
Lyndon School, Conwy
Manor Preparatory School, Oxfordshire
Mansfield Preparatory School,
    Nottinghamshire
Marymount International School, Surrey
Mount St Mary's College, Derbyshire
New Hall School, Essex
Northbourne Park School, Kent
Northcote Lodge, SW11
Oakhill College, Lancashire
Oswestry School, Shropshire
Our Lady's Preparatory School, Berkshire
Oxford Tutorial College, Oxfordshire
Queen Victoria School, Perthshire
Royal Alexandra and Albert School, Surrey
Rydes Hill Preparatory School, Surrey
St Aubyn's, East Sussex

St Bees School, Cumbria
St Columba's College, Hertfordshire
St Crispin's School, Leicestershire
St Edmund's Junior School, Kent
St Hilary's School, Surrey
St Joseph's Convent, Derbyshire
St Joseph's in the Park, Hertfordshire
St Margaret's School for Girls,
 Aberdeenshire
St Mary's Westbrook, Kent

St Michael's, Devon
St Michael's School, Kent
St Ursula's High School, Bristol
The Schiller Academy, SE1
Shebbear College, Devon
Slindon College, West Sussex
Stanbridge Earls School, Hampshire
Steephill School, Kent
Woodcote House School, Surrey
Worth School, West Sussex

Level 3

Ashgrove School, Kent
Attenborough Preparatory School,
 Nottinghamshire
Avon House, Essex
Ballard Preparatory School, Hampshire
Basil Paterson Tutorial College, Lothian
Belmont Grosvenor School,
 North Yorkshire
Bow School, County Durham
Bromsgrove School, Worcestershire
Carleton House Preparatory School,
 Merseyside
Cliff School, West Yorkshire
Clifton College, Bristol
Collingham, SW5
Copthorne School, West Sussex
Culford School, Suffolk
Dagfa House School, Nottinghamshire
Danes Hill Preparatory School, Surrey
Derby Independent Grammar School,
 Derbyshire
Duke of York's Royal Military School, Kent
Duncombe School, Hertfordshire
Durlston Court, Hampshire
Elmwood Montessori School, W4
Eversfield Preparatory School,
 West Midlands
Giggleswick School, North Yorkshire
The Hampshire Schools (Kensington
 Gardens), W2
The Hampshire Schools (Knightsbridge
 Under School), SW7

The Hampshire Schools (Knightsbridge
 Upper School), SW7
Hampstead Hill Pre-Preparatory & Nursery
 School, NW3
Harpenden Preparatory School,
 Hertfordshire
Hazlegrove (King's Bruton Preparatory
 School), Somerset
Hillcroft Preparatory School, Suffolk
The King's School, Cheshire
King's School, Somerset
The King's School, Nottinghamshire
Laverock School, Surrey
Lochinver House School, Hertfordshire
Lubavitch House Senior School for Girls,
 N16
Luckley-Oakfield School, Berkshire
Malvern College, Worcestershire
Monkton Combe School,
 North East Somerset
Mostyn House School, Cheshire
The Mount School, NW7
The New Beacon, Kent
New West Preston Manor Nursery School,
 West Sussex
Newlands School, Tyne and Wear
North Cestrian Grammar School, Cheshire
The Park School, Somerset
Playdays Nursery/School and Montessori
 College, SW19
Pocklington Montessori School, East
 Riding of Yorkshire

Princethorpe College, Warwickshire
Prior Park Preparatory School, Wiltshire
Ramillies Hall School, Cheshire
The Royal High School,
    North East Somerset
The Ryleys, Cheshire
St Andrew's School, East Sussex
St Andrew's School, Kent
St Anne's Nursery & Pre-Preparatory
    School, Hampshire
St Anselm's, Derbyshire
St Aubyn's School, Devon
St George's School, Edgbaston,
    West Midlands
St Hilda's School, Essex
St John's School, Essex
St Margaret's School, Essex
St Mary's Preparatory School,
    Roxburghshire

St Peter & St Paul School, Derbyshire
Sancton Wood School, Cambridgeshire
Seaford College, West Sussex
Seaton House, Surrey
South Hills School, Wiltshire
Staines Preparatory School Trust,
    Middlesex
Strathallan School, Perthshire
Talbot Heath, Dorset
Taunton School, Somerset
Thorpe House School, Buckinghamshire
Wentworth College, Dorset
West Buckland Preparatory School, Devon
West Buckland School, Devon
Wheelgate House School, Cornwall
Worksop College, Nottinghamshire
Wychwood School, Oxfordshire
Wycliffe Junior School, Gloucestershire
Yarrells School, Dorset

Unspecified

Brentwood School, Essex
Canbury School, Surrey
Cherwell College, Oxfordshire
Chilton Cantelo School, Somerset
Cumnor House School, West Sussex
d'Overbroeck's College, Oxfordshire
Davenies School, Buckinghamshire
Dollar Academy, Clackmannanshire
Great Ballard School, West Sussex
Hatherop Castle School, Gloucestershire
The Junior School, St Lawrence College,
    Kent

King's School, Devon
Marlin Montessori School, Hertfordshire
Milton Abbey School, Dorset
Norfolk Lodge Nursery & Preparatory
    School, Hertfordshire
Notre Dame Preparatory School, Norfolk
Oundle School Laxton Junior,
    Cambridgeshire
Priory School, Isle of Wight
St Teresa's Preparatory School, Surrey
Taverham Hall, Norfolk
The Tuition Centre, NW4

Attention Deficit/Hyperactivity Disorder

Level 1

Brackenfield School,
    North Yorkshire
Cambridge Arts & Sciences (CATS),
    Cambridgeshire
Ellesmere College, Shropshire
Kelly College, Devon

Long Close School, Berkshire
Northampton Christian School,
    Northamptonshire
Rossall School, Lancashire
St Margaret's Junior School Convent of
    Mercy, West Sussex

Level 2

All Hallows, Somerset
Arnold School, Lancashire
Ashbourne PNEU School, Derbyshire
Bedgebury School, Kent
Belmont (Mill Hill Junior School), NW7
Bentham Grammar School, Lancashire
Broadwater Manor School, West Sussex
Catteral Hall, North Yorkshire
Dorchester Preparatory School, Dorset
Dover College, Kent
Essendene Lodge School, Surrey
The Fen Preparatory School, Lincolnshire
Forres Sandle Manor, Hampshire
Green Hill School, Worcestershire
Halstead Preparatory School, Surrey
Haylett Grange Preparatory School, Pembrokeshire
Heathcote School, Essex
The High School of Dundee, Angus
Hordle Walhampton School, Hampshire
Kilgraston (A Sacred Heart School), Perthshire
King William's College, Isle of Man
Kingswood College at Scarisbrick Hall, Lancashire
Lyndon School, Conwy
Mansfield Preparatory School, Nottinghamshire
Northbourne Park School, Kent
Northcote Lodge, SW11
Nottingham High School, Nottinghamshire
Oswestry School, Shropshire
Our Lady's Preparatory School, Berkshire
Queen Victoria School, Perthshire
Royal Alexandra and Albert School, Surrey
St Columba's College, Hertfordshire
St Joseph's Convent, Derbyshire
St Margaret's School for Girls, Aberdeenshire
St Mary's Westbrook, Kent
St Michael's, Devon
St Ursula's High School, Bristol
The Schiller Academy, SE1
Shebbear College, Devon
Slindon College, West Sussex
Stanbridge Earls School, Hampshire
Steephill School, Kent
Woodcote House School, Surrey
Worth School, West Sussex

Level 3

Attenborough Preparatory School, Nottinghamshire
Avon House, Essex
Bow School, County Durham
Bradford Grammar School, West Yorkshire
Chinthurst School, Surrey
Copthorne School, West Sussex
Dagfa House School, Nottinghamshire
Derby Independent Grammar School, Derbyshire
Dulwich College, SE21
Durlston Court, Hampshire
Elmwood Montessori School, W4
Eversfield Preparatory School, West Midlands
Giggleswick School, North Yorkshire
The Hampshire Schools (Kensington Gardens), W2
The Hampshire Schools (Knightsbridge Under School), SW7
The Hampshire Schools (Knightsbridge Upper School), SW7
Hampstead Hill Pre-Preparatory & Nursery School, NW3
Hull Grammar School, East Riding of Yorkshire

King Edward VII and Queen Mary School, Lancashire

The King's School, Cheshire

King's School, Somerset

Ladymede, Buckinghamshire

Lochinver House School, Hertfordshire

Monkton Combe School, North East Somerset

Mostyn House School, Cheshire

The Mount School, NW7

New Hall School, Essex

North Cestrian Grammar School, Cheshire

Playdays Nursery/School and Montessori College, SW19

Pocklington Montessori School, East Riding of Yorkshire

Ramillies Hall School, Cheshire

The Royal High School, North East Somerset

The Ryleys, Cheshire

St Andrew's School, East Sussex

St Andrew's School, Kent

St Anne's Nursery & Pre-Preparatory School, Hampshire

St Anselm's, Derbyshire

St Aubyn's School, Devon

St Clare's, Oxford, Oxfordshire

St George's School, Edgbaston, West Midlands

St John's School, Essex

St Mary's Preparatory School, Roxburghshire

St Peter & St Paul School, Derbyshire

Seaford College, West Sussex

South Hills School, Wiltshire

Staines Preparatory School Trust, Middlesex

Talbot Heath, Dorset

Taunton School, Somerset

West Buckland Preparatory School, Devon

West Buckland School, Devon

Wheelgate House School, Cornwall

Worksop College, Nottinghamshire

Wycliffe Junior School, Gloucestershire

Unspecified

Canbury School, Surrey

Cherwell College, Oxfordshire

Cliff School, West Yorkshire

d'Overbroeck's College, Oxfordshire

Davenies School, Buckinghamshire

Dollar Academy, Clackmannanshire

Hatherop Castle School, Gloucestershire

The Junior School, St Lawrence College, Kent

Milton Abbey School, Dorset

Newlands School, Tyne and Wear

Norfolk Lodge Nursery & Preparatory School, Hertfordshire

Notre Dame Preparatory School, Norfolk

Oundle School Laxton Junior, Cambridgeshire

Priory School, Isle of Wight

Taverham Hall, Norfolk

Wycliffe College, Gloucestershire

Autism

Level 1

Ackworth School, West Yorkshire

Danes Hill Preparatory School, Surrey

Ealing Montessori School, W3

The Japanese School, W3

St Mary's Westbrook, Kent

Woodside Park International School, N11

Level 2

The Elms, Worcestershire
Langley School, Norfolk
Mansfield Preparatory School,
  Nottinghamshire
Pocklington Montessori School, East
  Riding of Yorkshire
Royal Alexandra and Albert School, Surrey
Wilton Grange School, Hartlepool

Level 3

Avon House, Essex
Dagfa House School, Nottinghamshire
Dorchester Preparatory School, Dorset
Elmwood Montessori School, W4
Hampstead Hill Pre-Preparatory & Nursery
  School, NW3
The King's School, Nottinghamshire
Lochinver House School, Hertfordshire
North Cestrian Grammar School, Cheshire
Orchard House School, W4
Playdays Nursery/School and Montessori
  College, SW19
The Royal High School,
  North East Somerset
The Ryleys, Cheshire
St Andrew's School, Kent
South Hills School, Wiltshire
Taunton School, Somerset

Unspecified

Barnardiston Hall Preparatory School,
  Suffolk
Newlands School, Tyne and Wear
Norfolk Lodge Nursery & Preparatory
  School, Hertfordshire

Cerebral Palsy

Level 1

Airthrie School, Gloucestershire
Danes Hill Preparatory School, Surrey
St Joseph's Convent, Derbyshire

Level 2

Alcuin School, West Yorkshire
Ashbourne PNEU School, Derbyshire
The Fen Preparatory School,
  Lincolnshire
Glen House Montessori School,
  West Yorkshire
Hampstead Hill Pre-Preparatory & Nursery
  School, NW3
Hethersett Old Hall School, Norfolk
Hordle Walhampton School, Hampshire
Leeds Girls' High School,
  West Yorkshire
Mansfield Preparatory School,
  Nottinghamshire
Polam Hall, County Durham
St Margaret's School for Girls,
  Aberdeenshire
St Ursula's High School, Bristol
Vernon Lodge Preparatory School,
  Staffordshire

Level 3

Avon House, Essex
Bellan House Preparatory School,
    Shropshire
Culford School, Suffolk
Dorchester Preparatory School, Dorset
Elmwood Montessori School, W4
Green Hill School, Worcestershire
King William's College, Isle of Man
Laverock School, Surrey
Lochinver House School, Hertfordshire
Moreton Hall, Shropshire
The Mount School, NW7
New Hall School, Essex

The Park School, Somerset
Playdays Nursery/School and Montessori
    College, SW19
St Andrew's School, East Sussex
St Andrew's School, Kent
St Mary's School, Cambridgeshire
Sir William Perkins's School, Surrey
South Hills School, Wiltshire
Taunton School, Somerset
Upton House School, Berkshire
Worksop College, Nottinghamshire
Wychwood School, Oxfordshire
Wycliffe Junior School, Gloucestershire

Unspecified

Canbury School, Surrey
Cranford House School, Oxfordshire

Marlin Montessori School, Hertfordshire
Newlands School, Tyne and Wear

Delicate

Level 1

Ealing Montessori School, W3
St Margaret's Junior School Convent of
    Mercy, West Sussex

Stanbridge Earls School, Hampshire
Thornton College Convent of Jesus and
    Mary, Buckinghamshire

Level 2

All Hallows, Somerset
Cokethorpe School, Oxfordshire
Dorchester Preparatory School, Dorset
Dulwich College, SE21
The Fen Preparatory School, Lincolnshire
Flexlands School, Surrey
Friends' School, Essex
Hamilton College, Lanarkshire
Kilgraston (A Sacred Heart School),
    Perthshire

Langley School, Norfolk
Lochinver House School, Hertfordshire
Manor Preparatory School, Oxfordshire
Mansfield Preparatory School,
    Nottinghamshire
Notre Dame Preparatory School, Surrey
Polam Hall, County Durham
St Dominic's School, Staffordshire
St Peter's School, West Sussex
Wilton Grange School, Hartlepool

Level 3

Avon House, Essex
Bellan House Preparatory School,
    Shropshire

Chase Academy, Staffordshire
Cliff School, West Yorkshire
Collingham, SW5

Dunedin School, Lothian
Edward Greene's Tutorial Establishment, Oxfordshire
Elmwood Montessori School, W4
Elstree School, Berkshire
Hillcroft Preparatory School, Suffolk
Ipswich School, Suffolk
The King's School, Nottinghamshire
Kingsley Preparatory School, West Midlands
The Mount School, NW7
New Hall School, Essex
New West Preston Manor Nursery School, West Sussex
North Cestrian Grammar School, Cheshire
Playdays Nursery/School and Montessori College, SW19
The Royal High School, North East Somerset
Royal School Haslemere, Surrey
The Ryleys, Cheshire

St Andrew's Montessori School, Hertfordshire
St Andrew's School, East Sussex
St Andrew's School, Kent
St David's School, Middlesex
St Gabriel's School, Berkshire
St James's School, Worcestershire
St Joseph's in the Park, Hertfordshire
St Margaret's School, Essex
St Mary's School, Cambridgeshire
Sancton Wood School, Cambridgeshire
Slindon College, West Sussex
South Hills School, Wiltshire
Stonar School, Wiltshire
Talbot Heath, Dorset
Taunton School, Somerset
West Dene School, Surrey
Wheelgate House School, Cornwall
Wycliffe Junior School, Gloucestershire

Unspecified

Cambridge Tutors College, Surrey
Cranford House School, Oxfordshire
First Impressions Montessori Schools, Hertfordshire
Marlin Montessori School, Hertfordshire
Newlands School, Tyne and Wear
Norfolk Lodge Nursery & Preparatory School, Hertfordshire

Notre Dame Preparatory School, Norfolk
St Nicholas House, Hertfordshire
St Ronan's, Kent
St Teresa's Preparatory School, Surrey
Shebbear College, Devon
Wentworth College, Dorset
Winterfold House, Worcestershire

Down's Syndrome

Level 1

The Japanese School, W3

Level 2

The Fen Preparatory School, Lincolnshire
Mansfield Preparatory School, Nottinghamshire

Pocklington Montessori School, East Riding of Yorkshire
St Andrew's Montessori School, Hertfordshire

Level 3

All Saints School, Norfolk
Avon House, Essex
Dorchester Preparatory School, Dorset
Elmwood Montessori School, W4
Emmanuel School, Devon
Hampstead Hill Pre-Preparatory & Nursery School, NW3
Lochinver House School, Hertfordshire
Mostyn House School, Cheshire
Playdays Nursery/School and Montessori College, SW19
Rainbow Montessori Nursery School, N6
St Andrew's School, Kent
South Hills School, Wiltshire
Taunton School, Somerset

Unspecified

First Impressions Montessori Schools, Hertfordshire
Marlin Montessori School, Hertfordshire
Newlands School, Tyne and Wear
Norfolk Lodge Nursery & Preparatory School, Hertfordshire

Dyscalculia

Level 1

Abbotsholme School, Staffordshire
Airthrie School, Gloucestershire
Ampleforth College, North Yorkshire
Avon House, Essex
Bredon School, Gloucestershire
Cambridge Arts & Sciences (CATS), Cambridgeshire
Clifton College, Bristol
Danes Hill Preparatory School, Surrey
Emmanuel School, Devon
Hazlegrove (King's Bruton Preparatory School), Somerset
Kingswood House School, Surrey
Llandovery College, Carmarthenshire
Long Close School, Berkshire
Magdalen Court School, Devon
Moreton Hall, Shropshire
Northampton Christian School, Northamptonshire
Oswestry School, Shropshire
St Anne's Nursery & Pre-Preparatory School, Hampshire
St Bees School, Cumbria
St David's College, Conwy
St John's School, Devon
St Joseph's in the Park, Hertfordshire
Seaford College, West Sussex
Stanbridge Earls School, Hampshire
Winterfold House, Worcestershire
Woodside Park International School, N11

Level 2

The Abbey School, Gloucestershire
Aldenham School, Hertfordshire
Amberfield School, Suffolk
Arnold School, Lancashire
Ascham House School, Tyne and Wear
Ashbourne PNEU School, Derbyshire
Ballard Preparatory School, Hampshire
Battle Abbey School, East Sussex
Bedford School, Bedfordshire
Bedford School Study Centre, Bedfordshire
Bedgebury School, Kent
Beech Hall School, Cheshire

Belmont Grosvenor School,
North Yorkshire
Brambletye School, West Sussex
Broadmead School, Bedfordshire
Brooklands School, Staffordshire
Castle House School, Shropshire
Catteral Hall, North Yorkshire
Chinthurst School, Surrey
Clayesmore Preparatory School, Dorset
Cokethorpe School, Oxfordshire
Collingham, SW5
Connaught House, W2
Copthorne School, West Sussex
Coventry Preparatory School,
West Midlands
Dorchester Preparatory School, Dorset
Dover College, Kent
Dulwich College, SE21
Durlston Court, Hampshire
Ealing Montessori School, W3
Edward Greene's Tutorial Establishment,
Oxfordshire
Ellesmere College, Shropshire
Elstree School, Berkshire
Essendene Lodge School, Surrey
Eversfield Preparatory School,
West Midlands
The Firs School, Cheshire
Forres Sandle Manor, Hampshire
Giggleswick School, North Yorkshire
Glen House Montessori School,
West Yorkshire
Great Ballard School, West Sussex
Green Hill School, Worcestershire
Greenbank, Cheshire
Hamilton College, Lanarkshire
The Hampshire Schools (Kensington
Gardens), W2
Hampstead Hill Pre-Preparatory & Nursery
School, NW3
Harvington School, W5
Haylett Grange Preparatory School,
Pembrokeshire
The High School of Dundee, Angus
Highfield Priory School, Lancashire

Hillcroft Preparatory School, Suffolk
Hollygirt School, Nottinghamshire
Holmwood House, Essex
Hordle Walhampton School, Hampshire
Hurst Lodge, Berkshire
Kelly College, Devon
Kilgraston (A Sacred Heart School),
Perthshire
King's School, Somerset
Kingswood College at Scarisbrick Hall,
Lancashire
Langley Preparatory School & Nursery,
Norfolk
Langley School, Norfolk
Leicester Grammar Junior School,
Leicestershire
Lochinver House School, Hertfordshire
Lyndon School, Conwy
Malvern College, Worcestershire
Manor Preparatory School, Oxfordshire
The Margaret Allen School, Herefordshire
Millfield Preparatory School, Somerset
The New Beacon, Kent
New Hall School, Essex
Newlands Manor School, East Sussex
Newlands Preparatory School, East Sussex
Northampton Preparatory School,
Northamptonshire
Northbourne Park School, Kent
Northcote Lodge, SW11
Nottingham High School,
Nottinghamshire
Oakhill College, Lancashire
Our Lady's Preparatory School, Berkshire
Oxford Tutorial College, Oxfordshire
Pinewood School, Wiltshire
Polam Hall, County Durham
Port Regis, Dorset
Prior Park Preparatory School, Wiltshire
Queen Victoria School, Perthshire
Ramillies Hall School, Cheshire
Rossholme School, Somerset
The Royal High School,
North East Somerset
Rupert House, Oxfordshire

The Ryleys, Cheshire
St Anselm's, Derbyshire
St Antony's-Leweston School, Dorset
St Aubyn's, East Sussex
St Aubyn's School, Devon
St Columba's College, Hertfordshire
St Crispin's School, Leicestershire
St Dominic's School, Staffordshire
St Edmund's Junior School, Kent
St James Independent School for Boys (Senior), Middlesex
St Joseph's Convent, Derbyshire
St Margaret's School for Girls, Aberdeenshire
St Martin's Preparatory School, North East Lincolnshire

St Mary's Preparatory School, Roxburghshire
St Mary's School, Dorset
St Michael's, Devon
The Schiller Academy, SE1
School of St Mary and St Anne, Staffordshire
Shebbear College, Devon
Slindon College, West Sussex
Steephill School, Kent
Taunton School, Somerset
Terrington Hall, North Yorkshire
Tettenhall College, West Midlands
Trent College, Nottinghamshire
Wheelgate House School, Cornwall
Wycliffe Junior School, Gloucestershire

Level 3

Arden Lawn, West Midlands
Ashdown House School, East Sussex
Ashgrove School, Kent
Bentham Grammar School, Lancashire
Bramcote School, North Yorkshire
Bromsgrove School, Worcestershire
Bronte House School, West Yorkshire
Dagfa House School, Nottinghamshire
Derby Independent Grammar School, Derbyshire
Downside School, North East Somerset
Duncombe School, Hertfordshire
Edenhurst School, Staffordshire
Elmwood Montessori School, W4
Haileybury, Hertfordshire
Hartlebury School, Worcestershire
Huddersfield Grammar School, West Yorkshire

Longwood School, Hertfordshire
Mostyn House School, Cheshire
Orchard House School, W4
Playdays Nursery/School and Montessori College, SW19
Queen's College Junior and Pre-Preparatory Schools, Somerset
St Andrew's School, East Sussex
St Andrew's School, Kent
St Aubyn's School, Essex
St George's School, Edgbaston, West Midlands
St Hilda's School, Essex
St Michael's School, Kent
St Peter's School, West Sussex
Talbot Heath, Dorset
West Buckland School, Devon
Westmont School, Isle of Wight

Unspecified

Barnardiston Hall Preparatory School, Suffolk
Cherwell College, Oxfordshire
Cransley School, Cheshire
d'Overbroeck's College, Oxfordshire

Dollar Academy, Clackmannanshire
Frensham Heights, Surrey
Gresham's Preparatory School, Norfolk
The Hampshire Schools (Knightsbridge Upper School), SW7

Hatherop Castle School, Gloucestershire

The Junior School, St Lawrence College, Kent

King's Hall School, Somerset

Lomond School, Argyll and Bute

Milton Abbey School, Dorset

Norman Court Preparatory School, Wiltshire

Notre Dame Preparatory School, Norfolk

Oakwood School, West Sussex

Prior Park College, North East Somerset

Priory School, Isle of Wight

Ryde School, Isle of Wight

Sacred Heart Preparatory School, Bristol

St Hugh's School, Oxfordshire

St Lawrence College, Kent

St Mary's School, Oxfordshire

St Nicholas House, Hertfordshire

Dyslexia

Level 1

Abbotsholme School, Staffordshire

Airthrie School, Gloucestershire

Avon House, Essex

Belmont (Mill Hill Junior School), NW7

Bradfield College, Berkshire

Bramcote School, North Yorkshire

Bredon School, Gloucestershire

The Brigidine School, Berkshire

Cambridge Arts & Sciences (CATS), Cambridgeshire

Cameron House, SW3

Canford School, Dorset

Chiltern Tutorial Unit, Hampshire

Clifton College, Bristol

Craigclowan Preparatory School, Perthshire

Ditcham Park School, Hampshire

The Dominie, SW11

Dulwich Preparatory School, Cranbrook, Kent

Ellesmere College, Shropshire

Elstree School, Berkshire

Emmanuel School, Devon

Eton College, Berkshire

Felsted School, Essex

Grenville College, Devon

Haileybury, Hertfordshire

Hazlegrove (King's Bruton Preparatory School), Somerset

King's School, Somerset

Kingsley Preparatory School, West Midlands

Kingswood House School, Surrey

Llandovery College, Carmarthenshire

Long Close School, Berkshire

Magdalen Court School, Devon

Mayville High School, Hampshire

Merchiston Castle School, Lothian

Millfield Preparatory School, Somerset

Moreton Hall, Shropshire

Mostyn House School, Cheshire

New Hall School, Essex

Northampton Christian School, Northamptonshire

Northampton Preparatory School, Northamptonshire

Oswestry School, Shropshire

Prestfelde Preparatory School, Shropshire

Princethorpe College, Warwickshire

Prior's Field School, Surrey

Rossall School, Lancashire

The Royal High School, North East Somerset

St Anne's Nursery & Pre-Preparatory School, Hampshire

St Anselm's, Derbyshire

St Bees School, Cumbria

St Brandon's School, Somerset

St David's College, Conwy

St Edward's School, Oxfordshire

St James's School, Worcestershire
St Joseph's in the Park, Hertfordshire
St Margaret's School, Lothian
St Mary's Westbrook, Kent
St Swithun's School, Hampshire
Seaford College, West Sussex
Shiplake College, Oxfordshire
Staines Preparatory School Trust, Middlesex
Stanbridge Earls School, Hampshire

Thornlow Preparatory School, Dorset
Westminster Cathedral Choir School, SW1P
William Hulme's Grammar School, Greater Manchester
Winterfold House, Worcestershire
Wolverhampton Grammar School, West Midlands
Worksop College, Nottinghamshire
Wrekin College, Shropshire

Level 2

Abbey Gate School, Cheshire
The Abbey School, Gloucestershire
The Abbey, Suffolk
Aberdeen Waldorf School, Aberdeenshire
Aberlour House, Banffshire
Ackworth School, West Yorkshire
Acorn School, Gloucestershire
Akiva School, N3
Alcuin School, West Yorkshire
Aldenham School, Hertfordshire
The Alice Ottley School, Worcestershire
All Hallows, Somerset
All Saints School, Norfolk
Amberfield School, Suffolk
Ampleforth College, North Yorkshire
Arnold House School, NW8
Arnold School, Lancashire
Ascham House School, Tyne and Wear
Ashbourne PNEU School, Derbyshire
Ashdell Preparatory School, South Yorkshire
Attenborough Preparatory School, Nottinghamshire
Austin Friars School, Cumbria
Ballard Preparatory School, Hampshire
Ballard School, Hampshire
Bangor Grammar School, County Down
Barfield School, Surrey
Barlborough Hall School, Derbyshire
Barnard Castle School, County Durham
Basil Paterson Tutorial College, Lothian
Baston School, Kent

Battle Abbey School, East Sussex
Bedford School, Bedfordshire
Bedford School Study Centre, Bedfordshire
Bedgebury School, Kent
Belfast Royal Academy, County Antrim
Bellan House Preparatory School, Shropshire
Belmont Grosvenor School, North Yorkshire
Bentham Grammar School, Lancashire
Bilton Grange, Warwickshire
Birkdale School, South Yorkshire
Blundell's School, Devon
Bodiam Manor School, East Sussex
Bosworth Independent College, Northamptonshire
Bow School, County Durham
Box Hill School, Surrey
Brambletye School, West Sussex
Brighton College Prep School, East Sussex
Broadmead School, Bedfordshire
Broadwater Manor School, West Sussex
Bromsgrove School, Worcestershire
Bronte House School, West Yorkshire
Brooklands School, Staffordshire
Caldicott, Buckinghamshire
Cambridge Centre for VIth Form Studies (CCSS), Cambridgeshire
Carleton House Preparatory School, Merseyside
Casterton School, Cumbria
Castle House School, Shropshire

Caterham School, Surrey
The Cathedral School, Cardiff
Catteral Hall, North Yorkshire
Chard School, Somerset
Chase Academy, Staffordshire
Cheam School, Berkshire
Chinthurst School, Surrey
Chiswick and Bedford Park Preparatory
    School, W4
Christ College, Powys
Churchers College, Hampshire
Claremont School, East Sussex
Clarendon Cottage School, Greater
    Manchester
Clayesmore Preparatory School, Dorset
Cleve House School, Bristol
Clewborough House School at Cheswycks,
    Surrey
Cliff School, West Yorkshire
Clifton Hall, Lothian
Cokethorpe School, Oxfordshire
Colchester High School, Essex
Collingham, SW5
The Compass School, Lothian
Connaught House, W2
Conway Preparatory School, Lincolnshire
Copthorne School, West Sussex
Coventry Preparatory School,
    West Midlands
Coworth Park School, Surrey
Craig-y-Nos School, Swansea
Craigholme School, Glasgow
Culford School, Suffolk
Dagfa House School, Nottinghamshire
Dallington School, EC1V
Dean Close School, Gloucestershire
Derby Independent Grammar School,
    Derbyshire
The Dormer House PNEU School,
    Gloucestershire
Dorset House School, West Sussex
Dover College, Kent
Downside School, North East Somerset
Duke of Kent School, Surrey
Duke of York's Royal Military School, Kent

Dulwich College, SE21
Duncombe School, Hertfordshire
Dunhurst (Bedales Junior School),
    Hampshire
Durham High School For Girls, County
    Durham
Durham School, County Durham
Durlston Court, Hampshire
Eagle House, Berkshire
Ealing Montessori School, W3
Eastbourne College, East Sussex
Edenhurst School, Staffordshire
Edward Greene's Tutorial Establishment,
    Oxfordshire
The Elms, Worcestershire
Epsom College, Surrey
Essendene Lodge School, Surrey
Eton End PNEU, Berkshire
Eversfield Preparatory School,
    West Midlands
Farleigh School, Hampshire
Farlington School, West Sussex
The Fen Preparatory School, Lincolnshire
The Firs School, Cheshire
Flexlands School, Surrey
Fonthill Lodge, West Sussex
Forres Sandle Manor, Hampshire
Framlingham College Junior School,
    Suffolk
Friends' School, Essex
The Froebelian School, West Yorkshire
Fyling Hall School, North Yorkshire
Gad's Hill School, Kent
Gateway School, Buckinghamshire
George Heriot's School, Lothian
Giggleswick School, North Yorkshire
Glen House Montessori School,
    West Yorkshire
The Grange, Worcestershire
The Grantham Preparatory School,
    Lincolnshire
Great Ballard School, West Sussex
Green Hill School, Worcestershire
Greenbank, Cheshire
Greenfield School, Surrey

The Mount Junior School, North Yorkshire
Mount School, West Yorkshire
Mount School, Worcestershire
Mount St Mary's College, Derbyshire
The New Beacon, Kent
Newlands Manor School, East Sussex
Newlands Preparatory School, East Sussex
Newlands School, Tyne and Wear
North Cestrian Grammar School, Cheshire
Northbourne Park School, Kent
Northcote Lodge, SW11
Northwood College, Middlesex
The Norwich High School for Girls GDST, Norfolk
Nottingham High School, Nottinghamshire
Oakhill College, Lancashire
Oakhyrst Grange School, Surrey
The Oratory Preparatory School, Berkshire
Orchard House School, W4
Oriel Bank High School, Cheshire
Osho Ko Hsuan School, Devon
Our Lady's Convent Junior School, Oxfordshire
Our Lady's Convent Preparatory School, Northamptonshire
Oxford Tutorial College, Oxfordshire
Pinewood School, Wiltshire
Plumtree School, Nottinghamshire
Pocklington Montessori School, East Riding of Yorkshire
Polam Hall, County Durham
Port Regis, Dorset
Primrose Montessori School, N5
Prior Park Preparatory School, Wiltshire
Queen Elizabeth's Hospital, Bristol
Queen Victoria School, Perthshire
Queen's College Junior and Pre-Preparatory Schools, Somerset
The Querns School, Gloucestershire
Ramillies Hall School, Cheshire
Raventhorpe Preparatory School, County Durham
Ripon Cathedral Choir School, North Yorkshire
Rossholme School, Somerset

Royal Alexandra and Albert School, Surrey
Royal School Haslemere, Surrey
The Royal Wolverhampton School, West Midlands
Rugby School, Warwickshire
Rupert House, Oxfordshire
Rydes Hill Preparatory School, Surrey
The Ryleys, Cheshire
St Agnes PNEU School, West Yorkshire
St Andrew's Montessori School, Hertfordshire
St Andrew's School, East Sussex
St Andrew's School, Surrey
St Antony's-Leweston School, Dorset
St Aubyn's, East Sussex
St Aubyn's School, Devon
St Catherine's School, Surrey
St Columba's College, Hertfordshire
St Crispin's School, Leicestershire
St David's School, Middlesex
St Dominic's School, Staffordshire
St Edmund's Junior School, Kent
St Faiths School, Cambridgeshire
St Gabriel's School, Berkshire
St George's College, Surrey
St George's School, Suffolk
St Helen's College, Middlesex
St Hilary's School, Surrey
St Hilda's School, Essex
St Hilda's School, West Yorkshire
St Ives School, Surrey
St James Independent School for Boys (Senior), Middlesex
St John's School, Devon
St John's School, Essex
St Joseph's College, Suffolk
St Joseph's Convent, Derbyshire
St Katharines Preparatory School, Fife
St Leonards School & St Leonards VIth Form College, Fife
St Margaret's School, Devon
St Margaret's School for Girls, Aberdeenshire
St Martin's, NW7

St Martin's Preparatory School, North East Lincolnshire
St Mary's Preparatory School, Lincolnshire
St Mary's Preparatory School, Roxburghshire
St Mary's School, Dorset
St Mary's School, Cambridgeshire
St Michael's, Devon
St Peter & St Paul School, Derbyshire
St Philip's School, SW7
St Piran's School, Cornwall
St Piran's Preparatory School, Berkshire
St Richard's, Herefordshire
St Ursula's High School, Bristol
Salterford House School, Nottinghamshire
Sancton Wood School, Cambridgeshire
Sandhurst School, West Sussex
Sandroyd, Wiltshire
The Schiller Academy, SE1
School of St Mary and St Anne, Staffordshire
Shebbear College, Devon
Slindon College, West Sussex
South Hills School, Wiltshire
Southbank International School, Hampstead, NW3
Steephill School, Kent
Stewart's Melville College, Lothian
Stoke College, Suffolk
Stonar School, Wiltshire
Stourbridge House School, Wiltshire
Strathallan School, Perthshire
Surbiton Preparatory School, Surrey
Talbot Heath, Dorset
Taunton School, Somerset
Teesside High School, Stockton-on-Tees
Terrington Hall, North Yorkshire

Tettenhall College, West Midlands
Thornton College Convent of Jesus and Mary, Buckinghamshire
Thorpe House School, Buckinghamshire
Tockington Manor School, Bristol
Tormead School, Surrey
Trent College, Nottinghamshire
Underhill - Junior School to Sutton Valence, Kent
Unicorn School, Surrey
Upton House School, Berkshire
Vernon Lodge Preparatory School, Staffordshire
Walthamstow Hall, Kent
Warlingham Park School, Surrey
Waverley School, Berkshire
Wellingborough School, Northamptonshire
Wellington School, South Ayrshire
Wellington School, Somerset
Wells Cathedral School, Somerset
Wentworth College, Dorset
West Buckland Preparatory School, Devon
Westmont School, Isle of Wight
Wheelgate House School, Cornwall
White House Preparatory School, Berkshire
Whitehall School, Cambridgeshire
Wilton Grange School, Hartlepool
Wimbledon College Prep School, SW19
Woodcote House School, Surrey
Woodleigh School, North Yorkshire
Worth School, West Sussex
Wycliffe Junior School, Gloucestershire
Wylde Green College, West Midlands
Yarrells School, Dorset

Level 3

Arden Lawn, West Midlands
Ashdown House School, East Sussex
Ashgrove School, Kent
The Belvedere School GDST, Merseyside
Bolton School (Girls' Division), Lancashire

Brackenfield School, North Yorkshire
Bradford Grammar School, West Yorkshire
Bramley School, Surrey
Bristol Grammar School, Bristol
Burgess Hill School for Girls, West Sussex

Charterhouse, Surrey
Elmwood Montessori School, W4
Eltham College, SE9
Eveline Day School, SW17
Francis Holland School, SW1W
Haberdashers' Aske's School, Hertfordshire
Harpenden Preparatory School, Hertfordshire
Hartlebury School, Worcestershire
Hornsby House School, SW12
Huddersfield Grammar School, West Yorkshire
Ibstock Place School, SW15
Ipswich School, Suffolk
Kelly College, Devon
The King's School, Kent
The King's School Senior, Hampshire
Lansdowne Sixth Form College, W2
Leicester Grammar School, Leicestershire
Longwood School, Hertfordshire
Lubavitch House Senior School for Girls, N16
Mander Portman Woodward, West Midlands
The Mount School, NW7
Mount Zion (Christian Primary) School, Bristol
Nottingham High School Preparatory School, Nottinghamshire
The Park School, Somerset
Playdays Nursery/School and Montessori College, SW19
Queen Elizabeth's Grammar School, Lancashire

Rainbow Montessori Nursery School, N6
St Andrew's School, Kent
St Aubyn's School, Essex
St Clare's, Oxford, Oxfordshire
St George's School, Edgbaston, West Midlands
St Margaret's Junior School Convent of Mercy, West Sussex
St Margaret's School, Essex
St Martin's School, West Midlands
St Mary's School, Buckinghamshire
St Michael's School, Kent
St Peter's School, West Sussex
School of St Helen & St Katharine, Oxfordshire
Seaton House, Surrey
Sir William Perkins's School, Surrey
Sutton High School GDST, Surrey
Trentvale Preparatory School, North Lincolnshire
Trinity School, Surrey
Wells Cathedral Junior School, Somerset
Wellspring Christian School, Cumbria
West Buckland School, Devon
Westwood, Hertfordshire
Widford Lodge, Essex
Withington Girls' School, Greater Manchester
Woodford Prep & Nursery School, Cheshire
Woodside Park International School, N11
Wychwood School, Oxfordshire
Yehudi Menuhin School, Surrey

Unspecified

Arundale Preparatory School, West Sussex
Ashville College, North Yorkshire
Barnardiston Hall Preparatory School, Suffolk
Beech Hall School, Cheshire
Bethany School, Kent
Bootham School, North Yorkshire
Brentwood School, Essex

Cambridge Tutors College, Surrey
Canbury School, Surrey
Cherwell College, Oxfordshire
Chilton Cantelo School, Somerset
Clifton College Preparatory School, Bristol
Cobham Hall, Kent
College Saint-Pierre, Essex
Collingwood School, Surrey

Copthill School, Lincolnshire
Cottesmore School, West Sussex
Cranford House School, Oxfordshire
Cransley School, Cheshire
Cumnor House School, West Sussex
d'Overbroeck's College, Oxfordshire
Dame Johane Bradbury's School, Essex
Danes Hill Preparatory School, Surrey
Davenies School, Buckinghamshire
Dean Close Preparatory School,
    Gloucestershire
Dollar Academy, Clackmannanshire
Dorchester Preparatory School, Dorset
Egerton-Rothesay School, Hertfordshire
Emscote House School and Nursery,
    Warwickshire
Exeter Tutorial College, Devon
Fairfield School, Leicestershire
Fairstead House School, Suffolk
Fernhill School, South Lanarkshire
Filgrave School, Buckinghamshire
Finborough School, Suffolk
First Impressions Montessori Schools,
    Hertfordshire
Foremarke Hall, Derbyshire
Frensham Heights, Surrey
The Glasgow Academy, Glasgow
Godstowe Preparatory School,
    Buckinghamshire
Grace Dieu Manor School, Leicestershire
Grantchester House, Surrey
Gresham's Preparatory School, Norfolk
Hatherop Castle School, Gloucestershire
Hawkesdown House School, W8
Heath Mount School, Hertfordshire
Hellenic College of London, SW1X
High March School, Buckinghamshire
Highfield School, Hampshire
Hilden Grange School, Kent
The Junior School, St Lawrence College,
    Kent
Kelly College Junior School, Devon
Kent College, Kent
The Kerem School, N2
King's Hall School, Somerset

King's School, Devon
Lathallan School, Angus
Leaden Hall, Wiltshire
Leeds Girls' High School,
    West Yorkshire
Licensed Victuallers' School, Berkshire
Littlefield School, Hampshire
Lomond School, Argyll and Bute
Lucton Pierrepont School, Herefordshire
Malsis School, North Yorkshire
Marlin Montessori School, Hertfordshire
Micklefield School, Surrey
Milton Abbey School, Dorset
Moorlands School, Bedfordshire
Mount House School, Devon
The Mount Senior School,
    North Yorkshire
Norfolk Lodge Nursery & Preparatory
    School, Hertfordshire
Norman Court Preparatory School,
    Wiltshire
North Bridge House Lower School, NW1
Notre Dame Preparatory School, Surrey
Notre Dame Preparatory School,
    Norfolk
Oakwood School, West Sussex
The Old Vicarage School, Derbyshire
Orwell Park, Suffolk
Oundle School Laxton Junior,
    Cambridgeshire
Our Lady's Preparatory School,
    Berkshire
Oxford High School GDST, Oxfordshire
Parsons Mead, Surrey
Portland Place School, W1B
Presentation College, Berkshire
Prior Park College, North East Somerset
Priory School, Isle of Wight
Ruckleigh School, West Midlands
Ryde School, Isle of Wight
Sacred Heart Preparatory School, Bristol
St Bede's School, East Sussex
St Bernard's Preparatory School,
    Berkshire
St Edmund's School, Kent

St Hugh's School, Oxfordshire
St Joseph's Convent School, Berkshire
St Joseph's School, Nottinghamshire
St Lawrence College, Kent
St Mary's Hall, East Sussex
St Mary's School, Oxfordshire
St Nicholas House, Hertfordshire
St Teresa's Preparatory School, Surrey
Scarborough College, North Yorkshire
Scarborough College Junior School,
    North Yorkshire
Sedbergh School, Cumbria
Sevenoaks Preparatory School, Kent
Shaw House School, West Yorkshire
Sherborne House School, Hampshire
Sherborne School, Dorset
Stanway School, Surrey

Stoke Brunswick, West Sussex
Stonelands School of Ballet & Theatre Arts,
    East Sussex
Stowe School, Buckinghamshire
Surrey College, Surrey
Taverham Hall, Norfolk
Terra Nova School, Cheshire
The Tuition Centre, NW4
The Vale School, SW7
Wellington College, Berkshire
West House School, West Midlands
Westholme School, Lancashire
Whitford Hall & Dodderhill School,
    Worcestershire
Woodhouse Grove School, West Yorkshire
Wycliffe College, Gloucestershire
York House School, Hertfordshire

Dyspraxia

Level 1

Abbotsholme School, Staffordshire
Bredon School, Gloucestershire
The Brigidine School, Berkshire
Cambridge Arts & Sciences (CATS),
    Cambridgeshire
Cameron House, SW3
Clifton College, Bristol
The Dominie, SW11
Ellesmere College, Shropshire
Emmanuel School, Devon
Eton College, Berkshire
Haileybury, Hertfordshire
Hazlegrove (King's Bruton Preparatory
    School), Somerset
King's School, Somerset
Kingsley Preparatory School,
    West Midlands
Kingswood House School, Surrey
Llandovery College, Carmarthenshire
Mostyn House School, Cheshire
Northampton Christian School,
    Northamptonshire
Oswestry School, Shropshire

Prestfelde Preparatory School, Shropshire
Rossall School, Lancashire
The Royal High School,
    North East Somerset
St Anne's Nursery & Pre-Preparatory
    School, Hampshire
St David's College, Conwy
St Edward's School, Oxfordshire
St Helen's College, Middlesex
St James's School, Worcestershire
St John's School, Devon
St Joseph's in the Park, Hertfordshire
St Margaret's School, Lothian
Stanbridge Earls School, Hampshire
Thornlow Preparatory School, Dorset
Thornton College Convent of Jesus and
    Mary, Buckinghamshire
Westminster Cathedral Choir School,
    SW1P
William Hulme's Grammar School,
    Greater Manchester
Winterfold House, Worcestershire
Woodside Park International School, N11

Level 2

The Abbey School, Gloucestershire
Aberdeen Waldorf School, Aberdeenshire
Akiva School, N3
Alcuin School, West Yorkshire
Aldenham School, Hertfordshire
All Hallows, Somerset
All Saints School, Norfolk
Ampleforth College, North Yorkshire
Arnold House School, NW8
Arnold School, Lancashire
Ascham House School, Tyne and Wear
Ashbourne PNEU School, Derbyshire
Attenborough Preparatory School,
	Nottinghamshire
Avon House, Essex
Ballard Preparatory School, Hampshire
Barnard Castle School, County Durham
Basil Paterson Tutorial College, Lothian
Battle Abbey School, East Sussex
Bedford School, Bedfordshire
Bedford School Study Centre, Bedfordshire
Bedgebury School, Kent
Beech Hall School, Cheshire
Bellan House Preparatory School,
	Shropshire
Belmont (Mill Hill Junior School), NW7
Bilton Grange, Warwickshire
Birkdale School, South Yorkshire
Brambletye School, West Sussex
Broadwater Manor School, West Sussex
Brooklands School, Staffordshire
Cambridge Centre for VIth Form Studies
	(CCSS), Cambridgeshire
Carleton House Preparatory School,
	Merseyside
Chase Academy, Staffordshire
Cheam School, Berkshire
Chinthurst School, Surrey
Christ College, Powys
Claysmore Preparatory School, Dorset
Cliff School, West Yorkshire
Cokethorpe School, Oxfordshire
Colchester High School, Essex
Collingham, SW5

Connaught House, W2
Copthorne School, West Sussex
Coventry Preparatory School,
	West Midlands
Dallington School, EC1V
Dean Close School, Gloucestershire
Dover College, Kent
Downside School, North East Somerset
Dulwich College, SE21
Dunhurst (Bedales Junior School),
	Hampshire
The Elms, Worcestershire
Essendene Lodge School, Surrey
Eton End PNEU, Berkshire
The Fen Preparatory School, Lincolnshire
The Firs School, Cheshire
Flexlands School, Surrey
Forres Sandle Manor, Hampshire
Friends' School, Essex
The Froebelian School, West Yorkshire
Gad's Hill School, Kent
Gateway School, Buckinghamshire
George Heriot's School, Lothian
Giggleswick School, North Yorkshire
Glen House Montessori School,
	West Yorkshire
The Grange, Worcestershire
Great Ballard School, West Sussex
Green Hill School, Worcestershire
Greenbank, Cheshire
Greenfield School, Surrey
The Hall School, NW3
Halstead Preparatory School, Surrey
Hamilton College, Lanarkshire
The Hampshire Schools (Kensington
	Gardens), W2
The Hampshire Schools (Knightsbridge
	Under School), SW7
The Hampshire Schools (Knightsbridge
	Upper School), SW7
Harecroft Hall School, Cumbria
Haresfoot Preparatory School,
	Hertfordshire
Harvington School, W5

St Margaret's School for Girls, Aberdeenshire
St Martin's Preparatory School, North East Lincolnshire
St Mary's Preparatory School, Roxburghshire
St Michael's, Devon
St Piran's School, Cornwall
St Piran's Preparatory School, Berkshire
St Ursula's High School, Bristol
Sandroyd, Wiltshire
Shebbear College, Devon
South Hills School, Wiltshire
Southbank International School, Hampstead, NW3
Steephill School, Kent
Terrington Hall, North Yorkshire
Tettenhall College, West Midlands
Thorpe House School, Buckinghamshire
Tockington Manor School, Bristol
Trent College, Nottinghamshire
Underhill - Junior School to Sutton Valence, Kent
Upton House School, Berkshire
Waverley School, Berkshire
Wellingborough School, Northamptonshire
West Buckland Preparatory School, Devon
Whitehall School, Cambridgeshire
Wimbledon College Prep School, SW19
Woodcote House School, Surrey
Woodleigh School, North Yorkshire
Worth School, West Sussex
Wycliffe Junior School, Gloucestershire
Yarrells School, Dorset

Level 3

Arden Lawn, West Midlands
Ashgrove School, Kent
Barfield School, Surrey
Belmont Grosvenor School, North Yorkshire
The Belvedere School GDST, Merseyside
Bentham Grammar School, Lancashire
Bosworth Independent College, Northamptonshire
Brackenfield School, North Yorkshire
Bradford Grammar School, West Yorkshire
Bramcote School, North Yorkshire
Bristol Grammar School, Bristol
Bromsgrove School, Worcestershire
Bronte House School, West Yorkshire
Burgess Hill School for Girls, West Sussex
Charterhouse, Surrey
Copthill School, Lincolnshire
Culford School, Suffolk
Dagfa House School, Nottinghamshire
Derby Independent Grammar School, Derbyshire
Duncombe School, Hertfordshire
Dunedin School, Lothian
Durlston Court, Hampshire
Edenhurst School, Staffordshire
Edward Greene's Tutorial Establishment, Oxfordshire
Elmwood Montessori School, W4
Eltham College, SE9
Eversfield Preparatory School, West Midlands
Farlington School, West Sussex
Haberdashers' Aske's School, Hertfordshire
Hampstead Hill Pre-Preparatory & Nursery School, NW3
Harpenden Preparatory School, Hertfordshire
Hawley Place School, Surrey
Huddersfield Grammar School, West Yorkshire
Hurworth House School, County Durham
The King's School, Kent
The King's School, Nottinghamshire
Longwood School, Hertfordshire
Moreton Hall, Shropshire
The Mount School, NW7
New Hall School, Essex

New West Preston Manor Nursery School, West Sussex

Northampton Preparatory School, Northamptonshire

Orchard House School, W4

The Park School, Somerset

Playdays Nursery/School and Montessori College, SW19

Queen Elizabeth's Grammar School, Lancashire

Queen's College Junior and Pre-Preparatory Schools, Somerset

St Andrew's Montessori School, Hertfordshire

St Andrew's School, East Sussex

St Andrew's School, Kent

St Aubyn's School, Essex

St Brandon's School, Somerset

St George's School, Edgbaston, West Midlands

St Hilda's School, Essex

St Margaret's School, Essex

St Michael's School, Kent

St Peter & St Paul School, Derbyshire

St Peter's School, West Sussex

Sancton Wood School, Cambridgeshire

The Schiller Academy, SE1

Seaford College, West Sussex

Seaton House, Surrey

Shiplake College, Oxfordshire

Slindon College, West Sussex

Staines Preparatory School Trust, Middlesex

Strathallan School, Perthshire

Talbot Heath, Dorset

Taunton School, Somerset

Teesside High School, Stockton-on-Tees

Wellington School, South Ayrshire

Wells Cathedral Junior School, Somerset

Wells Cathedral School, Somerset

Wentworth College, Dorset

West Buckland School, Devon

Westwood, Hertfordshire

Wheelgate House School, Cornwall

Wolverhampton Grammar School, West Midlands

Woodford Prep & Nursery School, Cheshire

Worksop College, Nottinghamshire

Wychwood School, Oxfordshire

Unspecified

Airthrie School, Gloucestershire

Ashville College, North Yorkshire

Barnardiston Hall Preparatory School, Suffolk

Bootham School, North Yorkshire

Brentwood School, Essex

Catteral Hall, North Yorkshire

Cherwell College, Oxfordshire

Chilton Cantelo School, Somerset

Clifton College Preparatory School, Bristol

Cobham Hall, Kent

Cottesmore School, West Sussex

Cranford House School, Oxfordshire

Cumnor House School, West Sussex

d'Overbroeck's College, Oxfordshire

Danes Hill Preparatory School, Surrey

Davenies School, Buckinghamshire

Dollar Academy, Clackmannanshire

Egerton-Rothesay School, Hertfordshire

Filgrave School, Buckinghamshire

First Impressions Montessori Schools, Hertfordshire

Foremarke Hall, Derbyshire

Frensham Heights, Surrey

Godstowe Preparatory School, Buckinghamshire

Gresham's Preparatory School, Norfolk

Hatherop Castle School, Gloucestershire

Hellenic College of London, SW1X

High March School, Buckinghamshire

Highfield School, Hampshire

The Junior School, St Lawrence College, Kent

The Kerem School, N2
King's School, Devon
Malsis School, North Yorkshire
Marlin Montessori School, Hertfordshire
Merchiston Castle School, Lothian
Milton Abbey School, Dorset
Mount House School, Devon
Norfolk Lodge Nursery & Preparatory School, Hertfordshire
Norman Court Preparatory School, Wiltshire
Notre Dame Preparatory School, Norfolk
Oakwood School, West Sussex
Orwell Park, Suffolk
Oundle School Laxton Junior, Cambridgeshire
Princethorpe College, Warwickshire
Prior Park College, North East Somerset
Ryde School, Isle of Wight

Sacred Heart Preparatory School, Bristol
St Bede's School, East Sussex
St Hugh's School, Oxfordshire
St Lawrence College, Kent
St Mary's School, Oxfordshire
St Mary's Westbrook, Kent
St Nicholas House, Hertfordshire
St Teresa's Preparatory School, Surrey
Scarborough College, North Yorkshire
Scarborough College Junior School, North Yorkshire
Stoke Brunswick, West Sussex
Stowe School, Buckinghamshire
Taverham Hall, Norfolk
Terra Nova School, Cheshire
The Tuition Centre, NW4
Vernon Lodge Preparatory School, Staffordshire
York House School, Hertfordshire

Emotional/Behavioural Difficulties

Level 1

Cambridge Arts & Sciences (CATS), Cambridgeshire
The Grange, Worcestershire

Moira House Girls' School, East Sussex
St Margaret's School, Lothian

Level 2

Akiva School, N3
Ashbourne PNEU School, Derbyshire
Beech Hall School, Cheshire
Belmont (Mill Hill Junior School), NW7
The Fen Preparatory School, Lincolnshire
Gateway School, Buckinghamshire
King William's College, Isle of Man
Ladymede, Buckinghamshire
Langley Preparatory School & Nursery, Norfolk

Mansfield Preparatory School, Nottinghamshire
Queen Victoria School, Perthshire
St Margaret's School for Girls, Aberdeenshire
St Piran's School, Cornwall
Shebbear College, Devon
Steephill School, Kent
Wilton Grange School, Hartlepool

Level 3

Aberdeen Waldorf School, Aberdeenshire
Arnold House School, NW8

Avon House, Essex
Bangor Grammar School, County Down

Derby Independent Grammar School, Derbyshire
Dunedin School, Lothian
Edward Greene's Tutorial Establishment, Oxfordshire
Elmwood Montessori School, W4
Kilgraston (A Sacred Heart School), Perthshire
The King's School, Nottinghamshire
Lochinver House School, Hertfordshire
Longwood School, Hertfordshire
Lubavitch House Senior School for Girls, N16
Notre Dame Preparatory School, Surrey
Oriel Bank High School, Cheshire
Playdays Nursery/School and Montessori College, SW19
Royal Alexandra and Albert School, Surrey

The Royal High School, North East Somerset
The Ryleys, Cheshire
St Andrew's School, Kent
St Anne's Nursery & Pre-Preparatory School, Hampshire
St Aubyn's School, Devon
St Peter & St Paul School, Derbyshire
Seaford College, West Sussex
South Hills School, Wiltshire
Strathallan School, Perthshire
Tashbar Primary School, Greater Manchester
Taunton School, Somerset
West Buckland School, Devon
Wheelgate House School, Cornwall
Whitehall School, Cambridgeshire

Unspecified

Barnardiston Hall Preparatory School, Suffolk
Cambridge Tutors College, Surrey
d'Overbroeck's College, Oxfordshire
Dollar Academy, Clackmannanshire
Le Herisson, W6

Norfolk Lodge Nursery & Preparatory School, Hertfordshire
Northampton Christian School, Northamptonshire
Notre Dame Preparatory School, Norfolk

Epilepsy

Level 1

Cambridge Arts & Sciences (CATS), Cambridgeshire
Canford School, Dorset
St Edmund's Junior School, Kent
St George's School, Suffolk

St Margaret's Junior School Convent of Mercy, West Sussex
St Margaret's School, Lothian
Thornton College Convent of Jesus and Mary, Buckinghamshire

Level 2

All Hallows, Somerset
Bellan House Preparatory School, Shropshire
Clayesmore Preparatory School, Dorset
The Fen Preparatory School,

Lincolnshire
Glen House Montessori School, West Yorkshire
Langley School, Norfolk
Mansfield Preparatory School, Nottinghamshire

The Margaret Allen School, Herefordshire
Polam Hall, County Durham
Royal Alexandra and Albert School, Surrey
Royal School Haslemere, Surrey

St James Independent School for Boys
(Senior), Middlesex
St Ursula's High School, Bristol
Wilton Grange School, Hartlepool

Level 3

Aberdeen Waldorf School, Aberdeenshire
Avon House, Essex
Bangor Grammar School, County Down
Bolton School (Girls' Division), Lancashire
Bradford Grammar School,
West Yorkshire
Bristol Grammar School, Bristol
Burgess Hill School for Girls, West Sussex
Christ College, Powys
Cliff School, West Yorkshire
Collingham, SW5
Culford School, Suffolk
Dagfa House School, Nottinghamshire
Danes Hill Preparatory School, Surrey
Derby Independent Grammar School,
Derbyshire
Dorchester Preparatory School, Dorset
Dulwich College, SE21
Duncombe School, Hertfordshire
Edward Greene's Tutorial Establishment,
Oxfordshire
Elmwood Montessori School, W4
Friends' School, Essex
Green Hill School, Worcestershire
Hampstead Hill Pre-Preparatory & Nursery
School, NW3
Heathcote School, Essex
Hurst Lodge, Berkshire
Ipswich School, Suffolk
Kilgraston (A Sacred Heart School),
Perthshire
Ladymede, Buckinghamshire
Lochinver House School, Hertfordshire
Longwood School, Hertfordshire
Luckley-Oakfield School, Berkshire
Lyndhurst School, Surrey
Monkton Combe School,
North East Somerset

Moreton Hall, Shropshire
New Hall School, Essex
Nottingham High School,
Nottinghamshire
Nottingham High School Preparatory
School, Nottinghamshire
Playdays Nursery/School and Montessori
College, SW19
Rainbow Montessori Nursery School, N6
The Royal High School,
North East Somerset
The Ryleys, Cheshire
St Andrew's School, East Sussex
St Andrew's School, Kent
St Anne's Nursery & Pre-Preparatory
School, Hampshire
St David's School, Middlesex
St George's School, Edgbaston,
West Midlands
St James's School, Worcestershire
St Margaret's School for Girls,
Aberdeenshire
St Martin's School, West Midlands
St Mary's School, Cambridgeshire
St Peter's School, West Sussex
School of St Helen & St Katharine,
Oxfordshire
Shebbear College, Devon
Shiplake College, Oxfordshire
Slindon College, West Sussex
South Hills School, Wiltshire
Stonar School, Wiltshire
Strathallan School, Perthshire
Talbot Heath, Dorset
Taunton School, Somerset
Wentworth College, Dorset
Wycliffe Junior School, Gloucestershire
Yarrells School, Dorset

Unspecified

Ashville College, North Yorkshire
Canbury School, Surrey
Davenies School, Buckinghamshire
Felsted School, Essex
Kelly College, Devon
Kingsmead School, Merseyside
Langley Preparatory School & Nursery, Norfolk
Lathallan School, Angus

Malsis School, North Yorkshire
Norfolk Lodge Nursery & Preparatory School, Hertfordshire
Northampton Christian School, Northamptonshire
Notre Dame Preparatory School, Norfolk
St Clare's, Oxford, Oxfordshire
St Dominic's Priory School, Staffordshire
St Mary's School, Oxfordshire

Hearing Impairment

Level 1

Merchiston Castle School, Lothian
St George's School, Suffolk

St Margaret's Junior School Convent of Mercy, West Sussex
St Margaret's School, Lothian

Level 2

Akiva School, N3
All Hallows, Somerset
Ashbourne PNEU School, Derbyshire
Beech Hall School, Cheshire
Brackenfield School, North Yorkshire
Clayesmore Preparatory School, Dorset
Cliff School, West Yorkshire
Dorchester Preparatory School, Dorset
Glen House Montessori School, West Yorkshire
The Grange, Worcestershire
Howell's School, Denbighshire
The Japanese School, W3
Ladymede, Buckinghamshire
Lochinver House School, Hertfordshire
Mansfield Preparatory School, Nottinghamshire

The Margaret Allen School, Herefordshire
Playdays Nursery/School and Montessori College, SW19
Polam Hall, County Durham
Queen Victoria School, Perthshire
Royal Alexandra and Albert School, Surrey
St Bees School, Cumbria
St Joseph's in the Park, Hertfordshire
St Margaret's School for Girls, Aberdeenshire
Sancton Wood School, Cambridgeshire
Stanbridge Earls School, Hampshire
Stonar School, Wiltshire
Wilton Grange School, Hartlepool
Wimbledon College Prep School, SW19

Level 3

Aberdeen Waldorf School, Aberdeenshire
Amberfield School, Suffolk
Arnold House School, NW8

Attenborough Preparatory School, Nottinghamshire
Bangor Grammar School, County Down
Basil Paterson Tutorial College, Lothian

Unspecified

Bethany School, Kent
Bootham School, North Yorkshire
Cambridge Tutors College, Surrey
d'Overbroeck's College, Oxfordshire
Davenies School, Buckinghamshire
Felsted School, Essex
Foremarke Hall, Derbyshire
Gresham's Preparatory School, Norfolk
Hellenic College of London, SW1X
High March School, Buckinghamshire
King Edward VII and Queen Mary School,
    Lancashire
Le Herisson, W6
Loretto Junior School, Lothian
Malsis School, North Yorkshire

Micklefield School, Surrey
Mount House School, Devon
New West Preston Manor Nursery School,
    West Sussex
Northbourne Park School, Kent
Notre Dame Preparatory School,
    Norfolk
Parsons Mead, Surrey
Prestfelde Preparatory School, Shropshire
Prior Park College, North East Somerset
St Margaret's School, Devon
St Teresa's Preparatory School, Surrey
Whitford Hall & Dodderhill School,
    Worcestershire
York House School, Hertfordshire

Moderate Learning Difficulties

Level 1

Bramcote School, North Yorkshire
Bredon School, Gloucestershire
Cambridge Arts & Sciences (CATS),
    Cambridgeshire
Emmanuel School, Devon
Grenville College, Devon
Kingsley Preparatory School,
    West Midlands
Magdalen Court School, Devon
Merchiston Castle School, Lothian
Millfield Preparatory School, Somerset

Northampton Christian School,
    Northamptonshire
Oswestry School, Shropshire
St Anne's Nursery & Pre-Preparatory
    School, Hampshire
St Brandon's School, Somerset
St Joseph's in the Park, Hertfordshire
St Margaret's School, Lothian
Shiplake College, Oxfordshire
Woodside Park International School,
    N11

Level 2

Akiva School, N3
Alcuin School, West Yorkshire
All Hallows, Somerset
All Saints School, Norfolk
Amberfield School, Suffolk
Ampleforth College, North Yorkshire
Arnold House School, NW8
Ashbourne PNEU School, Derbyshire
Barfield School, Surrey

Beech Hall School, Cheshire
Bellan House Preparatory School,
    Shropshire
Belmont Grosvenor School,
    North Yorkshire
Bow School, County Durham
Brooklands School, Staffordshire
Cambridge Centre for VIth Form Studies
    (CCSS), Cambridgeshire

Trent College, Nottinghamshire
Upton House School, Berkshire
Waverley School, Berkshire
Wellington School, South Ayrshire
West House School, West Midlands
Wheelgate House School, Cornwall

Whitehall School, Cambridgeshire
Wilton Grange School, Hartlepool
Wimbledon College Prep School, SW19
Wycliffe Junior School, Gloucestershire

Level 3

Aberdeen Waldorf School, Aberdeenshire
Avon House, Essex
Brackenfield School, North Yorkshire
Bronte House School, West Yorkshire
Copthill School, Lincolnshire
Copthorne School, West Sussex
Danes Hill Preparatory School, Surrey
Derby Independent Grammar School, Derbyshire
Duncombe School, Hertfordshire
Dunedin School, Lothian
Elmwood Montessori School, W4
Hillcroft Preparatory School, Suffolk
Homewood Independent School, Hertfordshire
The Jordans Nursery School, W6
The King's School, Nottinghamshire
Llandovery College, Carmarthenshire

Lochinver House School, Hertfordshire
Longwood School, Hertfordshire
Our Lady's Convent Preparatory School, Northamptonshire
The Park School, Somerset
Playdays Nursery/School and Montessori College, SW19
Rainbow Montessori Nursery School, N6
St Andrew's School, Kent
St Margaret's School, Essex
St Peter's School, West Sussex
Seaford College, West Sussex
Shrewsbury House School, Surrey
South Hills School, Wiltshire
Summer Fields, Oxfordshire
Widford Lodge, Essex
Woodford Prep & Nursery School, Cheshire

Unspecified

Barnardiston Hall Preparatory School, Suffolk
Brentwood School, Essex
Canbury School, Surrey
College Saint-Pierre, Essex
Cottesmore School, West Sussex
Cranford House School, Oxfordshire
Edenhurst School, Staffordshire
Egerton-Rothesay School, Hertfordshire
Eilmar Montessori School & Nursery, Middlesex
Fairstead House School, Suffolk
Felsted School, Essex
Fernhill School, South Lanarkshire
Foremarke Hall, Derbyshire

Great Ballard School, West Sussex
The Hampshire Schools (Kensington Gardens), W2
Harpenden Preparatory School, Hertfordshire
Heswall Preparatory School, Merseyside
Ingleside PNEU School, Gloucestershire
The Junior School, St Lawrence College, Kent
King's School, Devon
Kingsmead School, Merseyside
Le Herisson, W6
Leaden Hall, Wiltshire
Leeds Islamia Girls' School, West Yorkshire
Malsis School, North Yorkshire

Marlin Montessori School, Hertfordshire
Micklefield School, Surrey
Mount Zion (Christian Primary) School, Bristol
Norman Court Preparatory School, Wiltshire
Notre Dame Preparatory School, Norfolk
Orwell Park, Suffolk
Oundle School Laxton Junior, Cambridgeshire
Prior Park College, North East Somerset
Priory School, Isle of Wight
St Hugh's School, Oxfordshire
St Joseph's School, Nottinghamshire
St Lawrence College, Kent

St Mary's Preparatory School, Roxburghshire
St Mary's School, Oxfordshire
St Mary's Westbrook, Kent
St Teresa's Preparatory School, Surrey
Shaw House School, West Yorkshire
Stoke College, Suffolk
Stowe School, Buckinghamshire
Taverham Hall, Norfolk
The Tuition Centre, NW4
Welsh School of London, NW10
Whitford Hall & Dodderhill School, Worcestershire
Woodhouse Grove School, West Yorkshire
Worth School, West Sussex
Wycliffe College, Gloucestershire

Physical Impairment

Level 1

Oakhill College, Lancashire
St Joseph's in the Park, Hertfordshire
St Margaret's Junior School Convent of Mercy, West Sussex

St Margaret's School, Lothian
Thornton College Convent of Jesus and Mary, Buckinghamshire

Level 2

Alcuin School, West Yorkshire
All Hallows, Somerset
Ashbourne PNEU School, Derbyshire
Beech Hall School, Cheshire
Cliff School, West Yorkshire
Cokethorpe School, Oxfordshire
Derby Independent Grammar School, Derbyshire
The Fen Preparatory School, Lincolnshire
The Firs School, Cheshire
Flexlands School, Surrey
Glen House Montessori School, West Yorkshire

Kilgraston (A Sacred Heart School), Perthshire
Long Close School, Berkshire
Manor Preparatory School, Oxfordshire
Mansfield Preparatory School, Nottinghamshire
Oxford Tutorial College, Oxfordshire
Polam Hall, County Durham
Queen Victoria School, Perthshire
Royal Alexandra and Albert School, Surrey
St George's School, Suffolk
Wimbledon College Prep School, SW19

Level 3

Bangor Grammar School, County Down

Bellan House Preparatory School, Shropshire

Bentham Grammar School, Lancashire
Bolton School (Girls' Division), Lancashire
Burgess Hill School for Girls, West Sussex
Chinthurst School, Surrey
Colchester High School, Essex
Copthill School, Lincolnshire
Dorchester Preparatory School,
 Dorset
Downside School,
 North East Somerset
Dulwich College, SE21
Durham School, County Durham
Edward Greene's Tutorial Establishment,
 Oxfordshire
Elmwood Montessori School, W4
Eversfield Preparatory School,
 West Midlands
Giggleswick School, North Yorkshire
Hartlebury School, Worcestershire
Hazlegrove (King's Bruton Preparatory
 School), Somerset
Heathcote School, Essex
Hurst Lodge, Berkshire
Hurworth House School,
 County Durham
King Edward VII and Queen Mary School,
 Lancashire
King William's College, Isle of Man
King's School, Somerset
Kingsley Preparatory School,
 West Midlands
Laverock School, Surrey
Lochinver House School,
 Hertfordshire

Longwood School, Hertfordshire
The Mount School, NW7
New Hall School, Essex
Nottingham High School,
 Nottinghamshire
Oriel Bank High School, Cheshire
The Park School, Somerset
Playdays Nursery/School and Montessori
 College, SW19
Port Regis, Dorset
The Royal High School,
 North East Somerset
The Ryleys, Cheshire
St Andrew's Montessori School,
 Hertfordshire
St Andrew's School, Kent
St Anne's Nursery & Pre-Preparatory
 School, Hampshire
St Clare's, Oxford, Oxfordshire
St David's School, Middlesex
St George's School, Edgbaston,
 West Midlands
St Martin's School, West Midlands
Sancton Wood School,
 Cambridgeshire
Stonar School, Wiltshire
Talbot Heath, Dorset
Taunton School, Somerset
Trinity School, Surrey
Wentworth College, Dorset
Westwood, Hertfordshire
Wycliffe Junior School,
 Gloucestershire

Unspecified

Ashville College, North Yorkshire
Bootham School, North Yorkshire
Eilmar Montessori School & Nursery,
 Middlesex
Great Ballard School, West Sussex
High March School,
 Buckinghamshire
Leaden Hall, Wiltshire

Licensed Victuallers' School, Berkshire
Lomond School, Argyll and Bute
Lyndon School, Conwy
Malsis School, North Yorkshire
The Margaret Allen School,
 Herefordshire
Micklefield School, Surrey
Notre Dame Preparatory School, Norfolk

Prior Park College, North East Somerset
St Margaret's School, Essex

St Teresa's Preparatory School, Surrey
Sherborne School, Dorset

Profound/Multiple Learning Difficulties

Level 1

St Margaret's School, Lothian

Level 2

Royal Alexandra and Albert School, Surrey

Level 3

Elmwood Montessori School, W4
Lochinver House School, Hertfordshire

Playdays Nursery/School and Montessori
    College, SW19
St Andrew's School, Kent

Unspecified

South Hills School, Wiltshire

Severe Learning Difficulties

Level 1

St Anne's Nursery & Pre-Preparatory
    School, Hampshire

St Joseph's in the Park, Hertfordshire
St Margaret's School, Lothian

Level 2

Beech Hall School, Cheshire

Royal Alexandra and Albert School, Surrey

Level 3

Elmwood Montessori School, W4
Lochinver House School, Hertfordshire
Playdays Nursery/School and Montessori

College, SW19
St Andrew's School, Kent
St George's School, Suffolk

Unspecified

South Hills School, Wiltshire

Specific Learning Difficulties

Level 1

Airthrie School, Gloucestershire
Avon House, Essex
Bramcote School, North Yorkshire
Bredon School, Gloucestershire
The Brigidine School, Berkshire
Craigclowan Preparatory School,
    Perthshire
Danes Hill Preparatory School, Surrey
Emmanuel School, Devon
Haileybury, Hertfordshire
Hazlegrove (King's Bruton Preparatory
    School), Somerset
King's School, Somerset
Kingsley Preparatory School,
    West Midlands
Kingswood House School, Surrey
Llandovery College, Carmarthenshire
Long Close School, Berkshire
Magdalen Court School, Devon

Mayville High School, Hampshire
Merchiston Castle School, Lothian
Millfield Preparatory School, Somerset
Moreton Hall, Shropshire
New Hall School, Essex
Northampton Preparatory School,
    Northamptonshire
Prestfelde Preparatory School, Shropshire
St Anselm's, Derbyshire
St Bees School, Cumbria
St David's College, Conwy
St Edward's School, Oxfordshire
St James's School, Worcestershire
St Joseph's in the Park, Hertfordshire
St Margaret's School, Lothian
Stanbridge Earls School, Hampshire
Thornlow Preparatory School, Dorset
Winterfold House, Worcestershire
Woodside Park International School, N11

Level 2

The Abbey School, Gloucestershire
Akiva School, N3
Aldenham School, Hertfordshire
The Alice Ottley School, Worcestershire
All Hallows, Somerset
All Saints School, Norfolk
Amberfield School, Suffolk
Ampleforth College, North Yorkshire
Arnold School, Lancashire
Ashbourne PNEU School, Derbyshire
Ashdell Preparatory School,
    South Yorkshire
Ballard Preparatory School, Hampshire
Barfield School, Surrey
Battle Abbey School, East Sussex
Bedgebury School, Kent
Beech Hall School, Cheshire
Belmont (Mill Hill Junior School),
    NW7
Bentham Grammar School, Lancashire

Birkdale School, South Yorkshire
Bromsgrove School, Worcestershire
Carleton House Preparatory School,
    Merseyside
Castle House School, Shropshire
Caterham School, Surrey
Catteral Hall, North Yorkshire
Cheam School, Berkshire
Chiswick and Bedford Park Preparatory
    School, W4
Christ College, Powys
Claymore Preparatory School, Dorset
Cliff School, West Yorkshire
Cokethorpe School, Oxfordshire
Colchester High School, Essex
Coventry Preparatory School,
    West Midlands
Dallington School, EC1V
Dean Close School, Gloucestershire
Dorchester Preparatory School, Dorset

Dover College, Kent
Downside School, North East Somerset
Dulwich College, SE21
Duncombe School, Hertfordshire
Dunhurst (Bedales Junior School),
    Hampshire
Durlston Court, Hampshire
Eaton House School, SW1W
Edward Greene's Tutorial Establishment,
    Oxfordshire
The Firs School, Cheshire
Forres Sandle Manor, Hampshire
Gateway School, Buckinghamshire
George Heriot's School, Lothian
Giggleswick School, North Yorkshire
Glen House Montessori School,
    West Yorkshire
The Grange, Worcestershire
Green Hill School, Worcestershire
Greenbank, Cheshire
Halstead Preparatory School, Surrey
Hamilton College, Lanarkshire
Hampstead Hill Pre-Preparatory & Nursery
    School, NW3
Haresfoot Preparatory School,
    Hertfordshire
Heathcote School, Essex
Hethersett Old Hall School, Norfolk
The High School of Dundee, Angus
Highfield Priory School, Lancashire
Hillcroft Preparatory School, Suffolk
Holme Grange School, Berkshire
Hurst Lodge, Berkshire
Kilgraston (A Sacred Heart School),
    Perthshire
King Edward VII and Queen Mary School,
    Lancashire
The King's School, Gloucestershire
Kingsland Grange, Shropshire
Kingsmead School, Merseyside
Knighton House, Dorset
Ladymede, Buckinghamshire
Langley Preparatory School & Nursery,
    Norfolk
Langley School, Norfolk

Laverock School, Surrey
Littlegarth School, Essex
Lochinver House School, Hertfordshire
Loretto Junior School, Lothian
Lyndon School, Conwy
Malvern College, Worcestershire
Malvern Girls' College, Worcestershire
Manor House School, Devon
Manor Preparatory School, Oxfordshire
Mansfield Preparatory School,
    Nottinghamshire
The Margaret Allen School,
    Herefordshire
Marymount International School, Surrey
Moorfield School, West Yorkshire
Newlands Manor School, East Sussex
Newlands Preparatory School,
    East Sussex
Northbourne Park School, Kent
Nottingham High School,
    Nottinghamshire
Oakhill College, Lancashire
The Oratory Preparatory School,
    Berkshire
Oriel Bank High School, Cheshire
Oxford Tutorial College, Oxfordshire
Pinewood School, Wiltshire
Polam Hall, County Durham
Port Regis, Dorset
Primrose Montessori School, N5
Queen Victoria School, Perthshire
Ramillies Hall School, Cheshire
Raventhorpe Preparatory School, County
    Durham
Rossholme School, Somerset
Royal Alexandra and Albert School,
    Surrey
Royal School Haslemere, Surrey
The Ryleys, Cheshire
St Andrew's Montessori School,
    Hertfordshire
St Andrew's School, East Sussex
St Aubyn's, East Sussex
St Aubyn's School, Devon
St Columba's College, Hertfordshire

St Crispin's School, Leicestershire
St David's School, Middlesex
St Edmund's Junior School, Kent
St George's School, Suffolk
St Ives School, Surrey
St James Independent School for Boys
　(Senior), Middlesex
St Katharines Preparatory School, Fife
St Margaret's School, Devon
St Margaret's School for Girls,
　Aberdeenshire
St Martin's School, Middlesex
St Mary's Preparatory School,
　Roxburghshire
St Mary's Preparatory School,
　Lincolnshire
St Mary's Westbrook, Kent
St Michael's, Devon
St Peter & St Paul School, Derbyshire
St Piran's Preparatory School, Berkshire
St Ursula's High School, Bristol
Sancton Wood School,
　Cambridgeshire
Sandroyd, Wiltshire

The Schiller Academy, SE1
School of St Mary and St Anne,
　Staffordshire
Shebbear College, Devon
Slindon College, West Sussex
Southbank International School,
　Hampstead, NW3
Strathallan School, Perthshire
Terrington Hall, North Yorkshire
Tettenhall College, West Midlands
Thornton College Convent of Jesus and
　Mary, Buckinghamshire
Thorpe House School,
　Buckinghamshire
Trent College, Nottinghamshire
Waverley School, Berkshire
Westmont School, Isle of Wight
Wheelgate House School, Cornwall
Whitehall School, Cambridgeshire
Wilton Grange School, Hartlepool
Wimbledon College Prep School,
　SW19
Worksop College, Nottinghamshire
Wycliffe Junior School, Gloucestershire

Level 3

Brackenfield School,
　North Yorkshire
Chinthurst School, Surrey
Copthill School, Lincolnshire
Copthorne School, West Sussex
Culford School, Suffolk
Dagfa House School,
　Nottinghamshire
Dunedin School, Lothian
Elmwood Montessori School, W4
Eveline Day School, SW17
Farlington School, West Sussex
Huddersfield Grammar School,
　West Yorkshire
Ibstock Place School, SW15
Longwood School, Hertfordshire
Mostyn House School, Cheshire
The Mount School, NW7

Mount Zion (Christian Primary) School,
　Bristol
Notre Dame Preparatory School, Surrey
Orchard House School, W4
Playdays Nursery/School and Montessori
　College, SW19
St Andrew's School, Kent
St Hilda's School, Essex
St Margaret's Junior School Convent of
　Mercy, West Sussex
St Mary's School, Cambridgeshire
St Michael's School, Kent
St Peter's School, West Sussex
Stonar School, Wiltshire
Talbot Heath, Dorset
Upton House School, Berkshire
Wentworth College, Dorset
West Buckland School, Devon

Unspecified

Aberdeen Waldorf School, Aberdeenshire
Barnardiston Hall Preparatory School, Suffolk
Chilton Cantelo School, Somerset
Cranford House School, Oxfordshire
Cumnor House School, West Sussex
d'Overbroeck's College, Oxfordshire
Dollar Academy, Clackmannanshire
The Dominie, SW11
Egerton-Rothesay School, Hertfordshire
Eilmar Montessori School & Nursery, Middlesex
Ellesmere College, Shropshire
Filgrave School, Buckinghamshire
First Impressions Montessori Schools, Hertfordshire
Godstowe Preparatory School, Buckinghamshire
Great Ballard School, West Sussex
Gresham's Preparatory School, Norfolk
High March School, Buckinghamshire
King's School, Devon
Lathallan School, Angus
Lomond School, Argyll and Bute
Malsis School, North Yorkshire
Norman Court Preparatory School, Wiltshire
Notre Dame Preparatory School, Norfolk
Orwell Park, Suffolk
Oundle School Laxton Junior, Cambridgeshire
Priory School, Isle of Wight
Sacred Heart Preparatory School, Bristol
St Antony's-Leweston School, Dorset
St Edmund's School, Kent
St Hugh's School, Oxfordshire
St Mary's School, Oxfordshire
Scarborough College, North Yorkshire
Stowe School, Buckinghamshire
Wetherby School, W2

Speech and Language Difficulties

Level 1

Bellan House Preparatory School, Shropshire
Brackenfield School, North Yorkshire
Danes Hill Preparatory School, Surrey
The Dominie, SW11
Kingsley Preparatory School, West Midlands
Magdalen Court School, Devon
Northampton Christian School, Northamptonshire
St Joseph's in the Park, Hertfordshire
St Michael's School, Kent
Stanbridge Earls School, Hampshire
Thornlow Preparatory School, Dorset
Woodside Park International School, N11

Level 2

Akiva School, N3
All Hallows, Somerset
Ashbourne PNEU School, Derbyshire
Bedgebury School, Kent
Beech Hall School, Cheshire
Bramcote School, North Yorkshire
Bredon School, Gloucestershire
Broadmead School, Bedfordshire
Brooklands School, Staffordshire
Claremont School, East Sussex
Clayesmore Preparatory School, Dorset
Cliff School, West Yorkshire

Clifton Hall, Lothian
Cokethorpe School, Oxfordshire
Dorchester Preparatory School, Dorset
Downside School, North East Somerset
Emmanuel School, Devon
Essendene Lodge School, Surrey
The Fen Preparatory School, Lincolnshire
The Firs School, Cheshire
Glen House Montessori School,
    West Yorkshire
The Grange, Worcestershire
Green Hill School, Worcestershire
Hamilton College, Lanarkshire
Hampstead Hill Pre-Preparatory & Nursery
    School, NW3
Heswall Preparatory School, Merseyside
Hillcroft Preparatory School, Suffolk
King Edward VII and Queen Mary School,
    Lancashire
King's School, Somerset
Ladymede, Buckinghamshire
Langley Preparatory School & Nursery,
    Norfolk
Lochinver House School, Hertfordshire
Long Close School, Berkshire
Lyndon School, Conwy
Manor House School, Devon
Mansfield Preparatory School,
    Nottinghamshire
The Margaret Allen School,
    Herefordshire

Northampton Preparatory School,
    Northamptonshire
Oakhyrst Grange School, Surrey
Oriel Bank High School, Cheshire
Port Regis, Dorset
Royal Alexandra and Albert School, Surrey
St Andrew's Montessori School,
    Hertfordshire
St Andrew's School, East Sussex
St Andrew's School, Surrey
St Aubyn's, East Sussex
St Columba's College, Hertfordshire
St David's School, Middlesex
St Hilary's School, Surrey
St James Independent School for Boys
    (Senior), Middlesex
St Margaret's Junior School Convent of
    Mercy, West Sussex
St Michael's, Devon
St Peter & St Paul School, Derbyshire
Sancton Wood School, Cambridgeshire
Steephill School, Kent
Warlingham Park School, Surrey
Wheelgate House School, Cornwall
Whitehall School, Cambridgeshire
Wilton Grange School, Hartlepool
Wimbledon College Prep School, SW19
Woodleigh School, North Yorkshire
Wycliffe Junior School, Gloucestershire
Wylde Green College, West Midlands
Yarrells School, Dorset

Level 3

Avon House, Essex
Ballard Preparatory School, Hampshire
Belmont (Mill Hill Junior School),
    NW7
Bentham Grammar School, Lancashire
Dallington School, EC1V
Elmwood Montessori School, W4
Eveline Day School, SW17
The Froebelian School, West Yorkshire
Hazlegrove (King's Bruton Preparatory
    School), Somerset

The Jordans Nursery School, W6
Longwood School, Hertfordshire
New Hall School, Essex
New West Preston Manor Nursery School,
    West Sussex
Notre Dame Preparatory School, Surrey
Playdays Nursery/School and Montessori
    College, SW19
Polam Hall, County Durham
Rupert House, Oxfordshire
The Ryleys, Cheshire

St Andrew's School, Kent
St George's School, Suffolk
St Margaret's School for Girls,
  Aberdeenshire
St Mary's Westbrook, Kent

St Peter's School, West Sussex
Shebbear College, Devon
Strathallan School, Perthshire
Upton House School, Berkshire
Wentworth College, Dorset

Unspecified

Canbury School, Surrey
Cobham Hall, Kent
Cumnor House School, West Sussex
First Impressions Montessori Schools,
  Hertfordshire
Haresfoot Preparatory School,
  Hertfordshire
High March School, Buckinghamshire
King's School, Devon
Kingswood House School, Surrey

Malsis School, North Yorkshire
Marlin Montessori School, Hertfordshire
Norfolk Lodge Nursery & Preparatory
  School, Hertfordshire
Notre Dame Preparatory School, Norfolk
Prestfelde Preparatory School, Shropshire
St Crispin's School, Leicestershire
Salterford House School, Nottinghamshire
School of St Mary and St Anne,
  Staffordshire

Tourette Syndrome

Level 1

Kingsley Preparatory School,
  West Midlands

Level 2

Howell's School, Denbighshire
St George's School, Suffolk

St Ursula's High School, Bristol

Level 3

Bradford Grammar School, West Yorkshire
Culford School, Suffolk
Dorchester Preparatory School, Dorset
Edward Greene's Tutorial Establishment,
  Oxfordshire
Elmwood Montessori School, W4
Hartlebury School, Worcestershire
Lochinver House School, Hertfordshire
The Park School, Somerset

Playdays Nursery/School and Montessori
  College, SW19
Prior Park Preparatory School, Wiltshire
Royal Alexandra and Albert School, Surrey
The Ryleys, Cheshire
St Andrew's School, Kent
St Columba's College, Hertfordshire
Wentworth College, Dorset
West Buckland School, Devon

Unspecified

Dollar Academy, Clackmannanshire

Visual Impairment

Level 1

Magdalen Court School, Devon
St Margaret's Junior School Convent of
  Mercy, West Sussex

St Margaret's School, Lothian

Level 2

Akiva School, N3
All Hallows, Somerset
Bedgebury School, Kent
Beech Hall School, Cheshire
Burgess Hill School for Girls,
  West Sussex
Cliff School, West Yorkshire
Collingham, SW5
Dorchester Preparatory School, Dorset
Edward Greene's Tutorial Establishment,
  Oxfordshire
The Fen Preparatory School,
  Lincolnshire
Flexlands School, Surrey
Glen House Montessori School,
  West Yorkshire
The Grange, Worcestershire

Kingsland Grange, Shropshire
Ladymede, Buckinghamshire
Lyndon School, Conwy
Maldon Court Preparatory School,
  Essex
Mansfield Preparatory School,
  Nottinghamshire
The Margaret Allen School,
  Herefordshire
Oxford Tutorial College, Oxfordshire
Polam Hall, County Durham
St Bees School, Cumbria
St Joseph's in the Park, Hertfordshire
Salterford House School,
  Nottinghamshire
Stanbridge Earls School, Hampshire
Wilton Grange School, Hartlepool

Level 3

Bangor Grammar School, County Down
Basil Paterson Tutorial College, Lothian
Bolton School (Girls' Division), Lancashire
Copthill School, Lincolnshire
Danes Hill Preparatory School, Surrey
Derby Independent Grammar School,
  Derbyshire
Duncombe School, Hertfordshire
Elmwood Montessori School, W4
Green Hill School, Worcestershire
Hurworth House School, County Durham
King's School, Somerset
Lochinver House School, Hertfordshire
Longwood School, Hertfordshire
Lyndhurst School, Surrey
Merchiston Castle School, Lothian

The Mount School, NW7
New Hall School, Essex
Nottingham High School,
  Nottinghamshire
Playdays Nursery/School and Montessori
  College, SW19
Royal Alexandra and Albert School, Surrey
The Royal High School,
  North East Somerset
Royal School Haslemere, Surrey
The Ryleys, Cheshire
St Andrew's Montessori School,
  Hertfordshire
St Andrew's School, Kent
St Clare's, Oxford, Oxfordshire
St David's School, Middlesex

St George's School, Edgbaston, West Midlands
St Margaret's School, Devon
School of St Helen & St Katharine, Oxfordshire
Shrewsbury House School, Surrey
Stonar School, Wiltshire

Sutton High School GDST, Surrey
Teesside High School, Stockton-on-Tees
Wentworth College, Dorset
West Dene School, Surrey
Westholme School, Lancashire
Westwood, Hertfordshire
Wycliffe Junior School, Gloucestershire

Unspecified

Belfast Royal Academy, County Antrim
Hillcroft Preparatory School, Suffolk
Howell's School, Denbighshire

Malsis School, North Yorkshire
Wheelgate House School, Cornwall

Wheelchair access

Level 3

Hurworth House School, County Durham

Unspecified

Alcuin School, West Yorkshire
Arden Lawn, West Midlands
Attenborough Preparatory School, Nottinghamshire
Ballard School, Hampshire
Bute House Preparatory School for Girls, W6
Canford School, Dorset
Churchers College, Hampshire
Copthill School, Lincolnshire
Danes Hill Preparatory School, Surrey
Darul Uloom London, Kent
Dover College, Kent
Dulwich College, SE21
Dulwich Preparatory School, Cranbrook, Kent
Dunedin School, Lothian
Eilmar Montessori School & Nursery, Middlesex
Elmwood Montessori School, W4
The Fen Preparatory School, Lincolnshire
Flexlands School, Surrey

Fonthill Lodge, West Sussex
The Grange, Worcestershire
Hampstead Hill Pre-Preparatory & Nursery School, NW3
Hartlebury School, Worcestershire
Heathcote School, Essex
Homewood Independent School, Hertfordshire
Hornsby House School, SW12
Kingsley Preparatory School, West Midlands
Langley School, Norfolk
Le Herisson, W6
Long Close School, Berkshire
Longwood School, Hertfordshire
Lord Wandsworth College, Hampshire
New Hall School, Essex
The Oratory Preparatory School, Berkshire
Playdays Nursery/School and Montessori College, SW19
St Andrew's Montessori School, Hertfordshire

PART FIVE: REFERENCE SECTION

5.1
Index of Establishments Classified by Special Need

(Independent and Non-maintained Special Schools and Colleges only)

Note: Schools listed in bold specify that the heading under which they appear is a principal special need.

Asperger Syndrome

Alderwasley Hall School, Derbyshire
Aran Hall School, Gwynedd
Banham Marshalls College, Norfolk
Birkdale School for Hearing Impaired
　Children, Merseyside
Breckenbrough School, North Yorkshire
Brewood Education Centre, Kent
The Camphill Rudolf Steiner Schools,
　Aberdeenshire
Chelfham Mill School, Devon
Chelfham Senior School, Devon
Church Hill School, Norfolk
Cotswold Chine School, Gloucestershire
Cruckton Hall, Shropshire
Delamere Forest School, Cheshire
Derwen College, Shropshire
Dilston College of Further Education,
　Northumberland
Don Buss Learning Centre Primary, Kent
Don Buss Learning Opportunities, Kent
Doncaster College for the Deaf,
　South Yorkshire
Doucecroft School, Essex
Eden Grove School, Cumbria
Exeter College, Devon
Fairfield Opportunity Farm, Wiltshire
Farleigh College, North East Somerset

Finchale Training College, County Durham
Fortune Centre of Riding Therapy, Dorset
Grateley House School, Hampshire
Green Laund F.E. Centre, Derbyshire
Harmeny School, Lothian
Helen Allison School, Kent
Hereward College, West Midlands
Home School of Stoke Newington, N16
Hope Lodge School, Hampshire
Ivers, Dorset
Kisharon Day School, NW11
Lambs House School, Cheshire
Lindeth College of Further Education,
　Cumbria
The Link Primary School, Surrey
Linkage Further Education College,
　Lincolnshire
The Marchant-Holliday School, Somerset
Minstead Training Project, Hampshire
The Mount Camphill Community,
　East Sussex
The National Star Centre's College of
　Further Education, Gloucestershire
NCH Action for Children,
　Vale of Glamorgan
The New Learning Centre, NW6
Nugent House School, Lancashire

Oakwood Court, Devon
Ochil Tower (Rudolf Steiner) School,
  Perthshire
Overley Hall School, Shropshire
Parayhouse School, W12
Peterhouse School for Pupils with Autism,
  Merseyside
Philip Green Memorial School, Dorset
Philpots Manor School, West Sussex
Pield Heath School, Middlesex
Pontville School, Lancashire
Potterspury Lodge School,
  Northamptonshire
Priors Court School, Berkshire
Queen Alexandra College of Further
  Education, West Midlands
RNIB Redhill College, Surrey
The Robert Ogden School,
  South Yorkshire
Rossendale Special School, Lancashire
St Andrews School, Norfolk
St Dominics School, Surrey
St Elizabeth's School, Hertfordshire
The St John Vianney School, Cheshire

St John's College, East Sussex
St Loye's College, Devon
St Mary's School, East Sussex
St Rose's School, Gloucestershire
St Vincent's School, Merseyside
Southlands School, Hampshire
Starley Hall, Fife
Strathmore House and Florence Villa,
  Staffordshire
Sunfield, West Midlands
Swalcliffe Park School, Oxfordshire
Thornhill Park School, Tyne and Wear
Underley Garden School, Lancashire
Wargrave House School, Merseyside
Weelsby Hall Further Education College,
  North East Lincolnshire
West Kirby Residential School,
  Merseyside
Whitstone Head School, Devon
Woodcroft School, Essex
Yateley Industries for the Disabled Ltd,
  Hampshire
Yorkshire Residential School for the Deaf,
  South Yorkshire

Attention Deficit Disorder

Appleford School, Wiltshire
Aran Hall School, Gwynedd
Belgrave School, Bristol
Breckenbrough School, North Yorkshire
Brewood Education Centre, Kent
Bryn Melyn Group, Gwynedd
The Camphill Rudolf Steiner Schools,
  Aberdeenshire
Cedar House School, Lancashire
Centre Academy, SW11
Chaigeley School, Cheshire
Chartwell House School, Cambridgeshire
Chelfham Mill School, Devon
Cotswold Chine School, Gloucestershire
Delamere Forest School, Cheshire
Don Buss Learning Centre Primary, Kent
Don Buss Learning Opportunities, Kent

Eastwood Grange School, Derbyshire
Eden Grove School, Cumbria
Exeter College, Devon
Fairley House School, SW1P
Fortune Centre of Riding Therapy, Dorset
Grateley House School, Hampshire
Harmeny School, Lothian
Hillcrest Pentwyn School, Herefordshire
Hillside School, Fife
Kings Manor Education Centre, East Sussex
Lindeth College of Further Education,
  Cumbria
Linkage Further Education College,
  Lincolnshire
Loddon School, Hampshire
Lowgate House School, Cumbria
The Marchant-Holliday School, Somerset

Minstead Training Project, Hampshire
The Moat School, SW6
Muntham House School, West Sussex
NCH Action for Children,
    Vale of Glamorgan
The New Learning Centre, NW6
Nugent House School, Lancashire
Overley Hall School, Shropshire
Owlswick School, East Sussex
Parayhouse School, W12
Philip Green Memorial School, Dorset
Philpots Manor School, West Sussex
Pield Heath School, Middlesex
Pontville School, Lancashire
Raddery School, Highland
Riverside School, Cumbria
St Dominics School, Surrey
St Edwards School, Hampshire

The St John Vianney School, Cheshire
St John's College, East Sussex
St Phillip's School, North Lanarkshire
Spring Hill School (Barnardo's),
    North Yorkshire
Starley Hall, Fife
Sunfield, West Midlands
Swalcliffe Park School, Oxfordshire
Underley Garden School, Lancashire
Underley Hall School, Lancashire
Unicorn School, Oxfordshire
West Kirby Residential School, Merseyside
Whitstone Head School, Devon
Witherslack Hall, Cumbria
Woodcroft School, Essex
Woodlands School, Dumfries & Galloway
Yateley Industries for the Disabled Ltd,
    Hampshire

Attention Deficit/Hyperactivity Disorder

Appleford School, Wiltshire
Aran Hall School, Gwynedd
Barnardo's Lecropt Project, Stirling
Bessels Leigh School, Oxfordshire
Breckenbrough School, North Yorkshire
Brewood Education Centre, Kent
The Camphill Rudolf Steiner Schools,
    Aberdeenshire
Cedar House School, Lancashire
Centre Academy, SW11
Chaigeley School, Cheshire
Chelfham Mill School, Devon
Cotswold Chine School, Gloucestershire
Coxlease School, Hampshire
Cruckton Hall, Shropshire
Delamere Forest School, Cheshire
Don Buss Learning Centre Primary, Kent
Don Buss Learning Opportunities, Kent
Eden Grove School, Cumbria
Exeter College, Devon
Fairley House School, SW1P
Grateley House School, Hampshire
Harmeny School, Lothian

Hesley Village College, South Yorkshire
Hillcrest Pentwyn School, Herefordshire
Hillside School, Fife
Kings Manor Education Centre,
    East Sussex
Kisharon Day School, NW11
Lindeth College of Further Education,
    Cumbria
Linkage Further Education College,
    Lincolnshire
Linn Moor Residential School,
    Aberdeenshire
Loddon School, Hampshire
Lowgate House School, Cumbria
The Marchant-Holliday School, Somerset
Muntham House School, West Sussex
NCH Action for Children,
    Vale of Glamorgan
The New Learning Centre, NW6
Nugent House School, Lancashire
Oakbank School, Aberdeenshire
Oakwood Court, Devon
Overley Hall School, Shropshire

Ovingdean Hall School, East Sussex
Parayhouse School, W12
Philpots Manor School, West Sussex
Potterspury Lodge School,
  Northamptonshire
Raddery School, Highland
Riverside School, Cumbria
Rossendale Special School, Lancashire
St Dominics School, Surrey
The St John Vianney School, Cheshire
St John's College, East Sussex
St Phillip's School, North Lanarkshire
The Sheiling School, Bristol
Starley Hall, Fife

Sunfield, West Midlands
Swalcliffe Park School, Oxfordshire
Underley Garden School, Lancashire
Underley Hall School, Lancashire
Unicorn School, Oxfordshire
Weelsby Hall Further Education College,
  North East Lincolnshire
Westwood School, Kent
Whitstone Head School, Devon
Witherslack Hall, Cumbria
Woodcroft School, Essex
Woodlands School, Dumfries & Galloway
Yateley Industries for the Disabled Ltd,
  Hampshire

Autism

Aran Hall School, Gwynedd
Beech Tree School, Lancashire
Broomhayes School, Devon
Broughton House College, Lincolnshire
Camphill Blair Drummond Trust, Stirling
The Camphill Rudolf Steiner Schools,
  Aberdeenshire
Church Hill School, Norfolk
Cintre Community, Bristol
Coleg Elidyr, Carmarthenshire
Corbenic Camphill Community, Perthshire
Cotswold Chine School, Gloucestershire
Cruckton Hall, Shropshire
Daldorch House School, East Ayrshire
Delrow College, Hertfordshire
Dilston College of Further Education,
  Northumberland
Doucecroft School, Essex
Exeter College, Devon
Fairfield Opportunity Farm, Wiltshire
Fortune Centre of Riding Therapy, Dorset
The Forum School, Dorset
Fullerton House School, South Yorkshire
Green Laund F.E. Centre, Derbyshire
The Hatch, South Gloucestershire
Helen Allison School, Kent
Hesley Village College, South Yorkshire

Hill House School, Hampshire
Homefield Residential College,
  Leicestershire
**Honormead School for Children with
  Autism, Staffordshire**
Hope Lodge School, Hampshire
Ivers, Dorset
Kisharon Day School, NW11
Kisimul School, Lincolnshire
Lambs House School, Cheshire
Lindeth College of Further Education,
  Cumbria
The Link Primary School, Surrey
Linkage Further Education College,
  Lincolnshire
Linn Moor Residential School,
  Aberdeenshire
Loddon School, Hampshire
Longdon Hall, Staffordshire
Loppington House Further Education &
  Adult Centre, Shropshire
MacIntyre School Wingrave,
  Buckinghamshire
MacIntyre School Womaston, Powys
Meldreth Manor School,
  Hertfordshire
Mordaunt School, Hampshire

The Mount Camphill Community, East Sussex
Nugent House School, Lancashire
Oakwood Court, Devon
Ochil Tower (Rudolf Steiner) School, Perthshire
Orchard School, Shropshire
Overley Hall School, Shropshire
Pengwern College, Denbighshire
Pennine Camphill Community, West Yorkshire
Peredur Trust, Cornwall
Peterhouse School for Pupils with Autism, Merseyside
Philpots Manor School, West Sussex
Pield Heath School, Middlesex
Portfield School, Pembrokeshire
Priors Court School, Berkshire
Purbeck View School, Dorset
Radlett Lodge School for Autistic Children, Hertfordshire
RNIB Redhill College, Surrey
The Robert Ogden School, South Yorkshire
Rowden House School, Herefordshire
Royal Blind School, Lothian
Royal School for the Deaf (Manchester), Cheshire
The Ryes School, Suffolk
St Christophers School, Bristol

The St John Vianney School, Cheshire
St John's College, East Sussex
St Joseph's School, Surrey
St Mary's School, East Sussex
The Sheiling Curative Schools, Hampshire
The Sheiling School, Bristol
Southlands School, Hampshire
Spring Hill School (Barnardo's), North Yorkshire
Strathmore House and Florence Villa, Staffordshire
Stroud Court, Gloucestershire
Struan House School, Clackmannanshire
Sunfield, West Midlands
Sutherland House School (Primary Department), Nottinghamshire
Sutherland House School (Secondary Department), Nottinghamshire
The Sybil Elgar School, Middlesex
Thornhill Park School, Tyne and Wear
Wargrave House School, Merseyside
Weelsby Hall Further Education College, North East Lincolnshire
The Wessex Autistic Society, Portfield School, Dorset
Westwood, Staffordshire
Wilsic Hall School, South Yorkshire
Woodcroft School, Essex
Yateley Industries for the Disabled Ltd, Hampshire

Cerebral Palsy

Beaumont College of Further Education, Lancashire
Birtenshaw Hall School, Lancashire
Bridge College, Cheshire
Burton Hill School, Wiltshire
The Camphill Rudolf Steiner Schools, Aberdeenshire
Chailey Heritage School, East Sussex
Coney Hill School, Kent
Craig-y-Parc School, Cardiff
Dame Hannah Rogers School, Devon

Delrow College, Hertfordshire
Derwen College, Shropshire
Doncaster College for the Deaf, South Yorkshire
East Park Home School, Glasgow
Exeter College, Devon
Exhall Grange School, Warwickshire
Finchale Training College, County Durham
Fortune Centre of Riding Therapy, Dorset
Fourways Assessment Unit, Greater Manchester

Furze Mount, Conwy

The Grange Centre for People with Disabilities, Surrey

The Hatch, South Gloucestershire

Henshaw's College, North Yorkshire

Hereward College, West Midlands

Hinwick Hall College of Further Education, Northamptonshire

Holly Bank School, West Yorkshire

Hornsey Conductive Education Centre, N10

Ingfield Manor School, West Sussex

Ivers, Dorset

Kisharon Day School, NW11

Langside School, Dorset

Linkage Further Education College, Lincolnshire

Loppington House Further Education & Adult Centre, Shropshire

Meldreth Manor School, Hertfordshire

Mordaunt School, Hampshire

Nash College of Further Education, Kent

National Institute of Conductive Education, West Midlands

The National Star Centre's College of Further Education, Gloucestershire

Oakwood Court, Devon

Ovingdean Hall School, East Sussex

The Papworth Trust, Cambridgeshire

Parayhouse School, W12

Pengwern College, Denbighshire

Penhurst School, Oxfordshire

Pennine Camphill Community, West Yorkshire

Percy Hedley School, Tyne and Wear

Philpots Manor School, West Sussex

Pield Heath School, Middlesex

Portfield School, Pembrokeshire

Portland College, Nottinghamshire

Queen Alexandra College of Further Education, West Midlands

Queen Elizabeth's Training College, Surrey

RNIB Alwyn House, Fife

RNIB Redhill College, Surrey

RNIB Rushton Hall School, Northamptonshire

RNIB Sunshine House School, Merseyside

RNIB Sunshine House School, Middlesex

Royal Blind School, Lothian

Royal School for the Deaf (Manchester), Cheshire

Rutherford School, Surrey

Rutland House School, Nottinghamshire

St Christophers School, Bristol

The St John Vianney School, Cheshire

St Margaret's School, Surrey

St Mary's School, East Sussex

St Rose's School, Gloucestershire

St Vincent's School, Merseyside

seeABILITY (formerly Royal School for the Blind), Surrey

Sense East, Cambridgeshire

The Sheiling Curative Schools, Hampshire

Spring Hill School (Barnardo's), North Yorkshire

Stanmore House Residential School, South Lanarkshire

Treloar School, Hampshire

Vranch House School, Devon

Weelsby Hall Further Education College, North East Lincolnshire

Woodcroft School, Essex

Yateley Industries for the Disabled Ltd, Hampshire

Yorkshire Residential School for the Deaf, South Yorkshire

Delicate

Birtenshaw Hall School, Lancashire

Breckenbrough School, North Yorkshire

Calder House School, Wiltshire

The Camphill Rudolf Steiner Schools, Aberdeenshire

Dame Hannah Rogers School, Devon

Delamere Forest School, Cheshire
East Park Home School, Glasgow
Exhall Grange School, Warwickshire
The Hatch, South Gloucestershire
Hereward College, West Midlands
Hillside School, Fife
Kings Manor Education Centre,
    East Sussex
Langside School, Dorset
Linkage Further Education College,
    Lincolnshire
The National Star Centre's College of
    Further Education, Gloucestershire
Oakwood Court, Devon
Ochil Tower (Rudolf Steiner) School,
    Perthshire

Parayhouse School, W12
Pennine Camphill Community,
    West Yorkshire
Philip Green Memorial School, Dorset
Philpots Manor School, West Sussex
Pield Heath School, Middlesex
St Dominics School, Surrey
St Mary's School, East Sussex
St Rose's School, Gloucestershire
St Vincent's School, Merseyside
Spring Hill School (Barnardo's),
    North Yorkshire
Treloar School, Hampshire
Weelsby Hall Further Education College,
    North East Lincolnshire

Down's Syndrome

Beaumont College of Further Education,
    Lancashire
Bridge College, Cheshire
Camphill Blair Drummond Trust, Stirling
The Camphill Rudolf Steiner Schools,
    Aberdeenshire
Cintre Community, Bristol
Corbenic Camphill Community, Perthshire
Delamere Forest School, Cheshire
Derwen College, Shropshire
Dilston College of Further Education,
    Northumberland
Easter Auguston Training Farm,
    Aberdeenshire
Exeter College, Devon
Fairfield Opportunity Farm, Wiltshire
Fortune Centre of Riding Therapy,
    Dorset
The Hatch, South Gloucestershire
Henshaw's College, North Yorkshire
Hereward College, West Midlands
Hinwick Hall College of Further
    Education, Northamptonshire
Ivers, Dorset
Kisharon Day School, NW11

Kisimul School, Lincolnshire
Lindeth College of Further Education,
    Cumbria
Linkage Further Education College,
    Lincolnshire
Loppington House Further Education &
    Adult Centre, Shropshire
Minstead Training Project, Hampshire
The Mount Camphill Community,
    East Sussex
Nash College of Further Education,
    Kent
Oakwood Court, Devon
Orchard School, Shropshire
Overley Hall School, Shropshire
The Papworth Trust, Cambridgeshire
Parayhouse School, W12
Pengwern College, Denbighshire
**Philip Green Memorial School,
    Dorset**
Philpots Manor School, West Sussex
Pield Heath School, Middlesex
RNIB Redhill College, Surrey
Rowden House School, Herefordshire
St Elizabeth's School, Hertfordshire

The St John Vianney School, Cheshire
St John's College, East Sussex
St Joseph's School, Surrey
St Mary's School, East Sussex
The Sheiling Curative Schools, Hampshire
The Sheiling School, Bristol
Spring Hill School (Barnardo's), North Yorkshire

Strathmore House and Florence Villa, Staffordshire
Sunfield, West Midlands
Weelsby Hall Further Education College, North East Lincolnshire
Wilsic Hall School, South Yorkshire
Woodcroft School, Essex
Yateley Industries for the Disabled Ltd, Hampshire

Dyscalculia

Appleford School, Wiltshire
Beaumont College of Further Education, Lancashire
Belgrave School, Bristol
Brewood Education Centre, Kent
Calder House School, Wiltshire
Centre Academy, SW11
Cruckton Hall, Shropshire
Doncaster College for the Deaf, South Yorkshire
East Court School, Kent
Edington and Shapwick School, Somerset
Exeter College, Devon
Finchale Training College, County Durham
Fortune Centre of Riding Therapy, Dorset
Hereward College, West Midlands

Home School of Stoke Newington, N16
The Knowl Hill School, Surrey
Mark College, Somerset
The Moat School, SW6
Moor House School, Surrey
The New Learning Centre, NW6
Overley Hall School, Shropshire
Philpots Manor School, West Sussex
Portland College, Nottinghamshire
St Dominics School, Surrey
St Joseph's School, Surrey
Treloar School, Hampshire
Unicorn School, Oxfordshire
Woodcroft School, Essex
Yorkshire Residential School for the Deaf, South Yorkshire

Dyslexia

Alderwasley Hall School, Derbyshire
Appleford School, Wiltshire
Beaumont College of Further Education, Lancashire
Belgrave School, Bristol
Bessels Leigh School, Oxfordshire
Birkdale School for Hearing Impaired Children, Merseyside
Breckenbrough School, North Yorkshire
Brewood Education Centre, Kent
Bridgend College, Bridgend
Bruern Abbey School, Oxfordshire

Caldecott Community, Kent
Calder House School, Wiltshire
The Camphill Rudolf Steiner Schools, Aberdeenshire
Centre Academy, SW11
The Charmandean Dyslexia Centre, Buckinghamshire
Chartwell House School, Cambridgeshire
Cintre Community, Bristol
Cruckton Hall, Shropshire
Delamere Forest School, Cheshire
Derwen College, Shropshire

Doncaster College for the Deaf,
South Yorkshire
East Court School, Kent
Eden Grove School, Cumbria
Edington and Shapwick School, Somerset
The Enham Trust, Hampshire
Exeter College, Devon
Exhall Grange School, Warwickshire
Fairley House School, SW1P
Finchale Training College, County Durham
Fortune Centre of Riding Therapy, Dorset
Frewen College, East Sussex
The Grange Centre for People with
Disabilities, Surrey
Harmeny School, Lothian
Hereward College, West Midlands
Hillcrest Pentwyn School, Herefordshire
Home School of Stoke Newington, N16
Kings Manor Education Centre, East Sussex
The Knowl Hill School, Surrey
Lindeth College of Further Education,
Cumbria
Linkage Further Education College,
Lincolnshire
Maple Hayes Hall Dyslexia School,
Staffordshire
The Marchant-Holliday School, Somerset
Mark College, Somerset
The Moat School, SW6
Moon Hall School, Surrey
Moor House School, Surrey
More House School, Surrey
Muntham House School, West Sussex
NCH Action for Children,
Vale of Glamorgan
The New Learning Centre, NW6
Northease Manor, East Sussex

Nugent House School, Lancashire
**Nunnykirk Centre for Dyslexia,
Northumberland**
Oakwood Court, Devon
The Old Rectory School, Suffolk
Overley Hall School, Shropshire
Ovingdean Hall School, East Sussex
Owlswick School, East Sussex
Pennine Camphill Community,
West Yorkshire
Philpots Manor School, West Sussex
Portland College, Nottinghamshire
Queen Elizabeth's Training College, Surrey
Raddery School, Highland
RNIB Redhill College, Surrey
RNIB Vocational College, Leicestershire
St Andrews School, Norfolk
St Dominics School, Surrey
St Edwards School, Hampshire
St Elizabeth's School, Hertfordshire
St Joseph's School, Surrey
St Loye's College, Devon
St Mary's School, East Sussex
Thornby Hall School, Northamptonshire
Unicorn School, Oxfordshire
Weelsby Hall Further Education College,
North East Lincolnshire
The West of England College for Students
with little or no sight, Devon
Whitstone Head School, Devon
Willoughby Hall Dyslexia Centre, NW3
Woodcroft School, Essex
Wychbury House Residential School, Devon
Yateley Industries for the Disabled Ltd,
Hampshire
Yorkshire Residential School for the Deaf,
South Yorkshire

Dyspraxia

Alderwasley Hall School, Derbyshire
Appleford School, Wiltshire
Beaumont College of Further Education,
Lancashire

Belgrave School, Bristol
Birkdale School for Hearing Impaired
Children, Merseyside
Blossom House School, SW20

Brewood Education Centre, Kent
Bruern Abbey School, Oxfordshire
Bryn Melyn Group, Gwynedd
Calder House School, Wiltshire
The Camphill Rudolf Steiner Schools,
Aberdeenshire
The Charmandean Dyslexia Centre,
Buckinghamshire
Cruckton Hall, Shropshire
Delamere Forest School, Cheshire
Doncaster College for the Deaf,
South Yorkshire
East Court School, Kent
Edington and Shapwick School, Somerset
Exeter College, Devon
Fairfield Opportunity Farm, Wiltshire
Fairley House School, SW1P
Finchale Training College, County Durham
Fortune Centre of Riding Therapy,
Dorset
Frewen College, East Sussex
Grateley House School, Hampshire
Hereward College, West Midlands
Hillcrest Pentwyn School, Herefordshire
Home School of Stoke Newington, N16
Kings Manor Education Centre,
East Sussex
The Knowl Hill School, Surrey
Linkage Further Education College,
Lincolnshire
Maple Hayes Hall Dyslexia School,
Staffordshire
Mark College, Somerset
The Moat School, SW6
Moor House School, Surrey
Nash College of Further Education,
Kent
National Institute of Conductive
Education, West Midlands

The National Star Centre's College of
Further Education, Gloucestershire
NCH Action for Children,
Vale of Glamorgan
The New Learning Centre, NW6
Northease Manor, East Sussex
Oakwood Court, Devon
Overley Hall School, Shropshire
Parayhouse School, W12
Philip Green Memorial School, Dorset
Philpots Manor School, West Sussex
Pield Heath School, Middlesex
Portland College, Nottinghamshire
Potterspury Lodge School,
Northamptonshire
Rossendale Special School, Lancashire
Royal Cross Primary School, Lancashire
St Andrews School, Norfolk
St Dominics School, Surrey
St Elizabeth's School, Hertfordshire
The St John Vianney School, Cheshire
St John's Catholic School for the Deaf,
West Yorkshire
St Joseph's School, Surrey
St Mary's School, East Sussex
St Rose's School, Gloucestershire
The Speech, Language & Hearing Centre,
NW1
Treloar School, Hampshire
Unicorn School, Oxfordshire
Weelsby Hall Further Education College,
North East Lincolnshire
Whitstone Head School, Devon
Willoughby Hall Dyslexia Centre, NW3
Woodcroft School, Essex
Yateley Industries for the Disabled Ltd,
Hampshire
Yorkshire Residential School for the Deaf,
South Yorkshire

Emotional/Behavioural Difficulties

Ballikinrain Residential School,
Stirling

Balnacraig School, Perth and Kinross
Banham Marshalls College, Norfolk

Queen Elizabeth's Training College, Surrey
Raddery School, Highland
Red Brae School, South Ayrshire
Ripplevale School, Kent
Riverside School, Cumbria
RNIB Alwyn House, Fife
Rossendale Special School, Lancashire
Royal School for the Blind, Merseyside
The Ryes School, Suffolk
St Edwards School, Hampshire
St Francis Day Boy Unit, Glasgow
St Phillip's School, North Lanarkshire
Seafields School, North Ayrshire
Seamab House School, Perth and Kinross
seeABILITY (formerly Royal School for the Blind), Surrey
Sense East, Cambridgeshire
The Sheiling Curative Schools, Hampshire
The Sheiling School, Bristol
Sheridan House Child & Family Therapy Unit, Norfolk
Snowdon School, Stirling
Spring Hill School (Barnardo's), North Yorkshire
Springboig St John's, Glasgow
Starley Hall, Fife

Strathmore House and Florence Villa, Staffordshire
Stroud Court, Gloucestershire
Sunfield, West Midlands
Swalcliffe Park School, Oxfordshire
Talbot House Independent Special School, Tyne and Wear
Taxal Edge School, Cheshire
Thornby Hall School, Northamptonshire
Underley Garden School, Lancashire
Underley Hall School, Lancashire
West Kirby Residential School, Merseyside
Westgate College, Kent
Westwood School, Kent
Whitstone Head School, Devon
William Henry Smith School, West Yorkshire
Witherslack Hall, Cumbria
Woodcroft School, Essex
Woodlands School, Dumfries & Galloway
Wychbury House Residential School, Devon
Yorkshire Residential School for the Deaf, South Yorkshire

Epilepsy

Aran Hall School, Gwynedd
Banstead Place Brain Injury Rehabilitation, Surrey
Beech Tree School, Lancashire
Birtenshaw Hall School, Lancashire
Bridge College, Cheshire
Bryn Melyn Group, Gwynedd
Camphill Blair Drummond Trust, Stirling
The Camphill Rudolf Steiner Schools, Aberdeenshire
Chelfham Mill School, Devon
Cintre Community, Bristol
Coleg Elidyr, Carmarthenshire
Coney Hill School, Kent
Corbenic Camphill Community, Perthshire

Cotswold Chine School, Gloucestershire
Cruckton Hall, Shropshire
Dame Hannah Rogers School, Devon
The David Lewis School, Cheshire
Delamere Forest School, Cheshire
Derwen College, Shropshire
Dilston College of Further Education, Northumberland
East Park Home School, Glasgow
Exeter College, Devon
Exhall Grange School, Warwickshire
Fairfield Opportunity Farm, Wiltshire
Finchale Training College, County Durham
Fortune Centre of Riding Therapy, Dorset
Fullerton House School, South Yorkshire

Furze Mount, Conwy

The Grange Centre for People with
Disabilities, Surrey

The Hatch, South Gloucestershire

Henshaw's College, North Yorkshire

Hereward College, West Midlands

Hinwick Hall College of Further
Education, Northamptonshire

Holly Bank School, West Yorkshire

Ivers, Dorset

Kings Manor Education Centre, East Sussex

Kisimul School, Lincolnshire

Langside School, Dorset

Lindeth College of Further Education,
Cumbria

Linkage Further Education College,
Lincolnshire

Loddon School, Hampshire

Loppington House Further Education &
Adult Centre, Shropshire

MacIntyre School Wingrave,
Buckinghamshire

MacIntyre School Womaston, Powys

Meldreth Manor School, Hertfordshire

Mordaunt School, Hampshire

Nash College of Further Education, Kent

The National Star Centre's College of
Further Education, Gloucestershire

NCH Action for Children,
Vale of Glamorgan

Oakwood Court, Devon

Ochil Tower (Rudolf Steiner) School,
Perthshire

Orchard School, Shropshire

Overley Hall School, Shropshire

The Papworth Trust, Cambridgeshire

Parayhouse School, W12

Pengwern College, Denbighshire

Penhurst School, Oxfordshire

Pennine Camphill Community,
West Yorkshire

Philpots Manor School, West Sussex

Pield Heath School, Middlesex

Portfield School, Pembrokeshire

Portland College, Nottinghamshire

Queen Alexandra College of Further
Education, West Midlands

Queen Elizabeth's Training College, Surrey

RNIB Redhill College, Surrey

RNIB Rushton Hall School,
Northamptonshire

RNIB Sunshine House School, Middlesex

RNIB Sunshine House School, Merseyside

RNIB Vocational College, Leicestershire

Rowden House School, Herefordshire

Royal Blind School, Lothian

Rutherford School, Surrey

Rutland House School, Nottinghamshire

St Christophers School, Bristol

St Dominics School, Surrey

St Elizabeth's School, Hertfordshire

St John's College, East Sussex

St Loye's College, Devon

St Margaret's School, Surrey

St Mary's School, East Sussex

St Piers, Surrey

St Rose's School, Gloucestershire

St Vincent's School, Merseyside

seeABILITY (formerly Royal School for the
Blind), Surrey

Sense East, Cambridgeshire

The Sheiling Curative Schools, Hampshire

The Sheiling School, Bristol

Spring Hill School (Barnardo's),
North Yorkshire

Stanmore House Residential School,
South Lanarkshire

Strathmore House and Florence Villa,
Staffordshire

Stroud Court, Gloucestershire

Thornby Hall School, Northamptonshire

Treloar School, Hampshire

Weelsby Hall Further Education College,
North East Lincolnshire

The West of England College for Students
with little or no sight, Devon

Westgate College, Kent

Woodcroft School, Essex

Yateley Industries for the Disabled Ltd,
Hampshire

Hearing Impairment

Beech Tree School, Lancashire
Birkdale School for Hearing Impaired Children, Merseyside
Brewood Education Centre, Kent
Bridgend College, Bridgend
Camphill Blair Drummond Trust, Stirling
The Camphill Rudolf Steiner Schools, Aberdeenshire
Corbenic Camphill Community, Perthshire
Delrow College, Hertfordshire
Derby College For Deaf People, Derbyshire
Derwen College, Shropshire
Dilston College of Further Education, Northumberland
Doncaster College for the Deaf, South Yorkshire
Exeter College, Devon
Exhall Grange School, Warwickshire
Fairfield Opportunity Farm, Wiltshire
Finchale Training College, County Durham
Fortune Centre of Riding Therapy, Dorset
The Grange Centre for People with Disabilities, Surrey
Hamilton Lodge School for Deaf Children, East Sussex
The Hatch, South Gloucestershire
Henshaw's College, North Yorkshire
Hereward College, West Midlands
Hinwick Hall College of Further Education, Northamptonshire
Homefield Residential College, Leicestershire
Jordanstown Schools, County Antrim
Langside School, Dorset
Lindeth College of Further Education, Cumbria
Linkage Further Education College, Lincolnshire
Loppington House Further Education & Adult Centre, Shropshire
The Mary Hare Grammar School for the Deaf, Berkshire

Meldreth Manor School, Hertfordshire
Northern Counties School for the Deaf, Tyne and Wear
Ovingdean Hall School, East Sussex
The Papworth Trust, Cambridgeshire
Parayhouse School, W12
Penhurst School, Oxfordshire
Pennine Camphill Community, West Yorkshire
Philpots Manor School, West Sussex
Portland College, Nottinghamshire
Queen Alexandra College of Further Education, West Midlands
Queen Elizabeth's Training College, Surrey
RNIB Redhill College, Surrey
RNIB Vocational College, Leicestershire
RNID Poolemead, North East Somerset
Royal Cross Primary School, Lancashire
Royal National College for the Blind, Herefordshire
The Royal School for Deaf Children Margate, Kent
Royal School for the Blind, Merseyside
Royal School for the Deaf, Devon
Royal School for the Deaf (Manchester), Cheshire
Royal School for the Deaf, Derby, Derbyshire
Royal West of England School for the Deaf, Devon
Rutherford School, Surrey
Rutland House School, Nottinghamshire
St John's Catholic School for the Deaf, West Yorkshire
St Loye's College, Devon
St Margaret's School, Surrey
St Mary's School, East Sussex
St Vincent's School, Merseyside
seeABILITY (formerly Royal School for the Blind), Surrey
Sense East, Cambridgeshire

The Speech, Language & Hearing Centre, NW1

Stanmore House Residential School, South Lanarkshire

Treloar School, Hampshire

Trengweath School, Devon

Weelsby Hall Further Education College, North East Lincolnshire

The West of England College for Students with little or no sight, Devon

Westgate College, Kent

Woodcroft School, Essex

Yateley Industries for the Disabled Ltd, Hampshire

Yorkshire Residential School for the Deaf, South Yorkshire

Moderate Learning Difficulties

Banstead Place Brain Injury Rehabilitation, Surrey

Beaumont College of Further Education, Lancashire

Belgrave School, Bristol

Birkdale School for Hearing Impaired Children, Merseyside

Birtenshaw Hall School, Lancashire

Bladon House School, Staffordshire

Bramfield House, Suffolk

Brewood Education Centre, Kent

Bridge College, Cheshire

Broomhayes School, Devon

Bryn Melyn Group, Gwynedd

Burton Hill School, Wiltshire

Camphill Blair Drummond Trust, Stirling

The Camphill Rudolf Steiner Schools, Aberdeenshire

Cerrig Camu, Gwynedd

Chailey Heritage School, East Sussex

Chelfham Mill School, Devon

Chelfham Senior School, Devon

Cintre Community, Bristol

Coleg Elidyr, Carmarthenshire

Corbenic Camphill Community, Perthshire

Cotswold Chine School, Gloucestershire

Coxlease School, Hampshire

Crowthorn School (NCH Action for Children), Lancashire

Cruckton Hall, Shropshire

Dame Hannah Rogers School, Devon

The David Lewis School, Cheshire

Delamere Forest School, Cheshire

Delrow College, Hertfordshire

Derby College For Deaf People, Derbyshire

Derwen College, Shropshire

Dilston College of Further Education, Northumberland

Doncaster College for the Deaf, South Yorkshire

Dorton College of Further Education, Kent

Easter Auguston Training Farm, Aberdeenshire

Eastwood Grange School, Derbyshire

Eden Grove School, Cumbria

Exeter College, Devon

Fairfield Opportunity Farm, Wiltshire

Finchale Training College, County Durham

Fortune Centre of Riding Therapy, Dorset

Good Shepherd Centre, Renfrewshire

The Grange Centre for People with Disabilities, Surrey

Green Laund F.E. Centre, Derbyshire

Harmeny School, Lothian

The Hatch, South Gloucestershire

Henshaw's College, North Yorkshire

Hereward College, West Midlands

High Close School (Barnardo's), Berkshire

Hillcrest Pentwyn School, Herefordshire

Hillside School, Fife

Hinwick Hall College of Further Education, Northamptonshire

Holly Bank School, West Yorkshire

Homefield Residential College, Leicestershire

Ivers, Dorset

Kibble School, Renfrewshire
Kings Manor Education Centre, East Sussex
Kisharon Day School, NW11
Lambs House School, Cheshire
Lindeth College of Further Education, Cumbria
The Link Secondary School, Surrey
Linkage Further Education College, Lincolnshire
Linn Moor Residential School, Aberdeenshire
Loppington House Further Education & Adult Centre, Shropshire
Lufton Manor College, Somerset
MacIntyre School Womaston, Powys
Meadows School (Barnardo's), Kent
Minstead Training Project, Hampshire
The Mount Camphill Community, East Sussex
Nash College of Further Education, Kent
NCH Action for Children, Vale of Glamorgan
The New Learning Centre, NW6
Oakwood Court, Devon
Ochil Tower (Rudolf Steiner) School, Perthshire
Overley Hall School, Shropshire
Ovingdean Hall School, East Sussex
Owlswick School, East Sussex
The Papworth Trust, Cambridgeshire
Parayhouse School, W12
Pengwern College, Denbighshire
Pennine Camphill Community, West Yorkshire
Philip Green Memorial School, Dorset
Philpots Manor School, West Sussex
Pield Heath School, Middlesex
Pontville School, Lancashire
Portfield School, Pembrokeshire
Portland College, Nottinghamshire
Queen Alexandra College of Further Education, West Midlands
Queen Elizabeth's Training College, Surrey
Riverside School, Cumbria
RNIB Condover Hall School, Shropshire

RNIB Redhill College, Surrey
RNIB Rushton Hall School, Northamptonshire
RNIB Sunshine House School, Middlesex
The Robert Ogden School, South Yorkshire
Royal Blind School, Lothian
Royal School for the Blind, Merseyside
Royal School for the Deaf (Manchester), Cheshire
The Ryes School, Suffolk
St Andrews School, Norfolk
St Edwards School, Hampshire
St Elizabeth's School, Hertfordshire
St Francis Day Boy Unit, Glasgow
The St John Vianney School, Cheshire
The St John Vianney School, Greater Manchester
St John's College, East Sussex
St John's RC School, Essex
St Joseph's School, Surrey
St Mary's School, East Sussex
St Phillip's School, North Lanarkshire
St Piers, Surrey
St Rose's School, Gloucestershire
St Vincent's School, Merseyside
seeABILITY (formerly Royal School for the Blind), Surrey
Sense East, Cambridgeshire
The Sheiling Curative Schools, Hampshire
The Sheiling School, Bristol
Solden Hill House, Northamptonshire
Spring Hill School (Barnardo's), North Yorkshire
Springboig St John's, Glasgow
Strathmore House and Florence Villa, Staffordshire
Stroud Court, Gloucestershire
Swalcliffe Park School, Oxfordshire
Thornby Hall School, Northamptonshire
Treloar School, Hampshire
Underley Garden School, Lancashire
Underley Hall School, Lancashire
Vranch House School, Devon

Weelsby Hall Further Education College, North East Lincolnshire

West Kirby Residential School, Merseyside

The West of England College for Students with little or no sight, Devon

Westgate College, Kent

Westwood School, Kent

Whitstone Head School, Devon

Woodcroft School, Essex

Woodlands School, Dumfries & Galloway

Wychbury House Residential School, Devon

Yateley Industries for the Disabled Ltd, Hampshire

Yorkshire Residential School for the Deaf, South Yorkshire

Physical Impairment

Banstead Place Brain Injury Rehabilitation, Surrey

Beaumont College of Further Education, Lancashire

Beech Tree School, Lancashire

Birtenshaw Hall School, Lancashire

Bridge College, Cheshire

Burton Hill School, Wiltshire

The Camphill Rudolf Steiner Schools, Aberdeenshire

Cerrig Camu, Gwynedd

Chailey Heritage School, East Sussex

Coney Hill School, Kent

Corseford School, Strathclyde

Craig-y-Parc School, Cardiff

Dame Hannah Rogers School, Devon

The David Lewis School, Cheshire

Derby College For Deaf People, Derbyshire

Derwen College, Shropshire

Doncaster College for the Deaf, South Yorkshire

The Enham Trust, Hampshire

Exeter College, Devon

Exhall Grange School, Warwickshire

Finchale Training College, County Durham

Fourways Assessment Unit, Greater Manchester

Furze Mount, Conwy

The Grange Centre for People with Disabilities, Surrey

Henshaw's College, North Yorkshire

Hereward College, West Midlands

Hinwick Hall College of Further

Education, Northamptonshire

Holly Bank School, West Yorkshire

Hornsey Conductive Education Centre, N10

Kings Manor Education Centre, East Sussex

Lancasterian Special School, Greater Manchester

Langside School, Dorset

Linkage Further Education College, Lincolnshire

Love Walk, SE5

Meldreth Manor School, Hertfordshire

Mordaunt School, Hampshire

Nash College of Further Education, Kent

National Institute of Conductive Education, West Midlands

The National Star Centre's College of Further Education, Gloucestershire

Northern Counties School for the Deaf, Tyne and Wear

Orchard School, Shropshire

The Papworth Trust, Cambridgeshire

Penhurst School, Oxfordshire

Portland College, Nottinghamshire

Queen Alexandra College of Further Education, West Midlands

Queen Elizabeth's Training College, Surrey

RNIB Manor House, Devon

RNIB Redhill College, Surrey

RNIB Rushton Hall School, Northamptonshire

RNIB Sunshine House School, Middlesex

RNIB Sunshine House School, Merseyside
RNIB Vocational College, Leicestershire
RNID Poolemead, North East Somerset
Royal School for the Blind, Merseyside
Royal School for the Deaf (Manchester), Cheshire
Rutherford School, Surrey
Rutland House School, Nottinghamshire
St Elizabeth's School, Hertfordshire
St Loye's College, Devon
St Mary's School, East Sussex
St Rose's School, Gloucestershire
St Vincent's School, Merseyside
seeABILITY (formerly Royal School for the Blind), Surrey
Sense East, Cambridgeshire

Stanmore House Residential School, South Lanarkshire
Treloar School, Hampshire
Trengweath School, Devon
Vranch House School, Devon
The West of England College for Students with little or no sight, Devon
The West of England School and College for Pupils with little or no sight, Devon
Westgate College, Kent
Woodcroft School, Essex
Yateley Industries for the Disabled Ltd, Hampshire
Yorkshire Residential School for the Deaf, South Yorkshire

Profound/Multiple Learning Difficulties

Annie Lawson School, Berkshire
Beaumont College of Further Education, Lancashire
Beech Tree School, Lancashire
Birtenshaw Hall School, Lancashire
Bridge College, Cheshire
Broomhayes School, Devon
Camphill Blair Drummond Trust, Stirling
The Camphill Rudolf Steiner Schools, Aberdeenshire
Coney Hill School, Kent
Craig-y-Parc School, Cardiff
Dame Hannah Rogers School, Devon
East Park Home School, Glasgow
Holly Bank School, West Yorkshire
Kibble School, Renfrewshire
Langside School, Dorset
Linn Moor Residential School, Aberdeenshire
MacIntyre School Wingrave, Buckinghamshire
MacIntyre School Womaston, Powys
Meldreth Manor School, Hertfordshire
Mordaunt School, Hampshire
Nash College of Further Education, Kent

The National Star Centre's College of Further Education, Gloucestershire
Northern Counties School for the Deaf, Tyne and Wear
Ochil Tower (Rudolf Steiner) School, Perthshire
Pengwern College, Denbighshire
Penhurst School, Oxfordshire
Pield Heath School, Middlesex
Portfield School, Pembrokeshire
RNIB Condover Hall School, Shropshire
RNIB Rushton Hall School, Northamptonshire
RNIB Sunshine House School, Merseyside
RNIB Sunshine House School, Middlesex
Rowden House School, Herefordshire
Royal Blind School, Lothian
Royal School for the Blind, Merseyside
Royal School for the Deaf (Manchester), Cheshire
Rutherford School, Surrey
Rutland House School, Nottinghamshire
St Christophers School, Bristol
St Margaret's School, Surrey

seeABILITY (formerly Royal School for the Blind), Surrey
The Sheiling Curative Schools, Hampshire
The Sheiling School, Bristol
Stanmore House Residential School, South Lanarkshire
Sunfield, West Midlands

Trengweath School, Devon
Vranch House School, Devon
The West of England College for Students, Devon
Westgate College, Kent
Woodcroft School, Essex

Severe Learning Difficulties

Annie Lawson School, Berkshire
Aran Hall School, Gwynedd
Beaumont College of Further Education, Lancashire
Beech Tree School, Lancashire
Birtenshaw Hall School, Lancashire
Bladon House School, Staffordshire
Bridge College, Cheshire
Broomhayes School, Devon
Broughton House College, Lincolnshire
Burton Hill School, Wiltshire
Camphill Blair Drummond Trust, Stirling
The Camphill Rudolf Steiner Schools, Aberdeenshire
Cerrig Camu, Gwynedd
Chailey Heritage School, East Sussex
Coleg Elidyr, Carmarthenshire
Corbenic Camphill Community, Perthshire
Cotswold Chine School, Gloucestershire
Dame Hannah Rogers School, Devon
The David Lewis School, Cheshire
Derby College For Deaf People, Derbyshire
Derwen College, Shropshire
Dilston College of Further Education, Northumberland
East Park Home School, Glasgow
Exeter College, Devon
Fairfield Opportunity Farm, Wiltshire
Fortune Centre of Riding Therapy, Dorset
Fullerton House School, South Yorkshire
Furze Mount, Conwy
Green Laund F.E. Centre, Derbyshire
Henshaw's College, North Yorkshire
Hereward College, West Midlands

Hesley Village College, South Yorkshire
Hill House School, Hampshire
Hinwick Hall College of Further Education, Northamptonshire
Holly Bank School, West Yorkshire
Homefield Residential College, Leicestershire
Hope Lodge School, Hampshire
Ivers, Dorset
Kisimul School, Lincolnshire
Lambs House School, Cheshire
Langside School, Dorset
Linkage Further Education College, Lincolnshire
Linn Moor Residential School, Aberdeenshire
Loddon School, Hampshire
Loppington House Further Education & Adult Centre, Shropshire
Lufton Manor College, Somerset
MacIntyre School Wingrave, Buckinghamshire
MacIntyre School Womaston, Powys
Meldreth Manor School, Hertfordshire
Nash College of Further Education, Kent
Oakwood Court, Devon
Ochil Tower (Rudolf Steiner) School, Perthshire
Orchard School, Shropshire
Overley Hall School, Shropshire
Pengwern College, Denbighshire
Pennine Camphill Community, West Yorkshire
Philip Green Memorial School, Dorset

Pield Heath School, Middlesex
Portfield School, Pembrokeshire
RNIB Condover Hall School, Shropshire
RNIB Redhill College, Surrey
RNIB Rushton Hall School,
 Northamptonshire
RNIB Sunshine House School,
 Middlesex
RNIB Sunshine House School,
 Merseyside
The Robert Ogden School, South Yorkshire
Rowden House School, Herefordshire
Royal Blind School, Lothian
Royal School for the Blind, Merseyside
Royal School for the Deaf (Manchester),
 Cheshire
Rutherford School, Surrey
The Ryes School, Suffolk
St Christophers School, Bristol
St Elizabeth's School, Hertfordshire
St John's College, East Sussex
St John's RC School, Essex
St Joseph's School, Surrey

St Piers, Surrey
St Rose's School, Gloucestershire
seeABILITY (formerly Royal School for the
 Blind), Surrey
Sense East, Cambridgeshire
The Sheiling Curative Schools, Hampshire
The Sheiling School, Bristol
Spring Hill School (Barnardo's),
 North Yorkshire
Stanmore House Residential School, South
 Lanarkshire
Strathmore House and Florence Villa,
 Staffordshire
Stroud Court, Gloucestershire
Sunfield, West Midlands
Weelsby Hall Further Education College,
 North East Lincolnshire
The West of England College for Students
 with little or no sight, Devon
Westgate College, Kent
Westwood, Staffordshire
Wilsic Hall School, South Yorkshire
Woodcroft School, Essex

Specific Learning Difficulties

Appleford School, Wiltshire
Banham Marshalls College, Norfolk
Banstead Place Brain Injury Rehabilitation,
 Surrey
Barnardo's Lecropt Project, Stirling
Belgrave School, Bristol
Bessels Leigh School, Oxfordshire
Blossom House School, SW20
Bridgend College, Bridgend
Broomhayes School, Devon
Bruern Abbey School, Oxfordshire
Calder House School, Wiltshire
Camphill Blair Drummond Trust, Stirling
The Camphill Rudolf Steiner Schools,
 Aberdeenshire
Cedar House School, Lancashire
Corbenic Camphill Community, Perthshire
Cotswold Chine School, Gloucestershire

Crookhey Hall School, Lancashire
Cruckton Hall, Shropshire
Delamere Forest School, Cheshire
Derby College For Deaf People, Derbyshire
Dilston College of Further Education,
 Northumberland
Doncaster College for the Deaf,
 South Yorkshire
East Court School, Kent
Edington and Shapwick School, Somerset
Exeter College, Devon
Fairfield Opportunity Farm, Wiltshire
Fairley House School, SW1P
Farney Close School, West Sussex
Fortune Centre of Riding Therapy, Dorset
Green Laund F.E. Centre, Derbyshire
Harmeny School, Lothian
Hereward College, West Midlands

Hillcrest Pentwyn School, Herefordshire
Hillside School, Fife
Hinwick Hall College of Further
    Education, Northamptonshire
Home School of Stoke Newington, N16
Kibble School, Renfrewshire
Kisimul School, Lincolnshire
The Knowl Hill School, Surrey
Lindeth College of Further Education,
    Cumbria
The Link Primary School, Surrey
Linkage Further Education College,
    Lincolnshire
Loppington House Further Education &
    Adult Centre, Shropshire
Lowgate House School, Cumbria
MacIntyre School Wingrave,
    Buckinghamshire
Maple Hayes Hall Dyslexia School,
    Staffordshire
The Marchant-Holliday School, Somerset
The Moat School, SW6
Moon Hall School, Surrey
Mordaunt School, Hampshire
More House School, Surrey
Nash College of Further Education, Kent
NCH Action for Children,
    Vale of Glamorgan
Northease Manor, East Sussex
Nugent House School, Lancashire
Nunnykirk Centre for Dyslexia,
    Northumberland
Oakwood Court, Devon
Ovingdean Hall School, East Sussex
Pennine Camphill Community,
    West Yorkshire

Pield Heath School, Middlesex
Queen Elizabeth's Training College,
    Surrey
RNIB Redhill College, Surrey
Royal Cross Primary School, Lancashire
Royal National College for the Blind,
    Herefordshire
Royal School for the Deaf (Manchester),
    Cheshire
St Andrews School, Norfolk
St Dominics School, Surrey
St Mary's School, East Sussex
St Vincent's School, Merseyside
Spring Hill School (Barnardo's),
    North Yorkshire
Strathmore House and Florence Villa,
    Staffordshire
Treloar School, Hampshire
Trengweath School, Devon
Underley Garden School, Lancashire
Underley Hall School, Lancashire
Unicorn School, Oxfordshire
Weelsby Hall Further Education College,
    North East Lincolnshire
Westgate College, Kent
Whitstone Head School, Devon
Wilsic Hall School, South Yorkshire
Witherslack Hall, Cumbria
Woodcroft School, Essex
Woodlands School, Dumfries & Galloway
Wychbury House Residential School,
    Devon
Yateley Industries for the Disabled Ltd,
    Hampshire
Yorkshire Residential School for the Deaf,
    South Yorkshire

Speech and Language Difficulties

Alderwasley Hall School, Derbyshire
Appleford School, Wiltshire
Banham Marshalls College, Norfolk
Banstead Place Brain Injury Rehabilitation,
    Surrey

Barnardo's Lecropt Project, Stirling
Beaumont College of Further Education,
    Lancashire
Beech Tree School, Lancashire
Birkdale School for Hearing Impaired

St John's Catholic School for the Deaf, West Yorkshire
St John's College, East Sussex
St John's RC School, Essex
St Joseph's School, Surrey
St Mary's School, East Sussex
St Piers, Surrey
St Rose's School, Gloucestershire
St Vincent's School, Merseyside
The Sheiling Curative Schools, Hampshire
The Sheiling School, Bristol
The Speech, Language & Hearing Centre, NW1
Stanmore House Residential School, South Lanarkshire
Stroud Court, Gloucestershire

The Sybil Elgar School, Middlesex
Treloar School, Hampshire
Vranch House School, Devon
Weelsby Hall Further Education College, North East Lincolnshire
West Kirby Residential School, Merseyside
The West of England College for Students with little or no sight, Devon
Westgate College, Kent
Wilsic Hall School, South Yorkshire
Woodcroft School, Essex
Woodlands School, Dumfries & Galloway
Yateley Industries for the Disabled Ltd, Hampshire
Yorkshire Residential School for the Deaf, South Yorkshire

Tourette Syndrome

Aran Hall School, Gwynedd
Brewood Education Centre, Kent
The Camphill Rudolf Steiner Schools, Aberdeenshire
Chelfham Mill School, Devon
Chelfham Senior School, Devon
Cotswold Chine School, Gloucestershire
Delamere Forest School, Cheshire
Eden Grove School, Cumbria
Grateley House School, Hampshire
Hereward College, West Midlands
Linkage Further Education College, Lincolnshire
NCH Action for Children, Vale of Glamorgan
Nugent House School, Lancashire

Oakwood Court, Devon
Overley Hall School, Shropshire
Philpots Manor School, West Sussex
Pontville School, Lancashire
Potterspury Lodge School, Northamptonshire
RNIB Sunshine House School, Middlesex
Rossendale Special School, Lancashire
Rowden House School, Herefordshire
Royal Blind School, Lothian
St Elizabeth's School, Hertfordshire
St Mary's School, East Sussex
Starley Hall, Fife
West Kirby Residential School, Merseyside
Whitstone Head School, Devon

Visual Impairment

Banstead Place Brain Injury Rehabilitation, Surrey
Beech Tree School, Lancashire
Brewood Education Centre, Kent

Bridgend College, Bridgend
The Camphill Rudolf Steiner Schools, Aberdeenshire
Chailey Heritage School, East Sussex

Coney Hill School, Kent
Corbenic Camphill Community, Perthshire
Derby College For Deaf People, Derbyshire
Derwen College, Shropshire
Doncaster College for the Deaf,
   South Yorkshire
**Dorton College of Further Education,
   Kent**
Exeter College, Devon
Exhall Grange School, Warwickshire
Fortune Centre of Riding Therapy, Dorset
Henshaw's College, North Yorkshire
Hereward College, West Midlands
Jordanstown Schools, County Antrim
Langside School, Dorset
Linkage Further Education College,
   Lincolnshire
Linn Moor Residential School,
   Aberdeenshire
Loppington House Further Education &
   Adult Centre, Shropshire
Meldreth Manor School, Hertfordshire
Mordaunt School, Hampshire
Nash College of Further Education, Kent
The National Star Centre's College of
   Further Education, Gloucestershire
**Northern Counties School for the Deaf,
   Tyne and Wear**
Ovingdean Hall School, East Sussex
Penhurst School, Oxfordshire
Pennine Camphill Community,
   West Yorkshire
Pield Heath School, Middlesex
Portfield School, Pembrokeshire
Portland College, Nottinghamshire
Queen Alexandra College of Further
   Education, West Midlands
Queen Elizabeth's Training College, Surrey
RNIB Alwyn House, Fife
RNIB Condover Hall School, Shropshire

RNIB Manor House, Devon
RNIB New College, Worcestershire
RNIB Redhill College, Surrey
**RNIB Rushton Hall School,
   Northamptonshire**
RNIB Sunshine House School, Middlesex
**RNIB Sunshine House School,
   Merseyside**
RNIB Vocational College, Leicestershire
RNID Poolemead, North East Somerset
Royal Blind School, Lothian
Royal London Society for the Blind, Kent
**Royal National College for the Blind,
   Herefordshire**
Royal School for the Blind, Merseyside
Royal School for the Deaf (Manchester),
   Cheshire
Rutherford School, Surrey
Rutland House School, Nottinghamshire
St Elizabeth's School, Hertfordshire
St Loye's College, Devon
St Margaret's School, Surrey
St Mary's School, East Sussex
St Rose's School, Gloucestershire
St Vincent's School, Merseyside
**seeABILITY (formerly Royal School for
   the Blind), Surrey**
Sense East, Cambridgeshire
Stanmore House Residential School, South
   Lanarkshire
Treloar School, Hampshire
Trengweath School, Devon
**The West of England College for Students
   with little or no sight, Devon**
**The West of England School and College
   for Pupils with little or no sight, Devon**
Westgate College, Kent
Woodcroft School, Essex
Yorkshire Residential School for the Deaf,
   South Yorkshire

Wheelchair access

Annie Lawson School, Berkshire

Banham Marshalls College, Norfolk

The St John Vianney School, Cheshire
St John's Catholic School for the Deaf, West Yorkshire
St Loye's College, Devon
St Margaret's School, Surrey
St Mary's School, East Sussex
St Rose's School, Gloucestershire
St Vincent's School, Merseyside
seeABILITY (formerly Royal School for the Blind), Surrey
Sense East, Cambridgeshire
Snowdon School, Stirling

The Speech, Language & Hearing Centre, NW1
Stroud Court, Gloucestershire
Treloar School, Hampshire
Unicorn School, Oxfordshire
Vranch House School, Devon
The West of England College for Students with little or no sight, Devon
The West of England School and College for Pupils with little or no sight, Devon
Woodcroft School, Essex
Yateley Industries for the Disabled Ltd, Hampshire

5.2
Council for the Registration of Schools Teaching Dyslexic Pupils (CReSTeD)

Registered charity number 1052103
Information supplied by CReSTeD, April 2001

CReSTeD (the Council for the Registration of Schools Teaching Dyslexic Pupils) produces a twice yearly (Spring and Autumn) register of schools that provide for dyslexic children. The aim is to help parents and those who advise them to choose a school that has been approved to published criteria. CReSTeD was established over eleven years ago - its main supporters are the British Dyslexia Association and The Dyslexia Institute. Schools wishing to be included in the Register are visited by a CReSTeD consultant whose report is considered by the CReSTeD Council before registration can be finalised.

Consulting the Register should enable parents to decide which schools they wish to approach for further information. Dyslexic students have a variety of difficulties and so have a wide range of special needs. An equally wide range of teaching approaches is necessary. CReSTeD has therefore grouped schools together under four broad headings which have recently been renamed to avoid giving the impression of hierarchy, ie one group of schools should not be considered 'better' than another. The categories are designed to help parents match their child's needs to an appropriate philosophy and provision.

The four categories of the schools are described below:

Specialist Provision (SP) schools are specifically established to teach pupils with dyslexia and related specific learning difficulties.

The other three categories offer special help to dyslexic children within or alongside mainstream provision:

Dyslexia Unit (DU) schools offer a designated unit that provides specialist tuition for a small group or individual basis, according to need;

Specialist Classes (SC) schools teach dyslexic pupils in separate classes within the school for some lessons (often English and Mathematics);

Withdrawal System (WS) schools help dyslexic children by withdrawing them from appropriately selected lessons for specialist tuition.

A school in one category may also offer the sort of care found in a different, less intensive category. For example, a Dyslexia Unit category school may offer a Withdrawal System. If a school seems appropriate in other ways, parents should check directly with the school.

CReSTeD only examines the adequacy of a school's provision for dyslexic pupils. Registration with or approval by other educational associations, or status with the department Local Education and Employment (DfEE), Office for Standards in Education (Ofsted) or the Local Education Authority, takes account of a school's general competence and administration.

A free copy of the Register can be obtained by contacting CReSTeD on 01242 604852 or by email at **admin@crested.org.uk**, or by writing to The Administrator, Greygarth, Litttleworth, Winchcombe, Cheltenham, GL54 5BT. Alternatively, visit the website at www.crested.org.uk

SPECIALIST PROVISION SCHOOLS – SP

These cater for dyslexic students whose difficulties are most severe. These students are a small section of the dyslexic population and do not relish close liaison with non-dyslexic colleagues because they are seen to fail very publicly in the curriculum. They prefer to be in a school where everyone has a similar difficulty. These schools are small in size, with small classes, offering a whole school approach and a broad, balanced but suitable restricted curriculum which ensures a high level of individual skills directed teaching, using multi-sensory principles.

Appleford School
Shrewton, Salisbury, Wiltshire SP3 4HL
Tel: (01980) 621020
Independent; rural; boarding, weekly
boarding and day
90 boys and girls 7–13

Brown's School
Cannock House, Hawstead Lane,
Chelsfield, Orpington, Kent BR6 7PH
Tel/Fax: (01689) 876816
Independent; rural; day
33 boys and girls 6–12

Calder House School
Colerne, Bath, Wiltshire SN14 8BN
Tel: (01225) 742329
Independent; day
32 boys and girls 5–13

Centre Academy
92 St John's Hill Battersea, London
SW11 1SH
Tel: (020) 7738 2344
Independent, city, day
55 boys and girls 8–18

The Dominie
142 Battersea Park Road, London
SW11 4NB
Tel: (020) 7720 8783
Independent; city; day
32 boys and girls 6–13

East Court School
Victoria Parade, Ramsgate, Kent CT11 8ED
Tel: (01843) 592077
Independent; town; boarding, weekly
boarding and day
67 boys and girls 8–13

Edington and Shapwick School
Shapwick Manor, Shapwick, Bridgwater,
Somerset TA9 9NJ
Tel: (01458) 210384
Independent, rural; boarding, weekly
boarding and day
169 boys and girls 8–17

Fairley House School
30 Causton Street, London SW1P 4AU
Tel: (020) 7976 5456
Independent; city; day
95 boys and girls 6–12

Frewen College
Brickwall, Northiam, Rye, East Sussex
TN31 6NL
Tel: (01797) 252494
Independent; village; boarding; day
69 boys 11–17

Knowl Hill School
School Lane, Pirbright, Surrey GU24 0JN
Tel: (01483) 797032
Independent; village; day
40 boys and girls 7–16

Laleham School
Northdown Park Road, Cliftonville,
Margate, Kent CT9 2TP
Tel: (01843) 221946
Local education authority; edge of town;
boarding, weekly boarding and day
104 boys and girls 9–16

Mark College
Mark, Highbridge, Somerset TA9 4NP
Tel: (01278) 641632
DfEE Beacon School; independent, rural;
boarding, weekly boarding and day
80 boys 10–16

Moon Hall School
'Feldemore', Holmbury St Mary, Dorking,
Surrey RH5 6LQ
Tel: (01306) 731464
Independent; rural; weekly boarding and
day
80 boys and girls 7–13

More House School
Moons Hill, Frensham, Farnham, Surrey
GU10 3AP
Tel: (01252) 792303
Independent; rural; boarding, weekly
boarding and day
150 boys 9–16

Northease Manor School
Rodmell, Lewes, East Sussex BN7 3EY
Tel: (01273) 472915
Independent; rural; weekly boarding and
day
85 boys and girls 10–17

Nunnykirk Centre for Dyslexia
Netherwitton, Morpeth, Northumberland
NE61 4PB
Tel: (01670) 772685
Independent; rural; boarding and day
40 boys and girls 9–16

The Old Rectory School
Brettenham, Ipswich, Suffolk IP7 7QR
Tel: (01449) 736404
Independent; rural; boarding, weekly
boarding and day
48 boys and girls 7–13

Sunnydown School
Portley House, 152 Whyteleafe Road,
Caterham, Surrey CR3 5ED
Tel: (01883) 342281
Local education authority; edge of town;
weekly boarding and day
74 boys 11–16

The Unicorn School
Stroud Court, Oxford Road, Enysham
Oxfordshire, OX8 1BY
Tel: (01865) 881820
Independent, village, day
36 boys and girls 6–12

DYSLEXIA UNIT – DU

DU schools are larger and offer education to a limited number of dyslexic students in an *ordinary education setting*. These schools usually operate an initial screening system to ensure that the dyslexic student intake can cope with the breadth and pace of curriculum development, and that the facilities offered by the unit are appropriate to meet the less serious special needs of these students.

Abbotsholme School
Rocester, Uttoxeter, Staffordshire ST14 5BS
Tel: (01889) 590217
Independent; rural; boarding, weekly boarding and day
235 boys and girls 9–18

Avon House School
490 High Road, Woodford Green, Essex
IG8 0PN
Tel: (020) 8504 1749
Independent; edge of town; day
280 boys and girls 2–11

Bethany School
Curtisden Green, Goudhurst, Cranbrook,
Kent TN17 1LB
Tel: (01580) 211273
Independent; rural; boarding and day
280 boys and girls 11–18

Bloxham School
Bloxham, Near Banbury, Oxfordshire
OX15 4PE
Tel: (01295) 720222
Independent; rural; boarding and day
385 boys and 44 girls 11–18

Clayesmore Preparatory School
Iwerne Minster, Blandford Forum, Dorset
DT11 8PH
Tel: (01747) 811707
Independent; village; boarding and day
260 boys and girls 5–13

Clayesmore School
Iwerne Minster, Blandford Forum, Dorset
DT11 8LL
Tel: (01747) 812122
Independent; rural; boarding and day
305 boys and girls 13–18

Clifton College Preparatory School
The Avenue, Clifton, Bristol BS8 3HE
Tel: (0117) 973 7264
Independent; edge of town; boarding, weekly boarding and day
400 boys and girls 8–13

Cobham Hall
Cobham, Gravesend, Kent DA12 3BL
Tel: (01474) 823371
Independent; rural; boarding and day
190 girls 11–18

Ellesmere College
Ellesmere, Shropshire SY12 9AB
Tel: (01691) 622321
Independent; rural; boarding and day
410 boys and girls 9–18

Ercall Wood Technology School
Golf Links Lane, Wellington, Telford,
Shropshire TF1 2DU
Tel: (01952) 417800
Local authority; town; day
825 boys and girls 11–16

Fulneck School
Fulneck, Pudsey, Leeds, West Yorkshire
LS28 8DS
Tel: (0113) 257 0235
Independent; semi-rural; boarding, weekly
boarding and day
424 boys and girls 3–18

Grenville College
Bideford, Devon EX39 3JR
Tel: (01237) 472212
Independent; rural town; boarding and day
380 boys and girls 8–18

Hillcroft Preparatory School
Walnut Tree Manor, Haughley Green,
Stowmarket, Suffolk IP14 3RQ
Tel: (01449) 673003
Independent; rural; day
86 boys and girls 2–13

Holmwood House School
Lexden, Colchester, Essex CO3 5ST
Tel: (01206) 574305
Independent; edge of town; boarding and
day
338 boys and girls 4–13

Hurst Lodge
Bagshot Road, Ascot, Berkshire SL5 9JU
Tel: (01344) 622154
Independent; town; boarding, weekly
boarding and day
160 girls 2–18, 40 day boys 2–11

Kingham Hill School
Kingham, Chipping Norton, Oxfordshire
OX7 6TH
Tel: (01608) 658999
Independent; rural; boarding, weekly
boarding and day
210 boys and girls 11–18

King's School Rochester
Satis House, Boley Hill,
Rochester, Kent ME1 1TE
Tel: (01634) 843913
Independent, city, boarding, weekly
boarding and day
340 boys and girls 13–18

**Kings School Rochester,
Preparatory School**
King Edward Road, Rochester
Kent ME1 1UB
Tel: (01634) 843657
Independent, city, boarding,
weekly boarding and day
230 boys and girls 8–13

Merchiston Castle School
Colinton, Edinburgh E13 0PU
Tel: (0131) 312 2200
Independent; edge of town; boarding; day
390 boys 8–18

Newlands Preparatory School
Eastbourne Road, Seaford, East Sussex
BN25 4NP
Tel: (01323) 892334
Independent; edge of town; boarding,
weekly boarding and day
200 boys and girls 2–13

New Hall School
Chelmsford, Essex CM3 3HT
Tel: (01245) 467588
Independent, town, day
250 boys and girls 4–11
boarding, weekly boarding and day
370 girls 11–18

Roundhay School
Gledhow Lane, Leeds LS8 1ND
Tel: (0113) 293 7711
Local education authority; city; day
1192 boys and girls 11–18

St David's College
Llandudno, Conwy LL30 1RD
Tel: (01492) 875974
Independent; rural; boarding, weekly
boarding and day
210 boys and girls 11–18

Sibford School
Sibford Ferris, Banbury, Oxfordshire
OX15 5QL
Tel: (01295) 781200
Independent; rural; boarding, weekly
boarding and day
320 boys and girls 5–18

Sidcot School
Winscombe, North Somerset BS25 1PD
Tel: (01934) 843102
Independent; rural; boarding, weekly
boarding and day
74 boys and girls 3–8, 405 boys and
girls 9–18

Stanbridge Earls School
Romsey, Hampshire SO51 0SZ
Tel: (01794) 516777
Independent; boarding and day
184 boys and girls 11–18

Stowford College
95 Brighton Road, Sutton, Surrey
SM2 5SJ
Tel: (020) 8661 9444
Independent; urban; day
70 boys and girls 7–16+

St James's School
West Malvern, Worcestershire,
WR14 4DF
Tel: (01684) 560851
Independent, semi-rural, boarding,
weekly boarding and day
120 girls 10–18

Thornlow Preparatory School
Woodsford House, Connaught Road,
Weymouth, Dorset DT4 0SA
Tel: (01305) 785703
Independent; rural; boarding, weekly
boarding and day
70 boys and girls 3–13

SPECIALIST CLASSES – SC

These schools meet the needs of dyslexics in the ordinary classroom through support, differentiation of the curriculum, and special tuition within the classroom setting; or, where necessary, through limited withdrawal. Many of these schools are maintained and can call on the expertise of the psychology and special needs support services of the education authority.

Bodiam Manor School
Bodiam, Robertsbridge, East Sussex
TN32 5UJ
Tel: (01580) 830225
Independent; rural; day
170 boys and girls 2–13

Box Hill School
Mickleham, Dorking, Surrey RH5 6EA
Tel: (01372) 373382
Independent; edge of town; boarding,
weekly boarding and day
268 boys and girls 11–18

Brontë House School
Apperley Bridge, Bradford, Yorkshire
BD10 0PQ
Tel: (0113) 250 2811
Independent; edge of city; boarding,
weekly boarding and day

Danes Hill School
Leatherhead Road, Oxshott, Surrey
KT22 0JG
Tel: (01372) 842509
Independent, rural, day
800 boys and girls 3–13

The Hugh Christie Technology College
Norwich Avenue, Tonbridge, Kent
TN10 4QL
Tel: (01732) 353544
Local education authority; town; day
1100 boys and girls 11–18

King's School Junior School
Ely, Cambridgeshire CB7 4DB
Tel: (01353) 660730
Independent; small city; boarding, weekly
boarding and day
320 boys and girls 8–13

King's School, Ely
Ely, Cambridgeshire CB7 4DB
Tel: (01353) 660700
Independent; small city; boarding, weekly
boarding and day
400 boys and girls 13–18

Llandovery College
Llandovery, Carmarthenshire SA20 0EE
Tel: (01550) 723000
Independent; town; boarding; weekly
boarding; day
220 boys and girls 11–18

Mayville High School
35 St Simon's Road, Southsea, Hampshire
PO5 2PE
Tel: (023) 9273 4487
Independent; city; day
55 boys 4–11, 193 girls 4–16

Mount St Mary's College
Spinkhill, Derbyshire
S21 3YL
Tel: (01246) 433388
Independent, rural, boarding, weekly
boarding and day
285 boys and girls 11–18

Newlands Pre-Preparatory and Nursery School
Eastbourne Road, Seaford, East Sussex
BN25 4NP
Tel: (01323) 896461
Independent; edge of town; day
150 boys and girls 2–8

Ramillies Hall School
Cheadle Hulme, Cheadle, Cheshire
SK8 7AJ
Tel: (0161) 485 3804
Independent, edge of town, boarding
weekly boarding and day
89 boys and girls 4–13

Slindon College
Slindon House, Arundel, West Sussex
BN18 0RH
Tel: (01243) 814320
Independent; village; boarding, weekly
boarding and day
110 boys 11–18

St Elphin's School
Darley Dale, Matlock, Derbyshire
DE4 2HA
Tel: (01629) 733263
Independent, rural, boarding, weekly
boarding and day
135 girls 5–16

WITHDRAWAL SYSTEM – WS

These are usually larger schools with only a very small minority of much less seriously affected dyslexic students enrolled. These schools offer a broad academic curriculum where individual needs are met by limited withdrawal, either within the working day, or outside the timetabled curriculum to an unsupported specialist teacher.

Hordle Walhampton School
Lymington, Hampshire SO41 5ZG
Tel: (01590) 672013
Independent; rural; boarding, weekly
boarding and day
177 boys and girls 7–13

Monkton Combe School
Bath BA22 7HG
Tel: (01225) 721102
Independent; village; boarding, weekly
boarding and day
346 boys and girls 11–18

Mowden Hall School
Newton, Stocksfield, Northumberland
NE43 7TD
Tel: (01661) 842147
Independent; rural; boarding, weekly
boarding and day
170 boys and girls 4–13

Newlands School
34 The Grove, Gosforth, Newcastle upon
Tyne NE3 1NH
Tel: (0191) 285 2208
Independent; city; day
252 boys 3–13

Prior Park Preparatory School
Cricklade, Calcutt Street, Wiltshire
SN6 6BB
Tel: (01793) 750275
Independent; edge of town; boarding,
weekly boarding and day
187 boys and girls 2–13

St Bede's School
Bishton Hall, Wolseley Bridge,
Staffordshire ST17 0XN
Tel: (01889) 881277
Independent; rural; boarding, weekly
boarding and day
130 boys and girls 3–13

St Bees School
St Bees, Cumbria CA27 0DS
Tel: (01946) 822263
Independent; village; boarding, weekly
boarding and day
300 boys and girls 11–18

Windlesham House School
Washington, Pulborough, West Sussex
RH20 4AY
Tel: (01903) 873207
Independent; rural; boarding
290 boys and girls 4–13

Woodhouse Grove School
Apperley Bridge, West Yorkshire
BD10 0NR
Tel: (0113) 250 2477
Independent; edge of town; boarding,
weekly boarding and day
555 boys and girls 11–16

Woodleigh School
Langton Hall, Langton, Malton, North
Yorkshire YO17 9QN
Tel: (01653) 658215
Independent; rural; boarding, weekly
boarding and day
55 boys and girls 7–13

5.3

Useful Addresses and Associations

Action for Blind People
14–16 Verney Road
London SE16 3DZ
Tel: (020) 7635 4800
Fax: (020) 7635 4900

Services include an information and advice
service, including welfare rights advice and
a national mobile service. Publications
include "Disability Living Allowance for
visually impaired children" and "Young
people in full-time education: a guide for
visually impaired people" (benefit
information).

Action for Sick Children
300 Kingston Road
Wimbledon
London SW20 8LX
Tel: (020) 8542 4848
Helpline: (0800) 074 4519
Contact: P Moreton, Librarian

Aims to join parents and professionals in
promoting high quality health care for
children in hospital and at home.
Services include: library and information
service, publications, research and a
branch network which offers advice and
support.

Advice Service Capability Scotland (ASCS)
11 Ellersly Road
Edinburgh EH12 6HY
Tel: (0131) 313 5510
Fax: (0131) 346 1681

Advisory Centre for Education (ACE) Ltd
1C Aberdeen Studios
22–24 Highbury Grove
London N5 2DQ
Tel: Advice Lines (020) 7354 8321
Monday–Friday 2–5pm

The Advisory Centre for Education is an
independent national education advice
centre which offers free and confidential
telephone advice to parents every weekday
from 2–5pm on 020 7354 8321. Over 200
parents phone weekly with questions about
their children's education. ACE helps
explain the school system, formal
procedures, and aspects of education law,
particularly in the areas of admission and
exclusion appeals, and special educational
needs issues. ACE has a full range of
publications described in a free publication
leaflet and offers training to parents groups,
governors, LEA officers and teachers.
Contact the business line (020) 8354 8318
for these services or write to ACE at the
above address.

Afasic
69–85 Old Street
London EC1V 9HX
Helpline: (0845) 355 5577
Administration (020) 841 8900
e-mail: info@afasic.org.uk
Website: www.afasic.org.uk

Afasic represents children and young
adults with speech, language and
communication difficulties and supports
and provides information to parents/carers
and professionals.

Association of Educational Psychologists
26 The Avenue
Durham, DH1 4ED
Tel: (0191) 384 9512
Fax: (0191) 386 5287
Secretary: D Webster, BA, Msc

Trade union and professional body
representing educational psychologists.

**Association of National Specialist
Colleges (NATSPEC)**
PO Box 358
Grimsby DN34 4YA
Tel/Fax: (01472) 594014
email: chriswberry@ntlworld.com
Secretariat: Chris Berry

NATSPEC member colleges seek to offer
the widest choice of innovative, high
quality, cost-effective and appropriate
further education and training, in
residential or day settings, for young
people and adults with learning difficulties
and/or disabilities.

**Association for Spina Bifida and
Hydrocephalus (ASBAH)**
National Centre
42 Park Road
Peterborough PE1 2UQ
Tel: (01733) 555988
Fax: (01733) 555 985
e-mail: gillw@asbah.org

Executive Director: Andrew Russell, MA
Specialist Education Advisers: Four advisers cover England, Wales and Northern Ireland.

ASBAH provides information, advice and advocacy for people with Spina Bifida and or Hydrocephalus, promotes strategies which reduce their dependence on others, and funds medical and psychological reasearch.

The Association of Workers for Children with Emotional and Behavioural Difficulties
Charlton Court
East Sutton
Maidstone
Kent ME17 3DQ
Tel: (01622) 843104
e-mail: awcebd@mistral.co.uk

Website: www.awcebd.co.uk
Administrative Officer: Allan Rimmer

The Bobath Centre For Children with Cerebral Palsy –
Registered Charity No. 229663
250 East End Road
London N2 8AU
Tel: (020) 8444 3355
Fax: (020) 8444 3399
Consultant Paediatrician:
Dr Andrew Lloyd Evans MA, MD, FRCP

The Bobath treatment concept was developed by Dr and Mrs Bobath in the 1940s and is a holistic interdisciplinary approach involving occupational physio- and speech and language therapists. Treatment provided on an individual basis (outpatient only), and therapists teach

parents and carers how to continue therapy at home/or in school. A letter of referral is required from the child's consultant paediatrician or general practitioner giving full medical history and birth details. Letters should be addressed to the Director. On the basis of this information an application for funding may be made to the NHS. When the Centre has been notified in writing that its fees will be met, a consultation or course of treatment will be offered. If you would like further information this may be obtained from the Appointments & Funding Organiser.
The Centre organises post-graduate training courses in the Bobath treatment approach for physio-, occupational and speech and language therapists who are working with children who have cerebral palsy.
Details may be obtained from the Course Organiser.
For a list of the Centre's publications and teaching films please send a s.a.e. to the address above.

Break, Special Needs, Special Care (Registered Charity No. 286650)
7a Church Street, Sheringham
Norfolk NR26 8QR
Tel: (01263) 822161
Fax: (01263) 822181
email: office@break.charity.demon.co.uk
Contact: Geoffrey Davison

Break provides holidays and respite care for children and adults with learning disabilities and other special needs.
Full 24-hour care and a varied holiday programme, including outings, are provided. Special dietary requirements can be met. Centres are fully accessible, have numerous aids and adaptations, heated indoor swimming pool and adapted bus with wheelchair lift.

Breakthrough Deaf-Hearing Integration
National Office, Alan Geale House
The Close, Westhill Campus
Bristol Road
Birmingham B29 6LN
Tel: (0121) 415 2289
Text: (0121) 415 2289
Fax: (0121) 415 2323
Contact: Gill Winstanley,
National Services Manager

Developing innovative work between deaf and hearing people of all ages through partnership. Operates through four regional centres, London, Southern Counties, West Midlands and the North East (Gateshead) offering a programme of Contact, Information and Training. Meetings and activities vary in each region. For further information contact

	Text	Telephone
London	020 8853 2683	020 8853 5661
Southern Counties	01252 313 882	01252 313 882
West Midlands	0121 415 5900	0121 472 5488
North East	07977 257 668	01967 648 195

British Association of Teachers of the Deaf (BATOD)
21 The Haystacks, High Wycombe
Buckinghamshire HP13 6PY
Tel: (01494) 464 190
email: secretary@batod.org.uk
Website: www.batod.org.uk
Hon Secretary: Mr Paul Simpson

The British Association for Teachers of the Deaf (BATOD) is the only Association representing the interests of Teachers of the Deaf in this country. BATOD promotes the educational interests of all hearing-impaired children, young people and adults and safeguards the interests of Teachers of the Deaf. Nationally, conferences are organised to develop the professional expertise of Association members and to promote issues connected with the education of hearing-impaired children. There are seven Regions which organise workshops and activities locally. Courses and conferences are open to non-members. Associate membership is open to those who are not qualified Teachers of the Deaf.

British Colostomy Association
15 Station Road, Reading
Berkshire RG1 1LG
Tel: (0800) 328 4257
Fax: (0118) 956 9095
email: sue@bcass.org.uk
Website: www.bcass.org.uk

British Deaf Association
1–3 Worship Street
London EC2A 2AB
Tel: (020) 7588 3520
Fax: (020) 758 3527

The BDA's Education Office works to raise educational opportunities for all deaf people nationally, from birth to old age, and also empowers young deaf people to enjoy their youth to the full through education, access to information and pride in their identity. It campaigns for the provision of British Sign Language during all phases of education and represents BDA membership views on committees and working groups. It provides consultancy for LEAs and other information for individuals.

British Dyslexia Association
98 London Road
Reading RG1 5AU
Tel: (0118) 966 8271
Fax: (0118) 925 1927
email: info@dyslexiahelp-bda.demon.co.uk
Website: www.bda-dyslexia.org.uk
Helpline/Information Service 10am–12.45pm & 2pm–4.45pm weekdays

British Epilepsy Association
New Anstey House, Gate Way Drive
Leeds LS19 7XY
Tel: (0113) 210 800
Helpline Tel: (0808) 800 5050
Website: www.epilepsy.org.uk

British Institute for Brain Injured Children
Knowle Hall, Knowle Bridgwater
Somerset TA7 8PJ
Tel: (01278)648 060
email: info@bibic.org.uk
Family Service Manager: Mrs Caron Lane

Teaches the parents of brain injured children programmes of stimulation therapy which they carry out at home in order to improve their children's abilities. Initially three days are spent at the Institute for assessment, evaluation and teaching. The family then returns at four-monthly intervals for reassessment and programming adjustment. Periods of specialised treatment therapy are offered when appropriate.

British Institute of Learning Disabilities (BILD)
Wolverhampton Road, Kidderminster
Worcestershire DY10 3PP
Tel: (01562) 850 251

BILD works towards improving the quality of life of people with learning difficulties.

The British Kidney Patient Association
Bordon
Hampshire GU35 9JZ
Tel: (01420) 472 021
Contact: Mrs Elizabeth Ward, OBE

The BKPA was founded in 1975 by Elizabeth Ward, whose son was diagnosed with kidney failure at the age of 13 years. At that time there was no national association concerned with the plight of Britain's kidney patients. Now kidney patients can turn to the BKPA for support, advice and, perhaps more importantly, financial help and a much needed break with their families at the BKPA holiday dialysis centres. The work of the BKPA falls roughly into two halves engendered by two quite separate needs: on the one hand the material and physical needs of the patients and their relatives, and on the other the necessity to lobby for more and improved facilities and increased governmental funding, so that all parents may benefit from improvements in technology and pharmaceutical achievements.

British Psychological Society
48 Princes Road East
Leicester LE1 7DR
Tel: (0116) 254 9568

The British Psychological Society is the professional body incorporated by Royal Charter to maintain standards for the profession of psychology in the United Kingdom. The Directory of Chartered Psychologists, published by the Society, contains the names and addresses of those Chartered Educational Psychologists who have chosen to publish and their availability to provide psychological services, including services for parents and children with Special Educational Needs.

The British Stammering Association
15 Old Ford Road
London E2 9PJ
Tel: (020) 8983 1003 (3 Lines)
Helpline: (0845) 603 2001
Fax: (020) 8983 3591

Schools' Liaison Officer Tel/Fax:
(01606) 77374 (Visits and training
arranged without charge)

The BSA is the largest charity in Europe
helping children who stammer. It provides
free information for parents, teenagers and
teachers, and a counsellor is available to
discuss specific problems. It also offers a
mail-order service on specialist
publications and a video pack for teachers.
The Schools' Liaison Officer is able to offer
training to education staff, and advice and
guidance on oral assessment for public
examinations to schools and parents.

Brittle Bone Society
30 Guthrie Street
Dundee DD1 5BS
Tel: (01382) 204446
Fax: (01382) 206771
Helpline: 08000 282459
email: bbs@brittlebone.org
Website: www.brittlebone.org

The Society seeks to promote research into
the causes, inheritance and treatment of
osteogenesis imperfecta and similar
disorders characterised by excessive
fragility of the bones. It also provides
advice, encouragement and practical help
for patients and their relatives living with
difficulties caused by brittle bones.

Cancerlink
11–21 Northdown Street
London N1 9BN
Tel (Admin): (020) 7833 2818
Fax: (020) 7833 4963
Freephone Cancerlink: (0808) 808 0000
Groups Line: (020) 7520 2603
(Training, Information & Development for
Cancer self help and support groups)
email: cancerlink@cancerlink.org.uk

Cancerlink provides telephone guidance
and support to people affected by cancer,
their families, friends and professionals
produces a wide range of publications
concerned with the emotional and practical
aspects of living with cancer and acts as a
resource for over 700 cancer self help,
support groups and organisations across
the UK

**Centre for Studies on Inclusive Education
(CSIE)**
1 Redland Close, Elm Lane, Redland
Bristol BS6 6UE
Tel: (0117) 923 8450
Fax: (0117) 923 8460

Advice and publications for parents
wishing their children with special needs to
be included in mainstream schools.

The Child Psychotherapy Trust
Star House, 104–108 Grafton Road
London NW5 4BD
Tel: (020) 7284 1355
Helpline: (020) 7485 5510
Fax: (020) 7284 2755
email: cpt@globalnet.co.uk
Website:
www.childpsychotherapytrust.org.uk

Launched in 1987, the Child
Psychotherapy Trust is a national charity
dedicated to increasing the number of child
psychotherapists available throughout the
UK to treat emotionally damaged children,
adolescents and their families. It is
convinced of the benefits of treating
emotional difficulties early, before they
become entrenched.
The Trust publishes a range of material
including a series of *Understanding
Childhood* leaflets, written by child
psychotherapists, for parents, carers and
people working with children and families,
which aim to promote understanding of

children's emotional health, development and behaviour. They also publish a newsletter available for £10 per year. The Trust supports and manages various outreach projects, but does not itself offer psychotherapy or referral services.

Children's Legal Centre
The University of Essex, Wivenhoe Park
Colchester
Essex CO4 3SQ
Tel: (01206) 873820 Advice Line
Tel: (01206) 872466 General Enquiries
(Mon–Fri 10am–12.30pm & 2–4.30pm)

CLAPA (Cleft Lip and Palate Association)
235–237 Finchley Road
London NW3 6LS
Tel: (020) 7431 0033
Fax: (020) 7431 8881
email: info@clapa.com
Website: www.clapa.com
Chief Executive: Gareth Davies

CLAPA was set up in 1979 as a partnership between parents and professionals involved with the treatment of Cleft lip and/or Palate to provide specialist support for parents, the growing child, the adolescent and the adult. As well as practical parent-to-parent support services, CLAPA runs a helpline, dispatches feeding equipment, publishes a range of information leaflets, organises workshops for health professionals and, through its 50 branches, raises money towards facilities for local hospital treatment.

Contact a Family
209–211 City Road
London EC1V 1JN
Tel: (020) 7608 8700
Fax: (020) 7608 8701
email: info@cafamily.org.uk
Website: www.cafamily.org.uk

Support for families who care for children with disabilities and special needs. The organisation also publishes "The Contact a Family Directory of Specific Conditions and Rare Syndromes in Children".

Council for the Advancement of Communication with Deaf People
Durham University Science Park
Block 4, Stockton Road
Durham DH1 3UZ
Tel: (0191) 383 1155
Fax: (0191) 383 7914
Text: (0191) 383 7915
email: durham@cacdp.demon.co.uk
Chief Executive: Miranda Pickersgill

CACDP aims to improve communication between deaf and hearing people by the development of curricula and examinations in communication skills. CACDP offers certification in British Sign Language, Lipspeaking, Communication with Deafblind People and Deaf Awareness, and carries out the selection, training, monitoring and registration of examiners.

Council for Disabled Children
8 Wakeley Street
London EC1V 7QE
Tel: (020) 843 6061

The Council for Disabled Children is an independently elected council established under the aegis of the National Children's Bureau. The Council promotes collaborative work between different organisations providing services and support for children and young people with disabilities and special educational needs.

CReSTeD (Council for the Registration of Schools Teaching Dyslexic Pupils)
Registered Charity No: 1052103
Greyarth, Littleworth
Winchcombe
Cheltenham GL54 5BT
Tel/Fax: (01242) 602689
Administrator: Ms Christine Manser

The CReSTeD register is to help parents and those who advise them to choose schools for dyslexic children. Its main supporters are the British Dyslexia Association and the Dyslexia Institute who, with others, established CReSTeD to produce an authoritative list of schools, both maintained and independent, which have been through an established registration procedure, including a visit by a CReSTeD-selected consultant. For a list of schools see pages 503–511

Cystic Fibrosis Trust
11 London Road
Bromley
Kent BR1 1BY
Tel: (020) 8464 7211
Fax: (020) 8313 0472
email: enquiries@cftrust.org.uk
Website: www.cftrust.org.uk

The Cystic Fibrosis Trust Support Service provides emotional, practical, and financial advice to families who have a child with CF and adults with CF. The full-time staff are supported by a network of trained volunteer workers who operate on a local basis. The Trust offers advice on welfare benefits, insurance, employment, holidays, housing, equipment and other matters.

Council for the Registration of Schools Teaching Dyslexic Pupils

- There are over 1000 independent schools that offer help to dyslexic pupils

- Only those on the CReSTeD Register have received visits from a CReSTeD Consultant to ascertain if the school fulfils the criteria set by the CReSTeD Council

- CReSTeD is a charity set up to offer some initial guidance to parents who are seeking a school for their dyslexic child.

- The Register is available free of charge (please send an A5 envelope with 31p stamp) from the CReSTeD Administrator, Greygarth, Littleworth, Winchcombe, Cheltenham, Glos GL54 5BT; Tel: 01242 602689. Or visit our web site on www.crested.org.uk

Disability Alliance
Universal House, 88–94 Wentworth Street
London E1 7SA
Office (minicom available):
(020) 7247 8765
Fax: (020) 7247 8776
**Rights advice helpline (minicom
available):** (020) 7247 8763
The helpline is open on Monday 2–4pm
and on Wednesday 2–4pm

The Disability Alliance is committed to
breaking the link between poverty and
disability. It provides information to
disabled people about their entitlements,
and campaigns for improvements to the
social security system and for increases in
disability benefits.
It publishes the *Disability Rights Handbook*
and three issues of the *Disability Rights
Bulletin* every year, as well as other
publications and information briefings.
The Disability Alliance also runs training
courses on benefits and provides a free
telephone helpline.

The Disability Law Service
39–45 Cavell Street
London E1 2BP
Tel: (020) 7791 9800
Minicom: (020) 7791 9801
Fax: (020) 7790 9802
email: advice@dls.org.uk

Provides a broad range of free legal advice
and assistance on education, children and
many other matters specifically for disabled
people, their families and carers.

Disability Sport England
Unit 4G
784–788 High Road
Tottenham
London N17 0DA
Tel: (020) 8801 4466
Fax: (020) 8801 6644
email: sharon@dse.org.uk

DSE aims to provide, develop and
co-ordinate opportunities in sport and
recreation for people with disabilities. We
co-ordinate 12 National championships
and over 200 regional events for people
with all disabilities.

Disabled Living Foundation
380–384 Harrow Road
London W9 2HU
Helpline: (0845) 130 9177
Minicom: (020) 7432 8009
Fax: (020) 7266 2922
email: advice@dlf.org.uk
Website: www.dlf.org.uk
Head of Services: Mary Queally

The Disabled Living Foundation is a
national charity, which aims to provide
advice and information on equipment to
enable disabled and elderly people manage
daily living activities. Its services are open
to all: disabled people, carers, relatives,
students and professionals working in the
disability field.
The organisation runs a telephone, letter,
email enquiry service and an equipment
demonstration centre. It also publishes a
range of fact sheets.

Dogs for the Disabled
(Registered Charity No 700454)
The Frances Hay Centre
Blacklands Hill, Banbury
Oxon OX17 2BS

Tel: (01295) 252 600
Fax: (01295) 252 688
email: dfd@dial.pipex.com

Specially-selected dogs are trained to
perform tasks which disabled people find
difficult or impossible. Tasks include
retrieving articles, opening and closing
doors, activating light switches and helping
people with a balance problem to rise from
a chair or walk independently of other aids.
Dogs are trained to suit individual needs
providing independence, security and
companionship.

Down's Syndrome Association
155 Mitcham Road
London SW17 9PG
Tel: (020) 8682 4001
email: info@downs-syndrome.org.uk
Website: www.downs-syndrome.org.uk

The Down's Syndrome Association is the
only national charity, covering England
Wales & Northern Ireland, which works
exclusively with people with Down's
Syndrome. It exists to provide support,
information, advice and counselling to
people with Down's Syndrome, their
parents/carers, families and those with a
professional interest. The Association has a
network of parent-led branches and
groups, a national office and resource
centre in London and resource centres in
Belfast & Cardiff.

Dyslexia Institute (Head Office)
133 Gresham Road, Staines
Middlesex TW18 2AJ
Tel: (01784) 463851
Fax: (01784) 460747
Executive Director: Mrs E J Brooks

Through its national network of 25 centres and over 120 outposts the Dyslexia Institute offers assessments and specialist teaching programmes, as well as a wide range of courses and resource materials for all teachers. Staff also provide advice and counselling to dyslexic individuals and their families. The Dyslexia Institute's professional body, the Dyslexia Institute Guild, publishes a membership journal, "Dyslexia Review" and organises an annual symposium.

The Dyslexia Institute (Scotland)
74 Victoria Crescent Road, Dowanhill
Glasgow G12 9JN
Tel: (0141) 334 4549
Contact: Mrs Elizabeth Mackenzie

The Institute in Scotland provides psychological assessment, specialist teaching, short courses and teacher training to postgraduate diploma level.

Dyspraxia Foundation (Registered Charity No. 1058352)
8 West Alley, Hitchin
Herts SG5 1EG
Tel: (01462) 455016
Helpline: (01462) 454986
Fax: (01462) 455052

Dyspraxia is an impairment or immaturity of the organisation of movement, perception and thought, sometimes known as "Clumsy Child Syndrome". The Foundation offers advice, information, support, professional and parental conferences and much more.

Eating Disorders Association
First floor, Wensum House
103 Prince of Wales Road, Norwich
Norfolk NR1 1DW
Helpline: (01603) 621414
Mon–Fri 9am–6.30pm
Youth Helpline: (01603) 765050

Mon–Fri 4pm–6pm (18 years & under)
Admin: (01603) 619090
Media: (01603) 624310
Fax: (01603) 624915

The Eating Disorders Association offers information and understanding through telephone help-lines, guidelines, newsletters and a national network of self-help groups for people with anorexia or bulimia, their families and friends. Telephone helplines operate on 01603 621414 (Mon–Fri 9am–6.30pm). The Youth Helpline operates Mon–Fri, 4pm–6pm, on 01603 765050 and is specifically for callers aged 18 years or under. Membership includes a newsletter every quarter.

Electronic Aids for the Blind
Suite 4B, 71–75 High Street
Chislehurst
Kent BR7 5AG

Tel: (020) 8295 3636
Fax: (020) 8295 3737

A national charity helping blind and partially sighted people of all ages to achieve their fullest potential by awarding partial grants and arranging fund-raising appeals to third parties to purchase specialist or suitably-adapted equipment for personal use where no statutory obligations exist and where there is financial hardship.

emPOWER
c/o Limbless Association
Rehabilitation Centre
Queen Mary's Hospital
Roehampton Lane
London SW15 5PR
Tel: (020) 8788 1777
Fax: (020) 8788 3444
email: enquiries@empowernet.org
Website: www.empowernet.org

A consortium of users of prosthetics, orthotics, wheelchairs and electronic assistive technology which campaigns for a "natural look" based on individual needs.

ENABLE
6th Floor, 7 Buchanan Street
Glasgow G1 3HL
Tel: (0141) 226 4541

ENABLE can provide information and legal advice about educational issues affecting children with learning disabilities in Scotland. It has a network of local branches across Scotland offering mutual support to parents and runs a range of services including housing for adults with complex difficulties, employment training and support, day services and family-based respite care.

Family Fund Trust
PO Box 50
York YO1 9ZX
Tel: (01904) 621115
Text Tel: (01904) 658085
Fax: (01904) 652625
Information Manager: Allison Cowen

The purpose of the Family Fund Trust is to ease the stress on families who care for very severely disabled children under 16, by providing grants and information related to the care of the child. Further details are available from the Information Office at the above address.

The Foundation for Conductive Education
The National Institute of Conductive Education,
Cannon Hill House
Russell Road, Moseley
Birmingham B13 8RD

Tel: (0121) 449 1569
Fax: (0121) 449 1611
email: foundation@conductive-education.org.uk
Website: www.conductive-education.org.uk
Monday–Friday, 9.00am–5.00pm

A national charity formed in 1986 "to establish and develop the science and skill of Conductive Education in the UK". The National Institute of Conductive Education provides direct services to children and adults with motor disorders; cerebral palsy, multiple sclerosis, Parkinson's disease, children with dyspraxia and those who have suffered strokes and head injuries. Through a system of positive teaching and learning support, Conductive Education maximises its control over bodily movement in ways that are relevant to daily living.
The National Institute also undertakes research and offers a comprehensive range of professionally oriented, skills-based training courses at all levels. Covers UK and overseas.

FYD (Friends for Young Deaf People)
London & South East Embassy
East Court Mansion
College Lane
East Grinstead
West Sussex RH19 3LT
Tel: (01342) 323444
Minicom: (01342) 312639
Fax: (01342) 410232
Ethnic Minority Officer: Omeima Mudawi

The aim of the FYD is to promote an active partnership between deaf and hearing people which will enable young deaf people to develop themselves and become active members of society.

The Guide Dogs for the Blind Association
Hillfields
Burghfield Common
Reading RG7 3YG
Tel: (0870) 600 2323
Contact: Philippa Ireland
email: guidedogs@gdba.org.uk

Helen Arkell Dyslexia Centre
Frensham
Farnham
Surrey GU10 3BW
Tel: (01252) 792400
email:
general_enquiries@arknellcentre.org.uk
Director: Mrs Gail Goedkoop

A registered charity providing
comprehensive help and care for children
with specific learning difficulties,
including assessment, tuition, speech and
language therapy and short courses as well
as teacher training and schools support.
Financial help is available. Specialist books
on dyslexia for parents and teachers are
available by mail order.

Hornsey Conductive Education Centre
54 Muswell Hill
London N10 3ST
Tel: (020) 8444 7242

Provides Conductive Education for
children with Cerebral Palsy, and courses
for professionals working with children
who have Cerebral Palsy in mainstream
education.

**Hyperactive Children's Support Group
(HACSG)**
71 Whyke Lane
Chichester
West Sussex PO19 2LD
Tel: (01903) 725182
Fax: (01903) 734726
Contact: Mrs Sally Bunday

**I CAN (Invalid Children's Aid
Nationwide)**
4 Dyer's Buildings
Holborn
London EC1N 2QP
Tel: (0870) 010 4066
Fax: (0870) 010 4067

I CAN is the national educational
charity for children with speech and
language difficulties. The charity integrates
education and therapy services to help
children from pre-school to
school-leaving age reach their full
potential.

In Touch
10 Norman Road
Sale
Cheshire M33 3DF
Tel: (0161) 905 2440

Information and contacts for all types of
special needs in children. Newsletters and
publications available.

**Independent Panel for Special Education
Advice**
4 Ancient House Mews
Woodbridge
Suffolk
IP12 1DH
Tel: (01394) 380518
Co-ordinator: John Wright

IPSEA provides:
- Free independent advice on LEAs' legal
  duties towards children with special
  educational needs.
- Free professional second opinions for
  parents who disagree with an LEA's
  assessment of their child's special
  educational needs.
- Free representation at the Special
  Educational Needs Tribunal for parents
  who want to appeal against an LEA
  decision.

The Institute for Neurophysiological Psychology
4 Stanley Place
Chester
Cheshire CH1 2LU
Tel: (01244) 311414
Director: Peter Blythe
Co-Director: Sally Goddard-Blythe

Established in 1975 to research into the effects of central nervous system dysfunctions on children with learning difficulties, and to develop appropriate CNS remedial and rehabilitation programmes. INPP can diagnose what underlies dyslexia, dyspraxia and other specific learning difficulties, and then devise an appropriate physical correction programme to be done each day at home or school. The children are regularly monitored, and as the basic causes are corrected the children begin to benefit from teaching and the educational process.

LADDER
National Learning and Attention Deficit Disorders Association
95 Church Road, Bradmore
Wolverhampton
West Midlands WV3 7EW
Tel: (01902) 569280
Fax: (01902) 566166
Founder and Chairman: Stan Mould

LADDER was the first and is now the premier national registered charity in the ADD/ADHD field in this country which provides up to date information on the disorder, and a true multi-disciplinary approach based on medication, psychological and educational interventions. LADDER is in regular contact with the few professionals working in the field in the UK, as well as many of those abroad. They also have links with

American and Australian groups. The Association has a large library of information and has held educational meetings for parents and professionals in various places. Other meetings are planned as information is expanding throughout the country.

Learning Development Aids
Duke Street, Wisbech
Cambridgeshire PE13 2AE
Tel: (01945) 463441
Fax: (01945) 587361

The Leukaemia Care Society
14 Kingfisher Court
Venny Bridge
Pinhoe
Exeter
Devon EX4 8JN
Tel: (0345) 673203 (Local call rate)
Chief Administrative Officer:
Mrs S J Brown
email: leukaemia.care@ukonline.co.uk
Website: www.leukaemiacare.org

Supports children, and their families, suffering from leukaemia and allied blood disorders. Information is available from the Exeter office.

Limbless Association
Roehampton Rehabilitation Centre
Roehampton Lane
London
SW15 5PR
Tel: (020) 8788 1777
Fax: (020) 8788 3444
email: enquiries@limbless-association.org
Website: www.limbless-association.org

Information on a disabled football team run in co-operation with Wimbledon Football Club also available.

Makaton Vocabulary Development Project (MVDP)
31 Firwood Drive
Camberley
Surrey GU15 3QD
Tel/Fax: (01276) 61390/681368

Makaton Vocabulary is a language programme which provides basic means of communication and encourages the development of language and literacy skills in children and adults with learning and communication difficulties. The MVDP provides training and advice for parents, carers and children who wish to use Makaton through a national network of local and regional tutors. A wide range of resource materials is also available from the MVDP: these include books of signs and symbols, videos, pictures, guidelines and computer databases.

Marfan Association UK
Rochester House
5 Aldershot Road
Fleet
Hampshire GU13 9NG
Tel: 01252) 810472
Fax: (01252) 810473
Chairman/Support Co-ordinator:
Mrs Diane L Rust

Marfan Syndrome is an inherited disorder of connective tissue, which may affect the eyes, skeleton, lungs, heart and blood vessels and may be life-threatening. The Marfan Association UK exists to support those with the condition, providing educational material about Marfan Syndrome for both medical and lay sectors and encouraging research projects.

MIND (National Association for Mental Health)
15–19 Broadway
London E15 4BQ

Tel: (020) 8519 2122
Information Line: (020) 8522 1728 & (0345) 660163
email: contact@mind.org.uk
Website: www.mind.org.uk
Chief Executive: Judi Clements

MIND, the leading mental health charity, works for a better life for people in mental distress, campaigning for their right to lead an active and valued life. Founded in 1946, MIND has become the largest charitable provider of quality community care and an influential voice on mental health issues.

Muscular Dystrophy Campaign
7–11 Prescott Place
London SW4 6BS
Tel: (020) 7720 8055
Fax: (020) 7498 0670

The Muscular Dystrophy Group is the national charity funding research into treatments and cures for the muscular dystrophies and allied muscle wasting conditions. The Group also supports adults and children affected by these conditions with expert clinical care and grants towards equipment. The charity relies on voluntary donations to fund its work.

National Association for Gifted Children
Elder House, 540 Elder Gate
Milton Keynes MK9 1LR
Tel: (01908) 673677

NAGC provides services and support to gifted children, their families and those involved in their education through its information service, branch activities, counselling services and in-service training. It works to increase awareness and understanding of the social, emotional and education needs of gifted children and to improve provision.

**National Association of
Independent and Non-Maintained
Special Schools (NAIMS)**
c/o Holly Bank School
Far Common Road
Mirfield
West Yorkshire WF14 0DQ
Tel: (01924) 490833
Fax: (01924) 491464
Secretary: Mr S Hughes

**The National Association for
Special Educational Needs
(NASEN)**
NASEN House
4/5 Amber Business Village
Amber Close
Amington
Tamworth B77 4RP
Tel: (01827) 311500
Fax: (01827) 313005

email: welcome@nasen.org.uk
Hon General Secretary: Sue Panter

The National Association for Special
Educational Needs promotes the
development of children and young
people with special educational needs,
and influences the quality of provision
through strong and cohesive policies
and strategies for parents and
professionals.

The National Autistic Society
393 City Road
London EC1V 1NG
Tel: (020) 7833 2299
Fax: (020) 7833 9666
email: nas@nas.org.uk

The National Autistic Society aims to offer
families and carers information, advice and
support, to improve awareness amongst

key decision-makers, professionals and the general public, to provide training and to promote research into autism. The Society currently owns and manages six schools for children with autism offering daily, weekly, termly and 52 week a year placements. Local affiliated autistic societies run a further nine schools. The society also runs the Centre for Social and Communication Disorders which provides a diagnosis and assessment service.

National Children's Bureau
8 Wakeley Street
London EC1V 7QE
Tel: (020) 7843 6000
Fax: (020) 7278 9512
Website: www.ncb.org.uk

National Deaf Children's Society
15 Dufferin Street
London EC1Y 8PD
Information & Helpline: (020) 7250 0123 (voice and text)
Tel: (020) 7251 5020 (fax)

The National Deaf Children's Society is the leading national charity especially concerned with the needs of deaf children and their families. The society provides advice on education and welfare, health, technology and audiology and publishes information on all aspects of childhood deafness.

National Reye's Syndrome Foundation of the UK
15 Nicholas Gardens
Pyford
Woking
Surrey GU22 8SD

The National Autistic Society

The National Autistic Society seeks to meet the needs of children across the autistic continuum from those diagnosed as having Asperger syndrome or Autism to children with severe challenging behaviour. Provision varies from Day through to Weekly, Termly and full 52 Week boarding.

Broomhayes School
Kingsley House, Alverdiscott Road, Bideford,
North Devon, EX39 4PL
Tel: 01237 473 830   Fax: 01237 421 097
E mail: Broomhayes@nas.org.uk
Principal: Barbara Dewar
Type of School: Mixed, Full boarding and day

Daldorch House School
Sorn Road, Catrine, East Ayrshire, KA5 6NA;
Tel: 01290 551666   Fax: 01290 553399
E mail: Daldorch@nas.org.uk
Principal: Shona Pinkerton
Type of School: Mixed, Full boarding and day

The Helen Allison School
Longfield Road, Meopham, Kent, DA13 0EW;
Tel: 01474 814 878   Fax: 01474 812 033
E mail: Helen.Allison@nas.org.uk
Principal: Jacqui Ashton-Smith
Type of School: Mixed, Weekly boarding and day

Radlett Lodge School
Harper Lane, Radlett, Hertfordshire, WD7 9HW;
Tel: 01923 854 922   Fax: 01923 859 922
E mail: Radlett.Lodge@nas.org.uk
Principal: Lynda Tucker
Type of School: Mixed, Weekly boarding and day

Robert Ogden School
Clayton Lane, Thurnscoe,
Rotherham, South Yorkshire, S63 0BE
Tel: 01709 874 443   Fax: 01709 870 701
E mail: Robert.Ogden@nas.org.uk
Principal: Andrea Hull
Type of School: Mixed, Weekly boarding

The Sybil Elgar School
Havelock Road, Southall, Middlesex, UB2 4NR;
Tel: 020 8813 9168   Fax: 020 8571 7332
E mail: SybilElgarSchool@nas.org.uk
Principal: Chloe Phillips
Type of School: Mixed, Termly, Weekly boarding and day

Further details can be obtained from:
Director of Services: The National Autistic Society,
Church House, Church Road, Filton, Bristol BS34 7BD
Tel: 0117 974 8400   Fax: 0117 987 2576

THE NATIONAL
AUTISTIC SOCIETY

Tel: (01932) 346843
Fax: (01932) 346843
Contact: Mr Gordon Denney

Reye's Syndrome is a children's disease that affects the liver and brain. It is an acute disorder which affects children when they seem to be recovering from a viral illness. The National Reye's Syndrome Foundation of the United Kingdom was formed to provide funds for research into the cause, treatment, cure and prevention of Reye's Syndrome and Reye-like illnesses, to inform both the public and medical communities, and to provide support for parents whose children have suffered from the diseases.

Network 81
1–7 Woodfield Terrace
Chapel Hill
Stansted
Essex CM24 8AJ
Tel: (01279) 647415
Fax: (01279) 814908
National Co-ordinator: John Pashley
Administrator: Val Rosier

Network 81 is a national organisation supporting parents through the assessment and statementing process contained in the Education Act 1996. Services offered include a national helpline, literature for parents, and links with local Network 81 groups and other organisations. Individual, family and group membership is available.

OAASIS
Office for Advice, Assistance, Support and Information on Special Needs
Brock House
Grigg Lane
Brockenhurst
Hampshire SO42 7RE

Helpline: (09068) 633201*
Fax: (01590) 622687
email: oaasis@dial.pipex.com
Website:
www.hesleygroup.co.uk/oaasis.htm
Co-ordinator: Lesley Durston

OAASIS is an information and advice centre set up by the Hesley Group, an independent company running nine residential special schools and colleges. It offers advice, information and training days on many learning disabilities, including ADHD, Asperger Syndrome and autism. OAASIS also produces a range of literature on these disorders, from free Information Sheets, to its 'First Guide to …' series, for which a small charge is made.
Write to OAASIS or telephone the helpline* if you would like information about any aspect of special education, an information pack, publications list, forthcoming training day dates, or if you would like to go on the OAASIS mailing list.
(*calls to the Helpline cost 60p a minute)

Paget Gorman Society (Registered Charity No 1008041)
2 Downlands Bungalows
Downlands Lane
Smallfield
Surrey RH6 9SD
Tel: (01342) 842308
email: PruP@compuserve.com
Website: www.pgss.org

Advice and information for parents and professionals concerned with speech and language-impaired children. The Society runs courses in Paget Gorman Signed Speech (PGSS). Publications and a video are available.

Perthes Association
15 Recreation Road
Guildford
Surrey GU1 1HE
Tel: (Admin): (01483) 534431
Tel: (Helpline): (01483) 306637
Fax: (01483) 503213
email: admin@perthes.org.uk
Website: www.perthes.co.uk

The Association advises families of children suffering from Perthes' Disease and associated conditions in all parts of the British Isles and abroad. Perthes' Disease (a potentially crippling disease of the hip) is a form of osteochondritis, which affects 5.5 per 100,000 children (mainly boys) between the ages of 2 and 15 years. Perthes Association volunteers are at the end of the telephone line for any worried or distressed parents, will visit them if possible or put them in touch with a family living locally.

The Physical & Sensory Service
The Education Centre
Church Street, Pensnett
West Midlands DY5 4EY
Tel: (01384) 818001
Fax: (01384) 814241
Head of Service: Annette Hope

Rathbone
Head Office
Churchgate House, 56 Oxford Street
Manchester M1 6EU
Tel: (0161) 236 5358
Fax: (0161) 238 6356
Special Education Advice Line:
(0800) 917 6790

A national charity working for and on behalf of people with learning difficulties. Provides a wide range of services including youth and adult training, residential services, and advice and information services. Our

helpline provides advice on special needs education, statementing and exclusions.

REACH – Association for Children with Hand or Arm Deficiency
25 High Street, Wellingborough
Northamptonshire NN8 4JZ
Tel: (01933) 274126
email: reach@reach.org
Website: www.reach.org.uk

REACH: National Advice Centre for Children with Reading Difficulties (Registered Charity No 297694)
California Country Park
Nine Mile Ride, Finchampstead
Berkshire RG40 4HT
Tel: (0118) 973 7575 (Voice and text)
Helpline: (0845) 604 0414
Fax: (0118) 973 7105
email: reach@reach-reading.demon.co.uk
Website: www.reach-reading.demon.co.uk
Director: Beverly Mathias
Information Officer: Desmond L Spiers

REACH provides a resource and information centre for those who work with children whose disability, illness or learning problem affects their reading, language or communication. The centre contains both printed books and books on tape and video, plus microelectronic equipment and software. The collections are for reference only.

Royal Association for Disability and Rehabilitation (RADAR)
12 City Forum
250 City Road
London EC1V 8AF
Tel: (020) 7250 3222
email: radar@radar.org.uk
Minicom: (020) 7250 4119
Website: www.radar.org.uk

Information on all aspects of disability.

Royal College of Speech and Language Therapists
2 White Hart Yard
London SE1 1NX
Tel: (020) 7378 3013
Fax: (020) 7403 7254

The Royal National Institute for the Blind (RNIB)
224 Great Portland Street
London W1N 6AA
Tel: (020) 7388 1266
Fax: (020) 7388 2034
Website: www.rnib.org.uk
Director General: Ian Bruce
Director of Education and Employment: Eamonn Fetton

RNIB supports blind and partially-sighted children and their families by providing information and advice, books and magazines, schools, education centres, training and support for families.

The Royal National Institute for Deaf People
19–23 Featherstone Street
London EC1Y 8SL
Tel: (0808) 808 0123 – Helpline
Textphone: (0808) 808 9000 – Helpline
Fax: (020) 7296 8199
Chief Executive: James Strachan

The Royal National Institute for Deaf People (RNID) is the largest charity representing the 8.7 million deaf and hard of hearing people in the UK. As a membership charity, we aim to achieve a radically better quality of life for deaf and hard of hearing people. We do this by campaigning and lobbying vigorously, by raising awareness of deafness and hearing loss, by providing services and through social, medical and technical research.

Royal Society for Mentally Handicapped Children and Adults (MENCAP)
123 Golden Lane
London EC1Y 0RT
Tel: (020) 7454 0454
Website: www.mencap.com
Chairman: Brian Baldock CBE
Chief Executive: Fred Heddell CBE

- Mencap provides services for, and campaigns with, people who have a learning disability, their families and carers in England, Wales and Northern Ireland. Mencap is the UK's largest disability charity. It is a membership organisation.
- Mencap's leisure arm, Gateway, runs clubs for over 60,000 people around the country.
- *Viewpoint*, the monthly newspaper of the learning disability world, is available on subscription.

SCET (Scottish Council for Educational Technology)
74 Victoria Crescent Road
Glasgow G12 9JN
Tel: (0141) 337 5000
Fax: (0141) 337 5050
Development Officer: Mrs M Watson

- Advice on the use of technology for those with special needs.
- Development of software for special needs.

SCOPE
Cerebral Palsy Helpline
PO Box 833
Milton Keynes MK12 5NY
Tel: (0808) 800 3333

Scope exists to help all people with cerebral palsy and related disabilities.

Scottish Down's Syndrome Association
158–160 Balgreen Road
Edinburgh EH11 3AU
Tel: (0131) 313 4225
Fax: (0131) 313 4285
Website: www.sdsa.org.uk
Educational Liaison Officer:
Cecilie Mackinnion

**The Scottish Society for Autism
(Formerly Scottish Society for
Autistic Children)**
Hilton House
Alloa Business Park
Whins Road
Alloa
Clackmannanshire FK10 3SA
Tel: (01259) 720044
Fax: (01259) 720051
Website: www.autism-in-scotland.org.uk

SSAC is the leading provider of services for
autism in Scotland. They run Struan House
School, the only accredited school for
autism in Scotland (both residential and day
pupils); residential and specialist day
services for adults; the only respite care
centre for autism in the UK; nationwide
family support services; training for carers
and professionals; support self-help groups
and local societies; and produce
information and a members' magazine.
They undertake community care
assessments and give guidance on diagnosis,
assessment and care management. Advice
on all aspects of autism is available from
their professional staff.

Scottish Spina Bifida Association
190 Queensferry Road
Edinburgh EH4 2BW
Tel: (0131) 332 0743
Fax: (0131) 343 3651
Chief Executive: Andrew H D Wynd

The Scottish Spina Bifida Association seeks
to increase public awareness and
understanding of individuals with Spina
Bifida/Hydrocephalus and allied disorders.
It aims to secure provision for their special
needs and those of their families.

Royal National Institute for the Blind

Services for visually impaired children

RNIB offers a range of services to blind and partially sighted children and young people, their families and the professionals who work with them, including:

- Special schools for blind and partially sighted children, including those with additional disabilities
- Advice on equipment and technology to help children at home and at school
- Support, advice and information for parents and families

**For more details call RNIB Education & Employment
Information Service on tel: 020-7388 1286**
or check www.rnib.org.uk
Registered charity no 226227

RNIB

Scottish Support for Learning Association
Registered Charity Number: SE026546
2403 Paisley Road West
Glasgow G52 2QH
Tel: (0141) 883 6134
Secretary: Christina Brownlie

SENNAC: Special Educational Needs – National Advisory Council
Pett Archive & Study Centre
Toddington
Cheltenham
Gloucestershire GL54 5DP
Hon General Secretary: Mr John Cross

Sense, The National Deafblind & Rubella Association
11–13 Clifton Terrace
Finsbury Park
London N4 3SR
Tel: (020) 7272 7774
Fax: (020) 7272 6012
Minicom: (020) 7272 9684
email: enquiries@sense.org.uk
Website: www.sense.org.uk

Sense is the national voluntary organisation supporting and campaigning for people who are deafblind, their families, their carers, and professionals who work with them. People of all ages and with widely varying conditions use Sense's specialist services. Founded as a parents' self-help group in 1955, Sense is now the leading national organisation working with deafblind people.
Sense:
- offers advice, help and information to deafblind people and their families;
- supports families through a national network and local branches;
- runs holiday programme for deafblind children and adults;
- education, residential, respite and day services;
- communicator-guides and one-to-one intervenor support;
- training and consultancy.

Sense West
Midlands Area
Princess Royal Centre
4 Church Road
Edgbaston
Birmingham B15 3TD
Tel: (0121) 687 1564 (voice and text)
Fax: (0121) 687 1656

Sense West provides a regional advisory service to families, deaf-blind people and professionals working with them, an adult service department offering a range of residential provision and learning opportunities based on individual need for deaf-blind and multiply disabled sensory impaired adults, and a Training and Consultancy Service offering advice, assessment and training to people involved with the education and care of deaf-blind children and adults. In addition they also provide a day service for deaf-blind people in the Birmingham area and an information service.

The Sequal Trust
(Special Equipment and Aids for Living)
3 Ploughmans Corner
Wharf Road
Ellesmere
Shropshire SY12 0EJ
Tel/Fax: (01691) 624222

A national charity which aims to assist severely physically disabled people by providing special electronic/electrical communication equipment. SEQUAL is run by severely disabled people who themselves use a variety of electronic equipment and is dedicated to the improvement of conditions for its members and other disabled people.

The SIGNALONG Group
Communication & Language Centre
North Pondside
Historic Dockyard
Chatham
Kent ME4 4TY
Tel: (01634) 819915 (Enquiries & sales)
Tel: (01634) 832469
(Training & development)

SIGNALONG is a sign-supporting system based on British Sign Language intended to promote communication in learning disabilities and autism. The charity has devised a uniform method of presenting signs with drawings and descriptions, and has published the widest range of illustrated signs in Britain, catering for all ages and abilities. Manuals contain full signing instructions, but training advice is also provided, both by SIGNALONG staff and by independent accredited tutors. SIGNALONG works with other organisations to developed symbol resources and to promote total communication to enable understanding and expression of choice.

Skill –
National Bureau for
Students with Disabilities
Chapter House
18–20 Crucifix Lane
London SE1 3JW
Tel: (020) 7450 0620
Fax: (020) 7450 0650
Information Service:
(0800) 328 5050, (0800) 068 2422

(Info Service Minicom)
Monday to Friday 1.30–4.30pm
email: info@skill.org.uk
Website: www.skill.org.uk
Director: Ms B Waters
Information Service Manager:
Mr M Sissons

Skill is a voluntary organisation which aims to develop opportunities for young people and adults with any kind of disability or learning difficulty – in further, higher and adult education, in training and employment.

Special Needs Advisory Project Cymru (SNAP)
45 Penarth Road, Cardiff CF1 5DJ
Tel: (029) 2038 8776
Fax: (029) 2038 8776
email: snapcym@aol.com.uk

SNAP Cymru offers information and support to families of children and young people who have, or may have, special educational needs.

Tourette Syndrome (UK) Association
PO Box 26149
Dunfermline
KY12 9WT
Tel/Fax: (01892) 669151
email: enquiries@tsa.org.uk

The UK Federation for Conductive Education
c/o Horton Lodge School
Rudyard, Nr Leek, Staffordshire ST13 8RB
Tel: (01538) 306214
Hon Secretary: Mrs A Loton

SKILL

Skill (National Bureau for Students with Disabilities) is a charity that advises disabled people on how to access post-16 education, employment, training, and volunteering opportunities. It does this principally by operating a website and freephone helpline. Skill also works behind the scenes informing and influencing policy makers.

Skill's freephone helpline: *0800 328 5050 (voice)*
    0800 068 2422 (text)
Skill's website: *www.Skill.org.uk*

Skill has up-to-the-minute information about applications, universities' and colleges' facilities for disabled people, and how to get support, grants and benefits.

5.4
Bibliography

The following list has been compiled with the kind assistance of editorial contributors and offers suggested further reading on many aspects on special educational needs.

General

"The Code of Practice for the Identification and Assessment of SEN"

"Special Educational Needs: A Guide for Parents"

"Meeting Special Educational Needs – a programme of action"

"Meeting Special Educational Needs – a programme of action" – a summary, also available in braille, on audio-cassette and in British Sign Language

All the above publications are available from the Department for Education and Employment (DfEE), tel. 0845 602 2260

"Children with Special Educational Needs – Assessment Law and Practice"
J Friel
Jessica Kingsley Publishers
ISBN 185 302460 0

"Telephone Helplines Directory"
Telephone Helplines Association
61 Grays Inn Road, London WC1X 8LT
Tel: 020 7248 3388
£15.00

"Statements: A Handbook for Parents"
Network 81, 1–7 Woodfield Terrace
Chapel Hill, Stansted, Essex CM24 8AJ
Tel: 01279 647415

"How and Why Children Fail"
Edited by: Ved Varma
Jessica Kingsley Publishers
£13.99
ISBN 185 302186 5

"ACE SEN Handbook"
Advisory Centre for Education (ACE)
Tel: 020 7354 8318
£8.00 Plus postage

"Tribunal Toolkit"
Advisory Centre for Education
Tel: 020 7354 8318

"Taking Action: Your Child's Right to Special Education – the definitive guide for parents, teachers, advocates and advice workers"
J White and I Rubain
ISBN 184 190010 9

"Disability Rights Handbook"
(26th Edition)
A guide to rights, benefits and services for all people with disabilities and their families
Disability Alliance
Universal House
88–94 Wentworth Street, London E1 7SA
Tel: 020 7247 8776
Fax: 020 7247 8765
£12.50 or £8.50 for people on benefit
ISBN: 094 1903335000

"Children First"
Royal Association for Disability and
Rehabilitation (RADAR)
Publications Department
12 City Forum, 250 City Road
London EC1V 8AF

"Challenging Decision"
A practical guide to decision making and
the appeal process for social security
benefits
Disability Alliance, 2000
ISBN 0946336873
£4.00

"Children in Difficulty: a Guide to
Understanding and Helping"
J Elliot and M Place
Routledge, 1998
ISBN 0415144590

"Disability Living Allowance - A Guide and
Checklist"
A user-friendly guide to disability living
allowance
Disability Alliance
Tel: 020 7247 8776
Fax 020 7247 8765
ISBN 1903335027

"Hope for the Journey – Helping children
through good times and bad. Story building
for parents, teacher and therapist"
C R Snyder, D McDermott, W Cook and M
A Rapoff
Westview Press, 1997
ISBN 0813331560

"Spelling: Remedial strategies"
Diane Montgomery
Cassell, 1997
ISBN 0304329746

"Understanding and Supporting Children
with Emotional or Behavioural Difficulties"
P Cooper (Ed.)
Jessica Kingsley, 1999
ISBN 1853026662

For students aged 16+ with disabilities

"After Age 16 – What Next?"
The Family Fund, PO Box 50
York YO1 2ZX
Tel: 01904 621115

"COPE Directory: Compendium of
post-16 education and training in
residential establishments for young
people with special needs"
Lifetime Careers (Wiltshire)
7 Ascot Court, Whitehorse Business Park
Trowbridge, Wiltshire BA14 0XA
Tel: 01225 716024

"The Association of National Specialist
Colleges Directory 1997 and 1998 and
1999"
A directory of colleges with specialist
provision for disabled students
£5.00 from NATSPEC
Contact: Olive Ralphes, Trevor Villa
School Lane, St Martins
Oswestry SY11 3BX

"Guide to Training and Benefits for
Young People"
Published by Youthaid, 322 St John Street
London EC1V 4NT
Tel: 020 7833 8499
Email: youthaid@gn.apc.org
ISBN 1907658202
£6.00

"Taking Action! Your Child's Right to
Special Education"
J White and I Rubain
ISBN: 1841900109

"Your Future Needs Assessment"
(Scotland Only)
Published by the Special Needs Forum of
Children in Scotland
Contact: Children in Scotland
5 Shandwick Place, Edinburgh EH2 4RG
Tel: 0131 228 8484
Fax: 0131 228 8585
£2.95

A range of publications covering all aspects
of education for disabled students is
available from SKILL, The National Bureau
for Students with Disabilities
Chapter House, 18–20 Crucifix Lane
London SE1 3JW
Tel: 0800 328 5050 (voice) or
0800 068 2422 (text)

Higher education

"UCAS Handbook"
Available from UCAS or careers offices.

"UCAS Helpline"
Tel: 01242 227788
Minicom: 01242 225857
Website: www.ucas.ac.uk

"The Big Offical UCAS Guide to University
and College Entrance"
UCAS Sheedon and Ward

"Into HE: a guide to Higher Education for
people with disabilities"
Skill, Chapter House, 19–20 Crucifix Lane
London SE1 3JW
Tel: 0800 328 5050 (voice) or
0800 068 2422 (text)

ADD/ADHD

"The AD/HD Handbook. A guide for
parents and professionals on attention
deficit/hyperactivity disorder"
A Munden and J Arcelus
Jessica Kinsley
ISBN 1853027561

Autism/Asperger's Syndrome

"The Autistic Spectrum: A Guide for
Parents and Professionals"
Lorna Wing
Constable, 1996
ISBN 0094751609

"Children with autism and Asperger
syndrome: a guide for practitioners and
carers"
Patricia Howlin
Wiley, 1998
ISBN: 0471983284

"Autism: The Facts"
Simon Baron-Cohen and Patrick Bolton
Oxford University Press, 1993
ISBN: 0192623273

"Asperger's Syndrome: A Guide for parents
and Professionals"
Tony Attwood
Jessica Kingsley Publishers 1997
ISBN 1853025771

"Meeting the Needs of Children with
Autistic Spectrum Disorders"
R Jordan and G Jones
David Fulton, 1999
ISBN 1853465828

A range of books, booklets and videos on autism and Asperger's Syndrome is available from the National Autistic Society, 393 City Road, London EC1V 1NG
Tel: 020 7833 Fax: 020 7837 9666
And also from OAASIS
Brock House, Grigg Lane
Brockenhurst, Hampshire SO42 7RE
Tel: 0891 633201 (helpline)
Fax: 01590 622687

Cerebral Palsy

A range of publications on cerebral palsy is available from SCOPE.
Cerebral Palsy Helpline
PO Box 833
Milton Keynes MK12 5NY
Tel: 0808 800 3333
Fax: 01908 321051
Email: Cphepline@scope.org.uk

Cystic Fibrosis

A range of publications on cystic fibrosis is available from the Cystic Fibrosis Trust
11 London Road
Bromley, Kent BR1 1BY
Tel: 020 8464 7211
Fax: 020 8313 0472.

Down's Syndrome

"Down's Syndrome – The Facts"
Mark Selikowitz
Oxford University Press, 1997

"New Approaches to Down's Syndrome"
Edited by Brian Stratford and Pat Gunn
Cassell, 1996

"The Development of Language and Reading Skills in Children with Down's Syndrome"
Sue Buckley, Maggie Emslie
Gilly Haslegrove, Pat leProvost
University of Portsmouth, 1993

"Meeting the Educational Needs of Children with Down's Syndrome"
Gillian Bird and Sue Buckley
The Sarah Duffen Centre
University of Portsmouth, 1994

"Supporting Support Assistants –
A Practical Handbook for SENCOs in Mainstream Primary and Secondary Schools"
Stephanie Lorenz, 1996

"Supporting Special Educational Needs in Secondary School Classrooms"
Jane Lovely
David Fulton Publishers, 1995

Dyscalculia

"Mathematics for Dyslexics:
A Teaching Handbook"
2nd edition
Chinn and Ashcroft
Whurr
ISBN 1861560435
£22.50

"Sum Hope – Breaking the Numbers Barrier"
Steve Chinn
Souvenir Press
ISBN 0285634550

CD-ROM
"What to do when you can't learn the times tables"
Dr S Chinn

Available from
Mark College
Mark, Somerset TA9 4NP
£29.99 + £1.95 p&p

Dyslexia

For parents:

"Dyslexia: A Parent's Survival Guide"
C Ostler, 1999
Ammonite Books
ISBN 1869866134

"Overcoming Dyslexia (A straightforward guide for families and teachers)"
B Hornsby
Macdonald & Co
ISBN 0091813204

"The Scars of Dyslexia (Eight case studies in emotional reactions)"
J Edwards, 1995
Cassell
ISBN 0304329444

"Susan's Story (An autobiographical account of my struggle with words)"
S Hampshire, 1990
Corgi
ISBN 0552135860

"This Book Does not Make Sens, Cens, Sns, Scens, Sense"
J Auger
Better Books

"Reversals"
E Simpson
Gollancz

Dyslexia – General

"Dyslexia: 100 Years On"
Miles T & E, 1999
Open University Press
ISBN 0335200346

"Dyslexia in Children"
Fawcett & Nicholson
Harvester Wheatsheaf

"The Pattern of Difficulties"
Miles T R
Whurr

"Developmental Dyslexia"
Thompson M E
Whurr

"Dyslexia: A Cognitive Developmental Perspective"
Snowling M
Blackwell

"Dyslexia: Speech and Language: A Practitioner's Handbook"
Snowling & Stockhouse
Whurr

"Psychological Assessment of Dyslexia"
Turner M
Whurr

"Specific Learning Difficulites (Dyslexia): Challenges & Responses"
Pumfrey & Reason
Routledge

"Dyslexia: A Practitioner's Handbook"
Gavin Reid
Wiley
ISBN 0471973912

Teaching

"Dyslexia: A Teaching Handbook"
Thompson & Watkins
Whurr
ISBN 1861560397

"Learning Difficulties in Reading & Writing"
NFER
Nelson

"Specific Learning Difficulties (Dyslexia):
A Teacher's Guide"
Crombie M
Jordanhill College of Education

"Dealing with Dyslexia"
Heaton & Winterson
Better Books, 1996
ISBN 1897635575

"Together for Reading"
Smith, Shirley & Visser, 1970
Nasen
ISBN 0906730805

"Children with Special Learning
Difficulties"
Tansley & Pankhurst
NFER Nelson

"Reading Writing & Dyslexia:
A Cognitive Analysis"
Ellis A, 1984
Lawrence Erlbaum
ISBN 0863770037

"Children with Special Needs"
Chasty & Friel
Jessica Kingsley

"Instrumental Music for Dyslexics:
A Teaching Handbook"
Ogelthorpe S
Whurr

"Mathematics for Dyslexics:
A Teaching Handbook"
Chinn & Ashcroft
Whurr

Resources

"Learning to Learn"
Malone S
Nasen
ISBN 1874784434

"Alpha to Omega"
Hornsby & Shear, 1999
Heinemann
ISBN 0435103881

"Spotlight on Words"
Aitken G, 1970
Robinswood Press
ISBN 1869981510

"Easy Type"
Kinloch R, 1994
Egon Publishers
ISBN 0905858905

"New Phonic Blending Kit"
Learning Materials Ltd

For the older student:

"Help for the Dyslexic Adolescent"
E G Stirling
St David's College, Llandudno

"Use Your Head"
T Buzan, 1999
BBC
ISBN 056337103X

"Study Skills: A Pupil's Survival Guide"
C Ostler
Ammonite Books

"Adult Dyslexia: Assessment,
Counselling and Training"
McLoughlin, Fitzgibbon & Young
Whurr, 1993
ISBN 1897635354

"Dyslexia at College"
D Gilroy & Prof T Miles, 1995
Routledge
ISBN 0415127785

A range of publications and videos is available from The Dyslexia Institute
133 Gresham Road, Staines
Middlesex TW18 2AJ
Tel: 01784 463851
Fax: 01784 460747

"How to Detect and Manage Dyslexia"
P Ott
Heinemann, 1997
ISBN 0435104195

"Living with Dyslexia"
B Riddick
Routledge. 1997
ISBN 0415125014

"The Dyslexia Handbook 2001"
A Series of articles on different aspects of dyslexia.
British Dyslexia Association
ISBN 1872653316
£9.50 (including postage)

Dyspraxia

"Developmental Dyspraxia"
2nd Edition
Madeleine Portwood
£17.50 (inc p&p)

"Take Time"
Mary Nash-Wortham and Jean Hunt
£11.00 (inc p&p)

"Dyspraxia –
A Handbook for Therapists"
Michele Lee and Jenny Taylor
£7.00 (inc p&p)

All the above are available from
The Dyspraxia Foundation
8 West Alley, Hitchin
Hertfordshire SG5 1EG
Tel: 01462 455016,
Fax: 01462 455052.

"Praxis Makes Perfect"
A Dyspraxia Foundation Publication
£7.50 (inc p&p)

Epilepsy

Articles:

"Epilepsy, Learning and Behaviour in Children"
F M Besal
In "Epilepsia" 36 1:1995 58–63
Raven Press, New York

"Established antiepileptic drugs"
M Brodie et al
In "Seizure" 1997 6: 159–174

"Behaviour problems in children with new-onset epilepsy"
D W Dunn et al
In "Seizure" 1997 4:283–287

"Educational Attainment in Children and Young People with Epilepsy"
P Thomson
In "Epilepsy and Education –
A Medical Symposium on Changing Attitudes to Epilepsy in Education"
Edited by Jolyon Oxley and Gregory Stores
Published by Labaz Sanofi UK Ltd
London 1986

Gifted Children

"Gifted or Able"
Peter Young and Colin Tyre
Oxford University Press
ISBN 0335099963
£10.99

"Challenge of the Able Child"
David George
David Fulton Publishers
ISBN 1853463469
£12.99

"Supporting the Child of Exceptional
Ability at Home and at School"
S Leyden
David Fulton, 1998
ISBN 18534516X

The National Association for Gifted
Children (NAGC) publishes a range of
publications and newsletters for its
members.
Contact the NAGC
Elder House, 540 Elder Gate
Milton Keynes, MK9 1LR
Tel: 01908 673677
Fax: 01908 673679

Muscular Dystrophy

"Muscular Dystrophy: The Facts"
Alan E H Emery
Oxford University Press, 2000
ISBN 0192632175

"Childhealth Care Nursing: Concepts,
Theories and Practice"
Edited by B Carter and A K Dearmun
Blackwell Scientific, 1995
ISBN 0632036893
£19.99

"Children with Muscular Dystrophy in
Mainstream Schools"
Factsheet available from the
Muscular Dystrophy Group
7–11 Prescott Place, London SW4 6BS
Tel: 020 7720 8055

Speech and Language difficulties

AFASIC Publications

"Supporting Your Child's Speech and
Language": 12 booklets – price from £1–£2,
full set £12.50

"Glossary Sheets on Speech and Language
Impairments": 26 individual sheets which
explain terms used to describe children
with speech and language impairments
(35p each, £8.00 for the full set)

"Accessing Speech and Language Therapy
for your child – a Guide to the Law"

"Choosing a School – an AFASIC Guide to
Educational Options for Children with
Speech and Language Impairments"
£1.75

Other publications

"Activities for Speaking and Listening and
Confidence in Communicating"
Two publications – Part I (ages 3–7)
Part II (ages 7–11)
Heather Anderson, Frances Graham and
Alison Constable
£4.50

"Help me speak – a parent's guide to
speech and language therapy"
J Barrett
Souvenir Press, 1994
ISBN 0285631802

"Rachel – the 'write' to speak"
S Capelin
Minerva Press, 1998
ISBN 1861066341

"Children with Language Impairment:
an Introduction"
M Donaldson
Jessica Kingsley Publishers, 1995

"Trouble Talking: a guide for parents of children with speech and language difficulties"
J Law and J Elias
Jessica Kingsley Publishers, 1996
ISBN 1853022535

"Let Me Play; Let Me Speak"
D Jefree and R McConkey
Souvenir Press, 1996

"It Takes Two to Talk: a parent's guide to helping children communicate"
A Manolson
Window Press

"Dyspraxia – A Guide for Teachers and Parents"
K Ripley, B Daines and J Barrett
David Fulton, 1997
ISBN 1853464449

All the above publications are available from AFASIC –
Unlocking Speech and Language
347 Central Markets
Smithfield
London EC1A 9NH
Tel: (020) 7236 3632 (helpline)
Fax: (020) 7236 8115

"Communication Difficulties in Childhood"
Law, Parkinson and Tamnhe
Radcliffe Medical Press, 1999

"Elementary Mathematics and Language Difficulties – a book for teachers, therapist and parents"
Eva Grauberg
Whurr, 1997

Spina Bifida and Hydrocephalus

"Teaching the Student with Spina Bifida"
Fern L Rowley – Keith & Donald H Reigel
Paul Brookes Publishing Co,
ISBN 10557660646

"Living with Spina Bifida"
Adrian Sandler MP
University of North Carolina Press, 1997
(obtainable from Trevor Brown Associates,
Tel: (020) 7388 8500
ISBN 1080782352X

"Spinabilities: A Young Person's Guide to Spina Bifida"
Edited by Marlene Lutkenhoff
Woodbine House (USA) &
Sonya Oppenheimer
ISBN 0933139867

"Children with Spina Bifida and/or Hydrocephalus"
(Association for Spina Bifida and Hydrocephalus)
ASBAH House, Peterborough
ISBN 090668711X

"Hydrocephalus and You"
Rosemary Bachelor and Leonie Holgate
ASBAH, Peterborough, 1999
ISBN 090 6687128

"Hydrocephalus Information Pack"
ASBAH, Peterborough, 1999
ISBN 0906687128

"Current Concepts in Spina Bifida and Hydrocephalus"
Carys Bannister & Brian Tew
MacKeith Press
Distributed by
Blackwell Scientific Publishers Ltd
ISBN 0901260916

"The Statementing Process for
Children with Special Educational
Needs"
Peter Walker
ASBAH, Peterborough

"LINK"
Bi-monthly magazine of ASBAH
obtainable from ASBAH House
Titles available from ASBAH
42 Park Road
Peterborough PE1 2UQ,
Tel: 01733 555988
Fax: 01733 555985

Gilles de la Tourette Syndrome

"Tourette Syndrome: the facts"
Mary Robertson and Simon Baron-Cohen
Oxford University Press, 1998
ISBN 019852398X
£9.99

"Teaching the Tiger: A Handbook for
Individuals Involved in the Education of
Students with Attention Deficit Disorders,
Tourette Syndrome or Obsessive-
Compulsive Disorder"
Marilyn P Dornbush & Sheryl K Pruitt
Hope Press

Visual Impairment

"Visibility", "Eye Contact"

Both journals published three times a year
by the Royal National Institute for the
Blind.
Subscription: £9.00 for three issues.
Contact: Karen Porter
RNIB Education Information Service
224 Great Portland Street
London W1N 6AA
Tel: 020 7288 1266.

A range of books and videos covering the
needs of visually impaired children and
visually impaired children with additional
needs is available through the RNIB Book
Sales Service. For a catalogue contact:
Des Johnson
RNIB National Education Services
Garrow House, 190 Kensal Road
London W10 5BT
Tel: 020 8968 8600
Fax: 020 8960 3593

Glossary of Abbreviations

Learning Difficulties

ADD	Attention Deficit Disorder
ADHD	Attention Deficit/Hyperactivity Disorder
ASP	Asperger Syndrome
AUT	Autism
CP	Cerebral Palsy
DEL	Delicate
DOW	Down's Syndrome
DYC	Dyscalculia
DYP	Dyspraxia
DYS	Dyslexia
EBD	Emotional and Behavioural Difficulties
EPI	Epilepsy
HI	Hearing Impairment
LD	Learning Difficulties
MLD	Moderate Learning Difficulties
PH	Physical Impairment
PMLD	Profound and Multiple Learning Difficulties
SLD	Severe Learning Difficulties
SP&LD	Speech and Language Difficulties
SPLD	Specific Learning Difficulties
TOU	Tourette's Syndrome
VIS	Visual Impairment
W	Premises should be suitable for wheelchair access

Associations and Accrediting Bodies

ARC	Association for Residential Care
AWCEBD	The Association of Workers for Children with Emotional and Behavioural Difficulties
BDA	The British Dyslexia Association
CReSTeD	Council for the Registration of Schools Teaching Dyslexic Pupils
ECIS	European Council of International Schools
FEFC	Further Education Fundraising Council
HMC	The Headmasters' and Headmistresses' Conference
IAPS	The Incorporated Association of Preparatory Schools

ISA	The Independent Schools Association
ISC	The Independent Schools Council
ISI	The Independent Schools Inspectorate
ISIS	The Independent Schools Information Service
NAIMS	The National Association for Independent and Non-maintained Schools
NASEN	The National Association for Special Educational Needs
NASS	The National Association for Voluntary and Non-maintained Special Schools
NATSPEC	The National Association of Specialist Colleges
SHMIS	The Society of Headmasters and Headmistresses of Independent Schools

MAIN INDEX

K